An Unholy Brew

An Unholy Brew

Alcohol in Indian History and Religions

JAMES McHUGH

OXFORD
UNIVERSITY PRESS

OXFORD
UNIVERSITY PRESS

Oxford University Press is a department of the University of Oxford. It furthers the University's objective of excellence in research, scholarship, and education by publishing worldwide. Oxford is a registered trade mark of Oxford University Press in the UK and certain other countries.

Published in the United States of America by Oxford University Press
198 Madison Avenue, New York, NY 10016, United States of America.

Library of Congress Cataloging-in-Publication Data
Names: McHugh, James (James Andrew) author.
Title: An unholy brew : alcohol in Indian history and religions / James McHugh.
Description: 1. | New York : Oxford University Press, 2021. |
Includes bibliographical references and index. |
Identifiers: LCCN 2021027066 (print) | LCCN 2021027067 (ebook) |
ISBN 9780199375943 (paperback) | ISBN 9780199375936 (hardback) |
ISBN 9780197603031 (epub) | ISBN 9780197603048 | ISBN 9780199375950
Subjects: LCSH: Drinking of alcoholic beverages—India. |
Alcoholic beverages—India. | Alcoholic beverages—History. |
Drinking of alcoholic beverages—Religious aspects. |
Drinking of alcoholic beverages—History. | Alcoholism—Religious aspects.
Classification: LCC GT2883.I4 M34 2021 (print) | LCC GT2883.I4 (ebook) |
DDC 394.1/30954—dc23
LC record available at https://lccn.loc.gov/2021027066
LC ebook record available at https://lccn.loc.gov/2021027067

DOI: 10.1093/oso/9780199375936.001.0001

1 3 5 7 9 8 6 4 2

Paperback printed by Marquis, Canada
Hardback printed by Bridgeport National Bindery, Inc., United States of America

To Mat

Contents

List of Figures ix
Acknowledgments xi

Introduction 1

Aperitif: *Surā*, the Prototypical Liquor of India 19

ROUND ONE: DRINKS AND DRINKING

Cup 1: *Surā* Made from Grains 27

Cup 2: Sugarcane, Wine, Toddy, and Other Drinks 44

Cup 3: *Surā* Brewing and Public Drinking 76

Cup 4: Luxurious, Erotic Drinking in Literary Texts 111

Cup 5: Drink, Health, and Disease in Āyurvedic Texts 145

ROUND TWO: DRINK AND RELIGION

Cup 6: Drink in Ritual, Myths, and Epic 165

Cup 7: The Filth of Grain and the Pain of Drink: Morality, Vice, and Law 188

Cup 8: *Surā* Regained: Drink in Tantra 245

Cup 9: Firewater and Corpse-Reviver: Alcohol in Later Sanskrit Sources 280

Digestif: What Do We Do about This Stuff That Makes Everything Go Awry? 286

Appendix: Soma, *Ancient Drugs, and Modern Scholars* 289
Notes 297
Bibliography 363
Index 389

Figures

3.1: Possible image of a *surā* shop in the Asura realm from the *Saṃsāracakra* in Cave 17 at Ajanta. 101

© Ajanta Archives of the Saxon Academy of Sciences and Humanities, Research Centre "Buddhist Murals of Kucha on the Northern Silk Road," photograph Andreas Stellmacher. I thank Monika Zin for sharing this image with me.

4.1: Couple embracing with a cup, from Cave 3 at Badami, late sixth century. 115

Photo © James McHugh 2014.

4.2: Standing drinking couple, with stumbling woman. Mallikārjuna Temple at Pattadakal, eighth century. 118

Photo © James McHugh 2014.

4.3: Couples drinking with attendants present, Virūpākṣa Temple at Pattadakal, eighth century. 133

Photo © James McHugh 2014.

7.1: Indra appears with the jar before the king in an image of the *Kumbha Jātaka*. From Borobudur, Java. 225

From Krom (1920–1931, vol. 1: Reliefs, Serie 1.(B).a. Plaat VII, image 59). I thank the University of Chicago Library, and especially librarian Laura Ring, for allowing me to take this photo.

8.1: The Goddess Surā/Vāruṇī with nine cups and nine vessels, Kangra 1810–1820 (Losty 2019, 72). She also emerges from the water. Despite the fact that some details such as the lotus, the heads, the freshwater setting are not as in the text, I believe this is quite likely to be Surā. 262

Credit: Steven Kossak, The Kronos Collections. I thank Siddhartha Shah for alerting me to the existence of this image and Kurt Behrendt for helping me obtain this copy and permissions.

Acknowledgments

Many people have helped directly and indirectly with this multifarious project, from scholars to brewers. I am especially sad that my Ph.D. advisor Anne Monius died before the book was finished and I could not share it with her—I raise my glass to Anne.

First, I wish to thank my friend and mentor Stephanie Jamison for all her support and advice over the last few years. The thoughtful anonymous readers of the proposal and draft at Oxford University Press were enormously helpful in bringing some shape and order to what started out as a rather unwieldy project and I am grateful for all their diligent work. The University of Southern California also generously provided an opportunity for two scholars to read the book at a later stage, Patrick Olivelle and Projit Mukharji, whom I thank for their excellent comments and suggestions. I also thank all my colleagues and the graduate students in my department who attended this manuscript discussion event, and who offered many useful suggestions.

I also thank the many people who helped me in various ways in India, listed here roughly in the order I consulted with them: Dr. Shajahan at the Government Ayurveda College, Trivandrum; Dr. Rajagopalan at Kerala University; Mr. Balakrishnan Unni and Mr. Shashi Unni at Vasudeva Vilasam Ayurveda; T. K. Devanarayanan in Thrissur; Mr. V. S. Sunil Kumar, MLA; and Dr. Sivakaran Namboothiri at Sreedhary Ayurvedic Centre. At Sitaram Ayurveda, Kerala: Dr. Sankaranarayanan, Dr. R. Vighnesh Devraj, Dr. V. M. Wilson, and Dr. V. Neelakandan. At Vaidyaratna: Dr. G. Krishnadas. Arshad Faiz in Hyderabad. At the Tribal Museum Bhubaneswar: Baidar Murmu, Dr. Purusottam Pattanail, Mr. Nilamadhaba Kanhar. Mr. Jai Chacko in Mankotta. And John Mathew, Chandrahas Choudhury, Vivek Benegal. Also, Jatin Nayak in Bhubaneswar. In Kolkata: Protima Dutta, Rajarshi Ghose, Gautam Bhadra, Debasish Bose, Santanu Mitra, Arun Nag. At Shaw's Bar: Gour Chandra Shaw and Shibaji Shaw. Also, Debasis Bose, Abhik Ray, Amritendu Roy, Gautam Bhadra. In Jaipur: Surendra Bothra, Jyoti Kothari, and at Dhanvantari Aushadhalaya, Dr. Vimlesh Sharma, Mr. Vishvabandhu and Thakur Man Singh Kanota.

In China several people helped me observe and learn about brewing Shaoxing wine, which helped me think in new ways about large scale *surā* brewing. I thank my interpreter Mr. Shi Pu, and Mr. Kim whom I thank for all his time and generosity. I also thank all the brewers and guides I met at the following breweries: Guyue Longshan, Yuewangtai, Jianhu, and Kuaijishan.

The following people kindly read all or sections of the book and/or shared their own writing, images, and translations with me: Kurt Behrendt, Erik Braun, Phyllis Granoff, Ludwig Habighorst, Betsey Halpern, Lilian Handlin, Shaman Hatley, Maria Heim, Jiri Jakl, Sonam Kachru, Jesse Knutson, Finn Moore Gerety, Jason Neelis, Eva Schinzel, Gregory Schopen, Harald Wiese, Dominik Wujastyk, Monika Zin, Kenneth Zysk. In the USA, Canada, and Europe I also thank: Daud Ali, Lou Amdur, Vitus Angermeier, Stefan Baums, James Benn, Lisa Bitel, Willem Bollée, Joel Bordeaux, Gudrun Bühnemann, Beatrice Chrystall, Whitney Cox, Christopher Fleming, Rich Freeman, Adam Golab at Bent Water Brewing, Samuel Grimes, Andrea Gutierrez, Eric Gurevitch, Lilian Handlin, Johnna Tyrrell, Frank Korom, Christophe Laudamiel, my liver, James Mallinson, Mark McClish, Patrick McGovern, Arthur McKeown, Deonnie Moodie, Ernie Ocampo (for supplying basi), Nithya Raman, Laura Ring, David Roman, Nicolas Roth, Richard Salomon, Alexis Sanderson, Tom Sapsford, S. R. Sarma, Siddhartha Shah, Oktor Skjaervo, Walter Slaje, Donald Stadtner, Somdev Vasudeva, Linda Wootton, Thomas Zumbroich.

In order to shorten this book, I cut several longer sections to publish as articles, and the basic findings of these articles are now merely sketched in the book. Also, in some other cases my translations in this book also appear in articles, particularly in several articles that are reviews and surveys of the topic of drugs and alcohol in India. I thank all the editors and publishers of these journals for permitting me to reuse those translations, and for letting me briefly summarize my detailed research articles in this book. I also thank all the anonymous peer reviewers at those journals whose comments helped refine the conclusions of this large project as a whole.

Research for this book was supported by the USC Dana and David Dornsife College of Letters, Arts and Sciences, the USC Society of Fellows in the Humanities, as well as by generous grants from the National Endowment for the Humanities and from the American Council of Learned Societies.

At Oxford University Press I thank my editor Cynthia Read for her enormous patience in supporting and guiding this project, and also Rachel Gilman for all her work on the editorial process. Ursula DeYoung (independent editor) did an excellent job of cleaning up a very messy, overwrought manuscript. And Katherine Ulrich did an excellent, thorough job of the final copyedits. In India, Haripriya Ravichandran managed the production process brilliantly.

Finally, I thank my family for all their support over the years: my parents Celia and Damian, and Peter, Cordelia, and Elly. I also thank Mat for sharing drinks over the years.

Introduction

bhabhabhramati kiṃ mahī lalalalambate candramāḥ
kṛkṛṣṇa vavada drutaṃ hahahasanti kiṃ vṛṣṇayaḥ |
śiśīdhu mumumuñca me vavavavaktram ity ādikam
madaskhalitam ālapan haladharaḥ śriyaṃ vaḥ kriyāt ||

"Why is the earth whiwhiwhirling and why so lolololow the moon?
Krikrishna, tetell me right now why the Vrishnis hohohowl?
Shusugar-wine, lelelet go of my mumumumouth . . ."
May drunk-stammering Balarāma the Plough-bearer grant you blessings.

—Puruṣottamadeva[1]

We should begin the book in a bar. Shaw's Bar in Kolkata is one of the oldest bars in India, founded by an Indian family in 1872. Housed in a lofty shed from a long-gone market, male-only Shaw's has marble floors and tabletops, Burmese teak tables, and an army of twenty-six efficient uniformed waiters who serve pegs of whisky and rum as well as bottles of beer to a crowd of politicians, writers, actors, and retired military men, among others. The waiters also dish out small trays of snacks: chickpeas and chopped ginger—the house drinking snack. In 2014 Mr. Gour Chandra Shaw, whose family has been running the bar for four generations, showed me round and proudly related the history and traditions of this institution, where patrons share tables with whoever arrives, and where a varied crowd has enjoyed drink and conversation for well over a century.

Reading the country's newspapers, though, one might get the impression that much drinking in India consists of mass poisonings. And the various political and social movements to ban or restrict the trade in liquor in South Asia are too numerous and complex to consider here.

When I mention to people in the USA that I'm writing a book about alcohol in pre-modern India, they often ask, "But was there much alcohol in ancient India?"[2] Surveys of alcohol use in world histories are not typically much help, unless you're interested in the origins of Indian Pale Ale. Meanwhile, there is no shortage of books on *soma*, the "mystery drug" of ancient India.

An Unholy Brew. James McHugh, Oxford University Press. © Oxford University Press 2021.
DOI: 10.1093/oso/9780199375936.003.0001

Why do so few people know anything of the history of alcohol in India as compared with, say, that of ancient Rome, which many people, at least in Western countries, think of as a drinking culture? First, very few people in Europe and America study early Indian history. And the study of ancient and medieval India in the West is often concerned with matters more conventionally religious, philosophical, and literary. Popular Western interest is typically focused on the religious aspects of premodern India, especially on practices like meditation and yoga, as the shelves of American bookshops demonstrate (which is not in any way to denigrate excellent scholarship on such topics). The *Kāmasūtra* is an exception, but that text is often presented in a distorted or sensationalized way. Whereas for classical Greece and Rome, earthy social history is common—"courtesans and fishcakes," brothels in Pompeii, and so on—this sort of history writing about ancient India is relatively rare in Europe and America. Of course there are many exceptions. Gregory Schopen has shown that the lives of monks, nuns, and other Buddhists in ancient India were frequently far more worldly than previous scholars suggested. My agenda here, however, is not to correct previous scholarship on drinking in premodern India; there has been too little work done for that to be needed, and most people have almost no preconceived ideas about the topic, apart, perhaps, from a general awareness that certain groups did not drink. Rather I wish to fill the enormous, often unnoticed, gap in histories of alcohol and drinking where India is concerned. Thus one main aim of this book is simply to collect, translate, and communicate data about drinking in India.

Substances that we nowadays call "drugs" are another matter entirely. Western scholarship has often presented India as an exotic land of drug consumption and mystical states, less noteworthy for alcohol than for substances such as *soma*, cannabis, and opium. So, while drinks are largely absent, drugs are prominent in Western visions of India's past. Fischer-Tiné and Tschurenev describe this "editing out of the role of drink" as originating in the efforts of a diverse set of actors from the nineteenth century onward.[3] Many Indian nationalists, along with their Western allies, such as missionaries and devotees of Indian religious sects, presented the perceived problems of Indian drinking as being due to European influence, while the "Oriental state" was imagined as permitting unrestrained indulgence in drugs—a view that was important among British colonial administrators.[4] This Western view of Indian drug-taking was not entirely critical, and certain imagined "Oriental drug habits" (and altered states of consciousness in general) attracted people to the region and the culture, as they still do today.[5]

As an alternative to this vision, I provide in this book a detailed survey of drinks, drinking, and ideas about drinking in premodern India, based mainly on Sanskrit sources. It is impossible to be comprehensive when dealing with such a wide-ranging topic. The period covered is long and surviving texts numerous.

Moreover, I am not an expert in many of the subfields involved here, such as the Vedas or Hindu law. I focus on ancient, early medieval, and later medieval South Asia, starting with the Vedas and continuing until the early to mid-second millennium CE. At the end of the book I look briefly at the afterlife of some drinks and ways of talking about drinks, for example in Sanskrit texts from the eighteenth century. I have not used texts in classical Tamil, nor in other vernacular and literary languages such as Bengali; nor have I dealt with drink and Islam. I consider some visual evidence, though very much in the light of texts, as I am no art historian. In writing this book, I came to realize that drinks and drugs often need to be considered together, so there are shorter sections included on betel and cannabis. (King Soma has a tendency to steal the limelight, so I discuss *soma* in an Appendix.) In some cases I give a detailed chronological account of a topic, but in other cases I discuss only a few case studies, such as those concerning Jainism, Tantra, and medicine.

Sometimes academics call a book "descriptive" in a derogatory way, implying that there is little theory or no thesis. This book is very descriptive. It is necessary to excavate, reconstruct, and contextualize a mass of data before anyone can begin to analyze any subject. Also, when writing about over two thousand years of history in a vast region, it would be strange to expect a single thesis to emerge. Nevertheless, I offer various specific analyses and conclusions throughout the book.

Some Notes about My Approach

What Can We Do with the Evidence?

This book is based on texts, mostly in Sanskrit and related languages. Many of these texts are literary or scholastic, abounding in conventions, standard lists, stock characters, and motifs that I explain throughout the book. Many of the texts had a long and varied afterlife, often in tandem with scholarly commentaries composed centuries later.

Given this evidence, a text-focused approach to the history of drinking in India is relatively easy. That is to say, we're on safer ground when thinking about the history of ideas and textual traditions. Given the clarity of some of the descriptions we have of making drinks, I also think it is possible to get some sense of the material culture of making drinks, at least for a few times and places. It's much harder, however, to infer from our texts what was going on socially in the worlds when they were being written and read. Readers not familiar with the study of India in these periods might be unaware of how limited the historical archives are for writing certain types of history. By contrast, in his social history of the English alehouse, Peter Clark draws on the rich materials available to historians of England. He writes that in one unlicensed premises in Leicester, on a Saturday night in October 1607, we know that there were present two slaters, a laborer, a butcher, a weaver, and others, some of whose names we know too.[6] Accessing such historical detail is utterly inconceivable for the Indian equivalent of such a place in, say, the first millennium CE, and for most of the second millennium too. Thus writing a detailed social or material-culture history of India is exceptionally difficult.

In addition, the dates and origins of many of our surviving textual sources are poorly understood, such that an estimated date within a few centuries is quite common for some texts. One should not be overly pessimistic, however, and we do know more about certain works. But we possess nothing like dated monastic accounts and inventories, nor detailed autobiographies or diaries. There are many inscriptions, such as records of land donations, and these have been of some use here, though they're not enormously informative with regard to alcohol. We do have a large number of texts in many other genres for the period under consideration—literary, legal, philosophical, and medical texts, along with ones on statecraft and erotics. However, if we're also interested in thinking about the social history of drinking (as I am, with many qualifications) using these texts is difficult. But we might cautiously assume that some basic common features of drinking in the texts were also features of practice—for example, drinking out of individual cups as opposed to shared jars with straws; group-drinking at festivals; drinking at places that brewed and sold drink. And, taking a few such basic elements, we might then compare these features to better documented drinking cultures, tentatively imagining a social and economic history of drinking in India.[7] But the more material we consider in our triangulation, the vaguer our conclusions become in terms of time and place. Thus Rajendralal Mitra, who wrote so eloquently of drinking in India, would be irritated by the many "hypotheses hedged in by flimsy pretenses of 'it seems,' 'it is probable' . . ." that litter this book.[8]

Even when texts are clear about drink and can be placed historically, they need to be treated with caution. James Benn writes of China that one "has to admit that textual evidence is not necessarily an accurate indicator of what people in premodern times actually consumed or how they did so. Let us remember, for example, the case of the history of noodles in China. Although scholars of culture and foodways pored over the surviving texts, they could not discover any trace of noodles earlier than sources from the Eastern Han (25–220 CE). However, a recent archaeological discovery of a bowl with noodles still contained within it has obliged us to push back the date of noodle consumption to Neolithic times (about 4,000 years ago)."[9] Such a point is valid, though I would qualify it: the discovery of a Neolithic bowl of noodles *does* mean that there were noodles in that one time and place, but it by no means implies that noodles were common in China from the date of the excavated bowl. You would need more evidence to make that case.

Yet, perhaps the glass is half full. Particularly with technical materials such as recipes, incomplete evidence arguably sometimes implies the existence of a set of embodied, unstated, assumed practices that we might now be more aware of when looking at other types of evidence. There are various ways in which we can try to get a sense of where such gaps lie in our data and what might have filled them. We might try recreating these recipes today, in a manner similar to scholars who practice the experimental history of science. For example, in attempting to recreate James Prescott Joule's experiments to determine the mechanical equivalent of heat, historian of science Heinz Otto Sibum was able to highlight just how essential Joule's distinctive practical skills were to performing these experiments in an accurate manner, skills that he possessed largely thanks to his background in beer brewing.[10] Although I have tried to recreate some of the simpler recipes we possess for early Indian drinks (with very mixed successes), I have found more useful to emulate the methods of ethno-archaeology, observing various fermentation methods in person (in India and China) and reading widely about traditional methods for making alcoholic drinks in a number of cultures. Such comparative work is valuable both for understanding technical processes and sometimes for enriching our ability to imagine the social processes surrounding drink culture. This sort of work certainly allowed me to shake off many of my assumptions about brewing based on English beer manufacture. Then, becoming conscious of the implied skills of brewers of the drink called *surā* may focus our attention on other texts that do hint at the nature and value of such tacit knowledge, as when we read in a Buddhist legal text of woman who ruins a large batch of drink she is making for a wedding, which drink is saved, however, by a Buddhist nun who *does* have the right skills—but the social and economic implications of the nun's skills are not without significance.

To summarize the discussion thus far: given the limited nature of our evidence and my interest in examining and comparing a wide range of sources, from technical recipes to poetic descriptions of drinking bouts, this book somewhat eludes clear classification in terms of standard categories of scholarship. But if pressed to state the nature of this book in such terms I would say that it is a literary and intellectual history of drinking in India, with considerable reflection on the material culture of various drinks, along with some tentative explorations of the social and economic history of drinking. Where materials are contextualized, this is more in terms of connecting some parts of alcohol culture to others, for instance our understanding of recipes to legal texts, and I have not in general found it easy to relate this material to wider processes of historical change, to regional tendencies, and to political history, though other scholars might do a better job of that. Finally, I also view many of the Indian materials presented in this book as innately clever and interesting ideas in themselves, as a collection of new and original ways to think about relations between humans, intoxicating substances, and intoxication.

Words

The range of words for alcoholic drinks in Sanskrit is both impressive and confusing. A search for "liquor" in an online version of Apte's *Practical Sanskrit English Dictionary* brings up dozens of words for such drinks, many of which I never even mention in this book. Unfortunately, one can't rely on dictionaries for the exact meaning of Sanskrit words for alcoholic drinks, so for this book and several related articles I've done a lot of philological work—close, comparative reading of texts, and consulting works of historical linguistics—to get a sense of how we should understand these words: what they refer to (which is often a constellation of somewhat similar drinks), what they connote (e.g., rich or poor people drinking), how they are used in different genres, and how their meaning changes over time (e.g., the word "*vāruṇī*" is generic in poems and specific in medicine, where it starts out as a grain-based drink and later sometimes means palm toddy).

It is not strictly correct to say the dictionaries are wrong or even vague when it comes to the names of drinks, as some English (and German) entries may reflect changes in Sanskrit usage in India. In discussing drink in *dharmaśāstra*, the great legal scholar Kane uses "wine," "rum," and quite often "liquor."[11] For the Sanskrit word "*surā*," Monier-Williams gives "spirituous liquor, wine (in ancient times 'a kind of beer')." All these options for translating the word have some value. To compare, H. T. Huang chose to translate a Chinese word for an alcoholic drink as "wine," in order to convey in English the antiquity of this drink, mentioned in the ancient classics and associated with rituals—for which "wine" is a good fit.[12] However this ancient Chinese drink was made from grains, so something is lost as well as gained here. "Beer" is imperfect too, as these Chinese drinks were quite unlike European beer. And what do we do with Monier-Williams's translation "spirituous liquor"? I am far from convinced that distillation was present in South Asia in the period when many of the texts I shall discuss were composed, as I explain elsewhere.[13] Yet to call *surā* a "spirituous drink" in English is by no means entirely incorrect: for a nineteenth- or twentieth-century Indian scholar writing in Sanskrit, *surā* sometimes *was* a distilled liquor, as we shall see in Chapter 9. No doubt the *paṇḍit*s, as well as more recent Indian lexical works consulted by early European scholars, understood *surā* to be a distilled drink, which means that Monier-Williams's definition is correct, at least for a certain time and place.

Even for a given period or genre in which a word seems to have a narrow meaning and a tangible material referent, it can be hard to render it in English. In a study of a clay tablet listing brewing terms in Sumerian and Akkadian, Hartman and Oppenheim wrote that "an extensive and complicated nomenclature . . . was evolved by the brewers, which is highly difficult, if not impossible, to render into a modern language. Technical processes that are apparently quite simple . . . are subject to exceedingly exact terminological differentiations. . . . Each of these specific processes (and many others) was essential if a brew was to be manufactured which was clearly defined in taste, strength, and color. And each of these steps was identified by a specific technical term. . . . Further complications are caused by regional and diachronic differences in this nomenclature."[14] These are exactly the sorts of difficulties we have with words for drinks, drink components, and brewing processes in India.

Drinks are not just substances; they also have varied cultural and social meanings. Lager and champagne are made of different substances, in different places, by different methods. On top of that, swigging lager has a very different connotation from raising a glass of champagne. So, in many cases in this book, I interpret the material nature of a drink alongside its social, aesthetic, and cultural connotations, as for example with *maireya*.

Another complication is that the meanings of words (and the meanings of drinks) change over time. Take the English word "beer." A common story one hears about the history of words for beer explains that "beer" refers to a hopped drink (as opposed to unhopped "ale"), and the word in this sense became common in the sixteenth century.[15] Yet in the eighteenth century, usage changed and "ale" referred to strong beer, and in the nineteenth century "ale" was sometimes used for drinks made with lighter-colored malt, as in "India pale ale." In Old English, however, "ale" was the common word for an alcoholic drink made from malt, and "bēor" may have been used for a sweeter, stronger drink; it was also sometimes used for other varieties of alcoholic drink. Today, "ale" is often used in marketing for beers perceived to be made in a traditional manner: "real ale." Finally, we have root beer and ginger beer, and a beer called "barley wine."

Sanskrit words for drinks likewise changed over the centuries and had varied technical, legal, and medicinal usages, as well as all manner of other connotations. Some words, given in common lexica, are used in poetic texts for reasons of metrics and alliteration. It is unlikely, moreover, that people at the local *surā* house were ordering drinks in Sanskrit, nor did brewers probably speak classical Sanskrit. So, much of the surviving terminology is artificial, literary, or academic, interacting with vernaculars in all sorts of ways that are difficult to establish. Sometimes Sanskrit words might relate somehow to the vernacular words used in a given time and place, but sometimes the Sanskrit language of drink might offer a scholarly alternative universe that had little to do with everyday usage. Still, some educated people immersed in Sanskrit would have used it to write and talk about alcohol culture, whether they drank or not.[16]

The challenges become even more complex when we look at words for intoxicating substances in general, like English "drug," and for states of intoxication and inebriation. In South Asia during the period under consideration, there is no concept of a substance equivalent to alcohol or ethanol. This is why I have chosen mostly to avoid "alcohol" in discussing the drinks in this book (though I have kept things simple in the book's title). Rather, certain drinks, including *soma*, were understood to have the power to intoxicate, a state commonly designated with words derived from the Sanskrit root √*mad*, which can mean among other things "to be drunk" or "to be intoxicated" when applied to a state produced by alcohol, as well as referring to states of exhilaration, joy, and elation.[17] Elephants in rut are also "intoxicated" (*matta*). A number of words that often have the sense of madness (e.g., *unmāda*) and carelessness (e.g., *pramāda*) are derived from the same root, though, as with most Sanskrit words, all these terms have a wide range of meanings.[18] Steven Collins has noted that in one Pali Buddhist text, drunkenness is given as one form of madness (caused by drink, *pāna-*) in a list of the causes of eight varieties of madman (*-ummattako*), so at least in that one classification of mental states there is some overlap between madness and drunkenness.[19] As we'll see later in the book, the concept of negligence or heedlessness (*pramāda*) also plays an important role in some Buddhist texts on the morality of drinking. But this book is not the place to explore all these concepts in depth, and I focus mainly on states caused by fermented drinks and some non-fermented intoxicants.[20]

The most general Sanskrit term to denote drinks that create a drunken state is *madya* "intoxicating [drink]." Translating this word is hard. "Inebriating drink" is clumsy to my ear. "Intoxicating" contains the unfortunate "toxic" element that is not present in the Sanskrit word, though at least in English this is a common word, applicable to various substances and states and lacking any "toxic" associations in everyday usage. I also use "drink" in the sense of alcoholic drink, a usage paralleled in Sanskrit. And I have used "liquor" as a generic term for drink, though this is not ideal as it can suggest distilled drinks to some people. As with my use of the English word "intoxicated," these translations are merely placeholders that allow us to think about mental states and substances in English, while also paying attention to the nuances of the Indian words. On a related note, I have decided not to use the word "entheogen" in this book, since using this word assumes from the outset a lot of connections between drugs, what we might nowadays call mystical states, and religion. "Entheogen" is a word best used in conclusions, if used at all.

In many contemporary Western societies, drink—and especially drink considered as a drug—is associated not only with intoxication but with addiction. Indeed, the concept of drugs and addiction go hand in hand for many people. In her essay "Epidemics of the Will," Eve Sedgwick wrote of the philosophy and development of the modern ideology of addiction.[21] In a pervasive modern framing of drug consumption, taking drugs is not simply an act; consumers themselves are a *type*, with a distinctive identity: addicts.[22] Pathologized addiction has now been extended from drugs to food, sex, shopping, exercise, and other activities, so that the object pursued by the addict can no longer be defined automatically as a foreign substance or even an unhealthy behavior. Rather, addiction today is found in "the structure of the will that is always somehow insufficiently free, a choice whose voluntarity is insufficiently pure."[23] Inseparable from our modern concept of addiction, therefore, is the search for a reified, absolute free will, a pure voluntarity, thwarted at every turn, ironically, by the apparent tendency of voluntary acts to become compulsory addictions. Related, but more polemical in nature, is the recent popular-scientific description of the addict as having a "hijacked brain" that has been chronically, pathologically altered by drugs, which thereby foster uncontrollable, compulsive consumption.[24] Again, in this scenario, the people suffering though drug use have lost control of their will, though this way of talking about drugs shifts agency to the substance consumed (and thus justifies a crusade against the drugs themselves and those who produce or trade them). This is *not* to say, however, that people do not actually experience and suffer from addictions of various sorts. Rather I mean that the language and ideas we often use to talk about, demarcate, and understand this complex phenomenon very much belong to a certain time and place, and shape our thinking and ability to act in certain ways.

The connection between the word "addiction" and modifications of the will is long established in English-language texts. Rebecca Lemon writes of the concept of addiction in early modern England, when the word described an "overthrow of the will" and was applied both to familiar modern "addictions," such as to alcohol and tobacco, as well as to God.[25] In the latter case, addiction was an exclusive and zealous dedication of the self to God as a form of devotion, the binding over of a person's will to God, for both "addiction and devotion are forms of service."[26] This addiction, to God or to alcohol, was entered into freely and "represents an exercise of will even in the relinquishing of it."[27]

Why explain all of this? First, I want to be clear on why I avoid the concept of addiction in this book. The word is far too loaded, connected to a constellation of modern, mostly Western ideas about free will, ethics, neuroscience, pathology, and political rhetoric. Second, articulating some of these modern ideas here offers a useful foil to display what is distinctive in Indian thinking about intoxicants and intoxication. Third, becoming more conscious of *our* notion of addiction exposes the fact that most of us, often unknowingly, are embedded in a complex, culture-specific discourse about drugs and their effects—a way of understanding, talking about, and acting with regard to drugs, alcohol, and many forms of behavior that has countless economic, medical, legal, racial, and personal repercussions. This network of ideas, language, and practice regularly manifests itself in literature, television, and film, and is even given an erotic twist in the names of perfumes that conjure sexual irresistibility (Addict, Opium).

Intoxicants and intoxication in early India are likewise part of a web of words, practices, ideas, and associations. Although accounts of intoxication and drink in the texts I analyze in this book vary considerably, we shall see how premodern South Asian ideas about people and drink are often different from ours today.[28] Admittedly, sometimes people in these texts are *attached* to drink and intoxication, and repeatedly seek out drink *with desire*, and thus "addiction" is by no means a terrible translation for some Sanskrit concepts.[29] But in the Indian texts, this will or desire to drink has not in most cases been "hijacked" by the powers of the substance itself. The drinkers' relationship to the intoxicant has not changed them so that they are now compelled to take it. In many of the texts intoxicated people's desires and intentions may well be transformed, but this is part of a multitude of other changes: drunks perceive differently (e.g., a black drink as a bee); they interpret what they see in a jumbled manner (e.g., mother as lover, lover as mother); they react in confused ways (e.g., both laughing and crying); their bodies change (e.g., flushed faces, stumbling); their inhibitions are dissolved; and their sense of right and wrong is muddled. Intoxication confuses people and heightens their confused experience of the world. Yet, drunks in these texts typically choose and desire to become drunk—hence some legal discussions of purposeful versus accidental drinking. Although drunk people are not their usual selves—a concept implied by the fact that a son is not responsible for the drink debts accrued by the father—drunk intoxication in our sources is not simply a removal or take-over of the will. Drunks may sometimes be said to be "*like* possessed people," but they are not actually possessed. People in the texts exercise their will to ingest a substance that causes intoxication (*mada*), and the resulting state places them in a world of new, changed perceptions, conceptualizations, and reactions. Yet they can still exercise their own will to do other things in this state; for example, they can desire, uninhibitedly, to kiss their lover's face reflected at the bottom of a glass (but, amusingly or sadly, the face is not actually there). Rather than control the drinker, liquor in these texts often removes the bonds and fetters of everyday life, unleashing the drinker. Imagine purposefully driving the chariot of your body, mind, and senses into a vast city of illusions and distorting mirror mazes, where you feel as if you can do anything. It can be very enjoyable in there, but also damaging. And some people might really want to go back for more.

We need to approach this topic with an open mind, as the very ontology of drinks and intoxication is different in the sources that I explore. For us a unity underlies the variety of intoxicating drinks because they all contain alcohol. Some people, moreover, argue that there is a neurological basis common to a variety of addictions. By contrast, in early India, both drink and intoxication were often characterized by multiplicity. Some texts explain that different (alcoholic) drinks all share the property of causing *mada*, intoxication, but others describe the many different types of *mada* itself. *Intoxicants and intoxication take multiple forms* in these texts, and this theme is explored in an array of genres of texts over a long period. Surā, sometimes a goddess with many arms carrying many drinks, and Intoxication, sometimes a demon lurking in many entities, mutually define each other. They are both innately multifarious and innately confusing. Compared to these Indian concepts, Western categories for such substances and states seem simplistic and rigid. This is another reason why I avoid trying to line up the Indian materials with modern ideas ("they discovered alcoholism two thousand years ago!"), for this would only impoverish our understanding of this impressive tradition, a collection of texts and ideas that we might even view as a resource of novel ways of thinking about and even actually dealing with intoxicating substances and intoxicated people (ourselves and others).

It is not the case that *anything goes*, however. Surā only has so many arms, and there were limits to the complexity and variety of liquor and intoxication in any given time, place, and social context. And when the penance for Brahmins drinking liquor, to give one example, could involve drinking boiling hot liquid until they died, it was important to define the contours of these substances and concepts, changeable as they may be. This explains, broadly speaking, the purpose of some of our texts where we meet the nitty-gritty of intoxicating substances, lists of drinks, ingredients, discussions of fermentation times, permitted additives, and other factors. If liquor is multiple, variable, and potent, and some people cannot drink, we need to establish precisely what counts as liquor.

Another translation problem: Sanskrit names for plants are notoriously confusing. Suggested modern equivalents for a single Sanskrit word are often numerous and inconsistent. Moreover, Projit Mukharji writes of the problems of "retro-botanizing" in the study of ancient plant names, a process that "reproduces a problematic divide—that between 'nature' as an ahistorical universal and 'culture' as a historical and regional variable."[30] He notes that historians of science have argued that botany is also historically contingent.[31] Does that mean we should not attempt to line up Sanskrit words with modern botanical names, as I have sometimes done in this book? The dangers of retro-botanizing are variable: we're on safer ground with rice than with certain herbs, never mind with plants that feature only in mythology. I don't think it unreasonable to translate some Sanskrit grain words as "a sort of grain, maybe barley" or what seem to be

Sanskrit words for coconut palm trees as "coconut palms." Such practices enable us to write a more nuanced economic history, drawing on what we know today about how people make palm toddy, for example. Putting modern scholarship into productive conversation with older texts does not imply that you assume one side embodies universal truth and the other is quaint, primitive indigenous lore, at the best blindly shuffling around the contours of science. The same applies to the way people dealt with liquor in the absence of the concept of alcohol—we are all finding ways to talk about these things, and the way we do so says a lot about all of us. Moreover, tentatively identifying some plants does not exclude writing about the other connotations of these words in the texts. And by accepting that certain words refer to distinct things, like words for grapes or opium, I can make more useful arguments about how people assimilated new substances into pre-existing intellectual frameworks, relating the Indian texts to images, archaeology, and texts from other parts of the world. So, while Mukharji's critique is valuable, you have to pick your fights, and in this book I will indulge in careful retro-botanizing.

Previous Scholarship

There is no other academic book on the general history of alcohol and drinking in early India, but there are some good articles.

One of the best, and the earliest I have used in this book, is by Rajendralal Mitra (1822–1891).[32] Mitra, from Kolkata, came from a prominent family. In addition to studying Indian languages and Persian, he immersed himself in the study of Greek, Latin, English, and German. In 1846 he was made secretary and librarian of the Asiatic Society of Bengal, and ultimately became the first Indian president of this institution. As a historian and philologist he wrote prodigiously on many topics. His work includes analytic studies, such as his article on the history of alcohol in India, alongside erudite editions of numerous texts. He was no stranger to controversial topics, once publishing a famous article on "Beef in Ancient India,"[33] and he wrote that "The Earliest Brahmin settlers were a spirit-drinking race, and indulged largely both in Soma beer and strong spirits."[34] It appears that Mitra himself was fond of a drink.[35] Though dated in some ways, his papers on drinking in ancient India remain thorough and useful resources for this topic, and his work is also a window on how ancient Indian drinking looked to an erudite Indian scholar in the nineteenth century.

Several other South Asian scholars have discussed alcohol in premodern South Asia, though this is not the place for a full bibliography. Historian Om Prakash provides copious data on liquor, as well as other substances like sugar, in his *Economy and Food in Ancient India*. Likewise, the late scholar of Indian food K. T. Achaya has much to say about drink.[36] Some excellent works by Indian scholars on the cultural history of India "as seen in various texts" are also useful for studying drink.[37] For drink in the Vedic period, Madhavi Bhaskar Kolhatkar's book on *surā* and the sacrifice has been invaluable.[38] For later periods, which I cover only briefly here, an article by Prasun Chatterjee is highly recommended—though that topic deserves a whole book.[39] For legal matters, I rely on the magisterial work of P. V. Kane.[40]

Works on alcohol in India by Western scholars include a thorough article on drink by the Finnish philologist Pentti Aalto, as well as a study of the concept of intoxication in Hinduism by Oliver Hellwig, this latter article introducing some statistical analysis of Sanskrit texts.[41] Also, Ludwig Habighorst amassed an excellent collection of miniature paintings (later than most of the material in this book) of drugs and alcohol that has been published.[42] The many scholars who have researched *soma* have produced a sophisticated body of work, and there are a number of good studies on various drugs.[43] All of these works have been useful in locating some of the primary sources pertinent to this book—though I shall not cite them at every turn, for reasons of space (and in many cases I encountered these sources in my own research too). The many works by Patrick Olivelle on Indian law and culture and by G. J. Meulenbeld on Indian medicine have been foundational to my primary research. Jiri Jakl has been working on a book on alcohol in pre-Islamic Java, and timing was such that I was able to share early drafts of many of the chapters in this book (especially on drinks) with him. Once both our books are published this should open the way to more comparative work.

I have also read extensively about the history of drugs and alcohol in other times and places, from Mexico to China, and this has informed my thinking in many places. Again, for reasons of space, I will not give a complete bibliography of those materials, though I should highlight Peter Clark's exemplary social history of the English alehouse and Michael Dietler's stimulating work on alcohol and feasting.[44] For understanding traditional fermentation methods, Keith Steinkraus's work has been invaluable.[45] For ancient alcoholic drinks, the writings of Patrick McGovern are inspiring, and although the materials in this book are not as old as the archaeological evidence he discusses, I hope this book is a complement to his work.[46]

Is This Book Offensive?

Some readers may worry that this book is offensive or provocative, given the subject matter. If and when those people read it, they will appreciate that this is not the case. This book is as much a study of the complexities of abstinence in Indian religion and culture as of the various ways in which people appreciated drink (though to understand abstinence properly, you must study drinks and drinking too). Ironically, other readers may be irritated by my caution in reflecting on the nature of "ancient psychedelics" and by my accepting, for example, a probable relatively late date for when cannabis became a prominent drug in South Asia.

Truly, my motivation for writing this book was not to sensationalize nor to debunk. I was frustrated by the inadequate or nonexistent accounts of alcohol in early India in global surveys of alcohol and drinking, along with the vague definitions of drinks in Sanskrit dictionaries. I started this project by looking at a chapter on a drinking party in a twelfth-century text called the *Mānasollāsa*, and I soon realized that I was not equipped to understand this world of recipes and processes. But if anything emerges from this book, it's that alcohol has always been complicated in South Asia. Throughout the region's history there have been many drinks, many ways of drinking, many attitudes toward intoxication, and various sophisticated reasons for abstaining. Even people who do not drink will be impressed by the ingenious methods that people in India devised to transform starches and sugars into intoxicating liquids.

The one thing I'm confident will irritate quite a few people, scholars and others, is that I question the presence of alcoholic distillation in ancient India. In particular, I have enormous doubts about John Marshall's so-called "still," an object illustrated in many a book and reconstructed in museums.[47] I believe that alcoholic distillation was not practiced in South Asia on any appreciable scale, if at all, until approximately the twelfth century CE, and I'm not at all convinced by the archaeological evidence discussed by scholars such as Marshall, Allchin, and Mahdihassan.[48] Whenever I talk about alcohol in India at a conference, someone inevitably mentions this ancient "still," and many people of all stripes are evidently quite attached to the idea of it. Rather than burden readers with a lengthy and negative digression on the topic, I ask that those who are interested please see my article about the issue for my reasoning.[49] Informally speaking, however, I must explain that my doubts about ancient distillation do not stem from a desire to denigrate the history of technology in South Asia—indeed, this whole book proves otherwise. To be frank, when I started writing this book I was excited about the "still" myself. I had visions of complex fermented drinks being distilled with all manner of herbs, spices, flowers, and resins into potent elixirs. But on closer inspection of the "still," I just couldn't bring myself to believe the archaeological arguments, nor any of the textual arguments associated with the archaeology. Fortunately, the positive evidence about complex saccharification and fermentation technologies more than make up for this for me, as someone who is personally enthusiastic about drinks.

One more thing: readers not familiar with Sanskrit texts might find the manner in which they often reflect a male gaze within the context of a patriarchal society quite shocking—certainly there are many materials in this book where women are presented as pleasure objects (or even as desireable-but-problematic vices) for men. And the assumed reader of texts is very often male (and high class). In many genres, this is simply how things are, often in the long term, though, as noted already, exactly how these fantasies and textual conventions relate to social history mostly eludes us. I have tried, however, where possible to amplify what little we can say about women in these texts, and, more generally, the topic of alcohol introduces us to a lot of people, cultural achievements, and contexts that are typically not emphasized or celebrated in scholarship on early India.

Translations, Organization, and Chapters

I discuss many genres, a range of topics, and a long historical period in this book. I work with primary texts in a variety of Indian languages, though mainly Sanskrit. Some translations are by other scholars; some I have done myself. Many of the texts belong to genres best studied by specialists, and thus sometimes I've used the translations of experts, modifying some words for drinks, drinking, and drunken states. This in no way suggests that the previous translations are defective but is simply because I want to be consistent with certain crucial words. Realistically, were I to do my own translations in such cases I could only really be said to be *retranslating*, and everyone who knows this field would be perfectly aware of this. In some cases, although there is already an excellent translation, I've done my own, usually because a particular passage offers such rich evidence that I feel it's important to provide a fresh, drink-centric version. In other cases I've done new translations, often far clunkier than previous ones, in order to present a literal, transparent version of the text in English. In quite a few cases there were no previous translations. Where I present other people's translations, I have also closely examined the original text in my analysis. For reasons of space I have mostly not included quotations from the texts in their original languages. Chapter and verse references are given in the endnotes.

I've tried to make this book accessible to several audiences: scholars of India who may not know much about the history and technology of alcohol; scholars of drugs and alcohol who may know little about South Asian history, culture, languages, and religions; and, last but not least, anyone who is interested in the topic. Of course, writing an academic book and trying to make it accessible to several audiences requires constant explanation of terms and contexts. Unfortunately, such glosses make the book longer, and in formulating such definitions there is a danger of being vague, inaccurate, or behind the times. However, I believe it is worth the risk if it makes this book a little less forbidding. On a related note, I have used diacritics for the "estates," *varṇa*s, of classical Indian social theory, apart from in the case of the "Brahmin" *varṇa*, as I have found the somewhat more correct "Brahman" can be quite confusing to non-specialists, who I hope might also appreciate this book.

Although I have sometimes attempted to contextualize and historicize the materials discussed (in a way that may seem rather primitive to people who study other regions and periods), I am not trying to describe a complete arc of the history of alcohol in India. There are a few more defined patches of time, and blurred, several-century-long moments of change, and a few stories, structures, and attitudes that endure over a long time. But readers should not try to extract a comprehensive picture from this book. That would require a lot more work and may not always be possible. This book is a rough map to several aspects of thinking and writing about drink and drinking in South Asia over almost two millennia.

The book is arranged in order of increasing complexity: I begin with the basic nature of various drinks and deal with more sophisticated, theoretical aspects of drinking cultures toward the end. Echoing an Indian style of chapter nomenclature found in a text such as the *River of Kings* (*Rājataraṅgiṇī*), in which the chapters are "Waves," and also corresponding to the nine drinks offered by the goddess Surā (Liquor) in a myth we'll examine later in the book, I have divided the book into nine "Cups" (though for clarity I'll sometimes refer to them as "chapters").

The book is also divided into two parts, or "Rounds." In Round One, I discuss the material nature of the drinks themselves and various drinking practices. In order to make this book of a reasonable length, I decided at a late stage to place much of the material on the drinks themselves in a series of articles and simply to summarize my main findings here. Interested scholars can refer to the articles for details of how I came to my conclusions and for many more primary sources.[50] I apologize for the inevitable, rather embarrassing number of self-citations.

To set the scene of drink culture in early India, I preface Round One with an "Aperitif" in the form of an amusing Buddhist story about two men who discover liquor.

Cup 1 focuses on the ancient, prototypical drink of premodern South Asia: *surā*. The word "*surā*" means a lot of things, but as a named drink in ancient texts it often refers to a drink brewed from cereal grains. I examine a very early "recipe" for *surā* from a text on Vedic rituals. Then I examine later discussions of grain-based *surā* from a variety of sources, up through the twelfth century CE.

Sugar lies at the heart of Cup 2. Whereas the drinks in Cup 1 involve processing a grain into a sugar that can then be fermented to make alcohol, the drinks in this Cup do not require that step. In some cases they even ferment spontaneously, as with toddy or grape wine. For that reason I consider most other early South Asian drinks in this chapter: sugarcane drinks, drinks called *āsavas*, *ariṣṭas*, and *maireya*, grape wine, palm toddy, honey mead, and jackfruit wine, as well as non-alcoholic, flavored drinks. I also discuss another substance here—betel (*pān*).

I then explore brewing and drinking. Cup 3 contains a study of *surā* breweries and *surā* shops, institutions analogous in some ways to the alehouses of premodern England. Here I analyze texts on communal drinking, public places where people both made and sold drinks to all comers, and festivals and fairs. Savory snacks were essential to all drinking cultures in early India, and I consider those here too. Open, public drinking is sometimes represented as "common" and morally dubious, and thus many of the sources I examine have a humorous or moralizing tone—they are not high poetry. One of the problems that arises in this book is the connection between social drinking contexts, textual genres, and moral perspectives. Can we determine anything about the ancient Indian *surā* houses from these biased sources?

A more elevated literary style goes hand in hand with what we might call more elite drinking. In Cup 4 I explore a range of texts on such drinking, which often involves servants, privacy, precious vessels, imported wine, erotic encounters, intense literary moods, and perfumed betel. Again, the conventions of genre are very much in evidence here, so this chapter is more a guide to those features of literature than a study of practice. Here I also look at ancient Indian "wine talk" and consider some didactic passages on how to drink properly, including a few from the *Kāmasūtra*. In addition, I examine the small number of Sanskrit texts devoted primarily to the pleasures and purposes of drinking.

Sticking with the question of how best to go about drinking, in Cup 5 I look at a sample of medical texts that deal with drink and drinking, in order to give the reader a taste of āyurvedic medical theories on how to drink correctly. These texts also discuss how drink affects the mind and body and how to treat people when drink makes them ill.

In Round Two, I discuss various theories about drinking—second-order reflections on liquor. How is drink presented in early Indian mythology, law, and ritual? As in the book as a whole, I progress in this section from simpler matters toward the materials and subjects that require the most background knowledge, such as law, morality, and Tantric rituals.

Many texts—moral, legal, medical, and Tantric—refer to the use of drink in a certain Vedic ritual, as well as to a number of myths and narratives connected to drink. In Cup 6 I explore the use and significance of drink in the Vedas, and I also briefly present the most common stories associated with drinking. These are of intrinsic interest, but it is also essential to know these stories and frameworks in order to understand the remainder of the book. Note that this chapter presents only an assortment of reference materials, rather than a complete collection.

Cup 7 contains a lengthy account of various approaches to drink and drinking that we today might classify as ethical or legal, often for religious reasons.

I begin with the Vedas, investigating what they have to say about the morality of drinking. Then I move on to explore texts that present drinking more as a vice of kings than as a sin—a practice to be moderated rather than shunned. Then I examine Hindu, Buddhist, and Jain legal and moral texts on drinking. The amount of material I could have considered here is vast, and I analyze only a tiny sample. In the case of texts concerning Brahmins and other Hindus, I give a historical account of the development of laws on drinking, but for Buddhism and Jainism I merely sketch some better known rules and theories. Finally, I examine some texts that satirize the morality (or hypocrisy) associated with drinking and abstinence.

Drink, like sex, in Tantric rituals tends to attract popular attention. In Cup 8 I present a brief, simplified account of how drink was used in a selection of Tantric rituals, mainly as presented in some (though by no means all) Hindu Tantras, and in particular in the writings of Abhinavagupta. This is difficult material, especially for those with no previous knowledge of the topic, so I've endeavored simply to give readers a small sense of how drink was used in some of these rituals and how some premodern Indian scholars explained this ritual use of liquor. Additionally, I explore a somewhat later text that contains a spectacular description of the personified goddess of liquor: Surā (and her nine cups). This text also mentions cannabis, and I use that as an opportunity to discuss that drug along with opium, considering some ways in which new substances were incorporated into Indian religious and intellectual traditions.

In Cup 9 I make a few brief observations on what happened next to the drinks, ideas, narratives, and rituals discussed in this book. These later changes are really a topic for another book and a different scholar, but it is interesting to note a few aspects of the long afterlife of ancient Indian drinking, especially as studies of alcohol in the colonial period don't typically focus on certain more esoteric Sanskrit sources from this time.

Finally, in the Digestif, I make some general observations.

Aperitif

Surā, the Prototypical Liquor of India

Surā is unquestionably the most important alcoholic drink of early India. It's mentioned in our earliest sources, the Vedas. Surā personified—the gender of this word in Sanskrit is feminine—is a goddess with her own mythology and iconography. Although in many religious and legal texts *surā* is a morally ambiguous substance, it (or "she") was the most conceptually significant alcoholic drink in ancient, early, and later medieval South Asia. Indeed, the importance of *surā* resonated in some circles through the eighteenth and nineteenth centuries CE.

As one would expect, the word "*surā*" is loaded with meanings. First, *surā* is a generic type of drink made with cereal grains. Sometimes grain-based *surā* drinks have other names, as "porter" refers to a type of beer. And in some legal and ritual texts, *surā* was carefully redefined to cover drinks made of other substances, such as sugarcane. "*Surā*" also frequently has a general sense of any intoxicating drink or liquor, what we nowadays call alcoholic drinks made by fermentation.[1] Anyone who has studied Sanskrit will have come across the word *surā*, though it's easy to feel confused about exactly what it means. To complicate matters more, unlike wine in Italy today, despite the word's ubiquity in older texts, people from India or visiting India may not have come across a drink called *surā*, nor any drinks that resemble the *surā*s of early India, at least not in urban bars.[2]

What was grain *surā* made of, how was it made, and what was the finished product like? When I started work on this book, the nature of *surā* seemed relatively straightforward: in the narrowest usage of the word, it was an alcoholic drink made from grains or starches of some sort, so a type of beer; this contrasted with alcoholic drinks made from sugary raw materials, such as grapes or sugarcane. Yet on closer examination, I realized that, just as with beer and wine in Europe, *surā* has taken on many forms over the centuries in the vast region of South Asia. This complexity is evident even from our meager surviving written sources. The historical reality of *surā*-type drinks must have been even more spectacularly varied.

Before we enter the complicated world of *surā*, let's begin with a story about how humans invented, or rather discovered, *surā*. This story is part of a

An Unholy Brew. James McHugh, Oxford University Press. © Oxford University Press 2021.
DOI: 10.1093/oso/9780199375936.003.0002

previous-birth story about the Buddha, a genre of text called *Jātakas*. This one is called the *Kumbha Jātaka*, or "Previous-Birth Story of the Jar."[3] Ascertaining the exact date of the text is difficult. This passage is from the prose narrative part of the *Jātaka*, which at the latest took its final form around the fifth or sixth century CE.[4] For our purposes, an approximate date of the early to mid-first millennium CE is sufficient. We'll return to this *Jātaka* later in the book to see what it has to say about the dangers of drinking, but for now we'll simply look at how *surā* is made, what sort of people make it, and what it does to people:

> In the past, when Brahmadatta was reigning as king in Benares, a forester, an inhabitant of the kingdom of Kāsī, called Sura [a masculine form of the word *surā*, the drink in question] went to the Himalaya to look for goods. A tree had grown there, and at a point that was the height of a man it was divided into three. In between the three parts there was a hole the size of a *surā* jar (*surācāṭi-*), and when it rained this filled with water. Surrounding this were chebulic myrobalan (*harīṭakī*),[5] emblic myrobalan (*āmalakī*),[6] and black pepper (*marica*) plants, and their ripe fruit broke off [into the hole]. Close to this was some rice growing wild. Parrots collected the ears of rice from there and sat eating them on the tree, and, while they were eating, winter paddy (*sāli*)[7] and dehusked rice (*taṇḍula*) fell in there. And thus, brewing/cooking (*paccamāna*) by the heat of the sun, the water became a red (*salohitavaṇṇaṃ*) color.[8] In the hot season thirsty flocks of birds drank this and, intoxicated, fell at the base of the tree, where, after sleeping for a short time, they flew off chirping. And palm-civets (*rukkhasunakha*),[9] monkeys, and other animals also behaved in the very same way.
>
> The forester saw this, and thinking, "If this were poison they would die, but after sleeping a short while they go on their merry way—this is not poison," he drank some himself, became intoxicated, and got the desire to eat meat. Then he made a fire, killed the partridges, chickens, and so on that had fallen at the base of the tree, cooked them over the embers, and, waving one hand around in the air and eating meat with the other, stayed right there for one or two days. Near that place lived an ascetic called Varuṇa. One day the forester approached him, and then it occurred to him, "I should drink this drink together with the ascetic!" He filled a bamboo tube and, taking cooked meat, went to the leaf-hut, saying, "Sir, please drink this drink," and, both eating meat, they drank.
>
> And so, on account of being discovered by Sura and Varuṇa, that drink got the names "*surā*" and "*vāruṇī*" [common names for *surā* the drink].
>
> The pair of them, thinking "Now, here's a scheme!" filled bamboo tubes and took them by means of a carrying pole to a neighboring town, and had it announced to the king that "The drinking-house men (*pānāgārikā*)[10] are here!" The king sent for them, and they brought him the drink. And then the king

drank it two or three times and was intoxicated—this was only enough for him for one or two days. So he asked them: "Is there more?"

"There is, your Majesty."

"Where?"

"In the Himalayas, your Majesty."

"So then, bring it."

They went there, and, having brought it back once or twice, they thought, "We cannot constantly go." Noting the additive mixture (*sambhāre*), bundling up the bark of that tree, etc., they made all the herbal additive mixture (*sabbasambhāre*) and made *surā* in the town. The townspeople drank *surā* and became careless/negligent (*pamādam āpannā*) and miserable (*duggatā*), and the town seemed deserted. The drinking-house men fled that place and went to Benares and had it announced to the king that "The drinking-house men are here!" The king sent for them and gave them wages, and they made *surā* there too, and in the same way that town was also destroyed. They fled from there to Sāketa, and from Sāketa they went to Sāvatthi.

At that time there was a king called Sabbamitta ["Friend to Everyone"] in Sāvatthi, and he showed them favor, asking, "What are you in need of?" They said, "The money for the herbal additives, and rice flour (*sālipiṭṭhena*), and five hundred jars (*cāṭi*),"[11] and [the king] had everything given to them. They prepared *surā* in five hundred jars and tied one cat next to every jar in order to guard the jars.[12] They [the cats] were suffering, and at the time when [the *surā*] was taken out, they drank *surā* flowing in the bellies of the jars and fell asleep drunk.[13] Some mice came along, ate their ears, noses, whiskers, and tails, and went away. The superintendents announced to the king, "The cats died after drinking *surā*." The king, thinking, "They must be poison-makers," had the two men's heads cut off. They died while saying, "It's *surā*, your Highness! It's a sweet/innocuous (*madhura*) drink, your Highness!"[14] After he had them executed, the king gave the order: "Smash the jars." But the cats, after digesting (*jiṇṇāya*) the *surā*, got up and wandered around, playing. Having seen them, they [the superintendents] announced it to the king. The king said, "If this were poison they would have died—it must be an innocuous drink (*madhura*), so let's drink it," and he had the town decorated, and had a pavilion made in the royal courtyard. And, sitting down on the royal couch, on which a white parasol had been erected, in the ornamented pavilion, surrounded by a group of favorites, he began to drink *surā* . . .[15]

At which point the god Indra, who is here the Buddha in a previous birth, appears on the scene carrying a jar (*kumbha*) of *surā* and gives a speech on the evils of drink, in a passage we'll examine later in this book.

From the description of the spontaneous production of alcohol and the entrepreneurial men who discover this new drink, hawking it around the country and destroying town after town, through the image of the mouse-ravaged, drunkard cats, this story entertains as well as educates. The long speech on the evils of drink that Indra delivers next is far more sobering.

This story is framed within another, probably later "story of the present," composed as an introduction to the *Jātaka* prose story "of the past":

> The Master [i.e., the Buddha], dwelling at Jetavana, related this about five hundred *surā*-drinking women who were friends of Visākhā. Now, when a *surā* festival (*surāchaṇe*) was announced at Sāvatthi, when their husbands had stopped celebrating the festival, these five hundred women who had prepared strong ["sharp"] *surā* (*tikkhasuram*), said, "Let us enjoy the festival,"[16] and all went to see Visākhā and said to her, "Friend, let's enjoy the festival!" and when she said, "This is a *surā* festival—I shan't drink *surā*," they said, "You offer a gift to the Supreme Buddha, and *we* will celebrate." "Fine," she agreed, and taking their leave she invited the teacher and gave a great donation . . .[17]

Women, married householder women, are brewing here. This was for a *surā* festival, which their husbands were enjoying.[18] Although the story provides a fitting occasion for the Buddha to upbraid the women when they get drunk, dance, and sing in front of him,[19] there are many other ways in which one could have set up such a story, and it is notable that female brewers and drinkers, as well as drinking festivals, feature here. Of course this may arise more from conventional representations of gender than from actual practice; it may be a warning against unleashed lascivious women who get drunk and behave "shamefully" in public. Yet we should not ignore the fact that in a number of sources we'll see female brewers and drinkers depicted as routine, if not very "respectable," features in the world of the texts.

The story of the two men discovering *surā* tells us a lot about *surā* the drink. It does not offer a technical recipe, but we get a good sense of the basic ingredients and process, which was presumably what people were expected to know about *surā* at that time and place, just as a writer now might describe beer as being made from barley, hops, yeast, and water, omitting the complexities of the brewing process. The text also has echoes of terminology associated with *surā* in texts on monastic law. Not only is *surā* brewing probably simplified here, but the story shows how people might have imagined a primeval *surā*. We also learn how people imagined the ripple effects of *surā*: first the discovery of this strange drink, then how it got two of its common names, then the eventual trade in *surā*, then social chaos, and, finally, humans receiving divine wisdom on the dangers of drinking. The story implies that there was a peaceful time when there was no *surā*. Its discovery went hand in hand with violence (killing the sleeping animals), desire for pleasure and profit, and expanding social destruction. Even the men who discovered *surā* met an unfortunate end. Thus, it seems, concerns about drinking have been around for almost as long as drink itself.

In this Buddhist text, it is humans who create *surā*. They are driven by unwholesome desires, and they make the world a worse place. *Surā* in this story occurs naturally, in a mundane manner, and is discovered by an ordinary, greedy man called Sura. This contrasts with the divine origin of *surā* in many Hindu texts, as well as with a narrative in which Kṛṣṇa's brother Balarāma encounters Liquor personified in a tree hollow.[20] Despite these contrasts, however, Indra's speech on the evils of drink in the Buddhist text has much in common with Hindu and Jain texts on the vice of drinking. Thus the resemblances between this passage and other texts and religious traditions are various and complicated.

If we read the parable as a social critique, then the perceived problem here is drinking large quantities of *surā* at festivals and in royal drinking bouts—periodic disruptions of productivity and responsibility. We're not dealing with a problem like today's medicalized phenomenon of alcoholism. Significantly, *surā* is not represented as bad in itself. It is delightful to those who drink it; the problem lies in what it makes you do and neglect when drunk.

The invention of beer-like drinks still fascinates scholars of the history of alcohol. The most famous discussion of the topic was a lively symposium called "Did Man Once Live by Beer Alone?" in *American Anthropologist* in 1953, in which scholars discussed whether the first domesticated cereals were used for making bread or beer.[21] In this book I have no intention of stepping into those debates. Readers should consult the works of Patrick McGovern for that.[22] Here I discuss drinks and drinking as attested in later, more documented periods. I shall, however, note two important points here. First, the ancient *surā* recipes that we'll see in the next chapter are early, detailed accounts of making an alcoholic drink from grains, and archaeologists might find them of interest. Second, the "bread or beer?" question is not entirely pertinent in the South Asian case. Many, if not most, *surā*s were probably fermented in the form of a grainy mash, not as a filtered "wort"; filtering instead took place after fermentation. Also, some early medical texts classify alcoholic drinks alongside other types of fermented grain gruels.[23] Thus, in early South Asia, porridgy, fermented grain mixtures, ranging from sour rice gruels to the alcoholic *surā* mash, are all members of a complex family of fermented grain preparations, which would have been nutritious whether or not they were intoxicating. So the question of "bread or beer" does not seem to apply here, at least in this historical period.

ROUND ONE
DRINKS AND DRINKING

CUP 1
Surā Made from Grains

Brewing with Grains

Surā is the alcoholic drink mentioned in the earliest Indic sources, such as the *Ṛgveda*. Although, as noted, "*surā*" (f.) has a number of meanings, in its narrowest sense it refers to a fermented alcoholic drink made from grains.[1] Thus, as in ancient Mesopotamia, the primary alcoholic drink in the earliest Indian written sources was made from grains.

Making alcohol from grains is not straightforward. Fermenting sugars, as with grape juice, is simpler in theory, especially in a traditional setting where microorganisms present in the environment, such as yeasts, convert the sugars into alcohol. With grains, you need to convert the starch to sugar before any significant alcoholic fermentation can take place.[2] This saccharification requires enzymes, and humans have exploited various sources for them from ancient times (while not, of course, using the concept of "enzymes" until recently). In European brewing, sprouted, malted grains (especially barley) are used. These contain saccharifying enzymes, and are sometimes mixed with another, unmalted, adjunct grain that the malts then also saccharify. In much of Asia, saccharifying molds are used, often in conjunction with yeasts and other microorganisms, to achieve saccharification and fermentation simultaneously (e.g., in Chinese *huang jiu*). These microorganisms are often stored in the form of "cakes" that have been inoculated and dried, sometimes with herbs added, and frequently this sort of brewing is achieved in a solid or semisolid state. Cooked rice, for example, might be inoculated with a "ferment" cake; the combined substances then liquefy during fermentation, so that the final drink drips out or is squeezed out of the residual mass. Understanding this latter point is vital to understanding how *surā* was made. Over its long history, Indic *surā* brewing has exploited both malted grains and molds for saccharification, as we'll see later. Finally, human saliva has been used to saccharify grains, as in Peruvian *chicha*, though this method was not used for *surā*.[3]

Many traditional or premodern methods for alcoholic fermentation are complex, with several stages and ingredients, all known by distinct words. People brewing with these methods understood the processes in completely different ways from our modern understanding of enzymes, yeast, et cetera. "Traditional" German beers pride themselves on simplicity and purity, but ancient drinks were

An Unholy Brew. James McHugh, Oxford University Press. © Oxford University Press 2021.
DOI: 10.1093/oso/9780199375936.003.0003

by no means always simple and "pure," as archaeologist Patrick McGovern has shown.[4] If we approach descriptions of making *surā* with modern or Western brewing theories in mind, we may fail to see what is going on, so here we'll briefly consider some traditional forms of brewing in India and elsewhere.

Apong is a drink made by the Mising people of Northeast India.[5] One variety of *apong* is made by adding ashes of rice husks to cooked rice, along with starter cakes. The semisolid mixture is fermented in a jar and then placed in a cone-shaped bamboo basket lined with leaves and suspended over a vessel. Water is poured over the mixture, and the *apong* drips out of this filter cone.

Another, simpler drink, *handia* or *haria*, is brewed in parts of Odisha and West Bengal. This drink is made by mixing small starter cakes (made with rice flour and herbs that have been mixed and left to develop certain flora with fermenting powers) called "*ranu*" to cooked rice. The mixture is fermented in jars and can then be strained, or diluted and then strained.[6]

Sudanese *merissa* is made with sorghum, which is treated in several ways: fermented, toasted, re-fermented, half-cooked into a paste, and well-cooked into a paste. Notably, in this brewing process the substances and preparations at every stage are referred to by different words.[7] Like these traditional methods of brewing, ancient Indian brewing is often complex and quite unlike European beer brewing, with its own distinctive terminologies.

Surā in Vedic Sources

As we'll see later, *surā* is sometimes denigrated in the Vedas, a collection of ancient Sanskrit texts that contain hymns, liturgies, ritual instructions, and some metaphysical speculation.[8] By contrast, *soma*, an apparently psychoactive, not fermented or alcoholic drink (which I discuss in an Appendix), is the most prestigious drink in these texts, offered to the gods and shared with them in some major rituals. *Surā*, however, is only *both* ritually brewed and offered to gods in a ritual called the Sautrāmaṇī, which I'll examine later in the book. Here, I just consider the brewing process given for this ritual.

How do we know about this ancient drink? Fortunately there are several sets of detailed instructions for brewing *surā* in ritual manuals, *Śrauta Sūtra*s, associated with Vedic rituals. The sacred utterances, mantras, used in the Sautrāmaṇī ritual and two hymns in the *Atharvaveda* also allude to the stages and components of *surā* brewing.[9]

What I shall for convenience's sake call "Vedic *surā*" is made according to a set schema, a set list of ingredients, and a relatively fixed set of equipment. Later *surā*s were made with a quite different, simpler schema. Although the recipes in the *Śrauta Sūtra*s vary in how they interpret (and update?) the schema given in the older liturgies, all versions are recognizable brewing processes, and we might even infer some aspects of the process implied by the brewing schema contained in the oldest sources. As regards dates, the *Atharvaveda* that mentions this schema probably dates from a little before 1000 BCE.[10] The earliest known "recipe" is in the *Baudhāyana Śrauta Sūtra*, of uncertain but early date, perhaps around 500 BCE.[11]

The elements of *surā* in Vedic sources—both the liturgy and the instructions in ritual manuals—are as follows:

1. a principal grain or grains.
2. "*māsara*," often interpreted in the *Śrauta Sūtra*s as a mixture of liquid with a toasted grain product.
3. "*nagnahu*," sometimes obtained ready-made, maybe some sort of starter. Interpretations in the ritual manuals vary.
4. "*tokman*" and "*śaṣpa*," which are sprouted grains, probably functioning like malts to saccharify the grains.

Compared to many forms of traditional brewing, this is not a complex set of elements. These things are obtained or prepared; ground, roasted, or cooked separately; and then put together, at which point they transform into *surā*. Separately they do not become *surā*, but together they do, and I suggest that this is why the word for fermentation (*saṃdhāna* and related forms) in this and later contexts also means "putting together." For example, in the *Āpastamba Śrauta Sūtra* the moment when the *surā* components are put together is called "the time of putting together" (*saṃdhānakāle*), which simultaneously means "when [the *surā*] is fermented/brewed."[12] *To brew is to assemble in Sanskrit*, and *surā* is thus an intrinsically compound substance.

When the ingredients are put together, we should assume that they are semisolid, cooked grains with other additives.[13] This mass is then placed in a structure called a *kārotara*, in some places described as a hide-lined bamboo frame. Sometimes the *surā*-to-be is put in a *kārotara* placed over a pot to drip into as it ferments, set by a fire. Sometimes the fermenting mixture is placed in a hide-lined pit, the *kārotara* is immersed in this, and the liquefied fermented mixture oozes up (as with the bamboo *yongsu* used in Korean brewing). I'm convinced that the liquefied mixture, the fluid, that emerges from the fermenting grain mass is the substance, also a drink, called *parisrut*, which is then filtered in/into another type of pot (*sata*) to make the finished *surā*. This *parisrut*, "flowing around," *surā*-to-be is thus an intermediate substance comparable to Japanese *doburoku*—unfiltered *sake*. Texts from this early period in India also mention a substance called *kīlāla*, connected to *surā* brewing, made using grains and herbs and apparently sweet. Perhaps it was a product of a process that involved more saccharification than fermentation, like Japanese *amazake*, or a product made with the lees after straining.[14]

Here is the version of *surā* brewing given in the *Baudhāyana Śrauta Sūtra*:

> BŚS 17.31... Then they pound half of the paddy [rice with the husk on]. Then, placing an earthen pan upon the *gārhapatya* fire[15] they parch the other half [of the paddy]. Such of these as burst open become *lājā*. Such, indeed, as do not burst open, they are *tarī*. Placing a new jar (*navāṃ kumbhīm*) over the *gārhapatya* fire, they cook it [rice] like moist/wet rice (*prodakam ivaudanaṃ*) [in it]. Then they pour it [i.e., the wet-cooked rice] out into a [pot called] *kaṭhina* or *pājaka* and hang up [that pot]. Then they pound the parched ones (*bhṛgṇān*). Of those, they scatter the ones that are small and the *tarī* [i.e., unburst roast paddy] into the scum/overflowings (*utseke*) [of the rice now in the hung-up pot?] This is called *māsara*. One should then take a measuring vessel (*mānam*) and measure out one [measure] of *śaṣpa* [spouted barley], two of *tokman* [sprouted rice], three of *lājā* [the popped rice], and four of *nagnahu*. Then he completes the cooked rice by scattering with those powders and besprinkling with the *māsara* [liquid]. 17.32 And recite *mantras*...[16]
>
> 17.32 continued... Then, taking the stool along the east of the *āhavanīya* fire[17] he puts it down towards the south. He puts the support (*iṇḍva*) upon the stool (*āsandī*), the jar (*kumbha*) upon the support, and the *kārotara* [fermentation-drainage structure] on the jar. Then he heaps up the cooked rice [presumably mixed with the other ingredients] all around the *kārotara*. Having covered it [*kumbha? kārotara?* both?] he touches it [uttering] the *mantra*... Mixed, it remains for three [nights]. [For] it is said in the *Brāhmaṇa* "The *soma*, which is purchased, remains (undisturbed) for three nights."[18]

Another section, probably somewhat later in date,[19] explains some of the technical terms:

> The *surā* for the Sautrāmaṇī [sacrifice] is a quarter *kiṇva* or a fifth. "*Śaṣpa* and *tokman*" [mean] *śaṣpa* is of barley and *tokman* is of rice, and *nagnahu* is urad lentils (*māṣāḥ*). Then the *kārotara* should be made of wood or of split bamboo (*vaidala*) or clay, and it should be covered with hide (*carman*) on all sides.[20]

Kiṇva is the word for the fermentation agent used in later *surā* brewing, and it may here denote the collection of ingredients added to the cooked grains. The authors here may have intended to explain an already archaic terminology with words that later dominated descriptions of brewing in Sanskrit. The *māsara* infusion of toasted grains makes sense as a way to deliver color and flavoring evenly in a solid-state fermentation process; if a liquid wort had been used, the brewers could have added dry materials directly, as one can with hops.

After three nights, the fermented mixture is filtered in a vessel lined with a hair sieve and used in the ritual.[21] *Surā* was sometimes said to be reddish, as we saw in the "Previous-Birth Story of the Jar." In one hymn that describes *surā* brewing in the *Atharvaveda*, where we also read of the process involving sprouted grains (*tokman*, *śaṣpa*) and *nagnahu* starter (?), it is said that a blood-red substance (*rudhiraṃ*) is in the *surā* jar, that the drinkers are red, and that drinking incites them to violence (the hymn invokes *surā* to intoxicate and cause violence), something we also see associated with *surā* and drinking in the long term.[22] Perhaps the ruddy color of this early *surā* is from the toasted grains in the *māsara*. Note that *surā* is not distilled here—the instructions are clear, and there is no need to postulate stills to explain all of the steaming, dripping, and flowing of the fluids. Also, a distilled drink would not be colored unless someone added substances like herbs, or color-imparting molecules were imparted by storage containers.[23]

Other *Śrauta Sūtras* define the process and components of brewing *surā* in several ways, perhaps because of distinct traditions, whether of brewing or ritual practice, but I think it reasonable to conclude that this earliest form of brewing used cooked grains, to which were added a starter, perhaps an infusion of toasted grains, plus sprouted grains that probably functioned as malts. The *nagnahu* may have functioned like the ferment cake starters that we see in Asia today, though that is hard to be sure. Certainly some of the components here must have aided fermentation, and it is possible (though most uncertain) that there was fungal saccharification in addition to that produced by the malts. The grains used were probably rice, barley, and perhaps a sort of millet, though equating ancient words for grains with modern grains is fraught with difficulties. One might argue that the *Śrauta Sūtras*' descriptions of brewing were distorted to fit the older ritual terminology (or to echo elements of the *soma* rite), but there are significant commonalities among the instructions that seem to reflect a cultural memory of the process, if not a ritualized preservation of the older techniques. Moreover, this is such a plausible brewing method that I don't think it has been adjusted enormously to echo the *soma* process, which is profoundly different in terminology and method.

At this point I should briefly introduce *soma*. Although the exact nature of the *soma* plant is much debated, the basic method of preparing the *soma* drink is clear. *Soma* was made with plant stems that were wetted and crushed with stones. The expressed juice was filtered and mixed with milk, with no time to ferment. Therefore, it was prepared in a manner somewhat like the Polynesian drink called *kava*. *Soma* is raw and does not need time to "transform" after the combination of several essential components. (For a short introduction to *soma* aimed at non-specialists, with more detailed comments on the theories that it might have been alcoholic, see the Appendix.) Despite the major differences between *soma* and *surā*, some features of the Vedic brewing instructions for *surā* may indeed have been adjusted or highlighted to create parallels with *soma* pressing, which is compared explicitly to *surā* brewing in the liturgy of the Sautrāmaṇī ritual (see Chapter 6).

Vedic *surā* was a complex grain preparation, and although the exact nature of its components must remain uncertain, it definitely used sprouted grains, no doubt as saccharifying malts, like the beers produced in ancient Mesopotamia.[24] Around the time of the *Atharvaveda* (c. 1000 BCE), this appears to have been the dominant method used for brewing, though by the late first millennium BCE onward, the process may have given way to the "*kiṇva* process," as suggested by the reference to that substance in the passage given earlier. Later *surā* brewing uses this simpler *kiṇva* process, and from the ingredients listed in later sources we can infer that later *surā* was mostly made along the lines of grain-based drinks found elsewhere in Asia, with no malts involved.

It is worth repeating that from the point of view of the brewers (who did not, of course, think in terms of enzymes or microorganisms), *surā* was made by taking a number of non-intoxicating items, putting them together, and leaving them until they became fluid and intoxicating.

The Variety of Later *Surās*

Surā made from grains continued to be a major category of drink for a long time, with many varieties described in our sources, including texts on statecraft, medicine, and a guide to royal conduct, among others.

In these later texts, the Vedic brewing schema vanishes. The newer method uses grains and the fermenting agent *kiṇva*. Since these are the primary ingredients, and since the recipe we possess for *kiṇva* does not contain malts, we can infer that *kiṇva* was probably like modern Asian microbial inoculants that both saccharify and ferment. Grains and *kiṇva* are put together, and, as we've seen: to put together is to ferment. There was no concept of alcohol as a substance appearing, but rather an understanding that a new property arises when certain things are combined/fermented. In some recipes, an additive called *saṃbhāra* is used. Cognate with the *sambar* of South Indian cooking, this term, seen in the "Previous-Birth Story of the Jar" and also in texts on cookery, refers to an herb/spice additive mixture, somewhat like the "gruit" added to British beers before the introduction of hops.[25] As for the herbs, both in the *kiṇva* and the *saṃbhāra*, we should be very wary of always assuming there is some scientific or other rationale that makes obvious sense to us today for their presence in these mixtures, whether this be to do with color, flavor, fermentation, or even psychoactive properties. Especially for the *saṃbhāra* additive mixture, I think flavor, fermentation, and perhaps some folk-pharmacological notions (such as English "tonic") were understood to be the primary purpose of the herbs, as indicated by the fictional *saṃbhāra* of pepper and myrobalans we saw earlier in the "Previous-Birth Story of the Jar" (*Kumbha Jātaka*).

A Sanskrit text on statecraft called the *Arthaśāstra* contains a chapter about the state Superintendent of Liquor (*surā*), which we will return to often.[26] The *Arthaśāstra* is our earliest detailed source on the production and consumption of intoxicating drinks, early medical sources being vague on the details. The *Arthaśāstra* might arguably be read as a realistic account of the production of liquor in early India.[27] Patrick Olivelle suggests that the sources used to compose the earlier parts of the text (such as the passage on brewing) date from between the middle of the first century BCE and the middle of the first century CE.[28] As for location, the section we're dealing with here was probably composed in North India, and we may tentatively place it toward the west, around today's Gujarat and northern Maharashtra.[29] The *Arthaśāstra* was evidently popular for some centuries, being known to authors producing a variety of texts, from the *Kāmasūtra* to literary texts in the early to middle centuries of the first millennium CE. By the ninth century CE, however, writers seem to have become largely ignorant of this text.[30]

As one would expect from a text concerned in part with economic matters, there is an emphasis in the *Arthaśāstra* on what materials are used and in what quantity. Six principal drinks are described, including two types of *surā*. Note in the translations that follow that *droṇa*, *āḍhaka*, and *prastha* are units of measurement. These are Olivelle's translations, modified, with the breaks added for clarity:

> With regard to *medaka* [a type of grain *surā*], *prasannā* [a type of grain *surā*], *āsava* [sugar and juice based], *ariṣṭa* [sugar-based medicinal liquor], *maireya* [sugar-and-spice liquor with secondary fermentation], and *madhu* [grape wine]:
>
> One *droṇa* of water,
> half an *āḍhaka* of dehusked rice,
> and three *prasthas* of *kiṇva*
> is the mixture (*yoga*) for ***medaka***.
>
> Twelve *āḍhakas* of crushed grain (*piṣṭa*)
> and either five *prasthas* of *kiṇva* or the additive mixture (*saṃbhāra*) of its class
> mixed with the peel/bark and fruit of *kramuka*[31]
> is the mixture for ***prasannā*** ["clear"].[32]

We also get the quantities for "starter" (*kiṇva*) and herbal additive (*saṃbhāra*):

> One *droṇa* of urad dal (*māṣa*) pulp, either raw or cooked, and one third more than that of dehusked rice, mixed with one-*karṣa* portions of the ingredients beginning with *moraṭā*,[33] is the composition (*bandha*) of *kiṇva*.
>
> For *medaka* and *prasannā* [the two types of grain *surā*], the mixture (*yoga*) for the additive mixture (*saṃbhāra*) consists of five *karṣas* each of . . . (a list of herbs).
>
> *Kaṭaśarkarā*[34] mixed with *madhuka* decoction/extract produces a clear color.[35]

Kiṇva consists mainly of lentils and grains, with many herbs, and the additive mixture is just herbs. *Prasannā* means "clear," and the final mixture is used for clarifying *prasannā* or perhaps both drinks. The last two herbs in the *saṃbhāra*, the additive mixture, are types of pepper, also used in a drink called *maireya* (discussed later). Black pepper (*marica*) was in the *surā* that the hunter discovered in the tree trunk in the "Previous-Birth Story of the Jar." So some drinks in this period might have been spicy. We also learn:

> The mixture of raw materials (*yoga*) for *prasannā* is used for white *surā*.[36]

And a few lines later:

> Householders should be permitted to produce white *surā* during festive occasions, and for medicinal purposes *ariṣṭa* or other kinds. During festivals, fairs, and excursions, he [the Superintendent of *Surā*] should grant a *surā* license (*saurika*) for four days.[37]

White *surā* is probably a simpler drink and could be made on a small scale by householders engaged in intermittent brewing. Perhaps it was a non-clarified drink, and one commentator states that it differs from *prasannā* (clear) *surā* in that it lacks the herbal additive (which may well have added color).[38]

After this comes a line with a list of adjectives that refer to several types of *surā*, though there has been some disagreement, even among commentators, about how many types of *surā* are in question here.[39] I present my own tentative translation:

> Mango *surā* has a high proportion of juice, or great *surā* has a high proportion of seed (*bīja*),[40] or has herbal additive.[41]

These drinks are defined in terms of varying amounts of additives, and one by the addition of mango juice. Then the chapter gives a lengthy list of herbs that can clarify jars of these kinds of *surā* for the king, as well as instructions to add a quantity of sugar syrup (*phāṇita*) in order to increase sweetness.[42]

Several grain *surās* with different names and different ingredients are mentioned here, some called *surā* and some not. And the title of this chapter in the *Arthaśāstra* uses the word "*surā*" in the broad sense of "liquor." The main components of *surā* in this context are grains, water, starter (*kiṇva*), and sometimes an herbal additive (*saṃbhāra*), as well as clarifying additives. Some *surās* are apparently complex drinks made on a large scale. White *surā*, in contrast, is made by householders in a few days. Given the existence of a *surā* called "clear" (*prasannā*) and the additives that clarify the drink, we know that drinkers probably appreciated the visual appearance of *surā*.

We learn nothing of brewing methods or tools here, but combining this text with other descriptions and our knowledge of brewing methods, we can imagine the process. Presumably, cooked grains were mixed with a previously prepared inoculant-ferment (*kiṇva*), perhaps along with herbs, which might have been made into a decoction. After fermentation, the drink was probably extracted by dripping, squeezing, filtering, and maybe dilution. Possibly the herbs were added at that stage. Sometimes it was clarified. No malt is used in the *surā* described here, only grains and *kiṇva*, so saccharification must have been achieved through molds. The special permit for householders to make white *surā* for festivals (*saurika*) was granted for just four days, the number of days needed to make a weaker rice beer such as *handia* today (assuming the permit applied to production).

The amounts of grain and other materials listed here would produce relatively large volumes of *surā* and other drinks, if we include typical relative quantities of water, and this is only the basic unit of production.[43] Also, the *kiṇva* and *saṃbhāra* were made on a large scale, presumably to create a supply ready for use.

The Remarkable Ferment—*Kiṇva*

Kiṇva was thought to be a remarkable agent, a quality perhaps reflected in its etymology.[44] It was added to grains, and these two components, neither of them intoxicating, nevertheless became an intoxicating drink. Rice plus rice just makes more rice, or sour moldy rice after a few days. Rice plus *kiṇva*, managed correctly, makes a mind-befuddling substance, a desirable drug, a strictly forbidden intoxicant. With no concept of alcohol/ethanol as a new *substance* appearing in the liquor, the combination of grains and *kiṇva* appeared to develop a new property, somewhat like our concept of an emergent property: the power to intoxicate. By contrast, a sugary liquid such as sugarcane juice ferments when left to its own devices (though one can still use additives). And *soma* is always *soma*, whether a plant or a pressed drink. *Surā*, however, arises from things that are not *surā*, and comes into being gradually (with a halfway state/substance called *parisrut* in early sources).

In the *Arthaśāstra*, the Superintendent of *Surā* organizes the trade in *surā* (probably in the sense of "liquor") and *kiṇva*.[45] We also learn that "women and children should do the gathering of [materials for] *surā* and *kiṇva*."[46] Although *kiṇva* ingredients were relatively ordinary, preparing it probably required skill, and given its spectacular powers, it was a commodity that had to be regulated.

The concept of *kiṇva* was important, similar to the concept of a "catalyst" today. *Kiṇva* ferment-starter was valuable as a model for understanding other things because it was an essential part of a compound of entities that, once assembled, developed new but predictable properties. In particular, *kiṇva* is mentioned in accounts of the Cārvākas, a frequently reviled group of philosophical materialists who are said to have denied the existence of God, souls, and rebirth. A famous fourteenth-century doxographical text, the *Sarvadarśanasaṃgraha*, explains that this group argued that consciousness arises from the elements alone, in the form of a body, without the addition of an extra, imperceptible, soul-like entity: "In that case the elements, earth and the rest, are the four elements; from them alone, transformed into the form of a body, consciousness is produced, as the power to intoxicate [is produced] from *kiṇva* [when *surā*-components are assembled]."[47]

The materialists' statements, or at least the statements attributed to them by other writers, often have a satirical flavor, anti-brahminical and anti-Hindu. Either they were audacious, or there was a wry, almost masochistic, rhetorical ingenuity in the orthodox demonization of them. One can read this image of consciousness being like *surā* as similarly polemic: not only does it suggest that mind/consciousness is merely a product of the elements, but it envisions consciousness emerging from the material elements just as the boozy power of *surā* arises from ferment and grains. *Surā*, forbidden to Brahmins, is thus presented as a perfect model for understanding a key attribute of the absolute/soul in several Hindu philosophical systems. Liquor, it should be remembered, was associated with sensuous pursuits, as was betel-chewing, and Cārvākas apparently used the production of a red color from the components of betel as a similar model.[48] These analogies are thus especially fitting, since the materialists were often represented as privileging the pursuit of pleasure.

A brewing analogy not involving *kiṇva* also occurs in a Jain explanation of the manner in which subtle particles bond to the soul, becoming "karmic matter." This bonding and transformation into karmic matter takes place automatically in the presence of activities and passions, trapping the immaterial soul in the world of rebirth.[49] Akalaṅka (an eighth-century-CE Digambara Jain) explains that particles become karmic matter when in the presence of a soul with passions, quite spontaneously, like fermentation:

> Just as there is a transformation into the state of liquor (*madirā*) for various liquids,[50] seeds, flowers, and fruits placed in a certain type of vessel . . .[51]

Likewise particles of matter (*pudgala*) that are in a particular location—namely where there is a soul—transform (*pariṇāma*) into karmic matter (*karma*) though the power of passions (*kaṣāya*). It simply happens like that, just as the fermentation does. The emphasis on the special fermentation vessel, interestingly, is not something we've seen elsewhere in the discussions of making *surā* and other drinks. It is possible that the comparison of a process driven by the passions to the production of (sensuous) liquor was deliberate.

Medical Sources on *Surā*

Texts on medicine and pharmacology list numerous types of grain drinks like *surā*, though it is only in the later commentaries on these texts that we learn more details of their composition, and of course these later explanations may differ from how the drinks were understood at earlier periods. The *surā*s listed constitute part of the *materia medica* of traditional Indian medicine, Āyurveda, along with other fermented drinks that I'll consider in Cup 2. Thus the medical and pharmacological texts focus on their pharmacological properties. *Surā*s made from different ingredients were understood to have distinctive medical properties.

Āyurvedic literature is vast, but let's consider just a few examples.[52] *Suśruta's Compendium* (*Suśrutasaṃhitā*) is a foundational text of Indian medicine. This text evidently developed over a long time, from some centuries BCE through the centuries before 500 CE.[53] In the section on liquid substances (*dravadravya*), there is listed a group of intoxicating drinks (*madyavarga*).[54] The first drink is grape wine (*mārdvīkam*), followed by a drink derived from dates, *khārjūram*.[55] *Surā* is the third drink in the list, though the root text doesn't tell us anything about its composition. "Plain" *surā* is followed by other varieties, for which are given only names and pharmacological qualities. I have put the commentary of Ḍalhaṇa, writing in North India much later, in the late twelfth century CE, in brackets.[56] Ḍalhaṇa understands some of these *surā*s as a product of sedimentary layers, with the dregs (*bakkasa*) coming last:

> *Surā* [commentary: "*Surā* has a red, *lohita-*, color, is a little cloudy with grist, ferment, and sediment."]

White *surā* ["White *surā* is produced from the roots of white *punarnavā*[57] and other herbs, grist of paddy, and ferment. It is well known as '*katolī*.'"]

Prasannā ["*Prasannā* is the supernatant layer of *surā*, the uppermost clear part."]

Barley *surā* ["This is *surā* made from barley and ferment."]

Madhūlakam [Ḍalhaṇa suggests that this word can refer to a small type of wheat, or "monkey-hand grass," *markaṭahastatṛṇa*, and quotes the seventh- or eighth-century-CE commentary of Jejjaṭa,[58] which states that this is an unfermented drink made from mahua flowers: "which has not become an intoxicating drink and is made from mahua flowers."]

ākṣikī ["That made with peel of *akṣa*," i.e., *vibhītaka*, *Terminalia bellirica*. "Some call it '*valkikī*.'"]

kohala ["*Kohala* is made from cooked barley flour, *saktu*,[59] '*kauhalikā*' in the common language. Others, however, say it is *surā* made from cooked rice, which is what the *Pauṇḍra* people call '*kāñcanālī*.'" (*Pauṇḍra* can be loosely understood as Bengali.)]

jagala ["*Jagala* is the lower sediment of intoxicating drink that is discharged separately. According to others, *surā* made from *kiṇva* and cooked rice is *jagala*."]

bakkasa, "dregs" ["*Bakkasa* is just non-liquid *jagala*, merely *kiṇva* and herbs."][60]

Note that white (*śvetā*) *surā* and *prasannā* are also prominent drinks in the *Arthaśāstra*, though whereas *prasannā* in the *Arthaśāstra* has a specific composition, Ḍalhaṇa defines it simply as a clear top layer.

The explanation of *surā* varieties as different settling layers (as opposed to ingredients) is explicit in the *Śārṅgadharasaṃhitā* by Śārṅgadhara, probably of the thirteenth or fourteenth century CE.[61] This text—not a commentary—was a popular work on medicine and pharmacy, notable for discussions of topics that formed part of the medical culture of a later period, in particular alchemical features and the examination of the pulse.[62] Here, in a chapter on making fermented preparations (*saṃdhānakalpanā*), we read:

That which is produced from the fermentation of well-cooked rice is called *surā*. The supernatant part is *prasannā* ["clear"]. *Kādambarī* is denser than that, and under that it is called *jagala*, and *medaka* is denser than *jagala*. With the essence

(*-sāra*) removed, it is *vakkasa* [or *bakkasa*, "dregs"]. And *surā* seed (*surābījaṃ*) is *kiṇvaka*.[63]

Prasannā is the supernatant fluid at the very top in this explanation. The word used here, *maṇḍa*, implies a top layer, a scum or "cream" of sorts, and thus we are most likely dealing with refinement by vertical settling. The other types of *surā* are progressively denser or thicker and are found below each other. When all the liquids are removed, the remaining substance (dregs or lees) is called *vakkasa* or *bakkasa*. Finally, *surā* seed is called *kiṇva(-ka)* ("ferment") in this text. One wonders to what extent this reflects a tradition of separating *surā* into five separate layers, or if this is an attempt at a comprehensive rationalization of the many types of *surā* in earlier classical medical texts. Also, were parts of this scheme retained or adapted in the terminology of distilled drinks—another form of separation?[64] Indeed, given the approximate date he was working, Śārṅgadhara may well have known about alcoholic distillation.

To conclude: Sanskrit medical texts such as those we have just seen list the greatest number of types of *surā*, and although many of the commentarial explanations were written later, it is evident that at the period in which the root texts were composed, numerous *surās* were known, made in different ways with different ingredients, and considered to have distinct medicinal properties. *Surā* as mentioned in the early texts was probably made using *kiṇva*, as it was elsewhere in post-Vedic texts. Later medical texts emphasize that in some cases different varieties were formed from different settling layers (something also implied by the dregs being the last type of *surā* listed in the *Suśruta*).

Surā for Pleasure in the Twelfth Century

To conclude what is truly a superficial survey of surviving texts about grain *surās*, let's look at *surā* in a text called the *Delight of the Mind*, the *Mānasollāsa*. In 1131 CE in South India, the Kalyāṇa Cāḷukya, King Someśvara III, composed (or orchestrated) this large Sanskrit text.[65] It is an encyclopedic work covering all aspects of royal life, from choosing ministers to arranging elephant combats. The topics are often treated in remarkable detail, and in the latter part, in a section on games (*krīḍās*), we find a description of a drinking session that the king would enjoy with a group of women—a passage to which we shall return often.

The chapter describes several drinks, but the author is particularly concerned with the methods of making *surā*. *Surā* is not first in the list of drinks but is described after some verses on a sugarcane drink. The author discusses two types of *surā*, "pale" and "black":

[Pale *Surā*:]

Dry and grind to a powder fox-tail millet (*priyaṅgu*) that has been placed in water.[66]

Mix sorghum gruel (*yavanālayavāgū*)[67] with that powder.

Place more grist (*piṣṭa*) of the same sort in a jar (*ghaṭe*) abundantly. Having dried boiled rice (*odana*), mix it with that ground grain.

Put the aforementioned gruel in that grist and boiled rice.

Place that in jars and keep it in a sheltered place. Warmed for a day and a night and sprinkled [with water?], the grist has the odor of intoxicating drink (*madyagandhi*).

This is called *lavaṃ* and is an intoxicating *surā*-seed (*surābīja*).

Add ten-fold of drinking water to that and filter it (*gālayet*), or alternatively surround it with cloth and filter the pure/clear liquid (*nirmalaṃ rasa*).

In this way, using rice (*śāli*), wheat (*godhūma*), barley (*yava*), millet (*śyāmāka*), or kodo millet (*kodrava*), one makes the grist-based *surā* called "pale," which is agreeable and tasty.[68]

[Black *surā*:]

Thoroughly bruise the clean bark [or "rind"] of [the plants] *majjanā* [?], *yava* [barley?],[69] *ghoṇṭāka*,[70] and *rohiṇī*,[71] boil them [in water], and then afterward dry in the sun.[72] Powder fermented grain gruel (*kulmāṣakam*) and mix it together with that powder.

Having separately made grist from sorghum (*yavanāla*), mix it together [with all that]. Mix it together again in a bamboo tube and cover it for a long time, with heat (*soṣmaṇā*)—for three nights or five nights, until it turns black.[73]

Then an expert should add water according to the quantities [used] for *surā*-seed. Having stirred it, cover it and lay it down well-concealed.

Thus one prepares black (*kṛṣṇa*) *surā*, which possesses odor, dark color, and flavor, which especially produces drunkenness, and which possesses bitter and sweet flavors.[74]

These are probably our most detailed recipes for *surā*. We also get a sense of how the ferment component was produced for black *surā*, with herbs and powdered, fermented gruel. Note that a distilled alcoholic drink cannot be black unless the color is added after distillation. The blackness here may be from the heating/cooking, a Maillard reaction of sorts, or perhaps the (postulated) mold involved was black, as one sees in fermenting rice when *awamori* liquor is made in Okinawa today.[75] Again, the visual appearance of the drinks mattered.

A variety of grain drinks is something now associated with the Himalayas and the Northeastern states of India, but here we see evidence of a complex tradition of grain drinks in the South. It would be interesting to learn whether such *surā*s are still made or have been in living memory in South India.[76]

Conclusion

Although largely absent from surveys of alcohol history, and confusing to many scholars of early India, *surā* as made from grains was highly developed as a drink and discussed in many texts in premodern India.

Like "beer" or "ale" in Europe, the word "*surā*" covers a number of drinks (setting aside the other meanings of the word). There were many *surā*-type drinks, produced using several processes for well over two millennia in a vast region—and this is what we know from our surviving evidence alone. *Surā* made from grains was likely associated with local agricultural production (as opposed to, e.g., imported wine). Experts brewed more complex forms, and householders brewed simpler versions for occasions such as festivals. So long as grains and other basic materials were available, the only difficulty in obtaining *surā* was developing the skill to make it well. So, insofar as *surā* was a commodity, the value was based on local agricultural labor and on skill in brewing and *kiṇva* preparation. We should bear these factors in mind when considering the social, religious, and legal status of grain *surā* later in the book. Also we should consider the manner of producing *surā* when comparing it to imported wine, and even to *soma*—an imported herb prepared in an exclusive arena by a class of ritualists.

After the period of *surā*s made to the "Vedic schema," grain *surā*s were made with ferment (*kiṇva*). The production of intoxicating power from the combination of these simple materials was seen as remarkable. *Surā* was not distilled in early periods—the descriptions of the brewing process show that to be the case, as do the many references to its color. Indeed, the color of *surā* mattered quite a lot: ruddy, white, clear, and black. It's hard to know how strong *surā* was; it could have varied from a mild drink like *handia* (~ 0.78–1.38% alcohol) to the strength we see in Japanese *sake* (up to 20% alcohol).[77] *Surā* was often flavored with herbs and spices.

Understanding *surā* enriches the way we interpret other materials, such as legal texts. Yet we should also consider the intrinsic interest of *surā*, the (mostly) lost, great drink of ancient and early medieval India, a drink that brought countless people great aesthetic pleasure, enlivened their social lives, and afforded respite, though no doubt it brought conflict, poverty, and sickness too. Imagine if, in two thousand years, wine had vanished from France. Arguably the wine of France would deserve some sort of memorial as a great drink: it would be worth celebrating and simply *describing*. Even hypothetical-future-teetotal French people would be hard pressed to deny that. We should reflect on the lost aromas, flavors, and colors of these varieties of *surā*, which were numerous at any given time in just one region, not to mention across South Asia, where different grains, microbial traditions, and methods must have thrived. These drinks changed over time from the earlier, complex malted drinks we read of in Vedic texts, to the twelfth century South Indian black *surā*.

What were these *surā*s really like? The array of grain-based drinks made in South Asia today is far removed in time from these drinks, but perhaps they can still give us some sense of the ancient brews. Liquors such as fresh, cool, rice-based *handia* from Odisha are made on a small scale in a short time period and are probably like the white *surā* once made for festivals. But they are probably unlike the varieties of *surā* made on a large scale by professionals in cities two thousand years ago. In addition to the sensory qualities we're familiar with from the malted beers of Europe, we should reflect on the many other flavors that can develop in grain-based drinks made with saccharifying molds, bacteria, and yeasts. Think of the madeira or sherry-like notes of Chinese "yellow wines" (*huang jiu*). Given the possibilities for making interesting drinks from grains, and considering the esteem in which these drinks were held in India (despite significant condemnation on religious and moral grounds), we can be confident that the *surā*s of early India were refined and complex, at least to the accustomed palate.

In the Sanskrit *Rāmāyaṇa* epic, the protagonist, Rāma, is compared at one point to the best *surā*—a comparison that might be surprising to some people today. Yet this comparison suggests that at an early period good *surā*, though forbidden to some, was esteemed as a fine substance. Rāma and Sītā are living in the forest when the ten-headed demonic *rākṣasa* Rāvaṇa comes to abduct Sītā, who has been left alone and defenseless. At first Rāvaṇa, a powerful king and demonic shape-shifter, takes on the guise of a Brahmin, but then he reveals his true identity to Sītā. Thus far polite and hospitable, she now expresses her disdain for Rāvaṇa. In a powerful speech, she compares her husband Rāma to the demonic Rāvaṇa:

> The difference between a lion and a jackal; the difference between a little stream and the ocean; the difference between the best *surā* (*surāgrya*) and sour gruel (*sauvīraka*)—that is the difference between Rāma (Dāśarathi) and you . . .[78]

The best *surā* is thus contrasted with a type of sour gruel (*sauvīraka*) made with rice or barley,[79] both *surā* and gruel being mixtures of grain and water that have been left to transform. But top-quality *surā*, the lion of fermented liquids, is used here as a benchmark for something infinitely more refined and prestigious than fermented gruel—like a fragrant Chinese yellow wine compared to a humble (though tasty) Bengali *pāntā bhāt*.

CUP 2
Sugarcane, Wine, Toddy, and Other Drinks

In ancient, early, and later medieval India, people—those who drank, that is—produced and consumed a huge variety of alcoholic drinks, possibly more than in any other world region. Take the twelfth-century *Delight of the Mind* (*Mānasollāsa*), in which we learned of pale and black *surā*s. This text also lists drinks made from sugarcane juice, from a sugar product called jaggery, from grapes, coconut water, mahua flowers, and jackfruit, and from the sugary sap of various palm trees.[1] In the absence of a concept of alcohol-as-substance, people who wanted to regulate or prescribe drinking faced a complex task, as can be seen from medical, legal, and even Tantric ritual texts.

This chapter is about sugar. *Surā* was made from grains, but the drinks in this chapter start with a sugary substance, such as sugarcane juice. In making drinks from sugars, there is no need for saccharifying agents like *kiṇva* and malt, though sugar-based drinks might still be made through complex processes using other starters and additives. Unlike starchy grains, sugary liquids are ready for alcoholic fermentation as they are. Without pasteurization, sterilization, and refrigeration, a sugary liquid will often ferment spontaneously, and this can happen quite quickly. Sweet palm sap becomes alcoholic toddy in a matter of hours. Therefore, in the ancient world, sweetness and the potential for inebriating properties went hand in hand. A sugary liquid might become intoxicating by accident, and so the abstinent had to exercise caution, informed by some knowledge of fermentation.

Drinks based on sugars appear early in the Indian textual record, though not as early as grain *surā*. Of course, it's likely that people made such drinks before we have records of them—remember, this book concerns what people wrote more than what they actually did. I will explore the main categories of such sugar-based drinks here. (Note that some of these sections are short summaries of longer studies published elsewhere.[2]) And I shall also consider non-alcoholic flavored drinks and the drug betel (or *pān*) in this chapter. Betel first appears in the textual record early in the first millennium CE, and it was soon thoroughly embedded in a world where all manner of drinks were common. This non-alcoholic substance rapidly became a prestigious item of consumption, especially in elite circles, and so it's vital to know something of betel in order to make sense of broader patterns of drug and alcohol consumption in early India.

An Unholy Brew. James McHugh, Oxford University Press.
DOI: 10.1093/oso/9780199375936.003.0004

Sīdhu, Sugarcane Wine

Drinks made from sugarcane are a notable feature of the early alcohol culture of South Asia.[3] By the early first millennium CE, such drinks were consumed alongside grain *surās*, grape wine, and betel nut; they form part of the distinctive intoxicant culture of the region. Unlike in Europe, where sugarcane products have been known from only a comparatively recent period,[4] sugarcane was well known in ancient India before the Common Era. Sanskrit texts mention several varieties of sugarcane, as well as numerous products derived from sugarcane juice.[5] This variety of sugars can be confusing to scholars, particularly as most people who speak only a European language don't possess words for many of these products (though sugar specialists, of course, have a more expansive vocabulary for their field). These many words attest to a complex sugar culture in India, much of which survives to this day. Even now one finds many varieties of the sugar called jaggery on sale in India, and often people have strong opinions about their virtues. It's unfortunate that sugar is often denigrated in the West nowadays, and that the jaggery varieties of South Asia are not as well known as, say, French cheeses or Italian olive oils.

Sugarcane can be chewed or crushed with a mechanical device to produce juice (*ikṣurasa*), which can be used raw or cooked. This juice can also be fermented to produce alcohol or processed into a range of more stable products by heating and evaporating the water. These resulting products, from syrup (*phāṇita*) to various solids, can then be diluted and fermented into liquor. Jaggery (*guḍa*) is made by reducing the juice until it forms solids, sometimes shaped into balls. The reduced juice can be beaten to make a soft brown mass of crystals (*khaṇḍa*).

These products are all unrefined sugars. When making refined sugars, the juice is heated until crystals form ("massecuite," *matsyaṇḍikā*), and then these crystals (*śarkarā*) are separated from the remaining matrix (similar to molasses, *kṣāra*) and sometimes recrystallized and cleaned to make larger, white crystals (*sitopalā*).[6] All of these products can be made into alcoholic drinks. The more refined versions require more labor and fuel, and drinks made from them were presumably more costly.

The drink primarily made from sugarcane juice, raw or cooked, was called *sīdhu* (also *śīdhu*), though sugarcane products were also used in many other drinks, as I discuss later. Some types of *sīdhu* were made with other, more refined sugar products, but the basic version may well have been made simply with the juice. The drink was not distilled, so *sīdhu* is not rum. It isn't mentioned in the Vedas, but it does appear in quite early texts, likely dated to a few centuries BCE and from just around the turn of the Common Era. *Sīdhu* features, for example, in the *Rāmāyaṇa* and the *Mahābhārata*, as well as the *Arthaśāstra*.[7] The date of the two epics is uncertain and much debated, but possibly they date from some centuries BCE or a little later.[8] As we shall see later, neither text definitively mentions grapes or grape wine, so they may well reflect an earlier culture of alcohol.

In the *Rāmāyaṇa*, the description of what the monkey general Hanumān sees when he enters the palace of the *rākṣasa* (loosely: a type of demonic being) Rāvaṇa includes the amazing food and drink of the drinking place (*pānabhūmi*). The list includes "vessels made of gold, gems, and silver filled with *śīdhu*."[9] A wind blows there too, diffusing beautiful smells of cooling sandalwood and garlands and also "of sweet-tasting *śīdhu*."[10] When Hanumān burns down the citadel of Laṅkā, the *rākṣasa* inhabitants are said to "have tremulous eyes from drinking *sīdhu*."[11] Although *rākṣasas* are fierce and bloodthirsty, *rākṣasa* aesthetics in the *Rāmāyaṇa* are far from common or repulsive, so we should not read these references to *sīdhu* as indicating that the drink is deemed lowly. Rāvaṇa's palace is extremely lavish, more Trump Tower than dive-bar. Note also that this luxurious drinking apparently takes place in the relative privacy of Rāvaṇa's palace—like the elite drinking that becomes common in later poetry. Rāvaṇa's drinking area (*pānabhūmi*),[12] his "private bar," is particularly interesting:

> Various divine clear *surās* (*prasannā*) and prepared (?) *surās* (*kṛtasurā*),[13]
> Sugar (*śarkarā-*) *āsavas* and honey mead (*mādhvīka*),[14] flower *āsavas* and fruit *āsavas*,
> each one sprinkled with various scented powders.[15]

This list begins with types of *surā*, including the more processed, "clear" *prasannā*, so *surā* in the *Rāmāyaṇa* is evidently sometimes a prestigious, refined drink. As we shall see later, the category of *āsava* is very flexible. There is no *sīdhu* in this list, but there are *āsavas* here made from refined *śarkarā* (crystal sugar) and from flowers and fruit.

In the *Mahābhārata* epic, *sīdhu* is less glamorous, and we hear of it being drunk by people characterized as degenerate, including people in Bactria.[16] The latter reference is notable, since, in later periods, regions in the northwest were primarily associated with grape wine. Was *sīdhu* perceived as a drink of *the other* in these early sources? Did an awareness of *sīdhu* as a drink from a peripheral region influence the portrayal of the drinking habits of the *rākṣasas* in the *Rāmāyaṇa*?

The medical text *Suśruta's Compendium* lists several types of *sīdhu*, including some made from jaggery, uncooked ("cold") sugarcane juice, herbs, and even mahua flowers (see "Mahua-Liquor" section later in this chapter).[17] Arguably, prototypical *sīdhu* is made from sugarcane products, possibly mainly from the juice, and other usages, like "mahua-*sīdhu*," are extensions.

People aged *sīdhu* as well as other drinks. The poet Kālidāsa, writing in the fourth century CE, mentions old or aged sugarcane wine in the *Raghuvaṃśa*:

> All the troubles of lovers were wiped away by the end of the hot season, which supplied fragrance, mangos breaking bud, old sugarcane wine (*purāṇasīdhuṃ*), and fresh *pāṭala* flowers.[18]

Here the drink is associated with the final part of the hot season. Later, we will read that it was best to drink aged liquors in the rainy season, as they were easier to digest, and perhaps the same applies at the end of the hot season.[19] Or maybe the drink was inevitably aged by this time, like grape wine in Europe by the spring? In the *Bālarāmāyaṇa* of Rājaśekhara (c. 900 CE), another poetic reference to old *sīdhu* wine evokes its color, in a description of the dawn in which the eastern sky "has a delightful color like aged *sīdhu*" (*purāṇasīdhumadhuracchāyaṃ*).[20]

So aged *sīdhu* was perhaps drunk at a certain season and had a notable color, as do so many drinks in this book. The color of *sīdhu* might have been there from the start, from herbs or the juice itself, or it might have come from the storage vessels, or even from oxidation (as with Madeira). Elsewhere we read that aged drink had a reputation for being potent, no doubt from having fermented longer. A satirical one-actor play called *The Lotus Gift* (*Padmaprābhṛtaka*), of uncertain date but probably from the first millennium CE, introduces an old man who has gone to great lengths to look young, with hair dyes, cosmetics, and plucking out his white hairs. He also defends the charms of old things in general: "Verily, old wine (*madhu*) is intoxicating!"[21]

Sīdhu is a distinctive drink of ancient India, with several varieties. Two thousand years ago, Europe did not have sugarcane drinks, nor, probably, did China at early periods,[22] whereas South Asians were making liquors from a variety of sugarcane products at that time, not to mention from the several varieties of sugarcane plants that we read of in early texts. As with grain *surā*, the eventual rise of distillation may have slowly effaced the distinctive qualities of these sugar wines (medicinal ones excepted), and the drink from the Philippines called *basi* is perhaps the closest thing made nowadays to the fragrant, colored "old *sīdhus*" celebrated by poets. *Basi* has the aroma of rum and sugarcane juice and tastes like a light, watery amontillado, very dry and a little tannic.

Mixed and Medicinal "Wines": *Āsava*s and *Ariṣṭa*s

It's easy to buy an *āsava* or an *ariṣṭa* in India today, as these drinks are still used in the traditional system of medicine called Āyurveda. Typically they're made according to recipes in authoritative old texts, with fermentation methods similar to those used many centuries ago, though often modern equipment is used. But whereas some *āsava*s were drunk for pleasure in the past, nowadays both of these drinks are entirely medicinal (with the exception of occasional abuse, especially where prohibitions are in force).

We saw *āsavas* in Rāvaṇa's drinking-place earlier. In the *Mahābhārata*, in a line that was important to legal scholars and that I examine later, we hear of Kṛṣṇa and Arjuna being drunk on what is most likely a honey-*āsava* (*madhvāsava*).[23] In these contexts and others, *āsava*s are drunk for pleasure. We read of several varieties, each based on a particular sugar source plus other ingredients: x-*āsava*, y-*āsava*.

The *Arthaśāstra* mentions both *āsava*s and *ariṣṭas*:

> The mixture of raw materials for *āsava* is a *tulā* of wood apple,[24] five *tulā*s of sugarcane syrup (*phāṇita*), and one *prastha* of honey. A quarter more is the best one, and a quarter less is the lowest quality.
>
> *Ariṣṭa*s are determined by doctors for each particular disorder.[25]

This *āsava* also has a special herbal additive mixture (*saṃbhāra*).[26] Later, in a discussion of when householders can make their own liquors, we learn that they can make *ariṣṭa*s for use as medicine (*auṣadhārthaṃ vāriṣṭam*).[27] Note that *ariṣṭa*s are absent from early descriptions of drinking for pleasure, such as Rāvaṇa's drinks, described earlier—evidently they were entirely used as medicinal wines.[28]

The *Arthaśāstra* gives only one recipe for an *āsava*, though several types are mentioned in other early texts, as we saw already. This type of *āsava* was apparently drunk for pleasure, since, by contrast, the medicinal nature of *ariṣṭa*s is stated explicitly. Yet *āsavas* are also plentiful in medical texts, and the *āsava* spans both domains in early periods. According to the *Arthaśāstra*, there are many types of *ariṣṭa*s, and doctors prescribed different compositions for different disorders. The *Arthaśāstra* does not give such formulas, as presumably these belong in medical literature. But this text does specify that the *āsava* in question is a mixed drink based on fruit, sugar, honey, and additives: it consists of one part fruit pulp with a large quantity of sugarcane syrup, a much smaller quantity of honey, and a complex herbal additive, no doubt with the correct proportion of water. The honey would have added flavor, and maybe yeasts to aid fermentation.[29] The basic ingredients of this drink were typical of a medicinal *āsava*, but as the earliest surviving detailed recipe for what one might call a "recreational *āsava*," this description also gives us a sense of what these drinks, so prized in the epics, might have been like in general: fruit extract (or other flavoring extract) plus a large quantity of a sugarcane product, a little honey, and a herbal additive. Many *āsava*s today are similarly made, but often without the honey;

moreover, no *dhātakī* flowers are mentioned in the *Arthaśāstra* recipe, whereas they are commonly used today. *Dhātakī* flowers (*Woodfordia fruticosa*, [L.] Kurz) are dried, red, somewhat tannic flowers used in many old recipes for fermented drinks. They're an essential additive in several of the drinks in the *Mānasollāsa*, and we shall see *dhātakī* flowers again later in this chapter. Indeed, these flowers are as closely associated with fermenting in India as hops with beer in Europe, and this applies from a quite early period.[30] When I observed fermented medicinal drinks being made in Kerala today, a large quantity of these dried flowers was placed on top of the sugar-liquid prior to a jar being sealed. This layer of *dhātakī* flowers sinks down over the course of fermentation, and my informants told me that it was "like yeast," though of course the flowers also contribute other factors to the process too.[31]

Nowadays āyurvedic experts typically define an *āsava* as an alcoholic fermented medicine in which the herbs used are *not* made into a decoction, whereas an *ariṣṭa* is a fermented medicine in which a decoction (herbs boiled in water) is added to the sugar base prior to fermentation. There is a clear statement of this same principle in the *Śārṅgadhara Saṃhitā* (written in the thirteenth or fourteenth century CE).[32] Following a general definition of the two medicinal drinks as produced by keeping [pharmacological] substances for a long time in liquids so they ferment,[33] it is stated:

> The intoxicating drink (*madya*) prepared from unboiled herbs and water is an *āsava*; an *ariṣṭa* is prepared with a decoction (*kvātha*).[34]

Medical texts list large numbers of these drinks.[35] Like the author of the *Arthaśāstra*, I will not deal with this huge variety, though we should consider at least one formula, a purgative *āsava* from *Suśruta's Compendium*:

> Three parts of a cooled decoction (*niḥkvātha*) of purgatives is prescribed, and two of sugarcane syrup (*phāṇita*), and this is boiled over fire again.
> When it is well prepared, cool it and place it in a jar that has been prepared.
> Taking into account the difference between the cold and non-cold seasons, after a month, when it has the odor of wine (*madhu*, or "of honey"), the flavor (*rasa*, probably a technical term here) has arisen, and [this] is the best *āsava*.[36]

The commentator Ḍalhaṇa (from the late twelfth century CE) explains that the sugar-and-herb mixture is reduced by a half (by boiling) and then cooled, as one cannot ferment it when hot. (Note that although this is an *āsava*, it *does* use a decoction.) Ḍalhaṇa also explains that the jar is prepared by washing and drying the inside, applying a paste of honey and long pepper, and fumigating the jar with agarwood smoke. He then clarifies that in the cold season, the fermentation takes a month with the jar placed in a heap of grain (*dhānyarāśau*), and only a fortnight in the warmer seasons.

*Āsava*s appear quite early in our textual record, being mentioned in the epics and the earliest medical literature, as well as the *Arthaśāstra*.[37] In essence the "recreational *āsava*" was a flexible mixed drink, not mixed, as with a cocktail, but fermented from a combination of ingredients—a sugar product, an herbal additive, and possibly honey, in addition to another substance that might give its name to the drink: "fruit *āsava*," "flower *āsava*," or even "*surā āsava*" (where *surā* was used in place of water).[38] This is the nature of a prototypical *āsava*, and in this sense the word "*āsava*" is similar to the English "country wine," which is made from all sorts of things: rhubarb, for example, or parsnips, with sugar added so the drink could ferment, yet still defined by the fruit (though we shouldn't forget that unrefined sugars impart plenty of flavor and color). *Ariṣṭa*s are similar drinks but were used only as medicine in early periods, and in traditional āyurvedic circles are said to be based on herbal decoctions.

If the word *āsava* is confusing, perhaps that tells us as much about *our* classifications of drinks as it does about ancient India. Take German beer produced according to purity laws, Japanese (*junmai*) sake, or "natural" wines—such drinks, often presented as traditional and conservative, are characterized by purity and simplicity. Among the middle class today, this purity is usually desired, not because it saves us from the toxic adulterants that were a risk in earlier periods, but because the purity is thought to promote the "expression" of the simple ingredients and even the land they grew in. Ancient brewing, by contrast, including the methods practiced in India, was often characterized by a promiscuous attitude toward additives and mixed drinks.[39]

Maireya, an Ancient, Spiced, Variable-Sugar Drink

At one point while writing this book, I went to a bar in Los Angeles and ordered a gin martini.[40] What arrived did not taste like gin. It was more like lemon vodka, or even a rectified spirit infused with that American olfactory icon, Irish Spring soap. For me this was beyond the pale of gin, though clearly the manufacturers ("citrus-forward") would not agree. But who gets to define what constitutes gin? And when does something no longer count as gin? According to one European law, gins need to be based on ethanol of agricultural origin, with flavoring preparations such that "the taste is predominantly that of juniper," but other additives and the base spirit are otherwise flexible.[41] My citrus-forward gin was therefore not a gin, at least legally speaking in some times and places (though a thicket of tediously novel, often unrecognizable gins has sprung up in recent years). Gin may be a flexible category of drink, yet, both for the law (in some countries) and for drinkers, there are essential ingredients and flavors. People know a gin when they see it. In this one respect, the ancient Indian drink called *maireya* may have been like gin. Maybe to us *maireya* seems like yet another sugar-and-herb *āsava*, but just as gin is not any old botanical-flavored distilled alcohol, so *maireya* was quite possibly a particular, recognizable type of drink, popular and prestigious in very early periods, from before the turn of Common Era until at least several centuries later.

Like the *āsavas*, *maireya* is mentioned early, in the grammar of Pāṇini (circa the fourth century BCE), the *Rāmāyaṇa* (of uncertain date, but probably several centuries BCE), and in the Buddhist monastic rule on not drinking (from probably a few centuries BCE).[42] A Vedic text on domestic rites, the *Mānava Gṛhyasūtra* (also of uncertain date, possibly some centuries BCE), pairs *maireya* with *surā* in a list of other paired substances, including flowers and fruit, offered to possession-causing supernatural beings called *vināyakas*.[43] Likewise, in the *Mahābhārata*, *maireya* is paired with *surā*.[44] Perhaps this pairing represents a spectrum of drinks, like the English "grape and grain," here representing a range of sugar-based and grain-based drinks. As we see later, this pair, "*surā* and *maireya*," is also a phrase used in some Buddhist texts on drinking.

The *Arthaśāstra* contains a list of ingredients for *maireya*:

> *Maireya* is a fermented decoction (-*kvātha*-) of *meṣaśṛṇgī* ["ram's horn"] bark, with jaggery as an additional additive (*pratīvāpa*), and with long pepper and black pepper as additive mixture (-*saṃbhāra*), or mixed with the three-fruit (*triphalā*) herb mixture.[45] Alternatively, the "three-fruit" additive mixture is for all the ones with jaggery added.[46]

The decoction must have been made by boiling the bark in water. This was then fermented with a sugar source, unspecified here, with extra jaggery added. This extra sugar may have sweetened the drink or perhaps occasioned a secondary fermentation, like the *dosage* in Champagne. A herbal mixture is also added. The exact order of these stages is not clear. In addition to the flavors of the base sugar and the jaggery, this drink would have been spicy from the pepper, and possibly astringent from *triphalā*. *Meṣaśṛṇgī* is probably an herb of which the leaves, when chewed, suppress the ability to taste sweetness (*Gymnema sylvestre* [Retz.] R.Br. ex Sm.).[47] None of these are flavors as we understand them today but are instead oral sensations or alterations of taste. *Maireya* made thus would have been a spectacular drink indeed: alcoholic, with rich flavors from a double dose of sugars, with spicy or astringent sensations, and possibly with a strange sweetness-killing effect.

The sugar base may have been a local product, though some of the spices might have been imported, such that this drink might have been both local and exotic, quite different from grape wine (which was apparently imported in many areas) or local grain *surā*. *Maireya* was a spiced, intensified drink that you could make almost anywhere from a variety of sources, so long as you had the spices and the jaggery, though it was undoubtedly more complicated to produce than some of the simpler drinks.

The way Pāṇini refers to *maireya* suggests that the base sugar of the drink was variable, so one might have made, for example, honey-*maireya* or jaggery-*maireya*.[48] Notably, a vinegar recipe in the *Arthaśāstra* that partly resembles the *maireya* recipe given earlier gives several options for the sugar base used prior to fermentation and souring: sugarcane juice, jaggery, honey, sugarcane syrup, *jambū* fruit juice,[49] or jackfruit juice.[50] Medical texts also mention *maireya*, and commentators in the first millennium CE and later define it as made from "multiple sources," not implying that it is made from a choice of sugar bases but rather that it involves a secondary fermentation of other, already fermented drinks, for example *surā*-and-*āsava*-and-jaggery.[51] Though it is not clear whether *maireya* was something commonly people made and drank in the period these commentaries were composed (e.g., Ḍalhaṇa in the late twelfth century CE), so this may be a purely academic definition, building on the notion that *maireya* is characterized by "multiple sources." In all these cases, however, a secondary fermentation is involved.

It appears that *maireya* was esteemed in early periods, and we might speculate that it cost more than simple *surās*, being complex and spiced, at least in the recipe quoted earlier. The *Rāmāyaṇa* contains several references to *maireya* and implies that it is a desirable form of liquor. For example, in the *Ayodhyakāṇḍa* a Brahmin sage, Bharadvāja, provides an amazing, magical feast for Bharata's soldiers. First he requests that all the rivers come together and flow with drinks:

> Let some flow *maireya*, and others well-prepared *surā*, and others cool water like sugarcane juice . . .[52]

Then there are further wonders:

> And ponds full of *maireya* surrounded by piles of tasty prepared meat, hot pots of venison, peacock, and chicken.[53]

When the sage asks the moon to provide food and drink for the feast, he asks for "drinks, *surā* and the rest" (*surādīni ca peyāni*),[54] no doubt meaning "all manner of drinks." When the feast has appeared, some trees transform into women and say, "*Surā* drinkers (*surāpāḥ*) should drink *surā*."[55] So possibly not everyone present is a *surā*-drinker. After enjoying the feast, the army becomes drunk, and members of Bharata's retinue say that "this is heaven." When the serving women leave, the men are "drunk, puffed up with liquor (*madirotkaṭā*)."[56]

To sum up, *maireya*, a prominent drink in early periods, was made from a variety of sugar bases (or fermented drinks) with a secondary fermentation (or *dosage* of extra sugar) and may have been distinctively spiced. It was a prestigious drink, something to serve at a fantasy feast, and also something to list as a prohibited drink in Buddhist monastic rules, in which its variable nature is usefully flexible from a legal standpoint (see Cup 7). Patrick McGovern has described archaeological finds of ancient, complex mixed drinks, "grogs."[57] As noted for *āsavas*, ancient drinks were by no means "pure and simple." In the case of *maireya* we have an example of one such drink along with some texts on how people understood and appreciated the drink. *Maireya*, though mixed and variable like McGovern's "grogs," was classed as one specific drink, known by one word (sometimes in compound, e.g., honey-*maireya*).[58] *Maireya* was deeply appreciated, and was no more a primitive, messy concoction for ancient Indians than gin is for us today.

Although *maireya* had a long afterlife, as seen by its prominence in texts and its frequent occurrence in lexica,[59] it seems that it eventually faded away as a pleasure-drink. It is not, for example, in the list of drinks in the twelfth-century *Mānasollāsa*. Perhaps it was absorbed into the general class of *āsavas*, and maybe it was also superseded in the practice and representations of elite drinking by that imported beverage, grape wine, not to mention by betel-chewing. Yet the spicy, variable, double-fermented *maireya* had its day in ancient India and was so esteemed that one still catches echoes of it in Buddhist chants today.

Grape Wine: Esteemed and Foreign, a New Classic

Grape wine is unlike any other of the drinks in this chapter.[60] Let us read what the *Arthaśāstra* has to say about it:

> "*Madhu*" is grape juice (*mṛdvīkārasa*). Its name, according to its place of origin, is Kāpiśāyana and Hārahūraka.[61]

We learn nothing here about the quantities of materials needed to make wine. Instead we get a definition. Grape juice (apparently the alcoholic variety) is called *madhu*, and vice versa. *Madhu* is named after its place of origin, and we learn of two such varieties: Kāpiśāyana wine comes from Kapiśa, which is near Begram in modern Afghanistan; the location of Hārahūraka is uncertain.[62] In the *Arthaśāstra*, which is concerned here with economics, what is important about wine is terminology, not pounds and ounces. That is because wine, unlike other drinks, is viewed as an import by the author of the text. How it is made is of no interest.

But getting the words right mattered. As we shall see several times in this book, "*madhu*" and several similar and related words (*mādhvī*, *madhu-āsava*, etc.) are a common source of drink-related confusion, both for me and for some traditional commentators. The word "*madhu*," which clearly means wine in the *Arthaśāstra* line, can also refer to honey and nectar. *Madhu* also means sweet, and as with most Sanskrit nouns it means a lot of other things too, not least of which is an epithet of *soma*! Given that *madhu* is such a common word, it's not surprising to see it carefully (re)defined here, and also in the section on the storehouse in the *Arthaśāstra*: "'*madhu*' is honey (*kṣaudraṃ*) and wine ["the thing from grapes," *mārdvīkaṃ*]."[63] As far as I'm aware, this is the earliest attested usage of *madhu* to mean grape wine (though a reference to a *madhu* "derived from fruit," *phalajaṃ*, in the *Mahābhārata* (MBh 2.47.11) perhaps hints at a usage, not unlike our [agave] "nectar," at an early period, with "grape nectar" being applied to what we call wine too).

From a much later period, we get a description of wine-making in the *Delight of the Mind* (*Mānasollāsa*):

> Press grape juice (*mṛdvīkarasa*), ferment it [some] days: this is grape *āsava* (*drākṣāsava*), which is pleasant, the favorite of young ladies.[64]

Unlike most other drinks, including many of those described in this book, there are no additives of any sort involved here; wine consists of just a single ingredient. It's not clear whether wine was made in South India in this period. To add to the confusion, Sanskrit words for grapes may well refer to dried grapes in some contexts (as in āyurvedic *drākṣāsava* today). Nonetheless, wine was innately simple when compared to complex drinks like *maireya* and the compounded *surā*. And in many places it probably appeared ready-made, as an import.

Grapes and wine are not mentioned in the Vedas nor in the epics, at least not in the critical editions.[65] Dating early texts is tricky, but it seems that the earliest references to grapes, mostly to grape drinks, are from the second or third centuries BCE. The word used in these early references is *muddikā* (Pali), *mṛdvīkā* (Sanskrit), or *muddiyā* (Prakrit). Except in the regions of Kashmir and Gandhāra, both the fruit and the drink were often regarded as foreign, even novel, in early periods in India, as we saw in the *Arthaśāstra* earlier. Kālidāsa (from probably the fourth century CE) associates grape wine with Persia, where there was indeed an ancient wine culture.[66]

Archaeological evidence of amphoras and torpedo jars suggests that grape wine was imported to India from both the ancient Mediterranean (the Roman world) and the Middle East, from the first century BCE up through the first millennium CE.[67] The wines mentioned in the *Arthaśāstra* probably came from the Northwest. We can safely assume that a jar of imported wine was far more costly and prestigious than one of local grain *surā*, and indeed wine appears to have been the drink of the elite, as we see throughout this book. Perhaps then it's not surprising that in Hindu law wine is less strictly prohibited than grain *surā*, where Kṣatriyas and Vaiśyas are concerned (though this all depends on how one interprets the ambiguous word *mādhvī*; see Cup 7).

Where forms of Indic culture were established and wine was produced, this drink was celebrated with local pride: "We live in the land of prestigious commodities." For example, the Kashmiri poet Bilhaṇa praises Kashmir, where grapes and saffron, both costly exotics elsewhere, thrived in one and the same village.[68] Relief sculptures from Gandhāra show scenes of wine production, evidently a valued part of the local economy.[69] Although those images may be inflected by Hellenistic styles of representation, elsewhere in India such images (as at Mathura)[70] and textual representations indicate not so much the *influence* of a Western drinking culture on India as the deliberate adoption of a costly foreign drink, along with some paraphernalia and imagery, by a culture in which drinking alcohol was already well established. Wine culture in much of ancient South Asia was thus more like the importation and consumption of French and German wine in early modern England. Similarly, one might compare wine imagery at Mathura to the Chinoiserie of tea paraphernalia in Europe at certain periods. And, for wine, if there are linguistic connections with wine-producing areas in Sanskrit and related languages, these areas may be Iranian and not Greek/Hellenized.[71]

Grape wine was an exceptional drink in early India, simple in composition yet exotic (in many areas) and prestigious. It was celebrated in Sanskrit poetry but is absent from the Vedas and epics—a new classic of a drink. Yet, unlike in England, where wine was also largely imported, the development of the prestige of wine was hampered in India by complex attitudes toward drinking, even among those who were religiously permitted to drink. As a luxury consumable, especially in public settings, it was overshadowed by a more universally acceptable newcomer, the perfumed betel quid.

Palm Toddy: Simple, Local, the *Surā* that Grows on Trees

Toddy is made from the sap of various species of palm tree and is still a common drink in parts of South Asia and elsewhere in the world. The sap is collected from the cut flower-stalk or from an incision in the trunk, depending on the species of palm used. The sap ferments naturally and rapidly. Clear, light-brown, sweet sap collected early in the morning becomes milky, sour, alcoholic toddy by midday. The drink is perishable, best drunk the day it is gathered, though it can be distilled to preserve it. The sap can also be prevented from fermenting by cold weather or a lime-paste smeared on the collecting vessel, making a sweet drink that, like sugarcane juice, can be processed to make sugars, such as the date-palm jaggery so popular in West Bengal in the cold months. The fresher the toddy, the sweeter and milder it is; several hours later, the toddy will be too far gone and sour to drink.

Like the smell of ambergris, the taste of toddy is unique and difficult to describe. There's a touch of yeast flavor, very little sweetness, and a slight, pleasant flavor one might describe as peptic, in an invigorating way. It's somewhat like Mexican *pulque*. Toddy is mildly intoxicating, like a weak beer. When it's well made, it can be quite a varied drink. Mr. V. S. Sunil Kumar, MLA, of Anthikad, Kerala, explained to me that toddy is like a thumb print: every toddy is unique.[72] The tappers all have their own styles, the fermentation varies for different tappers, and the climate, palm tree, and soil all affect the drink's taste. (Of course, it's likely that all the drinks I discuss in this book were as capable of nuance as modern toddy.)

In South Asia, several palm species are used for toddy, principally the palmyra (*tāla*, *Borassus flabellifer* L.), the coconut palm (*nālikera*, *Cocos nucifera* L.), the talipot palm (*tālī*, *Corypha umbraculifera* L.), and a type of date palm (*kharjūra*, *Phoenix sylvestris* L. Roxb.). Interestingly, in traditional Sanskrit plant theory, palm trees are classified as "grass-trees" (*tṛṇadruma*).[73]

Toddy may grow on trees, but several factors are involved in getting it. The person who climbs the tree, prepares the collection site on the tree, and collects the toddy is called a toddy tapper in English, and for some species of palm his job involves the highly skilled and dangerous work of climbing many tall trees every day, armed with sharp knives, other tools, and a collection vessel. Nowadays, at least for the coconut palm, the tapper prepares the cut stem by rhythmically tapping it with a lead-filled bone over several days, then sealing the cut stem with a special paste until the sap starts to run. Once the sap is running, the tapper hangs a pot on the stem and, twice a day, climbs the tree to collect the sap into another pot that hangs from his waist. For the date palm the process is different: an incision is made in the palm's trunk, making this process more like rubber tapping or maple-syrup production.

To make toddy one also needs to have permission to access the site of the tree and use the products of the tree. In the case of coconut toddy, cutting the flower will prevent the formation of coconuts, so the process is not without economic consequences—something that applies to many of the drinks in this book. A fragmentary Telugu inscription from 1303 CE, from the Nalgoṇḍa district in modern Telangana in South India, refers to a community of toddy sellers (*Īḍaṛa*) as one of the eighteen communities of the town who pay a contribution to a temple.[74] Grants regulated legal access to economically useful trees, as Sircar writes: "In the medieval copper-plate inscriptions of the Sena kings of East India, the gift land usually carried with it the following privileges . . . together with betelnut and coconut palms . . . The grants of the Candras of Bengal usually add 'together with mango and jackfruit trees.' The privileges of the donees in regard to the enjoyment of particular trees, indicated in these cases, were not enjoyed by ordinary tenants."[75] Likewise, land grants of the Pālas of eastern India typically include "with its mango and *madhūka* trees (*s-āmra-madhūka*)," and other inscriptions also mention the rights to the *madhūka* trees, which we shall consider later.[76] One land grant from Odisha, probably from the twelfth century, uses the phrase "with the palmyra palms" (*satālakaḥ*), which are also included in some land grants for forest areas.[77] Thus, when alcohol (along with other things) is made from trees, the rights to access the trees and exploit them are often regulated.

Before we examine texts about toddy, I should sound some notes of caution. First, one can make an alcoholic drink out of dates, which are also produced by palm trees. And dates are long attested in South Asia, as far back as the *Yajurveda*.[78] Pliny mentions a "wine" made from dates in Parthia and India.[79] So if we see references to dates and date palms in connection with liquor, this does not necessarily refer to toddy. Also, people in premodern South Asia sometimes made an alcoholic drink out of coconut water, meaning the liquid inside the coconut, so words meaning "coconut liquor" do not necessarily refer to toddy. Further, people living and writing texts in a region where toddy was *not* commonly made might have been confused about how the drink was made, mixing up date drinks, coconut-water drinks, and toddy. Moreover, words change over time; consider "corn" in English, which can mean a number of Old World grains or simply "maize" in America. People writing commentaries and lexica, even quite early ones, who lived in a region where toddy was common, might sometimes have inferred a reference to toddy in a word that did not in fact refer to this drink at the time of composition.

Further, Kṛṣṇa's brother Balarāma is often represented as enjoying drink, and he is also said to possess a palmyra-palm banner.[80] Although in later periods the connection between Balarāma's love of drink and a toddy palm might have seemed obvious, there is no evidence of this conceptual link in the earliest sources. In early Sanskrit texts such as the *Rāmāyaṇa*, it appears that the palmyra palm, the *tāla*, was above all a proverbially tall object.[81] In the *Harivaṃśa*, a lengthy supplement to the *Mahābhārata*, there is an episode in which Balarāma and Kṛṣṇa confront a demon in a palmyra-palm forest.[82] The palm trees here are tall (*ucchrita*) and filled with fruits smelling so good that they're clearly delicious, like the nectar of immortality.[83] Mighty Balarāma shakes the trees to make the fruits fall (an action that requires a lot more strength than one might think).[84] However, a demon called Dhenuka, who has the form of an ass, lives in the forest of palmyras, protecting it. The demon finds Balarāma under the trees, looking like a banner himself (i.e., also tall),[85] but Balarāma defeats the demon by flinging him to the top of the palm tree. So, in this story, Balarāma shows his strength by shaking a palmyra and throwing a demon to the top of a tall tree, and his height is further emphasized by his resemblance to a banner or flagpole among these tall trees. The palmyras thus highlight Balarāma's strength and size in this narrative, and his conventional palmyra-palm banner evokes this episode and reminds people of how mighty he is. As for what Balarāma wants to take from the trees in this episode, it is not toddy but the sweet fruit. So references to Balarāma and palmyra palms in early texts are not necessarily references to toddy, tempting as it may seem to make the connection.[86]

Perhaps surprisingly to some, given the simple and "natural" nature of the drink, references to toddy in Sanskrit texts appear relatively late, though as with much in this book, its later appearance may tell us more about what people working in Sanskrit were interested in, or where they were living, than about South Asian drinking cultures themselves. As seen already, there are early references to palm trees, dates, and palmyra fruits (and what is probably date liquor, in *Suśruta's Compendium*),[87] but clear references to toddy are not found in these early sources.

There are no clear-cut references to toddy in the *Arthaśāstra*, nor in the epics, nor in *Caraka's* or *Suśruta's Compendia*, nor in the earliest legal texts. In the *Raghuvaṃśa* of Kālidāsa, from the fourth century CE, we read the following concerning King Raghu's soldiers in the country of Kaliṅga (approximately present-day Odisha), in a passage in which various items, including plants and drinks, are used to characterize regions covered in their conquests:

> Having prepared a drinking place (*-pānabhūmayaḥ*), the soldiers drank coconut *āsava* (*nārikelāsavaṃ*) using betel leaves (*tāmbūlīnāṃ dalaiḥ*), as well as their enemies' glory.[88]

This region is characterized by a distinctive alcoholic drink made from coconut palms, which might well be toddy. Precisely what is implied by "coconut *āsava*" is unclear, especially since we're dealing with a literary text here, not a pharmacological one. When it comes to material culture, especially of other lands, Sanskrit poets don't always show a close interest in the details. But here the coconut drink characterizes another region—it's seemingly exotic to Kālidāsa and his initial audience—and coconut toddy is not something one can trade over long distances (though palmyra toddy and date-palm toddy are made today in North India).

Toddy shows up clearly in Sanskrit legal and medical texts from approximately the mid-first millennium CE, and these sources treat the drink in different ways, for different reasons. From the mid-to-late-second millennium and onward, texts on Hindu law present ever-expanding lists of types of alcoholic drink. In the absence of a concept of ethanol/alcohol, banning alcoholic drinks was sometimes done case by case (a bit as we do with drugs today), and toddy appears in these lists.[89] Thus legal texts seek out and explicitly name new drinks, including toddy. As a drink that goes from being a sweet liquid to an intoxicating one in hours, it might be considered a borderline case.

Medical literature incorporates toddy in a quite different manner and apparently at a much later date. Take the *Śārṅgadharasaṃhitā* by Śārṅgadhara (of uncertain date, probably the thirteenth or fourteenth century CE).[90] After discussing varieties of *surā*, this text introduces a new and radical interpretation of the word *vāruṇī*, which is a synonym for *surā*, or one type of *surā*, in earlier texts:

> *Vāruṇī* is that which is brewed/fermented (*saṃdhitā*) with the juice of palmyra and date palms.[91]

Thanks to this redefinition of *vāruṇī*, toddy can now be read into all manner of older medical texts and finds a place in the classical *materia medica*.

There is another interesting candidate in the medical literature for an early reference to toddy, in a text called the *Hārītasaṃhitā*, dating from 700–1000 CE. Here several different intoxicating drinks are mentioned that appear to have been made from the palmyra palm (*tāḍamāḍarasodbhavā, tāḍamaṇḍikā*).[92] As in the legal literature, toddy is simply added to the list of types of alcoholic drinks, not hidden in the guise of an older word. This is perhaps no coincidence, as the classification of drinks in the *Hārītasaṃhitā* has echoes of a well-known legal classification of intoxicating drinks (from Manu).[93]

From twelfth-century South India, the *Delight of the Mind* (*Mānasollāsa*) describes both toddy and a fermented coconut-water drink:

> Place a lot of coconut water (*nārikelodakam*) mixed with *dhātakī* flowers inside a jar (*ghaṭodare*)—[this] is the best coconut wine (*nārikelāsavam*).[94]

Note the use of *dhātakī* flowers here, absent from the grape *āsava* recipe in the same text. The description of collecting toddy is extremely clear:

> Having cut the flower-tube (*kusumasthanalam*) of a *tāla* [palmyra palm], *hintāla* palm,[95] *tāpiccha*,[96] [or] *kharjūra* [date palm],[97] one should attach a pot to it for three watches [about nine hours total]. Take down the pot that is filled by the drops produced from the area that is cut—sprinkled with water, [this] is the intoxicating drink called *tālā*, etc.[98]

The fact that many different palms can be so exploited is noted.

Toddy is a local drink, confined to certain regions where the relevant palm trees thrive. Even within a toddy region, the drink cannot be transported too far. Spatially and temporally restricted and thus scarce elsewhere, nevertheless this perishable drink never became an exotic imported "palm wine of the South," except in poetic depictions of various regions. Surviving Sanskrit texts start to mention toddy frequently around the mid-to-late-first millennium onward (close philological examination of early Tamil texts for toddy words would be useful here), and toddy features in long legal lists of alcoholic drinks that we'll consider later. As we've seen, some of the medical texts find toddy in an old word for *surā*, *vāruṇī*, and it may not be a coincidence that this word is given such a meaning, as both grain *surā* and toddy were probably relatively cheap and intimately connected with the local agricultural economy. Toddy-as-*surā* is not palm "wine" at all, but rather "palm ale."

Mahua Liquor

Mahua liquor (*mādhvīka*, *mādhūka*) is unique to South Asia. It is made from the nectar-filled flowers of the mahua tree (*Madhuca longifolia*), a large tree that grows in central and North India and annually drops flowers on the ground, so that the labor of obtaining them consists simply of going to the trees and gathering them. As with toddy palms, such a resource led to the regulation of the right to collect the flowers, as attested by some of the land grants mentioned earlier. Mahua liquor is still made today, infused with water and jaggery, fermented and distilled, though typically on a small, rural scale. The tree can also be used for timber and the seeds for oil—in the *Arthaśāstra* these two uses are noted, but *madhūka* is not a source of sugar or liquor in that text.[99] The flowers, which can also be eaten, are often dried and stored, so that the drink can be made out of season. Although one assumes that this is a very ancient drink, distinctively Indian too, it never achieved a high profile in Sanskritic textual culture.[100] The flowers are mentioned relatively early, however, in a later Vedic text on domestic rites.[101] In the Pali Vinaya, *madhuka*-flower juice (*madhukapuppharasam*) is the only flower-based nonalcoholic drink that the Buddha forbids the monks to accept—perhaps because the flowers were so closely associated with an intoxicating drink.[102]

Mahua trees are often called *madhūka* in Sanskrit, and the drink is thus sometimes called *mādhūka*. In the web of *madhu*-like words connected to liquor in Sanskrit, references to this drink risk getting confused, lost, or inaccurately designated. The common word "*madhu*" can even refer to the mahua tree! And the word *mādhvī* can also refer to the same drink, at least according to some commentators, which is significant since that word is very important in Hindu legal texts.[103]

Let's start with a clear reference to the mahua drink, taken as before from the *Delight of the Mind*:

> Make a decoction in water with the *madhūka* tree flowers. That liquid, mixed into a *dhātakī* [flower] decoction, is called *madhuka āsava*.[104]

The drink is called an *āsava* in the broadest sense of the word. Mahua is listed here after coconut-water "wine" and before jackfruit "wine," and is thus grouped with other drinks made from trees.

Mahua liquor is also mentioned in the medical text *Suśruta's Compendium*. Here one type of *sīdhu* ("sugarcane wine") is said to be made from mahua flowers,[105] and in a list of sugarcane products there is a syrup made from mahua flowers (*madhūkapuṣpottham phāṇitam*), probably a reduced decoction of the flowers.[106] Thus, whereas toddy was assimilated as a *surā* synonym in some medical sources, in this early source mahua is closely associated with sugarcane, both as a syrup and as a fermented drink.

Perhaps mahua has a low profile in Sanskrit texts because, as today, mahua liquor was associated with rural, sometimes Adivasi ("tribal") communities, whose drinking cultures are less frequently represented in our sources. There is possible evidence for this theory in a reference to mahua in the seventh-century biography of King Harṣa, the *Harṣacarita* of Bāṇa. Here, in a passage about the Vindhya forest, there is a description of people who collect and trade forest products: honey, wax, peacock feathers, and "countless sacks of freshly pulled *dhātakī* flowers the color of ores."[107] There is also a forest village where the houses have "an abundance of mahua-flower *āsava* intoxicating-drink."[108]

In brief, mahua liquor, brewed from flowers (and nowadays distilled), is local, possibly pre-agricultural, and easily made on a small scale. It's no doubt one of the oldest drinks of India and is unlike any drink made elsewhere, yet until the present day it has never enjoyed much prestige.

Honey Mead

One common, ancient meaning of the word *madhu* is "honey." Yet, as we've seen, *madhu* (in the sense of wine) and several other drinks with *madhu*-like names are not made from honey. Sometimes what these *madhv*-esque words mean is ambiguous. Nonetheless, certain drinks in India were definitely made from honey, such as *madhvāsava* (*madhu-āsava*), at least as defined by Aruṇadatta (from the twelfth century CE),[109] who introduces yet another *madhu*-related word in his commentary on the *Aṣṭāṅgahṛdaya* of Vāgbhaṭa, perhaps to clarify the *madhu* confusion: "*Madhvāsava* (*madhu-āsava*): a type of intoxicating drink (*madya-*) called *mādhava* fermented from honey (*mākṣikeṇa sandhīyate*)."[110] This may also be the meaning of *madhvāsava* as seen in the *Mahābhārata* (5.58.5). It might have been a luxurious drink in early periods, honey being perhaps less abundant than sugarcane and grains. Yet mead is far less important in India than modern scholars trained to read *madhu* as "honey" might think given the frequency of *madhu*-words in these texts. Mead is an ancient drink of Europe, and there are historic-linguistic connections between "mead" and these *madhu* words, meaning that mead-readings tend to be more attractive to Western scholars. But we should resist this temptation in the absence of other evidence for something being a honey drink. There is also an interesting incident in the *Rāmāyaṇa* in which some monkey soldiers get drunk on honey, but I'll consider that later.

Jackfruit Wine (*Panasāsava*)

In the *Mānasollāsa*, jackfruit wine is described as follows:

> A skillful man should squeeze out crushed jackfruit into water. Mixed with *dhātakī* flowers and fermented, this is the best jackfruit *āsava*.[111]

Jackfruit wine is still made in South Asia today. Given contemporary descriptions, it must have been one of the more pungent drinks available.[112] Also, depending on how the wine was made, it was one way to make use of a vast harvest of jackfruit—an advantage that extends to some other fermented drinks too.

Although jackfruit wine is not mentioned in very early sources, there are hints that it may have been made then: a recipe for vinegar (similar to the recipe for *maireya*) in the *Arthaśāstra* could be fermented from a number of sources of sugar, including jackfruit.[113] Was jackfruit, then, used only to make vinegar, or was it also fermented for use as a liquor? If the latter was the case, why is it not mentioned in the section of the *Arthaśāstra* dealing with liquors? I can't answer this question, but it may point to a general discrepancy between the drinks people made in that era and the drinks they wrote about.

Non-Alcoholic Drinks

Many people in premodern India did not drink liquor, and even those who did so also drank other types of drink. It is absolutely *not* true that some people drank alcohol in premodern India because it was safer than water (or thought to be so). Nor does the "beer was safer than water" theory work for Europe in all premodern periods, beloved as this notion is to many people.[114] In India people drank water, and they were fussy about it, appreciating good water. For example, *Suśruta's Compendium* posits that the very best drink to have after food (*anupāna*) is rainwater.[115]

Many other types of non-alcoholic drinks were available too, including dairy products and flavored drinks. A number of sources discuss these drinks, including texts on Buddhist monastic law, on dietetics, on medicine, and in literary descriptions of food. This is not the place to explore in depth such a complex subject, but to give readers a glimpse of the world of non-alcoholic drinks in premodern South Asia, I'll look at one case study. The *Delight of the Mind* (*Mānasollāsa*) contains a section about food and cooking, which includes a recipe for a sweetened drink of curdled milk and fruit juice:

> Set up two stakes and tie a spotless cloth to them. With sticks, spread out some milk that you have curdled with a sour substance, that has white sugar added and is mixed with cardamom powder—you put this on the spread-out cloth and make it drip, pressing it evenly. Put that on there many times, until it becomes pure. You add roasted ripe tamarind fruit to it for color (*varṇārthaṃ*). This beverage, which has the name of whatever fruit juice you mix it with, is the best drink.[116]

As with many intoxicating drinks, the color is important. Also, sugar and flavors are added.

The next section of the text deals with drinking water.[117] First, we read that water should be taken with food for digestion and enjoyment, and at any other time to quench thirst. Then comes a list of nine types of drinking water, including river water, rain water, water from wells and dikes, and the "divine" (*divya*) water, which falls as rain combined with the sun's rays during the lunar asterism (*nakṣatra*) called Svāti; "divine" water is tasty and wards off all badness. And that's not all:

> Some acknowledge a tenth: that supreme tree-derived (*vārkṣaṃ*) drinking water, which is produced from the coconut (*nārikelasamudbhūtaṃ*), which is tasty/sweet (*svādu*), promotes sexual vigor (*vṛṣyaṃ*), and is pleasant (*manoharaṃ*).[118]

This drink is probably coconut water (the liquid found within coconuts), as opposed to unfermented sap.[119] Coconut water is an example of a slightly sweet drink that does *not* ferment so long as it remains stored in the coconut.[120] Another type of water, called "goose water" (*haṃsodaka*), is prepared by heating water in the sun in the day and cooling it by moon rays at night. And there is also a method for making a water-purifying herbal clay ball:

> A clay ball, mixed with long pepper (*kaṇā*) and nutgrass tubers (*mustaka*), kneaded with cardamom, vetiver, and sandalwood (*elośīrakacandana*), fired over charcoal of Acacia catechu (*khadira*), should be placed into pure water, which will remove all badness and be radiant—this ball-infusion is related by experts in water.[121]

In addition to this clay ball, Someśvara provides instructions for two perfuming infusions (*-vāsa*), one using mango juice and flowers and the other using powdered herbs. When it comes to drinking the water, a number of different vessels are described:

> Very cold, pure water should be brought, gently fanned, in clay water-pots that are smooth and have the ruddy beauty of coral, or in very pleasant leather vessels (*carmapātra*) that have been completely purified with the "three fruits" (*triphala*), and which have spouts[122] of silver, crystal, and gold that have many holes, [these vessels] being auspicious and wrapped in white cloth. [The king] should drink with golden drinking cups (*caṣaka*), or with "oyster shells" [small cups], or with lotus stems/fibers [*bisa*—perhaps as straws].[123]

Finally, Someśvara explains which types of water are suitable for each season, stating that the coconut "tree-related" water is to be consumed as one pleases.[124]

Thus, people did drink water in premodern India, along with all manner of other flavored non-alcoholic drinks, not to mention milk. The choice to consume intoxicating drinks was not motivated by fear of water or a bored palate.

Betel/*Pān*

We can't fully understand the drinking culture in premodern India without looking at betel (often called *pān*). Betel is still common in South Asia today, typically taken in the form of the leaf of *Piper betle* L. (a vine in the same family as black pepper) wrapped around some pieces of an areca nut, from the areca palm tree (*Areca catechu* L.). Powdered slaked lime is added, as well as astringent catechu. Nowadays people often take the quid or just the nut with tobacco. As in the past, other ingredients are added for flavoring, and the quid can also be presented in an ornamental fashion. The paraphernalia of betel is often beautiful: betel-nut cutters, lime containers, and all manner of vessels and trays. The quid is chewed and is a mild stimulant, staining the saliva and eventually the teeth red. An up-to-date monograph (or more than one) on betel in South Asian history is much needed.[125] Here I present simply a sketch of this drug, with a view to understanding how betel co-existed with alcohol.

Betel is not mentioned in the earlier Sanskrit sources. It is not in the Vedas or the epics. Yet it seems well established in texts composed in the fifth and sixth centuries CE. Two aspects of betel are of interest here. First, how did this new drug become embedded in Indian textual culture in such a short time? Second, how did betel compare with alcohol? That is, how did this new substance fare in an already complex world of drinking traditions and prohibitions? Arguably, as a habit that could be shared in public, betel-chewing filled a role that alcohol and tobacco occupied in other parts of the world. From the mid-first millennium CE onward, chewing betel was almost universally praised and thus forms a contrast with drink, which had a more ancient history but was by no means universally consumed, nor always esteemed among the people associated with our surviving texts.

Textual evidence suggests that betel became popular in South Asia in the early centuries of the Common Era, roughly around 300 CE. Maybe people were using it in South Asia earlier, but it is around this time that they started writing about it in sources that survive.[126] In the Sri Lankan *Chronicle of the Island* (*Dīpavaṃsa*), composed not long after 350 CE, there is a reference to the gods providing fragrant betel-vine toothsticks, areca nuts, and other adornments and dainties to King Aśoka.[127] Documents from Niya in the Tarim Basin in Central Asia, dating from the mid-third to mid-fourth century CE, mention gifts of betel (grape wine is also prominent in these documents).[128] The *Kāmasūtra*, perhaps from the fourth century CE, mentions betel.[129] These earliest clear references to betel demonstrate that it was present not only in India but also in Sri Lanka and Central Asia.

Another early reference to betel is in the Gupta-era Mandasor Silk Weavers' inscription of 473 CE.[130] This inscription, from Mandasaur in modern Madhya Pradesh, records the foundation and restoration of a temple to the Sun god by a guild of silk weavers, who had moved from the region of Lāṭa in modern Gujarat. The text is literary at times: the sun is said to be "very red ["coppery"] like the cheeks of drunk (*kṣībā-*) young women."[131] The guild is said to adorn the earth with a silk garment, and young women, though they may have golden necklaces, betel (*-tāmbūla-*), and flowers, are said not go to meet lovers until they are wearing a pair of silken garments.[132] At this date, therefore, betel was well-known enough to constitute part of the conventional adornments of women.

Earlier in this chapter, we read of betel leaves in the *Raghuvaṃśa* of Kālidāsa, probably from the fourth century CE, in the passage describing the soldiers drinking coconut *āsava* in the country of Kaliṅga (approximately present-day Odisha). The soldiers then march along a coast lined with fruiting areca palms (*phalavatpūgamālinā*).[133] For Kālidāsa, betel leaves and areca nuts characterize this region. The same account also associates other regions with various commodities: wine in Persia, saffron in the northwest, musk in the Himalayas, and agarwood in the far northeast.[134] These products henceforth feature as an almost classical set of luxury substances in Sanskrit texts, especially the perfumes.[135]

Given the period in which betel first appears in the historical record of India, we can analyze to some extent how a new drug was assimilated among a literate group of people with complex attitudes toward food and alcohol, at quite an early period. A new drink is easy enough to understand, but betel-chewing was apparently a new format entirely. Two early references to betel occur in the prose sections of two Pali *Jātaka*s, probably from the early to mid-first millennium.[136] In one we read of a perfumery shop (*sabbagandhāpaṇaṃ*)[137] that supplies betel (*tambūla-*)[138] along with perfumes and flowers. In the *Kāmasūtra*, a man-about-town keeps betel quids (*tāmbūlāni*) in his bedroom alongside flower garlands, lip wax, perfumes, and mouth-freshening citron peel.[139] In *Caraka's Compendium* there is a reference to the areca nut and betel leaf: in a section about the daily routine, betel is mentioned after toothsticks and tongue-scraping.[140] This text does not state, however, that "one should take a betel quid," but rather mentions a number of aromatic substances that one should keep in the mouth for purity, taste, and fragrance; the list includes areca nut/fruit (*-pūgānāṃ phalāni*), betel leaf (*patraṃ tāmbūlasya*), and the spices nutmeg, cloves, cubebs, camphor, and cardamom. Betel leaf is said to be good for the mouth and for bad breath in the *Suśrutasaṃhitā*, in which a similar list of ingredients is at one point prescribed as beneficial to take after a meal.[141] Again, betel here is not presented here as "taking a *pān*" like some sort of drug, but rather in a list of digestive, purifying, perfumed substances, taken "with betel leaf." Thus, betel was often classified with, or adjacent to, perfumes in this early period. This makes sense, as even today betel can be flavored with aromatics and will both perfume and color the mouth.

The *Great Compendium* (*Bṛhatsaṃhitā*) of Varāhamihira (c. 550 CE) contains a detailed passage on betel. This is a text on prognostication and astrology and treats many other topics too. The passage about betel comes at the end of a chapter on perfumery, again linking this substance with scents. Following a description of toothsticks, Varāhamihira explains:

> It inflames erotic desire, it reveals beauty, it imparts charm as well as mouth-fragrance, it creates vigor, and it destroys phlegmatic diseases—thus betel (*tāmbūlam*) has these and other qualities.
>
> Mixed with the proper amount of lime powder, it produces redness; [add] excessive areca nut (*pūgaphala-*), and there is a reduction in redness; with more lime powder, it gives the mouth a bad smell; more leaf gives a good smell.
>
> More leaf (*patra-*) at night is beneficial, and nut (*saphalaṃ*) in the day—doing otherwise than stated is quite ridiculous. Perfumed by cubebs, areca nut, *Phyllanthus acidus* fruit (*lavalīphala*),[142] and *pārijāta* perfumes,[143] [it] makes one pleased with the pleasures of passion.[144]

Betel, not mentioned at all in texts only a few centuries earlier, is well established here. Grouped with hair dyes, perfumes, and toothsticks, betel is classified as an adornment of the body that reddens and fragrances the mouth as well as producing amorous passion. To get the proportions of betel wrong is laughable and ridiculous (*viḍambanā*), implying that anyone cultured should know exactly how to prepare a good quid. The preparation (and remember, betel is a mixed product) is also assigned pharmacological qualities derived from the system of Āyurveda—more evidence that it has been thoroughly assimilated into the culture. Finally, betel should be perfumed with spices, further increasing its fragrance, its aesthetic and pharmacological complexity, its cost, and its prestige. Writing of the assimilation of tea, coffee, chocolate, and tobacco in Enlightenment Europe, Jordan Goodman describes a process of "Europeanization" as "an ongoing process of appropriation, development, and definition."[145] We might think of Varāhamihira, medical writers, and the authors of literary texts as engaging in a similar "Indianization" of betel, both in how they write about it and in the sheer fact that they include it among established materials and aesthetic modes.

By the Gupta period, one could consume imported wine, chew a betel quid, wear musk from the north, and use camphor from Southeast Asia in a newly forged and enduring Indic mode of luxury enjoyment. Thinking of betel as a "drug" makes it harder to understand its rapid incorporation. If, instead, we think of it as yet another mouth perfume, like camphor and nutmeg, it's easy to see how it fitted into a pre-existing system of perfumery, ultimately becoming a *framework substance*, along with which other aromatics (and later tobacco) were often taken. This consolidation of betel culture had already taken place by the time of Varāhamihira.

Was this new mouth-perfume subject to restrictions? Although often classified as a perfume or digestive-freshener, not everyone was supposed to use perfumes and garlands. Also, as I'll discuss later, betel was sometimes presented as an intoxicant or narcotic.[146] P. K. Gode and Andrea Gutierrez have both analyzed the prescription and prohibition of betel.[147] Broadly speaking, betel was associated with people (and deities) who lived a worldly life, enjoying the pleasures of the senses, and thus some later Hindu legal texts, from the late first millennium CE onward, specify that widows, ascetics, Vedic students, and people who are fasting should renounce betel.[148] These are roughly similar to those categories of people who might abandon adornment, perfumes, and so on as a sign of leaving behind a life of pleasures. Renouncing betel also correlates closely with states of celibacy.[149] Doing so presumably also reduces your attractiveness and allows you to avoid the heightened passions that betel can arouse. Betel-chewing, by contrast, was an index of the sensuous worldly life. Although the prohibitions appear in later *dharmaśāstra* texts, betel had clearly been assimilated into the framework of asceticism by that time: its use and prohibition line up with older prohibitions and permissions, such as those concerning garlands. Yet, as innocent and as sensuous as a garland, this new luxury drug (using the word in a broad sense) was available not just to Brahmins and kings; everyone could have betel, so long as they were not in certain types of ascetic states, and it was offered to deities in temple worship too. Betel was also allowed to Jain and Buddhist laypersons, who were required to abstain from liquor but not from sex or garlands.[150]

Betel is missing from earlier canonical texts, so it comes with very little history compared to alcohol. Arguably, when at a later date it's mentioned in *dharmaśāstra*, Hindu law, it was for purposes of clarification. This happens at the same period when Hindu legal texts began offering increasingly long lists of alcoholic drinks, probably as part of a process of accommodating legal theory to local practices. As betel wasn't specifically prohibited by caste or gender for people enjoying the worldly life, it was evidently a near universal social drug, with none of the controversies attending alcohol. In later periods, betel was highly praised. Some verses still quoted today, from the early to mid-second millennium CE, on the thirteen virtues of betel, conclude: "even in heaven these [virtues of betel] are rare!"[151]

As a sensuous pursuit, betel was sometimes associated with drink and the paraphernalia of arousal. We see this in the play *The Little Clay Cart* (*Mṛcchakaṭikā*) of Śūdraka. The date of this text is uncertain; while early, it was probably revised sometime after the fifth century CE.[152] The play contains a description of the activities taking place in the courtyards of a courtesan. In one, jewelers are at work:

> Wet layers of saffron are being dried;[153] tree-moss [?] is being liquefied;[154] sandalwood liquid is being carefully ground; blended perfumes are being mixed; betel [Prakrit: *tambolam*] with camphor is being given to the courtesans' lovers; people are looking at each other with side glances; there is laughter; *madirā* is constantly being drunk with hisses of pleasure; these male and female servants, and these other men who have disregarded their sons, wives, and wealth, are abandoned by the courtesans who have drunk the *madirā* from the *āsava* cups/pots (*āsavakaraa*)—they are all drinking![155]

Again, the connection of betel with perfumery is evident. And although betel was acceptable to people who shunned alcohol, that doesn't imply that it was never taken along with alcohol.

Even when depicted in a negative light, however, liquor and betel are different. When we see betel mentioned in a derogatory portrayal of a character, it's *not* because betel causes social pandemonium as alcohol does, but rather because taking *pān* was considered decadent, "fancy," even vain and affected, and connected to the pursuit of love. (Note, however, that this negative perspective is not standard in portrayals of the consumption of *pān*.) Consider the viciously satirical *Narmamālā* of Kṣemendra, composed around the middle of the eleventh century CE in Kashmir, which savages a caste of government scribes and officials (Kāyasthas), and which has been translated by Fabrizia Baldissera.[156] We read of the wife of a previously poor official who has recently become wealthy. Both she and her husband drink liquor, and he fills the house with jars of wine (-*madhughaṭā*-).[157] The husband's drinking is messy and laughable:

holding a jar of liquor (*madyakalaśa*)
between his knees,
repeatedly
he slowly sipped small amounts,
and thus drank a lot.[158]

And then:

Reeling from the liquor (*madyaghūrṇita*),
he trembled like a *vetāla* (corpse-animating demon)
who had taken possession (*āviṣṭa*) [of a corpse].[159]

He starts to move around spontaneously, just like the drunken hunter who discovered *surā* in the story at the beginning of this book:

The drunken (*kṣība*) *divira* [official/secretary] danced naked,
breaking his seat and his jar,
his body spattered by [black] dollops
from his rolling full inkpot.[160]

There is nothing charming or erotic about this man's drinking; he is a repulsive buffoon, a clumsy, nouveau riche, corrupt bureaucrat who drinks too much. His wife, by contrast, takes advantage of their new wealth to wear garlands and observes a "sacred vow" of cutting betel leaves (*tāmbūladalanavratā*).[161] Conceited, she reflects on her new life as follows:

The woman
who once drank rice water
—got by begging—
in a stone bowl
broken and pieced together again,
this very same woman now
drinks musk-wine (*kastūrikāmadhu*)
in a silver cup (*raupyapātre*).[162]

Unlike the gluttonous drinking of the husband, her drinking is associated with precious cups and wine perfumed with costly musk. The wife adorns her body and frequents her young male neighbors. She attracts libertines, who also adorn themselves and buy all the necessary paraphernalia of flirtation and seduction, having "spent prodigiously on perfumed oils, betel, incense, and the rest."[163] Discussing how to seduce her, these men note:

> Once social contact is born,
> one should offer her such things
> as flower garlands and rolls of betel leaves . . .[164]

Betel in itself does not cause bad behavior here, but rather, like perfumes, it is associated with activities sometimes conducted in a less than respectable manner. To give another example, Prabhāvatī, the admirably feisty wife in the humorous *Seventy Tales of the Parrot* (*Śukasaptati*), pops a betel quid into her mouth when, all adorned, she is about to leave the house for an amorous rendezvous. (Her wastrel husband has been sent away to redeem himself, having previously been ruinously attached to the classic vices of gambling, hunting, prostitutes, and intoxicating drink.)[165]

Whereas betel sometimes shared the stage with alcohol in private contexts, betel culture flourished in public settings because it was acceptable to so many people. In a society in which certain people ate separately and some people could not drink liquor, betel was perfectly suited to public consumption. Consider how tricky it would be to offer a public toast of alcohol in premodern India, or even in India today in some contexts. Betel could fill this social void. Drawing on inscriptional evidence, Daud Ali explains that in the Deccan, from the ninth or tenth century CE until the seventeenth century, betel and the related figure of the betel-bag bearer were of great consequence in royal rituals of welcome, social agreements, political alliances, and other contexts.[166]

To understand how people used and represented betel in the realm of royal power, let's consider a chronicle of the kings of Kashmir, the *River of Kings* (*Rājataraṅgiṇī*) of Kalhaṇa, from the twelfth century CE.[167] Here we see betel used in interactions with powerful people and associated with conspicuous consumption. Elite betel-chewers even adopted distinctive gestures and postures because they were constantly dealing with a betel-servant. At one point, King Jayāpīḍa's throne is usurped while he is away from Kashmir on a military expedition. Abandoned by his soldiers and dismissing his companions, he resolves to prove his power despite these setbacks. After arriving at a kingdom in the Bengal area, he goes to a temple to watch a dance performance. A dancer notices this handsome man and realizes that he must be a person of distinction:

> With astonishment she noticed that the hand of that distinguished-looking man reached, from time to time, quickly to the back of his shoulder.

She then thought: "Surely this must be a disguised king or a Rājaputra born from a great family."

"He is accustomed to take thus the rolled betel-leaves (*parṇavīṭikāḥ*) from [attendants] sitting at his back, and therefore his hand moves at every moment to the back of his shoulder."[168]

Similarly, South Indian images show a servant bearing a betel-bag standing behind the king.[169] The employment of a betel-servant was even subject to sumptuary rules.[170] From an earlier date, in the seventh-century prose poem by Bāṇa, *Kādambarī*, we read of a royal girl, brought from another king's harem to be the betel-box bearer and confidante for a prince.[171] When the same prince passes through the city streets, women flock to see him—a common motif—and one woman observes that he stretches out his hand, palm up, to ask for a *pān*.[172]

In the *River of Kings*, the dancer who spots King Jayāpīḍa's regal tic then slips pieces of areca nut (*pūgakhaṇḍān*, IV.430) into his grasping hand as a way to meet him, though later he resists her drunken advances.[173] Through this example of romantic detective work, we learn that the highly privileged had distinctive physical habits for taking *pān*, which visibly indicated their status. By contrast, although royal and high-class drinking has distinctive characteristics, it does not appear to reveal itself physically in such a distinctive manner.

The power of betel lies in both its exchange and its consumption, what Michael Dietler has called "commensal politics," the social consumption of substances as "a prime arena for the negotiation, projection, and contestation of power."[174] Betel was a perfumed, costly, mildly stimulating currency of social relations. Elite liquors, such as wine, had a limited scope for exchange and were shared among the elite only in private contexts, moments of intimacy depicted by poets and artists. Perfumed betel quids, by contrast, were (almost) universally acceptable and desirable. Significantly, betel also later thrived at Muslim courts.[175]

To offer betel was a powerful act of favor and hospitality. In the same chronicle of the kings of Kashmir, the *River of Kings*, when Prince Harṣa is approached by sixteen soldiers who are possibly intent on killing him,

He [Harṣa] called each of them by his name, offered them betel (*tāmbūlam*), and made them take their place in front of him.

They felt ashamed at this hospitable reception and, when taking betel, let go their weapons from their hands and the intent of murder from their minds.[176]

Not only does the act of accepting *pān* prevent the soldiers from holding their weapons, it also creates a debt of generosity and hospitality. Given that betel is presented as a luxury in this text, we can assume that these guards might never before have tasted such princely *pān* or been involved in such a prestigious and intimate exchange with a king.

This chronicle of Kashmir associates *pān* with the respectable upper classes and generally denigrates drinking and drinkers.[177] Yet, beyond its potential role in erotic intrigue, the expense of good betel also presented dangers. We have no explicit evidence for the price of betel, but it may sometimes have been costly. Possibly good leaves were not always available locally, and even if they were, just like today, leaves from certain regions may have been particularly desirable.[178] Thus we read that King Ananta, who was liberal in his expenditure and fond of *pān* (*priyatāmbūlaśīla*-), was almost ruined by the expense of buying betel from a certain Padmarāja, a foreigner who was a leaf procurer (*parṇaprāptika*-):[179]

> Then by selling *nāgarakhaṇḍa* and other such leaves, he almost had the king hand over the entire revenue of the land.[180]

Possibly these *nāgarakhaṇḍa* leaves were an expensive variety, possibly imported.[181] While Kashmir had local grapes and saffron, perhaps fresh betel leaves were a rarity.

Drinking was a vice, one that could ruin the king's character and health; excessive betel consumption, on the other hand, was respectable but could be economically ruinous. As a substance both precious and consumable (like perfume), betel was a good material for representing decadence. In the *River of Kings* we read this of one ruler:

> One time that king, most lavish in his youth, offered *pān* (*tāmbūla*) with pearls for areca-nut pieces.[182]

Again the problem is the expense, not intoxication. Betel can be decadent, but it does not lead to sin, at least no more than a garland might.

The flourishing of betel in a society with complex food and alcohol restrictions has similarities with the development of tea culture in Buddhist China. James Benn, writing of China, explains, "In the realms of knowledge exchange and aesthetics, the new commodity [tea] had a particularly noticeable effect. The aristocratic drinking party . . . had previously effectively excluded monks and devout lay-people from participating because of the precept against alcohol . . . Tea drinking, however, allowed monks and literati to meet on the same field and to share in the same aesthetic values, unthreatened by the dangers of intoxication . . . Monks and scholars thus discovered and promoted a mutually acceptable common ground in their new drug of choice."[183] In India, while some of the elite drank, the contexts in which they could do so with others were restricted.

Betel-chewing was a public, more inclusive (but still elite) form of consumption. Arguably, this situation has some similarities with cannabis consumption in the USA today, where cannabis is common and features in representations of many sections of society. Typically, however, cannabis in America is consumed by small groups in informal settings—set aside socially, temporally, and spatially from public life. When hosting a holiday party for your boss and colleagues, you wouldn't pass round that fancy Swarovski bong, a treasured wedding present. But you might offer Champagne.

Conclusions

People made a vast number of types of drink in early South Asia. As we've seen, even a single type of drink could include complex varieties. This is the case at any given time over a long period. Some drinks were simple in composition, like grape wine and toddy, and many were compounded from several ingredients. Some drinks were local, basic, and probably cheap. Some were local but more elaborate, containing spices and garnishes. Wine made from grapes stands out as the imported drink par excellence (at least in much of South Asia) and must have been unlike anything made locally when it first appeared on the scene. We'll never know what many of these drinks were like, though comparisons with drinks made today can give us some idea—modern *āsava*s, Chinese "yellow wine," and Filipino sugarcane *basi* in particular. One thing that stands out is the importance of a drink's appearance, as with the ruddy, white, black, and clear *surā*s. No doubt wine was also differentiated according to its color.

The words for drinks are as varied and complex as the drinks themselves. Some words, like *sīdhu* ("sugarcane wine"), have a relatively narrow field of meaning, and some, such as *āsava*, have a very broad application (alongside a narrow pharmacological definition). And of course there is the confusion of words related to or similar to "*madhu*." And we must not forget that many vernacular names would have been used for the drinks in practice.

Making, storing, and transporting drinks were also complex and varied processes, and in later chapters we'll see how different economic factors interacted with aesthetic, social, and legal attitudes toward drinking. Wine was apparently the only drink for which the place of production mattered. Other drinks were associated with certain regions, but even toddy from one place was not assigned a different name from toddy made in another. It's the *substance* of origin that marks each drink (other than wine), and sometimes the processing method (as with clear or aged drinks).

Wine was transported, requiring an exchange, possibly of money, and could be stored until used. With a cellar of jars, large quantities were available at any given moment. Other drinks, like *surā* and aged *sīdhu*, could also be stored. Toddy and some other drinks, by contrast, were available only soon after they were brewed. Distillation, when it appeared, must have changed everything, permitting previously perishable drinks to be stored and transported easily, and thus revolutionizing the economics of liquor and the skills required to produce it.

Why did people import wine when local drink was easy to produce? Why was India not largely a grain-*surā* culture? If people in India wanted more variety or craved a sugar-based drink, they already had one in the form of *sīdhu* or *maireya*, rendering grape wine even more redundant. To answer this question, I would argue that variety, taste, prestige, and a proximity to Iranian and Hellenistic cultures all played parts here. Even before the introduction of grape wine, a variety of drinks existed in India in addition to grain *surā*. Drinking was not just about intoxication but also about flavor. Drinks were like textiles, perfumes, or gemstones: variety, rarity, and luxury were highly appreciated. Possibly the varied geography, climate, and crops of South Asia played a part too. If we consider the wide area in which our texts were produced, we can't say, as Bottéro did for Mesopotamia, that the land condemned South Asia to manufacture and drink beer.[184] Moreover, as we shall see later, the brahminical tradition singled out grain *surā* as especially to be avoided, further hampering the development of a dominant culture of grain liquor, at least in elite circles.

With sugarcane a local crop and wine regions nearby—not to mention contact with Southeast Asia, the probable source of betel and many of its flavorings—the culture of intoxicants in India by the early to mid-first millennium CE was thoroughly varied. India in the first millennium CE was not an exclusively "beer civilization," nor a wine one, nor was alcohol the only common and highly developed drug (as we classify substances today). This prominence of both sugarcane drinks and betel is a distinctive feature of South Asian drug culture in the region's early period, quite unlike the drug cultures of China, the Middle East, or the ancient Mediterranean. Moreover, many powerful, literate people engaged in abstinence. This deep-rooted drug-complexity is reflected in literature, medicine, law, and other domains, though the enduring prominence of the word and concept *surā* is an echo of an ancient, formative time and place where grain drinks *were* apparently most significant. So, although pre-modern South Asia was most definitely not a "beer culture," *surā* is always the protagonist,[185] and plays many roles (as we shall see) in the more developed tradition. But unlike beer in Mesopotamia, *surā* the drink (the ancient grain drink) is most definitely not the drink of the gods, of priests, or of kings, whose tastes and habits are complex, involving other substances: from *soma*, to wine and *maireya* for Kṣatriyas, and later on, betel for everyone (who could afford it).

In ancient China, grain-based "wine" (*jiu*) played an important role in rituals and domestic consumption and was produced and enjoyed until the present day, so that the *jiu* drunk in practice, in classical poetry, and in rituals was a relatively similar substance in each case. By contrast, in India the most celebrated drug in classical, foundational religious texts, namely *soma*, was not produced and consumed outside Vedic rituals, leaving the preferred drinks of the gods and of many humans at odds, especially when we also consider brahminical restrictions on the consumption of *surā*—*soma*'s ancient antithesis. In later texts and rituals, however, the gods commonly enjoy a new elite "drug," betel, unknown in the Vedas. Thus, with betel, the consumption patterns of wealthy patrons, Brahmins, and (some) gods were once again aligned. (It is unclear to what extent poorer members of society had access to it.)

The actual drinking culture of South Asia must have been even more complex than what we can deduce from our surviving, patchy evidence. People in India manufactured a huge number of alcoholic drinks, managing the processes of obtaining sugars, fermentation, and flavoring in ingenious ways. Whether one approves of drinking or not, one can't deny that there should always be a chapter about premodern Indian drinks in any world history of alcohol.

CUP 3
Surā Brewing and Public Drinking

How did people in early India drink, and what did they write about modes of drinking? Did people drink alone or socially? Were there special drinking times, such as festivals and parties? Were there special drinking places? Were there people whom we might now call drink-professionals?

From the representations that survive, I have divided the topic of drinking into two parts. This chapter deals with public drinking, outside the home, in places like the *surā* shop ("alehouse") and at the festival. Such drinking seems to have been connected to a particular class of drinker and to certain drinks, often *surā*. It's often depicted as rowdy, though this characteristic may tell us more about the people writing and reading our sources than about the drinking itself. In Chapter 4, I consider the drinking associated with the wealthy, with privacy, erotics, and a literary, poetic style of representation. But the division is by no means absolute. And, again, the chapter division here is as much about textual genre as about practice.

Before I look at the Indian materials, let's briefly consider early English drinking culture, to get a sense of the nuances of drinking places and practices in a Western culture that may be more familiar to some readers. Although these distinctions were not rigid, in pre-industrial England there were three types of public drinking places, recognized in statute as well as common law:[1] Inns served wine, beer, and ale, and offered food and lodging in fashionable settings. Taverns sold wine to a prosperous clientele but lacked lodging. Alehouses sold ale or beer and offered basic food and lodging in simple settings for the "lower orders." All three types of institution underwent a complex development over the centuries.

Similarly, descriptions of drinking from early India were no doubt composed in a complex world. Styles of drinking and drinking places changed over time, and in such a large region there must have been much local variation. As with the word "tavern" in modern marketing language, some Sanskrit texts may for various reasons have continued to use archaic words and conventions that no longer related to life as it was lived "on the street."

Many of the texts on drinking in this chapter are literary, moralizing, or polemical. What can we do about this?[2] First, the polemics tell us a lot about the people who produced and propagated these texts, their attitudes toward drink, and what struck them as noteworthy about drinking practices. Thus it is eminently possible to write a literary and intellectual history of texts describing *surā* breweries and drink shops. But I am still interested in the possibility of writing,

An Unholy Brew. James McHugh, Oxford University Press. © Oxford University Press 2021.
DOI: 10.1093/oso/9780199375936.003.0005

even if only a rather cautious and attenuated, social and material-culture history of drinking in India. And arguably even highly stylized representations of drinking might feature elements—social and material—that were deemed basic to such contexts, both as depicted in art and as experienced in practice. To take an example from popular American culture, the cantina full of aliens in the first *Star Wars* film may well be intentionally weird, but it is also, in many respects, a typical American bar or a cantina as represented in, say, cowboy films. And in some respects it is not enormously unlike some actual bars in the Americas.

Such modern bars—in film and in reality—include, among other elements, a literal *bar*: a flat counter behind which the bartenders stand and the drinks and vessels themselves are displayed. But bars are not an inevitable feature of all drinking places in all times and places. Bars of this kind first appeared in England, at least, in the early seventeenth century.[3] We can be fairly sure that premodern Indian drinking places did *not* have bars, but they did probably feature proprietor-brewers who sold drink and snacks to a mixed bunch of customers seated or standing in drinking areas, much as one sees in a toddy shop today. They also probably had distinctive signs or banners. Thus, although our sources are far from documentary in style, I am open to the idea that some elements of the descriptions they contain, as with the alien *bar* in *Star Wars*, can sometimes serve as loose guides to features of drinking in practice (though other scholars might, perfectly reasonably, be more skeptical, taking such assumed, typical "realia" merely as common literary conventions, similar to the ubiquitous glass walls of TV-show hospital rooms).

Brewing and the *Surā* Trade in the Earliest Sources

Vedic texts contain possible hints of the drinking culture of early periods, when grain-based *surā* was probably the principal alcoholic drink. In the *Ṛgveda* there are references to the existence of *surā* and also a tricky reference to the house of a *surā*-possessor where there is what may be a leather *surā* container.[4] A later Vedic text contains a list of various figures in society, symbolic (not actual) victims in a hypothetical human sacrifice, who are offered to various deified principles.[5] This list mentions a *surā*-maker (*surākārám*) associated with a substance called *kīlāla*. This word, found in texts from before the Common Era, refers to a drink related to *surā*, which was perhaps sweet and might have some connection to milk products.[6] Although we lack details here, we can at least establish that a named member of society was associated with making *surā*. Also, the ancient recipes for *surā* in Vedic ritual texts, as well as the hymn about *surā* in the *Atharvaveda*, suggest that brewing was a highly developed process requiring skill and an array of resources: grains, malts, fire, special vessels and filters, and the elusive *nagnahu* (perhaps a starter). So in this period we have evidence of a labor-intensive, complicated brewing process and an example of a brewing specialist.

The Vedic *Vājapeya* ritual requires its participants to drink *parisrut*, which may be unfiltered *surā*.[7] The full ritual is complex, but it involves a chariot race, after which the participants drink *parisrut* that has been previously purchased.[8] Do we see hints here of communal male drinking associated with racing chariots? Such drinking would presumably be intermittent, associated with a particular event and a select group of participants. Also significant is the fact that one could obtain a ready-made *surā*-like preparation, by exchange.

In later Vedic texts on domestic rituals (*Gṛhya Sūtras*), we perhaps catch a glimpse of how *surā* was used at weddings. *Surā* is imbued with much symbolic meaning in these rituals. In the *Gobhila Gṛhya Sūtra*, prior to her wedding, a woman is sprinkled with *surā* by her friend. Oldenberg translates, "a friend should besprinkle her three times at her head, so that her whole body becomes wet, with Surā of the first quality, with [the formula] 'Kāma! I know thy name. Intoxication (*Mada*) thou art by name' . . . with the following two verses he should wash her private parts."[9] In another domestic ritual text (*Śāṅkhāyana Gṛhya Sūtra*), the bride-to-be is washed not with *surā* but with perfumed water.[10] Then, after she has been washed and dressed and her family priest has made offerings, the ritual continues: "After they have regaled four or eight women, who are not widows, with lumps of vegetables, *surā*, and food, these should perform a dance four times."[11] Then sweet mahua flowers are tied to her. *Surā* is thus present during the wedding, something we'll see again later. In the first instance the wife is sprinkled, accompanied by a mantra concerning *kāma* (desire) equated with intoxication, concepts associated with drinking over a long period. There is no sense in these texts that this is a transgressive rite. Women, it seems, conventionally drank *surā* and danced at weddings, all in an orthodox domestic ritual.

Surā is also added to an offering to female ancestors in a later Vedic text on domestic rites, and the announcement of funerary libations of a wife (or son) are recommended as a subterfuge to trick enemies into drinking large quantities of drugged liquor in the *Arthaśāstra*.[12]

To sum up, from Vedic sources we learn that there were *surā*-brewers and that people may have drunk *surā* at gatherings such as weddings and tournaments. We might assume that *surā* may have been produced in large quantities for such occasions. *Surā* in the Vedic texts is also connected to lust and intoxication. I will return to the meaning of *surā* in Vedic texts in Cups 6 and 7.

The Drinking House, the *Surā* Shop, and the Brewery

The most detailed description of the production and sale of liquor in ancient India that we possess is in the *Arthaśāstra*.[13] As noted earlier, this part of the text was probably composed around the turn of the Common Era. We learn of the duties of the Superintendent of *Surā*:

> He should have drinking-houses (*pānāgāraṇi*) built that have many rooms (*-kakṣyāṇi*), each with separate beds and seats, that have drink-indicators [menus? tallies? signs?],[14] where there are perfumes, garlands, and water, and that are comfortable according to the season. Secret agents placed there should note normal and unusual expenditures, and newcomers. They should note the ornaments, clothes, and cash of customers who are drunk or asleep. If these are lost, the traders (*vaṇij*) should give their value, and the same again as a punishment. But the traders should have their own charming female servants note the nature of newcomers, locals, and people with the appearance of Āryas when they are drunk or asleep in the secluded sections of the rooms.[15]

Though established by the Superintendent of *Surā*, these drinking-houses are run by traders/merchants, who sell drinks and maintain their rooms, furniture, perfumes, and seasonal paraphernalia. Secret agents, presumably disguised as workers or customers, keep an eye on newcomers and note exceptional expenditures, which might indicate that something dishonest is afoot. The landlord instructs his female servants/slaves (*dāsī*) to observe people. These women are attractive and can access the private areas where the secret agents can't spy. This type of spy-barmaid is quite different from the "alewife" we'll discuss later. The arrangement may imply that the customers are all male: the (male?) secret agents can observe the customers drinking in the more public places, but possibly only attractive women can access customers in the more intimate settings (though there is no suggestion of prostitution here, about which the *Arthaśāstra* is quite frank elsewhere). In its furniture, decorations, and service, this place resembles an English inn or tavern more than a common alehouse. Given that some customers are described as potentially asleep, we might wonder if one could stay the night—though they might simply be drunk. The *Arthaśāstra* elsewhere notes that "tipplers/brewers" (*śauṇḍika-*),[16] along with merchants of cooked meat and of cooked rice, should lodge people well known to them.[17]

This state-regulated inn is quite unlike the simple *surā* shops described in other texts. In all likelihood there were multiple types of drinking place, from small shelters to elaborate inns, just as England had inns, taverns, and alehouses. Nevertheless, it's hard to distinguish any consistent usage of Sanskrit words for drinking places corresponding to such a variety.

If the basic elements of an English pub are a name, a sign, a bar, a cellar, beer and other drinks, specially shaped glasses, bar snacks, a landlord, staff, and customers, then what were the basic elements of an ancient or early-medieval Indian drinking-house? Fortunately, there are several surviving depictions of drinking places that are consistent across a variety of sources.

Take the humorous comparison of a drinking-house to a Vedic sacrifice in a comic play called *Drunken Games* (*Mattavilāsaprahasana*). The play is from a relatively early date, the early seventh century CE, and we shall return to it several times.[18] Here a certain type of ascetic who likes a drink describes a drink-shop:

> My dear, look, look! This *surā* shop (*surāpaṇa*) equals the magnificence of a sacrificial enclosure. For here the flag-pole (*dhvajastambha*) is the sacrificial post; the *surā* is the *soma*; the drinkers (*śauṇḍā*) are the priests (*ṛtvijaḥ*); the drinking cups (*caṣaka*) are the soma-drinking vessels (*camasa*); the snacks (*upadaṃśa*), meat kebabs (*śūlyamāṃsa*), and so forth are the various oblations; the speech of drunkards is the *Yajus* mantras; the songs are the liturgical chants (*sāmāni*); the buckets (*udaṅka*) are the sacrificial ladles (*sruva*); the thirst is the fire; and the master of the *surā* shop (*surāpaṇādhipati*) is the sacrificial patron (*yajamāna*).[19]

Like the sacrifice, the *surā* shop here is an assemblage of people and things characterized by certain actions, including verbal ones. The location, a *surā* shop (*surā-āpaṇa*), may imply a simple affair like a chai stand or toddy shop today. There is a banner or sign (*dhvaja*). There are cups, buckets (or larger containers of some sort), and snacks, here meat on a spit or skewer and other snacks. Whereas in a sacrifice the offerings are put into the fire and also consumed by the priests, here thirst is the fire and the drinkers are the libation-pouring priests. Interestingly, the *surā*, which feeds the fire of thirst, is deemed the equivalent of *soma*. Yet *surā* is the antithesis of *soma*, and the author of these lines clearly had a sophisticated sense of how these substances related to each other in the orthodox view. This play elsewhere portrays what we might call proto-Tantric practices that transgress brahminical orthodoxy, and it's striking that the writer manipulates *surā* here to powerful humorous and literary effect (as opposed to the ritual, conceptual manipulation of alcohol in some forms of Tantra.)

This drinking place is owned by a landlord, just as a sacrificial patron pays for the sacrifice. The landlord no doubt enjoys the profits of the *surā* shop, just as the patron reaps the rewards of the sacrifice. Like a sacrifice, this place, with all its people and paraphernalia, is quite hectic, in this case with boisterous drunken conversation and singing. Apparently in such drinking places there was no physical bar, just a house or shelter where drinks were served from large vessels, along with snacks. As in several other descriptions, the people here may all be male, like the majority of personnel at a sacrifice; there is no equivalent mentioned here of the sacrificer's wife, although in the play this ascetic does have a female companion.

Brewing *surā* must have been hard work: imagine heaving a hide-lined bamboo frame into a pit filled with a fermenting grain, or boiling large pots of rice. We gain some sense of the challenges of the task from an early Buddhist Pali text, the *Upāli Sutta*. Here a man called Upāli wishes to debate the Buddha and describes how he will shake the Buddha about with his arguments:

> as a strong brewery worker (*soṇḍikākammakara*), placing a great brewer's basket (*soṇḍikākilañjaṃ*) into a deep pond of water and grasping the edges/corners, would drag it toward him and drag it this way and that . . . As a strong brewery rogue (*soṇḍikādhutta*), grabbing the [hair-]sieve (*vālaṃ*) by the edges/corners, would shake it off, shake it out, and throw it about . . .[20]

It's not clear what is going on here, nor does all the vocabulary correspond to terms seen elsewhere. The first man is a worker in a *soṇḍikā*'s establishment—that is to say a place where drink, probably *surā*, is made and sold—this being one of the several *śuṇḍā*-cognate forms associated with drink.[21] He grasps the edges of an object called a *kilañjā*, a word that can mean a fiber mat, a screen, a bundle, or a basket. Then this object is dunked into a pool of water, shaken, and dragged about violently. Might this be the process of wetting grains to malt them? Or perhaps the worker is simply washing grains or the mat/basket/bundle? A brewer's *kilañjā* is also mentioned in the Pali Buddhist *Saṃyutta Nikāya*, in which Māra, a demonic force of death and desire, takes on the form of a gigantic terrifying serpent, whose cobra-like hood is compared to a brewer's *kilañjā*,[22] leading one to think that the object is flat in profile and large, maybe a large woven tray or a woven flat basket. The second man in Upāli's comparison is a rogue associated with the brewery,[23] who no doubt drinks there (and maybe works there too, in a roguish manner). He grabs a sieve and shakes it around. In the Vedic descriptions of *surā*-making, filtering with a hair sieve comes at a late stage in processing the drink, and presumably this man is trying to extract as much drink from the sieve as possible. Or maybe he is drunk and playing with the object randomly, like a drunken student with a traffic cone? Despite this uncertainty, there are strong men present in *surā* breweries who labor proverbially vigorously using large objects.

The Drinking-House Banner

The drinking-house banner may seem insignificant—a mere sign for a pub—but in fact we can learn a lot from this object.[24] To scholars of Sanskrit, this banner will be familiar from Hindu law, where it features in punishments for drinking, being either carried as a penance or branded for punishment as an image onto the forehead. Punishment and penance in ancient India were often public acts, so the visibility and meaning of these marks mattered.[25] Older sources that mention these banners tell us nothing about what they were. For example, the *surā* banner (*surādhvaja*) appears for the first time in dharma literature in the *Baudhāyana Dharmasūtra*, dating from somewhere between the mid-second century BCE and the turn of the Common Era. In this text we're told that the king, who can't apply capital punishment to Brahmins, instead applies punishment (*daṇḍa*), branding the forehead of a Brahmin who has drunk *surā* (*surāpāna*) with the image of a *surā* banner—using a heated iron (*taptenāyasā*) to do so—and banishing him from the kingdom.[26] This same *surā*-banner punishment is common in later sources too.[27]

What sort of thing was the banner? When the king had a murderer branded, the image used was a headless body; heads separated from bodies generally, and unsurprisingly, were emblematic of murder and killing. For the *varṇa*-specific crime or sin of drinking *surā*, however, the older texts do not say that offenders were branded with a symbol such as a cup or jar, but rather with the sign or banner of a seller of *surā*. Later commentators tell us more: when discussing a penance that involves carrying an actual banner, the ninth-century commentator on *The Law Code of Manu*, Medhātithi, as well as other legal commentators, clarifies that the banner was a jar for intoxicating drink (and presumably the image of a jar when branded)—though they were writing much later than the first written references to such banners.[28]

Whatever the nature of the banner, the *surā*-drinking offender was branded with an image of a sign, a commercial sign. Effectively, the body of the offender was transformed into a walking *surā* advertisement, or even a *surā* shop personified. One is reminded of the Summoner in Chaucer's *Canterbury Tales*, whose garland transforms his head into the medieval sign called an ale-stake: "A gerland hadde he set upon his heed, As greet as it were for an ale-stake."[29]

Why would a *surā* shop have a sign? This might seem a strange question to us, who live in a world full of signs, but we should consider why a retail establishment would be so marked in ancient India. In medieval and early modern England, alehouses had signs, as did taverns and inns. Chaucer's alestake was a pole with a bush at the top, advertising that a brewing had taken place and that ale, perishable in those days, was temporarily available.[30] In a small village or a town with few visitors, presumably everyone knew where the *surā* shop was, so the sign might have been used to indicate the intermittent availability of ale. The sign might even have been a symptom of confusingly widespread brewing. As Judith Bennett writes of alehouses in England, in "a world where many households sold ale at least occasionally, a temporary sign of some sort . . . told potential customers that ale was available within."[31]

But this was not the only use of beer signage in England. Urban drinking establishments often had a red lattice or a checkers pattern painted on the wall, as one sees on the wall of the Sun tavern in Hogarth's engraving "Beer Street."[32] In a large city filled with new arrivals and travelers, such a sign indicated where to buy drink (compare it to a barber's pole). The *surā* sign of early India could have been this sort of sign, which would imply that *surā* shops were frequented by newcomers and travelers in populous urban settings, as is indicated in the *Arthaśāstra*.

Finally, the differentiation of access to *surā* in society leads us to another possibility: that the sign functioned as a warning of the presence of a highly defiling substance and indicated a structure that those forbidden to drink *surā* should avoid. Even if this was not the primary reason for such signs, they could well have functioned in this way for those who risked harsh consequences for drinking *surā*, especially in public.

A line in the *Mahābhārata* suggests that the *surā* sign was a proverbially prominent item of public display. This verse, about ostentatious, hypocritical piety, may also imply that such signs were constantly displayed:

> He who has a banner of righteousness forever raised up like a *surā* banner, but whose evil deeds are hidden, follows the cat observance.[33]

The "cat observance" refers to the following story: a cat once posed as a holy man (actually, a holy cat) to impress some mice, with the hope of eating them. But eventually they saw through his disguise and escaped his pious trap. Thus the "cat observance" indicates hypocritical and conspicuous behavior. There is a charming depiction of this story in a relief at Mahabalipuram.[34]

Although a retail sign may seem unremarkable today, the *surā* sign was conspicuous in ancient India—it may well have been the only retail sign—and any reference, visual or textual, to this distinctive object would have evoked participation in a practice, economy, and social class that, while evidently thriving, were by no means always celebrated in our surviving sources.

The Regulation of Brewing

Did people regulate the liquor trade—both brewing and sales—in early India? If so, in what ways, and why? The *Arthaśāstra* describes the ideal state regulation of drink production, trade, and drinking places: along with prostitution and the trade in salt, the sale of liquor in this text is a state monopoly.[35] The Superintendent of Liquor organizes the trade in *surā* and *kiṇva* (*surākiṇvavyavahārān*) through qualified officers.[36] Remember that, practically speaking, people could make *surā* more or less anywhere, needing only grains, fire, water, and *kiṇva* (starter)—the latter being so essential that it was also subject to regulation. Three sites of trade are mentioned: the fort (*durga*), the countryside (*janapada*), and the military camp (*skandhāvāra*). The text argues that there should be either single outlets (*mukha*) or multiple ones, and that the trade should be regulated according to the demands of sale and purchase.[37] Thus, in theory, a person could not just start brewing *surā* and selling it. Such unregulated outlets, in the *Arthaśāstra,* incur a fine of 600 *Paṇas*, whether the malefactors are involved in manufacturing, selling, or buying.[38] This policy would have concentrated the trade in certain spots, benefitting established brewers and making the transactions easier to monitor and tax.

Why regulate the liquor trade? What purpose did this state monopoly serve? Was it for revenue, or because an unrestrained liquor trade would have had implications for law and order? Perhaps both, for later in this *Arthaśāstra* chapter we read of the taxation of this idealized, state-regulated economy. First, however, we are told of the regulations on moving alcoholic drinks. This relates, no doubt, to the restrictions on the number of *surā* outlets. *Surā* should not be taken out of the village (*grāma*), nor stockpiled (*asaṃpātaṃ*)[39]—presumably a prohibition designed to prevent fluctuations in price and availability, as all the *surā* made was always put straight on the market.

Yet the text relates such unlawful movement or stockpiling to social order: uncontrolled drink has bad social consequences. People commissioned to do work might neglect it; Āryas might transgress the sort of restrictions one sees in *dharmaśāstra*; and "assassins might become emboldened."[40] That is to say, the lower classes might neglect their labor, which was undesirable for those who relied on it , and the higher classes might do things that threatened their respectability. Assassins would have been mainly a threat to the powerful, especially the king. The social dangers of drink thus differed according to class.

The chapter concludes with a recommendation that people drink at the drinking-house (or drink-house, *pānāgāram*).[41] This word implies a structure of some sort where both the selling and (probably) the manufacture took place. Drinkers, according to the text, should remain at this place, not spilling out into the town—a restriction one also finds today in many parts of the United States. The restrictions on taking drink away from a regulated outlet—effectively state "off-licenses"—do have exceptions: people known to be good and pure (*jñātaśauca*) can take various small quantities, though they have to be marked, perhaps with a seal (*lakṣitam*). The quantities in question were probably under a liter,[42] and it's not clear why five different volumes are specified in the text, though perhaps these were the standard measures of drink, like pints and half-pints in England?

The *Arthaśāstra* presents an ideal vision of a kingdom, but regardless of whether drinking was ever regulated in this manner (and some of the narrative sources suggest a less regimented reality), this vision of perfectly regulated drinking has notable features. First, despite the prohibition of drinking for Brahmins, there is no attempt in this ideal version to enforce complete prohibition, just various controls. Also, the way drink is regulated in the *Arthaśāstra* seems quite modern: centralized state control carried out by designated officers, restrictions on the number of outlets, and highly restricted off-licenses. As for revenue, duty on external and internal trade in liquor is mentioned elsewhere in this text: we learn that the state takes a one-tenth or one-fifteenth portion of the ferment (*kiṇva*), and a one-twentieth or one-twenty-fifth part of the intoxicating drink (*madya*).[43] In a somewhat unclear passage, we also read that some drinks, perhaps those not regulated by the state, were taxed at 5%.[44] Observe that the all-important *kiṇva* was taxed relatively highly compared to the finished product. It's not clear to what extent the state supervised brewing, aside from maybe enforcing the standards and ingredients that we saw earlier. Possibly the state issued permits for brewing and supervised measures and so on, with supervised brewer-landlords running their own drinking-houses and paying duty. Or did the state regulation extend all the way down to the servers in the drink-houses?[45]

Returning to the *Arthaśāstra*, there follows a passage on the recovery of stolen goods, a passage that seems out of place, though maybe drinking-houses were places where people exchanged stolen goods, or spent the profits from stealing.[46] We then learn that the price of liquor (*surā*) is fixed—people cannot sell it at a non-regulation price (*anargheṇa*).[47] As Kangle explains, if the price is too high, the seller is pocketing extra profit; too low, and there must be adulteration. Also, the state revenue is linked to the price of *surā*. Moreover, one cannot provide *surā* on credit (*kālikā*), though, as we'll see, there are hints that *surā* was sometimes so provided. In this case, the *Arthaśāstra* may reveal a policy honored more in the breach than in the observance.

These restrictions on pricing do not apply to spoiled (*duṣṭā*) drink. Bad *surā* could be sold elsewhere, or given as wages (*vetanam*) to slaves or workers, or given to beasts of burden as a "stimulating drink" (*pratipāna*), or fed to pigs as nourishment.[48] Paying people with spoiled *surā* suggests a system of mobilizing labor via rewards of drink, something commonly seen in other parts of the world.[49] Of course, if bad *surā* was used in this way, it would have reinforced a connection between certain classes and certain drinks. As for the animals' drinking habits, elsewhere in the *Arthaśāstra* we read that bullocks, cows, donkeys, and other animals are given a stimulating drink (*pratipāna*) that may contain *surā*, as are horses and elephants.[50] According to a later text on elephant lore, the *Mātaṅgalīlā*, the winter regimen for an elephant involves a warm stall provided with *surā*.[51] And in one Pali *Jātaka*, horses and donkeys are fed an intoxicating grape drink. While the "lowly" animals, donkeys, get a worse type of liquor and become intoxicated, the noble horses, served something resembling wine (at least in the prose part), remain calm.[52]

Then the *Arthaśāstra* presents regulations for domestic brewing. Householders (*kuṭumbinaḥ*) are allowed to make white *surā* (*śvetasurā*) for festivals.[53] Such domestic brewing for festivals and weddings may have been common and would have been almost impossible to prohibit in practice. Domestic brewing may even have been the older mode of production, culturally entrenched and hard to stamp out even with state regulation of public drinking-houses. This rule also implies that some householders—including women, as we'll see—were skilled at brewing at least of one type of *surā*. The text here also mentions that householders can make *ariṣṭa* for medical purposes, "or others [i.e., drinks]." *Surā* licenses (*saurikā*) for this sort of brewing lasted for four days, which may indicate how long large drinking festivals lasted, although exactly what is covered by a "*surā* license" is uncertain—brewing time, or drinking time, or both?[54] Certainly four days is a reasonable time to make a simple *surā*. Anyone without a license would pay a daily charge, which is not specified, implying that if one had the money, one could bypass getting a license to brew at short notice.[55] It is striking, though, that people who had no cash or surplus goods to use in a drink-house, yet who had grains and herbs at home, were still theoretically unable to obtain *surā* outside festival times.

Evidence of such regulations is rare, and the *Arthaśāstra* is our richest source. Did states actually organize the liquor trade like this? There is some inscriptional evidence for the regulation of liquor sales in early India.[56] The *Charter of Viṣṇuṣena*, from 592 CE, is a rare legal inscription from the early medieval period in which a feudatory king endorses the customary rules of a set of merchants in a community in western India.[57] Much of the terminology in this inscription is difficult, and even in the light of what we have learned in this book, the sections on liquor are not clear. In a section on miscellaneous fines, taxes, and fees, there are rules dealing with liquor, indigo, sugarcane, oil pressing, grain, ginger, bamboo, and spices. Thus the rules apply to a sizable part of the agricultural, manufacturing, and trading economy. If a significant portion of society drank and it was legal for them to do so, liquor would have been an important element of the local manufacturing economy, though possibly less suited to long-distance trade than dyes and textiles. As Clark has shown for early modern England, people engaged in large-scale pre-industrial manufacturing could become wealthy and powerful, and this may have applied in ancient and early medieval India too.[58]

Here are the rules concerning liquor from this inscription.[59] There may have been little or no distinction between the *surā* brewery and the *surā* shop, so the measures for *surā* retail may have applied to the same place in which it was fermented and stored (Translation of Wiese and Das, modified):

> Statutes 42–44:
> For the inspection of a vessel for liquor (*madyabhājana*), [the fee of] *rūpaka*s 5.
> For the first legal vessel [brewed], to the official *rūpaka*s 2½ [is to be given].
> If someone, without asking permission, brews[60] on a second day, he is obliged to pay twice that amount.

45:
For inspection of liquor equipment, *rūpaka*s 3, with respect to *dhārmika* [some sort of fee?],[61] *rūpaka* 1¼, and, as cession for the king, two quarter-measures of liquor.
[a difficult line on brass vessels]

47:
In the royal storehouse [or the royal tavern, *-gañje*], the guild's headman of the brewers (*kalvapālavārikeṇa*)[62] should not do anything else but what has to be measured by hand with quarter *śoṭīs*.

. . .

Statutes 66–70:
With respect to duty:
- On a vehicle [full] of liquor, 5 rupees. With respect to the *dhārmika* [fee], 1¼ rupees.

- For a load [of liquor?] whose carrier is a *khalla* [wineskin? – *khallabharakasya*], 1¼ rupees plus the *dhārmika* [fee].
- And on a yoke-net of a *kelā* [a measure of liquor?], half the tax of the above.[63]
- On a *pāda* jug, five *viṃśopaka*s plus the *dhārmika* [fee].

With respect to *kaṭu* liquor (*kaṭumadye* – strong? spiced?], 3 quarter-measures of *śīdhu* (sugarcane wine).

Despite the significant translation difficulties, these rules give us some sense of the liquor trade, particularly the complexity of liquor regulations. The main word for drink is *madya-*, the most generic term, referring to all intoxicating drinks. There is also a reference to a place where *surā* is made, and one fee is paid in the form of *śīdhu*, sugarcane wine. If we take *surā* here in the narrower sense of the word, meaning a grain drink, then the drinks mentioned correlate with raw materials mentioned in the statues: sugarcane and grains.

In this inscription it seems that we're dealing with the regulation of manufacture and sale rather than a state monopoly. First, there are required inspections (*avalokye*) of the vessels and the brewing place. The rule concerning brewing on a second day without permission implies that each stage required official permission (perhaps like the licenses in the *Arthaśāstra*). This may also be implied by the separate fees for inspecting the vessels (charged per vessel) and the brewery as a whole. It is possible that these inspections might have been established to maintain quality, preventing adulteration and other meddling, along with undeclared production and trade. The *Arthaśāstra*, by stipulating recipes, also suggests enforced brewing standards. Maybe the rule about the "first vessel" implies a fee paid for simply having an extra vessel, so that if people expanded their brewing operations they had to pay a duty on new equipment (and an increased volume of *surā*), in addition to the duty paid every time a batch was brewed. Uncertainties aside, it is clear that in this inscription the *production* of liquor, even on a small scale, was inspected and subject to fees.

In addition to the cash paid in duty in this time and place, a brewer had to cede some liquor to the king—another reason to keep the standards of brewing high. (Interestingly, in a Greek text from the mid-first century CE on trade in the Indian Ocean, the *Periplus Maris Erythraei*, the king takes some of the better wine being traded.)[64] Given the various fees, we can assume that the brewer needed to have liquid cash at hand. If we add up the costs of owning/renting and maintaining the place of brewing, buying large vessels and equipment, purchasing raw materials, and paying inspection charges such as these, large-scale brewing (possibly implied by the vehicle mentioned) would require the manufacturer to be affluent, with a complex cash flow and accounts, and possibly somewhat literate too, to keep records of this complex business.

The next regulations explain duties on transporting liquor and suggest that it was stored in vessels of different volumes (compare to the variously named sizes of barrel and bottle in Europe). Here we see a "wineskin" used for carrying liquor, something mentioned in Vedic sources too.[65] Finally there is a charge for trade in something called "pungent intoxicating drink." Notably, the charge for transporting "pungent" liquor is to be paid in sugarcane liquor—or maybe this is the quantity of sugarcane liquor used in making the pungent drink.

Despite the difficulties of the text, a picture emerges from this inscription of a merchant community in which the production and transport of liquor were closely regulated, generating revenue for the king through fees as well as tithes of liquor. The drink was transported in a variety of standardized containers, which implies that it was not highly perishable. All these fees would have raised the price for the consumer and made more work for the brewer and trader, though, as we know nothing about the alternatives, we should bear in mind that these regulations (and potentially others not mentioned here) may have been beneficial for the merchant community. Although we have only meager evidence, it not unreasonable to assume that, given the probable economic importance of liquor, such regulations were quite often in place.

Female Brewers

Several sources connect women to India's early drinking culture. In the *Arthaśāstra* we read that "women and children should do the gathering of [materials for] *surā* and *kiṇva*" (or possibly "*kiṇva* for *surā*").[66] This probably applies to the small-scale householder production covered in that sub-section. Elsewhere the *Arthaśāstra* explains that wives of brewer-traders (*śauṇḍika*) are permitted to travel freely, accompanied by men (i.e., not their husbands), so this was evidently a profession that required the wives to move at will and socialize with all manner of people, and possibly to sell drink and gather brewing materials too.[67] The *Law Code of Manu* portrays such unsupervised wandering (*aṭanaṃ*) and association with men as corrupting, just as drink itself (*pānaṃ*) is corrupting; these behaviors are part of a group of six "woman-corrupters" (*nārīsaṃdūṣaṇāni*) that somewhat correspond to the behavior of the brewing, dancing women in the Buddhist story of the jar.[68] The *surā*-selling, traveling, *kiṇva*-gathering, brewing-associated woman was apparently free of constraints by comparison to some other women, even if that meant she was not respectable in the eyes of some.

In the *Kāmasūtra*, from the Gupta period, there is a lengthy description of the duties of a sole wife (as opposed to a wife in a polygamous marriage), which tells us much about the workings of an ideal ancient Indian household:

> [The only wife is responsible for] the stocking of the jars of *surā* and the jars of *āsava*, as well as their usage, and she supervises buying and selling, as well as income and expenditure.[69]

This line comes after descriptions of foodstuffs and cooking and is followed by lines about her duties to her husband's friends and kin, possibly because it is with these friends that the drinks might be consumed. The first thing to note here is that the household has drink stocked: here the two basic categories of grain drinks (*surā*) and sugar-based drinks (*āsava*) that are stored in jars. It thus seems that the wife is in charge of overseeing the drink rather than making it herself. But this management still involves multiple skills: stocking the jars, which nevertheless possibly involved having the drinks made, and keeping track of consumption. She also has to supervise how the drinks are bought and sold, which suggests that a household's liquor stock might sometimes be sold.

There is an episode in the *Māhābhārata* in which women are involved with drink.[70] In the *Virāṭa Book*, the Pāṇḍava brothers are living incognito, and a man called Kīcaka becomes obsessed with their shared wife, Draupadī. She rejects his advances, but his sister, Sudeṣṇā, devises a plan to get Draupadī into Kīcaka's presence so that he can try again to seduce her. He has lots of food and drink prepared for a holiday (*parviṇīṃ*),[71] the drink being apparently *parisrut surā* (though there are many textual variants here).[72] His sister sends Draupadī to get some of the *surā*, saying that she wants a drink, and when poor Draupadī arrives Kīcaka tries to force himself on her. She escapes, and ultimately he is killed for his assault on her.

Several aspects of the story reflect early *surā* culture as seen elsewhere. First, Kīcaka commissions the *surā* for a periodic festival, and it may well be *parisrut*, the half-finished *surā* that we saw earlier. Draupadī's mistress wishes to drink some of the festive *surā* and sends her to get it. The connection of women and *surā* (drinking, collecting) also fits with what we see elsewhere.[73] This is Draupadī's second great humiliation; the first took place during a dice game. *Surā* and dice are classic vices (*vyasanas*) in India, and, as we'll learn later, they are abodes of intoxication (*mada*). When men are possessed by intoxication through dice or gambling, nothing good can come of it.

As an aside, we should note that the gambling in the *Mahābhārata* takes place in the assembly hall (*sabhā*), which, as Harry Falk has noted, was associated with drinking, gambling, and women as sexual objects (a vice also linked with *mada*), even in the late Vedic period.[74] And the *Sabhā* Book of the *Mahābhārata* does indeed contain a comparison of the intoxication of gambling to that of drinking (MBh 2.55.5, *madhu-* here presumably being mead?) These are all modes of behavior associated with the vices and practices of Kṣatriya men, especially kings, in later, classical formulations of society and morality, even when royal drinking is depicted as taking place in more cosmopolitan and luxurious contexts. We also perhaps get hints of this early drinking culture in the *Mahābhārata*, when Kṛṣṇa and Arjuna drink; in the feasts for soldiers in the *Rāmāyaṇa*, seen earlier; and even when the king sits down to drink *surā* in the story of the jar (told in the Apertif). These are examples of kingly, martial, male communal drinking, elite and powerful but not courtly, urban, and refined like the drinking of Gupta-period poetry. They may shed light on the tension that arises in the later, classical legal tradition, when the Kṣatriya is both Brahmin-like (as a twiceborn), and thus should shun *surā*, and yet is traditionally connected to certain drinking contexts—a tension ingeniously reconciled in the *Law Code of Manu*, which we'll examine later.

Returning to women and brewing, the Buddhist story of the discovery of *surā* was framed within another story in which a group of women make *surā* for a festival. The same story occurs with more elaboration in another Pali text, probably composed in Sri Lanka (*Dhammapadaṭṭhakathā*):

> Now on a certain occasion proclamation was made of a drinking festival to last seven days. Accordingly those women prepared *surā* for their husbands, and their husbands took part in the festival, carousing for a period of seven days. On the eighth day the drum went forth to announce the resumption of work, and they returned to their work.
>
> Those women thought to themselves, "We have not been permitted to drink *surā* in the presence of our husbands. Yet plenty of *surā* remains. Let us therefore drink it, but let us take care that our husbands shall know nothing about it."[75]

So they drink, get drunk, and are chastised by their friend Visākhā, a follower of the Buddha. Then they go home and pretend to be ill, to avoid being caught drinking by their husbands. But on another occasion they drink at a festival and sneak drink in pots/jars (*vārake*) into the monastery under large cloaks. When they get drunk, a deity possesses them and causes them to behave improperly in front of the Buddha,[76] at which he pronounces the verse "Why laughter, why joy? It [the world] is always burning! Will you not seek a light, you who are covered in darkness?"[77] Although we see again here the motif of the irresponsible drunken woman, we also get a sense that the preparation of drink was understood to be women's work, at least when brewed for special events such as a festival. Note that in this story the women are supposed to drink separately from the men and keep their drinking a secret (for fear of being beaten by their husbands).

We also possess a detailed narrative of women brewing for a wedding. Though Indian in origin, this story survives only in Tibetan, in a text on monastic discipline called the *Mūlasarvāstivāda Vinaya*, dating from the early centuries CE.[78] This narrative offers a vivid picture of domestic brewing, probably of a *surā*-type drink. A woman is to get married, and her mother is making an intoxicating drink of some sort. At a certain stage she warms the drink, which ruins it, so she approaches "the women who sold liquor" and orders a quantity of drink for the wedding. Then a Buddhist nun comes to the house for almsfood and offers to help save the batch of ruined drink. She inspects the pots and sees that it was ruined by warming, so she cools it by placing the jars on sand, wetting their sides, wrapping them with cloth, and fanning them. This makes the drink good again. Ultimately, however, her solution causes problems, for the mother of the bride refuses to pay for the drink she has ordered, all of which leads to the creation of a disciplinary rule stating that nuns cannot do the work of brewing.

This is a clear description of brewing, probably *surā*, with the vessels being kept at a cool, even temperature, probably embedded in sand, wrapped with (wet) cloth, and fanned. I have seen this use of sand and wet cloth wrappings in Kerala today, in the making of traditional *ariṣṭa*s and *āsava*s. From the story it seems clear that, ideally, the woman should brew the wedding drink herself, but there are also people, apparently women (though a man is mentioned too), who take orders for drink. And the nun, although not a brewer, is experienced at brewing, a process in which one vital skill was controlling the fermentation temperature, something also emphasized in early medieval China.[79] Although this was "woman's work," it is also presented as skilled work.[80]

Another story from the *Mūlasarvāstivāda Vinaya* depicts women using their brewing skills on a larger scale.[81] In this story a nun meets an affluent woman who explains that she purchased her clothes and jewelry by selling liquor. Afterward the nun meets a poor woman and asks her why she does not sell liquor to make money. The poor woman replies that she first needs the capital to purchase the merchandise, vessels, and a large house for drinkers. So the nun sets her up as a brewer and retailer, and her drinking-house becomes popular, making her rival liquor-sellers increasingly envious. When the king requires liquor, he summons all the liquor-sellers to him. His inspection makes people aware that a nun has set up a liquor business, which brings her order into disrepute, and so the Buddha creates a rule forbidding nuns to act as liquor-sellers.

It is striking how profitable brewing was perceived to be, and indeed as a simple form of manufacture it was no doubt a promising business. Whether nuns dabbling in brewing really was a problem, it was clearly a skill that some women were assumed to possess, perhaps because of their responsibilities during weddings and festivals, and offered one way for women to engage in business in ancient India, thus potentially achieving some economic independence. Maybe women were better suited to this particular business for certain social reasons? Gamburd writes that in some modern Sri Lankan drinking-houses, women have the domestic duty of serving; apparently they can more easily refuse requests for drink on credit, which Gamburd suggests may be because, in their own homes, they routinely refuse their husbands money for drink.[82]

Although the women's actions in the *Mūlasarvāstivāda Vinaya* are frowned upon, they are not presented as evil. On the contrary, the female brewers are presented as successful members of society; the only problem is that their work is incompatible with the monastic Buddhist life. The conflict arises from economic disruption within the community, not the women's association with liquor. The Buddha's injunction implies that the nunnery should remain separate from the local economy, rather than exploiting the traditional skills and knowledge of the nuns to compete with businesses outside.

These women brewers share some qualities with medieval English alewives, as well as women in other contexts who produce alcohol.[83] As Judith Bennett writes of fourteenth-century England, "brewing was—*by the low standards of women's work*—good work indeed."[84] Yet, as we'll see, brewing was not entirely women's work in India. We should not forget the vast differences between the archives dealing with brewing in early India and those from premodern England. The most detailed sources that point to female brewing in India are lifted from Buddhist texts in which the women brewers and drinkers are characters somehow requiring disciplining. (We see another side of this gendered motif later, when the liquor-associated woman is seen as sexually available.) Were female brewers actually common, or is the female brewer a literary notion, embodying vice and dangerous independence in order to frame a monastic rule or a story about the Buddha? I would argue that, despite the obvious biases of our sources, there is enough varied evidence extant to suggest that some women were indeed brewers in ancient India, profiting from skilled manufacturing based on common grains.

Drink on Credit

Although in the *Arthaśāstra* drink on credit was forbidden, it appears that this regulation was not always enforced or even present. Indeed, the very prohibition implies that there was demand for drink on credit. In a section of the *Arthaśāstra* on destroying an army through secret means, several of which involve drugged liquor, one method of tempting the enemy to consume poisoned goods is having agents don the guise of people who sell cooked meat, cooked rice, and flat bread, or of *surā* sellers/brewers (*śauṇḍika*), and announce their delicious wares as available on credit (*kālikaṃ*).[85] Apparently drink on credit would be irresistible, overriding any suspicions. From brahminical texts on dharma, starting quite early with the *dharmasūtras*, we learn that sons cannot inherit debts (*ṛṇa*) incurred through drinking or gambling.[86] The *Law Code of Manu* likewise states that a son is not responsible for his father's drinking debts.[87] So, while profitable, the liquor trade had its risks, and the state would not enforce dead men's drinking debts, making credit even riskier for the brewer.

In England credit and debts were a serious problem for ale-sellers. As Peter Clark writes of Canterbury between 1560 and 1640, "Of the 61 alehouse-keepers' inventories surviving from this period 15 record debts outstanding to the deceased . . . [A]mong poorer victuallers . . . uncleared debts amounted to half their personal estate."[88] Ancient India and early modern England were very different places, yet we can imagine that for the *surā* trader, preferring ready cash but forced sometimes to offer credit, unable to recover the debts of the deceased or destitute, life could be difficult. These forgotten Indian brewers worked hard to transform grains into good *surā*, sometimes ran up debts, and received significant social stigma in certain quarters for doing so.

The *Vāruṇi Jātaka*, the Buddhist "*Surā* Birth Story," gives some sense of the management of a fictional drinking house:

> Apparently Anāthapiṇḍaka had a friend who was a *surā* merchant (*vāruṇivāniko*). He prepared some strong/sharp *surā* (*tikhiṇaṃ vāruṇiṃ*), and he would sell it, accepting gold and money, and a crowd gathered. He commanded his apprentice, "Son, when you have taken the money, give [them] the *surā*," and went by himself to bathe. The apprentice, providing *surā* to the crowd, saw people time after time having salt crystals[89] brought to them, and eating [the crystals]. Thinking, "The *surā* must have no salt in it, I will put salt in it," he put a measure (*nāḷi*) of salt in the *surā* jar (*surācāṭiyaṃ*) and gave them the *surā*. They all filled their mouths with it and spat it out, asking, "What have you done?" He said, "I saw you having salt brought when you drank *surā*, so I mixed it with salt." Saying, "And that's how you ruined some lovely (*manāpaṃ*) *surā*,

> fool!" they scolded him, and, getting up one by one, they left. The *surā* merchant came back and, not seeing a single person, asked, "Where did the *surā* drinkers go?" He told him the reason . . .[90]

This merchant is a canny businessman (note that he is male, as is the apprentice), for he only accepts cash up front, which he specifies to his idiot apprentice. Despite this insistence on cash, his drink is good enough to attract crowds who both drink and eat salty snacks, or simply salt. The apprentice does not have a good understanding of the business, nor does he understand the common practice of drinking with salty snacks—maybe he is too young to have indulged in drinking? The story shows us how drinking places were assumed to work: the shop is owned by a man who prepares *surā* in jars and sells it for cash, avoiding the perils of credit, and who employs a (probably) younger apprentice at the shop. And the brewer values his reputation.

Drinking Snacks

Accompanying snacks (*upadaṃśa*) were inseparable from drinking, whether at the *surā* shop or in the bedrooms of the wealthy. They were clearly light refreshments, though, as opposed to full meals. Drinking was for drinking's sake and you have special salty, spicy snack foods to go with it. Typically we do not read of people drinking liquor to accompany and enhance meals, as with the European concept of "food and wine."[91] Drinking with snacks is still common in India today.[92]

In one Buddhist *Jātaka*, we read of drink-related food at a travelers' drinking place, one context where the food may have been more substantial than mere snacks, for people who were staying overnight:

> In the past, people of Aṅga and Magadha who were traveling from one to another country stayed from one day to the next at a house on the border of the countries, and drank *surā* and ate fish flesh (or "fish and meat"), and early in the morning yoked their vehicles and set out. When they went, a dung beetle, coming because of the smell of dung, saw the *surā* that was thrown away at the place they were drinking, and, thirsty for water, he drank it, got drunk, and climbed a pile of dung. When he climbed it, the wet dung slightly sank. He cried out, "The earth cannot hold me!"[93]

At this point an elephant comes along and is put off by the smell of dung/excrement, elephants in Indian literature being noted for their acute sense of smell. Our little beetle, his pride swelled by drunken "world-crushing" confusion, thinks the elephant is scared of him, so he challenges him to a fight. Irritated, the elephant says:

> I won't kill you with my foot, nor with my tusks or trunk, I'll kill you with my shit—the foul should be killed with the foul. . . . [And], dropping a huge lump of elephant-dung on his head and passing water, he took his life right there and entered the forest trumpeting.

This is not the only reference to animals inadvertently getting drunk in these stories: elsewhere some unfortunate crows get drunk on *surā* that people have left out as offerings for divine serpents (*nāgas*), as does a cunning jackal on offerings to beings called *yakṣas*.[94]

This travelers' rest is a rough, dirty affair, with animal dung, maybe even human excrement, and spilled *surā*, where people drank liquor and ate fish. Presumably such establishments were common—the *Arthaśāstra* indicates that drinking-houses were associated with travelers and foreigners. The beetle displays the classic features of the drunkard as represented in early India: in short, a general misalignment with reality. So, prior to being dispatched by a huge turd he shows confused perception, excited aggression, and immensely distorted confidence.[95]

In the *Kāmasūtra*, a list of drinks that people should consume at drinking bouts may reflect an ideal set of drinks deemed pleasant at that period, all taken with the ubiquitous snacks:

> There, the courtesans should have them [i.e., the men-about-town, *nāgarakas*] drink, and afterward they themselves should drink: wine (*madhu*), *maireya*, *surā*, and *āsava*, that have various bitter, spicy, and sour accompanying snacks (*upadaṃśa*), such as fruit and green vegetables that are salty.[96]

The commentator Yaśodhara (from the thirteenth century) explains:

> ". . . which have accompanying snacks," namely various, mostly salty and bitter things, as well as green and spicy moringa leaves (*śigruparṇa*) and so on.

Thus ideally one is able to serve several drinks and snacks—variety is appreciated.

There is a long list of different snacks in the chapter on drinking in the twelfth-century *Mānasollāsa* (*Delight of the Mind*). Although prepared for a royal occasion, these snacks are simple in their ingredients, and it is perhaps the sheer number offered that is fit for a king (in fact, for the king's ladies). The passage is not always easy, and I have deliberately refrained from imposing possible equivalences with modern Indian foods (e.g., pickles) in my translation:

> Having brought various intoxicating drinks in vessels of glass and clay, by way of drinking snacks (*upadaṃśārthaṃ*) one should have brought into the drinking place various types of meat roasted by fire; and tasty, [good-] smelling meats that have been cooked in cooking-dishes; and fragrant meats rich with brown mustard seed (*rājikā*)[97] and salt; and meats mixed with saffron,[98] citron, and fresh-ginger juice that have been fumigated (*dhūpitāni*) with asafoetida; various types of chewable solid food (*bhakṣyāṇi*) made of urad lentils (*māṣa*) and wheat; and delicious yoghurt-rice with various flavors; fruits sprinkled with the juice of *jambīra* lemon and of fresh ginger; and, one more thing, a lizard [?][99] from the forest that has been placed in salt water and has oil and mustard seed (*sarṣapa*) added to it; and camphor root (*karpūramūlakaṃ*),[100] fresh ginger, chebulic myrobalan,[101] as well as elephant's foot yam[102] and finger root/tuber (*velukanda*)[103] with brown mustard seed and salt; and the tuber of forest moringa (*vanaśigru*) with oil; large, appetizing, tasty, delightful onion bulbs with tamarind juice added and mixed with salt; tender, tasty asparagus sprouts[104] and *karir* capers[105] devoid of small ones[106] mixed with oil and with salt added; and black pepper, long pepper, royal citron (*rājamātuliṅgaṃ*), *tugām* [?],[107] *kataka*,[108] *kuṭajam*,[109] and bilva fruit[110] placed into salty water; chickpeas cooked in oil mixed with black pepper, and others roasted in hot sand; sweet, white chebulic myrobalan boiled in milk; and chickpeas with their sprouts all attached to each other, seasoned with a spice mixture (*saṃbhārasaṃskṛtān*) with mustard seed and salt added, and chickpeas on their own;[111] and that powder [mustard and salt? "their powder"?], with oil, mixed with slivers of fresh ginger; *balālaghulika* mix [?][112] with cumin powder (*ajāji*)[113] as well as urad lentils,[114] roasted/fried, boiled in salted water, with a chickpea/gram [flour?] shell[115] and crushed with the fingers, with bits of onion, and fumigated with asafoetida is the chewable solid food called *pūraṇa*,[116] which is soft, delicate, and fragrant . . .[117]

Strong flavors dominate: salt, peppers, and acids, as well as oil. The list begins with meats, then deals with fruits and vegetables, then chickpea preparations, and finally a filled patty. It is easy to see similarities with modern snacks, especially with the various chickpea preparations. Maybe some of these things were like modern pickles. Note that chilis had not yet arrived from the Americas, so pepper and ginger provided the pungency.

Far less appetizing are some radish-based snacks in a poetic metaphor comparing a battlefield to a drinking bout, an image that perhaps draws on the inflammatory, martial nature of drinking and ironically highlights the contrast between carousing and death:

> Row on row of tusks gleamed like radish drinking-snacks, fallen amid the horrible skull-sherds that were like goblets for Death's drinking parties.[118]

Even today, such items as fresh ginger slivers and spicy mixes that include black salt are common drinking snacks in India. A particularly good such snack that I saw prepared at the Royale Midtown hotel in Bhubaneswar consisted of julienned strips of fresh ginger doused in lime juice, salt, black pepper, chaat masala, and—updating the bar snack with that perfect addition, the chile—a few splashes of Tabasco sauce. Fresh ginger and boiled chickpeas are the house snack at Shaw's Bar in Kolkata.

The Ambience of the *Surā* House

What sort of people went to drinking houses? Why did they go, when, and what did they do there apart from drink? Did they sit or stand? A number of texts, mostly from the early or mid-first millennium CE, elucidate the conventions (entirely literary? somewhat rooted in practice?) of the *surā* house.

A satirical monologue, *The Kick* (*Pādatāḍitaka*) of Śyāmilaka, gives a vivid sense of a drinking house in a cosmopolitan, early medieval Indian city. This is a type of play called a *bhāṇa*, in which one actor speaks all the parts. It is set in the fifth century CE in the city of Ujjain and, if not composed then, was probably written shortly after that time.[119] The protagonist-narrator is a stock character known as a *viṭa*, a type of libertine perhaps translated as a "rake" or a "player." Charming, sociable yet lecherous, he is respected among courtesans and at gatherings/"salons" (*goṣṭhī*). He is generous yet economically dependent on others and is not ashamed of his lifestyle.[120] This libertine, parasite-rake wanders around Ujjain, in particular the courtesans' quarter, describing his encounters before he joins a gathering of other *viṭa*s.

Ujjain is filled with people from other regions and countries. When the rake arrives in the market, he observes the noisy metal-smiths, the flower-sellers (for garlands), the butchers, and how "the drinking-cup (*caṣaka*) moves about in drinking-houses (*pānāgāra*) and is drunk up."[121] He also sees gamblers who have won some coins make their way to the courtesans' quarter with servants carrying flowers, bread/cakes, meat, and *āsava* (*sāpūpamāṃsāsava*), presumably purchased in the marketplace.[122] The drinking-houses are in a market/shop area (*vipaṇi*) alongside traders, manufacturers, and places for gambling. So in this part of town you could purchase alcohol to take off the premises, as well as snacks and other paraphernalia required for an erotic encounter. The rake leaves the street of shops, passes some drinking-houses near a street of flower-sellers, and notices the following scene, presumably in a drinking-house (Dezsö and Vasudeva's translation, modified):

> Hey! Who is being celebrated here with Yodheyaka songs by drummers from Rohitaka, accompanied by cymbals and bamboo flutes? A wreath of yellow

amaranth flowers dangles from one of his ears as he draws up with his loincloth his threadbare, frazzle-hemmed upper-garment that covers his right side. One side of his buttocks is bared again and again as he dances, lifting up a liquor vessel (*madya-bhājanam*) with his left hand, and makes the drinking hall (*āpāna-maṇḍapaṃ*) laugh. *(looking)* Aha! I know! This fellow is the son of the Bactrian, the prime target of the ridicule of all rogues, the rooster of the courtesans' quarter: Mr. Steam! Upon my word, I've never seen him sober (*amattam*) or without a drink (*apītaṃ*), but at the same time, not even a halfpence ever rubs his hand. How can he manage this? *(reflects)* Bingo! I've got it! It is because he is obtrusive, shameless, and universally overbearing.

With a handful of drinking-snacks (*upadaṃśa-*), Mr. Steam plows into the circle of drinking dancers, danseuses, servants, and stablemen.[123]

Mr. Steam's exact posture is not quite clear, but evidently he is drunk, dancing with flowers on his head, and yanking up his clothes on one side to expose his buttocks while raising a vessel of liquor in his left hand. Then he takes a fistful of snacks and enters the mixed crowd of dancing drunks. Like the rake (*viṭa*), he is a sponger, yet he lacks sophistication, being a vulgar buffoon of foreign, northern origin. This drinking is public and urban, with a mixing of genders and classes, not so much erotic as raucous. In the play *Drunken Games* (*Mattavilāsaprahasana*), after the comparison of the drinking house to a Vedic sacrifice that we saw earlier, the singing and dancing drinkers are described in similar postures, with hitched and slipping garments—perhaps another literary convention.[124]

Despite restrictions on off-licenses in the *Arthaśāstra*, people did sometimes take drink elsewhere, as seen not only in *The Kick* but in another Buddhist *Jātaka*. Although the drinkers in this *Jātaka* are thieves, there is no suggestion that the *surā* itself is stolen; rather they are just going to continue drinking at home:

some thieves who had completed their work, having drunk *surā* in a *surā* shop (*surāpāne*), were taking more to their own house in a jar (*ghaṭa*) . . .[125]

Apparently, also, good liquor was something people might advertise. In another *Jātaka* we meet some *surā*-obsessed rogues who pose as *surā*-sellers:

At one time [some] *surā* rogues of Sāvatthi assembled and discussed: "Our *surā* money is gone, where might we get it from?" And then one cruel rogue said, "Don't worry, here's a plan!" "And how is that?" they said. "When Anāthapiṇḍika has put on his signet rings, is dressed in minister's robes, and is going to serve the king, we put a medicine that causes unconsciousness (*visaññīkaraṇabhesajjam*) in a bowl of *surā*, fit up a drinking gathering (*āpāna*) [place], and sit down.

> When Anāthapiṇḍika comes we call him, saying, 'Come over here, great treasurer!' and, [after] making him drink that *surā*, when he is unconscious, we take his rings and robes, and that will be the price of the *surā*!" They agreed, saying, "Okay," and having arranged things like that, when the treasurer came they went to meet him, saying, "Sir, please just come over here, we have here some extremely lovely (*atimanāpā*) *surā*. Drink a bit and go on your way." He thought, "Why would a stream-enterer, a disciple of the Noble One, drink *surā*? But, though I have no needs and am equanimous, I shall catch these rogues," and went to their drinking-ground (*āpānabhūmiṃ*) [and] observed their deeds.[126]

Then, of course, he catches them out, noting how they sit (*nisinnā*) in the drinking area (*āpānamaṇḍalaṃ*) praising their wares but dare not drink themselves, at which they all flee. This is a humorous moralizing story, so it does not offer a precise description of liquor-selling, but the notion of a makeshift drinking-area is notable. Is this a simple *surā* shop or just a semi-public area for a drinking gathering? The drugged *surā* is presented as particularly delicious, something that might tempt a wealthy royal officer, so evidently the idea of particularly tasty *surā* was current. And, as we see many times in this book, the drinking place is depicted as the haunt of morally suspect people. (As noted already, the *Arthaśāstra* also describes methods to drug people using doctored liquor.)

The *surā*-brewer/seller (*śauṇḍika*) features in the *Kāmasūtra* in a list of people who help courtesans meet with clients.[127] The *śauṇḍika* is grouped with people who, as Yaśodhara's commentary explains, are self-employed and enter people's homes—for example, washermen and perfumers. In the *Arthaśāstra*, in the chapter on spies, an agent disguised as a *śauṇḍika* attacks forest people after having drugged them while pretending to sell or present *surā* at rites for gods or ancestors, festivals, and fairs, yet again suggesting that *surā*-brewers were sometimes itinerant.[128]

A typical drinking-place probably had nothing like a bar but instead just one or more rooms, sometimes furnished. It seems the drink would have been served by servants or by the landlady or landlord. And there were evidently cups, larger storage vessels, and snacks on hand. In these ways, if our descriptions in any way reflect some real features, such places were probably quite like country liquor shops or toddy shops in India today.

There is very little evidence for the drinking postures in these places. When the rogues try to trick the minister into drinking drugged liquor, they sit at one point. The drinking-house described in the *Arthaśāstra* contains couches and beds, so perhaps people sat and lounged there; or the couches might have been used just for sleeping. Later I shall consider what appears to be a painting of a *surā* shop. In this painting the people selling the *surā* are seated in the shop and those receiving it are standing on the street, like many chai stands today. But other drinkers, the "northerners" illustrated at Ajanta, are seated to drink, and I will deal with the postures of couples drinking in private in the next chapter.[129]

In the "Previous-Birth Story of the Jar," the king sits on a couch before he drinks *surā*. Yet people are also said to dance and flail about when drunk (and collapse in the gutter). It is not clear whether the landlord or servers in the drinking-houses brought jars or filled cups to the drinkers. In the Ajanta image, the drink is being dished out into cups that the drinkers hold, and presumably people could not help themselves to the contents of the jars.

Where were the drinking houses located, spatially and demographically? The rowdy scene described here took place in the center of a large city, near a market. In the famous Sanskrit lexicon of Amarasiṃha, the words for drink-related matters are grouped in the *Śūdra Section* and precede the terms relating to gambling, thus connecting drinking with the *śūdra* (servant) class (*varṇa*) and their professions.[130] In the *Arthaśāstra*, however, in the description of the fort or walled city, the *surā* trade (*-surā- -paṇya*) lies in the southern direction, along with the trade in meat and cooked food/rice, prostitutes, dancers, and the Vaiśya (merchant) *varṇa* (*not* the Śūdra).[131] These are more ideals than descriptions, though; in the *Arthaśāstra* drink is a pleasure-commodity, and for Amarasiṃha it is a "lower"-class vice.

We have already seen references to groups of friends and acquaintances drinking together. In Kālidāsa's play *Śakuntalā*, from approximately the late fourth or fifth century CE, a police captain and a fisherman he has just accused of theft (in what turns out to be a misunderstanding) decide to go and have a drink to cement their new friendship: "our new friendship needs a *kādambarī* drink as witness. So let's go to the brewer-hall (*suṇḍiasālaṃ* = *sauṇḍikaśālaṃ*)."[132] Drinking is shown as vital in cementing a friendship for these two men, which gives us a rare positive insight into the attitudes associated with communal male drinking at *surā* shops, usually represented as the dubious solidarity of rogues.

Like the English alehouse, the drinking hall or *surā* shop might have been an appealing social space for some because it was "an alternative to, rather than an extension of, established family life."[133] The drinking-house offered neutral ground, away from in-laws, superiors, children, and spouses (and were presumably free from prying servants for the more wealthy people going to "inns").[134] Thus like a public house today, this place of leisure-drinking, the antithesis of productive labor, was both private and public. It was also a democratic place: drinking-houses were proverbially open to all comers, as we learn from two unpleasant verses in the Pāli *Jātaka*s that proclaim how women are like drinking-houses, roads, and rivers: available to all (yet another example of the connections between women, drink, and sex in these texts).[135]

A Painting of a *Surā* Shop?

I am persuaded that we possess an early painting of a *surā* shop, from the late fifth century CE. This painting is at the site of Ajanta, in Cave 17 (Figure 3.1) in an image of the Buddhist Wheel of Rebirth: a circle divided into sectors illustrating the different realms into which one can be reborn. Art historian Dieter

FIGURE 3.1 Possible image of a *surā* shop in the Asura realm from the *Saṃsāracakra* in Cave 17 at Ajanta.
© Ajanta Archives of the Saxon Academy of Sciences and Humanities, Research Centre "Buddhist Murals of Kucha on the Northern Silk Road," photograph Andreas Stellmacher. I thank Monika Zin for sharing this image with me.

Schlingloff has argued convincingly that in the sector showing the realm of the asuras ("anti-gods"), there is a depiction of a stall selling *surā*, complete with a number of round jars and two customers receiving *surā* in bowls.[136] Behind the stall is an enormous jar, which I believe may even be functioning visually as a sign, like the iconic *surā*-banner mentioned earlier, to indicate to the viewer (and the asuras) that *surā* is available.

Why would the asuras drink *surā*? Anyone with a knowledge of Hindu myth knows that the devas (gods) and asuras ("anti-gods," "demons") quarreled over another drink, *amṛta*, the nectar of immortality, at the churning of the milk ocean. As we shall see later in this book, *surā* was also produced in the churning of the ocean. So surely the asuras would want to drink nectar? Not, however, in a Buddhist context. Schlingloff points to another narrative in Buddhist sources concerning the asuras, the gods, and a drink. In this story, the asuras lived in heaven until they got drunk and were ejected. An expanded version explains:[137]

> Now at that time there were Asuras dwelling in the World of the Thirty-three [i.e. with the gods], and when they learned that the new gods had been reborn there, they prepared celestial drink for them (*dibbapānaṃ*). But Sakka [Indra] gave orders to his retinue that no one should drink thereof. The Asuras, however, drank freely and became intoxicated/careless (*pammajjiṃsu*). Thereupon Sakka thought to himself, "Why should I share my kingdom with these deities?" Forthwith, giving a sign to his retinue, he caused them to pick up the Asuras by the heels and fling them into the Great Ocean. So the Asuras fell headlong into the Ocean . . .[138]

Briefer but more relevant to Ajanta is a verse from the *Jātakamālā*, which, as Richard S. Cohen notes, is the "only text that can be indisputably shown to have been read at Ajaṇṭā," as there are other verses from it painted at the site.[139] This verse also shows that the motif of the asuras drinking was quite common in Buddhist texts (and maybe in the oral tradition too). Indeed, it appears that the asuras serve as a Buddhist stock example of drinkers who run into problems. The lines quoted here are from a speech that Śakra (i.e., Indra) makes about the dangers of drink. This is a Sanskrit version of the speech he delivers to the king in the "Previous-Birth Story of the Jar," which we saw in the Apertif:[140]

> The asuras were intoxicated from its bad effects, and the king of the gods stole their good fortune, and looking for salvation they plunged [or "drowned"] in the ocean—take this jar filled with that![141]

Another source explains the origin of the name "asuras," which can be understood to mean "the *surā*-less ones," as derived from their desperate cry—"We did not drink *surā*!"—when ejected.[142]

Thus it is likely that viewers with a Buddhistic background, aware of the proverbially fateful intoxication of the asuras, would see this painting as an image of a drink-shop, assuming that this is indeed the asura realm. Schlingloff describes the image as follows: "In the first shop . . . the proprietor occupies almost all the space in the shop, next to him there appears the head of a woman. In the background there are several pots in front of two bowls that are apparently full of rice. The shop proprietor has dipped a ladle into the first of the pots that stand in the foreground in order to pour the liquid from the pot into the drinking cups that the women standing in front of the shop are holding out."[143] Behind the shop we see cooking taking place, which may be the preparation of the *surā* itself or snacks. The large jar may be a fermentation vessel or, as I suggest, this highly visible image may be a sign advertising the *surā* shop, just as a large and obvious barrel might suggest a brewery in a European painting. If Schlingloff is correct, then this is a simple *surā* shop, with the brewing taking place around the back.[144] The customers carry cups, not pots big enough to take the *surā* home, so presumably they will drink it there. The two customers are women, and perhaps in the shop we see the *surā* brewer and his wife.

How does the drinking in this image relate to drinking in contemporaneous texts? The asuras are drinking in public, on the street. Women are buying their drink from a merchant and presumably drinking it at the shop, along with other customers. This is the sort of drinking we saw in the *Jātaka*s, where it is typically presented as less respectable. By contrast, in the painting of the heavenly sector adjacent to the painting of the asura realm, we see "high"-class drinking, probably of nectar, not liquor. In heaven the drinkers are seated as couples—the sort of drinking described as a prelude to making love in the *Kāmasūtra*, as we'll see in the next chapter. The gods drink nectar in the manner of the princes and men-about-town of *kāvya* poetry, while the drunk, careless asuras drink intoxicants (*surā*) like the "low-life" commoners we met in the Pali *Jātaka*s.

Festivals, Fairs, Picnics, and Parties

Fairs, festivals, parties, and weddings were all occasions for drinking. In the next chapter we shall look at literary accounts of elite drinking parties—semi-private versions of this sort of group-drinking—but for now let's consider more riotous public gatherings.

We've seen references to intermittent brewing for festivals and weddings, even perhaps for chariot races. In the "Previous-Birth Story of the Jar," when the women brew *surā* it is connected to a *surā* festival that their husbands have already enjoyed. The *Arthaśāstra* mentions brewing licenses for festivals, and there was the story of the Buddhist nun who helped a woman salvage the batch of liquor she had made for a wedding—not to mention the drinking, dancing women at the wedding in the Vedic text on domestic rites. Given so much diverse evidence, it is probable that such occasions for mass drinking were a social reality for some communities.

In the *Kāmasūtra*, in the account of the love life of the ruler (*īśvara*), we read how local women are seduced into entering the harem. First, the women are introduced to life in the harem during certain festive times, at which there were drinking parties for local women in the ruler's residence. Here a drinking festival merges with a royal drinking party:

> For the women of towns, cities, and market towns, at the *Aṣṭamīcandrikā* and *Kaumudī* festivals[145] and at Spring festivals there are generally games with the women of the harem in the residence of the ruler.
>
> At that time, at the end of the group drinking bout (*āpānaka*), the townswomen individually enter the women's apartments ("pleasure rooms"), according to their acquaintance with them, and, seated, they have stories, are honored and given drink, and they leave by nightfall.[146]

The *Aṣṭamīcandra* festival is the same day (as described elsewhere in the *Kāmasūtra*) that a man might intoxicate/drug a woman to achieve a "ghoulish" (*paiśāca*) type of marriage—the rape of an unconscious woman and *not* in any way considered a respectable form of marriage.[147] So it would seem that this festival was particularly associated with intoxication.

Many of the sources in this chapter emerge from a cultural world involving cities, but festivals may have been the main occasions for drinking prior to major urbanization, as well as in rural areas. Dietler writes, "[M]any traditional forms of alcohol (especially grain-based forms) have two important related characteristics. They are multi-step, labor-intensive products, and they are highly perishable. . . . This has clear implications for the labor requirements for sponsoring large drinking events (including the gendered structure of this labor), and it places clear restrictions on the ability to store or accumulate alcohol, and to transport it for trade. This means that the social value of these forms of drink resides in immediate and complete consumption in the context of a social *event*."[148] Possibly, in early periods and in the countryside, *surā* and festivals went hand in hand, prior to the development of the urban brewery. Certainly drinking in the epics tends to take place at festivals and parties, along with some private drinking among friends. Also, any group that did not drink, such as Brahmins or nuns, was conspicuously absent from such gatherings. If you shun *surā*, you exclude yourself from the carnival.

Drinking at a seasonal festival or wedding takes place on a set date, but we also read of more spontaneous drinking bouts, like parties. In the epics we see outdoor parties, boozy "picnics," which later become highly developed as an elite pursuit (or at least as a literary convention associated with sophisticated people).[149] In the *Mahābhārata*, the Andhaka and Vṛṣṇi clans—famous for their ultimate drunken mutual-destruction—hold a great festival (*utsava*) on a mountain, during which Arjuna sees and fall in love with Kṛṣṇa's sister Subhadrā.[150] Amorous excitement at festivals is a common theme. Here, among decorations, music, dancing, and crowds, Kṛṣṇa's brother Balarāma (Haladhara) is said to be wandering drunk (*kṣība*, a word that seems to be limited to alcoholic intoxication),[151] as are Pradyumna and Sāmba.[152] This event is not presented as a shameful mess but as a pleasant, romantically productive moment:

> [Balarāma] . . . wearing a forest-garland, drunk, like the peak of Kailāsa mountain, with dark blue clothes, sprinkled with intoxication [*mada*, a word that also significantly means "elephant must"] . . .[153]

At the ensuing wedding there are great group drinking bouts (*mahāpānaiḥ*).[154] Later we learn that Arjuna and Kṛṣṇa, avoiding the heat, make an outing to the river Yamunā, where there is a private royal party.[155] Surrounded by friends, they enter a pleasure-ground with trees, houses, garlands, gems, and tasty food. Everyone sports, the women playing in the forest, the water, and the buildings according to their desire. Some women dance, some shout, some laugh, and some drink the best *āsava*s. Some weep, some hit each other, some tell each other secrets. This is an early example of a particular genre, in which a group of beautifully adorned women go to a pleasure-ground outdoors, eat and drink, and engage in dancing, laughing, crying, and fighting, all perceived as an amusing spectacle by the few men present, who are barely described. We will see similar descriptions many times in this book.[156] This is not a rural *surā* festival but a private outdoor party for an elite group.

Even when we read of women going to a party on their own, it's not long before their antics are complimented by a male observer. In the *Mahābhārata*, in the story of Yayāti, a woman called Devayānī goes to the forest to play (*krīḍārthaṃ*) with some female friends, and there they drink honey mead (*madhumādhavīm*).[157] This drunken frolicking, secluded yet outdoors, renders Devayānī all the more attractive (and visually accessible) to Yayāti when he stumbles on the scene.

We also read of warriors drinking communally, taking a break from marching and fighting. Earlier, in the *Rāmāyaṇa*, we saw magical feasts with liquor prepared for soldiers. In another, particularly charming episode, the monkey (*vānara*) general Hanumān returns to his companions on the mainland and tells them that he has discovered where Rāma's wife Sītā is being held captive (by Rāvaṇa, whose liquor selection we examined earlier). Deciding to go tell Rāma the news, they pass a forest grove called the Madhuvana (Honey Forest).[158] This is no ordinary forest but is protected by Sugrīva, king of the monkeys, to whom Hanumān reports. It is guarded on his behalf by a powerful monkey called Dadhimukha, Sugrīva's maternal uncle. The monkeys, having asked permission from the elders in their own troop, gorge themselves on the "honey" in the marvelous grove. Readers will not need reminding of the confusions that attend the word "*madhu*" in the context of drinking. Here, apart from its intoxicating nature, the *madhu* is in all other respects honey, contained in large solid entities that can be collected and broken open, eaten, and the *madhu* inside drunk. There is even wax.[159] The *madhu* is a tawny (*-piṅgala*) drink, the same color as the monkeys.[160] Yet, judging from its effects, it is also intoxicating like liquor. Although *madhu* can mean mead, and also wine in later texts, I think it is simply supposed to be honey here, perhaps an unusual intoxicating honey as, after all, the grove is carefully guarded.[161] Or maybe for the *vānara*s honey is always intoxicating. Or maybe the honey is supposed to have naturally transformed to mead. Regardless, we should not forget that honey was probably less abundant than grains and sugarcane juice, whence the probable greater prestige of mead in early periods. This grove full of huge, intoxicating honeycombs would have held all the sugary appeal in ancient India that a fantasy candy factory with rivers of chocolate holds nowadays.

The monkeys' drunken behavior is like that of humans in Sanskrit texts, though with some monkey-like features. They sing, bow, dance, laugh, fall down, wander around, jump, and chatter.[162] Others support each other and jump from tree to tree. Singing, laughing, weeping, and shoving, they approach each other.[163] They even beat up Dadhimukha, the monkey guardian of the grove. Despite their antics, Hanumān gives them leave to enjoy themselves. This description emphasizes several themes that we see in representations of human drinking. The setting in a grove with drinkers singing, dancing, laughing, crying, and fighting resembles the scenes of women drinking (though these monkeys are male). The honey feast, so welcome to soldiers soon to enter a battle, recalls the martial drinking bouts seen elsewhere.[164] These similarities with human drinking, touched by monkey madness, make the scene charming and memorable.[165] For the reader or hearer of the *Rāmāyaṇa*, the frenzy in the Honey Forest provides light relief before the story gets serious and violent again.

Later Developments: Kalyapālas and the Rise of Distillation

What do we know about people who produced liquor in later periods? Roughly around the year 1000 CE, the Sanskrit word "*kalyapāla*" becomes prominent in inscriptions, lexica, and narrative texts. Kalyapālas are people, a caste it seems, involved in making drink—they are related to the modern Kalvārs. The word may be quite old, though it's not clear whether the early attestations of similar forms all refer to people connected to alcohol.[166] The word and related forms in Prakrits (*kallā*) may be derived ultimately from words connected with intoxication and liquor in South Indian, Dravidian languages.[167]

Recent forms of this word, such as Kalvār, refer to communities who practice distillation. So, when we read of Kalyapālas in older Sanskrit texts, does that mean we have evidence of distillers? No—especially since I believe that alcoholic distillation was not common in India until around 1200 CE. Just as "drivers" in the past did not drive motorcars, so the Kalyapālas in earlier times did not necessarily distill liquor, despite the word's later meaning. Also, whatever the origins of the word, these early forms do *not* mean anything on the lines of "burned-wine maker" (either in the Dravidian languages or as Sanskritized). It makes sense, however, that a community of liquor-makers would eventually adopt distillation, so the brewer Kalyapālas might well have become brewer-distiller Kalyapālas once alcoholic distillation became common.

We saw a reference to a Kalyapāla in the *Viṣṇuṣena* inscription, and such references become common from around the turn of the second millennium CE, when the word definitely has a sense related to liquor. There is a clear commentarial use of "*kalyapāla*" connected to drink from the ninth century, and lexica from the twelfth and thirteenth centuries CE also use this word in a liquor-related sense.[168] Inscriptions from the tenth to thirteenth centuries CE mention Kalyapālas as an economically powerful community that paid duty to support Hindu temples.[169] One Kalyapāla leader is a witness to a land grant.[170] In the tenth century CE, in the town of Sīyaḍoṇī in the modern Lalitput district, we learn from an inscription that the Kallapālas owned a market area (*haṭṭa*) in town for their trade.[171] In the same inscription, we learn of two occasions when merchants placed investments with the Kallapāla community, who were then expected to provide a regular revenue for the worship of the god (in one case specified as Viṣṇu). Evidently making *surā* was a solid source of profit, especially with a good injection of capital, something we saw in one of the stories about Buddhist nuns.[172] And clearly the profits of brewing were not deemed too tainted to use for worship. Betel-sellers (*tāmbūlika*) also feature prominently in the Sīyaḍoṇī inscription.[173] Evidently people were spending quite a lot of money on liquor and betel in the area around Sīyaḍoṇī in the tenth century.

We also read of a Kalyapāla in a Jain text composed in what is now Rajasthan in 1285 CE. Here someone takes fire from the hearth of a Kalyapāla to start a fire in the city.[174] This might suggest that the workplace of a Kalyapāla had the flammable characteristics of a distillery, yet we should be cautious: brewing grain drinks requires one to heat pots of liquids and grains. In twelfth-century London, for example, alehouses were considered a fire hazard and the city rulers ordered all alehouses to be built from stone.[175]

Although sometimes affluent, Kalyapālas are not always portrayed as respectable. In the twelfth-century chronicle of Kashmir, the *River of Kings* (*Rājataraṅgiṇī*), we read of a family of Kalyapālas who gained control of the throne in the early ninth century CE and are reviled by the author of the chronicle.[176] King Lalitāpīḍa had taken as a concubine a woman who was the daughter of a Kalyapāla called Uppa from a village called Ākhuva. She bore the king a son, Cippaṭajayāpīḍa, who became king. His maternal uncles, also Kalyapālas and described as "low born" (*akulīnāḥ*),[177] took control on the death of Cippaṭajayāpīḍa and installed their own puppet kings. Of King Śaṅkaravarman, descended from these Kalyapālas, we later read:

> Thus this [king], who did not speak the language of the gods [i.e., Sanskrit] but used vulgar speech (*apabhraṃśa*) fit for drunkards (*kṣībocita-*), showed that he was descended from a family of Kalyapālas.[178]

His Kalyapāla lineage here implies that this king was fundamentally uncultured, speaking low forms of language suited to drunks. Setting aside the author Kalhaṇa's distaste (he frowns on drinking and elevates betel),[179] it is notable that Kalyapālas became extremely powerful in Kashmir, despite the evident caste prejudices in certain circles.

Why did Kalyapālas rise to such prominence at this time? (assuming this impression is not just a product of our incomplete archives). Did brewing become more consolidated and organized, and brewers therefore more wealthy and influential? Or did an already wealthy community start engaging in economic activities associated with inscriptions, such as temple-related endowments, and as we saw in the *Rājataraṅgiṇī*? Are the later references to Kalyapālas connected to the rise of alcoholic distillation, which I believe became common roughly from around 1200?

Earlier I mentioned that the evidence for early stills in South Asia is more questionable than is often assumed, a matter I discuss in detail elsewhere.[180] Briefly stated however: on close consideration John Marshall's "still" excavated at Taxila was not found as a connected assemblage; Marshall assembled it himself from quite disparate finds, no doubt on the model of contemporaneous stills, in order to explain the function of just one of the vessels.[181] Allchin built on Marshall's hypothesis regarding the function of these vessels, and his textual evidence is not convincing.[182] Allchin likewise did not find a still assemblage but rather a large number of one type of vessel, with very few other parts. As for Mahdihassan, his methodology is so open that by his standards anyone can find evidence of stills in any time and any place.[183] Note that Kolhatkar, who also examined *surā* in detail, comes to the same negative conclusion as I do about ancient distillation.[184]

So when did alcoholic distillation appear in South Asia? The earliest explicit description of alcoholic distillation that I am aware of is from a medical text, the *Gadanigraha* by Soḍhala, a Gujarati, dating from around 1200 CE.[185] In this text one *āsava* recipe describes the distillation of an "*arka*," a Sanskritized word derived from Arabic to describe a distillate. To make this date (*kharjūra*) preparation, many plant products, including dates, emblic myrobalan, grapes, and *dhātakī* flowers, are all ground together with jaggery. Then the recipe describes the fermentation and distillation process:

> Put it [i.e., the herb-jaggery mixture] inside a capacious ghee-vessel (*ghṛtasya bhāṇḍe*),[186] and add one hundred and ten *prasthas* [a measure] of water, and put it in the earth for five days, and having ascertained that it is ready to be finished on the sixth day, it should be well attached in the middle part of a pair of devices (*yantra*) made from copper. Wash three hundred betel leaves and two thousand lotuses, and add them according to the method, and then, having sealed[187] the connection, place the device on a hearth. Then one should properly distill (*niṣkāśayet*) the *arka*, having put water on top of the device.[188]

The fine details are unclear, but certainly fermentation is taking place, and, when "finished," the liquid (or maybe the vessel) is placed with fresh leaves and flowers in the "middle part" of two copper vessels. The whole is placed on a fire, and an *arka*, distillate, is expelled or drawn out, with water condensing it.

It is absolutely clear that distillation is described here and that the liquid distilled is a fermented, sugar-based drink, so this is alcoholic distillation (of a specialized medicine, not a common liquor). An important point to note here is that, when Sanskrit texts mention alcoholic distillation, they are quite clear about it, using specific vocabulary: a distilled drink, *arka*, is made by distillation (*niṣ* √*kaś/kas*, caus. "expel").[189] From the seventeenth century or later, we have a whole treatise explicitly devoted to medicinal distillates, the *Elucidation of Distillates/Arrack* (*Arkaprakāśa*), which I shall consider at the end of this book.

Irfan Habib has written on distillation in medieval and early modern South Asia.[190] He presents an account of distillation that Zia Barani composed in 1357, in a text concerning the time of Sultan Kaiqubad (1286–1289): "the wine makers of Kol and Meerut brought [to Delhi] distilled (*chakānīda*) sweet-scented unfermented (*be-khammari*) arrack (*'arq*), two or three years old, filling wine flagons with it."[191] Habib also presents another passage from the same text that describes the reign of 'Alā'uddīn Khaljī, when the sale of wine had been prohibited and people "set up boilers (*bhaṭṭīs*) in their houses and made wine out of sugar (*qand*), and distilled it (*chakānidand*), drank it and sold it at high prices."[192]

We see here early evidence for the distillation of alcohol on a commercial scale. Habib also considers accounts of distillation by foreign visitors, Chinese and European. From these accounts, and from some discussed by Prasun

Chatterjee, it appears that in the fifteenth to seventeenth centuries people in South Asia distilled arrack from rice, sugar, and toddy.[193] Thus the old *surā* category, and perhaps *sīdhu* too, was transformed into the predecessors of what is now called "country liquor." Given the dates of these texts that mention distillation, alcoholic distillation for recreational drinking may have become common in South Asia from roughly the thirteenth century onward.

Conclusions

Although many sources we have examined abound in literary conventions, references in inscriptions to investments, profits, measures, and inspections accord with what we've read in the *Arthaśāstra* about festivals and drinking establishments, and are not unlike some aspects of drink culture described in more literary contexts. A picture thus emerges of the culture of brewing and public drinking in the first millennium CE. Brewing could be quite profitable. Ideally it was regulated in an urban setting. Drinking-houses ranged from large, urban, cosmopolitan inns to the common *surā* shop. The drinking place was easy to spot, marked by what was possibly the only retail sign in town. Both women and men were involved in the brewing and sale of liquor, and the brewer/trader was well integrated into society. Some people—at least those who drank—also brewed at home, possibly making simpler *surā* on a smaller scale for festivals, weddings, and parties. And tired soldiers liked to let off steam with a drunken feast if they got the chance.

Although some of the drinkers in our sources are depicted as rogues, the *surā* house and its denizens were not considered hateful, even by those who avoided drink. Even for the more moralizing narratives and their possible audiences, we should not assume that hearers of these tales always identified with the good guys. In fact, the *surā* shop seems to have been one of the few places in a small town where people, both men and women (the drinkers in the Ajanta image are female), could socialize out of the house, away from the family. At the shop they could spend money on a leisure activity (and get into debt), enjoying the various tasty calorific drinks available in early India. Many people shunned liquor, but there is no evidence that the authorities tried to suppress these revenue-generating institutions entirely. The drinking-house was, above all, a place of uninhibited socializing, free of the sort of people who might disapprove of one's drinking and one's class. Here we meet the well-connected policeman getting to know his new friend the fisherman over a cup of *surā*; the rogues trying to steal a minister's ring by drugging him with an irresistible treat, delicious *surā*; a woman thriving from her brewing business, funded by a local Buddhist nun; and finally the half-naked, drunkard son of a Bactrian flailing around with a handful of salty snacks, swigging from a jar of liquor, and thoroughly entertaining the rowdy crowd of drinkers in the marketplace.

CUP 4
Luxurious, Erotic Drinking in Literary Texts

> You can't even get the slightest whiff of liquor cups containing pieces of water-lily, that have circular waves stirred up by sprinkling with mango oil, with ripples agitated by the sighs of loving women; [drinking cups] that are shaped like dancing peacocks.[1]
>
> —*Dhūrtaviṭasaṃvāda*

A rake (*viṭa*) speaks to a wealthy merchant's son. The rake bemoans the restrictions imposed by a strict father—"a headache personified"—that prevent the son from gambling, watching cock-fights, and indulging in other pleasures, including these fantastic drinking cups: colored, perfumed, flavored, ornate, and shared with beautiful women. Like lovers in the monsoon, those who share these cups have the company of dancing peacocks. This enticing description from the play called *Conversation of Rogue and Rake* (*Dhūrtaviṭasaṃvāda*, from the early-to-mid-first millennium CE) is one of the more lavish descriptions I've encountered of erotic, urban, wealthy people's drinking in early India. Although this is a literary description, the cups may not be entirely imaginary, for many of the elements included here, such as the garnishes for the drink, are mentioned so frequently in our sources that they may reflect practice, or at least fantasies and aspirations.

This chapter is as much about genre as about drinking practices. Indeed, one challenge of this chapter is the sheer number of literary references to this sort of drinking. Verses on topics such as tasting drink on a lover's lips are so common that it's hard to know where to begin, so I will limit myself to outlining the main literary conventions and then looking at some striking descriptions of drinking. The practices described here are luxurious: wealthy, sophisticated people drinking from precious vessels, not in the *surā* house in the market but at home, in palaces, in courtesans' mansions, and at lavishly staged drinking parties. Such drinking is often erotic, sometimes charmingly messy, but rarely seedy or criminal, and is thus the respectable face of drinking in early India, from an elite point of view. The public *surā* house is often the setting for a moral tale in

An Unholy Brew. James McHugh, Oxford University Press.
DOI: 10.1093/oso/9780199375936.003.0006

plain language, but luxurious drinking is a foil for scenes of romantic pleasure in a poetic mode.

Can we get any sense of the social history of elite drinking? This is a tricky question given the limited types of evidence we possess. Imagine if the only sources we had for writing a history of upper-class drinking in eighteenth-century France was a large collection of rococo paintings. With few exceptions, our evidence for elite drinking in India is similarly wrapped up in conventions and artifice. Nevertheless, there are useful ways of thinking about this material. First there is a bare-bones empirical reading—recall the *Star Wars* cantina—in which you accept some elements of the representations as having probably applied at certain times and places: costly vessels, imported wines, drinking in domestic settings with servants, the use of betel and perfumes, drinking while seated on couches. We see all these things in the *Kāmasūtra*, in poetry, and in visual images. Such drinking is quite like the *surā* house, only private, and these are your servants, your couches, and your precious cups.

It's also possible that living in a world filled with these representations made people inclined to emulate these modes of drinking, or at least to construe their own drinking as being like these artistic versions—this being a matter of formation, refined sensibility, and speech. Art historian Meredith Martin writes of the politics of pastoral architecture—the way in which, in seventeenth- and eighteenth-century Europe, literary contexts and settings were reproduced through buildings, props, landscapes, animals, and people.[2] Such courtly, literary, pastoral worlds were then inhabited, and a regal-pastoral mode performed. The most famous such case is Marie-Antoinette's model hamlet at Versailles. These pastoral playgrounds, in turn, inspired the literary world, in a dialectic of practice and discourse that was a powerful aesthetic articulation of a particular regal and political persona. Catherine de' Medici's model farm and dairy at Fontainebleau projected a woman and regent, married to her new homeland, fertile, domestic, and stable, "the mother of our Gods, the French Cybele," as Ronsard described her in a poem meant to be read aloud by the royal children, possibly at her model farm.[3]

As the poet Ronsard celebrated Catherine de' Medici as Cybele, so we'll see King Someśvara III depicted as the master of ceremonies (and sole audience) at a luxurious drinking session characteristic of those found in Sanskrit *belles lettres*. As literature or as highly affected practice, this play (*krīḍā*), or participatory pleasure game, is a gilded take on the regular festival.

If the idea of people staging parties in the manner of literary scenes is too far a stretch, we can at least agree that some drinkers were surrounded by images of such drinking. By the mid-first millennium CE, literate wealthy people and those associated with royal courts lived in a world where such drinking was (1) prescribed, complete with the correct terminology, in texts like the *Kāmasūtra*;

(2) represented in literature; and (3) depicted in the visual arts. Betel-chewing, wealthy wine-drinkers could pursue these pleasures knowing that, when done in a certain way, they were aesthetically aligned with respected treatises, poems, and paintings.

The Man-About-Town and the World of the *Kāmasūtra*

Let's start with the *Kāmasūtra*. This text, which is far more than a manual of sexual positions, was probably written in the third or fourth century CE and instructs one on how to flourish in the realm of *kāma*, pleasure, which includes sex.[4] The setting is urban, with a complex cast of stock characters, the principal one being the *nāgaraka*, the man-about-town, an educated householder who has access to exotic perfumes, all manner of food and drinks, fine furniture, even talking parrots. We find ourselves in a world full of precious things, imported scents, betel, and a variety of drinks, a world in which courtly culture and urbane manners were highly developed. The *Kāmasūtra* teaches one how to behave in this complex universe and how to appreciate it correctly. In wine appreciation today, you need to know tastes, smells, and other qualities of wine, as well as words for these tastes, smells, wines, and so on. You must also understand what to do when drinking wine, particularly if you want to thrive socially in wine circles and feel confident that you're dealing correctly (outwardly *and* inwardly) with the Château d'Yquem that your host has served. So it is with the practices taught in the *Kāmasūtra*.

The drinking we see in the *Kāmasūtra* correlates to many (often rather artificial) literary descriptions and visual depictions. It forms a component of an enduring, cosmopolitan Indian aesthetic culture that took shape in the Gupta period. As Daud Ali writes, the period from roughly 350 to 750 CE, the "Gupta ecumene," was a "400-year period . . . which saw the development, crystallization and proliferation of a common political culture throughout all major regions of the subcontinent. Lineages and courts . . . adopted a series of cultural and political conventions which included . . . gestural, ethical, aesthetic and sumptuary practices which were distinctly courtly in nature."[5] While it seems that the focal point of luxury drinking was not the court (at least not the public life of the court), nevertheless we do see luxurious drinking in literature associated with the court.

Of course, some people condemned drinking as a vice. And some people, such as Brahmins, were strictly prohibited from drinking. Drinking is thus an aspect of cosmopolitan aesthetics that, while admired in poetry, was not for everyone in practice. The elite could all enjoy this sort of drinking in texts and images, yet only people of a certain class, who were allowed to drink and allowed to be seen drinking, could take part in the drinking culture itself.

In the *Kāmasūtra*, the man-about-town's bedroom contains a lot of pleasure paraphernalia, including lip salve, perfumes, peel of the citron fruit (*mātuluṅga-tvac*) used as a mouth freshener, betel quids (*tāmbūlāni*), and a spittoon (*patadgraha*).[6] This last object, also seen in art, is an additional sign that delicious betel is present, and that people's mouths are therefore colored and perfumed.[7]

How does this young man make love?

> The man-about-town, together with his friends and attendants, in a dwelling for sexual pleasure, in a prepared bedroom that has decorations of flowers and has been censed with fragrant incense, should approach a woman who has bathed and adorned herself, who has drunk the right amount / properly, with tender pacifying words and offering more drink.[8]

The thirteenth-century commentator Yaśodhara understands this passage as describing preparations (*saṃskāra*) for the sexual act. First there are preparations for the bedroom, where the sex will take place. Then there are the essential preparations of the woman, which, Yaśodhara states, are twofold, body and mind. The cosmetics prepare the body, for, as Yaśodhara explains, "Even seeing the woman when she is not adorned is forbidden." Then Yaśodhara states that "'who has drunk the right amount' means the preparation of the mind (*manaḥsaṃskāraḥ*). [This should be read as] Who has not drunk too much. Because that makes one unsteady." This is not a matter, therefore, of rendering the woman so drunk that she cannot refuse or consent. Then the man-about-town should offer the woman more drink, along with tender words. Yaśodhara explains that the second instance of drinking, which takes place with the man, is referred to as *saraka*, a word that also means a type of cup, which he has previously defined as the type of drinking that couples do, contrasted with the *samāpānam* or *āpānakam*, which Yaśodhara defines as communal, general drinking.[9] He also uses this term when listing attendants who should be present in the above scenario: "a betel-bearer, a loving-cup worker, and so forth." (*tāmbūladāyakasarakakarmāntikādibhiḥ*). So, at least as understood by this later commentator, there were distinct terminologies for varieties of drinking, the difference being the number of drinkers involved.

Then the couple drink again, converse, and enjoy music.[10] The man dismisses the retinue, offering them betel and fragrances, before the couple have sex. Afterward they bathe, separately and modestly, and reunite to sit and take that most important item of social interaction, betel. Then, when the man has smeared the woman's body with sandalwood or another unguent,[11] together they enjoy drink and food:

> And [the man-about-town] embracing her with his left arm, with a drinking cup in his hand (*caṣakahasta*), should have her drink while conciliating her. Or,

with water as a drink, they should both take morsels of food or something else, as suited to constitution and wholesomeness.

[There should be] clear meat broths, sour gruel, drinks along with fried-meat drinking snacks (*upadaṃśa*), mangoes, dried meat, sour citron pieces with sugar[12] such as are wholesome according to the region. Then, saying, "This one is sweet, or soft, or clear," and tasting them all, he should give her various things.[13]

This posture is exactly what we see in many visual depictions of couples drinking. Might we read early Indian images of this sort as representations of a specific moment in the love-making process, just before or just after? (It seems that their posture before the love-making is the same.) The basic iconography of two lovers, the man offering drink to the woman, dates at least as far back as the second century BCE.[14]

Here (Figure 4.1) is a typical image of this drinking posture, from Cave 3 at Badami. This posture allows the man to embrace the woman while offering drink and food with his pure right hand. Moreover, as we read in the *Mahābhārata*,

FIGURE 4.1 Couple embracing with a cup, from Cave 3 at Badami, late sixth century.

Photo © James McHugh 2014.

a man's left thigh was reserved for lovers to sit on, and the right for daughters.[15] The later visual images of this posture are contemporaneous with many of our texts and correlate closely to them, giving them a visible counterpart.[16] Most of all, these images reinforce the fact that drinking, like conversation and kissing, was an intrinsically social activity; indeed, one of the first things the hunter does in the *surā* origin tale, the "Previous-Birth Story of the Jar," is find a drinking companion.

We learn nothing about the particular type of drinks in the passages from the *Kāmasūtra* above, only that they are accompanied by snacks (*upadaṃśa*). But the foods here are spectacularly varied in flavor, texture, and appearance. As we'll see again later, talking about these flavor qualities seems to have been an expected part of the exchange.

The man-about-town also engages in group drinking. This is described earlier in the text, in the passage on his lifestyle. Following the description of his private activities comes a list of his social activities outside the house: religious festivals, salons, drinking gatherings (*samāpānaka*),[17] pleasure trips to gardens, and group games.[18] These are subsequently described in more detail:

> And there should be drinking gatherings (*āpānakāni*) in one another's residences.
>
> There, the courtesans should have them [the men] drink, and afterward they themselves should drink: wine (*madhu*), *maireya*, *surā*, and *āsava*, that have various bitter, spicy, and sour accompanying snacks, such as fruit and green vegetables that are salty.
>
> Trips to gardens (*udyānagamanaṃ*) are explained in this manner [i.e., like the drinking gatherings just described].[19]

The list of drinks here is very similar to the selection in the *Arthaśāstra*. This group drinking is unlike the general festival or the *surā* shop by the market. Here the man-about-town leaves his luxurious home (unless he is hosting the party) and goes to the relative privacy of another residence. Or, along with select others, he temporarily leaves the city for a well-planned drinking picnic.

In addition to the contrast between drinking in a couple and group drinking, there is a contrast between private and public drinking, wherever these forms of drinking take place. The *surā* shop and the village festival are the most public forms of drinking. By contrast, elite drinking tends toward privacy, which allows for uninhibited drinking for the upper-class people involved; sometimes, as an additional precaution, they send their servants and retinue away. Wealthy men's drunken ladies are for their eyes only. Whether in the city or in a screened area in the park, the upper classes restrict access to their erotically charged, confused, and vulnerable moments. Conversely, drinking in the marketplace, the alehouse, and at chaotic festivals is a public, visible unleashing of passions.

The Ideal Manner of Drinking

What else did luxurious drinking involve? Prior to drinking, some people performed a ritual of pouring drink mixed with water onto the earth, as an offering for supernatural beings.[20] In the *Delight of the Mind*, we read how the women bow to each other and splash some drink onto their heads with the ring finger of their left hands prior to drinking, though the rationale for this is not clear.[21] As far as I am aware, we have no record of any verbal toast or pledge.

In texts and images representing this mode of drinking, people often drink while seated. There are some images of standing couples drinking, in which the man holds the cup and offers it to an unsteady-looking woman. Possibly these evoke an outdoor setting, with dancing and stumbling, as opposed to the couches of the indoor party.[22] A standing image also provides a vertical composition and emphasizes the woman's inebriation and physical dependence on the male figure. The image shown here (Figure 4.2) is from the eighth-century Mallikārjuna temple at Pattadakal.

In images of seated drinkers, the cups are typically shaped like shallow bowls, with no visible foot, but in some earlier images, for example one of Balarāma from Mathura, the cups are shaped like chalices, each with a foot, and in some cases with a handle on the side.[23] As of the mid-first millennium CE, drinking cups are often called *caṣaka*s in these more luxurious contexts.[24] Sometimes they are also called *śukti*, which means "oyster shell" and probably implies a smaller bowl.[25]

An early medieval drinking bowl made of metal has survived, ostensibly excavated in Gilgit but possibly reflecting Kashmiri traditions of art.[26] In the center of this bowl is an image of a seated couple with the woman holding a bowl—a drinking scene inside a drinking bowl, as one sees in ancient Greece. Multiple texts mention vessels made from precious metals or colored glass, though no doubt in poetic texts the desire to list numerous precious metals or the full range of colors also played a role in such descriptions. The idea that a certain shape of vessel is technically ideal for tasting is entirely absent. Possibly the tendency to focus on the visual aspects of drinking was a product of and a stimulant for upper-class styles of drinking using colored glass and imported colored wines.

Finally, we have scattered references to drinking straws. There is a reference in a Vedic text to Indra drinking *soma* through a straw.[27] In the Pali *Jātaka* of "drinking with a reed" (*naḷapāna-*) we hear how the Buddha, in a previous birth

FIGURE 4.2 Standing drinking couple, with stumbling woman. Mallikārjuna Temple at Pattadakal, eighth century.

Photo © James McHugh 2014.

as a monkey, helped other monkeys drink from a pond that contained a dangerous demon by making the reeds there (*naḷadaṇḍaka*) hollow, so the monkeys could safely drink the water, as with a lotus-stalk/tube (*uppalanāḷa*).[28] These references all involve using straws in exceptional circumstances. A reference to more routine drinking with straws (routine for ghouls, that is) occurs in another comparison of a battlefield to a drinking scene, in which ghoul-lovers share a drink of blood-wine that they suck, as if with straws, through the trunks of elephants felled in battle.[29] In general, though, using straws seems to have been an exceptional way of drinking.

In some visual depictions, servants pour drinks from other vessels, jugs or ewers.[30] Presumably the process of taking the drink from the storage vessel required filters and secondary vessels in addition to cups. Yet making drinks does not always seem to have been servants' work in these circles, for preparing drinks, including intoxicating ones (*-āsavayojanam*), is one of the Sixty-Four Arts that should be studied, according to the *Kāmasūtra*.[31] Of course, luxury drinking was accompanied by the ubiquitous snacks.

Frequently in Sanskrit poetry the most desirable drinking vessel is your lover's mouth.[32] After all why should you drink your own drinks when you could drink them from each other's mouths during a kiss? In a story cycle from the first millennium, the *Bṛhatkathāślokasaṃgraha*, we learn:

> Liquor (*madirā*) intoxicates by its nature, how much more so when beautified by contact with a beloved's mouth.[33]

Extracting wine with a kiss also allows you to taste your lover's mouth-perfumes and scented betel. And the drink itself might have been perfumed too. In the epigraph to this chapter and elsewhere, we read of drinks garnished with flowers and aromatics. So emblematic are these garnishes of sensuous drinking that when, in the play *Much Ado about Religion* (*Āgamaḍambara*, from the late ninth century in Kashmir), we hear of a lax Buddhist monk with a lily in his drink, we know perfectly well what is really going on.[34]

The bawdy drama called the *Conversation of Rogue and Rake* (*Dhūrtaviṭasaṃvāda*) highlights the connection of drink, the great erotic enabler, with erotic professionals, courtesans. First we read that the wind from the brothel quarter is "infused with the perfume of garlands and *āsava*, like a sigh from the courtesans' quarter."[35] Later, a speaker defends spending money on courtesans. He explains that wealth and righteousness produce bodily pleasure (*śarīrasukham*). Therefore, not to spend your wealth on pleasure is a great waste, even a sinful ingratitude. If you've got it—good karmic rewards—you should enjoy it. The speaker then describes the greatest sense pleasures, all in terms of courtesans, going through the senses one by one: the sound of their sweet words, the touch of their bodies, the sight of their beautiful faces, and the scent of their hair filled with flowers, their clothes and lotus-like mouths, their intoxicated faces with red eyes (*tāmranetram*), and their sandal-smeared bodies.[36] As for the joy of taste:

> Drink (*pānaṃ*) is, as it were, the most reviled of liquids. On account of its being qualified by a courtesan, its enjoyment becomes pleasant. Remark, sir, the man who, in the courtesans' quarter, has drunk up liquor (*madirā*) that is hastily stirred up and whirled around, or falls from her mouth when she has drunk the rest, with her lips for a snack (*upadaṃśa*)—truly knows flavor (*rasa*)![37]

Ingeniously, the lips become the ubiquitous snack, and we see the notion that drink, though sometimes condemned, is an *aesthetically* superlative substance.

Drinking from a lover's mouth did have its risks: in the seventh-century *Harṣacarita* of Bāṇa we read how a certain "Pauravī, [killed] Somaka the Paurava lord by having him drink a mouthful of poison liquor (*viṣavāruṇīgaṇḍūṣa*), with her mouth smeared with an invisible antidote."[38]

Related perhaps to drinking from a lover's mouth is the convention that the *bakula* tree can flower only when its craving (*dohada*) is satisfied by being sprayed with intoxicating drink (often/always *sīdhu*?) from the mouth of a beautiful young woman. Effectively, the tree gets to take a drink from her mouth too.[39]

Classical Drunken Behavior

The materials in this chapter often depict drunk women as an amusing and attractive spectacle for a man in their midst (and for the reader or viewer of a play). We saw versions of this in the epics. In Sanskrit literary texts such behavior, often associated with elite outdoor parties, becomes a set piece for writers. The humans or other beings involved tend to be in some way remarkable: warrior monkeys, great heroes, royal consorts, divine pleasure beings. Such scenes are often erotic, associated with attempted seduction.

This sort of scene was codified in literary theory. In his foundational text on poetics, the *Kāvyādarśa*, while defining long "court-epic" poems (*mahākāvya*), Daṇḍin states that they should contain a description of a drinking party or wine-drinking (*-madhupāna-*).[40] Note, however, that the two poems I shall presently discuss were composed before this definition was created—and Daṇḍin's definition may even be based on the contents of the *Kirātārjunīya*, discussed later.[41] But we should never be surprised to see a drinking party in Sanskrit poetry. There is no space to list all such episodes here—two notable descriptions that I can't explore occur in the *Śiśupālavadha* of Māgha and the *Śrīkaṇṭhacarita* of Maṅkha.[42] Remember, also, that these scenes are far from documentary evidence of the reality of drinking. Also it is likely that the numerous names of the drinks in such scenes were frequently chosen for poetic effect.

Probably the earliest such passage in Sanskrit poetry (excluding the epics) is in the *Life of the Buddha* (*Buddhacarita*) by Aśvaghoṣa, dating probably from the first or second century CE.[43] Here the Buddha-to-be, a privileged prince, has just discovered that people can grow old, get ill, and die. His father, wishing more than ever to distract him from his ruminations, insists that he go on a trip to a grove in the city park (*purodyāna*) where a group of beautiful young women await him—a sort of party staged by his father.[44] When the prince arrives, the women start out shy, but "they quickly dropped their timidity under the spell of liquor and love (*madena madanena ca*)."[45]

The *Life of the Buddha* goes on as follows (Olivelle's translation):

> Surrounded, then, by those women,
> the prince strolled about the grove,
> like an elephant with a female herd,
> in a Himalayan grove.[46]

Some of the women press their bodies on him:

> One girl whispered in his ear,
> her mouth smelling of liquor (*āsava-*),
> her lower lip coppery red:
> "Listen to a secret!"
>
> . . .
>
> Another, pretending that she was drunk,
> repeatedly let her blue dress slip down.
> Flashing her girdle, she gleamed,
> like the night with lightning streaks.
>
> Some rambled hither and thither,
> with their golden girdles tinkling,
> displaying to him their hips,
> covered with fine see-through cloth.
>
> Others, grasping branches
> of mango in full bloom,
> bent down to expose breasts
> resembling golden pots.

. . .

One girl, wanting to start a fight,
grabbed a branch of a mango tree
and inquired, her speech slurred by drink:
"Whose flower is this?"

. . .

Then one girl, her eyes rolling,
Smelling a blue lotus bloom,
spoke to the king's son with words
that were somewhat blurred by drink . . .

. . .

Although seduced in this way,
he wavered not, nor rejoiced,
firmly guarding his senses,
and perturbed at the thought:
"One must die."[47]

As we shall see, drink and accidental nudity often go together, whether it is erotic or humiliating. Here we are outdoors and the prince is surrounded by many women, all approaching him in different ways, a bombardment of drunken flirts. As with other such passages, the reader gets an impression of eroticized chaos. Although it is a typical literary drinking scene, the situation also highlights the prince's indifference to such transient pleasures.

Another description comes from a poem called *Arjuna and the Hunter* (*Kirātārjunīya*) by Bhāravi, from roughly the sixth century CE.[48] The poem retells an incident from the *Mahābhārata* in which the hero, Arjuna, goes to the Himalayas to practice penances in order to win a boon from the god Śiva. As is often the case in Indian narratives, not everyone is happy when humans gain great powers through austerities, and some local foresters complain to the god Indra about the threat from Arjuna. To test Arjuna's determination, Indra sends his own courtesans, *apsaras*es, to seduce him. These beings travel with their partners, another type of divine being called *gandharva*s—pleasure-loving, male, musician demigods—and they all enjoy the pleasures of the mountain, hold a drinking party, and make love. After this, the *apsaras*es try to seduce Arjuna, but he is not moved. Again, this failed seduction nevertheless delights the reader, and the hero emerges as a man all the more determined to achieve his end.

The love-making begins at night. The setting sun is compared to the flush of intoxication, another commonly noted effect of drinking (Peterson's translation):

> Its great thirst quenched by deep draughts of lotus honey,
> drunk from cupped hands that were its rays, the
> sun turned red and sank low on the horizon, like a
> drunken man falling down.[49]

The women adorn themselves and settle down to wait:

> While awaiting their lovers, the women found no pleasure
> in flower garlands or fragrant sandalwood cream or
> wine (*madirā*). It is the presence of the lover that gives the
> accessories (*sādhana*) of love-making the power to charm.[50]

Recall that in the *Kāmasūtra* and its commentary, we saw drink and adornments as preparations for love. Then the drinking starts to affect the women, which makes for an uncertain start:

> The angry young women, en route to their lovers'
> houses, piqued by a quarrel, and brushing aside
> their girlfriends' advice, surrendered themselves to
> drunkenness, even though it defeated their purpose,
> making them unsteady and weakening their resolve.[51]

When they arrive, their mood changes and the love-making begins, inflamed by passion and alcohol:

> Whose handiwork could one see in those passionate
> women when, overcome by draughts of sugarcane-wine (*śīdhu-*), they
> joined their lovers, quickly losing their modesty and
> surrendering their pride—the work of the love god (Madana), the
> intoxicator, or of intoxication (Mada) itself?[52]

As we shall see later, Intoxication (Mada) is sometimes personified. The *apsarar*es and *gandharva*s continue making love. In the latter part of the description, drinks and their effects are the focus of many clever images and comparisons, and we see the most common themes associated with drinking in Sanskrit literature: the flower garnish, the mouth-cup, the intense emotions, the exposure of the body and the inner emotions.

The young men longed to drink in their lovers' smiling faces and the wine (*madhu*) laced with water-lilies. Both inflamed their passion, both offered new delights with each mouthful, and both only increased their thirst.

Lovemaking quelled anger; draughts of liquor (*vāruṇī*) ended love quarrels. The proud women made peace with their lovers, and the love god had no further need to aim his arrows at them.

With every draught (*madhu-vāra*), the young women relished every further instruction from the wine: "Quarrel with your young man! Be quick to relent! When he is stung, placate him with devotion!"

. . .

The wine (*āsava*) acquired a new flavor, it seemed, with each draught: first drunk by the women on their own, then given by their lovers with great tenderness, and later drunk together with their men.

Floating water-lilies quivered in the rippling wine in the goblet (*caṣaka*), their petals fluttering gently as though mimicking the graceful coquetry of the women's eyes and the charming play of their eyebrows.

The *gandharva* lovers, eager to taste the beloved's lip in a love bite, took greatest delight in wine quaffed (*madhuvāra*) from the goblets (*caṣaka*) that were their women's faces, where eyes blossomed like blue lotuses.

The right vessel confers greater distinction on the virtues of the virtuous. That is why the wine (*madhu*) drunk from the beloved's mouth was especially delicious.

When they saw, reflected in the jeweled goblets, how the wine (*madhu*) had washed the [red] lac from their lips and made the bite marks from their lovers' teeth, those bright red ornaments, shine so bright, the women esteemed the draughts even more.

> It erased the red gloss from the women's lips and made their eyes red with intoxication. It scented the nymphs' mouths, whose sweet scent intensified its fragrance. Was it by accident or by design that the liquor (*vāruṇī*) drunk by the *apsaras*es exchanged its attributes with theirs?[53]
>
> . . .
>
> The lovely flush of intoxication had spread all over their bodies, and yet it was in the women's faces, as in a mirror, that it found its clearest manifestation, in eyes red with passion and cheeks the color of coral.[54]
>
> . . .
>
> Suspicious of their lovers, the ladies thought, "He might leave me for another woman if I am befuddled with wine," and so they hesitated to drink (*madirā*) too much. Love sees dangers lurking everywhere.
>
> Delightful seclusion, the god of love, wine's intoxication (*madhumada*), moonlight, and union with their lovers—all this took the women's passion to new heights.[55]

The bodies and adornments of the female *apsaras*es are prominent here, while the male *gandharvas* are characterized by actions and enjoyment. The drink itself is also a notable actor: it instructs the *apsaras*es, is tasty and fragrant, dissolves cosmetics, makes the body and face flush red, intoxicates, and above all arouses desire. We also read of the typical vessel, the *caṣaka* cup, and there are references to draughts, cups (*-vāra*) of drink. The mouth, again, is prominent. Thus far we have seen lovers' mouths perfumed with citron peel, betel (noticeably absent here), with red lac coloring, used for biting and kissing, and transformed into living, pleasure-giving cups.

The passages above portray the attractions of drunk females prior to the failed seduction of a hero. A similar scene in the *Mānasollāsa* shows how a king "enjoys the earth."[56] Here we learn of the rationale for the royal drinking party. We have already examined the detailed recipes for intoxicating drinks and savory snacks given in this text. These are followed by a purely literary description of confused, flirting, drunken women. So, while the text lends itself to a more realistic, historicizing reading about the drinks themselves, it then dissolves into the conventions of literature.

At the start of the section, we learn the purpose of the women's drinking game:

> Now the game originating in the drinking of intoxicating beverages is related,
>
> In a grassy place in the forest, or on a sandbank by the river,
> in a garden filled with fruits and flowers, or in a pleasantly painted house,
> the king should have the womenfolk practice the game that arises from drinking liquor,
> for their happiness of mind and his own observation.[57]

These options allow for indoor and outdoor drinking parties, covering both options given in the *Kāmasūtra.* As with the gathering held for the Buddha-to-be, this event is held to entertain one observer. Though it is also for the pleasure of the women, they are directed to play the game by the king. After this short introduction, we learn about the drinks, which then arrive:

> Having brought various intoxicating drinks in vessels of glass and clay . . . he should have [the following] brought into the drinking place as drinking snacks . . .[58]

Probably these vessels are larger storage containers; the reference to glass here is noteworthy. Then:

> He [the king] should have lotus and blue water-lily leaves, plantain leaves,[59] and turmeric leaves placed in the drinking place (*pānasthāne*).
>
> And in the spot for drinking he should also have someone place glass drinking cups (*caṣakān*), food dishes (*sthālakān*) made of glass, and round pots (*karakān*)[60] made of that [i.e., glass], which are of various colors and shapes: the hue of sapphire, that have the radiance of the [yellow green] *gomedaka* gem,[61] the same hue as emerald, similar to the *vaiḍūrya* gem [blue/green], the color of clear rock crystal and the shade of [black] kohl, and with the luster of shining gold. And in the place for drinking wine (*madhupānasthāne*)[62] he should put food dishes and drinking cups (*caṣakāni*) prepared with gold and silver, and also small cups (*śuktikān*) made of gold.[63]

The drinks in this text are not made of anything especially rare, nor are they imported. But the drinks and snacks are distinguished by how they're served, in vessels made of precious metals and above all colored glass, which stands out as a prestigious material, maybe imported and thus linking the drinking culture to the Indian Ocean trade.[64]

Then the party starts:

> Then, lovingly, he should bring in the beloved women, covered in adornments, delightful to the eyes, slender-bodied, who captivate the heart, and he should have the women, who possess affection for each other, settle down in various places. On a sandy or grassy spot, inside a favorite bamboo thicket, in parks in the shade of trees, in the gardens of houses, with a private screen of cloth that is delightful in various colors, he should have these excellent women sit in a row according to their status.[65] In front of them the king should place splendid vessels (*pātrāṇi*), and the king should have glass, gold, and silver food dishes (*sthālāni*), drinking cups (*caṣakāḥ*), and small cups (*śuktīḥ*) put in front of his most beloved women in the proper manner. And the king should have women[66] carefully fill the drinking cups with intoxicating beverages (*madya*), *surās*, and also *āsavas* for the royal women to drink. He should have cooks (*sūpakāra*) serve (*pariveṣayet*) many types[67] of drinking snacks (*upadaṃśa*) in the vessels (*pātra*), describing each of the tastes, colors, and flavors. Then, having served the courses, they should depart.[68] The women should fill the *karaka* [round vessels] with the intoxicating drinks (*madya*) that are there.[69] And one should place a lotus in some vessels (*pātra*) full of *madhu*, in some a blue water-lily and in some *mallikā*-jasmine. Then, taking a vessel (*pātra*) full of *surā* in the hand, they should throw [or place, *kṣipeyuḥ*] drops of *madhu* on their heads with the ring fingers of the left hands.[70] Then, once they are given permission, the slender women, desirous of drink, respectfully bow to each other and joyfully drink the *surā* in the drinking cups (*caṣaka*). Having drunk ghee gradually and repeatedly they should drink the extremely intoxicating *surā*: white, with a pale liquid and sweet; black, sharp (*kaṭu*), and astringent;[71] and that made from sweet grapes (-*drākṣā*-); and other things characterized mainly by being slightly sharp,[72] as well as intoxicating drink made from palmyra palms and the rest. And then the women, while drinking *madhu*, should enjoy the snacks (*upadaṃśa*), fresh ginger and so forth; they should eat the chewable solid food, chew the chickpeas and so on, and savor the meats, describing the tastes, intense with flavors of pungent, sour, and so on, [and the] varied delightful intoxicating drinks that very much confuse the mind . . .[73]

This "party" has a quite formal start. The women are guided to their places and are surrounded by exquisite finery. Drinking is preceded by the ring-finger liquor-toss and a polite bow, as well as permission to start drinking and eating. Wherever the party takes place is surrounded by a private screen and the servers all leave. Again, upper-class group-drinking is concealed from the world. There is also some connoisseurship of the food and drink. Even the cook describes the various tastes of the food as he serves it.

They carefully describe the qualities of the *surā* (*kathayantyaḥ surāguṇān*), which, like the *madhu* word, may have a generic sense in this part of the text.[74] The women's drunken behavior is similar to that seen in the poetic texts discussed earlier, and I shall not quote the passage in full. It does, however, pick up on the colored *surā* mentioned in the part of the chapter that provides recipes, anchoring this literary material in the preceding realia:

> One woman, though drinking black *surā*—which was white from the brightness of her teeth—had not noticed the flavor and stopped drinking for a moment. One excellent lady, seeing *surā* that was black as hair in vessels that contained jasmine, was frightened to touch it because of mistaking it for a black bee.[75]

The women thus display the typical confusions of perception. Similarly, "[i]n the guise of drinking intoxicating drink, one woman joyfully kisses the face of her husband, standing nearby, that is reflected in the drinking cup."[76] Not only do the women see their lovers at the bottom of a glass, but the drink distorts their emotions and conduct, as described in a stylized passage very different from the recipes at the start of the section:

> Then, drinking liquor became for them like a relative, destroying sadness;
> An annihilator of worry, like gain; an increaser of affection like a friend;
> A remover of decorum, like anger; a destroyer of memory like confusion;
> Shameless like pain . . .[77]

We hear of the women's red cheeks and red eyes, garbled speech, and sluggish movements.[78] They laugh and cry for no reason, and also combine contradictory emotions and actions: they curse and bless at the same time, and weep while laughing.[79] One sings like a cuckoo; another joyfully dances with defective moves.[80] We are told that "one slim-bodied woman gapes in various ways as if possessed by a *graha* [a being that causes possession]"—another common comparison.[81] Their erotic confusion is directed toward the king, and they variously embrace him, kiss his cheek, and lift the hems of their skirts. Finally, the text returns to the king on his own, "like an elephant amongst female elephants" (*vaśāmadhye yathā dvipaḥ*).[82] He gleams with the pleasures of touch, caressed by the womenfolk, as described in a verse that exemplifies the poetic qualities of this passage (*śobhate sukhasaṃsparśāl lālito lalanājanaiḥ*).[83] The king plays for some time in this way, "like Kṛṣṇa with the cowherd women," increasing their lust from drinking *madirā*.[84] And thus the section ends.

Unlike the young Buddha-to-be, King Someśvara is fully engaged in the pleasures of the realm of rebirth, *saṃsāra*, and embraces these women, savoring their intoxication. Drink here is a good thing: it makes the women happy and transforms them into a multi-sensory, erotic spectacle for his amusement. Even when disturbances of the mind unleash anger and jealousy, these emotions simply emphasize the competition for his person among the women. Intoxicating drink heightens erotic social relations and also the enjoyment of other sensory pleasures. A drinking party produces a temporary excess of confused desire, and here the desire is guaranteed to focus on the king, though even then he is not defeated by seduction but lords it over the drunken ladies. Indeed, it appears that he remains sober throughout all of their antics.

Although reminiscent of a classical poem, the chapter in the *Mānasollāsa* is innovative, especially in its juxtaposition of recipes and poetry and the way it incorporates details about the drinks, like the black *surā*, into the poetic section. In many other literary texts, the drinks are of little importance aside from being intoxicating. They form part of a common set of cosmopolitan modes of representation—"sandalwood in the south," "saffron in Kashmir"—but one assumes that all manner of products and substances have been left out of the standard poetic picture. This is where the *Delight of the Mind* is innovative, for here the drinks do matter. The black and pale *surā* could well be a local and contemporary tradition, as there is nothing quite like them in other sources; it forms a local prop in this classical performance. Someśvara III and the women around him enjoy their party as the great heroes and *apsaras*es did in the semi-mythical past, yet strong black *surā* and local toddies feature in this chapter that alludes to the timeless world of poetry. The juxtaposition becomes less surprising when one notes that this text contains early examples of literary vernacular.[85] Here the vernacular drinks are confidently served at the party, pushing aside the rather bland, predictable cosmopolitans.

Did anything like this party ever take place? We'll never know, but in this text Someśvara III immortalized his court as a place where such events were staged.

Cellar-Keepers and Connoisseurship

The *Bṛhatkathāślokasaṃgraha* by Budhasvāmin (henceforth, for convenience, the *Great Story* by Budhasvāmin) is a fascinating source of information on life in early India.[86] The date of this text is uncertain, but it's probably from the first millennium CE.[87] It contains numerous references to drinking, but I will focus on two episodes that give an unusually vivid sense of the era's drinking culture.

The text concerns the adventures of a prince called Naravāhanadatta, who is often accompanied by a group of close male friends. The plot is too complex to explain here, but the translations are highly recommended to anyone interested. At many points in the story, things are not what they seem, people are in disguise, and motivations are quite different from what they appear to be. This applies to both of the episodes we are considering, in each of which a man drinks against his will. Yet in both episodes we ultimately discover that all is well; the drinking was part of a master-plan that serves the greater good, and the man did not do anything disreputable after all. In both episodes, the man drinks alcohol for the first time, and he is amazed by both the flavors and the effects of intoxication. In both episodes the desired result is an erotic encounter, the secret plan being in one case to consummate a marriage and in the other to make the man embrace a more worldly life.

In the first episode, the prince-protagonist is persuaded to drink by a "woman" he loves and has just married. In fact she is a type of being called a *vidyādharī* in the guise of a human woman. The ostensible reason for their marriage was that the woman had once prayed to a *yakṣa* (another type of non-human being) to become the prince's servant. At that time she agreed that if he granted her wish, she would offer him (the *yakṣa*) a drink after she married the prince. This *yakṣa*, a boozy tippler (*pānaśauṇḍena*), took the woman to the lord of *yakṣa*s, the god Kubera, who approved the deal.[88] Thus the woman is obliged to marry the prince in order to keep her promise to the *yakṣa*. At least, that's what the prince thinks is going on . . .

After the wedding, the woman returns to the prince's house and makes some offerings to Kubera and the *yakṣa*, who helped to make all this happen. In a manner typical of this narrative, the usual roles are reversed here, and the woman offers the man drink:

> There she worshiped the *yakṣa* along with the Lord of Wealth [Kubera], with flowers and other materials, and satisfied that very hard-to-satisfy one with an offering of drink (*pānadānena*).
>
> Taking a small cup (*śukti*) made of ruby, filled with wine (*madhu*) the color of liquid ruby, my lover then spoke to me: "This is the best of auspicious things, and it grants success in all affairs—the delicious leftovers (*śeṣā*) of the Lord of Wealth; please taste them."
>
> I said, "I don't even want to practice virtues if my respected father has not given permission, never mind a great vice!" Then she, firm in her zeal, left me unable to reply because of her lengthy irrefutable scolding, and she made me drink against my will. When I had drunk one small cup of wine (*-madhuśukti*), she smiled and asked me, "How does this drink taste?" and then I replied, "On drinking it, it had a sweet taste, and then a bitter aftertaste (*anusvāde*);[89] as it faded it was distinguished as slightly astringent and pungent." She said, "Clearly you have not experienced the flavor yet. Drink again," and at her command I drank again. When she asked, "How is it?" I said, "Why is my mind (*citta*) out of sorts?" She said, "Please taste just one more small cup, and your mind will soon be fine." When I had drunk it I saw trees, palaces, mountains, and other things,

> which, though immobile, were in motion, rapidly wavering around. And just as she made me drink—though unwilling—by urbane methods and scolding and so on, so I made her drink. Then, approaching forcefully, Intoxication and Lust made me do whatever they fancied. As the wedding we had performed to satisfy the *yakṣa* was fake, so she also performed a fake virginity.
>
> Then in the morning Hariśikha [a friend of the prince] came to the chamber, smelled that it was saturated with the odor of wine (*madhu*), and said, his mind agitated, "Prince, there appears to be a quite new smell here. I think that the princess made you drink against your will."[90]

There follows a discussion of whether the prince's drinking was right or wrong. Then another friend enters, dressed up in red cosmetics, red garlands, and red clothes. This man, Gomukha, is drunk and explains why he is dressed like this (though his account is also a strategic lie):[91]

> He said, "Your father's other wife called for me and in the presence of the king gave the order, 'Your brother has been indulging in drink at night, so, having yourself tasted the drink that is tasting good from the drink house (*pānagṛhāt*), you should have that which you like the taste of sent to your brother.'[92] And both the queens adorned me with their own hands and made me go to the drink-house (*pānāgara*), led by the Superintendent of Drink (*pānādhyakṣa-*). There, gradually tasting the various drinks (*pāna*), I, inebriated, sent you a succession [of drinks]. Therefore drink the Kāpiśāyana *āsava* free from concerns—you have been permitted to do so by your delighted parents, along with the ministers."
>
> Then I (the prince) spent days indulging in drink with my beloved and my circle of friends, with a delighted retinue . . .[93]

The prince is coerced to drink but is then concerned about his parents' permission. However, it turns out that his parents planned the episode to release his inhibitions (at least according to his friend).

The drink that his wife first offers him is not just any wine, but was the same wine offered to the *yakṣa* and his master, the Lord of *Yakṣa*s, Kubera. Later in the *Great Story* by Budhasvāmin, another prince visits an island inhibited by *yakṣa*s to find a certain female *yakṣa* (*yakṣī*), and this land is also quite boozy. Her father, who is playing dice, has a large belly and red eyes, and is drunk (*samadam*). The prince and the *yakṣī* drink divine wine (*divyasya madhunaḥ pānaṃ*) and make love.[94]

In the Buddhist caves at Ajanta, beings who are probably *yakṣa*s are depicted drinking, as elsewhere is the god Kubera, king of the northern direction in Buddhism as well as in Hindu sources.[95] Possibly some of the Ajanta paintings also depict beings who are elsewhere called "always-drunk" (*sadā-matta*) and "pitcher-in-hand" (*karoṭa-pāṇi*).[96] They are depicted drinking and dressed in the "northern fashion." In some cases the male *yakṣa*s are depicted drinking together (not with consorts), and they sometimes drink by swigging from jars. These are interesting visual depictions of raucous drinking, less frequently visually depicted than upper-class couples drinking.[97]

The above account of the prince's description of wine-tasting is unusual for early Indian sources. For the prince, the wine has a number of tastes—note that sensations like "pungent" and "astringent" were classed as tastes, *rasa*s, in Indian thought. He experiences these tastes in succession and possesses a vocabulary for each successive stage of tasting. His report of drinking wine, at least according to his wife, is not quite right, though the whole process of asking him about the flavor and driving him to taste more wine is also a clever plan to get him drunk.

The prince then describes his first experience of being drunk. He experiences a dizzy illusion in which immobile objects seem to move around rapidly; as so often in sources from early India, drink here is associated with visual confusion. He does not enjoy this experience, and his mind (*citta*) feels out of sorts. Finally, he loses his will to resist Intoxication and Lust.

Some other details stand out. There is the incriminating smell of drink. Later in the book we see formulas for hiding this smell. We also get a sense of how a wine cellar was run. The two queens dressed the prince's friend all in red, a color associated with passion and drink—was this a cellar-keeper's outfit?[98] Although placed in charge of tasting the wine, the man is accompanied by a royal officer, the Superintendent of Drink (*pāna*). This royal storehouse apparently contains grape wines (given the terms used and the color), which require the supervision of a professional. The friend is supposed to know what good wines taste like, implying that there were standards of good and bad. Finally, everyone discovers that the wine they were drinking was famous *Kāpiśāyana* wine, though here this is termed a type of *āsava*, no doubt used in a generic sense. (Remember, as with the other references, that *Kāpiśāyana* wine could be a literary device implying great wine rather than a reference to actual drinking practices.) Although the first night of drinking involved only the couple and was a prelude to sex, now the prince, his wife, and his male friends all drink together, in an example of the sociability of this prince and his circle, and perhaps reflecting how readers imagined such people—wealthy young men yet to take up power—passing the time and enjoying the pleasures of the senses.

This text rounds out our understanding of how the wealthy were imagined to engage in drinking. Young men were sometimes not supposed to drink as their fathers or parents might not approve, though not necessarily for reasons of religious law. We see that the wealthy might possess a storehouse for drink, managed

FIGURE 4.3 Couples drinking with attendants present, Virūpākṣa Temple at Pattadakal, eighth century.
Photo © James McHugh 2014.

by a special officer. Here the drink seems to be wine, imported, long lasting, precious, and appreciated for its complex tastes.

This text also contains several descriptions of communal drinking, both mixed and all-male. At one point the prince's friends all have disastrous wedding nights and assemble the following day to discuss what happened, mock each other, and drink.[99] This drinking, although no doubt taking place in privacy at an elite residence, is quite like what we might imagine in the predominantly male public drinking places, the inns and *surā* shops. After the bout, the same young men gather with their wives and share drinks while seated "in a drinking place/ground (*pānabhūmau*) more beautiful than a lotus pond."[100] They are instructed, "Each man should drink with a woman they do not mind drinking with, and each woman should drink with a man they do not mind drinking with."[101] This luxurious, semi-private drinking session of several men and women together reminds me of the scene depicted on a pillar in the eighth-century Virūpākṣa temple at Pattadakal in South India (Figure 4.3). Note the servants bearing drinks.

In another episode from the *Great Story*, we see a man coerced into drinking in order to relax about sensual matters.[102] This is frequently an important issue in early Indian narratives, connected with marriage and progeny. Earlier, we saw the Buddha-to-be's father stage a gathering to distract the young man from the idea of renouncing his princely career. (Note that in texts of this genre women never need to be nudged onto the path of sensuality by drink—frequently they are given drink so that they will abandon their coyness, but they never seem to be fundamentally averse to erotic pleasures in a socially problematic way.) The protagonist in this instance, Sānudāsa, was ruined by a good upbringing. As an only child conceived with difficulty, he was the focus of a lot of attention. First, his father gave him such thorough instruction that he knew nothing of the play of childhood. Then his teachers made him so disciplined (*vinīta*) that he was even shy around his own wife.[103] Now the king, Sānudāsa's parents, his friends, and his wife are all worried about this excessively sensible young man. So they devise a staggeringly elaborate plan to break his reserve.

First they must get him drunk. A friend of his invites Sānudāsa and his wife to join a group of friends and their wives by a lotus pool in a park (*udyānanalinīkūle*), where they have been playing, eating, and drinking. To convince Sānudāsa to come, the friend makes a short speech on the sinfulness of rejecting the karmic rewards of happiness and pleasure. Apparently the only way to get through to earnest, bookish Sānudāsa is by referring to religious notions of dharma, karma, and merit. Sānudāsa is no idiot, however, and he responds with a sharp speech on the dangers of kindling the fire of passion any more than necessary; he argues that sensuous pleasures are not the true rewards of religious merit and that, above all, it is disgraceful for a married woman to be seen eating, drinking, and possibly drunk in public. Therefore, *he* will reluctantly consent to go to the park and accept his sensuous rewards (though he will just watch), but *his wife* cannot possibly accompany him. Like some other episodes that I'll examine later, this passage gives us a sense of how some educated people enjoyed hearing humorous critiques of moral discourses and training.

Sānudāsa arrives at the park, having agreed to come on condition that he does not have to drink.[104] His friends are beautifully adorned. Sānudāsa's seat is fashioned from flowers, and he observes friends sharing wine with each other:

> And seated there I saw friends who had made their lovers drink and who were drinking wine (*madhu*) offered in the palms of the hands of their delighted lovers.[105]

Suddenly a man emerges from the lotus pond, carrying a cup made from lotus leaves, and joyfully exclaims, "Hey, I've got some blue-lotus nectar (*puṣkaramadhu*)," the ever-ambiguous word "*madhu*" here meaning "nectar/

honey" but also "wine."[106] The friends tell the man who has found the lotus nectar to be quiet about his discovery, as it is exceptionally rare, precious, and desirable. They mention "in passing" that since this incredibly tasty drink is not an intoxicating drink (*na ca madyam*), the sober Sānudāsa may drink it—and he does, experiencing the drink in his amusingly scholarly, analytic manner. As the editor Lacôte wrote, "Sānudāsa knows his Nyāya [logical philosophy] manual by heart!":[107]

> Because of its rarity and my friends' entreaties, when I heard it was not an intoxicating drink I drank that nectar. And I thought to myself, "Which of the six [flavors] could this be? There is no discernable similarity with sweet and the other flavors, nor can I undertake [to define it][108] by combining the six flavors, sweet and the rest—even for the omniscient it would be difficult to know the flavors here individually. So this should be understood to be a seventh delicious flavor, on tasting which even the nectar of immortality would seem flavorless." Then its flavor and smell, as well as my thirst, made me shameless, and quietly I said to Dhruvaka [his friend], "I am tortured by thirst." And I drank what he gave me. My normal mental state departed, and I wandered confusedly in the city park that was spinning rapidly like a wheel . . .[109]

Wandering drunk, Sānudāsa hears a woman and approaches her. He goes with her to her house. By an amazing coincidence she too has some blue-lotus nectar. He enters her bedroom, which smells of the rare blue-lotus nectar, and there offers his body to the woman, virtuously fulfilling her frustrated desires. Interested readers should read the rest of this story to see what happens next in the staged, sensuous education of Sānudāsa.[110]

In this tale we have yet another description of the subjective qualities of drink. Of course, if you had never drunk alcohol before, it would be hard to recognize its taste or effects, which is exactly what happens to Sānudāsa when he is duped into drinking "blue-lotus *madhu*." The taste is hard to define in terms of the classical list of tastes he has studied, nor does it make sense in terms of taste combinations, so this must be a new seventh taste, both uniquely delicious and baffling to his scholarly mind.

Also, although Sānudāsa has only just started to drink when he describes the nectar, this could be a rare example of drunk Indian scholasticism. "Wine talk" in these narratives is aligned with the classical theory of the senses and with the qualities of taste/flavor (*rasa*). But is that all there is to early Indian wine talk? What of a concept of taste that includes smell, an idea familiar today? Are these Sanskrit texts on wine talk imposing an intellectualized model on a more complex practice? One later description of wine from a text composed in Kashmir refers to more modalities than the scholastic flavors alone. In the introduction to the twelfth-century chronicle of Kashmir, the *River of Kings* (*Rājataraṅgiṇī*), one can find this description of Kashmir: "Learning, lofty houses, saffron, icy water, and grapes (*drākṣā*): things that even in heaven are difficult to find, are common there," grapes being a well-established, esteemed product of the region.[111] Although alcohol and drinking are generally depicted in a negative light in the *River of Kings*, at one point there is a striking description of good grape wine and the qualities that make it pleasant: flower-scented (*puṣpagandhi*), charming (*hāri*), light (*laghu*), and cool (*śītalam*) grape wine (*mārdvīkaṃ*), which is accompanied by fried meat (*bhṛṣṭamāṃsāni*).[112] The flower fragrance could be innate, or, more likely, this refers to the addition of flowers. Coolness is generally valued in Indian culture, for example the cooling qualities of sandalwood. Another text also suggests that the olfactory pleasures of food and drink were valued alongside their flavors. In the Jain *Epitome of Queen Līlāvatī* (from the thirteenth century) there is a discussion of the bad mental states and sins that can arise from an attachment to the sense of smell. Someone who is attached to fragrances (*nānāparimalāsakta*) will seek out betel scented with cardamoms, cloves, and other spices; milk perfumed with cardamoms, flowers, and camphor; wine; fragrant oranges (*nāgaraṅga*); mangoes; citrons; and other delicacies.[113] This list of edibles is followed by perfumes that are not eaten, such as garlands. The emphasis on the scented aspect of these edible items (recall that betel was often classed with perfumes) suggests that people may sometimes have separated the smells of edibles from the flavors in their analyses. Consider the experience of chewing a scented *pān* quid filled with rose jam (*gulkand*)—the sweet taste, the tactile cooling menthol, and the perfumed syrups stand out easily as separate sense modalities. Perhaps in a culture where the most delicious and valued foods were strikingly spiced and scented, it was easier to reify a scholastic distinction of taste versus smell in talking about food and wine. And perhaps descriptions of flavor qualities alone were not perceived as restrictive because there were also plenty of opportunities to speak of the fragrance of jasmine-scattered wine.

Returning to the *Great Story* by Budhasvamin: the erudite and now intoxicated Sānudāsa notices how the world seems to spin, and he wanders randomly, thirsting for more, becoming aroused and uninhibited, and finally liberated by alcohol from his previously unshakeable, overly analytic self-control. As with the other episode, Sānudāsa was tricked into drinking and his parents are complicit in the scheme,[114] so the man, though drunk, did not embark on the drinking out of his own desire, nor did he disobey his parents in taking to drink. Also, like the other episode, drinking encourages him to have sex, which is a good development.

What stands out the most in these scenes is the humor and camaraderie among a small group of friends,[115] along with the spectacular flavors of intoxicating drink, which in both cases appears to be grape wine.[116] Also, this topsy turvy narrative inverts the usual order of men having women drink to remove sexual inhibitions, and in doing so, and in reporting the thoughts of the men involved we perhaps get an insight into the *imagined* mental states of the people seduced in such scenarios—namely they are coy, inhibited (by internalized social morality), yet desirous, and they enjoy the experience when unleashed by drink. Is this how the women in such scenarios were imagined (by men?) to experience them too? Although the date of this text is uncertain, its representations of drinking and drinks have many echoes of the man-about-town in the *Kāmasūtra*, some of the images at Ajanta, and the increasingly complicated, *dharmaśāstric* legal opinions concerning wine and other drinks.[117] It is in this same approximate period, when we find increasingly complex literary and visual depictions of drinking, that Tantric rituals involving alcohol developed. Which is to say: such rituals took shape in a cultural and legal world in which educated people, abstinent or not, were by no means focused solely on brahminical abstinence, the dangers of royal vices, or the rogues at the *surā* shack, and where drink and drunkenness were complex affairs.

Treatises on Drinking for Pleasure?

Were there any texts devoted entirely to drinking, as there were to the art of perfumery—a drinking-*śāstra*? (Texts on fermented medicinal preparations are a separate matter.) The texts in Sanskrit and other Indian languages are so numerous that such questions are hard to answer, especially if we include unpublished manuscripts, not to mention the many texts we've lost. I am, however, aware of three texts dedicated exclusively to drink.

For one of these, we possess only a single, intriguing quotation. This occurs in a commentary on another text, in Mallinātha's late-fourteenth-century commentary on the *Meghadūta* of Kālidāsa. In the root text, in a description of the city of the *yakṣas*, these beings, accompanied by women, drink wine (*madhu*) produced by a magical wishing tree (*kalpavṛkṣa*), which is said to "result in sexual pleasure" (*ratiphala*).[118] The commentator Vallabhadeva reads the word in just that manner—the wine has the result of pleasure—and Mallinātha does likewise in his first comment on the word.[119] But then Mallinātha quotes what seems to be a recipe, composed in Sanskrit, for a "tasty, cool, wine (*madhu*) that incites Love, called '*ratiphala*', [that which has the result/fruit of sexual pleasure]." He indicates that this is a quotation from a text entitled the *Ocean of Liquor* (*iti Madirārṇave*).[120] I haven't been able to translate this challenging line satisfactorily, but it seems to involve a decoction containing mahua flowers along with a number of other ingredients that perhaps include palm toddy, jaggery, and various plants.[121] What was the *Ocean of Liquor*? Perhaps a medical text dealing with intoxicating drinks, though this recipe suggests that the text may have dealt with drinks for pleasure, or even with aphrodisiacs. The fragment was known to an erudite scholar in the fourteenth century and was composed in a complex meter. Such a form of composition is an especially tricky task when dealing with a recipe and may explain the obscure or ambiguous terms used for the ingredients. The "*Ocean*" in the title perhaps suggests that it was meant to be a comprehensive collection of recipes, or of all lore relating to drinking. The title probably also alludes to the mythical ocean of *surā*, which I'll discuss later. For now, the *Ocean of Liquor* must remain an intriguing mystery.

We also possess two texts that deal with the connections between drinking and the erotic life: *The Aphorisms on Taking Liquor* (*Kādambarasvīkaraṇasūtram*), attributed to the royal sage Purūravas (a king who was the lover of the *apsara* Urvaśī), which has a commentary, as well as *The Verse-Treatise on Taking Liquor* (*Kādambarasvīkaraṇakārikā*), attributed to the royal sage Bharata, and fortunately Eva-Marie Schinzel has translated and studied both texts.[122] We have no indication of when either text was composed, nor by whom, nor where. Manuscripts of these texts, kept at Kolkata, date from 1809 CE.[123] The text in verse is a detailed account of a session of love-making from start to finish and probably expands on the contents of the *sūtra* text.[124] It begins with drinking but quickly moves on to other matters, and is the nearest thing I've ever encountered in Sanskrit to literary pornography. The text begins:

> The nectar-like juice produced from grapes is called *kādambara* and arouses the penis . . .[125]

To start with drink and drinking is a distinctively novel structure for a text on erotics in Sanskrit. Note that the drink in question is grape wine.

The role of drink in the erotic life is more central in *The Aphorisms on Taking Liquor*. Composed in concise *sūtra* format, this text is very scholarly in tone. The commentary is also highly scholastic. In this text we see a focus on the utility, even the necessity, of drinking liquor for sex, including instructions on precisely when and how the presumed male reader should drink and have women drink for sexual purposes. I've translated the first four *sūtras* to give some sense of this text:

> [One should take intoxicating drink] on account of the necessity of consuming intoxicating drink in the sacrifice to Kāma [the god of love].

> This is because [drinking intoxicating drink] becomes the cause of indescribable joy in the arising of the joy of sex.

> Taking Varuṇa's daughter [Vāruṇī = Surā, i.e., liquor] is the supreme cause in the arising of an erection.
>
> When the thing-that-is-to-be-used that has the nature of the principal agent [i.e., an erection] is absent, there is no possibility of accomplishing the science of sexual pleasure.[126]

The text then explains the other benefits of drinking for sex, for example the delay of ejaculation and rendering intercourse painless for the woman.[127] Then we learn that drinking for sex is prescribed for youths and young men, but not for boys or old men. After that the *sūtras* treat the matter of who should drink. Kṣatriyas can drink any time, Brahmins only when authorized by the Vedas in certain sacrifices. Women can drink only in the company of lovers, and drink is only to be used in the "sacrifices of the god of love."

What is going on with this unusual text? I believe this erudite treatise is a complex, theoretical expansion of the instructions we saw in the *Kāmasūtra* on how a man should drink and have women drink as a prelude to good love-making.[128] As such, this text is far from anomalous. It is effectively a lengthy footnote to an established set of ideas, clarifying exactly how liquor is beneficial to the enjoyment of *kāma*. As we've seen in this chapter, literary references to drinking and love-making were common and respected in India. Yet, as we'll see later in the book, there are many genres of texts that condemn drinking as a vice or as an act forbidden for certain people. Arguably the co-existence of the literary celebration of drinking and the exhortation to drink prior to sex in the *Kāmasūtra* along with moral condemnations of drink as a vice or a caste-related sin created an intellectual division that would have been familiar to many: "My own *dharma* includes pleasure and sex, and we are encouraged to drink prior to sex in some authoritative texts (and people of my *varṇa* are permitted to do so)—yet drinking is a vice in other texts, and condemned in various ways in texts on dharma. How can I reconcile these materials?" I believe that these two texts bridge that very gap. That may be the internal logic behind the contents of these texts, but I have absolutely no idea who composed them, in what context, and who might have read them (presumably not a Brahmanical context?)

Conclusions

Sanskrit texts of a literary register describe a distinctive type of drinking. It shares quite a lot with the drinking prescribed in the *Kāmasūtra*, an authoritative guide to refined, sensuous pleasures. Yet drinking in the poems is often hyperbolic: beautiful nymphs, ruby vessels, astoundingly delicious drinks. In some cases the literary drinking scene helps the reader appreciate the hero at the center of the party: the Buddha-to-be is so alarmed by the fact of death that he rebuffs even those alluring drunken women, and Arjuna's resolve in his ascetic practices is such that he can't even be seduced by the *apsaras*es we saw at an erotic drunken party. King Someśvara III not only composed an encyclopedia of royal life and conduct, but he also knew how to direct a drinking excursion in every minute detail. His private amusements are just like an episode in a court epic poem.

Not all kings and protagonists are depicted as enjoying drinking. In some texts such depictions of kingly drinking are rare. In the *Harṣacarita* of Bāṇa, the king is not for the most part depicted as a drinker, and there is an allusion to King Harṣa abstaining from alcohol, in the form of punning descriptions of him.[129] One sees the same with the good kings in the *River of Kings* (*Rājataraṅgiṇī*) who rarely drink, and where the association of kings and drink is seen as a bad thing.[130] As noted in Cup 2, the consumption and sharing of betel is a far more prominent regal pursuit in that text.

Elaborate depictions of luxurious drinking events were an esteemed and enduring aesthetic phenomenon in medieval India. Among the people who studied and appreciated these texts, even those who would never touch a drop could gain pleasure from drink in the poetic mode, in scenes rich with the erotic, romantic mood (*rasa*). Indeed, quite a few people probably *only* ever experienced alcoholic intoxication through such descriptions, and the existence of this quite proper, literary spectatorship of drunkards, perhaps sometimes with imaginary, empathic intoxication, would be interesting to investigate further, using commentaries and texts that deal with the literary theory of *mada*, one of the transitory emotions, *vyabhicāribhāva*s (though I cannot consider these here for reasons of space). But we should not be at all surprised that many writers who presumably would have shunned drink in practice were fluent in the aesthetic qualities of drinking and intoxication. Liquor and drunkenness were never excluded from the world of words.

Consider the Jain Somadeva from the tenth century CE, who was fully aware of the benefits typically attributed to drink and composed a useful summary of the common praises of alcohol in his long prose-and-verse narrative, the *Yaśastilaka*, composed in 959 CE.[131] This is a vast and complex work, containing many subnarratives and much moral and philosophical material. At one point the protagonist, King Yaśodhara, has become disgusted by worldly life and defends the practices and attitudes associated with Jainism. Responding to him, his mother, a Hindu, defends her own religious and worldly practices. Commending the ways of drinking embraced by the masses, his mother describes such practices as follows:

> Mirrors for the amorous gestures of beautiful women, invigorators of Desire (*kandarpa*),

> Removers of the exhaustion of exercise, what wise man would try to give up intoxicating drinks (*madhūni*)?
> Women deprived of intoxicating drink are as good as dead in the opinion of experts in the erotic sciences . . .[132]

Yaśodhara's mother highlights drink's ability to intensify and inflame erotic desire, as well as assuage the pain and tiredness of exertion. Of course the readers of this verse, immersed in a Jain critique of such practices, would have seen many dangers in these "virtues." Nonetheless, in the realm of sensory pleasure and erotics it was hard to deny the role of drink, stated so thoroughly in *The Aphorisms on Taking Liquor*.

What social worlds might particular drinks, drinking, and intoxication construct, reify, differentiate, or parody in these literary texts?[133] I don't mean anything abstruse by this question; rather I'm referring to something we do frequently with drinks in our own era. Consider the case of Champagne. As Murdock Pemberton wrote in 1934, Champagne "is considered a gay drink, for celebrations, anniversaries, weddings, state affairs . . . [while] port and sweet wines are for slow drinking over philosophical talk."[134] Nor is Champagne just a sign of "celebration"; often Champagne-drinking itself partly constitutes an event. And Champagne-drinking works like this both in literature, film, and in practice.

Earlier, we saw the public drinking of "common" people. The *surā*-drinker at a festival enjoyed a period of intoxicated leisure—a period not of rest but of energetic feasting and heightened, mixed sociability, maybe with intoxicated sexual overtones. In the simple *surā* shop, largely free of the upper classes, drinking provided a temporary contrast with the place of labor, the home, and the extended family. No doubt the travelers' *surā* shops and inns were different again—rest stops for nourishment and, in the case of the larger urban inns, cosmopolitan places of intrigue. In descriptions of such drinking we read of a lot of men—the hunter who discovered beer, the husbands of the brewing wives, the rogues in the Buddhist tales. Though women also drink, and if the image at Ajanta is indeed of a *surā* shop they are drinking there too. In many of our sources, this sort of drinking is looked down upon. It's not that these people should be prohibited from drinking but that we, the assumed readers, are not like them. Just as celibacy means something only in a world where people have sex, so those who flaunted their pious abstinence needed to have drinkers in the same society (and in their narratives) to act as boozy, disreputable foils to their own moral self-control.

The drinking in this chapter is quite different. It constructs an idealized world for nurturing romance and humor. Even within the texts, the events are sometimes described as meticulously contrived. The reality of such events—if they ever did happen—may have been just as artificial as the texts. And the characters experiencing these gatherings are drunk, which creates a third layer of illusion. These are hyper-stylized, poetic descriptions of artifice-laden feasts attended by people whose perceptions have been altered by a drug. So disjointed are the scenes from regular life that they constitute an unthreatening arena for orgiastic behavior.

The erotic is central to this form of drinking, as the romantic, erotic literary mood, *śṛṅgārarasa*, is central to many of the poetic scenes (with some humor at times). The couple drinking in the house are in private, if we exclude the servants, who are literally in the background in a visual depiction. The house or park used for drinking is thoroughly prepared for the wine- and perfume-induced love-making. The larger, communal events are often held outside, like the festival, yet access to these events is restricted to the right sort of people, and the erotic aspect is again center stage. Thus privacy of sorts is central to this drinking. Dietler writes of what he calls diacritical feasts, which involve "the use of differentiated cuisine and styles of consumption as a diacritical symbolic device to naturalize and reify concepts of ranked differences in the status of social orders or classes."[135] These high-class drinking parties have such distinguishing features, and this may relate to the courtly or wealthy contexts in which some texts were produced.

Ideally, intoxication was an interactive state. If, as seen in both this and the previous chapter, drinking was considered a social activity, then the complex effects of drink and intoxication were mutually experienced: a drunk person, acting, thinking, and desiring in a transformed way, is usually perceived and described by another drunk person, whose own perceptions, intentions, and actions have *also* been changed by the drink. A drunken observer might describe a friend who is drunkenly flailing to shoo away a "bee" (which is really a drop of black *surā*) as "dancing," yet witnessing this "dance" might provoke not laughter or joy for the drunken observer, but tears. In this way, the nature of action fundamentally changes when two or more people drink together: the deeds people do change; the way a drunk participant in group-intoxication gives a narrative account of other drunkards' deeds is confused ("Is my drunk friend grasping? flailing? dancing? I can't tell—I'm wasted."), and the drunk observer's *reactions* to these actions-as-drunkenly-construed is topsy-turvy ("He is dancing! But that makes me want to fight him!").[136] They are in a new world. Perhaps some Buddhists might even have argued that this intoxicated mutual delusion is similar to what most of us experience, even when totally sober, in our unenlightened, emotionally chaotic lives of ignorantly craving and shunning entities whose true nature we utterly misunderstand. But the new world that comes into being for mutual drunkards is not always a bad thing in terms of theology—later we shall see one drunken, orgiastic Tantric party in which the drink-transformed participation in and contemplation of drink-transformed group behavior provides an uninhibited awareness of a sequence of phases in the divine cosmic process. Finally, adding another layer of confusion, it's possible that the readers of these poems about drunken interactions were not always sober.

Although men and women both need to be present at these sessions of erotic drinking, in many cases the drinkers and drunkards are women. (The *Bṛhatkathāślokasaṃgraha* is, as ever, an exception.) In the *Mānasollāsa*, the drunk women are not just participating in a staged drinking event—they *are* the performance, both for the king and for us, the readers. They have been selected and costumed to play the role of alluring drunk women, emulating scenes of Sanskrit poetry, just like the women in the park with the Buddha-to-be—a young man who wanted badly to see what such parks were like, since he had only heard about them in poetic lyrics.

It is worth noting here, by way of comparison, that the chaotic drinking sessions represented in these Indian texts differ somewhat from Bakhtin's carnival, "a pageant . . . without a division into performers and spectators . . ." where "everyone is an active participant . . ."[137] Rather, in our texts the drunk chaos, though it does obey its own carnivalistic laws with plenty of confusions and inversions, takes place for the contemplation of the spectator. Sometimes we do hear of a generally socially confused "carnival" *without* a protagonist-observer, but typically these are descriptions of festivals to be shunned by the controlled person (as we will see later in the discussion of Jain morality); they are carnivals *marked by the absence*, the non-participation, of certain individuals or communities. Or in the case of the Andhakas and Vṛṣṇis (see Chapter 6), a mutual drinking session where all participate is marked by mutual annihilation—here a carnival is like total social antimatter (and yet it is all still observed by Kṛṣṇa). Thus in most cases, the narrative of the Indian carnival is arguably related to define and preserve the hierarchies that ostensibly matter to those using our texts—and there is only a drunken suspension of hierarchies among the drunk people, who are, in any case, often presented as prone to unleashed conduct at other times too. Perhaps only in certain Tantric contexts (see Chapter 8) do we see an ideal of fully participatory suspension of hierarchies in an intoxicated setting.[138] But in general the drunk "carnival" as we read of it in Indian texts heightens distinctions: the voyeur, the seducer, the disaster-prone sinner, the prominently absent Brahmin or ascetic. Of course, this is not to say there were not actual festivals and even lost textual traditions that may have corresponded more to Bakhtin's model—but our surviving evidence, even when it celebrates drinking, maintains the differences of social positions: this party is primarily fun because all those messy drunken queens are all focused on *me*.

Can we relate these literary materials to changes in material culture? Although luxurious drinks and scenes of people drinking in semi-private spaces are present in early sources, such as the epics, it is only in the first few centuries CE, the Gupta period, that a distinctive set of drinking practices, along with certain substances and objects, becomes standard, even predictable, in literature and art. Such drinking, regulated by texts such as the *Kāmasūtra*, takes place in delightful surroundings with beautiful vessels (e.g., the *caṣaka* cup), grape wines, betel, and exotic perfumes. This consumption complex is what we see depicted at Ajanta and in many texts from this period onward: the pursuit of intoxicated pleasure surrounded by materials from Persia, Southeast Asia, and the Himalayas. The combination of imported wine, local sugarcane drinks, and perfumed betel was distinctively South Asian. Certain wealthier drinkers now lived in a world where someone emulating the life of a man-about-town had authoritative instructions on his lifestyle in carefully argued Sanskrit texts (*Kāmasūtra*, etc.), and where elaborate, respected models of (and for) erotic private drinking, visual and literary, were abundant and even formed part of a literary education.

Of course, even for those religiously permitted to drink according to highly orthodox texts, drink could still go wrong in various ways, and it is to the medical regulation of proper drinking that we now turn.

CUP 5
Drink, Health, and Disease in Āyurvedic Texts

Nowadays, if we think of alcohol in the context of medical practice, concepts such as alcoholism and addiction come to mind, or perhaps antiseptics. For some, drinking is a fundamentally pathological phenomenon and, in an ideal world, no one would drink.[1] This attitude co-exists with popular-science notions of connections between drink and good health, which are nevertheless presented as anomalous or pleasantly surprising.

In early India, scholars and practitioners of medicine took a different approach. We have already seen medical texts listing a variety of alcoholic drinks, along with recipes for fermented pharmacological preparations such as *āsavas* and *ariṣṭas*. Many early Indian medical texts also contain chapters about consuming intoxicating drinks, explaining, among other things, how to drink in a way that is both pleasurable and harmless. These are, in fact, some of our most detailed representations of idealized luxurious drinking from an early period. The texts also deal with the health problems of incorrect or excessive drinking, but that is not their sole focus. Nonetheless, while the medical texts sometimes present drinking in a positive light, they do *not* prescribe it as a universal practice. The authors explain it as a practice that can be injurious if badly regulated. The medical literature also explains how intoxicating drinks work on the mind and body, and we learn that alcohol was used as an anesthetic for surgical procedures.

In this chapter I'll present some highlights, not a comprehensive survey. I want the chapter to be accessible to non-specialists, so scholars and practitioners of Āyurveda must forgive me for general statements and simplifications.

A Perfect Drinking Session, According to Vāgbhaṭa's *Heart of Medicine*

To upset the balance of our modern-day prejudices, let's start with a description of the pleasures of proper drinking as given in an āyurvedic text.

The *Heart of Medicine* (*Aṣṭāṅgahṛdaya*) by Vāgbhaṭa probably dates from around 600 CE.[2] Vāgbhaṭa organizes his discussion of liquor into two chapters: symptoms/diagnosis (*nidāna*) of drink-related conditions, including

An Unholy Brew. James McHugh, Oxford University Press. © Oxford University Press 2021.
DOI: 10.1093/oso/9780199375936.003.0007

the qualities of drink and stages of intoxication, followed by therapy (*cikitsā*).[3] In the latter chapter, the discussion of treatment leads to a general praise of drink and a description of the ideal regime for drinking. Just after the general praise, Vāgbhaṭa explains:

> When extracting a deep foreign body ("thorn"), or in treatments with knives, caustics, and fire, a man who has drunk intoxicating drink (*-madya*) endures the doctor's torments with ease.[4]

Liquor can thus alleviate bodily pain, and the next verse praises intoxicating drinks for removing discomfort and increasing health (when used correctly, in moderation):

> It excites the digestion, is an appetitive, removes sadness and exhaustion—nothing is better than this, which imparts health, strength, and nourishment.[5]

Vāgbhaṭa concludes:

> Therefore a self-possessed man, having care for his life, should always drink [intoxicating drink], which is beneficial for those who use it directly and indirectly,[6] and is a supreme instrument of righteousness (*dharma-*).[7]

This is a strong statement and would have been striking to some readers in the past, especially those immersed in the Brahminical culture of abstinence. Vāgbhaṭa inverts the moral qualities associated with drinking in many of our Sanskrit sources, which suggest that drink upsets a person's sense of reality and judgment of right and wrong. We've seen that a touch of intoxicated chaos leads to excitement, humor, and romance; even writers who teach abstinence admit as much. But to describe liquor as a life-prolonging source o*f dharma* (righteousness, law, duty) for a self-possessed man, and as generally beneficial, is remarkable. For Vāgbhaṭa alcohol is clearly a wonderful substance, when used by a wise, controlled person.

His description of how one should drink (at least how a wealthy man should drink) is composed in poetic language and is worth translating in full. I've attempted to retain his style, with its cascades of description:[8]

> [*the setting*:]
> When he has bathed [and] paid homage to the gods, Brahmins, and his ancestors/elders (*guru*), and he has properly done his business and that of all his attendants, he should resort to the group-drinking place (*āpānabhūmi*), which is sprinkled with perfumed water and close to the food hall (*āhāramaṇḍapa*).

He should drink intoxicating drink (*madya*) on a finely bedecked, charming couch, joined by friends, servants, and lovely women, listening to his own fame being elevated out of this world by groups of story-tellers and bards,

[*the servers*:]
And [listening to] the flirtatiously beautiful song, accompanied by dance, of flirtatious women, with the soft sounds of musical instruments, and the little shaking bells of girdles, echoed by pet birds. [He takes liquor that] is simultaneously being circulated here and there by means of various vessels [?][9] made of gems and gold, moist with water, and that are wrapped in silk cloths that have various designs, [circulated] by beloved, delicate women who would disturb the minds of sages, with trembling eyes like the quavering eyes of deer, whose walk is unsteady—a magic spell to allure young men's minds—as they are weary on account of the weight of their breasts and buttocks, and as they are filled with fear of their master; who are drunk on youth and *āsava*, their minds occupied with flirty charm.

[*the drink*:]
[The drink is] being cooled by very cool breezes from palm fans and lotus leaves.[10] Just seeing [the drink] makes one submissive to the Mind-Born one [Kāma, the god of love]; how much more so tasting it! [And the drink] is perfumed with mango juice, camphor, and musk, garnished with radiant jasmine, is contained in little cups (*śukti*) of rock crystal, has ripples, and [ironically] has a lovely body, just like the Bodiless one [Kāma, the god of love, who also incites lust].

[*preparations for drinking*:]
And prior [to drinking] he eats *tālīsādya* powder, or an agreeable *elādika* powder, or an age-preservative, and then he has [drink] mixed with water offered to those beings who want it,[11] on a piece of ground that is well-anointed.

[*the manner of drinking*:]
[And then he drinks], steadily, prudently, never drinking too little or too much, doing absolutely everything with proper manners—that drink which is like the face of his beloved, in that its beauty is increased by the reflections of eyes that surpass [in beauty] bloomed dark-blue water-lilies, and which has captivated a crowd of bees [also: "wine drinkers"] by its fragrance.

[*food after drinking*:]
Having drunk a couple of cups (*caṣaka*) in this manner, then, having paid his regards to all his retinue, he goes to the dining place, where he should eat in

the presence of an excellent doctor, and here he should drink one or two more [cups], accompanied by meat, *āpūpa* cakes, ghee, fresh ginger, etc., and greens, together with black salt (*sauvarcala*), and at night he should drink only a little, to please his woman.

[*private drinking*:]
If a clever man in private, with his beloved on his lap, her body thrilling from his arms squeezing her, sweating, with bobbing breasts, does not have her drink a draught (*vāraṃ*) of sugarcane liquor (*śīdhu*), then why does he put up with the mostly troublesome business of a running a household?

That shared cup of liquor (*ṣaraka*), made most fragrant by contact with the mouth of his beautiful woman, is like a liquefied ruby that has the form of an *āsava*![12] Through the exhaustion of sex, intoxication arises for the one who drinks even a small quantity, so afterward, avoiding a decrease in vital energy [*ojas*], he should go to bed.

[*drinking, morality, and wealth*:]
Drinking liquor in this way, correctly, he is not deprived of the set of three [righteousness, wealth, and pleasure] and attains the ultimate joy in the insubstantial realm of eternal rebirth. It is an enjoyment of greatness that even the gods desire. If he does otherwise, his wealth is kindling for regret in times of misfortune; he is reviled by people who say "that prosperous man is devoid of enjoyment," and he is established as extremely miserly, someone whose business is hoarding. Therefore, always drinking drink in a regulated manner is beneficial for one who has overcome the willfulness of his pleasure-greedy senses.

This is the method for the wealthy. For those who do not yet have wealth, it is best to drink liquor moderately, as is suitable.[13]

Writers couldn't help but slide into the poetic mode when discussing the drinking of the wealthy. As with the party in the *Delight of the Mind*, this passage starts with the location. Then Vāgbhaṭa turns to the instruments by which the drink is served (women, vessels), before we learn of the drink itself (the object), and he finishes with the actions of the drinker, the subject. The drinker makes love, and Vāgbhaṭa explains the value of proper drinking in terms of the "set of three" areas of activity pertinent to the good life (*dharma*, *artha*, *kāma*). Vāgbhaṭa preempts suggestions that it might be better to abstain by explaining that if a wealthy man avoids the pleasure of drinking, he will regret it in times of hardship. Such a man will earn the criticism of others for being miserly and will suffer as a pleasure-shunning, reviled social object.

Vāgbhaṭa states explicitly that this is the mode of drinking for the wealthy (*vasumatām*). It's not just that taste reflects class but that this style of drinking costs a lot. Moreover, his claims apply only to proper drinking. Bad drinking is contrary in its effects, not just on health but on many other aspects of a person's life, as Vāgbhaṭa explains in a separate, cautionary section: while food taken improperly leads (only) to illness and death, drink used improperly destroys the "set of three," along with intelligence, courage/composure, and the sense of shame.[14]

Location matters too. When the man embarks on drinking, he moves to what is called a drinking area/ground, presumably in his own house. Like the bedroom in the *Kāmasūtra*, it is perfumed and adorned, only here there are performers singing the man's praises. Beautiful women sing and dance, and presumably another set of beautiful women, nervous in the man's presence, bring adorned vessels of drink. The drink is cooled by fans and served in small precious bowls. Before he drinks, the man doses himself with medicine—recall that the women in the *Delight of the Mind* also took ghee before drinking—and offers a mixture of drink and water to various supernatural beings by pouring it on the ground (maybe the ring-finger liquor-flick in the *Delight of the Mind* was a similar ritual?). The man has yet to take a sip of liquor.

His style of drinking is perfectly balanced in its quantity and decorum. Having consumed two cups, or *caṣakas*, he leaves his retinue at the drinking place and changes location again, going to the dining area, where he eats and drinks more, monitored by his physician. The food is salty and spicy, like typical drinking snacks, though note that this meal is eaten separately from the main episode of drinking, in both time and space, so that there is still somewhat of a separation between drinking liquor and eating a full meal. Then, in what may be a separate scenario, we find the man in private with his beloved on his lap, giving her a drink, just as in the *Kāmasūtra*. The actual lovemaking is not described beyond a reference to the ubiquitous drinking from the lover's mouth (or shared cup) and the fact that he should sleep after drink and sex to avoid decreasing his vital energy, *ojas*, a subtle substance that, elsewhere, is described as crucial to liquor's effects on the mind and body.

The exhortation to indulge in this sort of drinking to avoid social criticism recalls the passage we examined in which a man persuades his friend to drink on *dharmic* grounds. Yet whereas that scene was satirical, this advice is earnest, more like *The Aphorisms on Taking Liquor* (*Kādambarasvīkaraṇasūtra*), the author of which was similarly serious about drink as vital for sexual pleasure.

The *Heart of Medicine* also contains a charming description of the ideal seasonal regimen, which includes not just drink but foods, massages, surroundings, even women.[15] In the cool season of the year (*śiśira*), one should drink jaggery liquor (*gauḍa*), clear *surā* (*acchasurā*), and "plain" *surā*.[16] A second passage describes an ideal wintry scene:

> Together with friends, one should drink cheering, pleasant, healthy *āsavas*, *ariṣṭas*, sugarcane wine (*sīdhu*), grape wine (*mārdvīka*), [and] honey wine (*mādhava*) mixed with mango juice, tasting them as served by one's beloved, fragrant from contact with one's beloved's mouth, marked with the lotus eyes of the beloved; [and one should also drink] ginger water, heartwood water,[17] honey water, and nutgrass water.[18]

Evidently a wide range of drinks is suitable to winter drinking: several *surās*, which were no doubt grain-based, as well as drinks based on sugars and fruits.

For the hot season (*grīṣma*), Vāgbhaṭa states that "one should not drink intoxicating liquor (*madya*), or one should drink [only] a small amount."[19] In a text on literature called the *Kāvyamīmāṃsā*, the poet and critic Rājaśekhara (c. 900 CE) quotes a charming verse describing the cooling objects that people seek out in the hot season:

> A pleasant palace, the upper terrace flooded with moonlight,
> Watered-down liquor (*vāruṇī vārimiśrā*) that has been tasted by your lover,
> Garlands of trumpet flowers and *mallikā* jasmine on your neck,
> Oh, summer becomes winter in an instant![20]

So maybe diluted drink was sometimes acceptable in the hot season?

Returning to the *Heart of Medicine*: Vāgbhaṭa writes that in the rainy season one should take "aged (*cirantana*) wine (*madhu*) and *ariṣṭa*," and the commentator Aruṇadatta explains that this is because of the dangers of a sluggish digestion (*agnimāndyabhayāt*) in that season; it seems that aged drinks are easier to digest.[21]

Vāgbhaṭa's description is yet another authoritative Sanskrit model for correct drinking from the first millennium CE. This drinking is pleasurable, moral, measured, and good for one's health and social reputation. The drinker is a man, though he encourages women to drink so that they can join him in his pleasure. A man needs wealth to drink to this level of perfection, and a doctor has to be on hand, presumably one trained in these very texts.

Drinking, Intoxication, Disease, and Health According to *Caraka's Compendium*

The previous section may demonstrate what perfect drinking looks like, but many questions still arise. First, how does drink work, and exactly what does it do to a person? What are the stages of drunkenness? What should people with different physical constitutions drink? What medical conditions can drinking cause, and how does one treat them? In this section I explore these questions, as discussed in *Caraka's Compendium*.

The principal medical problem caused by drinking according to this text, *madātyaya*, means something along the lines of "intoxication-harm," "intoxication-danger," or even "intoxication-perishing" (also possibly, but less likely, is "excess intoxication"), though the first part of the compound word (*mada-*) has none of the "toxic" history of the English word "intoxication."[22] The term is sometimes translated as "alcoholism," but I have avoided this term; not only is it an anachronism, locating a recent Western medical concept in ancient Indian disease theory, but it might hinder our ability to appreciate the distinctive features of the condition described in these texts—an approach to medical drink-related problems that is different from ours today.

Caraka's Compendium, the *Carakasaṃhitā*, had a complex development. It probably dates from somewhere between the second/third century BCE and the fourth/fifth century CE. When I use such phrases as "the *Caraka* states . . ." it is only a convenient turn of phrase, simplifying a complicated textual situation. For our purposes, what matters is that the passages below were probably available in something like this form by the mid-first millennium CE, meaning that they were available at the time of the composition of many of the texts I discussed in the previous chapter.

With the *Caraka* we find ourselves again in a world of complex, regulated, high-class drinking, a world that can also be found in other texts on Āyurveda that contain similar discussions of drinking, namely: a classification of three stages of intoxication, variations of the drink-caused condition called *madātyaya* according to the three "humors" wind (*vāta*), bile (*pitta*), and phlegm (*kapha*), instructions on the best way to drink, and the notion that returning to drinking after a period of abstinence causes a particular medical condition.[23] The chapter on the treatment (*cikitsā*) of liquor diseases in *Caraka's Compendium* starts with a passage in praise of Surā (the drink and the goddess). This carefully argued apology for Surā draws on a number of ritual and mythological associations that we have yet to explore, so I'll discuss it later.

The *Caraka* then explains how to drink properly. This passage shares a lot with the one in Vāgbhaṭa's *Heart of Medicine* quoted earlier, so I won't translate it here (though note that the *Heart of Medicine* is of a later date than *Caraka*). As with Vāgbhaṭa's text, the drinker adorns both his body and his environment and is served drink in precious vessels by attractive women. He takes the liquor with various foods. As before, prior to drinking he offers drink to various beings:

> After having worshiped the gods, and having given the blessing, and having offered intoxicating drink (*madyam*) with water on the surface of the earth for those beings who are desirous of it (*arthibhyaḥ*) . . .[24]

For the eleventh-century commentator Cakrapāṇidatta,[25] the beings who desire liquor are Balarāma (see Cup 6), the goddess Caṇḍī, the beings called *yakṣas* whom we saw drinking earlier, and others. But what exactly is this offering? Harry Falk has linked the similar passage in the *Heart of Medicine* to Hellenized drinking practices, possibly depicted in some libation trays from the Gandhāra region.[26] But while there are some elements of foreign drinking habits in India, such as grape wines, some imagery, and possibly some words,[27] there is no reason to believe that the offering to the gods described in *Caraka's Compendium* and the *Heart of Medicine* is not an indigenous Indic practice. Drinking was well established in India prior to any foreign "influences." And the practice of making offerings to various beings by leaving food on the floor (*baliharaṇa*), which sometimes has to be cleaned first, was also well established in ancient Indian rituals.[28] Regardless, setting aside the question of origins, the connection of drinking to worship is significant, especially coming after the praise of Surā at the start of the chapter. A picture emerges of a drinking culture in which drinking and aspects of life that we now call religious were by no means incompatible.

The *Caraka* then describes the bodily preparations of the drinker according to his dominant "humor" (*doṣa*).[29] For example, a person dominated by "bile" (*pitta*)—a hot, fiery humor—needs to indulge in various forms of cooling prior to drinking.[30] As before, we read that these nuanced forms of drinking apply only to the wealthy (*vasumatām*).[31] We then read this:

> Intoxicating drink made from jaggery or ground grains (*gauḍipaiṣṭikam*) is generally best for people with wind constitutions, and for phlegmatic and bilious people grape wine and honey mead (*mārdvīkaṃ mādhavaṃ ca*) [are best].[32]

These drinks resemble a list of *surā* types that became prominent in texts on Hindu law, as I shall discuss later: that legal "threefold *surā*" included jaggery drinks, grain drinks, and ones based on honey and/or grapes ("*madhu*"-related drinks), though it's hard to establish any connection between the passages.[33]

Then comes a section on the general properties and actions of wine, as well as the nature of intoxication. The section starts with a description of drink as both medicinally harmful and beneficial:

> Intoxicating drink (*madyam*) is made of many substances, has many qualities, has many activities, and has the nature of intoxication (*mada-*), and this intoxicating drink is characterized both by good qualities and by faults. For the man who, delighted, drinks it in the correct manner, in the correct amount, at the right time, and with the right foods, according to his strength, intoxicating drink will be like the nectar of immortality. But intoxicating drink is like poison for the man who excessively eagerly (*prasaṅgāt*) drinks intoxicating drink as it

> is to hand [i.e., undiscerningly], and who is constantly engaged in harsh physical exertion.[34]

This is an especially clear statement of the general medical value and dangers of drink, quite distinct from the surrounding religious, moral, and legal issues. Much of the remainder of this chapter in the *Caraka* explains these variables. Bear in mind that since only a few people could afford to manage their drinking regimen in this way, poorer people could not help but risk drinking wrongly. Possibly the hard exertion mentioned here suggests that the drinking of manual laborers is inevitably harmful. As in the introductory praise of Surā (see Cup 7), intoxicating drink is compared to the nectar of immortality (*amṛta*), though for liquor to assume this divine form, it must take its proper place within an individual's lifestyle. Otherwise *surā* is poison, the antithesis of *amṛta* both practically and mythologically. Cakrapāṇidatta's commentary even notes that this chapter follows the one on treating poisoning because of the similarities of liquor-induced disease and poisoning.

How exactly does liquor make the body, mind, and senses intoxicated? The *Caraka* explains:

> Intoxicating drink (*madya*) enters the heart and disturbs the ten qualities (*guṇa*) of vital energy (*ojas*), with its own ten qualities, and transforms/perturbs the mind (*cetas*).[35]

So the action of intoxication takes place in the heart (*hṛdaya*), where the drink encounters a vital energy-substance called *ojas*. The human body, according to classical Āyurveda, consists of seven constituents—chyle, blood, flesh, fat, bones, marrow, and semen—and, to quote Jan Gonda, "The quintessence of these seven 'elements' is called *ojas* . . . It is situated in the heart, whence the main veins convey it through the whole of the body. It is the bearer of the vital function and constitutes the fundament on which the preservation of the body depends. Without *ojas* the elements of the body do not live; the vital powers . . . rest on this central entity . . . As long as it is upheld, the human being continues to exist, when it perishes, man passes away. Anger, hunger, sorrow, weariness are injurious to it; then man becomes timid, weak, lean, pale and sad. In extreme cases the decline of this central vital power results in death."[36] The qualities of drink are exactly contrary to those of *ojas*, so it disturbs this vital energy in a precisely directed way. After listing the opposed qualities (e.g. drink is light, *ojas* is heavy), the *Caraka* explains the significance of the location of this conflict of substances:

> The heart is said to be the location of the channels of food-essence (*rasa*), wind, and the other [bodily tissues and humors], and of the quality purity (*sattva*),

intellect (*buddhi*), the senses (*indriya*),[37] and the soul/self (*ātman*), as well as the primary vital energy (*ojas*). Intoxicating liquor drunk in excess and damaged vital energy [both] transform the heart as well as the bodily tissues (*dhātus*) located there.[38]

Setting aside the complexities of the classes of fluids and tissues, the basic picture here is clear. The heart is the hub of vital bodily tissues and faculties, as well as the site of *ojas*. When an intoxicating drink enters the heart, its *ojas*-antithetical qualities affect *ojas* strongly, and this interaction, along with the liquor itself, influences the other bodily factors, so that the body, the senses, and the mind are all transformed.

We then learn of the three stages of intoxication. These are explained in terms of the heart/*ojas* theory of drunkenness: In the first stage, the *ojas* energy-substance is not hurt/damaged (*avihate*) but the heart is awakened (*pratibodhite*). The commentator Cakrapāṇidatta points out that this refers to the intellect and other entities located in the heart. In the middle stage, the *ojas* is slightly damaged, and in the last stage it is damaged (or even "destroyed").[39] Drink made from ground grain, however, does not cause such extreme damage to the *ojas* because some of its opposing properties are not as powerful. This clarification is striking given that, in some Hindu legal texts, *surā* made from grains is forbidden for the greatest number of social classes and thus effectively the most broadly prohibited drink. According to the *Caraka*, by contrast, grain liquor is the mildest form of drink.[40]

Next the text defines intoxication and explains how the stages of intoxication affect a person's mental state and behavior. Note that the nuances of the words for the emotions here are difficult to capture precisely in English:

When the qualities of intoxicating drink enter the heart, there arises glee (*harṣa*), desire (*tarṣa*), extreme [or "sexual"] pleasure (*rati*), pleasure (*sukha*), and various changes that are pure (*sattvaṃ*), passionate, or dark and ignorant [*rājasatāmasāḥ*, i.e., the three *guṇa*s], which ends in loss of consciousness and sleep from excessive indulgence in intoxicating drink. This disturbance caused by intoxicating drink (*madya*) is referred to with the term "intoxication" (*mada*).

When intoxicating drink is drunk, three types of intoxication can be discerned: the first, the middle, and the final—we state these according to their characteristics.

The first intoxication is pleasant: it is thrilling and delightful; it displays the qualities of drink and food; it promotes music, song, laughter, and stories; and it

> does not rob you of intellect or memory; it does not disable your appreciation of the objects of the senses, and you sleep and wake contentedly.
>
> One should recognize these signs when the middle stage arises: at times memory, at times confusion; speech that is sometimes clear and sometimes unclear;[41] both coherent and incoherent conversation; wobbly walking; and erratic control of stance, drinking, and eating.
>
> [Here there is an exhortation not to progress to the third stage.]
>
> Reaching the third [stage of] intoxication, a man is inactive like cut timber; his mind is overcast with intoxication and confusion. Though alive, he is just like the dead; he is not aware of the pleasant objects of the senses, nor of his friends. He does not experience the intense/sexual pleasure (*rati*) for the purpose of which he drinks the liquor. What wise man would enter a state in which he does not recognize duty and that which is to be avoided, pain and pleasure in the world, or the beneficial and the harmful? Of all beings, he is one who is vile, reprehensible, and to be rejected, and because he is attached to drinking he will get a painful disease in the future.[42]

So: the first stage is entirely pleasant—it enhances one's experience and participation in pleasurable activities and has no adverse affect. The enhancement of sense pleasures is key to this stage. The second stage is mixed: the person in this stage is both in control and confused, and so this stage is similar to what we've seen in other texts, when people are laughing and crying, and confused about their experiences. The final stage is dull: the person lacks awareness and activity, nor is he able to make good judgments. This sort of intoxication is very bad for the health.

Here let us briefly consider another text that describes the stages of drinking. The *Nāṭyaśāstra* of Bharata (from possibly the third or fourth century CE) is an early, canonical text on dramaturgy.[43] The passage below describes how drunk intoxication (*mada*), a transitory emotion or *vyabhicāribhāva*, should be represented in a theatrical performance. The three stages are here called incipient (*taruṇa*), medium (*madhya*), and drawn out/inferior (*avakṛṣṭa*).[44] Three different type of people, varying according to their nature (*prakṛti*), react differently to intoxication in this scheme. Note that this is not a medical text; these are instructions on how to *represent* intoxication in drama. It is therefore apt that the description resembles literary descriptions of drinking:

> Some drunk people (*matta*) sing, some weep, and some laugh, some speak harsh language, and some sleep.

> The one with the best character sleeps, and the one with the middling nature laughs and sings, and the one with the lowest nature speaks harsh language and cries.
> The person with the best nature, in the stage of incipient intoxication, speaks with a smile, a pleasant emotion [or "sweet melody"]; the body is thrilled, with somewhat disordered speech and a delicate swinging gait.
> The one of middling nature, with medium intoxication, has unsteady, rolling eyes, loose, agitated waving of the arms, and a crooked, whirling/misplaced gait.
> The one of the lowest nature has lost his memory, has a completely impeded gait, is very disgusting with vomiting, hiccups, and phlegm, [and a] heavy, clinging tongue, and is spitting.[45]

Although the terms for these three types of intoxication imply a progression, in this text each stage correlates with the nature of the character representing it. The person of best character might sleep, not because he's been knocked out by too much drink but presumably because that way he will engage in no scandalous behavior. Even if this person does not sleep (which would be rather boring for someone *acting* drunk), he shows outward signs that correspond well with the first stage of drunkenness described in the *Carakasamhitā*: mild effects, nothing obnoxious, and a body that is thrilled/excited (*hṛṣtatanu*). The following stage, which applies here to people of a middling nature, is characterized by a loss of bodily control and whirling around. And in the third stage, associated with the lowest type of person, the mind and body are quite ruined and the person is rendered repulsive. But this highly intoxicated person is not unconscious, as we saw in *Caraka's Compendium*—presumably that would not make for a revealing performance on stage. In literary descriptions of drinking, and not just in plays, the outward signs are what we usually encounter, with far fewer subjective descriptions of the internal, mental experience. Whereas the *Caraka* treats the stages of intoxication separately from a person's nature and constitutional tendencies, in the dramaturgic text the character types and intoxication stages are somewhat fused, so that a certain type of intoxication displays a certain type of person. The *Caraka*, however, does briefly allude to such a correlation, stating that just as fire shows the nature of gold as best, worst, and middling, so "intoxicating drink manifests the nature of minds/characters (*sattva*)."[46]

In the next section of the *Caraka*, the dangers of drink are stated again, this time with a focus on how it affects the mind (*manas*): "And the mind is greatly disturbed by intoxicating drink, like a tree on a river bank by a great blast of wind."[47] Note that "mind" here may have been used in a narrower philosophical sense, found also in this text,[48] of an atomic corporeal entity responsible for introspection and switching between the various sense faculties; if that is the case, then the mind may be viewed here as literally knocked around by drink. This cautionary section concludes, "So those [who] thus know the faults of intoxicating drink vigorously condemn intoxicating drink."[49] Yet there is more to intoxicating drink than this, and the next section, on how to drink correctly, begins in this way: "However, in terms of its innate nature intoxicating drink is taught [as being] just like food—used in an unsuitable way it produces disease, and used suitably it is like the nectar of immortality."[50]

The *Caraka* then turns to the complexities of the proper manner of drinking, and its virtues. First, a general statement:

> Intoxicating drink drunk in the proper manner gives a pleasant intoxication and immediately produces a thrilling [of the body], gladness, thriving, good health, virility [or "semen"], and strength.[51]

As with the dangers of drink described earlier, the virtues are both mental and physical and take place rapidly after drinking. The mention of virility suggests that only male drinking is alluded to here. Then comes an expanded explanation of the many virtues of drink, which is worth quoting as it provides another good counterbalance to Indian texts that focus on drinking as a vice or a sin:

> [Intoxicating drink] promotes appetite and improves digestion, is good for the heart, purifies the voice and complexion, nourishes, fattens, strengthens, removes fear, grief, and fatigue, promotes sleep for insomniacs, awakens the voice of the dumb, makes the excessively sleepy wakeful, cures the constipation of the constipated, and removes the awareness of those pained by the troubles of imprisonment and punishment; and intoxicating drink itself drives away diseases that arise from intoxicating drink. It causes extreme pleasure, and increases delight and attachment with regard to perceiving the objects of the senses, and even for old people intoxicating drink causes merriment and cheer—for both young and old, there is nothing on earth comparable to the intense pleasure (*rati*) in the five agreeable objects of the senses [that happens] in the first stage of intoxication. Intoxicating drink taken in the proper manner is a source of rest (*viśrāma*) for this world of living beings who are suffering from many pains and afflicted by grief.[52]

Having begun, in the *Caraka*, with a praise of the divine nature of *surā*, followed by warning of the many dangers of liquor, we thus return to the notion that, if drunk in the correct way, liquor is a remarkable substance, especially with regard to things that we might call "of this world." Drink improves the health of the body, the pleasures of the senses, and allays bodily pain and mental anguish. Though it is not stated explicitly, we might say that drink highlights the good things and attenuates the bad things in the realm of rebirth, *saṃsāra*. Drink is a flawed, messy, temporary fix for a flawed, messy, transient world, and is therefore a valuable substance.

What is correct drinking, according to the *Caraka*? First, in order to drink properly (*yuktyā*) one needs to be aware of several factors: food, drink, disease, strength, time, the three humors (*doṣa*), and the three types of character (*sattva*).[53] Correct drinking thus requires considerable knowledge (or incredibly good luck).

We learn that there are three types of drinking gatherings (*āpāna*), classified according to the scheme of the three *guṇa*s, or qualities. This metaphysical notion is complex, and I won't discuss it in detail here. Put simply, the three *guṇa*s are fundamental metaphysical principles/qualities that we saw above in the classification of emotions: *sattva*, or purity, clarity, understanding; *rajas*, which is energy and passion; and *tamas*, inertia and darkness. The corresponding gatherings are described as follows:

> The drinking gathering characterized by clarity/purity (*sāttvika*) has perfumes, flowers, and song, is well prepared and not crowded,[54] is clean, with delicious food and drink, ever with sweet-sounding conversation, with pleasant drinking, [and] good intoxication; [it] increases delight and joy, and ends well. It does not produce the final stage of intoxication.[55] Those with a nature characterized by purity are not forced to enter a lowly state by the faults of intoxicating drink, for intoxicating drink does not powerfully seize the quality of purity by force. The [gathering] characterized by the quality of passion and energy (*rājasa*) has conversation that is generally agreeable or disagreeable, is at once clear and murky, is variable, generally does not end well, and is crowded. The drinking gathering characterized by inertia and darkness (*tāmasa*) is taught as devoid of delight, joy, and conversation. There is no satisfaction in eating and drinking, and it ends in confusion/stupor, anger, and sleep.[56]

No surprises here: the nature of each party is mostly determined by the type of drunkenness experienced by the people attending, which largely matches the three levels of intoxication seen earlier. The *Caraka* adds that at a drinking party one should find *sattvic* (pure, clear) companions and shun the *rajasic* (passionate, energetic) and *tamasic* (inert, murky) ones.

Here I should again emphasize one fundamental aspect of almost all the descriptions of drinking quoted in this book. Like conversation, kissing, and sex, drinking in early India was an intrinsically social phenomenon.[57] Just as one had to choose the ideal snacks and the right drink for the season, one also had to select the right companions—the people and the party were considered medically necessary. Choosing them required an understanding of human character traits, here classified according to the three *guṇa*s, and so this section ends with comments on ideal drinking companions (*sahāya*) and their virtuous, pleasant, and sensuous qualities: they are good-looking, esteemed by good people, devoted to the objects of the senses, and so on.[58]

Only after explaining how to drink properly does the chapter consider in detail the dangers of drink to the body and mind. It begins by stating, "Oh Agniveśa, now, below, I shall relate respectively the arising individual characteristics and treatment of *madātyaya* (intoxication disorder)."[59] These factors are mainly described according to a person's humor: whether he is dominated by wind, bile, or phlegm. The section is quite long, and in order to make the material more accessible I focus here on just a few aspects of the disorder as it affects people dominated by bile (*pitta*, sometimes translated as "choler"). Readers should bear in mind that a major quality of the bile humor is heat, though not necessarily literal, tactile heat. This is an abridged account; specialists in Āyurveda can refer to the original text in all its complexity.

We first learn the causes of bile-dominant (*pittaprāya*) intoxication disorder:

> The man who eats food that is sour, hot, and pungent, who gets angry, and is fond of fire and the heat of the sun, and takes an excessive amount of pungent/strong (*tīkṣṇa*), hot, and sour intoxicating drink will especially develop the intoxication disorder from bile, which is either quickly extinguished or kills for one with excessive wind humor.[60]

Note the several heat-related factors here. The symptoms are similarly hot:

> One recognizes the bile-dominant intoxication disorder for a person with a green/yellow (*harita*) complexion by means of thirst, burning sensation, fever, sweating, fainting, diarrhea, and agitation.[61]

We then learn that all types of intoxication disorder are caused by all three humors, but one should nonetheless focus on the humor perceived to be dominant. Perhaps surprisingly to us, the text suggests that one should treat the problems arising from incorrectly consumed liquor by administering the right liquor, in the correct amount.[62] In connection with this idea, we learn the pharmacological qualities of liquor (*madya*):

> Liquor (*madya*), sour by nature, is taught to have four "secondary flavors" (*anurasa*): sweet, astringent, bitter, [and] pungent, and there are the ten previously stated qualities (*guṇa*)—with these fourteen qualities liquor stands at the head of all sour substances (*amla*).[63]

As understood in the *Caraka*, liquor is really an incredibly complicated substance.

The treatment of an intoxication disorder, as noted, involves serving the correct liquor—sometimes with additions, special diets exploiting the system of medicinal meats that Francis Zimmermann has so eloquently described.[64] A range of other treatments was also recommended, involving massages, unguents, and special environments that were cool or hot depending on the disorder. Thus:

> In bile intoxication disorder, at the correct time one should give [the patient liquor] to drink made of sugar (*śārkara*) or else made of grapes, that contains a lot of water, that has the juices of *bhavya*,[65] dates, grapes, [and] *phālsā*[66] added, that contains pomegranate juice, is cool, sprinkled with the powder of cooked barley flour, and contains sugar . . .[67]

In addition to several other types of treatment, we learn of the many cooling treatments used in this case—an avalanche of conventionally cooling substances, and a fantastic vision of medical treatment for the wealthy:

> Cool food and drink, cool beds and seats; the touch of cool breezes and water; cool parks; the touch of linen, lotus, and lily, and of gems, and of pearls cool with sandalwood water, which are cool like the rays of the moon; and the touch of vessels made of gold, silver, and brass, full of cool water; wind puffs from ice-filled waterskins,[68] and [the touch] of women moist with sandalwood; with the wind from the best of sandalwood [trees?]—contact [with these] is taught in the case of bile intoxication disorder. And one should employ everything else that possesses a cool potency (*vīrya*). In the case of a burning sensation produced from intoxicating liquor, contact with the pleasant leaves of lotuses and lilies wetted with sandalwood water is beneficial. And varied stories are extolled, and the auspicious sounds of peacocks, and the sounds of rain clouds—these allay intoxication disorder. In the case of a burning sensation, the doctor should fashion fountain houses (*dhārāgṛhāṇi*) with showers from water-devices and air from wind-devices . . .[69]

Again, this medicinal description verges on the poetic: a cooling idyll staged by your doctor.

The *Caraka* mentions that if the treatment of administering more liquor—the "liquor method" (*madyavidhi*)—does not work, one should abandon it and use milk instead. But once this latter method is successful, one should then return to the liquor method, which is apparently the primary form of treatment.[70] A description is included of two extra disorders that arise when someone returns to liquor consumption after a period of abstinence, and then the chapter[71] ends with a single verse commending total abstinence: "The wise man who has abstained from all intoxicating liquor and who has conquered his senses is not affected by bodily or mental diseases."[72]

This chapter is written with a wealthy drinker in mind, who can afford to indulge in proper drinking and elaborate treatments if need be, yet here, at the end, is a nod to the abstinent. These wise people are said to be entirely healthy, and although we just learned of the mental and physical virtues of drink as well as the dangers, the chapter becomes irrelevant if you abstain altogether. For those who drink—and in Hindu law, plenty of people could if they so desired[73]—the *Caraka* provides a detailed guide to *managing* a powerful drug that is both beneficial and dangerous. As we see so often in premodern South Asia, alcohol is an ambiguous substance here, and there is plenty of (quite respectable) room for both the drinker and the teetotaler.

Conclusion: Perfect, Harmonious, Social Drinking for the Wealthy Man

Āyurveda recognized a complex disorder, taking several forms, that could result from drinking. This disorder had several causes and was by no means simply the result of drinking vast amounts of what we now call "alcohol." Rather, the wrong drinks taken in the wrong manner, the wrong season, the wrong quantity, and the wrong combination for a certain constitution produced the disorder. Drink alone, in other words, was not the problem. Indeed, an important treatment was the correct administration of more liquor. There is no suggestion that people with this condition had to abstain for life to be cured.

By now, it should be clear that a translation of this disorder as "alcoholism" obscures the richness of these medical theories (and this chapter really is a superficial survey.) The existence and nature of the illness described here implies that drinking could be done in a certain, correct manner. These texts lay out something like a dietetics of liquor, involving a huge number of factors, from the company one keeps to the raw materials used to make the drink. Some foundational Indian medical texts also praise the many and varied joys of correct drinking. Although the treatises state clearly that not everyone can take part in correct drinking, nevertheless the two sources we've examined here explicitly, even heavy-handedly, defend the practice of drinking and the virtues of drink, using the language of orthodox rituals, *dharma*, and mythology. Thus we should by no mean assume that such ways of thinking and writing about drink reside primarily within an abstinent ascetic or brahminical realm. As we see below, the picture is very complex and varied.

It is to such materials, including the two praises of *surā* found in medical texts, that we'll turn in the next section of the book.

ROUND TWO

DRINK AND RELIGION

Round Two of this book is different in scope and organization from Round One. Until now we've explored drinks, brewing, and drinking practices, but henceforth we'll turn to second-order ways of talking about and using drink. I will consider the place of drink in mythology; theories of the morality of drinking; and the ways in which people used drink in some rituals. For the most part the texts I'll examine are ones that nowadays we would class as religious in nature, so I call this part "Drink and Religion."

The collection of topics here is large and by no means coherent. We're dealing with multiple currents in several religions, quite a few rituals and myths, and a number of sophisticated legal and moral theories—and all this is only a sampling of the surviving material. These stories, texts, and practices all interact with each other in different ways. Rituals transgress laws that in turn were developed in the context of lifestyles defined by other, quite different rituals. Often themes crop up in several contexts, such as the Vedic Sautrāmaṇī ritual or the fatal fight of the Andhakas and the Vṛṣṇis, and thus the significance of these rituals and stories becomes ever more complicated.

I've organized my analyses of these varied materials in a progression, from those that can be explained on their own to those that can be understood only in terms of previously explained topics. For that reason, I've found it helpful to describe attitudes toward *surā* in the Vedas before Hindu laws concerning *surā*. And it makes sense to present Hindu laws on alcohol before looking at Tantric texts and rituals that transgress those laws. Myths are best presented before moral speeches that refer to those same myths. Even within the myths, there is an internal temporality: Surā has to come into being before she/it gets prohibited. In the following chapters and their subsections, I've given a chronological account as much as is possible. Nevertheless, given all the topics covered here, this part of the book is a bit more of a grab-bag than the first part, and readers can treat it as such.

In Cup 6, on rituals and myths, I start with the oldest topic, the Vedic Sautrāmaṇī ritual, and then explore a variety of myths and narratives, grouped to reflect continuities and connections (sometimes within mythological time). Some parts of this chapter are included for completeness and can be skipped by all but the most committed readers. The sections most essential for understanding the rest of book are the Sautrāmaṇī ritual, the origins of Surā at the churning of the ocean, the incident in which the sage Śukra prohibits *surā* for Brahmins, and the fateful fight of the Andhakas and Vṛṣṇis. One compensation for the eclectic nature of the materials in this chapter is that many of the stories are quite entertaining.

Cup 7, which focuses on morality and legal theory, is divided into several parts. The material here is arranged chronologically, starting with the Vedas, and also by religious tradition: Hindu, Buddhist, and Jain. I present ideas about drinking as a vice (as opposed to a grave sin) after the Vedas and before Hindu law. Such material is present in all discourses from the Vedas to the epics, in texts on statecraft as well as in religio-legal texts, yet it might easily be overlooked in light of more distinctively sectarian ideas about the morality of drinking. Placing it at the start of the chapter allows us to see how this strand of thinking about drink pervades a wide variety of texts. Finally, at the end of the chapter, I examine texts that contradict, ridicule, or satirize the religious moral-legal material. Effectively these texts are third-order discourses on drinking, further complicating an already elaborate landscape of ethical and religious ideas surrounding drinking in early India. These will leave us in a strong position to consider the practical and conceptual manipulations of drink in some forms of Tantric religion, which I explore in Cup 8.

Finally, in Cup 9, I briefly look at a few later developments in Indian drinking culture and theory, as presented in Sanskrit texts from the last few centuries.

CUP 6
Drink in Ritual, Myths, and Epic

In this chapter I'll explore the use of *surā* in one Vedic ritual along with the presence of drinking in mythic narratives. Much of the material in this chapter forms a repertoire of drink allusions that occur in several genres: medical, legal, moral, Hindu, Buddhist, Jain, and some Tantric texts. Knowing this material will enable us to interpret such allusions, and also understand some basic attitudes in ancient and early medieval India toward drink and intoxication as they pertained to myth and ritual.

Why Do People Offer *Surā* to Gods in a Vedic Ritual?

Let's start with some of the oldest material, the Vedas. Earlier, we read of *surā* being brewed to offer in a Vedic sacrifice called the Sautrāmaṇī.[1] Yet the mind-altering[2] drink people usually offered to the gods in Vedic rituals was *soma*, which was considered antithetical to *surā*. One Vedic text affirms that *soma* and *surā* are "the divine and the human."[3] Elsewhere *soma* is equated with truth and light, *surā* with falsehood and darkness.[4] As Stephanie Jamison writes, *surā* is a sort of "evil twin" to *soma*.[5] Or, as Malamoud has written, *surā* is the counterpart of *soma*.[6] So, in the realm of gods and humans dealing with gods (i.e., in the Vedic sacrifice), *surā* is usually kept out of the picture. This contrast in the Vedas is not, however, some sort of Manichaean absolutely-good-*soma* versus a pure-bad-*surā*, but rather a contrast between the intoxicating drink of the gods and that of humans. As we'll see below, in later texts on *dharma* that articulate the ideal order conduct for Brahmins, Brahmin-hood is closely associated with abstention from *surā*, and we see some of the roots of that rule in this contrast—for it was Brahmins above all whose livelihood theoretically involved dealing with the *soma*-drinking gods.

Given the contrary natures of the two drinks, offering *surā* to certain gods in the ritual called the Sautrāmaṇī might seem odd to anyone familiar with the system of Vedic sacrifices. Later writers, not just Hindus, sometimes referred to the anomalous nature of this ritual, meaning that this Sautrāmaṇī ritual was considered to be conceptually exceptional in later discussions of drink in law, morality, and certain Tantric rituals.

An Unholy Brew. James McHugh, Oxford University Press. © Oxford University Press 2021.
DOI: 10.1093/oso/9780199375936.003.0008

In the Sautrāmaṇī sacrifice, people offer *surā* (along with animals and various libations) to a pair of gods called the Aśvins, to the goddess Sarasvatī, and to the god Indra "Sutrāman" ("Indra of good protection"), from whom the ritual derives its name.[7] Stephanie Jamison explains, "*Sautrāmaṇī* is a healing or reinvigorating ritual, and, curiously, involves the drinking of *surā* . . . This ritual is prescribed for people in a number of circumstances, but the common thread that connects them is loss of strength or vigor."[8] For example, one performs this sacrifice for a person who has vomited or purged the *soma* drink (and is thereby weakened).[9] This purpose for the ritual perhaps explains why materials for making the *surā* should be purchased from a eunuch, a traditionally weak figure, and why, in the preparation of the *surā*, one adds the hairs of fierce strong animals—the wolf, the tiger, and the lion—to the cups.[10] Thomas Oberlies suggests that, in a postulated ancient (*Ṛgvedic*) form of the sacrifice, a mixture of *surā* and *soma* was offered, known by the portmanteau word *surā́ma*.[11]

Some texts relate a myth that highlights the connection between *surā* and the process of healing someone who has vomited *soma*. In this myth, of which there are several versions,[12] the god Indra makes an agreement with the *asura* ("anti-god") Namuci that Indra cannot slay Namuci "with anything dry or with anything wet, by day or by night."[13] In some cases we're told that this is because the two fought and Namuci gained the upper hand, prompting Indra to make the pact. Then Namuci gets Indra drunk with *surā* (Indra's usual drink being *soma*),[14] which robs him of strength, *soma*, and food. In another version, Indra drinks some *soma* that was not offered to him and explodes into a great number of materials, including all the components of the Sautrāmaṇī sacrifice. For example: "from his hips fire flowed and became *surā*, the essence of food."[15] Indra being thus impaired, the Aśvins and Sarasvatī heal him with a sacrifice. And these three, together with Indra, are the gods who receive the *surā* in the Sautrāmaṇī. In a third version, Indra is simply sick from drinking *soma* and is healed by the Aśvins with the Sautrāmaṇī sacrifice.[16] Once healed, Indra kills Namuci without breaking his oath by doing the deed at dawn (not day or night) and beheading him with foam (neither liquid nor solid). These are mythological explanations and models for why one performs the Sautrāmaṇī to restore strength, and also when someone has vomited *soma*. When ritually treating excessive *soma*, its counterpart *surā* serves the purpose of an antidote.[17]

Although reconstructed from later texts, these narratives also help us to understand a hymn in the *Ṛgveda*, a hymn that contains imagery of the processing of barley (*yava*) in an earlier verse, which is probably not insignificant where *surā* is involved. Indeed, the barley verse is recited as a mantra in the Sautrāmaṇī ritual, meaning that the hymn is connected to the ritual in both mythical content and ritual practice.[18] Although the details here aren't the same as in the above accounts, the basic themes are clear:

> 4. O Aśvins, having separated the surā-soma (*surāmam*) by drinking it in company with the asuric Namuci,
> you helped Indra in his deeds, O lords of beauty.
> 5. Like parents their son, both the Aśvins helped [you], Indra, through their wondrous skills and sage words.
> When with your powers you separated the surā-soma by drinking it, Sarasvatī healed you, bounteous one.
> 6. Let Indra be of good protection, of good help with his help, very gracious, affording all possessions.
> Let him thrust away hatred; let him create fearlessness. Might we be lords of good heroes in abundance.
> 7. May we be in the favor of him who deserves the sacrifice, in his propitious benevolence.
> Let Indra of good protection, of good help to us, keep hatred away even from a distance.[19]

Even in this extremely early text, the story of healing Indra provides the rationale and prototype for the ritual.

In later Vedic texts—including those in which we saw the instructions on brewing *surā*—we also learn of the sacred formulas, or mantras, that priests recite during that ritualized process.[20] The first part of the mantra below, until "I unite," is recited while mixing the components of *surā*. Then the mantra "Thou art the *soma*" is recited as the priest touches the vessel and drainage-structure containing the mixture that has been left to ferment:

> Thee, the sweet one with the sweet one, the strong one with the strong one, the immortal one with the immortal one, the honeyed one with the honeyed one, with the Soma I unite. Though art the Soma. Be prepared [literally, "be cooked"] for the Aśvins; be prepared for Sarasvatī; be prepared for Indra the good protector.[21]

Those involved in the ritual would have known that the assembled grains and other ingredients were now on their way to becoming sweet and intoxicating, so the mantra is apt. The words also connect the *surā*-to-be with the divine Soma (also sometimes "sweet"). In fact, the mantra ritually transforms the drink into *soma*, a suitable offering for gods.

Later in the ritual, broths are offered to the deities and more mantras are recited. These mantras clearly suggest one model of how the *surā*-offering ritual works to heal Indra's body: the ritual is a mantra-powered reverse-motion-sequence of the explosion of substances that occurred from Indra's body, or of the unloosening and robbing of Indra described in the myths. *Soma's* antithesis (i.e., *surā*) only works in the ritual when the dismemberment is "played backwards." Of course, the ritual can heal the body of the *patron* of this sacrifice too. In reading the following mantras let us not forget that all these brewing materials must have been vividly present to the senses of the ritual officiants. Note how the parts of the sacrifice correspond to, and rebuild, Indra's body parts, which is most appropriate given that brewing, fermentation, is also a matter of putting-together (*saṃdhāna*):

> That immortal form of him three deities [i.e., the two Aśvins and Sarasvatī], bestowing their gifts, have made with their powers. Just as his hairs [were produced] by malted grains of barley (*śáṣpa*) in great quantity, and by malted grains of rice (*tókman*), [so] the parched grains (*lājā́*) became like his skin and flesh.
>
> Therefore the two Aśvins, the two physicians [of the gods], move on the paths of Rudra, [and] Sarasvatī weaves the inner shape [of Indra]. With the *māsaras* [a liquid mixture of toasted grain] and with the *kārotara*-sieve [a bamboo and leather filter], they make his bones and marrow, on the skin of cows.
>
> Mindfully Sarasvatī, with the Nāsatyas [the two Aśvins], weaves the lovely, excellent, beautiful figure, just as the skillful *Nagnahu* [starter] [weaves] the red juice (*rásaṃ róhitaṃ*) with the foaming juice [*parisrútā*, unfiltered *surā*]—as the shuttle [weaves the cloth on] the loom.[22]

The mantras continue in this manner, meticulously reassembling the whole anatomy and powers of Indra (and the sacrificial patron) though ritual. Whereas in the previous mantras *surā* was praised and transformed into *soma*, now the components of *surā* are analogized to a healthy, vigorous body being put together, or "woven."[23] The principal agents of this assembling process are the deities who receive the sacrifice, though in the third verse the *nagnáhu* ferment/starter is the agent, weaving the red juice with the *parisrút*, the liquified *surā*-mash. All these materials, with their different textures and forms, now make up Indra's body. The remaining mantras assemble the organs, fluids, and powers of Indra, but in the mantras above the principal elements of brewing make up the basic body itself: its hairs, skin, flesh, bones, marrow (and form)—the parts of an ancient Indian "canonical creature" that Stephanie Jamison has described.[24] There are many ways in which we could theorize this complex of myth, liturgy, ritual action, and brewing technology, but, generally speaking it is clear that these mantras relate to the *surā* components, effecting a powerful god-rebuilding (and man-rebuilding) event in both mythological and localized/ritual space and time. Malamoud has written of Vedic sacrifices as "cooking the world."[25] In this ritual the participants brew a warrior-ruler.

It's interesting that *surā*'s role remains ambiguous in the ritual. Though it is compared to and transformed into *soma*, its power is still derived from its status as a counterpart to *soma* and the fact that it is compounded using all these materials. *Soma* is male (and a masculine noun), and *surā* is feminine. Malamoud writes that "the femininity of *surā* does not only come from the feminine gender of the term, nor from her role as a sexual partner of the masculine *soma*. It can also be seen in its composite character (it is made of several ingredients), whereas *soma* is simple: now in Vedic thought the feminine is frequently associated with the plural and the singular with the masculine . . . On the other hand it is explicitly claimed that in social symbolism . . . *surā* 'represents' the *viś*, the class of peasant producers, the subjects (*prajā*) 'eaten' by the 'eaters' who are the Brahmins and the Kṣatriya. Now within the large divisions of Indian society, the *viś*, the class of Vaiśyas, is the only one that is a feminine noun, and this is also the only one that is a group designated as a plural group, a multitude."[26] One might also speculate that early Indians connected the feminine nature of *surā* to the women who sometimes produced this drink in the domestic sphere, for it seems that the preparation of *soma*, by contrast, was a male affair. As Malamoud has famously noted, Brahmins were theoretically the cooks in ancient India. Brewing, however, was one realm of "cooking" in which (at least outside this ritual) Brahmins were presumably never the cooks.

Surā's status as an outsider in divine consumption was also important in the rituals of royal consecration in which a form of the Sautrāmaṇī can be included. Writing of this Malamoud suggests, "There is an all-encompassing order that implies and contains disorder; a light that does not banish, but rather embraces the darkness. The ritual that allowed the king of the gods to make reparations for the wrongdoing he had committed and suffered, and to reclaim possession of the totality of his being . . . the human king celebrates this ritual, not to be healed but because he wishes to appropriate to himself all rituals . . ."[27]

Usually *surā* was excluded from the realm of divine interaction. It belonged to the world of humans, with all their flaws. *Soma*, meanwhile, was a ritual drink with no place as a drug in society outside the sacrifice. But we must not forget the changing nature of ritual practices over time. Divorced from any social consumption and possibly difficult to obtain, the older *soma*-plant products might have eventually been replaced by various substitutes, ritualized placeholders rich in associations, like our concepts of "ambrosia" and "balm." *Surā*, though not offered in most Vedic rituals, was a common drink. The brewing process and the drink's effects on people were familiar, even to those who shunned it. In the long term, *surā* remained anchored in everyday practice while *soma* existed in a ritual, mythological realm. *Surā* thus remained thoroughly human, while *soma* became ever more divine and remote from everyday life.

The Origins of *Surā* at the Churning of the Ocean

Modern scholars accept the materials described in the previous section as some of our earliest textual evidence of *surā* in India. But what did religious traditions have to say about the origins of *surā*? In post-Vedic Hindu sources, *surā*, also the goddess Surā, is said to have appeared during the churning of the ocean—a famous Hindu myth found in the epics, Purāṇas, and other texts. Briefly, this myth relates how the gods (*deva*s) and the "anti-gods" (*asura*s or *dānavas*)[28] churned the ocean with a mountain, using a large serpent as a churning rope and twirling the mountain around as people traditionally do in India when churning milk with a churning stick to make butter or ghee. The gods and anti-gods do this in order to produce the nectar of immortality (*amṛta*), which emerges, like butter, from the churning. There follows a struggle over who gets to drink this elixir, and the gods win. Other significant things also emerge in the churning, including Surā. What happens to Surā next varies in different versions.[29]

In the *Mahābhārata*, as the gods discuss how they might get the nectar of immortality, the god Nārāyaṇa says:

> The bucket of the Ocean must be churned by both the Gods and the assemblies of *Asura*s. Then the Elixir shall spring forth when the Ocean is being churned. Churn ye the Ocean, O Gods, and ye shall find the Elixir, after ye have obtained all good herbs and precious stones.[30]

The gods go to Mount Mandara, which they plan to use as a churning stick, and they have a mighty snake, Ananta, uproot the mountain. The gods and *asura*s then persuade the king of Tortoises to be the foundation for the mountain, and they use another snake, Vāsuki, as the twirling-rope:

> So for the sake of the Elixir the *Asura*s and all Dānavas took hold of one end of the King of Snakes, and the Gods stood together at the tail . . . And as Vāsuki was forcefully pulled up and down by the Gods, puffs of fire and smoke belched forth from his mouth. The clouds of smoke became massive clouds with lightning flashes and rained down on the troops of the Gods, who were weakening with the heat and fatigue.[31]

The churning process is violent, crushing animals and starting fires, and eventually the juices of herbs and tree resins flow into the ocean. Then:

> with the milk of these juices that had the power of the elixir, and the exudation of the molten gold, the Gods attained immortality. The water of the ocean now turned into milk, and from this milk butter floated up, mixed with the finest essences.[32]

Ultimately the milk ocean yields the sun, the moon, the goddess Śrī (Fortune), the goddess Surā (Surā devī), an archetypal white horse, the gem that is placed in Viṣṇu's chest, and the god of medicine, Dhanvantari, carrying a white waterpot that contains the nectar of immortality.[33] In the *Mahābhārata*, Surā, Śrī, the moon, and the horse all follow the path of the sun and go to where the gods are. The *asuras* then try to take the nectar of immortality, and, to somewhat simplify the story, a struggle ensues. The gods get the nectar and drink it, causing a violent battle between the gods and *asuras*. The *asuras* lose and flee into the earth and the sea.

Recall that in the Buddhist myth of the banishing of the *asuras*, the struggle also arose over a drink. In that myth the *asuras* consume a "bad drink" (liquor) and are banished from heaven by Indra. Here they fail to drink a "good drink" and are similarly banished in the struggle for access to that drink. In the Buddhist story, the *asuras* show their true colors: they are beings not suited to heaven because they take liquor, the root of so much bad behavior. In the Hindu myth, on the other hand, they're not allowed to partake of a divine substance that only the gods possess, one that renders the gods immortal. In both versions and in the Vedic sacrifice, the gods are distinguished by what they drink (*soma*, the nectar of immortality) and by what they do not drink (liquor). Thus, while observant Buddhist humans may not share the *soma* of the gods in Vedic rituals, nevertheless, like the gods in the Buddhist myth, they *do* avoid liquor.

The above myth narrates the origin of Surā and, as such, describes events that occur before she/it was prohibited to Brahmins, which happens in a story that we'll see later. At this initial moment of her existence, she was neither cursed nor forbidden to anyone. Thus, in the *Mahābhārata* version, Surā goes to the gods. In the *Rāmāyaṇa* she is known by her other name, Vāruṇī, daughter of the god Varuṇa, the lord of the waters:

> After this, delight of the Raghus [Rāma], Varuṇa's illustrious daughter, Vāruṇī, was born. She, too, wished to be accepted.
>
> Heroic Rāma, the sons of Diti [i.e., *asuras*] would not accept Surā, the daughter of Varuṇa, but the sons of Aditi did accept her, for she was irreproachable.
>
> Because of this, the *daiteyas* came to be known as the *asuras*, while the sons of Aditi became the *suras*. Having accepted Vāruṇī, the gods were joyful and excited.[34]

Here the *initial* association of the gods and Surā explains a common Sanskrit word for god: "*sura*." Compare this with the description of the *asura*s crying out that they had not drunk *surā* and were "*a-surā*" (not having *surā*) in one version of the Buddhist story.[35] As for her acceptance by the gods, Surā is, after all, divine and offered in the Sautrāmaṇī sacrifice; she is not yet forbidden to any humans in this mythical time.

Even when the *asura*s take Surā, this is no victory. A later Hindu text, the *Bhāgavata Purāṇa*, presents Surā as a consolation prize for the *asuras*. The date of this text is debated, but for our purposes the second half of the first millennium CE will suffice, perhaps on the later side.[36] In this text, Surā appears after the goddess Śrī (Fortune), whom all the gods, *asura*s, and humans desire.[37] Śrī chooses Viṣṇu and disregards the *asuras*. They are dejected, until Surā arrives. 'Then the goddess Vāruṇī [Surā] arose, a lotus-eyed maiden, and the *asuras* accepted her with the permission of Hari [Viṣṇu/Kṛṣṇa].'[38]

Here Surā pales in comparison to Śrī, who chooses God; but the sad, shameless[39] *asura*s choose to accept Liquor, who is attractive and young though not as desirable as Fortune. With the *asura*s as runners-up, the theme of the *asura*s as losers is preserved, and the gods are unambiguously separated from Surā right from the start. Might this version reflect orthodox Hindu approaches to drink in later periods?

There are still more versions of the myth, in all of which Surā goes either to the gods or to the *asura*s, with the exception of one version in which she joins the king of *nāgas* [divine serpents], Ananta.[40] This serpent is sometimes said to be incarnated as Balarāma, Kṛṣṇa's brother, who, as we'll see later, is partial to drink.

In some versions, the goddess is called Madirā, a common and flexible word that refers to intoxicating drink in general (though the term was not adopted in technical legal contexts to the extent that *madya* was.)[41] One of the goddesses installed in the fortified city, according to the *Arthaśāstra*, is Madirā.[42] It's unclear if this goddess is the same as Surā/Vāruṇī of the churning myth, though there is clearly a connection.[43]

In a later context, when Surā had re-emerged as a vital component of some Tantric rituals, we see a more complex account of Surā's origins, but in these earlier, epic and purāṇic churning myths, we learn relatively little about her.

In premodern India, the myth of the churning of the ocean would have evoked the preparation and eating of food. After a struggle, the gods get to eat the nectar; a cosmic poison is swallowed and rendered safe by Śiva; Surā is allotted variously; and an eclipse-causing being tries to swallow the nectar (but is thwarted by the sun and the moon, and ever since he attempts to swallow—eclipse—them). In the process, access to these materials was distributed throughout the cosmos. This is what we might call a locative view of the universe and the important fluids (nectar, *surā*, poison) within it, a view "which emphasizes place."[44]

Surā is not outside this structure but rather has a special place within it. To echo Mary Douglas's famous definition of dirt,[45] what the texts instruct their readers to avoid is *surā* out of place—given the proper organization of the universe at a particular moment in cosmic time.

We learn more about the kin of Surā in the *Mahābhārata*, in a list of the origins of many beings and persons: 'Varuṇa's wife, the goddess Jyeṣṭhā, was born from Śukra, and she had a son, Bala, and Surā, a daughter of gods.'[46]

This text emphasizes Surā's relations to other persons rather than her appearance in the churning. Particularly notable here is her grandfather Śukra, who, as we'll see, later banishes *surā* the drink. Her connection to Varuṇa, however, is the most prominent of her kinship relations, especially given her alternate name, Vāruṇī, "daughter of Varuṇa."[47]

Some Sanskrit dramatic works mention the goddess Surā, typically in a humorous context. In *The Kick* (*Pādatāḍitaka*, from around the fifth century CE), we hear of a courtesan, a great dancer, who gives a flawed performance at the house of the Superintendent of Courtesans (*veśyādhyakṣa*), a man who is also a chamberlain (*pratīhāra*).[48] An interlocutor ascribes the courtesan's faulty dancing "to the goddess Vāruṇī," to which the protagonist adds, "It is right that the goddess Surā (*bhagavatī Surādevī*) is always present in the house of the chamberlain."[49] Here deified Surā is an elegant, humorous euphemism for drink itself, not a serious theological construct or an object of worship. Similarly, in the play about a drunken ascetic that we examined earlier, the *Mattavilāsaprahasana*, in which an ascetic and his consort approach a *surā* shop (humorously compared to a place of Vedic sacrifice), his consort observes of the sacred city of Kāñcī (Kanchipuram): "Sir, Kāñcī is faultlessly sweet like the Goddess Vāruṇī."[50] It is clear where their priorities lie.

In Hindu mythology, the gods won the nectar of immortality at the churning and the *asura*s lost. This is a clear victory over an unambiguously desirable drink, nectar. For Buddhists, in a myth that is less familiar today, the *asura*s are fond of liquor and thus get ejected from heaven, which afterward belongs only to the gods. Hindu versions vary as to who keeps Surā when she appears: sometimes she joins the gods, and in one text she is a consolation prize for the *asura*s. In these mythological frameworks, Surā is complex from the start. Later, *surā* is exiled and reviled. And then she is effectively redeemed, or at least given a new role that exploits her powers and complex past, in some Tantric rituals. Things are never straightforward with alcohol in Indian religions.

Cosmology: An Ocean of *Surā*

In the churning myth in the *Mahābhārata*, the ocean turns into milk. Other edible oceans also occur in Indian descriptions of the universe. These oceans are not just a quirk of ancient cosmology, the "seas of treacle and seas of butter" that Thomas Macaulay mocked in 1835.[51] Indeed, when understood as visions of realms of enjoyment and lists of pleasure-liquids, they seem far from absurd or childish.

Let's start with an early reference to bodies of delicious fluids. The *Atharvaveda* describes heavenly lakes of liquids that may anticipate the oceans of later sources: 'Ghee lakes, with honey banks and *surā* waters, filled with milk, water, and curd.'[52]

If one changes honey to sugarcane juice, one gets more or less the same bodies of tasty water that one sees in many later sources (our own salty ocean excepted).[53]

The flavorful oceans of later Hindu cosmography are on the same cosmic level as our world. Buddhists do not have edible oceans, as far as I know, but some Jain oceans have food-related names.[54] Willibald Kirfel studied the ways in which Hindu texts arrange the concentric rings of continents and oceans of the terrestrial realm (as opposed to heavens, hells, etc., which are on different vertical levels). Textual traditions give three different orders, yet there is always an ocean of *surā*. Despite the variations, the Surā Ocean (*Suroda*) always rings the outer edge of the *Śālmala* Continent.[55] According to some sources, the *Śālmala* Continent is named after a *śālmali* tree, which is the abode of Viṣṇu's mount, the bird Garuḍa. One list of oceans runs as follows:

1. Salt Ocean (*Lavaṇoda*, which surrounds our continent),
2. Sugarcane-Juice Ocean (*Ikṣurasoda*),
3. *Surā* Ocean (*Suroda*),
4. Ghee Ocean (*Ghṛtoda*),
5. Cream-Curd/Yoghurt Ocean (*Dadhimaṇdoda*),
6. Milk Ocean (*Kṣīroda*),
7. Sweet Water (*Svādūdaka*).[56]

Note that there is no *Soma* Ocean. Perhaps that would be out of place in this literally mundane list of liquids, though that most worldly of drinks, *surā*, fits well. In some texts the continents beyond ours, surrounded by these oceans, are places where life is easy and long, and where people enjoy the results of their actions (i.e., they are *bhogabhūmis*).[57] These are not heavens but paradisiacal places, and in that sense the oceans arguably play the same part that they did in heaven in the *Atharvaveda*.

Although the *Surā* Ocean, consisting of a substance forbidden to some in classical texts on Hindu law, might seem anomalous, I'm not aware of any discussion of that matter in the sources. Maybe the morality of materials was assumed to be different in other realms. After all, these are areas dedicated to the enjoyment of karmic results, not karmic action, so the potential to get drunk and commit evil deeds is not present. Such a notion recalls the non-inebriating heavenly rivers of wine in Islam.[58]

The Demon Intoxication

There is also a myth that explains the origin of Intoxication (Mada).[59] As with many of the stories discussed in this chapter, this myth concerns a dispute over access to a special liquid, namely *soma*.

One version of this story, in the *Mahābhārata*, begins with a seer named Cyavana, who has been performing austerities by a lake for so long that his body is encased in an anthill. One day a king comes to this spot with his retinue, including his beautiful daughter Sukanyā:

> And she, with pretty teeth, surrounded by her girlfriends, wandered there examining the delightful trees.
> Beautiful, youthful, amorous, and intoxicated (*madanena madena*),[60] she broke the most blossoming branches off the trees.
> The wise Bhārgava [the seer Cyavana] saw her left alone by her friends, adorned and wearing a single garment, wandering as if like lightning . . .[61]

This is a typical description of a drinking session in the forest, the sort of thing we have seen many times. Seeing a glint from the anthill, the princess prods a thorn into it, which of course hurts the seer's eye. Cyavana is angry and curses the king's soldiers with constipation. The king discovers that Cyavana is angry because of his daughter's offence and begs his forgiveness, which he agrees to accept on condition that he can marry the princess.

Cyavana marries Sukanyā, and she is a devoted wife. One day the two Aśvins see her nude after bathing and tell her she is too beautiful for her husband, a decrepit sage; she would surely be happier with one of them. She insists that she is devoted to her husband, so they offer to transform him into a handsome man—then, all things being equal, she can choose the one she prefers. The seer agrees, and after immersing themselves in water all three emerge looking young and beautiful. Yet Sukanyā still chooses Cyavana. Cyavana is delighted to be young and beautiful, as well as his wife's choice, and he tells the Aśvins that he will make them *soma* drinkers.[62]

Cyavana holds a sacrifice to offer *soma* to the Aśvins, but the god Indra stops him, saying that they are unworthy of *soma* (*na somārhau*)[63] because they are healers and servants and mingle among humans.[64] It's clear that *soma*, in this myth, belongs only in a fully divine context. The sage ignores Indra, however, and offers the *soma*, at which point Indra throws his thunderbolt at him. But Cyavana has great powers, gained from his austerities. He paralyzes Indra's arm and:

> Then, by the power of his austerity, the seer's sorcery became a great *asura* ["anti-god/demon"] called Mada [Intoxication], who was very strong and had a huge body that neither gods nor anti-gods could describe. His great mouth was terrible, with sharp-pointed teeth; one side of his jaw was on the earth, and the other in the sky. He had four teeth that were hundreds of leagues (*yojana*) long, and his other teeth were ten leagues [long]; they looked like ramparts and resembled the tips of spears. His arms were like mountains, both ten thousand [leagues] long; his eyes like the sun and moon; his mouth like Death. Licking his mouth with his tongue flapping and waving like lightning, his open mouth was horrible to behold, as if swallowing the world by force; furious, he ran at Indra, trying to eat him; he made the worlds resound with a great, horrible sound.[65]

Intoxication is vast and powerful, almost invincible, and he is hungry, characterized by a vast jaw, mouth, and teeth—reminiscent of the dazzling, terrifying vision of Kṛṣṇa in the *Bhagavad Gītā*. Mada is an *asura* here. Whereas Surā is beautiful and inclined to attach herself to both gods and *asuras*, Intoxication is destructive.

Indra's arm is still paralyzed. He agrees that from now on the Aśvins can have *soma* and begs for mercy. The seer calms down, but, as with all such demons, Intoxication does not simply vanish, so he needs to be assigned a role elsewhere:

> And, O King, that mighty one [the seer] shared out Mada [Intoxication] in drink (*pāne*), in women, in dice, and in hunting, where he had been created before many times.[66]

In this version Intoxication is contained by being divided among the classic vices that are "produced from desire/lust," vices that the texts exhort kings to avoid. Because Intoxication has apparently already been born in these contexts before, these vices are a safe, or at least predictable, place to put him.

In other versions, Intoxication ends up in different places. In an earlier, Vedic text he suffers a different fate:

> Now verily the monster Mada, the demon (*asura*) [of intoxication], became afraid and said: "Summon me not for nothing; dispose of me [somewhere]." They, thinking, "We will drink [him]," said, "Let us fetch hither *surā*, the sap of Varuṇa, for no one was ever injured, to hurt, in *surā*. There [into *surā*] do thou go away, O Mada." So this Mada, the demon, was deposited in surā (*sa eṣa mada āsuras surāyāṃ vinihitaḥ*).[67]

So here Intoxication enters *surā* alone, and this drink now contains a demonic entity that even Indra, the chief of the gods, fears.

Another contrast between the epic and the Vedic versions of this myth lies in the social implications, if we can take "social" to include the gods. Later in the *Mahābhārata*, the god Agni alludes to these events: the story, he notes, demonstrates that "the strength of the Brahmin [the seer] is greater than that of the Kṣatriya [Indra]."[68] In this interpretation, the story offers an idealized set of power relations between the two classes. On the surface it seems strange that a Brahmin would produce Intoxication, but this fits with the fact that Kṣatriyas, unlike Brahmins, are permitted (at least in later articulations) to drink liquor (*madya*) and are thus more vulnerable to its force. When, in the *Mahābhārata*, Intoxication is placed in the vices, they are the same vices commonly said, in literature on kingly conduct (*nīti*), to be a danger to kings and Kṣatriyas. The epic version of the Intoxication myth thus concerns Brahmin power and ritual knowledge versus kingly power and morality/vice.

The Vedic version is limited to the realm of ritual. Here the power struggle is said to illustrate the power of humans (Brahmins, seers) relative to that of the gods. As Agni says to Indra in the Vedic version, "They [the human seer] are better [stronger] than we . . . We [the gods] are born from these seers."[69] In this version Indra and the other gods flee after the conflict, leaving the seer with a godless sacrifice. Then the seer Vidanvat "sees" the *sāman* (chant/melody) that will bring Indra back to the sacrifice. Explaining the origin of this powerful chant is ostensibly the purpose of this version of the myth (which belongs to a school associated with the *Sāma*—sung—*veda*). It demonstrates the power of humans with respect to the gods in the context of sacrifice, and in particular of the Brahmins who chant the *Sāmaveda*. The status of kings and Kṣatriyas is not at stake here, nor is intoxication as a vice, for here Intoxication enters *surā*. In both versions, however, humans made *surā* intoxicating, and a human determined that the Aśvins can now drink the *soma*, despite Indra wishing otherwise.

Also, in both versions, Mada must then be banished for everything to work out as it should. Yet as at the end of many a horror film, the demon is not destroyed; instead it lurks inside certain common things, from which he can continue to work his terrible power.

The story of the demon Intoxication, while perhaps not familiar to many people today, was certainly known to the eleventh-century Kashmirian poet Kṣemendra.[70] He revives and expands the myth in his satirical *Kalāvilāsa* (*The Grace of Guile*). The text is a dialogue, in which a character called Mūladeva discusses bad qualities and traits with a young disciple—greed, pride, and so on, finishing with a discussion of virtue. In one chapter Mūladeva discusses the dangers of intoxication, *mada*. He interprets *mada* in very broad terms, describing several varieties, some of which can affect even those who don't drink alcohol, such as heroism-intoxication and wealth-intoxication. Also, the "intoxication of learning" (*śrutamada*), still familiar to many who work in academia, which is described in medical terms: where the eyes are red with slight anger and which makes a man unable to bear the mere voices of others, while he himself remains talkative.[71] Mūladeva concludes:

> But the intoxication of drink is the most base, the abode of all disgust, a great delusion.
> Though momentary, it immediately removes the merit earned in thousands of years.[72]

Kṣemendra then parodies two verses of the *Bhagavad Gītā* that describe the way the wise view the world: ironically, like spiritual insight, intoxication from drink does not differentiate between a Brahmin, a cow, an elephant, a dog, and a dog-cooker (a very "low"-caste person), nor between gold, mud, and stones. Which is to say, "Though he has attained the state of a yogin, the drunkard falls to hell of his own accord."[73] Kṣemendra's satire is astute, playing on the common understanding of drink as causing perceptual confusion, as well as highlighting the irony that this particular altered perspective on reality is thoroughly sinful. (As we shall see with Tantra, there were some contexts in which intoxication was valued for precisely the perceptual and cognitive changes it produces.) Kṣemendra adds that the drunkard is a mirror image of the realm of eternal rebirth (*sāṃsāra-*) because he exhibits confused and heightened emotions—crying, singing, laughing, running, wailing, getting confused, constantly changing—just like the unstable world of eternal rebirth and death. As Somdev Vasudeva points out, this frantic behavior also recalls certain mystical states (as well as possessed people, to whom drunkards are elsewhere compared).[74]

Kṣemendra then briefly relates the story of the creation of Intoxication (Mada), at the end of which Intoxication is placed in gambling, women, drink, and hunting, just as in the *Mahābhārata*. But Kṣemendra does not stop there. In his version, Intoxication also lives in the hearts (*hṛdaye*) of embodied living beings, restrained by their virtues.[75] He hides, moreover, "in the tongues of envoys and the learned," "in the teeth, hair, and clothes of the beautiful," and "in peacocks' tails." Kṣemendra concludes:

> Thus the great possessing-demon called Intoxication, an intense delusion that has many forms, forever dwells in the body of all beings, having become [inert and solid, like] wood.[76]

Kṣemendra here relates a very ancient myth, drawing on the stock literary and medical characteristics of a drunkard, yet he extends his interpretation ingeniously. Intoxication lies dormant in all manner of things, and although people might avoid the intoxication of drinking, the same demon and the same propensity to sin can emerge in many other activities, if unleashed by a relaxation of the cords of virtue (*guṇa*).[77] With Kṣemendra, this ancient myth feels almost classical. In his telling, the myth is an ancient, authoritative background that he ornaments with erudite allusions to produce a contemporary social satire.

Why *Surā* Is Out of Bounds to Brahmins

Thus far in mythological time, we've seen divine Surā arise from the ocean and learned how Intoxication became associated with her. Neither of these stories, however, explains why she came to be forbidden to certain people. Another myth explains this circumstance.

The story is related in the *Mahābhārata*, within the tale of King Yayāti, who married Śukra's daughter, Devayānī.[78] (Note that one of her sons, Yadu, is the ancestor of the Yādava clan, whom we'll meet later.) As is often the case, the gods and the *asura*s are arguing over the sovereignty of the universe. The gods select Bṛhaspati (the planet Jupiter) as their priest, and the *asura*s select Śukra (the planet Venus), so these two figures have the function of Brahmin priests.[79] In the battle for sovereignty, when the gods kill the *asura*s, Śukra can revive them using his vast knowledge. The gods' priest, Bṛhaspati, is not able to do likewise. This is of great concern to the gods, who decide to send a man called Kaca, the son of their priest, to study with Śukra and learn the art of reviving the dead. Kaca goes to Śukra and requests that he accept him as a pupil for one thousand years, and Śukra agrees to this. Everything goes well for five hundred years. Śukra's daughter, Devayānī, and Kaca get along very well (though chastely).

But then the *asura*s discover who Kaca is: the son of the gods' priest is living with Śukra, no doubt aiming to learn or steal the secret of reviving the dead! Finding Kaca herding cows alone one day, the *asura*s kill him. They cut him into tiny pieces and feed him to hyenas.[80] This elaborate method of disposing of the corpse is designed to prevent Śukra from reviving him. When Kaca fails to return, Devayānī is worried, but Śukra says that if he is dead he will call him and revive him, which he then does, using his magical reviving knowledge (*saṃjīvanīṃ vidyāṃ*).[81] So the threat to the *asura*s' upper hand in the struggle remains.

On another occasion, when Kaca goes to gather flowers for Devayānī, "the *asura*s, killing him a second time, burned him, ground him into powder, and gave him to the Brahmin [Śukra] in *surā*."[82] This is a far more ingenious method of disposal, for if Śukra revives Kaca he will explode Śukra's body in being restored.

Although Śukra is at first resigned to the death of Kaca, Devayānī persuades her father to revive him. So Śukra calls out to Kaca who, fearing for the life of his guru, replies to him quietly from Śukra's belly, where he now lies in pain, mixed with *surā*. He hints that Śukra should revive him, but Śukra explains that he himself will die if he does so. Devayānī is devastated by this dilemma: she loves both her father and Kaca. So Śukra offers to teach the art of reviving the dead to Kaca while Kaca is still inside his belly. Then, once he has been revived (killing his guru in the process), Kaca will in turn be able to revive Śukra with his new knowledge. Śukra teaches Kaca the secret, then revives him, and Kaca successfully revives his guru.

And now the *asuras*' evil plan has really backfired, for Śukra has thoroughly instructed Kaca in the secret of reviving the dead. At this point: .

> Led to deceit and a most terrible loss of consciousness because of drinking *surā*, and then seeing handsome Kaca whom he had drunk when deluded by *surā*,
>
> Then Śukra [here: Uśanas Kāvya] of great dignity, stood up enraged, desirous to act for the welfare of Brahmins and, being alarmed, spontaneously spoke this command:
>
> "From this day forth, whichever stupid Brahmin through folly shall drink *surā* will be despised in this world and the next as one devoid of righteousness, a Brahmin-killer.
>
> I have established this moral limit, a verbal boundary to the *dharma* of Brahmins in the whole world.
>
> May virtuous Brahmins, obedient to their gurus, the gods, and the people, all pay heed!"[83]

He summons the *asuras* and rebukes them, pointing out that their plan has failed. And Kaca returns to the gods.

When Śukra drinks the ashes of his pupil, we learn nothing about his state, but later, when he contemplates the horror of what happened, we're told that earlier he was not just deceived but also lost consciousness[84] and was stupefied/deluded (*mohita*) by the *surā*. This consequence is viewed as particularly dangerous for Brahmins, presumably because of the immense powers they are said to wield and their meticulous concern with ritual *dharma*. So Śukra makes a new rule: Brahmins shall not drink *surā*. If they do, it will be regarded as equivalent to killing a Brahmin—the most serious sin. After all, drinking did lead to the death of this Brahmin, namely Śukra. Although all the world is to take note of this new rule, it applies only to Brahmins. Yet the drink itself is not reviled in this text. *Surā*'s typical effects on people are mentioned, but Śukra does not blame the drink. Rather he establishes a new limit in the righteous conduct of Brahmins. The language used, etymologically, has spatial as well as moral/legal connotations, just as the equivalent terms do in English: *surā* is now beyond the pale, out of bounds for Brahmins.

As in the other myths explored in this chapter, a potent liquid has been assigned a new, enduring position in cosmic society, a status that also becomes constitutive for the persons involved: Brahmins. And who should be plying Śukra with the ruinous drink but *asura*s, whom we have seen connected to this drink already. Here, yet again, they lose their upper hand in a cosmic war through a failed plan involving *surā*. It is indeed a drink for the losers in cosmic society in these myths.

Both Śukra and Cyavana, who created Intoxication, are members of the same priestly clan of Brahmins, the Bhṛgus.[85] In both myths these Brahmins assert their autonomy, even their dominance—over gods, Kṣatriyas, and antigods. The Bhṛgus will not be pushed around by anyone. They will offer *soma* to whomever they want, and they will foil the evil, rather stupid plans of the *asura*s. Both men are threatened by powerful beings. In the resulting struggles, *surā* and Intoxication are powerful weapons. At the end of both stories, however, the Bhṛgu protagonists put *surā* and *mada* in their places. The question of who gets to drink *soma* and who can no longer drink *surā* are central in these Bhṛgu narratives, which, as Goldman notes, define "the group's place in the social and spiritual orders of brahmanical India."[86] The combined effect of the Bhṛgus' deeds in these stories is the orthodox status quo of these two drinks—*soma* and *surā*—in relation to gods, *asura*s, Brahmins, and Kṣatriyas. The drinks may be divine, but it is Brahmins who distribute them. The Śukra myth provides the final part of the picture, leaving us with the orthodox distribution of drinks that we have in our own time. What you drink defines who you are, and it was Brahmins who defined these boundaries of identity.

The changing reception of *surā* in brahminical traditions was presented as hypocritical by some opponents of Brahmin ideology, as we'll see later. There is also tension inherent in the Hindu concept of Surā the goddess. She is at once divine—the daughter of a god and accepted by the gods—and yet for the most part she is excluded from god-related patterns of consumption, and is often associated with the *asura*s, the enemies of the gods. The story of Śukra, however, opens up another perspective, that the *reception* of Surā, her acceptance and rejection by humans and other beings, is what varies; the drink/goddess is relatively straightforward. She does what she does, and people, gods, and *asura*s can take it or leave it. Arguably this introduces the possibility of rehabilitating her; perhaps one day Brahmins will recover their ability to accept and enjoy beautiful, powerful *surā*.

Balarāma and Liquor

The myths in the *Mahābhārata* that I discussed earlier in this chapter took place in the distant past, not in the "now" of the epic. But there is much within the main timeline of the epics that concerns drink. We must now consider Kṛṣṇa's brother, Balarāma, as well as the drunken self-destruction of Kṛṣṇa's clansmen, the Andhakas and the Vṛṣṇis.

We've already encountered Balarāma several times. He is the elder brother of Kṛṣṇa and carries a palmyra palm as a banner (though, as noted earlier, it may not always be connected to toddy); we also met him wandering drunk at a festival; and this book began with a verse in which drunk-stammering Balarāma is asked to provide blessings. The association between him and drink is not limited to written sources: early images of Balarāma often show him carrying a vessel for drink.[87] Moreover, in the *Arthaśāstra* agents disguised as ascetics devoted to Balarāma (Saṃkarṣaṇa) outwit people with a drugged drink; possibly they chose this disguise because such ascetics were associated with taking liquor.[88] This is not the place for a full exploration of Balarāma's connections to drinking, but we will look at a few more examples.[89]

One peripheral story describes how Balarāma met his beloved drink, here called Kādambarī. The word "*kādambarī*" (or *kādambara*) illustrates the complexity of alcohol terminology in Sanskrit. As we saw in the medical texts, *kādambarī* is one of the layers produced from the settling of *surā*. In practice, however, "*kādambarī*" was often used as a generic and flexible word for intoxicating drink, like "*madirā*" and "*vāruṇī*," especially in literary contexts. Thus, in one of the texts on drinking and erotics, we read that the juice of grapes is called *kādambara*.[90] The word suggests associations with the *kadamba* tree,[91] though in researching this book I did not see any recipes in the primary sources using parts of this tree for such a drink. The narrative here, however, provides one mythological explanation of the origin of this word.

The story comes from the supplement to the *Mahābhārata* called the *Harivaṃśa*, in which we learn the history of Kṛṣṇa.[92] In the vulgate of this text (not the critical edition), a story is included that explains why *kādambarī* the drink is called after the *kadamba* tree.[93] The episode depicts the start (or revival) of a lifelong association between drinking and Balarāma, who is sometimes said to be a partial incarnation of the divine serpent (*nāga*) Ananta—we encountered this snake earlier, uprooting the mountain used for churning the ocean. Significantly, *nāgas*, especially Ananta-Balarāma, are sometimes depicted drinking.[94] This story is similar in some respects to the Buddhist tale of the discovery of *surā*. Like the hunter in the "Previous-Birth Story of the Jar," Balarāma encounters drink while alone in the forest, drink that has spontaneously developed in a tree—a *kadamba* tree in this case. Whereas in the Buddhist tale the hunter and his friend hawk this evil drink around the land, thus lending their ignoble names to liquor, in the Balarāma story the drink is the goddess Vāruṇī herself, who has been waiting in the *kadamba* tree to serve Balarāma. The goddess and the others are his drinking companions here, and the scene is a romantic one:

> Then glorious, vigorous Balarāma (*Saṃkarṣaṇa*), looking like a mountain, wandered without Kṛṣṇa on the mountain peak. He sat down in the pleasant shade of a full-blown *kadamba* tree, being fanned by the pleasant, gently scented wind. And being refreshed there by this stream of wind, an odor produced from contact with liquor came, touching his nose.[95] Then thirst, produced of liquor (*vāruṇī-*), quickly entered him, and his mouth dried up like a drunkard's the day after. That mighty one was reminded of the ancient tasting of the nectar of immortality; then, thirsty and seeking intoxicating drink (*madirā*), he looked at the tree. Water that poured down from clouds in the rainy season had become delightful liquor (*madirā*) in a hollow of the blossoming tree. And he, that powerful one, overpowered with thirst, repeatedly drank it like one afflicted and, through folly, became unsteady in body. Drunk, his face had somewhat wavering eyes, with a reeling expression, looking like the autumn moon [i.e., bright white]. That which arose in the hollow in the *kadamba* tree is called "*Kādambarī*"; it is the embodiment of [the goddess] Vāruṇī, who is the churning stick of the nectar of immortality.[96] Knowing Kṛṣṇa's older brother to be drunk on Kādambarī, three divine women approached him, speaking sweetly: Madirā [liquor] embodied; and Kānti [beauty], beloved of the moon; and the goddess Śrī herself, the most excellent woman with the lotus banner. That goddess, her hands held forth in homage, approached Balarāma (*Rauhiṇeya*) who was bewildered, possessed of liquor [or "accompanied by Vāruṇī], and she [Vāruṇī] spoke these words: "Baladeva, heavenly lord, conquer the forces of the *daitya*s ["anti-gods"]! I, Vāruṇī, approach as your beloved wife. Hearing you had vanished forever into the [undersea] mare's mouth-fire, I wandered the earth as if my merit were exhausted, O bright-faced one! I dwelled on flower filaments, smeared on the mass of flowers, on fragrant creepers with clusters of flowers, O unshakeable one. In the cloudy season, I, fond of pleasure, concealed my own form, fused with the *kadamba* tree, seeking for you in your thirsty state. O sinless one, my father, Varuṇa, sent me, endowed with all excellence, to you, as at the churning of the nectar. As in the ocean and in the mare's mouth, I wish to be enjoyed by you—I hold you in esteem, my guru! I will not abandon you, O Ananta, even if you threaten me, O sinless one! I cannot bear to inhabit the worlds without you, O lord!"[97]

Then the other two goddesses address him. Beauty is also drunk and professes her love for him. Śrī provides him with his standard ornaments and garments—his single earring and dark blue silks.

Balarāma's encounter with Kādambarī is a love story, for Liquor has been pining for him. The two had met before, at the churning and apparently in the ocean, but, as is so often the case in Sanskrit literature, they were then separated. Balarāma too has been deprived, and as soon as he smells the distinctive odor of Liquor he becomes possessed by thirst—he is incomplete without his beloved. Now they are reunited, and she vows never to leave his side again. Brahmins may shun her, but she is welcome with this warrior, who does not just enjoy the taste of drink but loves Drink herself. Liquor's rightful place is by the side of mighty, plough-wielding Balarāma. The story has an enduring appeal, and in a later text the same story appears as a prelude to Balarāma's own *rasa* dance with the cowherd women, *gopīs*.[98]

Another passage, this time from the *Mahābhārata*, concerns Balarāma's drinking and offers a good opportunity to assess the chronology of drinks in the texts of early South Asia. When Arjuna has married Kṛṣṇa's sister Subhadrā, the people connected with Yudhiṣṭhira (Arjuna's brother) as well as those on Kṛṣṇa's side (the Andhakas and Vṛṣṇis) enjoy themselves with great drinking bouts (*mahāpānaiḥ*).[99] Just before this, in one manuscript tradition, we find the following passage:

> and then Baladeva [Balarāma], day and night, constantly [drank] wine (*madhu*) with his juniors, and excessively [drank] excellent Kāpiśāyana wine (*madhu*) made from grapes (*drākṣāprabhavam*), and pleasant *āsava* mixed with divine honey that was placed in vessels (*-bhājaneṣu*) made of ruby, sapphire, and other gems; and in drinking cups (*caṣakeṣu*) of the best gold and silver he drank *surā* . . .[100]

Balarāma leads this social, luxurious drinking. Although it's difficult to assign a date to the passage, the reference to wine—and to Kāpiśāyana wine at that—is telling. Also, the word *caṣaka* for "drinking cup" probably places this passage in the early-mid first millennium CE, at the earliest.[101] Kāpiśāyana is the precious imported variety of wine that we saw earlier; the word signifies "the best wine," like "Falernian wine" in classical poetry. Grape wine is most likely not mentioned elsewhere in the critical edition of the *Mahābhārata* (though honey *āsavas* are), and this passage thus brings Balarāma's drinking habits up to date with the prestigious drinks (or compositional repertoire) of a later period.[102] The drinkers, moreover, use cups and vessels made from gemstones, silver, and gold, another element found in the luxurious drinking of later literary texts.

Andreas Bigger has shown that Balarāma is not in fact frequently characterized as drunk in the *Mahābhārata*; rather, he is often described using words derived from the root "*mad*"—"intoxication"—in its broadest sense that includes frenzied passion and that, very significantly, also applies to rutting elephants (*matta*), who secrete a substance, musth, sometimes called *mada*.[103] The passage here, however, expands and complicates the presentation of Balarāma as a drinker in the epic, supplementing the sparse references in earlier versions. Evidently some people wanted to see more of this side of Balarāma, depicted in a way that reflected literary tastes of the early-mid first millennium CE.

Finally, let's look at some references from a later, highly literary poem. The *Śiśupālavadha* of Māgha (from the seventh or eighth century CE) concerns an episode from the *Mahābhārata* in which Kṛṣṇa and Śiśupāla come into conflict. Here, in a chapter describing a meeting in the council chamber (*sabhā*), Balarāma is described as follows (as translated by Dundas):

> By now Balarama was rolling his eyes; they were tinged
> with red from his drunken delight in wine, while their
> lids had been laved by Revati's moist kisses.
>
> . . .
>
> His breath was saturated with the aroma of wine (*madirā*), fragrant
> from being held in Revati's mouth as they kissed.[104]

Here Balarāma is not a warrior drinking with other warriors but instead bears the marks of "erotic drinking." Whereas the previous passage updated the types of drink he was being served, these verses portray Balarāma's style of drinking in the classical literary mode.

Balarāma's drinking, therefore, is chameleonic, adapted to whatever period or genre in which we find him. So what can we say about Balarāma and drink in general? First, the sheer fact that someone of such renown and status in epic and literary texts drinks liquor and gets drunk makes him an exemplar of acceptable, even admirable drinking. He is a warrior, a Kṣatriya—and, as we'll see, he is thus allowed to drink in the mature Hindu legal tradition so long as he avoids grain *surā*. He is immensely strong, and thus drinking is compatible with health and competence when done correctly. We often see him already drunk, fired up, intoxicated like an elephant in rut, and invincible. Balarāma is a mighty icon of (non-Brahmin) drinking culture, a passionate, elite warrior with rolling red eyes, moon-white skin, sapphire-blue robes, and a single gleaming earing.[105]

Krishna's Clansmen Are Destroyed by Drinking

Our final story tells us how drinking led the men of an ancient and important clan to kill each other. The people in question are the Yādavas, sometimes called the Andhakas and Vṛṣṇis, and this is the clan of Kṛṣṇa and Balarāma—though these two men are excepted from the slaughter. This story is frequently mentioned as an example of the dangers of drink, even for strong and noble people, and it is *the* proverbial tragic drunken misadventure mentioned in Sanskrit texts of many genres and periods.

The episode occurs toward the end of the *Mahābhārata*, when the great battle is over and the end of a world era approaches. Gāndhārī, the mother of the Kaurava brothers who were killed in the battle, has cursed Kṛṣṇa, declaring that he will be responsible for the killing of his own kin.[106] This mutual slaughter takes place thirty-six years later and is described in a short book, the *Mausalaparvan*, named after the club (*musala*) that plays a role in the killings. The place is Kṛṣṇa's city, Dvārakā, the capital of the Yādava clan.

It all starts with a joke that backfires. One of Kṛṣṇa's sons, Sāmba, has been adorned to look like a woman, and some Yādavas present him to some powerful visiting sages, asking them to name the sex of "her" future child. As we've learned already, sages are extremely powerful. The offended sages announce that Sāmba *will* give birth, but to an iron club by which the clan will destroy themselves. Kṛṣṇa and Balarāma will not be part of this slaughter, dying in other manners.[107] When Kṛṣṇa hears this, he recognizes that the destruction of the clan is coming. The next day, poor Sāmba does indeed give birth to an iron club. Attempting to escape their fate, the Yādavas crush it to powder and throw the powder into the ocean. Then an announcement is made in the city:

> From this day forth, *surā* and *āsava* are not to be made in all houses of the Vṛṣṇi-Andhaka clan here, by anyone living in this city.
> And should any man make drink clandestinely in any circumstances, he will be impaled on a stake he has made himself, together with his kin.[108]

I interpret this as a restriction on all grain-based and sugar-based drinks, and therefore on alcoholic drink altogether.

Despite these precautions, however, terrible omens appear and sinister Time/Death himself wanders in the town. Wishing to allow the curse to take its course, Kṛṣṇa suggests a journey to the ocean (*tīrthayātrām*), which turns out to be part pilgrimage, part festival.[109] The people prepare various things to eat and drink, including intoxicating drink (*madya*), and leave the city.[110] Installed on the coast with their food and drink, they start to enjoy themselves. The festival begins on an irreverent note when they offer food originally prepared for Brahmins, and which now reeks of *surā*, to monkeys.[111] Then the great group drinking bout (*mahāpānaṃ*) starts, with the sounds of hundreds of instruments and many dancers and actors.[112] Balarāma drinks, along with other Yādavas, in the presence of Kṛṣṇa (who appears not to drink).

Then one man, Sātyaki, rebukes another, Kṛtavarman, for his ignoble warrior conduct. The argument escalates, and Sātyaki ends up beheading Kṛtavarman with his sword in front of Kṛṣṇa.[113] He goes on to kill more men and is then assailed by others of the clan, who are "possessed by the intoxication of drink" (*pānamadāviṣṭāḥ*).[114] One of Kṛṣṇa's sons goes to Sātyaki's aid, but the two men are both killed in Kṛṣṇa's sight. Angered, Kṛṣṇa grabs a handful of grass that then becomes an iron club—the fateful club has returned.[115] With this he kills those before him. A general fight and slaughter breaks out, and any grasses the men grab become clubs. Sons kill fathers, and fathers kill sons. Thoroughly intoxicated/frenzied (*mattāḥ*), they destroy each other.[116] Kṛṣṇa, seeing his son Sāmba and other close kin killed, finishes the others off with his club, thus fulfilling the fateful curse and destroying all the men of the clan.[117]

Afterwards Kṛṣṇa returns to the city and arranges for the women to be protected. He then leaves and witnesses his brother Balarāma's "death": alone in the forest, Balarāma is in a state of yoga when a huge white serpent (*nāga*) emerges from his mouth. Kṛṣṇa also attains a state of yoga in the forest and is shot with an arrow by a hunter, who mistakes him for a deer.[118]

Within the narrative, all this destruction is necessary for the curse to be fulfilled. But when the episode is mentioned elsewhere, it is usually referred to as an example of tragic drunken loss. How do the story's events fit with drinking as represented in other early texts? First, drink is acceptable in this regal/warrior milieu. Yet it is still a cause of turmoil and violence, as we see when the people in the city, as a precaution, are forbidden to produce liquor. Then, when they all embark on the trip, the prohibition is abandoned for a festive occasion in a different location. This recalls the exceptional licenses for making drink mentioned in the *Arthaśāstra*. When the festival starts, it is called a great group drinking bout, and there is much dancing and music. Although temporarily prohibited in the city, the drinking at this festival is not considered sinful, as it would be for Brahmins. The drinking bout is thus *not* portrayed as an unusual and debauched event. Balarāma drinks, as do others, before the liquor loosens tongues and fighting breaks out.

But then these famous warriors, possessed by Intoxication, abandon *dharma*: fathers kill sons, and sons kill fathers. Even for those permitted to drink, and even for the most virtuous among them, intoxication is the cause of bad deeds because it creates a misalignment with reality and duty.

It is to this world of morality and duty, of *dharma*, that we will now turn.

CUP 7

The Filth of Grain and the Pain of Drink

Morality, Vice, and Law

In the *Mahābhārata*, in a speech on law and righteousness (*dharma*), a wise man called Vidura teaches the following:

> He who is afraid of doing what should *not* be done, of neglecting what *should* be done, and of untimely breach of counsel should not drink that which makes him drunk.[1]

In the same speech, the drunk man (*matta*) is mentioned first in a list of ten people who do not know *dharma* (righteousness).[2] Vidura also mentions other types of *mada*, "intoxication," which are similar to those in Kṣemendra's satirical version of the myth of demonic Mada: *mada* of knowledge (*vidyā-*), of wealth (*dhana-*), and of noble birth (*abhijana*).[3] These are the afflictions of people who are "stained" by *mada* (*madaviliptānām*). For good people, these same factors are practically and, rather ingeniously, *phonetically* the opposite of intoxication—they are forms of self-control (*satāṃ damāḥ*).[4]

With this speech Vidura neatly sums up the main problem with drinking as described in many sources from early India when it comes to morality, law, and social duty—that is to say, with *dharma*. A drunk person is inversely aligned with duty, doing not-to-be-done things and not doing things that should be done, as well as thoughtlessly botching complex social webs of discretion and loyalty. Where *dharma* is concerned, the drunkard's perceptual confusions and off-kilter laughing and crying are mere symptoms of a deeper moral misalignment with how they ought to act in the world. The lesson is to avoid drinking things that will make this misalignment happen to you.

In this chapter I present a survey of texts on the morality and legal theory of drink. What might otherwise seem abstruse legal distinctions should be easier to understand now that we're familiar with the contrast between grain *surā*, imported wine, and perfumed betel, just as nowadays we can easily reflect on the nuances of laws concerning moonshine, Champagne, and "handmade" vodka. We can even learn more about drinks and drinking practices from legal texts, though we should be wary of reading these materials as a window onto what people did (or were forbidden to do but did anyway). Not only do laws present

An Unholy Brew. James McHugh, Oxford University Press. © Oxford University Press 2021.
DOI: 10.1093/oso/9780199375936.003.0009

an idealistic vision of behavior and misbehavior, but, as Peter Clark writes, "Laws were often made to deal with localized or specific problems and simply to keep up governmental appearances; at all times legislation describes only a fractured image of social reality."[5] There is a regular legalistic announcement on the Chicago transit system that bans gambling—this local law exists not because authorities wish to suppress a general Chicagoan train-gambling tendency but rather because one specific gambling scam was common at a certain time.

I'll start with our earliest sources, the Vedas, before proceeding to texts on drinking as a vice—a passion of kings that needs to be moderated. Then I'll examine Hindu, Buddhist, and Jain texts on the laws and morality of drinking. At the end of the chapter, I present texts that challenge, satirize, or complicate the moral texts previously discussed.

The Vedas and Drink

Surā is mentioned in the *Ṛgveda*, which probably dates from the second half of the second millennium BCE.[6] Here the drink is associated with regrettable deeds, but we should be wary of assuming that it was prohibited to anyone in this earliest period—these hymns are not laws. Also, in one hymn we also hear of the benefits for the giver of the priestly gift at a Vedic sacrifice—"The benefactors won the right to the inner drinking of liquor (*antaḥpéyaṃ súrāyā*)"—which suggests that drinking was sometimes perceived as a good thing, though it's not clear what "inner drinking" implies.[7] The same verse mentions that "the benefactors won a bride who is richly dressed," so maybe the *surā* was associated with wedding rituals; certainly later Vedic texts on domestic rituals mention the use of *surā* in weddings.[8]

In one *Ṛgvedic* hymn, the poet addresses Varuṇa, god of commandments and of the authority of the king. Varuṇa is also associated with controlling the waters and, in later texts, is the father of the goddess Vāruṇī. The poet repents to Varuṇa, describing his misdeeds:

> This was not one's own devising, nor was it deception, O Varuṇa, [but rather] liquor (*súrā*), frenzy, dice, thoughtlessness.[9]

Note the association here of *surā* drinking with gambling, a related vice in later formulations. In another hymn there is a reference to the edible components of a *soma* sacrifice, which seem to create an internal disturbance:[10]

> When they have been drunk, they fight each other within the heart, like those badly intoxicated on liquor (*durmádāso ná súrāyām*).[11]

Thus *surā* incites violence, a common theme, as we've seen in the *Atharvaveda*.[12] Unlike *soma*, *surā* causes a *bad* form of *mada* here.

Another *Ṛgvedic* hymn, to Indra, reveals that habitual *surā*-drinkers don't respect that *soma*-drinking god. Stephanie Jamison explains that in this hymn, unusually psychological in tone, "the poet ponders the various different relationships that he and his people might have with Indra . . . with a brief and idiosyncratic characterization of some who don't have relationships with Indra":[13]

> You never take on a rich man for companionship. The booze-fueled (*surāśúvaḥ*) revile you.[14]

Surā clearly does not (usually) belong in a good relationship with Indra, yet it does belong in the gambling hall, as seen in some hymns from the *Atharvaveda* that reinforce the association with dice, another cause of "intoxication" (*mada*).[15] Yet in some *Atharvavedic* hymns *surā* is associated with entities said to contain glory and splendor (*varcas*, *yaśas*). Undeniably, *surā* has some attractions, even when it sometimes causes bad deeds:

> What glory (*yáśas*) [is] in the mountain, in the *aragárāṭas*, in gold, in cows, in *súrā* when poured out, [what] honey in *kīlā́la* [a sweet drink associated with *súrā*]—[be] that in me.[16]

Elsewhere, in a line similar to this, in another hymn *surā* (along with hills, mountains, cattle, and horses) is said to contain a figurative "honey."[17] The hymn as a whole requests union with glory—*varcas*—a valued concept connected to royal power in Vedic sources, and present in the water used in royal consecrations, which is, as Tsuchiyama writes, "imbued with the vitality inherent in the cosmic fluids of the heaven, or with the splendid power in the cosmic fire, the sun."[18] Notably, two of these *Atharvavedic* texts that mention *surā* in a more positive light were used in one version of the Sautrāmaṇī ritual to accompany the pouring out of *surā*.[19]

The splendor in *surā* was also said to be contained in desire-enticing entities later associated with the vices. In an *Atharvavedic* hymn connected to weddings, the Aśvins are asked to favor the woman with the glory (*varcas*) that is in dice, *surā*, cows, and the "backsides of courtesans."[20] As Whitney writes, the Aśvins here are asked to "give her all the attractions which these various seductive things are known to possess."[21] In another hymn, to produce mutual attachment between cow and calf, a man's connection to *surā*, along with meat, dice, and women (a list very close to the later, classic vices) is invoked as a model of intense attachment or "fastening."[22] Here *surā* is remarkably powerful, containing a splendor that generates passionate attachment in men (and that sometimes causes problems). For better or worse, *surā* in these hymns gets things happening in the human realm.

The association of *surā* with various misdeeds in these very early texts complicates our understanding of *surā* prohibitions. Although the ritual/structural explanation for *surā* prohibition is prominent in later Vedic texts (i.e., *surā* is the antithesis of *soma*), the *Ṛgveda* and *Atharvaveda* both present *surā* as bad for more mundane reasons. But there are two sides to things that cause *mada*, and *surā* was sometimes praised as impressively, dazzlingly attractive.

Later Vedic texts deal more with the relations of people and *surā* in ritual life (and priestly identity). An important issue here is keeping *surā* from Brahmins: "Therefore the Brahmin should not drink *surā* (*tasmād brāhmaṇaḥ surāṃ na pibet*)."[23] But, to complicate matters, various priests and the sacrificial patron were required to drink *surā* in the Sautrāmaṇī rite. There is evidence that some Brahmins were uncomfortable drinking *surā* even in such a ritualized context, and in the *Śatapatha Brāhmaṇa* we find a discussion of what to do with ritual *surā*:

> He drinks with [the mantra], "Whatever is mingled herewith of the juicy *Soma*,"—he thereby secures for him the essence [juice] of the effused [extracted] and the infused (*Soma*);—"which Indra drank with eagerness,"—for Indra, indeed, drank it with eagerness;—"that [essence] thereof [I drink] with propitious (*śiva*) mind,"—for unpropitious (*aśiva*), as it were, to a Brāhmaṇa is that drink, the Surā-liquor: having thus made it propitious (*śiva*), he takes it to himself;—"King *Soma* I drink,"—it is thus King *Soma* that comes to be drunk by him.[24]

Here we see the possibility of drinking *surā* once it has been ritually transformed into *soma*. The text adds alternate methods:

> Here, now, other Adhvaryus [a type of Brahmin priest in the ritual] hire some Rājanya or Vaiśya [i.e., not priests] with the view that he shall drink that [liquor]; but let him not do this; for, indeed, this *Soma*-drink falls to the share of the fathers and grandfathers of whoever drinks [the liquor] on this occasion. Having shifted three coals of the southern fire to outside the enclosing stones, he may there offer [of the liquor] with these [three] utterances . . .[25]

Other opinions circulated too.[26] In some texts the priests simply smell the *surā*—which is noteworthy in light of later prohibitions of smelling *surā* (which will be discussed later).[27]

In these texts, *surā* is already clearly articulated as something that Brahmins—Veda-knowing, (sometimes) *soma*-drinking priests—should not consume, with an exception being made for the Sautrāmaṇī ritual. By contrast, people considered to be Rājanya (chiefs, kings) and Vaiśya (concerned with trade and agriculture) can drink *surā*, according to some. Kṣatriyas (i.e., Rājanya) are said in another text to be produced from *surā*, which is the thoughtlessness (*mālvyam*) of Prajāpati (a creator figure).[28] Note that the fully developed *vaṛna* system of social classification is not found in the earliest Vedic texts, and even in later Vedic texts the system is still taking shape. Nevertheless, we see some patterns developing in terms of these roles, their designations, and the relationships of certain people to *surā*.

A connection between *surā* and violence is reiterated in later Vedic texts. In the *Śatapatha Brāhmaṇa*, in a discussion of adding the hairs of fierce animals to *surā* in the Sautrāmaṇī, it is stated, "He thus puts into the Surā what belongs to Rudra, whence by drinking Surā-liquor one becomes of violent (*raudra*) mind."[29] Also present is the theological dichotomy of *surā* versus *soma*, in which *surā* represents untruth, wickedness, and darkness, as opposed to *soma*, which represents truth, prosperity, and light.[30] Yet, despite the banning of *surā* for Brahmins and the association of *surā* with regrettable deeds, *surā* was, as noted, used in some later Vedic domestic rites, associated with marriage, women, and sexuality—a theme we see in the long term and something perhaps hinted at in the early references to the attractive splendor in *surā*.

There are several strands to the morality surrounding *surā* in these Vedic texts. First, we see the notion that drinking leads to violence and regrettable deeds, an idea present from the *Ṛgveda* onward. There is also the idea that *surā*, like dice and women, is extremely attractive to men (which can of course lead to violence, bad *mada*, and bad actions). Then there is the discourse in later texts about separating Brahmins and *surā*, which correlates to the opposition of *surā* and *soma* in Vedic ritual: the Brahmins, like the gods, are associated with divine *soma* as opposed to fighty, lustful, worldly *surā*. This tension, between a general worldly conception of drink as a vice and a prohibition framed in terms of theology and people's ritual roles, is also present in later Hindu texts on religious law.

The Royal Vice of Drinking—A Matter of Moderation

In this section I look at sources dealing with the dangers of drinking as a *vice*. Here drink is not stringently prohibited but rather, like gambling, is considered a practice that must not get out of control, especially where kings are concerned (though one text recommends total abstinence). In this context drink is not a sin, or a crime. As we saw in the *Atharvaveda*, *surā*, dice, and women contain splendor, and men can be strongly attached to them. But if a king drinks too much or too often, this can have disastrous consequences socially and politically. Moderation is key to the idea of vices, which we might nowadays think of as secular, social, or political problems.

"Vice" (also sometimes translated as "addiction" or "passion") is the English word most often used to translate the commonest Sanskrit word for these tendencies, *vyasana* (though other Sanskrit terms are sometimes used to denote the vices in lists of bad human tendencies).[31] Just like the lists of Deadly Sins in Western thought, there are standard lists of vices and sinful actions in early Indian texts. Henk Bodewitz defines these vices as "defects in one's character, wrong attitudes and passions," as opposed to "specific committed sins."[32]

As we saw earlier, three of the later classical vices (e.g., *surā*, dice, and lust for women) are associated with each other in the *Ṛgveda* and the *Atharvaveda*. Kingly vices are also found in the *Mahābhārata*. In the speech of Vidura quoted earlier, there are seven faults (*doṣa*) that destroy kings, the first four of which are women, dice, hunting, and drink.[33] Then come harshness of speech, harshness of punishment, and squandering wealth. Recall that the first four are the same things into which the demonic Mada, Intoxication, was deposited in the myth from the *Mahābhārata*. And another reference to that myth in the *Mahābhārata* explains that Cyavana's conjuring of Intoxication demonstrates the dominance of the Brahmin over the kingly Kṣatriya, who is apparently most threatened by Intoxication.

We also read of the vices (*vyasana*) that kings should avoid in the *Law Code of Manu*, probably from the second or third century CE.[34] (Manu's *Laws* contains a separate account of the sin of drinking, and we'll explore that material later.) According to Manu, ten vices arise from desire and eight from anger. This scheme is cleverly connected here to the three realms of human activity, *dharma*, *artha*, and *kāma*, in that attachment to desire-born vices (*vyasanas* from *kāma*) divorces the king from *artha* (wealth, power) and *dharma* (righteousness, law). Of the ten desire-vices, Manu states that the worst are drink (*pānam*), dice, women, and hunting—the four we saw earlier. Yet, though a king must not let desire and lust make him too attached to these things, there is no hint that drinking in moderation is bad or sinful.[35]

The *Arthaśāstra* likewise lists two classes of vices (*vyasana*), three from anger and four from desire, the latter being the same as Manu's most serious desire-based vices.[36] The section in question is most likely a later addition to the text, later than Manu.[37] As in the *Essence of Politics* (*Nītisāra*) discussed later, the *effects* of the vices are described. One notable problem associated with drinking here, and not mentioned elsewhere to my knowledge, is "attachment to skill in stringed instruments and singing, which destroys wealth." Is this because such skills were associated with the bedroom, seduction, or parties?[38] Bühnemann writes that the *vīṇā* is "played by several Hindu goddesses who are associated with the consumption of wine and intoxication."[39]

The *Arthaśāstra* contains a debate on the dangers of the vice of drink compared to those of the vices of women and gambling.[40] Kauṭilya concludes that drink is worse than women, but not as bad as gambling (which, he argues, is the worst vice). One scholar (Vātavyādhi), whom he quotes, claims that drinking is less serious than indulging in women, as drinking has some redeeming features: "But in the case of drinking (*pāne*), there is the enjoyment (*upabhoga*) of the objects of the senses, sound and so forth (hence the dangers of the lute?), giving gifts from love, paying respect to attendants, and removal of the exhaustion of work."[41] The author of this section of the *Arthaśāstra* disagrees with this positive assessment and gives a description of the dangers of drink that generally resembles the one found in the *Nītisāra* I quote later.

Yet vices have their uses according to the *Arthaśāstra*: one expert is quoted as saying that drinking can be exploited to tempt the prince and heir to rebel, thus testing him.[42] We also learn that a prince can be steered away from this vice by offering him what is no doubt an unpleasant "doctored drink" (*yogapāna*).[43] Later in the *Arthaśāstra* we read that debts run up through three of the vices (gambling, liquor, and love) need not be honored by the son or heir of the debtor.[44] The intoxicated debtor was apparently not himself, so the heir is not responsible for his deeds.

The *Essence of Politics* (*Nītisāra*) of Kāmandaki is an accessible and popular verse treatise on statecraft that collates and subtly innovates the political theory of early medieval India. It dates from sometime between the fifth and eighth centuries CE.[45] The author describes how vices (*vyasana*) can ruin the king and thence the state, drawing, in the case of drinking, on the repertoire of proverbially bad drunken episodes.[46] The *Essence of Politics* also mentions seven vices, classed according to their origin, with the now familiar four desire-vices:

> Harshness in speech and punishment, and the destruction of wealth—experts in the vices teach that these are the three vices that arise from anger.
>
> Hunting, gambling, women, and drink (*pānaṃ*)—these are the four vices that arise from desire (*kāmajaṃ*), as taught by experts in the vices.[47]

The results of abusing drink are:

> Vomiting, unsteadiness, loss of consciousness, nakedness, a lot of unrestrained chatter, sudden random calamities;[48]
>
> diminishing of life force; destruction of friendship; errors of intellect, learning, and judgment; dissociation with good people, and association with bad people; keeping company with worthless people;
>
> stumbling, tremors, drowsiness, and excessively frequenting women—these and more things constitute the vice of drink, very much reviled by good people.

> The Andhakas and the Vṛṣṇis, endowed with learning, morality, and strength, of untarnished reputation, went to their destruction through the fault of excessive drinking.
>
> And the blessed lord of yogis, the son of Bhṛgu, equal in intelligence to Bhṛgu, Śukra, ate his very own pupil because of extreme drink-intoxication.
>
> A man overpowered by drink becomes a person you cannot have dealings with, because he fails to engage in anything he engages in.
>
> A wise man can indulge freely in women and drink if in moderation, but not in gambling and hunting, as these are extreme vices.[49]

First come bodily and mental disturbances, together with behavior that causes public humiliation. Then we move to the bad social consequences. As examples, we read of two disastrous episodes: the Andhakas and Vṛṣṇis, and the sage Śukra, who drank his student's ashes. The author emphasizes that these drinkers were powerful and moral yet still undone by drink. Finally, a drinker is a messy wastrel who should be avoided, the zit on the pimple of uselessness.

From a similar period, a text on divination and rituals connected to military marches, the *Yogayātrā* by Varāhamihira (from the mid-sixth century CE), has some interesting things to say about the vices of kings, including drink.[50] Varāhamihira emphasizes the drunken confusion we see elsewhere: "He treats his mother like a wife . . . treats a well like a house . . . treats a king like a friend . . ." and so forth.[51] Nevertheless, Varāhamihira concludes that drinking is permissible when done on account of a visitation or a festival, or on the advice of a doctor, and when done discreetly, and so as not to injure the intellect.[52]

As should be clear by now, the vices apply particularly to kings, "Kṣatriyas" in the classical formulation. This does not imply that kings should therefore never drink, but rather that they should not become too attached to this pleasure and should drink in moderation. Drink ruins kings by damaging their bodies, minds, and reputations, and by bringing them into a circle of bad people. The same problems are described in texts that prohibit drinking altogether. For example, in some Buddhist texts, elements of the vice discourse and arguments for abstinence are closely aligned. Hindu and Jain laws add their own distinctive sectarian concerns.

I translate *vyasana* as "vice," but it's a complicated concept that we can understand in more than one way, as writers did in early medieval South Asia. Indeed, the classification and theorization of vices in the texts described here are strikingly well developed and varied.

In the famous collection of moral fables, the *Pañcatantra*, there is a sophisticated discussion and classification of royal *vyasanas*.[53] Here drink is one of a class of seven *vyasanas*, four of which arise from desire (*kāmaja*, including drinking) and three from anger (*kopaja*). These seven *vyasanas* are just one of five larger classes of root (*mūla*) *vyasanas*. The class that contains drink is in the root-*vyasana* called *prasaṅga*, meaning "attachment to, indulgence in, devotion to something." (Similarly, in the *Laws of Manu* the common root of the desire and anger *vyasanas* is said to be greed—*lobha*.)[54] The other classes of root *vyasanas* in the *Pañcatantra* are lack/want, revolt, affliction, and bad policy, showing that the scope of "*vyasana*" is sometimes very broad.

Drink and lust/desire belong together. Drink, itself desirable, inflames, fills with passion, is even sometimes red, a color associated with passion, and is a vital accessory to love-making—and hence ascetics must avoid it entirely. So isn't the attachment-rooted *vyasana*-of-desire simply an "addiction"? There is indeed some overlap with our modern-day concept of addiction, but there are also many differences.[55] In the Indian concept, the emphasis is not on the surrender or defeat of the will. Instead this is an active, repeated, desire-driven attachment to an object—*surā*, a woman, a deer, dice—that resists being totally mastered or satisfactorily attained. It's an intense passion that sets up a ruinous, endless chase (Buddhists might argue that most people's entire existences are characterized by a similar deluded chase).[56] The modern-day notion of a powerless "hijacked mind" that has become *dependent* on the object (e.g., a drug) has a different emphasis. And although, as we saw already, demonic Mada, Intoxication, is sometimes said to dwell in all four of these desire-*vyasanas*, *mada* is not possession but rather a transformed engagement with the world, a temporary frenzy. So the intoxicated king should rein himself in, stop himself doing this act, get his desires in order. The *vyasanas* associated with attachment/greed[57] have more in common with the seven deadly sins, particularly Lust, Greed, Wrath, and Envy. There is also something about the *vyasanas* of desire in particular that is strikingly concrete, as these "failings" involve the king doing a bodily action with respect to a physical entity (women, dice, drink, hunted animal). What "*vyasana*" does have in common with "addiction" and "sin" is that it is a variable and complicated concept, not easily translated, though I tend to favor "vice."

Although drinking is a major vice, literary texts do not abound in the drunken antics of kings, presumably because the king is often the protagonist and hero—he is more likely to be surrounded by charming tipsy women. In the chronicle of Kashmir, however, the *River of Kings* (*Rājataraṅgiṇī*), King Lalitāditya does get drunk along with the women of the harem one night (*madirākṣība*, IV.310) and orders his minister to have a certain town burned. The wise ministers stage a fake fire using horse fodder, and when the king sobers up he is filled with regret. Then the ministers tell him that the fire was staged, and he tells them never to follow orders that he gives while drunk.[58]

As we explore drink in what we classify as religious law, it will become apparent that the list of the four serious desire-vices that we've seen in this section resemble lists of major sins, such as the "great" sins given in some Hindu texts: killing a Brahmin, drinking liquor, stealing, and sex with a guru's wife.[59] Just like those sins, the royal vices deal with killing (hunting), the misuse of property (gambling), sexual behavior (women), and drinking (in excess). But where the vices are concerned, the king *can* do these things in a controlled way, at least according to some authors. And the consequences of the vices are worldly, related to the success or ruin of the king and kingdom, to *artha* as well as *dharma*. This is an expedient morality for the king and warrior, and the list of vices to avoid is emblematic of royal conduct (and misconduct) in the same way that codes enforcing abstinence from liquor are emblematic of Brahminhood.

Yet the lists of vices and of sins do contain what are arguably similar categories of deeds.[60] Setting aside the issue of the origins of these lists, I tentatively suggest we might see these sets of sins *and* of vices—sex, drinking, and so on—in their mature formulations functioning as a shared set of general categories that is variously adjusted for different groups of people. Sometimes the general category of deed is totally forbidden (Buddhist monks and sex), sometimes it is just restricted (kings and excessive indulgence in women). Sometimes transgression is seen as severe (as for Brahmins and drink) and sometimes less severe (Brahmins *smelling* drink).[61] The exact nature of the deed (murder; hunting), the scope of the category (all liquor; excessive liquor), and the perceived severity of transgression/prohibition is not uniformly intensified or attenuated for all the categories for a given group of people. Rather the sins/vices are individually adjusted in a manner that suits and even *defines* the group involved. Thus Brahmins are, among other things, partly defined by abstinence from drink, and Buddhist monks strongly defined by celibacy. Kings are defined as people who can indulge in all the categories of deeds so long as they do it with moderation (at least according to some texts).

To conclude, the lists of vices, dangers to kingly conduct, perhaps by extension to all Kṣatriya conduct, are richly theorized and contain echoes of themes (dice, *surā*) from early Vedic texts. Thus Brahminical and ascetic lifestyles by no means dominate thinking about drink in ancient India. Kings and warriors know a lot about dealing with intoxication, for better or worse, from our very earliest sources.

Normative and Legal Texts on Drinking from the Hindu, Buddhist, and Jain Traditions

Whereas the texts on drinking as a vice often suggested moderation, the texts that we'll examine now, texts that we would define as religious-legal today, mostly prescribe forms of total abstinence. If we use a broad definition of "normative or legal literature" from premodern India, the quantity of material available is enormous. I will examine just a few texts—Hindu, Buddhist, and Jain. Even this focused account is quite long, and readers should skip sections as they see fit.

The texts in this chapter are not laws as we think of them today. Rather they are theoretical, scholastic texts that list and sometimes justify duties and restrictions for certain groups of people. These texts present ideal models for how humans of a particular ritual group and/or social status (Brahmins, monks, Jain laypeople, et al.) ought to behave with regard to drink, offering examples of both good and bad conduct. Later Hindu texts, for example, discuss the intersections of caste, drinks, and other factors, providing a complex resource for thinking about what people should do, avoid, and how they should be punished or do penances in many situations. These texts are not just about actions but also about other texts, offering interpretations of key terms, ancient legal formulas, and reflections on the relative authority of other texts.

Hindu Laws on Drinking

There is an early statement of the sin of drinking *surā* in the *Chāndogya Upaniṣad*, from the seventh or sixth century BCE.[62] This passage is notable for mentioning three other sins later associated with drinking in Hindu law. (This is *śruti* because the *Upaniṣads* are Veda.) This is not a set of regulations, however. The verse is quoted after an explanation of the different paths a man can take when he dies. In order to avoid a foul rebirth, one should avoid certain actions:

> A man who steals gold, drinks *surā*,
> and kills a Brahmin;
> A man who fornicates with his teacher's wife—
> these four will fall.
> As also the fifth—he who consorts with them.[63]

We are not told to whom this applies, but it's likely that Brahmins are implied, as a king quotes this verse to a Brahmin, and the inclusion of a "teacher" implies Vedic studenthood, which in turn often, though not always, implies Brahminhood.

Dharmasūtras

Our next Hindu sources are the *Dharmasūtras*.[64] Composed primarily in concise aphorisms (*sūtras*), these texts probably date from the beginning of the third century BCE to around the beginning of the Common Era.[65] They deal with *dharma*, here meaning "accepted norms of behavior, ritual actions and rules of procedure, moral/religious/pious actions and attitudes (righteousness), civil and criminal law, legal procedure and punishment, and penances for infractions of *dharma*."[66]

As Olivelle writes, they "give us a glimpse, if not into how people actually lived their lives in ancient India, at least into how people, especially Brahmin males, were ideally expected to live their lives within an ordered and hierarchically arranged society."[67] The implied subject of most of the rules is a Brahmin male, and they cover his life from his Vedic initiation through his marriage, death, and ancestral offerings.[68]

What exactly does *dharma* mean here? To quote Olivelle again, the concept of *dharma*, a marginal concept in later Vedic literature, rose "to prominence within the religious discourse of India between the fourth and fifth centuries BCE in its assumption, along with other terms and symbols of royalty, by the newly emergent ascetic religions, especially Buddhism, and its use for an imperial theology by Aśoka in the middle of the third century BCE."[69] Over time, however, a Hindu tradition of hermeneutics called Mīmāṃsā developed a theological understanding of all *dharma* as being rooted in Vedic injunctions. In practice, however, much that is covered by texts on *dharma* is not contained in the Vedas, so that certain textual traditions (e.g., texts like the *Dharmasūtras*) and the practices of good people also came to be accepted as sources of *dharma*—though the rules relating to *dharma* were all supposedly contained in a now unavailable complete Veda. In the case of *surā*, as we saw earlier, prohibitions can indeed be found in the extant Veda, but those exhortations are arguably less central to Brahmin practice and identity than the prohibitions concerning *surā* to be found in later Hindu legal texts.[70]

In what is probably the earliest *dharmasūtra*, the *Āpastamba Dharmasūtra*, in a section on the life of a Vedic student who has returned home but (possibly) not graduated,[71] among the rules on food there is a total ban on intoxicating drinks: "All intoxicating drink is not to be drunk (*sarvaṃ madyam apeyam*)."[72] Moreover: "And likewise herbs for *kīlāla* [are forbidden]."[73] In Vedic texts "*surā*" is the commonest word for liquor: *surā* is used in the sacrifice, *surā* causes bad deeds, and *surā* is prohibited for Brahmins. Here a general term, "*madya*," is used, one that at least in later texts means all fermented alcoholic drinks. In addition, the word "all" is included, which reinforces the total ban on such drinks (and other *madya* substances, perhaps). Even herbs associated with *kīlāla* are forbidden—*kīlāla* being possibly a milder *surā*-like product, which is mentioned in other texts from before the Common Era, though it is not forbidden elsewhere, as far as I'm aware.[74] Perhaps this second rule is an attempt to dissociate the student from even the slightest whiff of *surā* culture.

The author of this text evidently understood brewing, for, when discussing items that Brahmins can never trade, the text lists sprouted rice and ferment (*tokmakiṇve*).[75] The next two items listed, long pepper and black pepper (*pippalimarīce*), are perhaps also forbidden owing to their use in brewing.[76] With its references to the sprouts (*tokma*) of Vedic brewing, the ancient *kīlāla* drink, and the *kiṇva*-ferment that dominates later brewing, this text encompasses two styles of brewing.

Elsewhere, though, in a section on acts that cause a loss of caste, Āpastamba mentions "drinking *surā* (*surāpānam*),"[77] a narrower restriction, closer to the terminology we see in other Brahminical sources. Āpastamba also describes a penance for the sin of drinking *surā*: "A man who drinks *surā* should drink burning hot *surā*."[78] Penances were voluntary ritual acts, designed to correct offences against moral order.[79] They had the power to repair the karmic damage of sinning as well as the social exclusion resulting from certain sins.[80] In addition to that fatal penance, Āpastamba quotes an opinion that such a sinner can undergo various hardships to remove the sin in three years.[81] The penance for drinking is listed alongside penances for three other major sins: killing a Brahmin, having sex with the wife of an elder/guru, and theft.

Those four *sins*, along with association with people who have done those sins, constitute the standard list of the "great sins," the *mahāpātaka*s, and serve as the principal framework for discussions of drinking in Hindu legal texts from this point onward. These sins not only have negative karmic consequences but also produce social exclusion (falling from caste).[82] Though *surā* was frowned upon in Vedic texts, references to drinking were not prominent there. Now, in a concise articulation of ideal conduct, drinking *surā* is put center stage with other sins that are destructive to Brahminhood.

The *Gautama Dharmasūtra* gives a rule for students, that intoxicating drinks are to be avoided, but adds that this applies specifically to Brahmins (*madyaṃ nityaṃ brāhmaṇaḥ*).[83] By implication, other students are allowed to drink? Gautama also lists drinking *surā* as a sin causing loss of caste, giving the same penance of drinking hot *surā*.[84] Yet he adds the qualification that there is a milder penance for inadvertent (*amatyā*) drinking of *surā*—thus bringing the question of intent into the picture.[85] Smelling the odor of a *surā*-drinker (*gandhāghrāṇe surāpasya*) also requires a penance—and indeed in later texts smelling *surā* becomes a "secondary" sin.[86] Gautama also adds a far milder penance for the sin of drinking *surā* (*surāpāna*) when the sin remains unknown to the public, as he does for other sins.[87] Again, sins, penances, and *surā*-avoidance are related to the public perception of the Brahmin community. Gautama also lists liquor-drinkers among the many types of people who are unfit to invite to ancestral-offering meals.[88]

The *Dharmasūtra*s of Baudhāyana and Vasiṣṭha come later, probably dating from after the mid-second century BCE and around the beginning of the Common Era respectively.[89]

With Baudhāyana, the regulations on drinking are expanded to deal with several other factors, such as *varṇa* ("class," sometimes translated as "caste") and gender. At the start of the text, Baudhāyana notes regional differences in conduct: actions may be acceptable in one region but not elsewhere (though he cites

Gautama's opinion that this moral relativity is not accepted universally).[90] In the north, one of the accepted customs is drinking *sīdhu*, sugarcane wine.[91] Recall that in the *Mahābhārata* the people of Madra and the Bactrians were characterized as drinking *sīdhu*. The word stands out in this *surā-madya*-centric textual world, as if all the laws were about "ale" and suddenly there was a regional exception for "cider."

The *Baudhāyana Dharmasūtra* is the earliest *dharma* text to mention the punishment (as opposed to penance) imposed for a Brahmin who drinks *surā*: branding with the *surā*-shop banner.[92] On the penances for drinking *surā*, Baudhāyana is similar to Gautama, but he quotes a verse stating that Brahmins, Kṣatriyas, and Vaiśyas (i.e., all the twice-born *varṇas*) who unintentionally drink *vāruṇī* (i.e., *surā*) need to undergo initiation again.[93] ("Twice-born" can refer to men who belong to *varṇas* who undergo an ceremony that permits them to study the Veda, i.e., Brahmins, Kṣatriyas, and Vaiśyas—though, rather ambiguously, the term is quite often a synonym of "Brahmin".) The same verses also impose a penance on someone who has drunk water that was left overnight in a vessel used for keeping *surā*. As with the penance for smelling a *surā*-drinker, the prohibition on *surā* increasingly takes on the characteristics of fastidious purity rules. The discourse of *surā* as a vice is absent here, and ritual purity, along with the overt separation of certain communities from *surā*, is ascendant.

Baudhāyana also discusses women and drinking, expanding and clarifying the scope of *dharma*. When a woman's husband (presumably a Brahmin or at least a twice-born) dies, she should abstain from honey, meat, intoxicating drink, and salt (*madhu-māṃsa-madya-lavaṇāni*—note the Ms) and sleep on the floor for a year—the implication being that in other circumstances she is permitted to partake of those four things.[94] Observe that the word used in this ascetic context is "*madya*," the generic term for liquor, and not "*surā*." Here we should recall the use of drink in domestic rites involving women, as well as the references to women preparing and consuming drink in early Buddhist texts. In a similar vein, in a section on marriage law in the *Arthaśāstra*, the woman who drinks when she is forbidden to do so must pay a fine, which also implies that women were not always forbidden to drink.[95]

When discussing purity, Baudhāyana notes various places and objects that are always pure, for example the hand of an artisan.[96] Without this qualification, life would be particularly difficult for Brahmins. All factories/workshops (*ākara*) are pure except *surā*-makers (*surākara*).[97] Given that *surā* and related substances are already forbidden for Brahmins, this explicit prohibition seems unnecessary—though perhaps, just as Catholic priests might avoid a lingerie department, Brahmins are required to steer clear of any place at all connected to *surā*.

The *Vasiṣṭha Dharmasūtra* foregrounds the grievous sins that cause loss of caste, including drinking *surā*.[98] It presents an even more nuanced treatment of penances for *surā*-drinking, dealing with intention as well as liquors other than *surā*. First, there are penances for "[deliberately] drinking an intoxicating beverage that is not *surā* and inadvertently [drinking] *surā* (*madyapāne tv asurāyāḥ surāyāś cājñāne*)."[99] The general term "*madya*" is contrasted with "*surā*" to clarify the legal status of the full range of drinks. In this case, drinking non-*surā* liquor (*madya*) on purpose is a sin of the same gravity as drinking *surā* by accident. Non-*surā* liquor is thus less condemned than *surā*, which is so forbidden that even unintentional drinking of it is a serious sin. Vasiṣṭha also gives instructions on self-purification after drinking water that has stood in a jar for an intoxicating beverage (*madyabhāṇḍa-*), and he finishes this section by turning to the most serious version of the sin of *surā* drinking: but if a twice-born repeatedly [drinks] *surā*, he should drink burning hot [*surā*]. It is said, "After death he is purified."[100] Not only does Vasiṣṭha mention the drinker's *varṇa*, the drink, and the intention behind the drinking, but it now matters if someone is a repeated *surā* drinker.

Then Vasiṣṭha describes the karmic result in the next life for the sin of drinking *surā*: one will have black teeth—an oral punishment for an oral sin.[101] In some Indian religious texts, sins are marked on the body in future births in a manner correlating to the body parts associated with the sin. Olivelle writes that, by extending the system of bodily marking for sins beyond the human practices of penance and punishment, "the upholders of the established order are able to anchor the moral and legal systems in the very working of the cosmos; they become naturalized."[102] However, what got naturalized in effect by these laws was the more "natural" side of penance and punishment, and the brand of the *surā*-shop banner, a product of social convention, is never reproduced on the cosmic level.

In a section on the purification of objects, we learn that earthenware (*mṛnmaya*) that has touched a variety of impure substances—including blood, urine, and intoxicating drink (*madya*)—cannot be purified by firing it again.[103] Liquor, in other words, is now being treated like any other impure substance.

Whereas Baudhāyana implicitly suggests that some women might drink liquor when married, the *dharmasūtra* of Vasiṣṭha clearly condemns Brahmin women who drink *surā*:

> When a Brahmin woman drinks *surā* (*surāpī*), gods do not lead her to the world of her husband; bereft of merits, she meanders in this very world and becomes a water creature or a pearl oyster living in water.
>
> . . .
>
> Half his body becomes out-caste when a man's wife drinks *surā*. No expiation is provided for someone half of whose body has become out-caste.[104]

The choice of words really matters in these texts. The woman, Brahmin in the first line and possibly twice-born in the second (or married into these classes), is obliged to emulate the *surā*-shunning practices of the community she belongs to. The rebirth as some sort of water creature is likely connected with the liquid nature of *surā*.

Finally, one penance in the *dharmasūtra* of Baudhāyana helps us see how Brahminical abstinence might have been experienced in a world where the production and availability of liquor was different from today. A purificatory observance, which can apply to someone who has drunk *surā* (among other sinners), involves drinking a gruel of barley (*yava*) for a period of time.[105] The Brahmin male observing this penance would find himself drinking gruel made of the very grains which, when malted and left for a few days (with the right additions), would make *surā*. One had to tread a narrow path between gruels and beers, and the main ingredients of *surā* were easily available in the very context where the drink was most forbidden. This also helps us to see why *kiṇva* was so important. The use of this ferment made the difference between a pure, respectable penance meal and the fatal penance of drinking boiling *surā*.

These early texts on *dharma* mainly regulate the lives and conduct of Brahmin males. Brahmins become ever more separated from even the smallest whiff of *surā* culture in these texts. In the earlier *dharmasūtra*s, the rules are quite simple—it's the later *dharmasūtra*s that analyze and expand the notion that "Brahmins should not drink *surā*," taking into account *varṇa*, gender, region, intention, and the drinks themselves. Yet the picture is not entirely consistent, nor would someone consulting one or more of these texts have a good sense of whether a king could drink grape wine, for example, or whether the king's wife could.

The move to encompass more people, drinks, and drinking scenarios in textual models of *dharma* has placed a lot of pressure on the word and concept of *surā*. *Madya*, "intoxicating/inebriating drink" potentially covers all alcoholic drinks, yet the tradition of early Hindu *dharma*, particularly the Brahminical *sin* of drinking and associated penances, is deeply rooted in the *surā* concept and language, and the scope of the term "*surā*" is the focus in many later Hindu discussions of drinking, as we see in the next section's discussion of Manu. A maxim associated with interpreting legal texts sums up why scholars needed to work on carefully defining *surā*: "in the case of an authoritative text that much only is to be accepted as covered by it which is expressed by the words used" (*yāvad vacanaṃ vācanikam*).[106]

Dharmaśāstra and the Law Code of Manu

The *Law Code of Manu*, or *Mānava Dharmaśāstra* (henceforth also "Manu," or "Manu's *Laws*") presents a complex and systematic account of *dharma* concerning liquor, with explanations for why drink is to be avoided. It's composed in verse, and Olivelle suggests that it was composed by one author, or at least that there was one "strong chairman with a committee of research associates."[107] The text was composed during the second or third century CE and has a clear agenda, namely the desire to re-assert Brahminical privilege in the face of significant patronage for Buddhists, and a drive to re-establish the alliance between kings and Brahmins.[108] This broadened context arguably explains the extended scope of this text with regard to drinking: the morality surrounding drinking for classes other than Brahmins is better clarified here than in the texts described in the previous section, as is the legal status of more drinks. One gets the impression that the author is engaging with a broader community, some of whom drank liquor. Manu treads a fine line between incorporating Kṣatriyas and Vaiśyas into the realm of *dharma* previously reserved more for Brahmins and creating space for established practices of drinking in other groups. Manu's nuanced perspective on drink informed scholarly, upper-caste Hindu reflections on this topic well into the second millennium CE. This text is probably the best-known *dharmaśāstra* today and also the most controversial, being a symbol of caste and gender oppression for some social and political movements in India.[109] For this reason it's worth highlighting at the outset that, while Manu has a Brahmin-centric agenda, he is relatively permissive when it comes to drink and does not push a teetotaling agenda on everyone (though being *omitted* from Manu's drinking regulations is hardly a mark of prestige).

Manu's most extensive discussion of drink comes in the chapter on penances for "great sins" that cause loss of caste.[110] After the list of main sins, he discusses secondary sins causing loss of caste, one of which is having sex with a woman who drinks intoxicating beverages (*madyapastrīniṣevaṇa*), thus reinforcing the social divide between drinking and non-drinking classes.[111] He also presents a category of lesser sins that cause exclusion from caste (*jātibhraṃśakara*), "milder" versions of the great sins: making a Brahmin cry; smelling liquor (*madya*) and substances that are not to be smelt; cheating; and sex with a man.[112]

In stating the penances for the sin of drinking *surā*, he makes some important comments:

> If a twice-born man in his folly (*mohāt*) drinks *surā*, he should drink boiling-hot *surā*; when his body is scalded by it, he will be released from that sin. Or, he may drink boiling-hot cow's urine, water, milk, ghee, or watery cow dung until he dies. Or, he may eat only broken grain or oil-cake once a day during the night for a full year, wearing a garment of hair, keeping his hair matted, and carrying a banner, in order to remove the guilt of drinking *surā*.
>
> *Surā* is clearly the filth of various grains; sin is also called filth (*surā vai malam annānāṃ pāpmā ca malam ucyate*). Therefore, Brahmins, Kṣatriyas, and

> Vaiśyas must not drink *surā*. It should be understood that there are three kinds of *surā*: one made from jaggery, another from ground grain, and a third from *madhu*. Just as drinking one of them is forbidden to the best of twice-borns [Brahmins], so are all. Intoxicating drink (*madya*), meat (*māṃsa*), and *surā* and *āsavas*[113] are the food of *yakṣas*, *rākṣasas*, and *piśācas*; they must not be consumed by a Brahmin, who eats the oblations to the gods. When a Brahmin is intoxicated, he may tumble into filth, blabber Vedic texts, or do other improper things. If the *brahman* [i.e., the memorized Veda] resident in a man's body is drenched with liquor even once, his Brahmin nature departs from him and he sinks to the level of a *śūdra*.[114]

Let's analyze this passage. Manu begins with the simple prohibition of *surā* and classic penance for drinking it—drinking hot *surā*. Yet he qualifies the drinking with *mohāt*—"out of folly or confusion." The term probably implies that the sinner has drunk intentionally but also out of stupidity.[115] Manu then gives other penances for this sin. Commentators explain that these are for lesser versions of drinking, such as unintentional drinking.[116]

Manu then states which liquors are prohibited for which classes. He first explains that *surā* is the filth (*mala*) of grains/food (*anna*), and sin is also called filth (*mala*).[117] This may also allude to the fact that brewing with saccharifying molds is a somewhat funky process, a controlled rotting. Then Manu names the three "twice-born" classes—Brahmins, Kṣatriyas, and Vaiśyas—as people who should not drink this grain-based *surā*.

After this Manu does something clever, momentous even, in the history of Hindu liquor laws.[118] He presents a new definition of the word "*surā*," including not just grain drinks but drinks made from jaggery[119] and *madhu* (*mādhvī*). These three, legally defined varieties of *surā* are forbidden to the "*best* of twice-borns," namely Brahmins, and thus implicitly they are *not* forbidden to Kṣatriyas and Vaiśyas.[120] The line is worth quoting again as we shall see variations of it several times later on:

> ***gauḍī paiṣṭī ca mādhvī ca vijñeyā trividhā surā* |**
> *yathaivaikā tathā sarvā na pātavyā dvijottamaiḥ* || Manu 11.95.

Which I translate very literally as:

> **Jaggery-based and grist-based and *madhu*-based: *surā* is understood as threefold.**
> Just as for the one [type], likewise all of them are not to be drunk by the best of twice-borns (= Brahmins).

The commentator Medhātithi (from the ninth century) explains, "The use of 'best of twice-borns' here has the purpose of permitting intoxicating drinks (*madyānujñānārtham*) for Kṣatriyas and Vaiśyas. And in the *Mahābhārata* the Bhāratas and Yādavas are described drinking intoxicating drink (*madya*) . . ."[121] Medhātithi then quotes the famous epic line that I consider later, describing the Kṣatriyas Kṛṣṇa and Arjuna as having drunk *madhvāsava*, which is certainly not made from grains, however we understand it.

Concise as Manu 11.95 may be, it ingeniously expands and clarifies the prohibition for Brahmins, while also bringing Kṣatriyas and Vaiśyas into the respectable fold of *surā*-abstinence, in a limited way. Śūdras (and presumably all other categories) are allowed to drink what they want, yet they are denigrated for drinking. Yet, according to other texts, Śūdras could still commit other types of offences with *surā*: they could disregard the regulations we saw for the *surā* trade in the *Arthaśāstra*, and they could violate the purity laws by causing a Brahmin to consume forbidden food or drink, including *surā*, the latter defilement being punishable by death according to some sources.[122]

Manu's definition of *surā* was developed over the centuries through textual additions, transformations, and commentarial interpretations. I shall resist exploring all the commentaries on this one verse—but consider just two facets of the discussion, the terms "jaggery-based" and "made from *madhu*." "Jaggery-based" might seem clear enough, but does it include liquor made from uncooked sugarcane juice, which is not jaggery though it comes from the same source? And what about *maireya* containing jaggery? *Surā* "made from *madhu*," Manu's *mādhvī surā*, is even more ambiguous, though this may have been deliberate.[123] The commentary of Medhātithi (possibly from Kashmir, a region associated with grapes and wine) interprets the phrase as meaning "grape wine," and others understand it as meaning mahua drink or honey mead, drinks that might have been associated with different regions and social groups.[124] Of course, legal ambiguity can be both desirably permissive and dangerously capricious.

Manu then turns to *madya*, "intoxicating drink," in general, explaining why drinking is bad and connecting some ideas that we saw in earlier texts on vices to the laws on drinking, particularly as it applies to Brahmins. We learn that *surā* and *āsava*s, as well as meat, are enjoyed by various "lowly" supernatural beings, and that the Brahmin who eats the food and drink offered to the gods should therefore not take alcohol. As we saw earlier in this book, the beings called *yakṣa*s are sometimes associated with drinking, and the other beings mentioned here are connected to drink in one medical text.[125]

Although Manu's vision of dharmic society involves surprisingly little prohibition of liquor for the populace at large, Brahmins are the exception. Not only should the Brahmin keep his body ritually pure because he shares in divine offerings, but if he gets drunk he will blabber the Vedas so that they can be heard by people who have no right to hear them, and do improper things.[126] Given that the memorized Vedas are in some way contained within the Brahmin, drinking *surā* effectively soaks these sacred texts in the impure, intoxicating filth of grains, causing the Brahmin's Brahmin-nature to depart from him permanently. The commentator Medhātithi explains here that the memorized Veda (*brahman*) lies in the heart, and in one medical text earlier we saw that the heart is precisely where liquor goes (bearing in mind that the "heart" is also somewhat of a mind concept). *Surā* thus stains and exposes to all ears the internalized Veda.

Later, Manu has more to say about drinking in a section that may be an early editorial interpolation. This verse supplements what Manu has said thus far with a statement on the drinker's intention:[127]

> When someone drinks *vāruṇī* inadvertently, he is purified only by undergoing Vedic initiation. If he drinks it intentionally, no penance is prescribed; its penance ends in death—that is the settled rule.[128]

Again, *surā* causes one's Brahmin-ness to vanish, even when drunk by accident. Not only is abstinence constitutive of Brahmin public morality, but its violation washes away that identity altogether. A tradition of abstinence common to other ancient ascetic groups (see Buddhism and Jainism sections later in this chapter) is thus thoroughly Vedicized, Brahminized.

There follow penances for various related sins such as drinking water that has been kept in a *surā* jar or intoxicating liquor vessel and for a *soma*-drinker who smells a *surā*-drinker, collating many previous developments in legal theory to create a rich resource for thinking about drinking.[129] As Medhātithi explains (on Manu 11.147), we now have several factors in play for Brahmins alone: drinking intentionally or not, drinking *surā* made from grains as opposed to other drinks. And Medhātithi introduces the issue of drinking once or repeatedly. The law has become very complex indeed, and Medhātithi here lays out six different scenarios combining these various factors.[130]

Another line from Manu is worth noting. In a section on forbidden food, at the end of a passage on eating meat, Manu makes the following general statement:

> There is no fault in eating meat (*māṃsa*), in drinking intoxicating drink (*madya*), or in having sex (*maithuna*); that is the natural activity (*pravṛtti*) of creatures. Abstaining from such activity, however, brings great rewards.[131]

These activities are permitted and even natural, though ideally avoided. This declaration seems to undo much of what Manu has stated elsewhere regarding drink, though, according the commentator Medhātithi, drinking *madya* here applies only to "Kṣatriyas and the rest," that is, everyone apart from Brahmins.

Madya, "intoxicating drink," is the most general term we see in these texts. The word denotes all liquor and makes a useful contrast with "*surā*" in its narrower senses. Yet I suggest that in some passages "*madya*" has other distinctive connotations. In the *Āpastamba Dharmasūtra*, we learned about the total avoidance of *madya* in a section on a Vedic student who has returned home.[132] In the *Dharmasūtra* of Gautama, the rule on *madya*-avoidance was also given for students. A student living with a guru is not only celibate but must also avoid all manner of other pleasures—perfumes, dancing, and so on—meaning that studenthood is a time of enhanced asceticism. The word *madya* was also used in describing the ascetic regime of the widow in Baudhāyana (though arguably there were alliterative factors at play there too).[133] Thus the word seems to have been used particularly in descriptions of liquor abstinence during specific ascetic periods in life, such as studenthood and initial widowhood (although the Brahmin is never permitted drink, student or otherwise). Then, in the line quoted, Manu lists *madya* with meat and sex as things that are common and natural but ideally avoided. I tentatively suggest, therefore, that *madya* sometimes has the connotation of an indulgence, as opposed to the caste-specific sin of drinking *surā*, which has roots in the ritual life of the Brahmin male. (*Madya* implies intoxication, whereas *surā* is a particular *substance* with ancient Vedic pedigree.)

Overall, Manu presents a lucid, comprehensive synthesis of most of the drink variables discussed in earlier dharma texts. He gives the ancient word "*surā*" an enduring new definition: a threefold nature expressed in one memorable verse. The verse very clearly brings two other classes, or *varṇas*, into the respectable, Brahmin-like fold of *surā* abstinence, while permitting them to continue drinking what were probably even more prestigious drinks at the time—wine, mead, *maireya*, and so on.[134] Manu is therefore permissive with respect to alcohol, at least where non-Brahmins are concerned, and this text sets a precedent for a wider Hindu legal discourse that lists many drinks that everyone apart from Brahmins can drink. What started out in the earliest texts as a rather narrow law concerning drinking *surā*, largely connected to a priestly lifestyle, has now become a general theory about all varieties of drinks for all the "upper" classes. At its heart of the law is the separation of Brahmins and *surā*, with echoes of this among Kṣatriyas and Vaiśyas. The other, "lower" classes are excluded from this respectable, *dharma*-text-regulated abstinence. Unless, of course, they elect to avoid drink, but that would be their own choice and would by no means include them in the prestigious classes of people who *must* abstain.

(In the following two subsections I explore some extra texts on Hindu law and drink. All but especially interested readers should skip ahead to the sections on Buddhism and Jainism.)

Later Dharmaśāstra Texts

I'll now present a sketch of some later texts and commentaries. The *Vaiṣṇava Dharmaśāstra* (or *Viṣṇusmṛti*) builds on Manu's writing on *surā*. Unusually, we know the time and place of the composition of this *dharmaśāstra* fairly well. It has a strong Vaiṣṇava (i.e., Viṣṇu-related) affiliation and was composed in Kashmir probably between the sixth and eighth centuries CE.[135] The verses on drink, however, were possibly added at a later period, between the seventh and twelfth centuries CE.[136] Whereas in Manu the permission to drink for Kṣatriyas and Vaiśyas was implicit, here there is an explicit statement that these two *varṇas* may "touch" these drinks. The verses are contained in a section on miscellaneous sources of impurity:

> Jaggery-based and grist-based and *madhu*-based: *surā* is understood as threefold.
> Just as for the one [type], likewise all of them are not to be drunk by twice-borns (*dvijātibhiḥ*).
> That which is made from mahua flowers, made from sugarcane, made from wood-apple,[137] made from jujube,[138] made from dates[139] and jackfruit, grape juice, made from honey, *maireya*, and produced from coconut[140]—these ten intoxicating beverages are impure for Brahmins, but Kṣatriyas and Vaiśyas are not defiled by touching them.[141]

Note that the first verse is taken directly from the *Law Code of Manu*, with the possible change of one word. If we accept the readings of Olivelle's critical editions, this text contains a significant modification, or at least reflects an alternative textual tradition. In this text, if we understand the ambiguous "twice-born" in its broadest sense, then all three twice-born *varṇas* are forbidden to drink all three types of *surā*.[142] And whereas the verse of Manu addressed only a limited number of types of drinks, at least without commentarial unpacking, the second verse here covers what must have been almost every type of non-grain drink available at the time. Possibly this expansion is due to regional variation and/or chronological changes in what people drank. The ten extra drinks are all forbidden to Brahmins, so for Brahmins this author has vastly expanded, or at least clarified, Manu's restrictions. Yet, like Manu, the author/compiler of these verses has simultaneously relaxed the rules for Kṣatriyas and Vaiśyas, at least if we understand the reference to "touching" as implying drinking, as does the seventeenth-century commentator Nandapaṇḍita.[143] Indeed, if we interpret the first verse as expanding the *surā* prohibition to all twice-borns, the next verse is necessary if Kṣatriyas and Vaiśyas are to be allowed to drink at all. Presumably the appeal of this interpretation of Manu was that now all twice-born *varṇas* had to avoid all types of *surā*, and Brahmins additionally had to avoid the other named drinks—a clear list that was easier to deal with than Manu's ambiguous terms. Yet, with this expansion, what do the two non-grain types of forbidden *surā* consist of? The longer list includes sugarcane, honey, and grapes! Not surprisingly, the commentator Nandapaṇḍita has to work hard to reconcile this inconsistency, and to make things even more complex the three types of *surā* are broken down into subvarieties in some texts, such as the *Hārītasaṃhitā*, that he quotes.[144] When glossing the longer list of drinks, he therefore explains the difference between such drinks as *forbidden* jaggery-*surā* and *permitted* sugarcane-*madya*, explaining that: "'made from sugarcane' (in the longer list) means produced from sugarcane—'jaggery-based' liquor excepted." Nandapaṇḍita quotes extensively from other sources, showing the extent to which commentary on the "threefold *surā*" had developed by his time, and how many texts Hindu scholars had at hand for discussing drink by the seventeenth century. We should bear in mind, however, that in Nandapaṇḍita's time alcoholic distillation was probably common. This may have introduced another distinction in people's minds—between arracks made from grains and non-distilled grain-drinks like *handia*, a distinction that must have applied to drinks made from almost all substances. Was "*surā*" possibly "hard liquor" by the seventeenth century?

A famous early-twelfth-century commentary by Vijñāneśvara (the *Mitākṣarā*) on a *dharmaśāstra* called the *Yājñavalkyasmṛti* provides us with an efficient summary of part of the problem, in a section on penances:

> Here we should consider this matter: does the word "*surā*" have the conventional meaning of the whole class of intoxicating drinks (*madyamātre*); or just the sense of the three: jaggery-derived drink, honey-derived drink, and grist-derived drink; or just the sense of ground-grain-derived drink?[145]

Note how Manu's threefold *surā* frames the discussion, in which Vijñāneśvara considers lists of drinks provided in other *dharmaśāstras*, including the list of ten "extra" drinks from the *Vaiṣṇava Dharmaśāstra* that we saw earlier.[146] He also quotes a list of twelve drinks from the *Pulastyasmṛti* (from possibly the mid-first millennium CE) of which only quotations survive, and which has not ten but twelve types of intoxicating drink (*madya*):[147]

> Jackfruit wine, grape wine, mahua drink, date drink, [palmyra palm?] toddy, sugarcane drink,
> Honey drink, *saira*,[148] *ariṣṭa* [a herbal drink], *maireya*, and the drink from coconut [water or sap?].
> One should know these eleven intoxicating drinks (*madyāni*) to be the same, but the twelfth, the *surā* intoxicating drink (*surāmadyam*), is the worst of all.[149]

Once again we see just how many drinks educated people were aware of in the first millennium CE in South Asia—and the project of listing and classifying these drinks was key to the Hindu laws concerning drinking. In the absence of a unifying concept of alcohol-as-substance, the best way to strive for legal clarity was to list all known drinks, just as we do with drugs today in the absence of a substance that unites them all. Ritually, medicinally, and legally, what intoxicating drinks were made of determined how they should be treated. Given that, for Kṣatriyas and Vaiśyas, the difference between a sin or a permitted pleasure came down to "grain or grape," Hindu legal scholars were obliged to treat all drinks in terms of their ingredients.

Returning to Vijñāneśvara:[150] having stated the problem and discussed the varieties of liquor, he mentions the passage from the *Mahābhārata* in which Kṛṣṇa and Arjuna have drunk intoxicating drinks ("Vyāsa also permits . . ."). Evidently this was a crucial example of permitted drinking for the Kṣatriya, possibly in the wake of Kumārila's analysis (see the following section). He discusses whether the prohibition and penance applies to children and the uninitiated before concluding:

> The drink made from ground grains is prohibited as of birth for the three *varṇa*s [i.e., Brahmins, Kṣatriyas and Vaiśyas]. And for Brahmins, the whole class of intoxicating drinks is also prohibited from birth. And for Kṣatriyas and Vaiśyas there is never a prohibition of intoxicating drinks made from jaggery and the rest [*gauḍyādimadya*, i.e., Manu's extended definition of *surā*]. For Śūdras there is no prohibition of drinking *surā*, nor a prohibition of intoxicating drinks.

To sum up, the earliest sources of Hindu law contain simple and clear rules that Brahmins should not drink *surā* (the *madya* term is seemingly more reserved for ascetic states), yet it was far from clear whether other drinks were covered by the word "*surā*." As the tradition developed, authors and commentators addressed this uncertainty, as well as the roles of intention, age, and gender. Later Hindu legal thinking on drink becomes very complex, covering a large part of society and all conceivable drinks. Throughout, Brahmins remain defined as people who must not take any liquor, but the remaining population was permitted to drink many types of drinks. Twice-born classes, initiated into the Vedic tradition, were prescribed Brahmin-like conduct with respect to *surā*, but not to other drinks. Grain *surā* was especially vilified, perhaps because of its central place in the earliest prohibitions, in the rituals of the Vedic priest. This category, which possibly included distilled versions at a later date, was permitted in these laws only to "lower" *varṇa*s in Hindu law. As we've seen, *surā* culture was quite advanced, yet in Hindu law this common drink went remarkably unlegislated, religiously at least, for what must have been the majority of the population in many times and places.

Drunken Role Models and How We Know Dharma

Manu's analysis of *surā* crops up in a famous discussion of ethics and epistemology. Mīmāṃsā is a Hindu philosophy concerned with how one should interpret texts, in particular the Vedas. The Mīmāṃsakas consider the Vedas to be a valid, eternal, authorless authority on *dharma*. They proclaim that they wish above all to know *dharma*, defined as "a desirable thing [*artha*] indicated by a scriptural command [*codanā*]."[151] Only the Vedas can be a source of knowledge of *dharma* as it involves the future and supernatural results of action, and thus cannot be known through perception, which gives knowledge only of present objects. This means that such knowledge as "Brahmins must not drink *surā*" can be derived only from scripture. However, not everything people ought to do is covered in the Vedas, at least what is still available of them. Hence, in the foundational *Mīmāṃsāsūtra*, there is a discussion of the status of human-authored "texts of recollection" (*smṛti*), such as the *Law Code of Manu*.[152] These are considered authoritative, since we can infer that the injunctions in them were derived from Vedic texts that are no longer available.

Another source of *dharma* knowledge is social custom, or the actions of good people (which should also theoretically align with the *dharma* in a Vedic text whether or not that is now accessible). But the social customs of good people might sometimes appear to infringe *dharma*. Kumārila (from the seventh century CE) discusses this problem in the *Tantravārttika*, a commentary on a commentary on the *Mīmāṃsāsūtra*: what can we do with reports of exemplary good people doing things that seem to infringe *dharma*? Kumārila presents an imaginary opponent who claims that since some good people do bad things, their actions should be rejected as a basis for *dharma*. One of the examples that this opponent mentions is from the *Mahābhārata*, when Kṛṣṇa and Arjuna are drunk on *madhvāsava* ("honey *āsava*," though you can read it as "wine and *āsava*" and might well do so after a certain date, when "*madhu*" was used for grape wine).[153] If these two men are indeed sinning, then the theory that the behavior of good people is in line with *dharma* is undermined. Kumārila, in response, must show that this episode aligns with texts on *dharma*, and even with the Vedas, in order to maintain that the deeds of good people are valid sources of information about what people ought to do, and not in conflict with Vedas (though note that Kumārila rejects the notion of a totally lost Veda).[154]

His explanation comes down to *varṇa* and to the beverage that Kṛṣṇa and Arjuna are drinking—which is to say, to Manu's version of *surā* law. In the *Mahābhārata*, when the Kauravas are discussing the possibility of avoiding a great war with the Pāṇḍavas, a man called Saṃjaya visits the Pāṇḍavas, one of whom is Arjuna, and who are supported by Kṛṣṇa. Saṃjaya then reports how Arjuna and Kṛṣṇa appeared when he found them:[155]

> Both were drunk on *madhvāsava*, both were smeared with sandalwood;
> wearing garlands and the best garments, they were both adorned with divine ornaments.[156]

In dealing with this line, Kumārila first refers to Manu. He explains that while grain *surā* is prohibited to all three twice-born *varṇas*, the drinks called *madhu* and *sīdhu*, made from grapes and sugarcane respectively, though prohibited for Brahmins, are not prohibited for Kṣatriyas and Vaiśyas.[157] Kṛṣṇa and Arjuna are intoxicated on *madhu* and *āsava*, which Kumārila interprets as wine and a sugarcane drink, so there is no transgression of *dharmaśāstric* law here.[158] Taking his argument to the ultimate authority, he argues that a particular Vedic text, read in light of Manu, implies that drink is prohibited for Brahmins but permitted for Kṣatriyas.[159] Therefore the actions of Kṛṣṇa and Arjuna on this point are, in fact, supported by the Vedas. Through analysis of the drinks themselves, combined with Manu's laws and a line from the Vedas, Kumārila demonstrates that these good people were not infringing *dharma*.

Kumārila's solution is clear and orthodox. Readers of this book could most likely have made the same points themselves, from what we have seen already. Kṣatriyas drinking in the epics are doing nothing legally wrong according to Manu and the Vedas. As we know, this does not mean that Kṣatriya drinking always ends well (i.e., it can be a vice), and of course the general idea that drinking was best avoided co-existed with the technicalities of the law.

Before we leave Hindu law, let's consider an aphorism:

> Woman, wine, wealth: *surā* is understood as threefold.
> One intoxicates when you merely see her, one when it is drunk, and the other through excessive hoarding.[160]

Ingeniously, the verse combines traditional vices (drink and women) with the types of *surā*. Manu's "threefold *surā*" must have been familiar to many scholars and students, and perhaps this line was intended to be humorous for such an audience. The three things listed intoxicate because they are *surā*, and they are called *surā* because they intoxicate. As with other ideas we'll encounter later on, this thought is woven on Manu's framework.

Buddhism and Drinking: Bad Conduct, Reputation, and Intention

Indian Buddhist texts on the morality of drinking are also extensive, and I shall give just a brief survey here. Some scholars of early Indian Buddhism use materials that survive only in Tibetan and Chinese, but I will not for the most part consider those texts. Fortunately, previous scholars have also explored liquor in Indian Buddhism, and I largely rely here on the sources they've highlighted.[161]

The Precept Concerning Drinking Liquor

Probably the most well-known Buddhist engagement with drinking is the moral precept (*śikṣāpada*) by which observant Buddhists undertake to abstain from drink. These Buddhist precepts guide moral behavior, and they constitute one of the foundations of spiritual attainment. There are three sets of precepts, which are vows to abstain from certain practices. The set of *five* precepts, taken by laypeople and monastics, consists of vows to abstain from (1) killing, (2) stealing, (3) sexual misconduct, (4) lying, and (5) intoxicating liquors. Building on these is a set of eight precepts taken by lay Buddhists who wish to undertake greater moral training. Monastics and novices (who are also subject to extra, monastic rules: *Vinaya*) take on a set of ten precepts that build on the first five, with slight modification.

In ancient India, abstinence from drink was an observance common to ascetics and certain groups of sexually and economically active laypersons, such as Brahmins, Buddhist laypeople, and Jain laypeople—a conspicuous distinction that separated these people from certain substances and social spaces.[162] Earlier I noted parallels of sorts between the classic vices (hunting, gambling, women, and liquor) and the great sins in Hinduism, suggesting that we see in these lists a shared set of moral topics inflected in different ways for different groups (with sometimes harsh speech or lying included too). In the Buddhist and Jain cases, abstinence from drink is an enhanced, publicly observable moral discipline for laypeople, a form of respectable conduct shared with monastics and ascetics.[163]

The Buddhist precept about drinking is the fifth one, in which a layperson or a monastic takes on the precept to abstain from "the state of heedlessness caused by [or "associated with"] the intoxicating drinks *surā* and *maireya* (*surā-maireya-madya-pramāda-sthāna*)."[164] This formula is translated in various ways in contemporary Buddhist texts, as a quick search of the internet will show, but such translations often elide or modernize the elements of *surā*, *maireya*, and *madya* for contemporary relevance. Here I am interested in how this phrase would have read in a world where people actually drank *surā* and *maireya*, or where *maireya* was perhaps an archaic yet somewhat familiar word, like "hock" in today's English.

This Buddhist formula is more complex than the earliest Brahminical regulations. Along with the ancient word "*surā*," "*maireya*" is included, a word and a drink that, as we saw earlier, appeared several centuries BCE and was prominent for many centuries. The Buddhist precept (also the monastic rule—see the following section) is thus markedly different from Hindu law, and right from the start, in words attributed to the Buddha, it includes two drinks, *surā* and *maireya* (though one Buddhist text has a threefold classification).[165] This terminology is striking. Imagine if one religious community followed the rule "thou shalt not drink ale" and another followed the rule "thou shalt not drink ale and wine." In their early forms, *surā* and *maireya* were very different drinks. *Surā* was made from grains and a starter. *Maireya* was a spiced, double-fermented, sugar-based drink, and it was ideally suited to a rule that might require flexibility in interpretation, as it could be made from a variety of sugars. *Maireya* belonged to a certain time-period too, bringing the rule in line with drinking that took place a few centuries BCE. The two drinks may even have had different social connotations—the grain *surā* of the drinking festival, shunned by Brahmins, and the prestigious spiced *maireya* of the royal feast. Also, the pair likely conveyed the full gamut of drink at a certain point, like the expression "grape and grain" in English—earlier we saw other references to "*surā* and *maireya*" in ancient sources where the pair does indeed seem to imply "all manner of drinks." The fact that the precept also contains the word *madya*, the general term for intoxicating drink sometimes used in Hindu law, which possibly has connotations of sensual indulgence, may further broaden the scope of this rule, in terms of both the actual substances covered and the connotations of those substances.[166]

The precept mentions "occasions/states of heedlessness" (the simpler monastic rule does not contain that phrase, nor the term *madya*), which makes explicit the notion that drink may lead to bad conduct. What one abstains from in the precept is thus far more complex than simply *surā*. One might even argue that, according to the precept, a person should abstain only from the heedless state of liquor-induced intoxication, and that mild, sensible intoxication is therefore permitted.[167] However, the scholar Vasubandhu, whose work I examine later, would not agree with such a permissive interpretation.

Buddhist Monastic Rules on Drinking

Buddhist monks and nuns abided by ten precepts, including the ones listed here (modified to include total celibacy), and they were also theoretically obliged to follow a code of monastic rules called the *Vinaya*. Again, these texts are not quite like modern laws. They include formulas for public recitation and lists of rules, with narratives and interpretive framing.

We've already seen some Buddhist monastic rules, in the narratives about nuns who meddled in brewing. In the Pali *Vinaya*, another story describes monks doing work that leads to behavior not fitting for them, leading them to be banished from the order.[168] The monks in question run a garden and workshop for making garlands, which they give to various women. The monks then sport with these women, eating, drinking liquor (*majjam*),[169] dancing, and singing, all while perfumed and garlanded. Thus they behave contrarily to some of the moral precepts in the longer list of ten taken by monastics. They also play a number of games that they're supposed to avoid. Daud Ali writes that what these monks do resembles the pastimes of the man-about-town in texts such as the *Kāmasūtra*.[170] As we've seen, liquor and love-making, along with bodily adornment, are often associated with each other in early India. In the longer lists of eight and ten Buddhist moral precepts, some of the rules after the first five concern exactly this sort of conduct, such as dancing and garlands. Thus, on the one hand, drink goes with sex, killing, and stealing or gambling in some classic lists of sins and vices (and in the five precepts). And simultaneously, for Buddhists, drink (as precept five of ten) could be seen as a "bridge" misdeed connecting those most serious deeds to indulgence in games, dancing, and perfumes. Drink leads to heedlessness and to serious sins connected with sex and killing, *and* it's characteristic of the non-monastic life of sensuous pleasures—garlands, dancing, and so on. Drinking is thus doubly unsuitable for monastics and other Buddhists in a strictly observant state.

In the Pali monastic code, *Vinaya*, associated with the traditions of Theravada Buddhism, the main rule concerning drink is less prominent than one might expect, given that it is precept number five. It occurs among certain rules that require expiation when broken (*pācittiya*). The 227 rules for monks and the 311 for nuns are classified according to their penalty for infringement. The first and worst offences are *pārākija*, requiring disrobing. The other categories are successively less serious. Indeed, fifth-century Buddhaghosa distinguishes between the first two categories (including the first four sins: sex, theft, killing, and lying) as matters of *śīla*, morality, and the remaining categories (including drinking liquor) as matters of *ācāra*, good external conduct.[171] Thus in the *Vinaya* drinking is not placed in the most serious category of offences.

The basic list of 227 rules for monks (*pātimokkhasutta*) is embedded in another text, the *Suttavibhaṅga*. The linguistic form of the *rule* on drinking suggests that it is an ancient formulation, meaning the *surā+maireya* compound is very old.[172] The rule is embedded in a story about the time when the Buddha first prescribed the rule; then we learn the rule itself, with additional conditions, an explanation, and exceptions.[173] This story is also found in several monastic codes and other Buddhist narratives,[174] but here I present the version from the Pali *Vinaya*.[175]

During the lifetime of the Buddha, in a certain town there lives a dangerous serpent-being (*nāga*). A venerable follower of the Buddha, Sāgata, withstands and counters all the *nāga*'s powers by means of abilities he has developed through spiritual practices. In a nearby town, Kosambī, lay followers of the Buddha hear about this impressive feat. One day the Buddha goes on an almsround in Kosambī with some other monks, including Sāgata. The laypeople approach the newly famous Sāgata and ask if there is anything rare (*dullabha*) and pleasant (*manāpa*) that they might offer to the monks. A group of six monks suggest "the clear [*surā*] called *kāpotikā*" (*kāpotikā nāma prasannā*)—not at that time a forbidden drink for monastics—and the generous laypeople therefore present (*paṭiyādetvā*) that drink in many houses, so that it can be offered to the monks on their alms-rounds. Sāgata is offered, and consumes, this rare drink in house after house, so much so that as he leaves town he falls down at the gate. The Buddha passes him and orders the monks to pick him up. At the monastery they lay him in front of the Buddha, but he turns around and falls asleep with his feet toward the Buddha—a most disrespectful posture. The Buddha questions the monks: Was Sāgata respectful previously? And what about now? Did he not come into conflict with the fierce serpent? But could he possibly do that now? Would he have lost consciousness if he had drunk only what ought to be drunk?

Following this discourse, the Buddha pronounces the rule: "For drinking *surā* and *maireya*, there is an expiation."[176] There follows an explanation of what is implied by "*surā*" and "*maireya*," including a list of *surā*s made from grain products (e.g., crushed-grain *surā*), which also contain *kiṇva*-starter and herbal additive (*sambhāra*). "*Maireya*" is said to imply *āsava*s made from flowers, fruits, honey, or jaggery (meaning sugar sources), with a herbal additive. As one would expect, the central contrast between *surā* and *maireya* is that *surā* is made from grain products and contains *kiṇva* (*kiṇṇa*). Drinking is said to occur if a person "drinks even with the tip of a blade of grass (*kusaggena*)."

There follows a legalistic statement of the possible permutations in terms of the drinker's knowledge and whether the drink is actually intoxicating. Here the nature of the drink is more important in deciding the seriousness of the offence than the intention of the drinker, meaning that drinking actual liquor when you think it's not liquor is a greater offence than drinking what is not liquor while thinking it is liquor. Finally, exceptions are listed: it's not an offence to drink a non-intoxicating drink that has the color, smell, and flavor of intoxicating drink (presumably when the drinker knows that it is not intoxicating). Nor is it an offence to drink liquor in a cooked broth, with cooked meat, with cooked oil, in emblic myrobalan syrup (presumably as medicine),[177] or as a non-intoxicating *ariṣṭa* (medicinal wine). Nor is it considered an offence if the drinker is insane, or if the person in question is the first to commit this offence (i.e., Sāgata).

As with the Andhakas and Vṛṣṇis, the story shows that even people we hold in esteem can be undone by drink. Yet, compared with the women who get drunk and dance around in the presence of the Buddha in the *Previous-Birth Story of the Jar*, Sāgata was only quietly and unconsciously rude. Technically, moreover, he was doing no wrong, as there was not yet a monastic rule against drinking. The good people of the town wanted to please the monks after Sāgata's combat with the serpent, and he was simply accepting alms.

The drink involved is a special variety, apparently clarified and called "*kāpotikā.*" Was this a real drink that people knew about in a certain time and place? The word may imply a color, so perhaps this was a satire on the color-named drinks seen elsewhere, such as white/black/clear *surā* ("Algernon opened the mauve Chartreuse . . .")?[178] It could even have been a sophisticated satire on Kāpiśāyana wine.[179]

The rule itself, spoken by the Buddha, is simpler than the precept about liquor—the offence lies in drinking *surā* or *maireya*, and there is no mention of "intoxicants" or "occasions of heedlessness." The rule is a simple prohibition, just as one sees in the early texts for Brahmins, only with the addition of *maireya*. Yet, whereas for Brahmins drinking *surā* is a serious sin, for Buddhist monastics drinking liquor is not an enormously grave offence—despite the similarities between the Buddhist precepts and the lists of sins in Hindu sources. If we set aside socially universal crimes such as murder, celibacy, rather than drinking, stands out as distinctively constitutional of the Buddhist monastic life according to these rules, with sex as the primary heinous offence that causes a falling in status.

The qualifications to the rule against drinking refer to other uses of liquor, in foods and medicines. Elsewhere in the Theravada monastic rules, monks are permitted to drink as medicine oil mixed with liquor, so long as they can't detect the liquor with the senses—in the event that there is a lot of liquor in the oil, they're allowed to use it as an unguent.[180]

Buddhism was adopted over vast regions of Asia, and the ways in which the rule and precept on intoxicating drinks were adapted and interpreted in other regions is a worthy subject of study.[181] To give just one example, in sixteenth-century Burma there was a controversy over the exact stage in production at which palm toddy becomes a forbidden (because intoxicating) drink.[182] In regions where palm toddy was a notable economic product and source of nutrition, this was an important question. A monk from Sri Lanka who was in Burma passed judgment on the matter, composing a text entitled the *Investigation of Surā* (*Surāvinicchaya*). The trouble arose from how to read sub-commentaries on the texts on monastic discipline. One party took it that only toddy prepared with the herbal additive mixture (*sambhāra*) mentioned in the rule was forbidden, while the other declared that even freshly dripped toddy was forbidden.[183] What's interesting is how the ancient term "*sambhāra*" (additive mixture) was so critical to the application of the rule here. In the absence of a concept of alcohol-as-substance or a good method for establishing and quantifying the intoxicating potency of liquors, the only options for ascertaining whether a drink was forbidden or not were (1) experiential, which was a problem for those not permitted to drink, and (2) strict, regulated attention to how the drink was produced and how this process related to the letter of the law. In the latter case, the timing of fermentation and the use of additives like *kiṇva* (starter) and *saṃbhāra* (additive mixture) assumed legal importance. Yet again, we see why ingredients mattered so much in legal texts on liquor.

Paying attention to the material culture of alcohol complicates how we understand ancient texts on law and morality. We can see something similar if we consider laws concerning drugs, alcohol, caffeine, or tobacco today: these laws exist in a web of medicine, economics, politics, chemistry, and regional conventions, as well as traditions of practice and usage. In the case of Buddhist monastic law, debates about intentionality and additives seem less like arcane scholasticism once we take into account what we know about drinks in this period, when there were no bottles of liquor clearly labelled with their *alcohol* content, nor any refrigerated, pasteurized drinks in no danger of becoming intoxicating.

(All but the most committed readers may skip forward now to the section on "The Dangers of Drink in Buddhist Narratives.")

Buddhist Scholastic Analysis of Drink and Drink Rules

There is a considerable commentarial literature on this precept and rule.[184] Among other topics, Buddhist scholastic debates on drinking tackle the question of what type of offence or sin is involved: precisely what makes drinking liquor a bad action?[185] Is drinking liquor intrinsically evil, the product of evil intentions, like murder? Or is drinking liquor simply a matter of breaking a rule, as when monks eat after midday and thus violate a vow, though the action of eating is not in itself reprehensible?[186] Related to this question is the issue of whether drinking is wrong in itself or wrong only because it leads to other wrongs.

Let's consider one example. Vasubandhu was a Buddhist philosopher of the Gupta period, probably in the fourth or fifth century CE.[187] He composed the *Abhidharmakośa* (*Treasury of the Abhidharma*), to which he also added an autocommentary. This large text is a systematic and detailed compilation of doctrine, stating the position of a non-Mahāyāna philosophy (with the commentary often defending another position). In explaining his own positions, Vasubandhu also describes other schools of thought.[188]

In the style typical of Indian scholarly writing, Vasubandhu often pits his own position against a hypothetical opponent and wins the argument in the end. In this case the dispute concerns whether someone who has drunk liquor has only broken a rule of discipline or has committed an innately bad action, like murder. Mark Tatz explains the legal distinction here: "Monastic trainings incorporate not only the natural (*prākṛta*) law that the monastic hold in common with the laity—not killing and so forth—but also special artificial or prescriptive (*pratikṣepaṇa*) legislation formulated in the monastic discipline (*vinaya*) to establish a lifestyle suited to the preservation of the teachings and the rapid attainment of liberation. Celibacy, poverty, group living and so forth are not a natural morality in the sense that not killing and stealing are."[189] Central to the argument is the fact that sometimes people take liquor for medical reasons and do not get drunk. Such a person—drinking for good intentions, not getting drunk, and not committing other sinful actions—is surely not doing anything bad, and therefore drinking is not universally, intrinsically evil in the way murder is. The other factor to consider is how we know deeds are prohibited—from the word of the Buddha. Thus, in the discussion to follow, Vasubandhu combines interpretations of the teachings of the Buddha with common-sense observations on how drink and drinking work in practice.

Vasubandhu's discussion in the autocommentary expands on a concise line on the precept for observant lay Buddhist disciples (*upāsaka*).[190] In this root text he states that among the conduct that laypersons undertake to avoid, only abstention from intoxicants relates to a breach of Buddhist rules while not being an intrinsic evil: "The only immorality related to violating a socially ordained rule (*pratikṣepaṇasāvadya*) [that the layman abstains from] is from intoxicating liquor (*madya*)." Why must lay Buddhist disciples abstain from this one "mere rule"? "In order to the keep the others [i.e., the rules about intrinsic evils like killing]." Thus, according to Vasubandhu: (1) drinking liquor is not evil by nature (*malum in se*), but rather is an infringement of a rule of conduct given by the Buddha (*malum prohibitum*).[191] Yet lay people must observe this precept because (2) drinking will lead people to commit other sins, ones that *are* evil in nature, like killing. Thus drinking liquor is an "occasion of sin" as well as what is called a *malum prohibitum* in common law. It is to be avoided because the Buddha has stipulated not to do it, but that rule is in place because drinking makes you do other sins. And this is unique among ("mere") *rules* because laypeople must observe it too in the five precepts—monastics follow all manner of other rules.

Earlier, I noted what seems like a discrepancy in Buddhist liquor laws: the precept itself is quite prominent, yet drinking is not classified as a grievous monastic offence if we compare it to something like killing (another prominent precept). One way of thinking about the ethical-theoretical issue at stake here is that Vasubandhu is addressing this apparent discrepancy. Among items of "mere" legislation, why is abstaining from drink listed among the set of five precepts the that laypeople also follow, the core commitments of morality? Now we know why: breaking this particular rule leads people on to commit acts that *are* evil by nature.

Vasubandhu goes into more detail in his autocommentary. He explains why his school (the Ābhidhārmikas) believe that drinking liquor (*madyapānam*) is reproachable because it transgresses a rule (i.e. is *pratikṣepaṇasāvadya*), and that it lacks the characteristics of actions reproachable by nature (i.e. is not *prakṛtisāvadya*). He states that actions by nature reproachable are committed with a defiled mind (*citta*), "but it is possible to drink intoxicating liquor with only medical treatment in mind, such that it does not intoxicate. Only when one drinks knowing it to be intoxicating (*madanīyam*) is the mind defiled."

At this point, hypothetical opponents (Vinayadharas, Vinaya experts) interject: "Intoxicating drink *is* reproachable by nature." How do they defend this stance, given Vasubandhu's argument about drinking liquor as a medicine? They quote the authoritative word of the Buddha—a strong argument indeed.[192] In the first passage they quote, the Buddha states that one can treat sickness by any means except sins of nature. In the second, the Buddha prohibits intoxicating drink for sick people, who must not drink liquor, even with the tip of a blade of grass. The two quotations together give the impression that the Buddha wanted to treat drinking liquor as a sin by nature. And the word of the Buddha overrides Vasubandhu's comments about consuming medicinal liquor without defiled thoughts. The opponents add that the Noble Ones (*āryas*) do not drink liquor, even in the next life, just as they do not kill in the next life.[193] Again, drinking lines up with sins of nature, like killing. Finally, along with murder and illicit sex, drinking is classed as a bodily misdeed in some scriptures.

Vasubandhu now deals with all these points: although sick people can disobey rules for the purposes of treatment—this is implied by the Buddha's comments—the ban on liquor for the sick is an exception to that flexibility, so that bad incidents associated with drinking can be avoided, particularly as there is no fixed rule decreeing what quantity of liquor is intoxicating (*madanīya-mātrâniyamanāt*). Presumably even sick people can do, think, and say bad things while drunk. And the difficulty in measuring a liquor's strength explains why the Buddha specifically forbids even a drop of liquor on the tip of a blade of grass. Yet this does not imply that innocent drinking is impossible. It is just impossible to *know* if a given act of drinking is harmless. Thus Vasubandhu's argument still stands. As for the Noble Ones who avoid all drink, *they* do so because they possess modesty, since drinking destroys awareness, and they don't take even a tiny amount, just as they would not take poison, but not because drinking is an innate sin like murder. Drinking, moreover, is classed in some scriptures as a bodily misdeed simply because it causes a state/occasion of moral heedlessness (*pramāda-*). In explaining this latter point, Vasubandhu gives a compelling reading of the precept in which "occasion of heedlessness" occurs.[194] This term, he says, is not used in the other precepts: one does not vow to give up the "heedlessness of killing"; rather you give up killing itself, because killing is an innately bad sin.[195]

Then Vasubandhu sets aside the ethical status of the precept and offers a commentary. What exactly does one undertake to abstain from when one abstains from *surā-maireya-madya-pramāda-sthāna*?[196] He starts with the drinks: "*Surā* is grain/rice *āsava* (*annāsava*)," using "*āsava*" in its broadest, least technical sense. *Maireya* "is a substance-"wine" (*dravyāsava*)," presumably made from things other than grains, so maybe including everything that is not grain *surā*.[197] As we saw earlier, *maireya* was considered a specific (though innately flexible) drink in earlier periods, but Vasubandhu interprets these two drinks as covering all types of liquor, somewhat like Manu's redefined *surā* but with a twofold starting point.

Why does the precept also include the word "intoxicating drink" (*madya*)? Vasubandhu explains: "At certain times these two [drinks, *surā* and *maireya*,] have yet to develop or have already lost the condition of being intoxicating." For example, sugarcane juice is allowed, but not once it has become an intoxicating drink.[198] He qualifies this statement with the following interesting comment: "areca nuts (*pūgaphala-*), *kodrava* grain, etc. also intoxicate, hence the use of [the words] '*surā* and *maireya*.'" He evidently intends to clarify that, although the previously mentioned drinks are to be avoided only when intoxicating (i.e., when they have become *madya*), not everything that can intoxicate will cause the forbidden heedless state, just these two classes of drinks.[199] Finally he explains that, although the phrase "occasion/state of heedlessness" is used here because drinking itself is "just" a rule, not an innate sin, nevertheless consuming liquor is in fact an occasion for all heedlessness (including committing innate sins).

Digression: Kodo Millet, Datura, and Narcotic Drugs

Vasubandhu's comment about areca and *kodrava* is worth a short digression. Given the approximate date of this text, its clear reference to betelnut is in line with references to this drug in other texts. Yet the notion that betel intoxicates is striking—elsewhere in the earliest references it's represented more like a digestive, refreshing mouth perfume. Intoxicating *kodrava*, the other exception he mentions, is kodo millet (*Paspalum scrobiculatum* L.), an intoxicant we haven't yet encountered. Writers in this era were clear about the difference between a fermented intoxicant and others, so he definitely does not mean kodo-millet beer. Rather, this grain sometimes becomes toxic, producing a condition known as kodua poisoning that we now understand to be related to a fungal contamination of the grains (contrary to what some might assume, ergot is not the most important contaminant responsible for this condition).[200] In one Indian medical text, the toxic property of kodo millet was understood to arise spontaneously in certain conditions, similar to the arising of intoxicating power of *surā* once its ingredients were assembled.[201] This tainted grain, however, was not taken for pleasure but was used as a narcotic poison, for both people and animals. "Narcotic kodo millet" (*madanakodrava*) is also mentioned in the *Arthaśāstra*, where it is used for various purposes related to the security and defense of the state. For example, it is placed in the entrails of dead animals to drug and perhaps kill dangerous beasts.[202]

Some other texts also group narcotic *kodrava* with substances like areca nut and cannabis, deeming it what we today might call a "drug-cause" of intoxication (*mada*). In a section of the Prakrit grimoire and formulary the *Girdle of*

Śiva (*Haramekhalā*, from the ninth or tenth century CE) on treating poisons, we find formulas for dealing with the *mada* arising from *kodrava*, datura, and areca nut, as well as for becoming immune to the unpleasant form of liquor-*mada*.[203] The *mada* of areca nut is said to consist of "extraordinary bristling of the body hairs, sweating, and mental confusion," and one formula to calm this condition involves drinking handfuls of cold water. Likewise, *mada* is described as being "like from consuming areca nut (*pūga*), *kodrava*, and *dhattūra* (datura)" in a twelfth-century commentary called the *Madhukośa* of Vijayarakṣita.[204] In the *Śārṅgadharasaṃhitā* (from the thirteenth or fourteenth century CE), in a comprehensive list of diseases (*roga*) distinct from the *mada* problems of liquor, and following a section on poisons, two drug-induced types of *mada* are listed:

> One *mada* is fourfold, with areca nut, cannabis (*-bhaṅgā-*), belleric myrobalan [*Terminalia bellerica* Roxb.], and *kodrava*. The other fourfold one, of *materia medica*, is produced from fruits, bark/peel, roots, and leaves.[205]

The fourteenth-century commentator Āḍhamalla notes that this *mada* is distinct from the *mada* of (alcoholic) *āsavas* and *ariṣṭas* (*āsavāriṣṭād bhinna*). Observe, moreover, how such lists expanded over time, with cannabis added in the early second millennium, which fits with other textual chronologies of that drug (see Cup 8).

Datura, mentioned in some of these lists, also deserves a few comments. The datura plant is an unusual case, for its genus is native to the New World, and so scholars are convinced that the plant was introduced to South Asia and other Old World regions.[206] Yet, strangely, there is convincing evidence of the presence of a datura species in South Asia, the Middle East, and the Mediterranean in some Indic and Arabic sources that predate the introduction of New World plants, meaning that datura was apparently somehow introduced far earlier than, say, tobacco or tomatoes.[207] Perhaps the earliest relatively narrowly dateable reference to datura in Sanskrit texts occurs in the *Kāmasūtra*, where it is used in a penis ointment (with pepper and honey) that puts your partner in your power, and we also learn there that, if the datura fruit is eaten, it renders people insane (*unmāda-*), though this insanity may be reversed.[208] Probably this latter use of the datura fruit was intended to confuse or discredit people for nefarious means. Aside from datura's use in medicine,[209] in at least one Tantric text it is used in rituals to harm people and cause types of destruction (*not* as some sort of mystical "entheogen").[210] I prefer not to apply a medicalizing explanation to these uses, along the lines of "the smoke from the datura in the ritual made them so high that they believed in the magic," since, for one thing, there are plenty of such rituals that do not use datura and were considered quite effective, and, for another, such explanations enormously underestimate how well people understood the effects of this drug. As we shall see later in Tantric texts, they would probably have explicitly stated if they were using datura to induce visions in such rituals. Also, the participants were no doubt quite capable of avoiding the state of being rendered insane or drugged by datura smoke. In terms of datura as a drug, we shall see later that it was classed as a type of *surā* in a late Tantric text, along with cannabis, and there is also evidence that it was added to some alcoholic drinks to strengthen them in the early twentieth century.[211] In general, the history of datura in India requires more work, but scholars should be open to the idea that it was not primarily used as a mystical "entheogen."[212]

From the cases of kodrava and datura, it's clear that, morality aside, not all *mada* was the sort of thing anyone would willingly pursue—there existed a category of bad narcotics and stupefying drugs (separate from fatal poisons), the kinds of substance you would use to knock out tigers and drive your enemies mad.

***

What are we to conclude from this Buddhist scholastic debate? Kieffer-Pülz suggests that Theravada Buddhist commentaries interpreting the drink precept as a matter of simply breaking a rule might correlate to a more liberal attitude toward drinking.[213] It's hard to make this argument for Vasubandhu, however, who is by no means liberal when it comes to drinking. For him the drink precept may be a rule, but it's no *mere* rule, as a person can't control how much liquor it takes to become intoxicated and, moreover, drunken intoxication is an occasion of all innate sins such as murder and sexual misconduct. Arguably this debate may have developed from traditions of legal textual interpretation, removed from social pressures. Vasubandhu's theory of drink as the root of other misdeeds does, however, implicitly furnish an internal, systematic explanation for why what is a relatively minor offence in the monastic rule also appears in the short list of five precepts taken by observant lay disciples.

The Dangers of Drink in Buddhist Narratives

In the *Previous-Birth Story of the Jar* (see Aperitif), just as the king is about to start drinking, the god Indra (Śakra/Sakka)—in this case the Buddha in a previous birth—steps in to save him. As illustrated by the story so far, if the king succumbs to drink, the world will ultimately be destroyed. Addressed to a king, Śakra's teachings here share a lot with the texts on drinking as a vice. For many Buddhists in ancient and early medieval India, this sort of text was probably far more accessible than the scholastic texts examined in the previous section.

In the Pali version of the story, the birth story begins with the appearance of Sakka (Śakra = Indra), and this is when the eponymous jar (*kumbha*) appears. There is also a Sanskrit version of the story that lacks the framing stories and starts with the descent of Śakra. This Sanskrit version is part of a literary text called the *Garland of Previous Birth Stories* (*Jātakamālā*) by Āryaśūra, possibly from the fourth century CE.[214] In both versions, Śakra assumes the form of a Brahmin when he descends. Carrying a jar full of *surā*, he floats in the air before the king, saying, "Buy this jar, buy this jar!" though at that point the king has no idea what's in the jar. It is relevant here that Brahmins are frequently depicted carrying water vessels and that the iconography of Indra sometimes includes a jar of the nectar of immortality—but this jar is a quite different affair.[215] We have visual depictions of this moment of suspense—the Brahmin with the mystery-jar standing before the king—for example, a relief at Borobudur in Java (Figure 7.1):[216]

Such visual images accentuate the ironies of this scene: a pious Brahmin standing before a king is actually Śakra/Indra carrying *surā*, of all things, and he is insistently hawking it to the king (with good motives, of course).

The king wonders who this Brahmin is and what he has in his jar. The Sanskrit *Garland* emphasizes that the king knows nothing about the dangers of drink, which Śakra, observing the world from heaven, finds alarming.[217] Śakra reflects that drink, though tasty at first, is a "delightful evil course" for those who "are averse to seeing its evil."[218] The king is not knowingly doing wrong in accepting the drink; he is ignorant of the impending moral and social dangers. He needs to be cured (*cikitsanīya*), *not* by a divine prohibition, but by education in the dangers of drink. The king's rejection of drink will then come from the king himself, and this moral lesson will save society, since all that is good and bad among the people originates in the king.[219] Presumably this can also be said of the moral

FIGURE 7.1 Indra appears with the jar before the king in an image of the *Kumbha Jātaka*. From Borobudur, Java.
From Krom (1920–1931, vol. 1: Reliefs, Serie 1.(B).a. Plaat VII, image 59). I thank the University of Chicago Library, and especially librarian Laura Ring, for allowing me to take this photo.

benefits of listening to the story. The similarities to the king-related vice discourse are clear.

The Sanskrit *Garland* elaborates on what Śakra finds when he descends to earth, where the king is "engaged in conversation on *surā*, *āsava*, sugarcane wine (*śīdhu*), *maireya*, and wine (*madhu*)."[220] This is a far greater variety of liquors than what is listed in the Pali version. The drinking scene in the Sanskrit *Story of the Jar*, set in the distant past of one of Buddha's previous lives, is furnished with a list of drinks not unlike those in the *Arthaśāstra*.

In both versions we then turn to the jar, and Śakra begins listing delicious and wholesome liquids, liquids the jar does *not* contain. Here is Śakra's description from the Sanskrit *Garland*:

> This isn't full of water from rainclouds, nor of water from sacred places, nor of fragrant nectar from lotus filaments, nor of choice ghee, nor of milk the hue of the beams from a cloudless moon on blooming lilies—but hear the power of the evil stuff that fills this jar.[221]

In both versions, Śakra then relates the problems that the liquid in the jar causes. In the Pali version, all the verses conclude with the Brahmin's (i.e., Śakra's) sales cry: "Buy this jar full of that [extremely dangerous thing]!"[222] perhaps paralleling the street cry of the men who discovered *surā*.[223] There are many similarities between the Pali verses and the Sanskrit, though the Sanskrit speech is shorter. Both deal with the humiliating events that befall an individual who drinks, the moral and economic risks to family and society, and the unpleasant rebirths that result from drinking. Both speeches allude to two disastrous drinking episodes: the self-destruction of the Andhakas and Vṛṣṇis[224] and the Buddhist story of the *asuras* ("anti-gods") being ejected from heaven for drinking.

Consider some extracts from the Sanskrit version. Śakra first describes the ways in which drinking liquor will impair a person's faculties, and the resulting behavior that will destroy his reputation:[225]

> It makes you lose mastery of your own mind, you wander with intellect destroyed, stupid like cattle, making your enemies hurt with laughter, and you even dance in public to your own mouth-drumming—this here [stuff], devoid of goodness, inside the jar is worth buying!
>
> When you drink it, you give up even your usual personal modesty, and, like a naked ascetic (*nirgranthavat*),[226] freed from the distress of the restraints of clothing, you boldly wander roads thronging with the people of the city—it is here ready to buy inside this jar![227]

> When they drink it, people sleep on the royal roads, smeared with food brought up by vomiting, their faces being licked by fearless dogs, unconscious—this most suitable purchase is placed here in the jar![228]

After the consequences for an individual, Śakra describes how drinking causes social disintegration, especially within the family.[229] He also mentions women's drinking here, in a relational context. When a man drinks, he destroys himself as well as his clan and his family, but women are primarily the cement of family-based society, existing more for others than for themselves:[230]

> When she uses it, weak from its intoxicating strength, [a woman] would even tie her parents to a tree, and would not consider the Lord of Wealth to be her husband—that [drink] is stored up, placed in this jar!
>
> Drinking it, the Vṛṣṇis and Andhakas lost their minds from intoxication, forgot[231] that they were kinsmen, and pulverized each other with clubs—that maddening thing is in this jar!
>
> Attached (*prasakta*) to which the most eminent of families, abodes of fortune are destroyed; it is the exterminator of wealthy families—that is in the pot, held up for sale![232]

There follows a generic condemnation summing up the dangers of liquor. A drunk person no longer knows nor can state what is truly the case (perception, epistemology, speech), nor what ought to be the case (duty, law). *Surā*—divine in Hindu myth—is an embodied (*mūrti*) curse:

> With conviction, you will say something as truth although it's untrue; delighted, you will do something as a duty, although it's prohibited; by its effect, you know good as bad and bad as good—this, like an embodied curse, is contained here in the jar![233]

After some more general dangers, we get the "reveal": Śakra announces what the terrifying substance in the pot actually is:

> Such is this intoxicating drink (*madyam*), O god-like king, known as "*surā*" in common parlance . . .[234]

Now that we know what the drink is called, Śukra discusses the currently invisible results from drinking it that will arise in future births:

> Those who use it, attached to bad deeds, fall into the terrible precipices of hell, are born as animals, or in the miserable state of being a hungry ghost—who indeed would even be willing to look at it?[235]

Not surprisingly, the king is convinced and gives up drink. In the Pali version, he has the *surā* jars broken—a rare hint at an ideal of a drink-free society. The king tries to offer a gift, but Śakra refuses, revealing his true identity as a god, and returns to heaven. He leaves the king reformed by his wise speech—but the Pali version adds, "Though, in Jambudvīpa [India, the part of the universe we live in], *surā*-drinking developed in due course."[236]

Buddhist narrative texts contain some of the longest descriptions of the many social dangers of drinking, even in very early periods.[237] Condemnations of drinking that resemble the vice discourse are found in other religious traditions, but this material is perhaps most developed in Buddhism. By contrast, in Hindu law the Vedic, ritual significance of *surā* plays an important role. And later Jain texts, while they also dwell on drinking as a cause of bad deeds, develop their own distinctive theory, namely that drinking is reprehensible because it is a form of violence.

Jainism: Ruinous Drinking and Killing Liquor-Beings

Jain literature on correct conduct is vast, as is the body of Jain narrative literature in which one could find references to drinking. Here I'll focus on a small sample of Jain materials relating primarily to lay conduct (*śrāvakācāra*), many of which are later in date than most of the sources examined in this chapter. These Jain discussions of alcohol share much with other traditions but nonetheless display distinctive tendencies, and it is these uniquely Jain attitudes toward liquor that I explore, along with distinctive Jain narratives.[238]

Jain ascetics are not to drink alcohol. As they live on alms, in practice this prohibition means not accepting alcohol when it's offered and avoiding occasions in which they might encounter alcohol.[239] The *Ācārāṅga Sūtra*, in a section on begging for food, explains the dangers to an ascetic of going to a feast (*saṃkhaḍiṃ*), where he might meet people who would offer him intoxicating drink (*soḍaṃ*).[240] Such an ascetic "might not find the [promised] resting-place on leaving the scene of entertainment and looking out for it; or in the resting place he may get into mixed company; in the absence of his mind or in his drunkenness he may lust after a woman or a eunuch . . ."[241] The setting in this text, which dates probably from the first or second centuries BCE, resembles others of that period, namely a temporary public feast where drinking takes place. Such events, often used as opportunities for drinking, lead to undesirable social mixing and sexual acts.

Many texts aim to distinguish observant adherents (Brahmins, monks, nuns, laypeople) from the sorts of people who attended these feasts. Yet the culture of festivals is presented as unremarkable here, and they are not condemned in themselves—only for certain people.

Technically speaking, abstinence from drink is embedded among the five (sometimes six) Great Vows taken by Jain ascetics.[242] Crudely stated, these concern killing, lying, stealing, sex, attachment/possessions, and eating after dark, but they do not include a vow against intoxicants. However, drinking liquor is included in a clause of the vow renouncing sexual pleasures, and one assumes that, at least in the later Jain tradition, when the conception of drinking liquor as a form of killing was clearly articulated, it was also implicitly included in the vow against killing.[243] Nevertheless abstinence from liquor is not explicitly mentioned in the Jains' Great Vows.

Jain laypeople are also prohibited from drinking liquor, and since they don't live by begging, theirs is an active abstention (the same applies to Buddhist laypeople). All types of intoxicating drink (*madya*) are prohibited.[244] Betel, classed as an item to be used once or consumed internally (i.e., an *upabhoga* or *bhoga*),[245] is not usually forbidden to Jain laypeople, and indeed it is used in certain lay rites.[246] Again, we see the near universal acceptance and prestige of betel in South Asia.

Jain texts from the early second millennium CE contain complex discussions of the dangers of liquor. For Jains of the Śvetāmbara sect, alcohol was covered by the rules relating to food, rules consistent with the attention Jains pay to the ethics of eating. Authorities also mention liquor in the context of trades one should avoid.

Hemacandra was a Śvetāmbara Jain polymath from Gujarat who lived in the twelfth century (1089–1172).[247] He provides a clear statement of Jain attitudes toward drinking in his *Yogaśāstra* (and autocommentary).[248] This text was popular, and some writers of the Digambara sect incorporated parts of it into their writings.[249]

With regard to livelihood, Hemacandra explains that lay Jains are forbidden to trade in alcohol and *dhātakī* flowers, which were used in many alcoholic drinks:

> Sale of lac, realgar, indigo, *dhātakī*, borax, etc. is called trade in lac—a seat of sin.
>
> Sale of unclarified fermented butter (*navanīta*), animal fat, honey, intoxicating drink (*madya*) and the rest, and sale of humans and animals is called trade in liquor (*rasa*)[250] or hair.[251]

The first materials are mostly coloring items. In his autocommentary, Hemacandra notes that realgar and borax kill those whose livelihood is transporting them (*vāhyajīva*), possibly because they are dangerous poisons.[252] He explains that *dhātakī* flowers and bark cause the fermentation of alcoholic drinks (*madyasandhānahetu*), and that the paste/sediment (*kalka*) of *dhātakī* is a cause of worms/creatures (*kṛmihetu-*), which one would presumably kill by drinking liquor (a topic addressed later). The second verse lists edible liquids connected to harming creatures, as well as the sale of living beings. The liquids are produced or consumed through violence: killing the beings that arise in the fermentation of butter, the killing of animals for fat, and the killing of bees for honey. In his autocommentary, Hemacandra explains that one should not sell alcohol, as it produces intoxication and contains creatures/worms that one kills (presumably) by drinking it (*tadgatakṛmivighāta*).[253]

Hemacandra also presents the bad results of intoxicating drink (*madya*), one of sixteen things one should not consume:

> III.8. Merely by drinking liquor (*madirā-*), a sophisticated man's reason flees, just as his lover flees on account of his misfortune.
>
> 9. Evil men, their minds out of control from drinking liquor (*kādambarī-*),[254] treat their mothers like lovers and their lovers like mothers.
>
> 10. The man whose mind is destroyed from liquor (*madya*) does not know himself from others—that pitiable man treats himself like a master and his master like a servant.
>
> 11. Thinking it to be a hole in the ground, dogs urinate in the gaping mouth of the drinker rolling, fallen at the crossroads like a corpse.
>
> 12. Sunk in savoring liquor-drinking, he sleeps naked at the crossroads and readily exposes his hidden intentions.[255]
>
> 13. Beauty, fame, intelligence, and fortune depart because of drinking liquor (*vāruṇī*),[256] just like multicolored painted compositions from soot in the air.
>
> 14. The *surā*-drinker dances frantically like a man possessed, howls like a sorrowful man, and rolls on the ground like one tormented by burning fever.
>
> 15. Liquor (*hālā*)[257] is comparable to deadly poison (*hālāhala*),[258] making the body limp, fading the senses, and causing a prolonged state of unconsciousness.
>
> 16. Discrimination, self-control, knowledge, truth, purity, compassion, and forbearance—liquor dissolves it all like a spark of fire [destroys] a haystack.
>
> 17. Liquor is the cause of sins. Liquor is the cause of calamities.
>
> So shun liquor as a diseased man shuns unwholesome things.[259]

As is common in such texts, the drinker's confusion of mind causes him to mix up external objects, people, and even himself, taking one thing for another. We also see a loss of decorum and of the sense of right and wrong, leading to undignified behavior in the eyes of others. And there are physical effects—unconsciousness and acting like a person possessed. The possession comparison, which we've seen elsewhere, is revealing, since in many ways the drunkard is not himself anymore, lacking his self-control. Hemacandra has no interest here in types of drinks. He uses a series of generic words for drinks, and the autocommentary glosses these words with other generic terms. Given that Hemacandra was also the author of Sanskrit lexica, this must have been a deliberate choice—liquor *in general* is the issue here.

Despite sharing much with texts in other traditions on the evils of drink, this passage is distinctively Jain. First, liquor is discussed along with other foods to avoid. The distinctive eating practices of the Jains were, and still are, well known. Also, as noted already, Hemacandra quotes in his commentary a verse stating that drinking harms living beings produced in the liquor, directly connecting liquor-abstinence to non-violence, *ahiṃsā*, a concept central to Jain ethics.

Other writers elaborate this latter idea. Thirteenth-century Digambara Jain author Āśādhara explains the sin of drinking in terms of the harm to sentient beings present in liquor:[260]

> If the souls (*jīvas*) in a drop of it spread forth, they would fill the whole universe. And, bewildered (*viklava*) by it, [souls] will struggle in this and other worlds. One should certainly give up that intoxicating drink (*kaśyam*).[261]
>
> When drunk, the multitude of souls in it with flavor-bodies all immediately die, and, along with the sin [of killing them], desire, anger, fear, confusion, and so forth arise.
>
> Observing a vow to abstain from intoxicating drink, like the thief Dhūrtila, one does not fall into danger. But drinking it, like Ekapād, and committing bad deeds, one sinks into misfortune.[262]

For Āśādhara, the sheer act of drinking kills countless beings—drinking is therefore murder and the root of destructive mental states.[263] After stating these dangers, Āśādhara refers to an exemplary pair, one an abstainer and one a drinker—Dhūrtila and Ekapād—prompting the reader to ask: who are these characters, and what is their story?

An earlier text, the *Yaśastilaka* (from the tenth century CE) by the Digambara Jain Somadeva, supplies these narratives, along with other observations on the evils of drinking.[264] This literary text, which we've seen already, contains narratives, discussions of correct conduct, and philosophical materials. Somadeva presents the tales of Dhūrtila and Ekapād in his account of a category of abstentions for householders (*gṛhastha*) that the Digambaras call the *mūlaguṇas*.[265]

Before telling the stories, Somadeva explains:

> All evils arise because of intoxicating drink (*madya*), the great source of mental confusion, that stands at the head of all sins.
> Confusing right and wrong, what sin would people not commit, [sin] that will cause them to wander astray in the vast forest of the world of eternal rebirth?
> The Yādavas were destroyed by intoxicating drink, the Pāṇḍavas by gambling: this story is very famous everywhere in this world.
> Indeed, embodied souls, arising and dying in great numbers in this world, in time become intoxicating drink (*madyībhavanti*) to confuse minds (*manomohāya*).
> If the living beings arisen in a single drop of intoxicating drink were to spread forth, without a doubt they would fill the whole world.
> The cause of mental confusion, the cause of misfortune—good people should ever give up intoxicating drink, which produces evil in this world and the next.[266]

Drinking confuses the mind, causes evil deeds, and plunges the drinker into misfortune in both this world and future rebirths. Given all this, it's not surprising that Somadeva mentions the drunken, self-destructive violence of the Yādavas (the Andhakas and Vṛṣṇis).[267] He also presents the possibility of being reborn as living beings who dwell in (or simply *are*) intoxicating drink, and who confuse people's minds. This is clearly a bad rebirth, and vast numbers of such beings are contained in just one drop of liquor. Somadeva does not say that drinking kills these beings, but that can be taken for granted. For Somadeva, when you drink alcohol, you swallow countless creatures intent on causing you suffering. It's as if you were murderously ingesting a swarm of microscopic hell-beings who will then cloud your mind and cause future pains. For these Jain writers, the drink itself can both suffer and cause suffering.

And now for the stories of Ekapād and Dhūrtila, which concern the harm that people inflict and endure when they drink.[268] The story of Ekapād focuses on moral decline from indulging in liquor (*madyapravṛtti*). Ekapād, a wandering ascetic (*parivrājaka*) is going to bathe in the Ganges when he meets some carousing Mātaṅga people (a group of low rank). They say they will kill him if he doesn't partake in one out of intoxicating drink, meat, or women (*madyamāṃsamahilāsu madhye*).[269] Ekapād reflects that eating even a small amount of meat would be a great sin.[270] Sex with a woman of this low class is likewise forbidden. But in the Vedic sacrifice called the Sautrāmaṇī, the "crest jewel of all sacrifices," drinking is enjoined, and drinking in that context is not classed as drinking *surā* (*ya evamvidhāṃ surāṃ pibati na tena surā pītā*).[271] Moreover, for Ekapād not only are Hindu scriptural injunctions concerning alcohol inconsistent, but the ingredients of *surā*—ground grains, water, jaggery, and *dhātakī* flowers (*piṣṭodakaguḍadhātakī-*)—are themselves pure (*viśuddhāni*).[272] Thus, though unwilling to drink and aware that he probably shouldn't do so, he hopes that drinking might not be *quite* as sinful as the other two acts. Once he drinks, however, his mind becomes confused, and he throws off his loin-cloth, eats meat, and makes love to a Mātaṅgī woman. Thus, on account of drinking, a religious ascetic (*not* Jain) descends into sin (and the Vedic Sautrāmaṇī sacrifice is implicated in the process.)

The tale of Dhūrtila deals with the virtues of ceasing to drink liquor (*madyanivṛtti*). Dhūrtila is one of a gang of five skilled thieves in the city of Valabhī. On a rainy night they go out and steal many valuables. Then, when dividing it up, they drink, fight, and kill each other. Not Dhūrtila, however, for he made a vow earlier that if he ever saw a (Jain) monk, he would not drink liquor for one day (*āsavavratam*). As it happened, he was observing this vow of sobriety when the other thieves drunkenly killed each other, and so, having survived this drunken slaughter, Dhūrtila shaves his head and becomes a monk. Even criminals are redeemed by abstention.

The Aesthetic Delights of Forbidden Liquor, and Satires of Morality

As we've seen, even among those who wished to avoid drink there was a vast range of voices. It's not surprising, therefore, that there were also all manner of reactions to anti-drinking rules and theories. Some writers used humor to criticize the laws against drink and the perceived hypocrisy of those who were supposed to abstain from drinking. Sometimes attitudes toward liquor were surprisingly complex, and some respected medical texts praised liquor outright.

In this section, I present a selection of such texts. These materials are by no means evidence of subaltern resistance. Rather, they were written and read by literate, elite people, whose voices *would* have been heard, though not everyone would have agreed with them.

Earlier, when dealing with medical literature, I mentioned two paeans to *surā* attached to discussions of drinking. Now we're in a good position to appreciate those passages. I begin with a later, simpler passage from the *Aṣṭāṅgahṛdaya* of Vāgbhaṭa:

> The one (or "she") which imparts the great splendor of the Aśvins, the strength of Sarasvatī, the vigor of Indra, and the might of Viṣṇu; which is the weapon of Kāma [Makaraketu] and the highest human good (*puruṣārtha*) for Balarāma [Bala]; which is offered into the mouth of the Brahmin and into the sacrificial fire in the Sautrāmaṇī ritual; which, along with Śrī, the moon, and nectar arose from the great ocean full of every herb when it was being churned by the gods and *asuras*; and which, with many forms—wine, mead, *maireya*, sugarcane wine, jaggery-drink, *āsava*, and the rest[273]—never quits the power of intoxication . . .[274]

Vāgbhaṭa draws on several major themes connected to drink in the Hindu "classics." Surā is presented as the sacred, primordial, desire-inciting goddess-drink of the gods, which occurs in many forms. The tension between the variety of alcoholic drinks (and drugs) and their perceived unity is an important theme in Indic thought we've seen again and again.

The praise of Surā in *Caraka's Compendium* draws on fewer themes but frames Surā in an even more orthodox manner. Some scholars have suggested that these verses should be attributed to Dṛḍhabala, who compiled and revised the *Carakasaṃhitā*, probably between 300 and 500 CE, which dates this passage to the Gupta era, when the major features of legal theories and literary expression for drinking had crystallized.[275] I provide an expanded translation of the ritual terminology for non-specialists:

> [That] which the gods together with the Lord of Gods [Indra] honored in former times; which is offered as an oblation in the Sautrāmaṇī sacrifice; which is consecrated [for offering] by priests of the ritual; which carries the sacrifice; by means of which Indra—very much brought low by drinking excessive *soma*, devoid of vital energy (*ojas*), and overcome by dark inertia (*tamas*)—was saved from that bad state. And which, high-minded sacrificers, seeing it, touching it, and preparing it, may use in the sacrifice for the success of the sacrifice, according to injunctions ordained in the Vedas; which has many specific varieties in terms of raw materials, processes, names, etc., and is of one type because of being universally characterized by intoxication; which unites the gods with supreme fortunate things in the form of the nectar of immortality, and does the same for the ancestors as the oblation for the ancestors (*svadhā*), and for twice-born classes as *soma*. Which is the great splendor associated with the Aśvins, the force associated with Sarasvatī, the vigor associated with Indra, and which, prepared and perfected (*siddhā*), is the *soma* in the Sautrāmaṇī sacrifice; which destroys sorrow, discontent, fear, and agitation; which has great power; which is joy (*prīti*); which is sexual pleasure (*rati*); which is speech (*vāc*); which is flourishing (*puṣṭi*); which is bliss [*nirvṛti*, possibly also "liberation"];

which is pleasure; called "*surā*" by the gods, *gandharvas*, *yakṣas*, *rākṣasas*, and humans—one should drink this *surā* in the proper manner.[276]

One couldn't imagine a greater contrast to the materials we've examined earlier in this chapter. The person who composed this was well-versed in Vedic learning. The Sautrāmaṇī here is not simply a place-holder for the concept of permissible drinking. Rather, the purpose and mythological background to the Sautrāmaṇī ritual were clearly present to this writer, who despite his evident knowledge of Vedic ritual, was an advocate of correct drinking.

Why is *surā* so excellent, according to this passage? Surā was also revered by the gods at a primordial moment, no doubt the churning of the ocean. We read that *surā* in the form of[277] other substances connects the gods, ancestors, and Brahmins (or the three twice-born classes) with good edible things, suggesting that *surā* is somehow a primordial potent drink that takes the form of substances typically enjoyed by these classes of being. We learn too that *surā* embodies powers and qualities associated with certain deities, the same ones connected to the Sautrāmaṇī sacrifice. *Surā* is equated with a number of abstract concepts, such as bliss, but we should note that many of these terms can be read as both concepts and divine personifications, in particular as goddesses, which of course includes Surā herself (the first two goddesses here, Prīti and Rati, are the wives of the Kāmadeva, the god of love).[278] Indeed, in the list of contents at the end of this particular chapter, this passage is said to concern the Goddess Surā (Bhagavatī Surā).[279]

In contrast to these pious apologies for *surā*, there were several satires written on both drinking and the morality surrounding drinking. Perhaps the most famous of these is the *Mattavilāsaprahasana* (*Drunken Games*), a one-act satirical play from the early seventh century CE, composed by King Mahendravikramavarman of the South Indian Pallava dynasty.[280] Christian Ferstl has observed that the play, set in the city of Kāñcīpuram, is a valuable early source for the doctrines, practices, and social history of an early ascetic Śaiva movement.[281] We shall look at some of those aspects later, but here I examine the character of a Buddhist monk.

This monk is desperately frustrated by his vow to abstain from drink. Far from having abandoned passion (*vītarāga*),[282] he is a greedy, sensuous fellow. When he first appears on stage, he is musing on the tasty alms of fish and meat that he received at a merchant's house.[283] He then reflects on the Buddhist monastic life, ironically celebrating what are in theory restrictions on sensuous pleasures: the monastery is a mansion (*pāsāda*); the beds—restricted in terms of permissible height—are nevertheless well-constructed; the monastic restriction on eating after midday is construed as a positive instruction to eat food in the morning; and the limitation to take only drinks after midday is no hardship, as the drinks are well-flavored.[284] The consumption of betel by Buddhist monastics is not here restricted, so this is another source of pleasure: the betel-wraps are perfumed with the "five perfumes." Finally, his robes are soft garments. Given the sensuous glamor of this Buddhist monastic life, the monk seems genuinely surprised that he can't have sex or drink alcohol (Lorenzen's translation, modified):

> But what I haven't seen are the rules for taking a wife or drinking liquor (*surā-*). Is it possible that the Omniscient One did not envision this? I suspect that these tired, evil Buddhist elders removed the rules about women and liquor from the holy books[285] out of their jealousy of us young folk. Where can I find an unmodified original text?[286] If I find it, I will gratify the community by making known to all the complete words of the Buddha.[287]

Most conveniently, the monk has forgotten the teachings and rules that deal with the very things he claims have been removed from the books. Of course, the humor depends on the audience having a basic knowledge of Buddhist practices, since these "luxuries," for example the beds, are associated with the *ten* precepts iconic of Buddhist monastic life, which also *most definitely* cover sex and drink. The passage perhaps also parodies the Indic scholarly practice of claiming that authority lies in texts that are lost or not available. It may even hint at the Tantric project of creating new revealed texts—texts that would contain permissions to drink and have sex.

Later, when the Śaiva ascetic accuses him of stealing his begging-bowl, the monk defends his honor in a way that reinforces all he has "forgotten" and misconstrued—a creed of irreproachability and sneaky booze-optimism:

> My lord, how can you say this? It is a precept that one should abstain from taking what is not given. It is a precept that one should abstain from false speech. It is a precept that one should abstain from sexual intercourse. It is a precept that one should abstain from taking a life. It is a precept that one should abstain from eating at inappropriate times. I take my refuge in the religion of the Buddha.[288]

Some readers might notice something a little odd here, and no doubt ancient audiences did too. Technically the abstentions that he lists are indeed Buddhist precepts. He lists five, giving the precept dealing with theft first, which makes sense as he has just been accused of theft. The next three precepts (false speech, sex, and killing) are correct, but he has reversed their familiar order, perhaps because he is not a very conscientious monk. The next precept, on eating at inappropriate times (i.e., not after midday) is indeed one of the ten precepts for monastics, but it is usually given as precept number six—and one would expect, in any case, that if a Buddhist monk recited *just five* precepts, the fifth would be the liquor precept. In this way, his technically correct but conveniently jumbled, cherry-picked presentation of the precepts enhances the irony when he then declares in self-defense, utterly contradicting himself in desperation: "What possible motive can there be for one who takes the Buddha's word as his authority (*pamāṇīkaraanto*) to grab a vessel of *surā* (*surābhāaṇaṃ*)?"[289]

It's important to realize that this is not a satire on sincere abstinence. The scene is amusing because this character, supposedly in control of his body, mind, and senses, is a bad monk. In part his faults are blamed on the loose discipline in his monastery. But his own hypocrisy, self-delusion, and greed also undermine his moral resolve.

As we saw earlier, people in early India appreciated sweet, flavored drinks, and Buddhist monks and nuns, forbidden to take liquor, were permitted sugary "medicines," namely honey (*madhu*) and sugarcane syrup (*phāṇita*), along with oil, ghee, and butter during the hours when otherwise they had to fast.[290] Monks were also permitted a number of sugary fruit-juices, though it's notable that the juice of mahua flowers (*madhukapuppharasaṃ*)[291] is specifically disallowed, presumably owing to its associations with liquor. The commentator Buddhaghosa (from the fifth century CE) wrote of how permissible mango-juice is to be made, with either raw or cooked mangoes.[292] The raw version is made by splitting tender mangoes, placing them in water in the heat of the sun, "cooking" them with sunshine, straining them, and mixing them with honey, sugar, camphor, and other items that have been received that day; the grape drink (*muddikā-pānaṃ*) is to be made in the same manner. It would be easy for drinks made in this manner to ferment a little, though not to the extent of drinks like *āsava*s and wines, which were aged for several weeks. Even if they did not ferment, they would have been quite tasty, probably far better than many people could afford to make.

These sweet drinks permitted to Buddhist monks after midday were objects of suspicion, all the more so in a world where sweet liquids could ferment rapidly. In the ninth-century Kashmiri satirical play *Much Ado About Religion* (*Āgamaḍambara*), a Vedic graduate and his pupil observe a Buddhist monastery that, as before, is far from austere. They notice the monks being served food and drink by attractive female servants:

> Boy: . . . And here they are bringing some drink, placed in a spotless jar (kalasa).
> Graduate: Here is wine (madhupānam) by another name, disguised by the word "cooked juice" (pakvarasa), and meat devoid of the three conditions. Oh, what severe asceticism![293]

One monk here even has a lily in his drink! Whereas in Sanskrit literature Buddhist nuns are often go-betweens for lovers, monks are bon vivants here. In both cases the Buddhist institutions are attacked because they're luxurious, a quality not intrinsically wrong in premodern India but at odds with monastic life.

Other concepts were also the object of drink-related satire. Earlier we saw the *Conversation of Rogue and Rake* (*Dhūrtaviṭasaṃvāda*). Here, in a satirically academic discourse on the virtues of actual pleasure over potential pleasure, the speaker, a rake (*viṭa*), questions the appeal of heaven (*svarga*), a place of karmic rewards in Hindu, Buddhist, and Jain texts.[294] If everything is made of gold in heaven, he argues, gold would no longer be special. Never sleeping would be quite dreadful. "And what about the speech of women, with syllables slurred by the intoxication of liquor (*vāruṇī*), coy, pleasant, and pleasing—where is that in a heaven devoid of drink?"[295] Again, this satire is complex. Perhaps this sort of heaven does seem a bit dull, but the rake, with his love of gold, naps, and liquor, also has limited aspirations. People watching this play would no doubt have been aware that the pleasures in heaven were supposed to be of a far higher order than a mere cup of wine.

Where there is hypocrisy about sobriety, there are methods to disguise drinking. Recall that the smell of liquor was (and still is) often considered incriminating. Earlier, in the *Bṛhatkathāślokasaṃgraha* ("Great Story") we read of the smell of wine filling a bedroom the next morning. At one point, also, the protagonist pretends to be a Brahmin but fools nobody as "his breath is saturated with the fragrance of *āsava*."[296]

Another text, the *Bhāvaprakāśa* is a North Indian treatise on medicinal substances (c. 1550–1590). Here, at the end of a section on alcoholic drinks, there is a formula for a mouth freshener that not only removes a naturally arising stink in the mouth but also eradicates the smell of liquor (*madya-*), garlic, and other substances, presumably forbidden ones.[297] In the *Haramekhalā*, a compendium of formulae for many purposes, one formula makes liquor become "like water":

> Liquor/*surā* (*madirā*) mixed with *kataka* [clearing nut][298] powder that has been mixed with ash of the external rind of the *ciñcā* fruit [tamarind] instantly becomes like water.[299]

The commentary on this verse explains that the odor of liquor disappears too.

Even where we might expect to see liquor utterly denigrated, this is not always the case. In Jainism, "*leśyā*s" are sorts of soul-taints or soul-colorings that reflect mental states and passions. For example, a virtuous person might develop the white *leśyā* for a certain duration. One early Jain text (*Uttaradhyāyanasūtra*) describes the other sensory qualities of these soul-colors.[300] The sensory qualities for good *leśyā*s are pleasant and unpleasant for bad *leśyā*s, at least as regards taste, smell, and touch. Thus the black *leśyā* smells worse than the corpse of a cow, dog, or snake, and the good *leśyā*s smell of fragrant flowers and perfumes being pounded.[301] The yellow (*pamha*)[302] *leśyā* is the second purest after the white, which tastes better than dates, grapes, milk, and crystal sugar:

> The flavor of the yellow one is better than the flavor of the best *vāruṇī* [i.e., *surā*], and of various *āsava*s, and the taste of wine (?) and *maireya* (*meraya*).[303]

It is especially striking, in a Jain context, that the second-best *leśyā* is compared favorably to the flavor of a number of alcoholic drinks, which were totally forbidden to Jains. The list, as with the presence of grapes in the list for the white *leśyā*, also confirms the approximate chronology of drink-words—*surā*/*vāruṇī*, *āsava*s, *madhu*-as-wine, and *maireya*, all of which are typically seen around the turn of the Common Era.

Finally, there is the notion that conduct varies in different regions. We saw one reference to this earlier, in a *dharmasūtra*. The following proverb illustrates the same idea:

> There is no offence in intoxicating liquor in Magadha, nor in that made from rice in Kaliṅga,
> In enjoying your brother's wife in Oḍra, nor in eating fish in Gauḍa.
> And also there is no fault in marrying the daughter of your maternal uncle in Drāviḍa country.
> The conduct in a given place is fixed by tradition.[304]

This does not mean that "anything goes," morally speaking, but rather that laws should accommodate regional tradition.

Drinking and abstinence were complex in early India. Abstinence, sometimes selective, was practiced for a number of reasons: scriptural prohibitions, regional or community traditions, the avoidance of vice. People who drank were probably aware of many stories and opinions that presented drink in a negative light. Perhaps, like smoking today, it was difficult to drink without at least some mental "baggage" in the background. Our evidence reveals little about attitudes toward drinking in communities who were less involved to the sorts of texts I use in this book, but we should be wary of envisioning the village *surā* shop as a place of untroubled drinking just because opposition to liquor in that world was not articulated in texts that survive. The proverbial drunken-disaster stories (and others) may have been well-known there too. Indeed, we should by no means assume that our surviving Sanskrit or Pali versions are the primary forms or contexts of these narratives—these are just materials that survive today, and which were appreciated in various ways in certain circles.

Conclusions

Drinking liquor makes you drunk, and when you get drunk you mess things up in a universal way. This sums up an attitude shared by Hindus, Buddhists, and Jains alike. This attitude wasn't always what we would nowadays call a religious stance. In the texts on vices, cautions against immoderate drinking served as good, practical advice for the flourishing life of a king and his subjects.

People writing about drinking and morality developed over time a varied body of reflections and laws. Sometimes we find a litany of bad things that happen when a person drinks, ranging from individual confusion and humiliation (naked exposure, like drunken Noah in the Bible) to social breakdown. The drunken mutual massacre of respected warriors in the *Mahābhārata* was a famous example of how drink can ruin anyone. This proverbial drunk disaster does not involve the sinful drinking of Brahmins but rather culturally and legally permitted (Kṣatriya) drinking gone horribly wrong.

Over time, different traditions developed distinctive articulations of the evils of drink. Some Jains treated it as a food to be avoided, in part because it makes you do bad things but also because drinking liquor is a violent act in itself. Some Buddhists emphasized that drinking provides an occasion for doing other bad things. Buddhists also had an ancient narrative tradition about drink, not to mention their own myth for how the *surā*-drinking *asura*s came to be expelled from heaven. Brahmin-centric and Hindu texts are initially concerned to separate Brahmins from *surā* partly for ritual-related reasons, but become ever more wide ranging in terms of drinks and society.

Conspicuous avoidance of all liquor was a common mark of various ascetic, highly-observant-lay, and ritual-focused lifestyles in ancient India, part of a set of restrictions on sexuality, liquor, incorrect use of money/property, and violence (and sometimes incorrect speech) that crop up in many different contexts. And, while celibacy is emphasized in some stages of a Brahmin's life, abstinence from drink is practiced throughout the life of a Brahmin, who is by no means an entirely ascetic figure in other respects: when married he can have sex, wear ornaments and garlands, and so on. But drink is one of the great sins that cause a Brahmin to fall from caste, a list that becomes prominent from the time of the *dharmasūtra*s onward. These *dharmasūtra*s are the very same texts in which, as Stephanie Jamison has written, the married-householder male Brahmin is first called a "*gṛhastha*" in Sanskrit, a word that implies "a man with a religious life equivalent to that of a wandering ascetic—but a religious life pursued and fulfilled within the context of a sedentary family existence."[305] Arguably, liquor abstinence in a married Brahmin's life was a recognizable part of this regime of domestic asceticism—hence the overlap of the liquor rule with practices of ascetic groups and those of other conspicuously disciplined laypersons such as Jains. Yet, in the mature Brahminical tradition this abstinence is not just a matter of domestic asceticism, but is also given a prominent and distinctive articulation connected to Vedic ritual propriety and caste identity. Nevertheless, just as sex is the norm and celibacy an exception, so arguably drinking is the norm—*surā* is of humans—and abstinence is the marked exception, ascetic, controlled, pure, or god-like.

Manu and later Hindu writers and commentators had to deal with the mismatch between the ancient *surā* concept and the range of drinks that later became available. And if they wanted their legal theories to have a broader scope, they had to accommodate their drinking regulations to a complex society. Their responses to this conundrum suggest that many people drank all sorts of things. We end up with a threefold *surā* and long lists of non-*surā* liquors, variously prohibited and permitted according to a drinker's place in the *varṇa* system. We might even compare the *surā* concept to the modern idea of a "drug," insofar as what people include in the category is highly contested and constantly redefined, and usage of the term changes from one context to another, with varying social and legal consequences. Writing about adoption law in an early-modern text from Kerala, Donald Davis argues that it exemplifies "a continuous process of accommodating, and translating idealized, yet incomplete *Dharmaśāstra* rules into a system of positive, practicable laws"; a process that accommodates "changing legal and religious standards into the *Dharmaśāstra* idiom."[306] Arguably, we see a similar process in the texts on *dharma* after the turn of the Common Era, though I'm not confident that we can produce a finely tuned theory of how these materials relate to what was going on in any particular time and place. We can say, however, that Indian legal texts were far from static—every major source examined in this chapter (and this is just the tip of the iceberg) had something distinctive to say. That the statements get more complex over time may well reflect the fact that the people involved in these debates were attempting an ever-increasing political and cultural integration, treating ever more drinks and local traditions.

It's vital to observe that abstinence from drinking was not a feature of all ancient presentations of *dharma*. As Olivelle writes, Emperor Aśoka in the third century BCE articulates what is effectively a universal *dharma* in his inscriptions—a *dharma* that is silent on crimes, being instead more concerned with "development of character, virtue, and spiritual growth."[307] Though Aśoka was a strong supporter of Buddhism, his version of *dharma* diverges strikingly from the Buddhist lay *dharma* given in the five moral precepts. Olivelle notes there "are only two common elements: truthfulness and not killing. Three central elements of the *pañcaśīla* [five precepts] are missing: sexual misconduct, theft, and abstention from alcoholic drinks . . . Even though it may have been promoted by and drew inspiration from the Buddhist Dharma, the ideology of Dharma that Aśoka was promoting had a different and broader intent then the propagation of the Buddhist religion."[308] Negative evidence is difficult to interpret, but this particular omission is quite noticeable. We might attribute the omission of references to sexual misconduct and theft to a general silence on crimes and offenses, but abstinence from drinking could conceivably have been included with the moral virtue of not lying and not killing—as we've seen in this chapter, temperance was commonly included in early lists of moral observances. Was it omitted because a *dharma* for all people in many widespread regions couldn't possibly promote abstinence, given that drink was acceptable for people in many social stations and groups? Certainly Aśoka's inscriptions displace "Brahminical exceptionalism" (and I might even add "ascetic and ascetic-adjacent exceptionalism") from any central or privileged position in his civil *dharma*.[309] Or does this omission strike us as noticeable *only* because we're so focused on ascetic and Brahminical regimes of *dharmic* abstinence? After all, recall that the earliest Vedas mention not only the *soma* cult but also a culture of drink, dice, and women, a culture that clearly has its attractions but may also go wrong, as we see in the epics and the *Arthaśāstra*.

The development of these moral and legal theories of drink does not necessarily imply a clampdown or a backlash. As with the recent regulation of commerce in cannabis in California, necessary since the drug's legalization in the state, the Indian boom in moral drink-regulation perhaps suggests that people in certain circles who *did* drink now had a vested interest in coming under the umbrella of *dharmic* morality and/or Sanskritic political-vice theory. Or perhaps a certain group, like Brahmins, wished to accommodate their ideology to the mores of certain communities who drank. Of course, it's hard to know exactly what was going on, but an increase in regulation does not always imply that there was a burgeoning "drink problem" needing to be controlled, nor that drinking was increasingly unacceptable. The expansion of laws may even imply the opposite, especially when they were aimed at a minority.

Complete prohibition in society was never really the explicit aim of these regulations. The fully developed Hindu theory corresponds to an idealized but complicated world, even a complicated universe, of people and other beings, some who drink and some who do not. The idea of a world where no one drinks is present but rare in Hindu texts, a fantasy of a society of perfect Brahmins.[310] Buddhists and Jains, by contrast, do aim at universal abstinence, at least for the observant in *their* communities.

From some perspectives, being abstinent was a disadvantage. The rule-following Brahmin, the pious Jain, and the precept-observant Buddhist (as well as various ascetics) were excluded from the drinking culture, which to the rest of the populace offered a convenient system of calories on credit. Consider also how long-distance travel must have differed for Brahmins, as compared to the classes who were permitted to eat, drink, and mingle socially at *surā* shops.

What can we do with these regulations as evidence for material culture and social history? To start with, we have the range of drinks, the appearance of betel in the record, the *surā*-shop banner, and the basic notion that being drunk in public was not respectable. Also present is the pervasive idea that drinking—sometimes qualified as excessive drinking—leads to bad results for people, individually and collectively. In the early period, the Brahmins, Buddhists, and Jains are distinguished by their abstinence. Later, Kṣatriyas and Vaiśyas also abstained from that most Vedic of drinks, grain *surā*, but could otherwise enjoy drinks like wine, which was in keeping with epic (*smṛti*) and literary precedent where drink often incites the non-Brahmin elite to enjoy the pleasures of *saṃsāra*. Some other communities were so frequently depicted drinking and enjoying drink festivals that, despite the bias of representations, we might infer that people did enjoy these pleasures.

Do the writings of foreign visitors help to give a sense of what was really going on? The Chinese pilgrim Xuanzang, writing of his travels in India in the seventh century CE, relates that Brahmins and monks take no liquor but do drink grape and sugarcane juice; Kṣatriyas take liquors made from grapes and sugarcane (*mādhvī*, *gauḍī*?); and Vaiśyas take "fermented spirits and unfiltered wines" (grain *surā*? non-*prasannā*? I'm using a translation from the Chinese, so we should ignore the implications of the word "spirits").[311] The low and mixed castes have no specific drinks in Xuanzang's description. Overall, his account looks suspiciously close to Manu's work. Does the description reflect practice, or was Xuanzang just relating the local *theory* of how drinks should be distributed in society (for a Chinese audience)?

The *Arthaśāstra* paints a completely different picture of liquor regulation. People sometimes brewed in large quantities, and the economics of drink must have been important to certain communities. The *Arthaśāstra* gives us a sense of how this economy was managed, as does the inscription we examined earlier, and we can assume that there were many legal standards and regulations connected to the world of brewing that we no longer possess today.[312]

It's likely, however, that in practice certain people, for example Buddhist monastics and Brahmins, were publicly marked as teetotalers (you could spot a *fake* Brahmin by his boozy breath). Many of the texts in this chapter address people who would typically have been abstinent, and so these laws may not have been designed to prohibit something that frequently happened in practice (as, for example, with a law preventing twenty-year-old Californians from buying beer) but rather may have served a rhetorical purpose, enshrining defining moral values for a community—a revered constitution aired in public or analyzed in a scholarly setting.[313]

The absence of a concept of alcohol as a substance helps us to understand some of the texts: When does a sweet liquid become intoxicating? What is the status of drinks made from X and from Y? Early Indian liquors were all produced by fermentation, yet even today the intoxicating power of something like freshly dripped toddy is uncertain, so it's useful to have named drinks in your reference books.

Can we relate the broader history and culture of drinks in ancient India to the legal texts of the time? Spicy, sugar-based *maireya* may well have been prestigious several centuries BCE. It's in this era that the Buddhist twofold prohibition of *surā* and *maireya* was propagated and publicly declared by laypeople and monastics alike. Brahmins might distinguish themselves by abstaining from *surā*, but *all* observant Buddhists avoided *surā* and *maireya* (theoretically speaking). Not to be outdone, Manu clarifies that the *surā* of the ancient *dharma* laws is in fact threefold, and he explains that *surā*-abstinence applies not just to Brahmins but to all twice-born classes. Of course the reality was more complex, but this gives us some idea of the sorts of interactions that may have occurred.

Probably better known to most people than the legalistic sources were the stories about drinkers and the litanies of drunken deeds. These texts may have informed a less legal-technical avoidance of drinking, as one still finds in many contexts today in India, shaped not so much by the religious laws as by local and family traditions. Thus, when people were ignorant of the academic minutiae of liquor law and moral theory in premodern India, they might still have practiced abstinence, according to various traditions—perhaps even more extensive abstinence than was technically required of them. This would explain the implied sense of surprise of the hypothetical opponent in the text in which Kumārila discusses the drinking of Kṛṣṇa and Arjuna.

What are the connections between drink, abstinence, and power? While many statements were made about the general evils of drink, the feared consequence was not typically political unrest. In Hindu texts, the prohibition of varieties of *surā* is reserved for the three twice-born social classes; other social classes are free to drink whatever they want. In the Pali *Jātaka* stories, though drinking is condemned, the drinkers are not depicted as hateful villains, nor on the verge of rebellion—they are more petty criminals. It might, in fact, have been more threatening to some of the economic and political elites if some of the drinking masses had adopted their own stringent forms of abstinence.

Perhaps, ultimately, the materials described here are just as much about the public virtues of abstinence as they are about the evils of drink. If we were to give some sort of functional explanation to these materials, we might say that texts on the sins and vices of drink were not devised by puritanical reformers who wished to control or criminalize an underclass; on the contrary, it was a mark of distinction to be threatened by the vices, as kings were, or to acquire the potential to commit serious sins by consuming *surā*. Of course, parallel to these articulations of abstinence is an exclusion, even a vilification-by-silence, of those whose drinking was utterly unregulated by these laws, whether those people chose to drink or not.

CUP 8
Surā Regained
Drink in Tantra

Introduction: Religious Drinking?

In the last chapter we met a Buddhist monk, a transparent, greedy buffoon frustrated because he isn't allowed to drink. Yet the protagonist of the same play, a certain type of mendicant, drinks as much as he can get, and the audience would have been aware that this was entirely permissible for him, given his religious status. Indeed, this short play, the *Mattavilāsaprahasana*, is all about his farcical attempts to recover a lost skull-bowl filled with kebabs (*śūlyamāṃsa-*), a skull he also uses for drinking.[1]

The mendicant is conversant with Hindu law and the Vedic sacrifice (as we saw earlier), yet he thrives in the *surā* shop. The common motifs of drunkenness are prominent in this play: his drunk female companion, thinking the world is spinning, staggers, and he attempts to support her; in the drinking house people dance and hitch up their garments. The mendicant, a devotee of Śiva, exclaims that the Goddess Vāruṇī (Surā) is the life of coquetry and amorous perturbation.[2] Drinking in this play is pleasurable, seedy, and humorous.

Who is this mendicant who drinks, and why does he drink? As with the gluttonous Buddhist monk in this play this is not necessarily a realistic account of such a figure. Lorenzen writes, "Kapalikas [skull-carrying mendicants] survived mainly in the literary and religious texts of their opponents as stereotypical villains, buffoons, or heretics."[3] Yet there were real Kāpālikas in ancient India, ascetics whose practices included drinking for ritual reasons. Also, people initiated in some practices as revealed in texts called Tantras engaged in the ritualized drinking of liquor. In this chapter I shall mainly focus on this latter "Tantric" drinking.

Kāpālikas were Brahmin male ascetics aiming at liberation from the eternal round of death and rebirth (though it appears females were also initiated).[4] The Kāpālika practices are earlier than Tantric Śaivism proper, which nevertheless has antecedents in the systems of the Kāpālikas (and related Lākulas), for the Kāpālika practices did include features associated with some later forms of

An Unholy Brew. James McHugh, Oxford University Press. © Oxford University Press 2021.
DOI: 10.1093/oso/9780199375936.003.0010

Śaiva Tantra (associated with Śiva) and Śākta Tantra (associated with Śakti, the Goddess), namely what are called the Mantramārga and Kulamārga divisions of Tantra. These features include erotic ritual with a companion, blood offerings, and consumption of liquor, among other practices.[5] The later, fully Tantric practices, however, were by no means limited to lifelong ascetics, nor always to Brahmins.[6] The Tantric rituals offered the reward of spiritual liberation or the attainment of supernatural powers.[7] Also, unlike the rituals of the full-time ascetic Kāpālikas, the Tantric rituals I discuss in this chapter were esoteric and practiced in secret alongside a public adherence to conventional, orthodox norms of conduct. Yet, despite the secret nature some Tantric practices, this humorous play and many other such literary episodes remind us that the *idea* of Śaiva practices involving impure materials was well established in the popular imagination.[8]

The Challenges of Examining the Role of Drink in Tantra

No book on alcohol in South Asian history and religion can ignore Tantra, especially since secondary scholarship and popular interest have often focused on its use of alcohol and other transgressive practices (e.g., "Tantric sex"). "Tantra" as a general term is a somewhat contested category in academic writing, and there are a vast number of texts and practices, Hindu, Buddhist, and Jain, that various scholars would categorize as somehow "Tantric." Tantric texts deal with many topics, primarily ritual practices aimed at attaining spiritual liberation and/or supernatural powers but also mantras (sacred sound formulas and syllables), theories of ritual, theologies/metaphysics, iconographic descriptions and visualizations of deities, and many other subjects, including snakes and demonic possession. Since the academic study of Tantra is a specialized field, I provide only a simple account of alcohol and Tantra here—a reading of selected texts from a liquor-centric perspective. There are several areas of Tantra I shall not touch on, such as Tantric Buddhism. In exploring drink in Tantra, I've relied on the work of other scholars, especially Alexis Sanderson.

I'd like this chapter to be somewhat accessible to people with little or no knowledge of Tantra, so I've included some basic explanations. I've also omitted a lot of material: there are many Tantric texts that discuss liquor that I don't examine, such as the *Kulārṇava Tantra*, which contains recipes for drinks, lists of drinks, and explanations of the use of certain drinks in rituals (e.g., "date-wine destroys enemies").[9] Nevertheless, I hope that my "liquor-reading" of a few Tantric texts will still be of interest to specialists, enriching the project of studying, translating, and editing Tantric sources by relating them to other fields of textual and cultural production pertinent to their development and interpretation.

Prohibited Substances in Some Tantric Rituals

In addition to a somewhat vague, broader use of the word "Tantra" encountered in some writing, Tantras are a category of text, which Sanderson describes in the case of Hindu Tantras as "an additional and more specialized revelation (*viśeṣaśāstra*) [than orthodox Hindu texts] which offers a more powerful soteriology to those who are born into this exoteric order. The Tantric rituals of initiation (*dīkṣā*) were held to destroy the rebirth-generating power of the individual's past actions (*karma*) in the sphere of Veda-determined values, and to consubstantiate him with the deity in a transforming infusion of divine power."[10] Tantric ritual systems and their antecedents developed from the early to mid-first millennium CE and eventually spread beyond India to Southeast and East Asia as well as to Tibet. Although followers of orthodox religions sometimes excluded Tantrics, the Tantrics themselves saw their systems as a hierarchically superior level of ritual and revelation. In addition to exoteric Tantric systems, often (though not always) overtly compatible with orthodox sensibilities, there were esoteric, secret forms of Tantra in which the initiates transcended conventional practice and perspectives—for example, by consuming meat, drinking liquor, and having sex with women they were forbidden even to touch according to caste *dharma*.

In the first half of this chapter, I focus on some of these esoteric forms of Tantra, especially as presented in the writings of the Kashmiri writer Abhinavagupta. But just how transgressive were these rituals in terms of the substances used? After all, we've already seen *surā* offered in one Vedic ritual. Let us consider the following, quite extreme example:

> The *mantra* master should flood excrement, urine, mingled semen and menstrual blood, and phlegm with liquor (*alinā*),[11] fill [a chalice made from] a human skull (*narakam*) [with them] after empowering it with the mantras [of the Yāga], and then drink [this mixture of the] five nectars and *wine (conj.).[12]

There is complexity in this impurity, a combination of the disgusting, universally impure (excrement, skulls) with a mode of consumption that would otherwise be permissible and desirable for many people—drinking "garnished" liquor. Drinking was forbidden to Brahmins, but it was by no means viewed as a repellent activity, as we've seen many times.[13] In this ritual, the only element *not* replaced by disgusting and impure substances is the liquor, forbidden to Brahmins but otherwise the most "normal" feature. On a Brahmin-centric level, everything here is prohibited (though not all repulsive), but aesthetically speaking, the *mixture* of elements is what would have been most disturbing within early-medieval drinking aesthetics, like a small turd bobbing, olive-like, in a martini.

It's all too easy to pay attention only to the transgressive elements of Tantric rituals while ignoring what they share with more conventional enjoyments. The *Jayadrathayāmala* describes a scene of orgiastic Tantric worship, which reads in parts like the description of a drinking party: the seats, fragrances, betel, food, and drink are all carefully prescribed.[14] The royal drinking party in the *Delight of the Mind* (*Mānasollāsa*), which we looked at earlier, is designed to produce a confused mess of intoxicated women for the king (and the reader) to contemplate. This Tantric orgiastic ritual is also an object of contemplation, but for different reasons. Here liquor is installed and worshipped as a god, Madyabhairava (Liquor Bhairava), Bhairava being a form of Śiva. As the drinking progresses, people become uninhibited and dance, laugh, vomit, faint, meditate, weep, copulate, and consume human body fluids. The ritualized orgy takes drunken, confused degeneration to an extreme. At the end of the ritual, the intoxicated Tantric assembly is treated as one entity, a fused mass of shining, expanding consciousness—intoxicated, joyful, and utterly uninhibited by conventional rules concerning impure matter and social mixing. The initiates present should *contemplate* this entity, and it is stated that by celebrating in this way an adept could achieve supernatural powers (*siddhi*s) and theological gnosis.[15]

As with the skull-cup of impurities described above, the underlying structure of this orgy is not shocking, just some of its elements (though much of the confused behaviour is quite conventional) and the possible presence of Brahmins. Yet the party is also infused with ritual elements and construed as an aestheticized mass of divine consciousness. Whether such orgies ever took place in real life or not (though there is some evidence they might have),[16] educated people either attending or reading about them would undoubtedly have been aware of representations of *non*-Tantric, sensuous drinking bouts. In the drinking party in the *Mānasollāsa*, the king effectively finds himself in a staged literary scene. Similarly, some transgressive Tantric rituals involved drinking in what has clear echoes of a high-class, literary drinking ambiance (the garnished cup, the party, the erotic confusion).

The above examples are both extreme forms of Tantric transgression. Intoxicating drink is also used in other ways in Tantric rituals, often in much simpler circumstances. The intensity of the transgression usually correlated to the ritual's level of esotericism.[17] Sometimes the deity was simply offered *surā*, and sometimes other offerings consumed by the initiate were sprinkled with liquor—a practice utterly forbidden for Brahmins. But these were all ritualized uses of liquor, involving purification rituals and consecration with mantras—nothing like a casual drink at the *surā* shop.

Tantric Scriptures on Liquor

Recall the praises of *surā* in medical texts that I discussed in the previous chapter. Those passages presented *surā* as divine and primordial, referring to several gods and myths as well as the Sautrāmaṇī ritual. Thus, at the time when the earlier Tantric texts were compiled, and even earlier, other texts were cleverly synthesizing Vedic, epic, and Purāṇic materials in defense of *surā*.

Thus, it may have been well known to many people that *surā* was divine, but in treating liquor, however, esoteric Hindu Tantra faced the more serious problem of how to bring *surā*-shunning Brahmins back into the *surā* fold, something a simple praise of *surā* could not achieve. On the other hand, a new divine revelation superseding the orthodox status quo would make their return feasible. After all, mythologically speaking, there was a time when this potent primordial intoxicant was not prohibited to Brahmins.

How do these new Tantric revelations defend or explain the use of liquor in rituals? Tantric Śaiva scriptures (as opposed to commentaries and synthetic summaries) contain some references to the meaning of intoxicating drink in rituals.[18] Some texts engage in semantic analysis, *nirvacana*, to explain and justify parts of the ritual. The *Kulasāra* clarifies:

> It is called *vāruṇī* (in the sense of "coming from or belonging to the god of the ocean, Varuṇa") because it was produced as such from the churning of the milk ocean. *Surā* [is so called] because it was drunk by the gods (*suraiḥ*).[19]

Such references would have been familiar to many, especially Hindus. The Tantric text Judit Törzsök translates here also justifies the use of *surā* by referring to the orthodox Vedic Sautrāmaṇī sacrifice,[20] the latter being a mythical precedent that Abhinavagupta also mentions.[21] But, interesting as these comments are as apologies for *surā* as a sacred offering-substance, they do little to explain what role *surā* plays in these particular rituals.

Surā is defined, very much in light of the *Law Code of Manu*, in a text called the *Brahmayāmala Tantra*:

> *surāpi trividhā proktā gauḍī paiṣṭī ca mādhavī.*[22]
> And *surā* is said to be threefold, jaggery-based, grist-based, and *mādhavī*.[23]

The rest of this section of the *Brahmayāmala* further expands what is covered by these three types of *surā*—giving recipes. The text thus aligns divinely revealed Tantric-ritual drinking with a range of liquors, and with drink law and theory, in a way that we would expect from a text that probably dates from the seventh or eighth century CE.[24] Drawing on Manu's framework and well-known myths, and sometimes involving a number of varied liquors, this Tantric ritual drinking looks thoroughly "of its time," a practice that drew on a range of contemporary intellectual and practical resources. And the rationale given in other texts for the use of liquor in Tantric rituals also reflects contemporaneous ideas about drinking.

The Ms

In some forms of Tantra, a distinctive way of classifying substances perhaps sheds light on the connotations of liquor and other substances—a set list of five offerings denoted by words beginning with "m" in Sanskrit, often known as the "five Ms" (*makāras*): intoxicating drink (*madya*), meat (*māṃsa*), fish (*matsya*), parched grain (*mudrā*), and sexual intercourse (*maithuna*).[25] Another list, the "three Ms," consists of intoxicating drink (*madya*), meat (*māṃsa*) and sex (*maithuna*).[26]

We've already seen lists of Sanskrit M-words associated with consumables and worldly, sensuous actions, such as in the *Law Code of Manu*:

> There is no fault in eating meat (*māṃsa*), in drinking intoxicating drink (*madya*), or in having sex (*maithuna*); that is the natural activity of creatures. Abstaining from such activity, however, brings great rewards.[27]

South Asian scholars of Tantra saw this parallel in terms of the Ms, too, and Jayaratha refers to the above verse in his commentary on Abhinavagupta's *Light on the Tantras* (*Tantrāloka*).[28] There are similar alliterative patterns of sensuous, morally valent Ms (and other labial consonants) in several other contexts.[29] The notion of the sensuous M is not limited to Hindu materials—a line in the Jain *Yaśastilaka* praises abstention from another "three Ms": "*madya-māṃsa-madhutyāgāḥ*"—intoxicating drink, meat, and honey.[30] The list from Manu was probably well known, and I would argue that the Tantric lists of Ms (three, then five) have antecedents in such lists and may even deliberately echo Manu's (or a shared tradition). Such Tantric assimilation and reinterpretation of stock phrases of Hindu law is attested elsewhere: the threefold *surā* in the *Brahmayāmala Tantra*, for example, adapts Manu's definition (or an intermediate text).

It's important to remember that Manu's three Ms are not prohibited; rather, he states that there is *no* universal prohibition on drink, meat, and sex (except in the case of Brahmins and liquor, *madya*). In the orthodox context, the verse from Manu reads as a statement of permission qualified by an encouragement to abstain from these things. Likewise, a list of sensuous Ms in the *Baudhāyana Dharmasūtra* names things that a widow should abstain from for one year. Thus, these Ms are often pleasures commonly enjoyed but avoided in a life of intensified discipline. So, alongside an emphasis on complete abstinence for Brahmins, the Tantric lists of Ms should perhaps be read as lists of sensuous things, which one should avoid if one is being especially disciplined and virtuous in the realm of conventional morality. It's not just the substances but also the *phonetic* forms given in Tantric revelation—the M-words—that evoke sensuous enjoyments. By contrast, impure and repulsive body fluids and excretions have different connotations in both law and the broader culture.

Abhinavagupta on Liquor

Let's now turn to some synthetic and exegetical texts from Kashmir that contain complex and sophisticated discussions of liquor in Tantra. The key figure here is Abhinavagupta, active circa 975–1025 CE, a scholar and theologian from Kashmir who composed works on both aesthetics and on Tantric theology and ritual.[31] His *Light on the Tantras* (*Tantrāloka*) is a vast summation of all aspects of Tantra, in particular the branch of Śaiva Tantra called the Trika, though he also attempts to integrate some less orthodox elements associated with the cult of Kālī taught in a Tantric branch called the Krama. I shall, in addition, consider a commentary on Abhinavagupta's *Light on the Tantras* composed in the thirteenth century CE by a scholar called Jayaratha.[32]

Abhinavagupta and Jayaratha both held a non-dualistic philosophy according to which, to quote Sanderson, "the true identity of oneself and all phenomena is the Lord (*īśvaraḥ*) defined as this all-containing, autonomous consciousness."[33] Seen from this point of view, there is no such thing as impurity, nor is a person essentially a limited, world-snared mortal, eternally being reborn. Liberation can be achieved through knowledge, gnosis, of the true nature of reality and thereby of one's self. Yet, as ritual was central to the Tantric traditions, scholars such as Abhinavagupta had to explain how these rituals worked in such a system: the "whole text of the ritual was . . . transformed into a series of variations on the theme of non-duality and the nondualization of awareness."[34] In many cases this gnosis was achieved by the "practice of nonduality," transgressing the (not ultimately real) limits, perspectives, and structures of orthodox norms of conduct. For example, a ritual in which Brahmins drank liquor was justified "by arguing that this practice of nonduality had been revealed by Śiva himself in his highest and most esoteric scriptures as the ultimate means of liberating consciousness from the contraction or inhibition which holds it in bondage."[35]

Abhinavagupta was not just a theologian; he was also well informed in other realms. In his work on aesthetics he demonstrated great learning, something shared with other Kashmiri Śaivas, "reflecting the importance of dance and music in their liturgies and the aestheticism of the Kaula mystical cults, which saw enlightenment not in withdrawal from extroverted cognition but in its contemplation as the spontaneous radiance of the self."[36] Abhinavagupta wrote quite a lot about liquor in various contexts, but I'll focus here on just a few passages.[37]

Above we saw that, in one revealed Tantric scripture, the Vedic Sautrāmaṇī ritual was mentioned as a precedent for the ritual use of *surā*. Abhinavagupta takes this point further. He states that the "anomalous" purity of *surā* in that Vedic ritual is emblematic of the non-objectivity and obvious relativity of the values of purity and impurity practiced in Brahminical orthodoxy.[38] When the true nature of all phenomena is that they are the Lord, the Absolute, how can anything be impure? If *apparent* properties of the conventional lived world, such as pure-versus-impure, are not *ultimate* properties of reality, maybe everything else is likewise a mere construction (of consciousness by consciousness—remember there is not really an ignorant, limited individual constructing all this, just the Lord, autonomous consciousness). Abhinavagupta thus draws on orthodoxy itself to undermine and reconstrue the orthodox viewpoint, raising us to an ultimate perspective. As Sanderson explains, "To object to the Sautrāmaṇī [Vedic liquor offering] and Paśubandha [Vedic animal sacrifice] rituals because there are general Vedic prohibitions against drinking alcohol and taking life would be as unreasonable as to object to the use of irregular verbs. The grammar lays down general rules to cover most cases and then gives specific rules to cover the exceptions. So does the corpus of ritual injunctions."[39] Both the ancient Sautrāmaṇī sacrifice and Tantric drinking are exceptions that were revealed in scripture.

For Abhinavagupta liquor is also ritually effective on another level—the level of the contraction and differentiation of absolute consciousness into gods, bodies, and other phenomena, including drinks. For the Absolute has projected our differentiated reality of time and space, while still maintaining its non-dual, timeless nature as consciousness.[40] The world of phenomena is thus not merely an illusion in this system. The ritual and cognitive system of Abhinavagupta's Tantra works within differentiated, manifest reality to allow practitioners both to overcome it and to enjoy it. In this way the very understanding of pleasure changes within the Tantric sect called Kaula (which was associated with the more extreme Tantric practices). It's worth quoting Sanderson at length here:

> [W]hen the objects of the senses are seen as things outside consciousness, to be appropriated and manipulated by the subject, then the senses are no more than the instruments of the state of bondage; but when the subject abandons this

> appetitive style of perception he experiences the objects of his senses within consciousness... This shift from the appetitive to the aesthetic mode of awareness is seen by Abhinavagupta as the divinization of the senses themselves, or rather as the recognition of their divine nature as projections of avenues of the blissful but egoless consciousness which is the underlying identity of all awareness... [W]here before they were starved by brahmanical restraint and fastidiousness—[now] they liberate consciousness into the realization of its all containing radiance and transparency.[41]

Liquor usage in Tantric ritual, despite the Vedic precedent, is impure for Brahmins according to orthodox law and is thus a useful tool for overcoming cognitive boundaries about the conventional world. But it's also an ideal ritual tool to use in this liberated mode of aesthetics for, as we've learned, drink is innately pleasant to taste; it enhances sensory experience of other phenomena, and it makes the drinker less inhibited in enjoying all manner of pleasures. Concerning the limited, orthodox perspective on drink and certain other substances, and their useful awareness-expanding effects, Abhinavagupta writes:

> Now, impurity [here] is to be understood in the terms of the unliberated and their [Vaidika][i.e., orthodox] scriptures...
>
> But in fact any [substance] that makes our awareness come to the fore from its [usual] state of suppression is suitable as an offering. For it is [this] emergence of awareness that constitutes bliss.[42]

Such suitable offerings include intoxicating drink, *kādambarī*, and sugarcane wine, so liquor in general (*madyakādambarīśīdhu-*)[43] as is taught in Tantric scriptures. The fact that, as with perfumes, one could obtain special types of liquor might even have rendered drink more valuable in these rituals for some practitioners. As we've seen, liquor was associated with the prelude and aftermath of making love, which produces some of the ritual "nectars" used in some Tantric rituals. By contrast, while an offering of blood might please some forms of the goddess, given her appetites, as well as being impure and thus useful for overcoming the inhibitions of orthodoxy—unless we are divinely or otherwise possessed it would not delight our senses or alter our mental states, nor is it sexually arousing.

Let's now examine what I think is Abhinavagupta's most revealing discussion of liquor, in the Kula ritual, along with the commentary of Jayaratha.[44] Abhinavagupta states the following:

> 29.10. In this sacrifice the knowledgeable should use a substance—prohibited in the series of scriptures—sprinkled with the left-hand nectar [i.e., liquor].[45]

Here the commentator Jayaratha quotes a verse stating that this refers to:

> . . . substances that people revile and are excluded on account of scriptural precepts; which are very repulsive and reprehensible.

This implies the less appetizing substances we saw in the skull-cup earlier—both repulsive and excluded. Turning to the "nectar," that is, liquor, Abhinavagupta focuses on the possible varieties:

> 11. And in the blessed *Brahmayāmala* [*Tantra*], it is stated that *surā* is the externalized juice/elixir (*rasa*) of Śiva. Without it there is no supernatural power or liberation. It is made with ground grain, honey, or jaggery (*piṣṭakṣaudraguḍais tu sā*).
>
> 12ab. It has feminine, neuter, and masculine forms, and the prior and subsequent furnish greater and lesser rewards (or "pleasures").

The line about the ingredients of *surā* should seem very familiar by now—it is yet another adaptation of Manu's definition, and perhaps also supposedly an adaptation of the *Brahmayāmala Tantra*'s version of Manu. We saw earlier how the *madhu*-related words for liquors can cause confusion, and thus Abhinavagupta wisely chooses to use a less ambiguous word (*kṣaudra*) that definitely means a drink made from honey. But why is he so keen to clarify this technical issue, excluding a word that might possibly mean grape wine? He continues:

> 12cd. But the thing produced from grapes (*drākṣotthaṃ*) is the supreme light (*tejas*), Bhairava (*bhairavaṃ*),[46] devoid of formation/differentiation (*kalpanojjhitam*).
>
> 13. In itself it is a pure elixir (*rasaḥ*) made of light, bliss, and consciousness (*prakāśānandacinmayaḥ*), ever beloved of gods[47]—on account of this one should always drink this one.

Abhinavagupta's unambiguous reference to "honey mead" in the threefold definition of *surā* has permitted him to isolate and elevate grape wine, which he explicitly names (though it is, in fact, included in *mādhavī* in the expanded *Brahmayāmala Tantra* definition). Wine is thus set apart from the three other types of *surā*, with their clear echoes of the orthodoxy of Manu, and the frustratingly uncertain "*madhu*" and related words are totally omitted. Abhinavagupta leaves no room for confusion. His statement may even imply that grape wine is not covered by Manu's orthodox definition of *surā*. Regardless, grape wine, now clearly defined, is here declared the supreme drink, the most powerful in ritual.

The commentator Jayaratha draws on a lot of material to explain these verses, and I'll present only selections here. He first quotes verses from other Tantric texts to justify these statements: *surā* is indeed the supreme Śakti; intoxicating drink (*madya*) is said to be Bhairava transformed into a liquid form; there is indeed no acquisition of liberation or supernatural powers without drink, which provides supernatural powers and liberation to the man who smells it, hears it, sees it, drinks it, and touches it.

Then Jayaratha turns to the varieties of liquor, explaining, "And it is twofold: manufactured/fabricated (*kṛtrimā*) and simple/natural (*sahajā*). The manufactured is threefold: made from grist, from honey, and from jaggery; and there is only one simple/natural one, produced from grapes . . ." Presumably the use of the word "manufactured/fabricated" (*kṛtrima*) refers to the processing and extra ingredients (herbal additives, *kiṇva* starters) involved in making the first three types of *surā* (as defined here).[48] Recall also that grain *surā* is intrinsically compounded. By contrast, grape wine is said to be "simple/natural/spontaneous" (*sahaja*), probably because wine-making is a spontaneous process that takes place with (theoretically) no additions. That is exactly how the *Delight of the Mind* (*Mānasollāsa*) defines grape wine—as grape juice that has been left for some time.[49] Regarding the genders, Jayaratha explains that relative to the masculine form of *surā*, the feminine and neuter have [greater] utility or enjoyableness, which makes sense of Abhinavagupta's statement that the feminine, the neuter, and the masculine forms give respectively greater and lesser rewards. Jayaratha also quotes a stanza explaining this distinction with respect to manufactured and simple/natural liquors:

> Grist-based, jaggery-based, and *madhu*-based *surā* is said to be manufactured/fabricated. It furnishes rewards to practitioners according to its being feminine, masculine, or neuter.

The first part of this verse again adapts Manu, but here the emphasis is not on *surā* as threefold but on these drinks being manufactured/fabricated. No doubt any educated person reading either the root text or the commentary would pick up on this similarity, though Manu-esque definitions of *surā* are so common as to be a routine occurrence in texts from that era.

What are we to make of the genders here? At least in their adjectival forms, these words are all feminine, being varieties of *surā* (f.). Perhaps the differentiation refers to common terms for drinks made from these bases, which are indeed of the three grammatical genders: *paiṣṭī surā* (f.), *madhu* (n.), and *sīdhu* (m.).[50] Or perhaps the question arises simply because a revealed text says that the drinks have those genders. John Dupuche suggests that in the world of subjects and objects—meaning the world *as perceived* by those who are still "bound"—things are designated by words with a grammatical gender.[51] The "I" in Sanskrit, however, has no gender, and from an enlightened perspective, where "all is I," there are no such objective differentiations. The lower, forbidden, threefold *surā* of Manu belongs to the world of subject and object, of grammatical gender, compounded-substances, and conventional moral norms. But wine, being natural and spontaneous, is like the Absolute Consciousness, at least when consecrated and consumed in Tantric rituals.

Unlike with Abhinavagupta's text, the verse I just quoted also presents us with the eternal problem of what "*madhu*" means. But having stated that these three drinks are fabricated, Jayaratha then quotes a verse about grape wine, and by juxtaposing the fabricated *surā*s with an explicit reference to grape wine, he clearly implies that the *madhu*-derived drink (*mādhvī*) in the previous verses refers to a honey drink:

> But grape wine is the sole spontaneous one; it is fire that has the nature of Bhairava ["the terrible"]—the supreme Lord is not feminine, not neuter, not masculine.

Again, grape wine, being uncompounded and produced from grapes alone, is like the Absolute. The three "lower," manufactured, compounded *surā*s are lined up with the three genders in a manner that limits them: they are conditioned, possess limits, as well as parts, by virtue of the composite, assembled nature of their production—just as gendered entities are also conditioned and limited. These "mixed" drinks are suitable only for attaining limited ritual goals. But the supreme Lord is beyond such distinctions, and wine, spontaneously fermenting from one unadulterated substance alone (grape juice), occupies the same place in the world of intoxicating drinks.

In this particular Tantric scheme, there are a total of four types of intoxicating drink (*madya*) that fall into two categories, one being supreme. If this is the correct interpretation, here we see classical legal definitions, fermentation technology, and cultural preferences all brought to play in ritual theory. For I don't think it's implausible that Abhinavagupta elevated the status of wine in ritual because he was from Kashmir, a region associated from early periods with grapes and wine.[52] Indeed, in the final verses of *Light on the Tantras* Abhinavagupta presents a praise of Kashmir in very much the same mode as seen in (non-Tantric) poems by Kashmiris,[53] who also praise Kashmir in terms of its admired products, grapes, wines, saffron and also citrus fruits:

> [Kashmir]: where wine (*madya*), Mahābhairava, gleaming with the four Powers, has the ruddy luster of oranges, the white hue of pale flowering wheat, the pleasing radiance of the golden color of spotless citrons bursting forth, and is brilliant with a dark luster the image of *kerīkuntala* plantain trees.[54]

> Melted by the Three-Eyed One's blaze of great anger, Kāmadeva's mass of [flower] arrows remains here, blooming in the guise of wine (*madya*)—how else does [wine], constantly producing passion, confusion, intoxication, and love fever, put the world in its power with the afflictions of love?

> Grape wine (*mārdvīkam*), which imparts bold confidence to the amorous words of lovers, and, unhindered, takes any fear out of [pursuing] sexual acts, and in which is present all the goddesses of the circle, endowed with splendor—there [in Kashmir] it instantly bestows power and liberation.[55]

The following verse (TĀ 37.45) describes the colorful glories of the saffron flowers of the region, which are likewise not just beautiful but constitute a veritable garden for rites of worship. And in a poetic portrait of Abhinavagupta by his contemporary Madhurāja he is described as seated with standing female attendants on both sides, who are bearing a cup of wine (*śivarasa-saraka*), a betel bag, a citron, and a lotus.[56]

Returning to Jayaratha, we turn now to the last set of properties of liquor that Abhinavagupta describes. Jayaratha explains that liquor is like mercurial elixir, or perhaps simply mercury, on account of its supreme fieriness (or energy/potency, *paratejastvāt*). This raises the question of whether he is referring to a distilled drink, or whether it's "fiery" because of its color, strength, and purity. As we'll see in the next chapter, one expert in Tantra writing in the eighteenth century describes *surā* as being made of the element *tejas*, fire, because of its flammability. And Jayaratha (though less likely Abhinavagupta) is from a late enough period that he might, in fact, have been describing a distilled drink. Jayaratha then quotes a verse on liquor being equal to mercury in its excellence and hierarchical supremacy.

He clarifies that one should not consume drink out of lustfulness and other such motives (*laulyādinā*) in the manner of "bound souls" (*paśuvat*), meaning those who have not received a liberating Tantric initiation and who drink for unenlightened pleasure. He even quotes a verse stating that drinking in this "bound" way will lead a Tantric adept to hell. But he also strengthens the injunction to drink liquor in rituals by noting that it's a sin *not* to drink it in that context (*apānāt pratyavāyo 'pi syāt*), quoting verses about this too. If we recall the orthodox Brahminical rules about drinking, this latter point highlights the transgressive—or transcendent—nature of Tantric practices as related to orthodox Hindu *dharma*—in this "left-hand" realm it is a sin *not* to drink liquor. And whereas in the previous chapter we read of penances exacted for the sin of drinking, in this Tantric text we learn that a man who does *not* drink in rituals must perform a penance (*prāyaścittī*).[57]

Drinking in certain rituals may be obligatory, but Jayaratha reminds us that drink is to be consumed only in connection with worshiping the pantheon (*yāgakālāpekṣayaiva yojyam*). Yet outside the realm of certain types of Tantric worship, there was a whole world of drinking, and Jayaratha quotes a revealing passage describing how drink is demarcated in use for those who are uninitiated—still fully immersed, in other words, in the conventional distinctions of caste-*dharma* drinking. These verses take the form of a dialogue with a goddess, and of all the materials in this chapter, they convey most explicitly where drinking in Tantric Śaivism stands in relation to other, mundane drinking:

> And from the time when it (i.e., liquor) was vilified by the preceptor of the Daityas (i.e., Śukra when he was tricked into drinking *surā* mixed with his powdered pupil), the distinction according to social classes (*varṇa*) has been specified. For Brahmins it is taught in revered tradition that it is for drinking in the Sautrāmaṇī sacrifice, for Kṣatriyas in the great battle, for Vaiśyas in rites of the land (or "work on the land"), for kinsmen in great festivals, for friends in gatherings, and for Śūdras around the cremation ground, and at weddings, and on the birth of a son. This is the partition of drinking for ignorant-minded beings, good lady. For those twice-borns (Brahmins, Kṣatriyas, and Vaiśyas, or "just" Brahmins), however, who are initiated in a Tantra of Śaṅkara (= Śiva) or in a Tantra of the Goddess, who are devoted to the commands of their guru, who are private and absorbed in recitation and worship, who are skilled in sacred and other knowledge, and being of revered intention, and who are not [doing it] out of lustfulness—[for those twice-borns] it is never forbidden, dear lady.[58]

Thus all the regulations and social traditions about drinking that we saw earlier are for the ignorant. They form yet another limitation, practical and gnostic, intrinsic to the "bound," conventional, orthodox life. And it all dates back to when Śukra reviled drink, which set in motion the differentiation of drinking according to social class (*varṇa*). But the twice-born who has undergone Tantric initiation and follows his guru's instructions is not bound by these restrictions. Drinking as prescribed in Tantric revelation—a newly revealed but perfectly valid irregular verb—is thus a redemption of liquor, beloved of gods. For, prior to Śukra's pronouncement, liquor was not vilified, or censured (*dūṣitam*). Still, the new allowance for Brahmins depends on several conditions: certain revealed scriptures that prescribe it, initiation by a guru into certain cults that practice drinking, and a particular ritual context. Tantric drinking is highly delimited.

Jayaratha then leaves the topic of who can drink and when, and turns to the role of drink in ritual, pointing out that intoxicating drink is necessary for the sacrifice to be effective, and that other impure substances need to be accompanied by liquor for the ritual to work. He quotes many verses to prove that, while the other substances are not necessary, if there is no liquor (*madya*, *ali*)[59] the ritual will be ineffective.

Society, Practice, and Mythology

For whom does all this apply? Just Brahmins, or other *varṇa*s too? As we saw earlier, in a common understanding of orthodox Hindu law based on Manu, only Brahmins are forbidden all liquor; other *varṇa*s are permitted it in varying degrees. Yet Manu states that even those who are permitted to drink would do better to abstain. So the cognitive/ritual efficacy of this systematic Tantric transgression hinges somewhat on the *varṇa* and/or attitude of the person doing the ritual. A Brahmin drinking liquor in a Tantric ritual is sinning by the standards of caste *dharma*, whatever the drink is made of. And a Śūdra was not doing anything transgressive in drinking, though it may have gone against his or her preferences. But could Śūdras, Kṣatriyas, and Vaiśyas be initiated into the Tantric systems? The situation is complex, though we know that Kṣatriyas could be initiated.[60] Several texts state that caste (*jāti*) is a mere fabrication (*kalpanāmātraṃ*).[61] Some texts state that Śūdras can be initiated, though this applies only to those who have chosen not to drink alcohol (*amadyapāḥ*).[62] Indeed, from the sources collected by Alexis Sanderson on this subject, it seems that Śākta Tantrics, who would have engaged in "fierce" practices, often rejected caste. Later sources giving lists of Tantric Gurus (*Nāthas*) list some who made liquor (*jātikalyapālaḥ*, *karavālaḥ*) along with Brahmins, Kṣatriyas, Vaiśyas, and Śūdras.[63] The liquor-makers are the same caste, *kalyapāla*, that we saw mentioned in the Kashmiri *Rājataraṅgiṇī*, in which kings who were descended from *kalyapāla*s were scorned.

Was ritual drinking transgressive for Kṣatriyas? Most texts on *dharmaśāstra* permitted some alcoholic drinks for this *varṇa*, but despite that legal permission, in "popular orthodoxy" and some local traditions, and according to the advice of Manu and others, abstinence might well have been viewed as the ideal of conduct. As we saw earlier in the *Rājataraṅgiṇī* chronicle of Kashmir, betel was emphasized as respectable for kings, while alcohol was typically presented in a negative light—and it was also seen as improper for kings to perform fierce Kaula rituals in that text.[64] This more generalized conventional morality, in which *good* people should abstain from drinking, might also have informed the meaning of liquor in Tantric Buddhism.[65] Brahmins were most constrained when it came to drink, but perhaps this was fortunate for them within Tantra, since that particular prohibition—obviously socially relative—made a good starting point for dismantling metaphysical inhibitions.

There is a tension, almost a contradiction (though a productive contradiction), in Abhinavagupta's and Jayaratha's project of interpreting alcohol. On the one hand, Tantras and their interpreters discuss liquor's importance on a sacred, cosmic, mythical level, also noting its use in an orthodox Vedic ritual. Yet they also emphasize the prohibition of drink, for this prohibition is vital to the cognitive/ritual performance designed to overcome the initiate's dualistic inhibitions. This means that *surā* is at least three things in these texts: (1) a substance prohibited by conventional caste *dharma*—on a human, contemporary, orthodox level; (2) a divine, *originally* permitted drink of myth, used in a Vedic ritual—on a cosmic, ancient, yet still orthodox level; and (3) the Absolute, Śiva, along with all other phenomena—on the ultimate level of Tantric revelation. In addition, *surā* is intoxicating, arousing, and aesthetically pleasing. From my brief, piecemeal survey we see that Abhinavagupta's project of interpreting drink in rituals works on all these levels. Drinking in Tantra is far more than just a transgressive act.

Liquor is unusually well placed to work on all these levels when compared to other materials. At the risk of being repetitive, for Abhinavagupta one purpose of using substances that are forbidden in orthodox life is to help people overcome inhibitions in how they experience reality, which prevent them from perceiving non-dual reality.[66] The forbidden nature of alcohol is well known to be socially relative, and thus liquor-prohibition is an easy boundary to break in dismantling a person's ideas about conventional reality. Liquor is also tasty. It loosens inhibitions. Flowers are delightful ritual offerings, but they are not forbidden. Other impure things, such as excrement, are forbidden to Brahmins, but they are not always suitable offerings for divine beings, nor is excrement intoxicating and thus inhibition-loosening in the same way as alcohol is.[67] Liquor is a substance of pleasure with a divine pedigree for which the orthodox Hindu proscriptions contain just the right amount of apparent internal contradiction to allow Tantric practitioners to realize the illusory, merely conventional distinctions that obscure and limit their gnosis of the Absolute. With the help of wine Absolute Consciousness knows itself, enjoying itself in the process.

The Goddess Surā in Later Texts

With Surā reintegrated into ritual life for initiates in certain Tantric traditions, some texts teach us more about her divine personification. Earlier we saw that Surā appeared in the myth of the churning of the ocean, but those ancient sources revealed little about her. Just as the Tantrics working in a more scholastic mode highlighted and theorized the many properties of liquor-as-substance, so Tantric texts in a more narrative, Purāṇic style elaborate on the myth of Surā the goddess.

There are several detailed iconographic descriptions of Surā in Sanskrit texts, as well as extant visual images, and Gudrun Bühnemann has produced a thorough study of this material.[68] Typically Surā (or Vāruṇī) in these sources has red skin, eighteen arms carrying a number of attributes, and a skull-cup seat, implying that *surā* is contained in a skull cup, not unlike the one we read about earlier. I focus here on another Tantric narrative of Surā in which we also discover a new intoxicating substance—cannabis—woven into the ever-accommodating framework of the churning myth. This text is from the late-medieval *Esoteric Teaching of the Goddess*, the *Devīrahasya* (also called the *Parārahasya*),[69] which teaches a Kaula system of Tantra (containing many "fierce" transgressive elements, as we saw in the previous sections of this chapter), though it does not teach the non-dualistic philosophy.[70] Note that I'm offering a liquor-reading of the text, not the interpretation of a scholar of Tantra. At least one painting (see Figure 8.1) would appear to depict Surā with the iconography of the *Devīrahasya*, and there may be more.[71]

The myth is presented as revealed by the god Bhairava, and, although the basic story was no doubt well-known, the richness of detail is unlike what we've seen before:[72]

Bhairava said:

> Now, O goddess, I shall relate the origin of Surā, O Maheśvarī,
> merely hearing[73] which one will gain the rewards of initiation.
> When the sea, the milk ocean, that supreme ocean, was being churned,
> the goddess Surā arose there, possessing the beauty of a maiden,
> naked, resembling the world-destroying fire, her face flashing with laughter,
> divine, with eighteen arms, carrying nine jars (*kumbha*),
> and also carrying nine cups (*pātra*),[74] her eyes reddish from liquor (*madirā*),
> covered in ornaments of various flowers, her hair loosened, with three eyes,
> wearing various bejeweled armlets, bowed by creeper-like pearl-strings,
> abounding in beauty because of her red rings,[75] bowed by lofty, swollen breasts,
> on her buttocks a girdle thread studded with a variety of gems,
> on a bejeweled lion-throne, imparting supreme bliss.
> Seeing that goddess, Brahma, Viṣṇu, and Maheśvara,
> the gods (*sura*), the anti-gods (*asura*), and *gandharva*s (celestial musicians), together with Īśvara and Sadāśiva praised her.[76]

Surā the goddess is beautiful, naked, and adorned with jewels, with the idealized body-type of women in classical Sanskrit literature and art. Her liquor-character is seen in her reddened eyes, laughter, and loosened hair. She imparts supreme bliss. Notably, the gods all praise her when she appears—her reputation is yet unsullied. She holds nine jars of drink and nine cups in which she will serve drink to the gods.

When drops of the drinks fall on the earth, they become the plants associated with intoxicating and pleasure-producing substances. (The process resembles

FIGURE 8.1: The Goddess Surā/Vāruṇī with nine cups and nine vessels, Kangra 1810–1820 (Losty 2019, 72). She also emerges from the water. Despite the fact that some details such as the lotus, the heads, the freshwater setting are not as in the text, I believe this is quite likely to be Surā.

Credit: Steven Kossak, The Kronos Collections. I thank Siddhartha Shah for alerting me to the existence of this image and Kurt Behrendt for helping me obtain this copy and permissions.

another set of myths recounting the creation of gemstones from the bodily tissues of a demon that were scattered over the earth.[77]) The first drink is given to Sadāśiva, who plays an important role later:

> [Cup 1.]
> Then Surā, with a pleased/bright (*prasanna-*) face, ready to grant a boon,
> first gave a divine cup filled with the juice of bliss (*ānandarasa-*)
> to Sadāśiva, O queen of gods. He bowed and accepted the vessel.
> A drop from the cup fell on the earth, and "jaggery creeper" (*guḍalatā*) came into being.
> From the falling of the drop, droplets were produced, and from them were
> produced by the thousand the varieties of sugarcane, the catechu trees,[78]
> the three pungent spices and the rest;[79] white crystal sugar and other
> types of sugar, areca-nut palms, [and] the betel-leaf vine flowed forth, O Maheśvarī!
> And this is called jaggery-based *surā* (*gauḍī*), made of these, which provides all things.
>
> [Cup 2.]
> Then, O Śivā, Surā gave the next cup to Īśvara.
> A drop from the cup fell on the earth, from which the *ahivallarī* ("snake-creeper"; betel?) was produced.
> And species of grape [vine?] (*drākṣā*) were produced a thousandfold from the droplets of the falling drop,
> And grapes (*mṛdvīkā*) and the rest, great purifiers, were produced, O great goddess.
> This is called grape *surā* (*mādhvī*), which furnishes all the supernatural powers (*siddhi*) in the practices of the Mahāvidyās.[80]
>
> [Cup 3.]
> Then she gave the next cup, filled with nectar of immortality, to Rudra.
> A drop from the cup fell on the earth, and the varieties of wheat (*godhūma*) came into being.
> From its droplets arose the varieties of grain (*dhānya*).[81]
> This surā is called grist-based (*paiṣṭī*), which imparts supreme bliss, O goddess![82]

These first three drinks, given to Śaiva deities, are the now-familiar "threefold *surā*" of the *Law Code of Manu*, based on jaggery, grapes (as with Abhinavagupta, "*mādhvī*" is rendered unambiguous in this context), and grain. Not only does Manu's threefold *surā* have a mythical, divine manifestation here, but the components of betel-chewing are incorporated. These substances are connected to the sugary drinks, the *gauḍī surā*, probably because sugar was sometimes used to flavor betel wraps. Betel has now found its place in a divinely revealed mythical past. In other contexts presented as a perfume rather than a drug, betel in this source is linked to *surā*.

The process of the drinks becoming human drugs has two stages. In some cases the first drops produce plants with names that I have not seen elsewhere, such as the "jaggery creeper" in the quotation's first cup.[83] Perhaps these are mythical plants, intermediary species between the divine materials of the drink and the mundane plants that we use to make drinks on earth. Or maybe the names allude in the most generic terms, almost like botanical families, to the plants that follow, according to whether they originate with the fruit, the flower, or other plant parts—so that the "jaggery flower" in the seventh cup of the passage implies "sugar-producing flowers."[84]

The updating of the mythical origins of intoxicants does not stop with betel:

> [Cup 4.]
> Then she gave the next cup to mighty Viṣṇu.
> A drop from the cup fell on the earth, and then, O beloved, cannabis (*saṃvit*; "consciousness/understanding") came into being;
> And from its droplets, O queen of gods, its varieties, "gold" (*kanaka*; possibly datura?) and the rest.
> And many other varieties were produced that increase intoxication (*madanavardhaka*).
> I call it "victoria" (*vijayā*; a common term for cannabis), *vaiṣṇavī* that imparts the supreme goal!
> Between cannabis (*saṃvit*) and *āsava* (liquors), cannabis is indeed the most important.[85]

Cannabis arises from the cup offered to Viṣṇu, which explains one of the names of this drug: *vaiṣṇavī* ("Viṣṇu-related-thing," f.). The status of cannabis is ambiguous—this is the fourth cup, presented after Surā has offered the other types of *surā*, and it's offered to Viṣṇu (in this Śaiva text), yet the drug is stated to be more important than alcoholic *āsava*s, in a stock line found in other Tantric texts (to be discussed later). Just as nowadays, cannabis apparently has many named varieties, and the plant performs the action of increasing intoxication (or "passion," *madana*).

After the three *surā*s and cannabis, the drops from the other cups become other types of drinks. The nature of these classifications is not clear in every case:

[*Cup 5.*]
The blessed Surā gave the next cup to Brahmā (Parameṣṭhin).
A drop from the cup fell on the earth, and quickly *parūṣaka* [*Grewia asiatica* L., a type of sour berry] came into being.
And from its droplets were produced varieties, *kṣaudrarasa* ["honey-juice"][86] and the rest.
This is called the supreme universal drink, O goddess.[87]

This could refer to drinks made from honey, or it could be another fruit to go with the *parūṣaka*, a variety called "honey-juice"—in which case this is the creation of drinks made from the fruits of plants other than grapes.

[*Cup 6.*]
Then she gave the next cup filled with the nectar of immortality (*amṛta*) to Indra.
A drop from the cup fell on the earth, and then the nutmeg (*jātīphalaṃ*) came into being.
And from its droplets were produced the varieties, emblic myrobalan (*āmalaka*)[88] and the rest.
Indeed that divine drink is said to be the elixir of life (*rasāyana*).[89]

The drops from cup six produce common flavoring spices, perhaps associated with herbal, medicinal drinks. This may also be the category of dried fruits used in drinks.

[*Cup 7.*]
Then, O lady-born-of-the-mountain, Surā gave the next cup to Guru (Bṛhaspati, preceptor of the gods/*devas*).
A drop from the cup fell on the earth, and then jaggery flowers (*guḍapuṣpa* – possibly mahua flowers)[90] [came into being], O Śivā.
From its droplets varieties arose, the coconut and the rest.
This drink is indeed the supreme elixir of life (*rasāyana*), O queen of gods.

[*Cup 8.*]
Then she gave the next cup, filled with the nectar of immortality, to Śukra (preceptor of the anti-gods/*asuras*, who later banishes Surā).
A drop from the cup fell on the earth, date trees came into being,
And from its droplets the varieties, almonds (*bādāmaka*?)[91] and the rest, were produced.
And that drink is also said to be divine and to produce contentment.

[*Cup 9.*]
Then she simultaneously gave another cup to the Sun and the Moon.
A drop from the cup fell on the earth, and the herb that revives the dead (*sañjīvanauṣadhi*) came into being.
And from its droplets various herbs were produced, O Śivā.
That very drink is said to be the supreme one, of general usage;
It imparts all things, O goddess, and imparts all eloquence.[92]

With these cups mahua-drink is possibly produced, as is toddy and the medicinal herbs used in the many herbal wines we saw earlier in this book. The organizational principle may be that the seventh cup creates sugar-producing flowers along with coconut toddy (tree-sugars?), the eighth cup creates dates, and the ninth cup creates herbs. But I suspect that the contents of these latter cups were contrived to fit the number of Surā's arms in her standard iconography.

Now that Surā has arisen, given drinks to the gods, and inadvertently provided humans with intoxicants, the gods are thoroughly delighted and praise her. They grant her a boon and even insist on the necessity of humans using *surā* in worshiping the gods. Of course this is a Tantric text, so there is an agenda behind this vision of prelapsarian *surā*-consumption:

Having given out the divine liquid (*rasa*), the goddess Surā vanished.
All those gods, Sadāśiva and the rest, filled only with the joy of Surā, O Supreme Goddess, gave a boon to Surā:
"Those who drink the supreme drink, producer of supreme joy,
will all go to the ultimate state (*paramaṃ padam*) that is eternal and unchanging.
He who, without jaggery-based (*surā*) drink, [and] without grape-based *surā* (*mādhvī*), worships [the goddess] Śivā (f.), [the god] Śiva, Nārāyaṇa, and Rudra, becomes a hell-dweller.
The non-initiated is a bound-soul (*paśu*), and without *surā* (*asura*) even the initiated is a bound-soul.
Therefore, O Śivā, having honored it in worship, the best Vaiṣṇava should drink jaggery-based [*surā*] (*gauḍī*), grape-based [*surā*] (*mādhvī*), and also grist-based [*surā*] (*paiṣṭī*), [and?] the best *āsava*. And all drink is good: in the absence of the first ones [mentioned, one should use] the following ones.
This is the supreme secret truth of Kaulas, the total essence of the Lord of Joy, to be protected/hidden like a close blood-relative.[93]

These verses declare that Manu's three types of *surā* are the best ones, and it does not mention cannabis, possibly showing the development of the text.

Here we see Surā accepted and praised by the gods, which establishes her essential nature as sacred and good. Yet in Tantric rituals described elsewhere in the same text, *surā* must he purified before being drunk. The *Esoteric Teaching of the Goddess* teaches how this came to be:

Bhairava said:

> Listen, O Goddess, I shall relate the supreme method for purifying *surā*. If a mantra-master does this in the Kali age, he will become fit for liberation.
> O Goddess, the commingling of substances that make a practitioner a sinner—by worshiping with those very [substances] when they are purified, he will enjoy rewards of supernatural powers or liberation.
> From the time that Surā attained renown in this world, all the gods (*sura*), O Goddess, Brahmā, Viṣṇu, Hara (i.e., Śiva), and the rest, had their inmost hearts filled with the joy produced by association with her.
> The *asuras*, *rākṣasas*, *yakṣas*, *gandharvas*, humans, and other beings also partook of divine *surā*, consecrated by purifying rituals using mantras.
> Over time the Goddess Surā had become located in a jar (*kalaśasthā*), O queen of gods,
> [And] when the world was tormented by the Kali [era], who had the form of Time (or a "black form"), O beloved one, she was cursed (*śaptā*) by Śukra, O queen of gods, on account of the killing caused by Kaca.
> Through the influence of the curse of Śukra, the gods Brahmā, Viṣṇu, Śiva, and the rest, and the Brahminical sages respectively cursed the goddess Surā. [And therefore] drinking Surā is known to be equal to slaying a Brahmin, O great goddess.
> When the gods cursed Surā, the Daityas were delighted, and when they drank *surā*, the Daityas expelled the gods led by Indra, devoid of strength, from heaven, O goddess.
> Then, with Indra at the fore, the gods performed a sacrifice. Sadāśiva and the rest appeared at that supreme sacrifice, O goddess, [saying,] "Choose a boon right now, whatever you desire, O chief of gods!"
> "Then we ask of you that we may quickly go to our own abode."
> Then, O goddess, Śukra honored Guru, O Śivā, and said, "Tasting a mere drop of *surā* on the tip of a blade of grass gives us satisfaction that we cannot get from hundreds of pots of the nectar of immortality. [But] she is cursed by Brahmā, Viṣṇu, and Śaṅkara (Śiva) . . . ," O goddess, "[and] without her [the gods] have become powerless and subjugated by their enemies."
> Then all the gods praised Śiva the unchanging Lord with great devotion, repeatedly prostrating [themselves]:
> . . . [Here the gods praise Śiva] . . .
> Thus they praised the great god Bhairava Śiva Īśvara, and all the gods, Brahmā, Viṣṇu, Hara, and the rest, then bowed down. Then a voice emerged from the

> sky from Him whose body consists of the five voids:[94] "This Surā is to be worshiped always by all those desirous of release, by this method, devotedly, properly, in regular order.
> I consist of the four Vedas, having the form of the *Ṛg*, *Yajur*, *Sāma*, and *Atharva* [*Vedas*], the soul of *mantra*s, the supreme self, Śiva, immutable.
> Having scrutinized the Vedas and assumed the meaning of the Vedas in the form of *mantra*, O Sadāśiva!, manifest the great *vidyā* (a sacred formula) called *kurukullā*[95] and the supreme revealed scripture (*āgama*) that has sixty-four parts; show the purification of Surā by the best humans in that [text]!"
> When the great voice produced by Śiva stopped, then the gods, bowed down in obeisance, praised the god Sadāśiva, saying,
> ... [Here the gods praise Sadāśiva] ...
> Thus praised, the great god, the great-souled, holy Sadāśiva, related the revealed scripture, the path of liberation for the great-souled.[96]

From these verses we learn that time is to blame for the current difficulties with Surā. She is rejected in the degenerate Kali era, having been cursed by Śukra in the episode we saw earlier. Here the gods also curse the goddess/drink, but then, unable to drink, they lose their strength, and the anti-gods who still drink *surā* are able to eject the weakened gods from heaven. This is a variant of the episode we saw earlier in the book, in which Surā was variously accepted or rejected by the gods (*sura*s) and anti-gods (*asura*s or *daitya*s). The ejection of the *surā*-deprived gods from heaven by the antigods is a striking inversion of the Buddhist myth in which the *asura*s are ejected because of their attachment to *surā*.

By means of a sacrifice, the gods in this myth receive a boon and can return to heaven, but their return does not solve the problem, for good people and gods can no longer drink the strengthening, joy-producing *surā*. It is Śukra the sage who presents this as an ongoing problem: the figure who cursed *Surā* in the first place now initiates the process by which it/she is redeemed. Śukra's reference to the joys of a drop of drink on the tip of a blade of grass subvert the phrase we saw in a Buddhist formula, in which monastics are forbidden to drink even a drop on the end of a blade of grass.

Reminded of the dangers of not being able to drink, the gods praise Śiva, at which point a voice sounds from the sky and informs Sadāśiva that he must reveal Tantric scriptures, in which there will be instructions on how to purify *surā*, thus allowing gods and humans to drink again and enabling the gods to retain their superior status. Nectar might give the gods immortality, but *surā* gives them strength, and apparently they much prefer *surā*. Note that it is Sadāśiva, hierarchically superior in this theology, who provides a new revelation and saves the other gods. The gods who get into trouble "with Indra at their head" are the Vedic pantheon, associated with the older, orthodox, prohibitive approach to alcohol. As to why people should use liquor in Tantric rituals, from this myth at least we learn that *surā* is not a ritual tool to achieve gnosis but simply a delightful, empowering drink beloved of the gods and, above all, prescribed in (some) Tantric revelations in order to renew access to it for both the gods and fortunate initiates.

The way alcohol is viewed and consumed within Tantra is fundamentally secondary, even of a third order. At every turn, drink is defined by its religious and cultural history. As with many new revelations that supersede earlier ones (e.g., Mormonism updating Christianity and Judaism), there is an implication that using *surā* in Tantric rituals is in fact a return to an earlier state, before she/it was cursed and separated from humans and gods. Returning to that state requires knowledge and ritual work, and it can be attained only by the initiated who have access to a special revelation.

The quoted passage from the *Esoteric Teaching of the Goddess* is ingenious. While expanding the mythology of drugs and alcohol to include substances used at this later period, it also successfully (1) explains the redemption of *surā* using the same mythic style as the better-known texts on how *surā* was cursed and prohibited; (2) acknowledges and adapts Manu's ubiquitous, orthodox threefold *surā* to include new substances; (3) explains the ritual means for the purification of *surā* so that people can consume it in this newly permitted manner (which section I omitted here); and (4) provides a sacred genealogy for the very texts that cover points (1) to (3).

Superficially, Indian religious texts may seem conservative, even static, in their approach to intoxicating substances, but close examination proves them to be dynamic in response to a changing world of alcohol and drugs. The process is particularly clear in the next case.

Enter Cannabis

Cannabis as an intoxicant, appears in Indian texts approximately a thousand years ago. To my knowledge, references to cannabis as a drug are most prominent in ritual and medical texts; it never gains the place of liquor in literary sources—though more work on later texts and vernacular sources could well change that assumption.[97] But the drug has a close association with India in the Western imagination, so it's worth pausing to discuss it. Wujastyk writes that today's authors sometimes "enlist pre-modern India as a shining example of a culture in which medicinal and psycho-active uses of cannabis were widespread and fully integrated not only into recreational and sexual life, but also into religious practice."[98] The same could be said for sexuality (see the many popular works on the *Kāmasūtra*) with an equal lack of accuracy, and I hope I haven't suggested in this book that there was a "golden age" of Indian drinking—drink is and always was a complicated issue in India.

There are some good studies of cannabis in premodern India, but one could still devote a whole book to the subject.[99] Here I offer a few observations and translations for the curious reader. Cannabis also serves as a useful comparison with alcohol and betel.

It's difficult to establish exactly when people in South Asia started to use cannabis for medical, mind-altering, and ritual purposes. The hemp plant has a number of uses, and people in South Asia have known hemp as a fiber plant from an early period, though this by no means implies that people were consuming it as a drug in ancient times, nor that the plants used then were psychoactive.[100] Some of the words that were used in later texts to refer to cannabis as a drug do also occur in earlier texts but, as we've seen in this book, the referents of many words for plants change over time, as with the word "corn" in English. Even if these old words do mean cannabis, the plant was not always used as a drug. (Recall that Europeans also used hemp for fiber long before they consumed the plant as a drug.) The word *bhaṅga* (not the feminine form, *bhaṅgā*, that is later used for cannabis) occurs in some Vedic texts, yet it's far from clear what the word refers to.[101] The same applies to the word *vijaya* (not *vijayā*) in the *Suśruta-saṃhitā*.[102] As Meulenbeld explains, only "when commentators give us additional, and reliable, information, or when the context enables us to decide, can we be sure whether *vijayā* refers to hemp or another plant."[103] Nor can one argue that early texts were quiet about the use of hemp as a drug because it was taboo or illegal—it simply wasn't, and early texts are very open about other plants and alcohol being used as intoxicants. There is no conspiracy!

One of the earliest clear references to cannabis as an intoxicating item of *materia medica* is in the *Cikitsāsārasaṃgraha* of Vaṅgasena (1050–1100 CE).[104] Other medical texts from the same period and a little later also mention it in a manner that probably indicates cannabis being used as a drug.[105] Locating these references geographically is tricky, but possibly some of these texts were composed in Bengal, near Delhi, and in Gujarat.[106] Once these clear references appeared, probably no earlier than 1000 CE, knowledge of the drug seemed to become relatively widespread.[107] Hellwig has analyzed the frequencies of words that probably refer to cannabis in Sanskrit texts, demonstrating that such references are far more common in the second millennium CE.[108] Of course, just because a substance or practice is not mentioned in Sanskrit texts doesn't mean that it wasn't present or used in earlier periods, but it does imply that it wasn't common (or commonly discussed) among people involved with Sanskrit texts. It's also possible that cannabis as a drug was used for a long time only in a restricted area and context (even if that was somewhere in South Asia), prior to being adopted swiftly over a wider area, as happened with coffee in the Middle East.[109] The same may apply to betel and grape wine. The old world was not static when it came to drugs. Anyone who is resistant to the idea that cannabis-used-as-a-drug might only have been adopted in many areas (including most/all of South Asia) at a relatively recent date might ask themselves: why is it easy to accept that one old world psychoactive substance previously limited to a restricted area—coffee—*was* relatively recently, quite suddenly widely adopted in the Middle East and Europe, whereas the possibility that something similar happened with cannabis-as-drug is harder to accept?

Sanderson writes, in the context of Tantra, "[it] is probable that the use of cannabis for spiritual intoxication was adopted following the example of Muslim ascetics in India such as those of the Madāriyya order, founded by Bādiʿ ad-dīn Shāh Madārī, an immigrant who settled in Jaunpur, where he died c. 1440 . . . an order notorious for its use of hashish."[110] Note that Sanderson writes here of cannabis's use in "spiritual intoxication"—the drug might have been taken for non-ritual, recreational, aphrodisiac, or medicinal purposes earlier. Nor was the use of cannabis as a drug in India *necessarily* a Muslim innovation. Indeed, given how little we know about the early history of cannabis in India, it may also have been used earlier for what we today would call religious purposes too. References to cannabis in a play called the *Dhūrtasamāgama* reveal something of attitudes to the substance in the early fourteenth century. Here cannabis (*indrāśana*) is carried by an ascetic in a special bag (*jhollia* = *jhaulika*); its scent is admired; it is treated as special, and, although carried by an ascetic, perhaps even emblematic of his ascetic status, other people are keen to get some.[111] There is also a description of its medicinal and other properties in this text. As things stand, however, we know little about cannabis consumption in India at the time of its first appearance in texts. More research is needed.

According to an alchemical text called the *Ānandakanda*, probably composed sometime after the twelfth or thirteenth century CE, cannabis was taken in a variety of social contexts, including by women, children, yogis, medical patients, and people suffering from impotence.[112] Of course, these early references may reveal only those instances in which people who composed and read Sanskrit texts encountered the drug, or the contexts in which they thought it most notable (compare to the "jazz cigarette").

Although cannabis was established at an earlier period as a medicinal drug in Islamic cultures, Franz Rosenthal writes that there is no evidence of the use of cannabis, hashish, "for pleasure and enjoyment" during the first four or five centuries of Islam.[113] There is even a legend related in an Arabic text by al-Badrī, completed in 1464 CE,[114] of an Indian shaykh from Bengal (hence "bang," according to this text), who was taught to use hashish by Satan speaking from the interior of his "idol," after which the use of Indian hashish spread elsewhere; in Arabic texts the drug was sometimes qualified with the adjective "Indian" (*hindī*).[115] Note how a Muslim writer connects it to Indian "idolatry" in the mid-fifteenth century. Similarly, though it was an ancient and established medicinal drug, opium is mentioned frequently in Persian literature only from the eleventh century CE onward, and is mentioned as being used for non-medicinal purposes in Iran only from the tenth century CE onward.[116] In this respect, the South Asian cannabis/opium culture appears to have experienced changes that were also taking place in the Arab and Persian drug cultures (and maybe elsewhere in the Indian Ocean) at approximately the same period. This is a topic that merits more (collaborative) research, with scrupulous attention to the dating and philology of primary sources.

Returning to Tantra: Sanderson explains that whereas most Śākta systems (related to the cult of the Goddess) used only liquor, in later Śākta systems from eastern parts of India cannabis was used in some Tantric rituals, ritually empowered by a mantra already used for liquor.[117] One relatively complex recipe in this eastern tradition called for other ingredients too: milk, water, grape juice, jaggery, and so on.[118] Apparently large quantities of cannabis were consumed and, although some texts state that one can consume either liquor or cannabis-drink in rituals, "the East-Indian tradition is in no doubt that cannabis is superior. This is stated in a verse-line frequently encountered in its texts: *saṃvidāsavayor madhye saṃvid eva garīyasī*, 'Of cannabis and wine it is cannabis that is the greater.' "[119] We saw this very line in the myth of Surā earlier, which possibly demonstrates that text's connection to the Eastern Indian tradition. But not everyone agreed that cannabis was superior: one Kashmirian commentator dismissed claims that cannabis enhances awareness.[120] It was possibly in the context of these debates, over the utility and value of cannabis in Tantric rituals, that some of the texts I'll now discuss took shape.

There were several varieties of cannabis, prepared in different ways, yet the drug may have lacked the prestige of the good grape wines that Abhinavagupta so admired, for cannabis was probably grown relatively locally, more herb than spice. Nor would prepared cannabis probably have been a costly substance, as betel sometimes was with its precious aromatics and paraphernalia. Moreover, with respect to Tantric rituals, although cannabis was eventually assigned a place in Hindu mythology, it arrived far too late to feature in the classical *dharmaśāstric* legal texts and thus lacked the potential to function as a transgressive substance—it could only be mind-altering. Unless, that is, someone defined it as a type of *surā*.

The lack of both *dharmaśāstric* legal status and any negative cultural associations might have formed part of the appeal of cannabis in various contexts. Certainly in later periods cannabis was sometimes the Brahminical drug of choice (when drugs were used at all). Uday Chandra Dutt, a nineteenth-century historian and botanist in India, wrote:

> On the last day of Durga pooja [an important Hindu holiday in the Bengal region] . . . it is customary for the Hindus to see their friends and relatives . . . After this ceremony is over it is incumbent on the owner of the house to offer his visitors a cup of bhang and sweet meats for tiffin . . . In Bengal it has latterly become the fashion to substitute brandy, but I well remember having seen in the days of my boyhood the free use of bhang among the better classes of people who would have shunned as a pariah any one of their society addicted to the use of the forbidden spirituous liquor.[121]

More recently, Carstairs studied a village in Rajasthan where the consumption of alcohol and cannabis was divided sharply along the lines of caste: "The Brahmans, on the other hand, were quite unanimous in reviling daru [alcohol] and all those who indulged in it . . . In their references to the use of bhang, the Brahmans were matter-of-fact rather than lyrical. 'It gives good bhakti,' said Shankar Lal . . . [and] he went on to define bhakti as the sort of devotional act which consists in emptying the mind of all worldly distractions and thinking only of god."[122]

The non-transgressive appeal of cannabis as a ritual intoxicant makes sense if we consider that some practitioners of Tantra might have felt uncomfortable using alcohol—it's important to keep in mind that, despite the earlier focus of this chapter, many forms of Tantra avoided alcohol totally. A text called the *Khecarīvidyā* contains a passage also attested in another text, the *Matsyendrasaṃhitā*, that is a Kaula praise of liquor, *madirā*. Yet, as James Mallinson writes, the version of this passage in the *Khecarīvidyā* is carefully "redacted to make it more palatable to orthodox practitioners of *haṭhayoga*," with all the references to alcohol changed, so that the text now praises Khecarī and *Śivabhakti* (devotion to Śiva) instead of liquor.[123] Mallinson also mentions another text that "cleans up" Kaula references (i.e., fiercely transgressive references) to alcohol.[124]

A later Tantric text from the Bengal region, the *Sarvollāsa Tantra*, which also contains recipes for cannabis preparations,[125] also gives two non-cannabis, non-alcoholic substitutes for intoxicating beverages (*madya*) in a discussion of the "five Ms" (in a quotation from the tenth- or eleventh-century *Bhāvacuḍāmaṇi*),[126] though it's important to note that these drinks are prescribed for people of a less advanced disposition, who are engaging in milder practices (*vibhāvasya . . . paśoḥ*). The first of these recipes is as follows: "Cook cow's milk over a fire, [and] date-palm sap—the jaggery from that [date sap] mixed with areca-nut powder is equivalent to an intoxicating beverage (*madyatulya*)."[127] As we saw earlier, in large doses areca-nut was considered an intoxicant.

Pratapaditya Pal writes that a popular sixteenth-century Bengali compilation, the *Tantrasāra* of Kṛṣṇānanda, also contains non-intoxicating liquor substitutes, along with a verse forbidding Brahmins to offer liquor in Tantric rituals.[128] Did the ritual use of cannabis flourish in such contexts, where orthodoxy-compatible substitutes for (originally) transgressive offerings were developed and disseminated? Certainly, as with tea in China and coffee in the Islamic world, a complex set of circumstances must have led to the development of what today we might call "religious cannabis," not the least of which was the appearance (or proliferation) of a strongly intoxicating, not fatally-toxic, non-fermented drug that was easy to produce in South Asia. Again, more research is needed to move beyond mere hypotheses.

The alchemical *Ānandakanda* also contains a myth explaining the origin of cannabis, together with a classification of its varieties.[129] This myth differs from that seen above, though the same motif appears of the stray drops of divine drinks becoming remarkable substances on earth. Here, Bhairava explains that part of his nature is fiery (*āgneya*) and part of the goddess's nature is cool/moist/*soma*-like (*saumya*).[130] The gods and *asuras* place all the herbs that are also fiery and moist into the ocean and churn it with the mountain. The fiery part of Bhairava becomes the terrible *hālāhala* poison that Bhairava swallows out of compassion for the gods and *asuras*.[131] The gods and *asuras* continue with the churning, and all the other items, including the goddess Lakṣmī and the nectar of immortality (*amṛta*), appear.[132] Note that there is no reference to the arising of Surā. The nectar of immortality is then distributed. As Bhairava consumes his portion, he makes a thundering noise from intense joy—and some fine drops of the nectar fall, from which a great herb (*mahauṣadhi*) arises. Bhairava nurtures it with nectar (*pīyūṣa*) from his own hand.[133] And this divine herb is eventually taken to earth.

What is the name of this divine herb, asks Bhairavī, and what are its potencies? Bhairava explains that there are four colors of cannabis: white in the Kṛta Yuga (the first world age), red in the Treta Yuga, yellow in the Dvāpara Yuga, and dark blue (*nīla*) in the Kali Yuga—the one we're living in now.[134] According to the *Ānandakanda*, there are also varieties with different numbers of leaves: one, three, five, six, nine, ten, eleven, and thirteen.[135] Bhairava then explains:

> The female form (*strīrūpā*) is a creeper (*vallī*) that bears fruits; the male form has the form of a tree. And the one with fruits causes intoxication (*mada*), fainting (*mūrcchā*), pleasure (*sukha*), and *sattva* (a quality of goodness, clarity, understanding, and purity).[136]

Bhairava then lists and explains its many names, including *vijayā* (conqueror, victoria), *bhaṅgī*, *gañjā*, and the rest.[137] He also provides detailed instructions on how to cultivate the plant—for example, the seeds should be sown with snake flesh—and describes some preparations of it.[138] The section concludes with the nine stages of excessive consumption:

> When there is excessive consumption of this root of supernatural attainment (*siddhimūlī*), perturbations arise. Listen to them, O Supreme Goddess! In the first stage, reddish eyes, dry tongue, lips, [and] palate, a dry nose-tip, hot breath . . .[139]

These symptoms, which even in the ninth stage (buzzing ears, fainting, fits and confusion, vomiting, inarticulate sounds, rolling on the ground, and miserable talk)[140] are not considered fatal, are to be treated with conventionally cooling substances—sandalwood, vetiver, camphor, and so forth.

Another text, the *Padmapurāṇa* (as quoted in the eighteenth-century *Haṃsavilāsa* of Haṃsamiṭṭhu), explains the nature, virtues, and uses of cannabis.[141] The passage in question may have been written earlier than the eighteenth century, though it's difficult to assign dates to sections of such complex texts as large Purāṇas, in forms attested at late periods and quoted in other sources.

The passage begins when Sanatkumāra, a son of the god Brahmā, asks the sage Nārada, "O sage! By what power is your mind always steady, always fixed on one point, joyful, and your eyes extremely red?"[142] The sage replies that the answer is very secret indeed, and was related to him by the god Śiva. Śiva first explained the manner of preparing the drug. The procedure is ritualized and accompanied by mantras. First one brings it into the house—implying that it is purchased or obtained elsewhere, though, as we've seen, special methods of growing it are also described in one text. Then the cannabis is made into a powder (*cūrṇayet*), shaken through a fine cloth, and roasted (*bharjayet*) over a gentle fire. Then one eats it, presumably in a drink or edible preparation. Śiva (the sage continues) then explained the potencies of cannabis:

> And this great herb is celebrated in this world as having three varieties: demonic (*rākṣasī*), human (*mānuṣī*), and divine (*daivī*)—one should pronounce their characteristics.
> If, on merely eating it, a man is helpless, a bound beast (*paśu*), with the quality of darkness and inertia, his knowledge gone,[143] gazing upward—for that man it is said to be demonic.
> And if, on merely being eaten, it makes a man desirous of erotic pleasure, it is proclaimed to be human for him.
> And if, on merely being eaten, it provides right knowledge, does not cause a pale face nor raised-up eyes—it is known as divine for him . . .[144]

These texts show that considerable work went into articulating many aspects of cannabis in just a few centuries—its sacred origin, cultivation, effects, and various qualities. Not long after people started to write about cannabis as a drug, including in Tantric rituals, it had emerged with a full, complex Hindu genealogy.[145]

Such a mythical incorporation of a novel substance was not limited to cannabis. The alchemical *Ānandakanda* also relates the origin of opium. This drug, which later became so important in Indian history, first appears in the Sanskrit textual record at a relatively late date, around the tenth or eleventh century CE.[146] Opium is presented in the *Ānandakanda* as a medicinal drug to treat diarrheal illness, among other things, *not* as a drug to be taken in ritual or other contexts for its intoxicating powers—though its intoxicating property is acknowledged, as it is stated that it imparts stupefaction/confusion (*mohadam*).[147] As with *surā* and cannabis, opium is said to have originated at the churning of the ocean, the source of so many substances that affect the body, both human and divine, in remarkable ways: the *hālāhala* poison, nectar of immortality, and various intoxicants. One common form of a Sanskrit word for opium is *ahiphena* (*ahi-phena*), "serpent-foam," a folk etymology of a foreign word[148] that no doubt has some connection to the following story:

> In the past, drops of sweat, together with poison, that arose from the mouth of [the serpent] Vāsuki when he was tired from the agitation of churning [the ocean] fell in another continent. Wherever they fell, they grew forth in the form of clumps of bushes, and people call the exudation produced in them opium ("foamless," "not-foam," *aphenaṃ*).[149]

The churning of the ocean was an almost inevitable choice when assigning this new intoxicant its mythical origins.

Despite the timeless aura of these narratives, we can see in the extensions of the churning myth an ingenious response to an ever-changing world of intoxicants by people producing and adapting mythical texts, just as the ritual, legal, and medical discourses constantly adapted to changing practices and new substances. Reading between the lines of the Sanskrit texts I've examined in this book, we can trace a culture of intoxicants that was not only complex at any one time but also constantly and rapidly developing. The introduction of tobacco, coffee, and tea, as well as the changes of the colonial period, took place in a world where people already had many resources for assimilating new substances and assigning them places in both the cosmic and the human realms. We should not see such assimilations as cynical exercises to present new drugs in an old guise, pretending that "they were there all the time." Rather, just as Manu's threefold *surā* became so common as to seem to be the true nature of *surā*, so these mythological frameworks were so deeply bound up with drugs and alcohol that for many writers and readers the construal of opium as "snake-foam" (*ahiphena*) would have seemed natural and expected, happening seamlessly and even unconsciously. As Whitney Cox observes of some southern Indian scholars of the second millennium, they "understood the world to be shot through with the tropes and topoi of the universe of discourse in which they spent much of their imaginative and intellectual lives. It was through works of language that they experienced the world at its most real."[150] In this case, it was through drugs, intoxicating substances endowed with divine origins in texts shot through with many of the threads we've seen in this book, that people could experience a temporary, transformed experience of reality.

Conclusions

While this chapter might seem dense at times, it is in fact just a superficial survey of only a few aspects of drink and drugs in selected Tantric texts. A drink-centric reading of these cases has nevertheless been productive. Just as the Tantric tradition supersedes earlier ones, so drink in Tantra builds on, adapts, and inverts a wide range of earlier ideas, laws, classifications, myths, and even literary modes of drinking. Hindu Tantric texts considered as a whole speak in all the idioms of classical texts where alcohol in concerned (where they deal with alcohol, that is).

Ronald Davidson has written of the drinking song of a Buddhist saint (Siddha) called Virūpa who is associated with Tantric traditions.[151] To my mind the song in question evokes the ambiance of the *surā* shop perfectly, and the associated social connotations of drinking are every bit as prominent in that case as the ritually transgressive ones. That song evokes public drinking, and the drink it describes is apparently of terrible quality. At the opposite end of the spectrum, some Tantric "orgies" were more like elite parties. And Abhinavagupta praises the qualities of grape wine, which we know was highly appreciated in some circles in Kashmir. The transgressive aspect of drinking is important, but liquor was exceptionally rich in uses and associations: erotic, tasty, mind-altering, sense-enhancing, inhibition-removing, expensive or common to mention just a few. Thus a passage from a Tantric text called the *Āgamarahasya*, the *Esoterium of Revelation* (as quoted in an eighteenth-century text), presents a picture of drunken erotics that fits perfectly with the conventions and imagery of the *Kāmasūtra* and other literary texts, as well as the visual motifs of drunken couples:

> Yogins (male), drunk with intoxicating drink (*madamattā*), fall on the chests of young women (*pramadā*),
> Confused with intoxicating drink (*mada*), Yoginīs (female) fall on the chests of men,
> And they mutually fulfill their desires,
> Transforming their hearts, so joy arises.[152]

Here Tantric drinking shares many of the conventions of the literary realm, in which drinking is sensuously productive: delicious drink creating erotic chaos.

There are several phases in the mythical history of the relations between humans (especially Brahmins), gods, and *surā*. Hindu Tantra, both the revelation and the practice, places itself at the most recent and final stage when it deals with liquor. Brahmins can now drink this potent holy brew, but only in a controlled, ritual manner. Yet the vicissitudes of human/divine/Surā relations have endowed Surā with far greater potency than she possessed at the start. When she arose, she was intoxicating and potent but quite unable to help humans shed their inhibitions concerning the Absolute, as she had not yet become prohibited and thus drinking was not transgressive. Her new role (at least as it is understood by Abhinavagupta and others) was unintentionally bestowed by the Brahminical tradition of Śukra, Manu, and others, who established and maintained the conventional orthodox drinking laws. The re-admission of Surā, however, has now been taught to humans by God in Tantric Texts. Of course, this cosmic drama has little relevance to some classes of humans, for whom drinking was always permitted in Hindu law. But from the Brahminical perspective, Tantra triumphantly presents Surā as restored to gods and humans, framed in rituals and mantras, and gnostically potent.

We might also speculate about the mundane aspects of Tantra. To practice it, people had to obtain all manner of vessels and substances. Brahmins would have had to figure out how to obtain (or even brew) liquor while retaining an outward appearance of orthodoxy. As with temples where liquor is offered today, the use of liquor in ritual (*not* always strictly Tantric) is not just shaped by the law and economy but may have played a minor role in shaping those realms. An inscription from South India, from the eleventh century CE in the reign of the Cola King Kulottuṅga I, from the temple of Kolaramma, records that a royal officer appointed a committee to allot paddy to various shrines in the temple, including the shrines of a Yoginī and Yogeśvara for whom intoxicating drink (presumably *surā* based on rice) was required: "One *kalam* of paddy for two *kalam* of intoxicating drinks for the worship of Yoginī and Yogeśvara."[153] In temples today where liquor is offered, a quantity is often returned to devotees as *prasād*, sanctified liquor, and this may also have been the case in earlier temples such as the one mentioned in this inscription.

That said, the period discussed in this chapter was *not* an age of promiscuous indulgence, abounding in "Kāma Sūtra temples" and other such fictions. For many people, this sort of Tantric ritual drinking would have been (and still is) better known from secondhand sources: literary and dramatic representations of Tantrics, meetings with or stories about living ascetics, and from temples and shrines where liquor was publicly offered to such deities as Kāla Bhairava, or the temple in the inscription above.[154] None of these practices or representations demonstrate a lax attitude toward drinking among the orthodox religious—if anything, liquor in Tantra was the exception that proved the rule of upper-caste public abstinence.

For some circles of theorists and ritualists, however, with the Tantric revelations *surā*, a beautiful, potent, divine intoxicant, was regained in both myth and practice. And what we might think of as an extended, positive theology of Surā developed for Brahmins and those who were allowed in the fold of their laws and frameworks.

CUP 9

Firewater and Corpse-Reviver

Alcohol in Later Sanskrit Sources

> There dids't thou gather in Parnassus clift
> This precious herbe, Tabacco most divine.[1]

What happened to all the drinks we've encountered in this book, and to these ways of writing and thinking about them? Did people continue to use this repertoire of concepts and narratives to incorporate other drugs in very changed historical circumstances? The answers to these questions could be the topic for another book, one I'm not qualified to write, but I will nonetheless give a few examples here of how ancient brewing methods and discourses were maintained and adapted until quite recent times, an aspect of the history of drugs and alcohol in more recent Indian history that is often overlooked.

People in South Asia still make many drinks that resemble the ones we've examined: medicinal *āsava*s and *ariṣṭa*s, palm toddy, mahua liquor, and rice drinks like *handia*, not to mention the many grain drinks still made in areas such as Assam and the Himalayan regions, some of which are distilled today. The rise of distillation may have effaced the earlier *surā*s and sugarcane drinks, though more detailed research is needed on drinks from approximately the twelfth century onward to prove that theory. Arguably, the Country Liquor shop often found in South Asia is the modern equivalent of the *surā* shop, usually selling one type of affordable drink for public consumption alongside spicy snacks. Country Liquor, or Indian Made Indian Liquor (IMIL)—the well-made sort, at least—is an underrated drink, in my opinion. Many modern drinking snacks have a lot in common with the earlier ones, and the sheer fact that people in India almost always complement their drinks with salty, spicy snacks may well be a survival of the ancient practice. Both betel and bhang are also still consumed.

Once distillation became common, how was this manifested in Sanskrit texts and other sources? The *Elucidation of Distillates* (*Arkaprakāśa*), dating from the seventeenth century CE or later, is a treatise on distilled medicines (*arka*).[2] The text is in the form of a dialogue between Rāvaṇa and his wife Mandodarī, where he relates the knowledge of this topic he received from Pārvatī. The knowledge

An Unholy Brew. James McHugh, Oxford University Press. © Oxford University Press 2021.
DOI: 10.1093/oso/9780199375936.003.0011

of making distillates, not all of them alcoholic, is thus given a divine origin. The world of distillates is highly developed in this text as a whole (and relations with Unani medical texts would be interesting to explore). In the *Elucidation of Distillates*, as in the much earlier *Gadanigraha* we saw above (c. 1200 CE), a distillate is called an *arka*, a Sanskritized form derived ultimately from Arabic.[3] Also, a specific Sanskrit verbal root is used for "distill" in the *Gadanigraha*, in the *Arkaprakāśa*, as well as in in a later perfumery text: the causative form of the verb *niṣ √kas* (also *kaś*), which means "to expel" or "to drive out."[4] Portuguese physician Garcia da Orta writing in the sixteenth century noted that in the Goa area, coconut toddy was called *surā* (*çura*), which was distilled to make what is called "*fula*," so no doubt *phūl*, "flower," and this, when mixed with the undistilled toddy, is called arrack (*orraqua*).[5] And for Rajendralal Mitra *surā* was most definitely a distilled drink, arrack.[6]

Govindadāsa, probably a Bengali, composed a lengthy treatise called the *Bhaiṣajyaratnāvalī*, most likely in the eighteenth century.[7] At the end of the chapter on aphrodisiacs there is a recipe for a complex distilled drink that is still available in India today: "Dead-Reviving *Surā*" (*Mṛtasañjīvanīsurā*) attributed to no other than the sage Śukra—"created by Śukra at the time of the battle of the gods and asuras."[8] It is of course Śukra who prohibited *surā* for Brahmins in the myth that highlights both his authority over *surā* and his amazing ability to revive the dead.[9] So here we have a distilled medical drink called *surā* (mainly jaggery based), said to be invented as an aphrodisiac medicine by no other than the corpse-reviving sage who banned *surā* for Brahmins in the first place. Whoever created this medicine was a master of the latest medical developments and fluent in the cultural grammar of liquor in the long Sanskritic tradition.

Nowadays starches are easily transformed into sugar and alcohol on an industrial scale, using enzymes and yeasts, but the ancient *kiṇva* method was economically significant until at least the early twentieth century. In an article from 1906, the chemist J. C. Ray (not to be confused with the author of *A History of Hindu Chemistry*) described the manufacture of rice-based alcohol at the government-controlled Central Distillery at Cuttack.[10] First, dehusked rice was steamed in an earthenware pot with a hole in the bottom. After around half an hour, this steamed rice was heaped up with other batches of steamed rice and mixed (at a ratio of 100 to 1) with a substance called *bakhar*—small balls of which were ground to powder before being added to the rice. This *bakhar* clearly resembled the herb-containing ferment-culture cake seen in many parts of Asia and was analogous to *kiṇva*. Ray notes that the ferment was "prepared and sold by a low-caste people of the hills of Orissa in the form of small balls about the size of a walnut," meaning that the people making the rice drink in the factory treated it as a ready-made entity.[11] The inoculated rice was placed in a basket for about twenty-four hours and then spread into circular cakes, each about an inch thick and weighing about two pounds, on a raised earth platform. Here the mold developed, and after three or four days the cakes were piled on each other for another four or five days, at which point the cakes were densely coated in black mold. The moldy cakes were then put with water into large unglazed earthenware vats, each with a capacity of 32 to 40 gallons and previously fumigated with burned straw, and the vats were half buried in the earth floor of a thatched shed. This is reminiscent of the dilutable *surābīja* in the *Mānasollāsa*, including the black *surā* mentioned in that text. After a day, an equal weight of freshly steamed rice was added to each vat. The total proportions were around 2.5 parts water to 1 of rice. After eight to ten days, when fermentation ceased, the mixture was distilled using an alembic apparatus. Ray also mentions another drink, *pachwai*, made in the same manner but not distilled. Some mind-altering herbs, such as cannabis and datura, were added to the *bakhar* used for *pachwai*.[12] In its finished form, this early-twentieth-century country liquor was basically distilled rice *surā* made on quite a large scale, in a manner resembling the methods implied by the lists of ingredients in the *Arthaśāstra*.[13]

What became of the Sanskritic discourse of drinks and drinking, which was regularly and ingeniously adapted to changing circumstances, even at early periods? It seems that for some people the discourse remained a living tradition through which to articulate ideas about liquor, even after political, cultural, and technical circumstances had dramatically changed and when distillation became common.

We find a late, fascinating discussion of drinking alcohol in a text called the *Transport of the Haṃsas* (*Haṃsavilāsa*), which Somadeva Vasudeva has studied.[14] The *haṃsa* is a bird, sometimes translated "goose" (and sometimes "swan"), but more important here than the zoological identity of the *haṃsa* is the metaphorical association of this word with the liberated soul. The word *haṃsa* is also a *mantra*. Composed in the second half of the eighteenth century in Vārāṇasi in North India, this text features two narrators who are "Haṃsas," the esoteric identities of a man called Miṭṭhu Śukla and his wife Bhūlī. Indeed, as Vasudeva explains, anyone initiated into the system taught in the *Transport of the Haṃsas* will become a Haṃsa (or Haṃsī, feminine). These two Haṃsas teach four forms of religious discipline ("yoga"), for high-caste initiates, of which the fourth and highest, royal yoga (*rājayoga*), is the cultivation of divine amorous joy called *rāsalīlā*—a practice then associated with devotional Vaiṣṇava traditions.[15] The *rāsalīlā* of the Haṃsas involves sex, alcohol, and cannabis, but this should not be understood as transgression, since the Haṃsas have taken pains to align their system with Hindu orthodoxy. As Vasudeva explains: "A major paradigm in the 'Transport of the Haṃsas' is the attempt to show the functional equivalence of Vedic practices and Kaula [a type of Tantric] practices: thus the consumption of *soma* in Vedic ritual is equated with the consumption of wine in Kaula ritual."[16]

In his erudite presentation of liquor, Haṃsa Miṭṭhu draws on many of the themes we've seen in this book: he quotes the long description of Surā distributing drinks and the verses in the *Rāmāyaṇa* on the arising of Surā at the churning of the ocean. He notes that, though cursed by the gods, Surā can be consecrated and made pure by certain mantras. He then describes *surā* in a remarkable way: "It is not made of the element water (*jalamayī*) but rather of the element fire (*tejomayī-*) because it burns in a lamp as oil does (*tailavad dīpake jvalati*)."[17] Evidently *surā* for Miṭṭhu is a distilled drink, perhaps similar to the one we read of earlier, in Cuttack. A highly distilled alcoholic drink will burn, and thus for Miṭṭhu *surā* is not like other water-based drinks that might be rejected as impure; it is a different substance entirely, made of the element fire. In this way he aligns the product of distillation with classical Indian elemental theory, adding this empirical proof of the fiery nature of *surā* to his other references, epic and mythological.[18]

These examples demonstrate a continuing mastery of the textual tradition and the ways in which people could still combine and interpret a huge range of materials in producing a "classical" argument. In the case of the medicinal "Dead-Reviving *Surā*," we see an active engagement with matter and technology, informed and framed by a flourishing competence in textual erudition and analysis, all of which is applied to a bottle of distilled aphrodisiac that one can still find on the shelves today.

What of drugs that appeared at an even later date? A Tantric compilation that we saw earlier, the *Sarvollāsa*, quotes a text called the *Niruttara Tantra* (a Śākta Tantra from eastern India), which has a rather remarkable definition of *surā*. Although the *Sarvollāsa* (and the quoted text) may have been first composed/compiled around 1400 (or in the sixteenth century),[19] the verse quoted here is presumably a later addition—assuming it's correct to understand the word *tāmrakūṭa* ("copper-peak") as tobacco. Such floating verses with various attributions are not rare.

> A Brahmin, having drunk *surā* with a heroic disposition (*vīrabhāva*, i.e., at a more advanced stage) should recite the mantra. If that [*surā*] is not available, the Brahmin should offer cow's milk repeatedly. Betel, tobacco (? *tāmrakūṭam*), *tvaritā* (some sort of cannabis?),[20] and *tāditā* (palmyra-palm toddy?), opium (*ahiphenaḥ*), date-palm juice (*kharjurasaḥ* – probably made into toddy), datura (*dhūstūraṃ*), and cannabis (*samvidā*). These eight *surā*s are taught, which give bliss to the practitioner.[21]

It's tempting to translate "*tāmrakūṭam*" as "tobacco," and one Indian scholar, Ganapati Ray, writing in 1911, did just that when he attempted to show the indigenous nature of tobacco in India, postulating that this word was an earlier form of Bengali *tāmāku* ("tobacco").[22] Ray may well have been correct that this word means tobacco, but the verses should in that case be assigned a date *later* than the introduction of tobacco to India. References to tobacco in Sanskrit do not imply that it was present in India prior to the introduction from the New World: all that's Sanskrit is not old. Not only do we encounter this word in a list of intoxicants, but it has a phonetic resemblance to tobacco words—somewhat distorted here perhaps, but that's not surprising given the tendency to use a semantically relevant form for such new, imported words, as we see with *ahi-phena*, "serpent-foam," for opium.[23] Moreover, *tāmrakūṭa* resembles the word *kālakūṭa*, one name for the poison produced in the churning of the ocean, that famous source of all intoxicants. Indeed, in another, similar verse that Ganapati Ray quotes, attributed to the *Kulārṇava Tantra*, *tāmrakūṭa* is listed after *kālakūṭa* in a list of drugs that also mentions opium.[24] *Tāmrakūṭa* is also given in a Bengali dictionary for "tobacco."[25]

That these verses, if they truly contain a word for tobacco, are a later addition to the text (or a respectable attribution) need not worry us. What's remarkable is that at some point someone composed this verse to incorporate all these drugs, possibly including tobacco, as types of *surā*, meant to impart joy to the Tantric practitioner. We saw the same method of assimilating new drugs into traditional forms with cannabis and also with toddy as *vāruṇī*. Whereas Manu broadened the scope of *surā* to include jaggery drinks and grape wine (or whatever he meant by *mādhvī*) in order to clarify orthodox conduct, and later legal texts massively expanded the lists of non-*surā* drinks, here we see a list of drugs classified as types of *surā* for entirely permissive reasons, though only within the restricted context of Tantric rituals that require *surā*. The ancient *surā*-concept thus thrived as an important framework for dealing with intoxicants until a very recent period in Indian, Sanskritic textual culture. If the text just quoted does indeed refer to tobacco, then "*surā*" also came to incorporate that drug, and even if the word refers to some other substance, Ganapati Ray's interest in this matter in 1911 shows how powerful the Sanskrit tradition was in Indian histories of substances: this ingenious, flexible tradition of assimilating drugs was invoked to prove the antiquity and indigenous origin of New World *materia medica* in colonial-period India.

The tricky case of *tāmrakūṭa* also demonstrates that the meticulous work of philology, historical linguistics, and critical editions is essential to the study of the history of drugs and alcohol in India. Is "*tāmrakūṭa*" a word for tobacco, and if so when did it appear in these texts? Are there references to grapes in the epics? Do some words for grapes, wine, and cups in India come from Iranian-language areas? When the *Laws of Manu* were composed, did they forbid the three types of *surā* to "twice-borns," with all the ambiguity that term includes, or to the less ambiguous "best of twice-borns"? The ability to answer such questions in a thematic book like this one depends entirely on good critical editions and works of historical linguistics. So I thank scholars for their hard work in those fields.

Several later Sanskrit texts mention a plant substance that is definitely tobacco.[26] The *Yogaratnākara*, possibly a South Indian text, from the first half of the eighteenth century, contains a detailed description of the plant.[27] The passage first lists a number of synonyms for it, several of which contain the element "smoke" (*dhūma-*). There is also the Sanskritized form *tamākhu*. The plant is physically described as having many seeds, many flowers, and other features. The text then enumerates the qualities of tobacco in the terminology of traditional medicine. These include causing intoxication, bile, and dizziness, as well as being an emetic and cathartic. Smoking tobacco is called "smoke-drinking," a term long used to refer to a method of taking medicinal preparations by inhaling smoke (though not technically "smoking" in the sense of smoking tobacco or other drugs for pleasure).[28] P. K. Gode analyzed a number of Sanskrit and Marathi sources from the seventeenth and eighteenth centuries that mention tobacco.[29] Some of these texts, of uncertain date, mention taking dried tobacco powder, chewing it with slaked lime (like betel) and also chewing it together with the components of betel, something still common today. Gode notes that a Persian/Sanskrit lexical text from around 1676 mentions tobacco as well as a *hookah* ("smoking-device").[30]

That same Persian/Sanskrit lexical text, the *Rājavyavahārakośa*, attributed to a certain Ragunātha Paṇḍita, minister of King Chhatrapati Shivaji, also contains an early reference to coffee, grouped with cannabis, opium, and perfumes but separate from liquor and betel.[31] Here coffee (the transliterated Persian is *kāhavā*) is defined in Sanskrit as "relaxation liquid-extract" (*viśrāmakaṣāyaḥ*).[32] It is listed in the *Bhogyavarga* section where it follows water and flavored drinks and is followed by what we could class as "drugs (mild and strong)" and "perfumes." Thus coffee is followed by opium; cannabis (in Indic-transliterated Persian: *kaiphaḥ*), which is said to be an intoxication substance (*madadravya*); drinking cups; water pipes (*dhūmayantraṃ*, "smoke device" = *guḍguḍī*); tobacco; perfume (*khuṣboya* = *sugandhidravya*); musk; ambergris; *covā* ("agarwood essence"); civet; a red powder called *gulālaḥ*; *attaraḥ*, which is said to be "flower essence" (*puṣpasāra*); *arka* (a distillate, e.g., rose water), which is defined as the essence of a substance (*vastusāra*); the rose (*gulābaḥ* = *makaranda*); saffron; and various floral oils. There follows, grouped quite separately, the department of alcohol, *śarābkhāna*, defined as *surāgāra*, or "*surā* house"; the person who serves alcohol (*śarābdār* = *surādātṛ*, "*surā* provider"); and then betel.

South Asia in all periods was evidently open to new substances that altered the mind, and the sorts of people who used the texts we've explored in this book were well equipped to classify and assimilate these substances. The words, classifications, myths, and frameworks people had at their disposal—for example, the meaning of "*surā*," or what we learn about the goddess Surā—also changed and developed in the process.

Digestif

What Do We Do about This Stuff That Makes Everything Go Awry?

I can't possibly suggest one main thesis about alcohol or drinking in India for the vast period covered in this book, but a few major points have emerged.

It's striking just how much there is to say about alcohol and drinking in India on the basis of surviving Sanskrit texts alone, never mind the materials I haven't considered, such as texts in other languages, archaeological data, and all the evidence we've lost (not to mention the numerous sources I cut in writing this book). Many types of drink were consumed in early India, as well as several other substances that today we would class as drugs. And every few centuries, it seems, there were major changes and additions to the list: grain *surā*, sugarcane drinks, grape wine, betel, cannabis, opium, tobacco, coffee. Even on the basis of our limited sources, it's evident that at any given time there were several modes of consuming these substances, and these modes must have changed over time. There must also have been regional variation. So much seems clear, even though our data is far from a mirror on practice. The constant evolution of the world of alcohol and drugs (some of which, like distilled alcohol, cannabis, and opium, were quite strong) complicates and attenuates the idea of a recent "psychoactive revolution" in the case of South Asia.[1]

Representations of drinking in texts and images were likewise varied at any one time, and they too changed. Think of how the myth of Mada, Intoxication, was reworked in various texts, or how different writers used the story of the Andhakas and Vṛṣṇis. In Sanskrit and related languages, words for drinks were numerous and shifting. "*Vāruṇī*" became toddy, "*āsava*" was both vague and specific (extremely specific today), and some specialized definitions of "*surā*" eventually included cannabis and betel. Drink and drinking were mentioned in many genres, each with its own conventions and approach to the topic. Within certain genres, such as medical or legal texts, certain words, phrases, narratives, theories, and attitudes formed a common repertoire over long periods, such as the Sautrāmaṇī sacrifice, the arising of Surā at the churning, and threefold *surā* with its many variations. The rate at which genres responded to changes in practice varied too.

An Unholy Brew. James McHugh, Oxford University Press. © Oxford University Press 2021.
DOI: 10.1093/oso/9780199375936.003.0012

Literary texts were mostly stuck with a standard palette of drink-words that crystallized around the early to mid-first millennium CE, but medical and legal texts showed greater adaptability. In the previous chapters we saw how texts in the mythical mode could also be innovative. And we must not forget that the status of drink even within cosmic, mythical time was not stable. Several texts locate us at a particular moment, when *surā* has a certain status and humans have access to particular revelations and laws concerning *surā*. Writers, redactors, and readers used these materials for different purposes: the Sautrāmaṇī could be a prestigious, ancient, and powerful ritual; or it might show the hypocritical inconsistency of Hindu scripture; or it could be an exemplary scriptural exception setting a precedent for the consumption of liquor in rituals given in a secondary revelation.

I would therefore make the perhaps uselessly general point that in South Asian texts from this vast, rather nebulous "early" period there is enormous complexity with regard to alcohol. Our sources show an immense array of drinks, drugs, modes of consumption, and styles of representation, along with great diachronic change. Indian writers were well aware of all this variety and articulated it using an ancient but ever-developing set of concepts, words, narratives, drink-motifs, and literary types. These stock resources by no means limited their ways of talking about drink, drugs, and intoxication, nor, as we've seen, did they inevitably place a Hindu or Brahminical imprint on the subject.

Much of the material in this book formed a set of ideas and texts associated with a literate elite, and it's hard to know from our sources how much these ideas animated other communities' engagement with these substances. Even among the elite, though from the very start there were negative assessments of drink, as a vice or a forbidden substance, there were also many positive depictions of drink and drugs.

For the philosopher William James, alcohol stimulated the mystic consciousness, being "the great exciter of the Yes function in man . . . It makes him for the moment one with truth . . . [while sobriety] diminishes, discriminates, and says no; drunkenness expands, unites, and says yes."[2] If forced to pass judgement on alcohol in early or premodern Sanskritic Indic thought, I would say that alcohol is the drug that, when taken in excess, makes everything go awry for the drinker—amiss, confused, misplaced, upset. The drinker's conception and evaluation of people (self and others), things, and deeds becomes topsy-turvy, and there is crying, laughing, and making love to the wrong person. Of course, sometimes the drunkard shakes off prudishness and makes love to the right person. When a person drinks a lot, everything is out of place, but only with regard to that individual, a phenomenon that causes problems for the drinker but is entertaining for observers. It is easy to take advantage of drunk people in a number of ways, given their confusion.

Drink is a worldly drug. Vedic authors were right that drink is thoroughly human. Drink enhances the senses, desires, and fears, resulting in pleasure and pain, in endurance and enjoyment of your karmic lot in life, or in committing destructive bad deeds. *Surā* reeks of *saṃsāra*. Certain communities in early India were marked by their abstinence from drink, but, like celibacy, abstinence gained meaning from its larger context, a world of many drinkers. Abstinent communities avoided the sins and pains of drink, but they also never experienced the varied, tipsy, intensified engagement that a drunk person has with other people and the world. This limitation transformed their own experience of life and the reputation of their communities. It also placed them outside many social spaces and forms of interaction. Fortunately, betel allowed the abstinent—at least those who could afford it—to enjoy communal consumption of a mild drug (at least as we classify substances today). Later, cannabis enabled abstinent communities (and gods) to take a strong intoxicant while still avoiding alcohol and the people and places associated with it.

Tantra came relatively late, both in our historical framework and in the cosmic biography of Surā. Some later Tantric authors actively navigated their places in two temporalities: the mythological timeline of *surā* and of divine revelations to humans, and the material world of their own era, when opium, betel, cannabis, and even distilled *surā* were becoming well-known intoxicants. Even in early Tantra, *surā* was understood through the reworked categories of Manu and the myth of the churning.

Of course, there's a lot we don't know. The many gaps in this book highlight areas where more work is needed, such as research using languages other than Sanskrit for the second millennium CE in South Asia; studies of drink and drugs in early Tamil sources; a review of drugs and alcohol in early Indian archaeology and art history; and more research on other substances (several books could be written on the history of betel and cannabis in India). But, despite the limitations of this book, and although our sources give only restricted glimpses of the subcontinent's drink culture at any one time and place, it should now be clear that South Asia has carried on a long, complex, and impressive engagement with this most remarkable of substances.

In the world of subject and object, of pleasure and pain, and of good and bad deeds, *surā* shuffles a person with respect to all these things. Given these powers of *surā*, for some people in some situations *surā* is pleasant, right, even useful. For others *surā* is wrong and destructive. In a human world where desire and anger sometimes align with what is right and sometimes do not, drink intensifies human relations: sex and violence, alliance and enmity.

Surā takes many forms. *Mada*, intoxication, too takes many forms: the exhilarated warrior-*mada* of Indra drinking *soma*, a sacred *mada* restricted to the gods and those who deal with them; the thrilled, charming, expansive *mada* of a playful drinking party; the frenzied, drunken slaughter of your own kin; the extravagant beauty of peacock tails, and the incessant booming opinions of vain, proud scholars.

APPENDIX

Soma, Ancient Drugs, and Modern Scholars

> To future historians, nothing will explain our behavior, except, and hear me out, a mass outbreak of ergotism caused by contaminated rye stores?
>
> —Patricia Lockwood[1]

The *soma* drink is the most famous ancient Indian drug. *Soma*, made from a plant called *soma*, is also a god, and a drink that was used as an offering to the gods in some Vedic rituals. *Soma* was celebrated at an early period, as shown in the hymns of the *Ṛgveda*. The preparation of *soma* is also described in later liturgical texts and ritual manuals. An analogous substance, *haoma*, is used in Zoroastrian rituals, and so scholars have considered ancient proto-forms of the *soma/haoma* tradition.[2] Even today, one can buy something called *soma* from Indian herb suppliers, and a plant called *soma* is used in modern performances of some Vedic rituals.

In many respects we know exactly what the *soma* drink was: a cold, pressed infusion of a plant. But there is much debate as to the identity of the plant used (though we know it would have been somehow psychoactive). *Soma* differs from alcoholic drinks in one important respect: the main psychoactive component of ancient liquors was the same as that of contemporary ones (i.e., ethanol), but scholars can't agree on the identity of the psychoactive component of *soma*.

In the earliest period that I consider in this book, the *soma* drink was the conceptual and ritual counterpart of *surā*, so its identity has some bearing on this book's main focus. My reason for exploring it in an appendix is that, somewhat to my irritation, when I give talks on alcohol in India to people outside my field, my audience's curiosity about *soma* tends to overshadow the subject of alcohol. Also, some scholars of ancient South Asia may have no desire to read any more on *soma*!

Theories about *soma* highlight the methodological problems of dealing with ancient descriptions of substances and experiences, and the historiography of *soma* studies offers a fascinating window onto different eras' theories about drugs, alcohol, and religion.[3] To paraphrase archaeologist Jacquetta Hawkes's comment on theories about Stonehenge: every age has the *soma* it deserves—or desires.[4] In reviewing R. Gordon Wasson's book containing the "mushroom theory" of *soma*, Huston Smith reports on the opinions of scholars ranging from Claude Lévi-Strauss to Robert Graves.[5] In my opinion, if the *soma* mystery is never solved, that will be no bad thing, since it's so productive of interesting research in every generation, and serves as an excellent foil for changes in theories about drug-induced religious experience.

Soma is a huge topic, and I will just introduce the matter here, focusing especially on its relation to the study of alcohol in India. I shall mention only a few of the many candidates for the *soma* plant.[6] But why does anyone care about the original *soma*? After all, we know how the drink was prepared, its ritual usage, and its ritual/mythological significance. Put crudely, some scholars think the nature of the *soma*-altered-mental-state at the "dawn" of Indian religion, in the Vedas, could be understood to have somehow sowed the seeds for the development of other theological and philosophical ideas. Huston Smith makes this sort of case: "Etymologically and otherwise Vedanta [a school of philosophy] is the 'culmination of the Vedas,' and the Vedas derive more than from any other single identifiable source from *Soma*."[7] Of course, not everyone makes such a strong case for *soma*'s significance; for some scholars, it simply constitutes a fascinating puzzle.

How might we identify this plant? We could look at plants called *soma* today, which is what some nineteenth-century scholars did. Then, since those plants were not psychoactive, they looked for something else in the drink to make up the difference. We could also consider descriptions in ancient texts of its form (e.g., stems) and origin (e.g., mountains)—though such texts were far from botanically accurate by our standards. We could consider the plant's apparent effects (a buzz or exhilaration—it's very hard to know the nuances of the words used) and the behavior in rituals that accompanied *soma* consumption (sometimes a *soma*-taker stayed up all night; sometimes he vomited). But just as there are many difficulties with the botanical identification of plants in ancient texts, so there are even greater problems in correlating ancient descriptions of people's experiences with recent descriptions of substance-induced mental and physical states. On top of all this, what counted as *soma* has changed over the years, and it may also have varied at early periods, so our question (and solution) should be framed narrowly: "What plant was most commonly used to make the *soma* drink in the early period of the *Ṛg Veda*?" Scholars of the *soma* problem are acutely aware of all these variables.

Let's begin with *soma*'s relation to alcohol: it was *not* a fermented alcoholic drink. As prepared in rituals, the (probably dried) *soma* stems were moistened with water, crushed, squeezed, and filtered, then mixed with milk and other substances to sweeten the resulting drink. Descriptions of the classical *soma* ritual sometimes mention curds or barley flour that might have been added after the drink was filtered. But the basic drink was a simple, cold water–extraction and was drunk relatively promptly. Rajendralal Mitra, writing in 1873, suggested that the *soma* drink was alcoholic because grain products were sometimes added to it.[8] However, given that the *soma* plants used in India in his time were evidently not psychoactive, Mitra was trying to understand how the *soma*-drink could have been psychoactive (also, as we saw earlier, Mitra had a somewhat irreverent agenda when it came to alcohol in ancient India).[9] In fact it's quite clear that *soma* was not fermented, though Mitra was not alone in claiming *soma* was alcoholic, and scholarship on *soma* forms part of the historiography of alcohol in India.[10] Pentti Aalto, for example, repeats the notion.[11] Other candidates that have been suggested for components of *soma* as an alcoholic drink are the Afghan grape and barley, which might supposedly have created something like beer, with the *soma* plant functioning like hops (this latter idea being Friedrich Max Müller's suggestion).[12]

Pursuing a different path, in 1894 Hermann Oldenberg suggested that the *soma* plant was a substitute for an Indo-Germanic mead drink.[13] Oldenberg wrote that frequent references in Vedic texts to the *soma* drink as "*madhu*" ("sweet," with the additional meaning of "honey" and, much later, "grape wine") attest to the transmission of an earlier "mead" terminology to a substitute drink.[14] In a similar vein, Georges Dumézil proposed that the original ambrosial drug of the Indo-Europeans was a beer-like drink, which was eventually replaced by the newer drug *soma*.[15] This proposed change in ritual drinking is intriguing, but it need not concern us now, in our exploration of alcohol and drugs *as attested* in South Asia. Also, this proto-liquor would have existed even earlier than the tradition of the Vedas, so it does not solve the problem of the Vedic *soma*.

Still, the difference between these sets of theories is important. One set proposes that there was a sacred alcoholic drink in ancient India inadequately described in the surviving texts, which misleadingly focused on a mere plant additive—on the hops, as it were—ignoring the beer. These theories of *soma*-as-alcoholic complicate the idea that Western discourses on India are dominated by the notion of alcohol as foreign, with India instead being the home of exotic drugs. The other set of theories—in which an ancient ritual involving an alcoholic drink traveled from beyond the region into South Asia, and at some point along the way a plant-drug was substituted for the alcoholic drink (either in South Asia or, as proposed more recently, in Central Asia)[16]—aligns with the discourse of alcohol as foreign in innately teetotal, "spiritual," drug-centric India.

If it wasn't an alcoholic drink, we must return to our earlier question: what was the original, psychoactive *soma* plant? Some nineteenth-century scholars were attentive to what native informants had identified as the *soma* plant, but as these plants are not psychoactive, and because the alcohol theory does not hold, people inferred that these plants are substitutes and thus started the search for the *true*, ancient, psychoactive *soma* plant.[17] One method of searching involves examining descriptions of the effects of *soma* alongside modern categories of drugs (e.g., "stimulant," "hallucinogen") and then searching for a plant containing that type of drug. The difficulty here is that the hymns of the *Ṛgveda* contain much complex imagery and symbolism, and, as Stephanie Jamison notes, "These ritual elements are also given cosmic dimensions."[18] Also, in the study of drugs the extent of social/cultural construction of experience and of the *reporting* of experience is contentious, to say the least.[19] Thus we should be cautious in interpreting the ancient descriptions of the "*soma* experience." Nevertheless, working with this and other types of evidence, scholars have proposed a variety of drug types as candidates for *soma*: stimulants (ephedra), hallucinogens with various other effects (fly agaric, Syrian rue, ayahuasca-analogous plants), and cannabis.[20]

In the *Ṛgveda*, *soma* is associated with a particular experiential state. Forms of the verbal root (√*mad*) associated with this state were also associated with gambling, and to describe the effects of alcohol.[21] But *soma* does not lead to confusion or regrettable deeds as *surā* does and is more associated with power and mastery. Indeed, *soma* gives the god Indra immense strength in his battle with his arch enemy. Hence the scholarly translation as "exhilarating" used in some Vedic contexts. Yet, as Jamison and Brereton write, the identity of the *soma* plant "affects the translation of some hymns and particularly the translation of the various forms of the root √mad."[22] So, how we understand and translate these *descriptions* of the *soma*-experience depends on how we understand the actual effects of a given drug/plant—intoxicated, thrilled, exhilarated, drunk? If the meaning of the Vedic Sanskrit words that describe the experience of "being on *soma*" is not fully determined, then translations and interpretations may import prior assumptions about the effects of a proposed plant/drug. It is hard to find English words for some sort of drug effect that do not evoke a certain state or substance (e.g., drunk, high, tripping). But we can hardly go about using such loaded translations of ancient *experiential* vocabulary to go about hunting for a modern *drug* that matches the description—that would be completely circular. As a rough working translation maybe we could use the extremely colloquial but usefully vague word "buzz" as a translation: *soma* buzz, alcohol buzz, gambling buzz. It does not tell you a lot about the feeling, but that is a good thing in this particular situation where precision limits and maybe distorts what we can think. There does seem to be some effect, but it is not clear precisely what that is from the texts alone.

In addition to many occurrences of forms of the root √*mad* in relation to drinking *soma*, some detailed experiential descriptions exist in the *Ṛgveda*, or at least passages that some people have read as such. One of the most famous *Ṛgveda* hymns including a description of taking *soma* is sometimes called "The Self-Praise of the Lapwing."[23] The identity of the speaker here is not certain, but translators Jamison and Brereton, following George Thompson, think that "the speaker is fundamentally the poet, but the poet consciously taking on the voice and identity of another entity or entities—in our view both that of a bird and that of a god, indeed of Indra."[24] The *soma*-drinker in this hymn is lifted up, with wings that seem to fill the cosmos:

> Because both world-halves are not equal to even one wing of mine . . .
> —have I drunk of the *soma*? Yes![25]

Who is speaking, and what exactly is happening? Given that this may represent the words of a god assuming the identity of a bird, we need to be careful how much we make of the verse, especially when looking for a matching drug-high. If we had dozens of such hymns, and almost all their references to *soma* described variations on such experiences, we would have more solid grounds for describing drug experiences reported over three thousand years ago. Sadly, we don't have such data.

Accepting these limitations, can we deduce anything useful about *soma* from the hymns? Even a superficial cross-cultural study of drugs and alcohol shows how many practices, behaviors, and reported experiences associated with drugs are contingent on social and cultural, rather than biological, factors. As Jan Houben writes, "Merely because Apollinaire (1880–1918) published the 'visionary' poem *Vendémiaire* in his collection *Alcools* we do not put the label 'hallucinogen' on alcohol."[26] Earlier in this book, we saw many references to a drug causing significant visual confusions and distortions: alcohol. And consider a Chinese poem from the ninth century CE:

> The fifth bowl purifies my flesh and bones.
> The sixth bowl allows me to communicate with immortals.
> The seventh bowl I need not drink,
> I am only aware of a pure wind rising beneath my two arms . . .
> I . . . ride this pure wind and wish to return home.[27]

The marvelous drink in these bowls is tea, though some of the imagery here recalls that of the lapwing hymn in the *Ṛgveda*.

Does *soma* even have to be what we consider a strong drug? We might productively compare *soma* to kava root (*Piper methysticum* G., Forst), traditionally consumed in some Pacific Ocean societies. Kava roots are sometimes exchanged in bundles as prestigious gifts; the roots are prepared by mashing or chewing them fresh or dried, adding water, and straining them, all of which can be associated with ritual practices and special implements.[28] Like *soma*, kava possesses a varied and complex mythology and plays an important role in ritualized social occasions. Yet kava is not always strong when consumed. As Vincent Lebot et alia note, "Given the plant's complex and subtle psychoactivity, it is difficult to categorize in the terms of common drug classification schemes . . . The psychoactive potency of the drug can vary considerably, from very weak to quite strong. Kava may induce sociability, feelings of peace and harmony, and, in large doses, sleep, or it may fail to produce relaxation and provoke nausea."[29] Kava use in these Pacific Ocean societies provides an enlightening model of a drug culture based on a substance processed in similar ways to *soma*. Though not strongly psychoactive, at least in the eyes of most modern Western people, kava is nevertheless highly valued and significant in these societies. Likewise, archaeologist Andrew Sherratt points out that where few intoxicating substances are available, a psychoactive effect that Westerners might think mild today would still be highly appreciated.[30]

Even putting aside the elusiveness of other people's subjective experiences, cultural expectations of how people should behave and what they should report when taking drugs vary, adding another layer of complexity to the task of extrapolating from *soma*'s effects to a given plant or drug. Given that *soma* was divine, restricted in use, and shared with the gods, its consumers' behavior and verbal articulation of their experiences were no doubt inflected by many considerations. When you drank *soma*, you ingested a god, who then affected your mind and body. And let's not forget that this was happening in a world with no tea, coffee, tobacco, or cocaine. Apparently the only other intoxicant was *surā*. It's quite striking, in fact, how little interest is shown in the *Ṛgveda* in the effects of *soma*. The poets, and no doubt their patrons, seem to have been more interested in the preparation process and the status associated with the drink.

Though I have little to add to the ongoing theories about *soma*, from studying alcohol and perfumes I can offer a few pertinent points. First, even if one had a time machine and went back to a *soma* ceremony in the period of the *Ṛgveda*, one might still have difficulty determining *soma*'s botanical identity. To illustrate: in 2009 I was studying perfumes in India, and in old Hyderabad I asked a few shopkeepers to show me agarwood. One traditional perfumer showed me several varieties of a dark, oily, fragrant wood. It looked like the "agarwood" one also sees on sale in, say, Dubai and is derived from a number of different species of trees from Assam and parts of Southeast Asia. Some of the samples might even have been fake. When I asked for agarwood at the shop of a merchant of Unani medicines (the traditional medicine of South Asian Muslims), he produced what appeared to be ebony or some other black wood, not fragrant and clearly different from what I'd seen elsewhere as agarwood. I have often related this story—not an unusual one in dealing with plant products in traditional contexts—to illustrate that, as a valued plant in the ancient world, "*soma*" may have covered many varieties of *soma*-similar plants, prepared forms of *soma*, and common *soma* substitutes, even in early periods. Houben notes that in later ritual texts, when "mountain *soma*" was not available, the local *soma* could be used.[31] This doesn't imply that the mountain variety was considered more authentic; it may just have been better.[32] And "better" might not imply more psychoactive, just more prestigious: compare fine Darjeeling tea with a cheap, drugstore caffeine pill. If we consider "*soma*" over a long period as a term more like "coffee," which can mean arabica, robusta, or chicory, or the Sanskrit "*candana*," meaning "sandalwood,"[33] which covers several plants, of which some varieties are considered better than others, this might help to settle, or rather diffuse, the problem of *soma*'s identity in any one context—for the problem is probably insoluble, even with a time machine.

But perhaps we do we have something like a time machine. In the 1990s, archaeologist Viktor Sarianidi published news of discoveries from Central Asia: ancient ritual complexes, possibly proto-Zoroastrian, dating from the early to late second millennium CE, in which vessels were found that contained ephedra, poppy, and cannabis.[34] As Houben observes, this was actual physical evidence of an early fire cult involving the preparation of a *soma*/*haoma*-type drink, along with actual plant remains.[35] However, a more recent examination of the contents of these vessels, by archaeologist Corrie Bakels, suggests that they contained not the remains of those drug plants but instead broomcorn millet (*Panicum miliaceum*).[36] These newer findings may disappoint scholars who are inclined to think that *soma* was an ephedra species, but the glass is half full, for millet and sorghum were components of many early grain-based alcoholic drinks, and some of the jars that Sarianidi found may thus have contained a type of beer (though more analysis is clearly needed).[37] This does not, however, imply that *soma* was possibly millet beer! It's a stretch even to say for certain that the contents of the jars should be considered an early, proto-*soma*/*haoma* drink. Future research may clarify this particular matter, but I'm confident that *soma* scholarship will continue indefinitely.

In many respects, *soma* is a curious case in the history of drugs. For one thing, it's so well-known yet famously absent—as if wine, mentioned so often in the Bible, were now a lost mystery drink. Also, *soma* was prestigious and sometimes described as an import, unlike *surā*, which was made from locally farmed grains. In Vedic texts, the use of *soma* is restricted to elite persons, and association with *soma* was a mark of distinction (though in later periods local substitutes were used, at which point the "trade" was ritualized). Yet *soma* did not share the fate of some other elite exotic drugs. Whereas wine in France trickled down from being an elite drink in the Bronze Age to being a locally produced common drink today, and rare tea, coffee, and chocolate in Europe all became increasingly common, *soma*-as-drug withered away.[38] Imports of it presumably ceased, local substitutes took over, and *soma* does not form a part of later Indic drug cultures, nor is there evidence of it being consumed outside rituals (and some medical contexts). On the other hand, imported wines in India were joined by betel, often perfumed with exotics such as camphor and musk. *Soma* differed from these novelties as it was an archaic drug, and its elite nature was tied up with its exclusive ritual use—at least in recorded periods. Perhaps for these reasons, in later Indic culture *soma* was prominent less as a "drug" than as a mythological figure or general concept, more like classical ambrosia than imported wine in medieval England. The ease with which substitutes were used, coupled with *soma*'s ritual exclusivity from an early period (with the rituals themselves becoming less common), may have contributed to *soma*'s strange transformation into a substance both famous and unknown, a mythical drug.

Setting the mystery of the plant aside, we should note that *soma* is very different from early alcoholic drinks. That the water-soaked *soma* stalks required pounding with stones is striking. Evidently *soma* was a tough substance—again, a comparison with kava root is useful. From this perspective, we know a lot about the *soma* drink, just as one can know a lot about "tea" without knowing anything about *Camellia sinensis* and caffeine. Unlike *surā*, *soma* was a raw preparation, and the main ingredient was not local—the best type of *soma* came from elsewhere. But the drinks did have some similarities: both involved the noisy labor of pounding, careful filtering, and the production of a water-based drink (though *soma* did not need to ferment). Whereas the preparation of *surā* evoked the familiar methods of the kitchen and the preparation of food, *soma* was a mysterious imported infusion, prepared only for the gods and some privileged people who shared it. Yet both drinks were squeezed out of a solid substrate and filtered, and both were made using a *process* (as opposed to a drink like toddy, which emerges from the tree almost ready to drink). The very word "*soma*" is probably derived from a root meaning "to press out"; as Elizarenkova notes, it "is a ritual denomination of substance, from which the juice is pressed out . . ."[39]

Charles Malamoud describes the centrality of cooking for the Vedic sacrifice, and in that context it's striking that *soma* was not cooked. Although it was offered to the fire, this part of the ritual occurred so that it could be consumed by the gods via the Fire (Agni); the portion that the humans drank was not cooked at any stage. *Surā*, by contrast, is thoroughly cooked—made from cooked grains and placed by the fire to ferment. This contrast emphasizes that the mind-altering drink of the gods was raw while that of men was cooked, though, as Malamoud points out, the exception makes perfect sense as Soma itself was considered a god, not just another oblation to be cooked (note that the Goddess-nature of *surā* was not developed in these early texts).[40]

Finally, drinking *soma* was not just about getting somehow intoxicated or exhilarated. Jarrod Whitaker writes of *soma* in the rituals of the *Ṛgveda* (*soma*'s earliest appearance in the Indic context), "[T]he hypothetical pharmacological effects of *sóma* are secondary—if not irrelevant—to the ritual and political symbolism and ideology underlying its use. The primary issue here is a matter of representation, not of the effects of a drug-induced experience."[41] Whitaker argues that the significance of *soma* is complex, connected to physical strength, manliness, and political power, as one sees with the warrior god Indra, the recipient of *soma*: "[A]s a ritually created substance, *sóma* plays a fundamental role in fusing divine and human realms in Ṛgvedic ritual performances and (literally) in a man's body, and in mapping Indra's identity and exploits into the idealized image of Āryan men, especially warriors and chieftains."[42] Seen in this light we might think of the ancient *soma* of the *Ṛgveda* more as a virile, military stimulant drug that is, in this case, shared with a chieftain god than as some sort of mystical hallucinogen (though, for all the reasons explained already, that by no means implies that the botanical *soma* of the *Ṛgveda* must contain what is nowadays called a "stimulant" by pharmacologists).

I shall leave *soma* now, unresolved but fascinating. Behind all the ancient texts and Vedic liturgies of *soma* and *surā* lies a world of blazing, smoky, wood fires, bundles of aromatic herbs, sometimes brought from afar, heaps of grains, sounds of pounding with heavy, wet stones, and heaving wooden tubs and clay jars filled with liquids, hot or cold, milky, porridgy, herbal, frothy and fermenting, and straining these drinks through hairy, woolly cloths to offer to the gods and drink oneself. In this context, it's not hard to understand the enthusiastic descriptions of divine *soma* from the *Ṛgveda*:

> The exhilarating drink of exhilaration, the *soma*, rushes into the filter
> beyond the waves,
> smashing aside the demons, seeking the gods.
> He runs into the tubs, he is poured around into the filter.
> He grows strong through the hymns at the sacrifices.[43]

Notes

Introduction

1. I have given preference in translating to preserving an approximate place of articulation (*Subhāṣitaratnakoṣa* no. 127).
2. I shall use both words for the region here, though by "India" I mostly do not refer to the modern nation-state. I often use "early" and sometimes "premodern" as convenient terms to cover what some scholars might call ancient, "classical," early, later early, later, and "plain" medieval. I mostly focus on approximate centuries rather than periods.
3. Fischer-Tiné and Tschurenev 2014, 1–3.
4. See, for example, James Mills's (2003) study of cannabis.
5. I modify my comments in McHugh forthcoming a.
6. Clark 1983, 125.
7. Though see Southworth's balanced comments on the assumptions (and dangers) of linguistic palaeontology (2005, Section 1.31–32).
8. As quoted by Sur (1974, 373).
9. Benn 2015, 22.
10. Sibum 1995. I thank Projit Mukharji for this reference.
11. HDŚ II.2, 791–799. I adapt comments from McHugh 2017.
12. Huang 2000, 149–150.
13. See McHugh forthcoming b. Also see "Later Developments" in Cup 3.
14. Hartman and Oppenheim 1950, 6–7.
15. See the OED, s.v. "beer" and "ale."
16. Studies of alcohol-related words in other Indian languages would be a useful contribution here—I am missing a lot of the picture.
17. For the exhilarating effects of *soma* see *The Rigveda*, trans. Jamison and Brereton, p. 31. Gambling can also produce this state in a person in the *Ṛgveda* (e.g., X.34.1). *Surā* produces a bad *mada* at *Ṛgveda* VIII.2.12 (and see Cup 7). Thus *mada* does not only apply to *soma*/*haoma* in early periods. Also early, Brough translates a line from the *Avesta* (*Yašt* 17.5) where there are several "intoxications" (*maδ*-), only one of which is from *haoma*, "Homage to Haoma, in that all other intoxications are accompanied by Frenzied Wrath with bloody club, while that intoxication which is Haoma's is accompanied by his own Aša (truth)." (Brough 1971, 331). Sanskrit √*mad* (to bubble, be glad, be drunk) is likely from Proto-Indo-European (PIE) *mad*-, meaning to drip, wet, fat, glossy, well fed (EWA Part 2, s.v. MAD citing Pokorny 694). English "mad" in the sense of insane is from a *different* root (Watkins 2011, s.v. mei-[1]). *Madhu*,

"honey," "wine," and related forms are from yet another PIE form connected to sweetness, honey, and mead (EWA Part 2, s.v. *mádhu-*; Watkins 2011, s.v. medhu-).

18. For both words MW also gives the sense of intoxication, but in this book as we shall see that plain "*mada/matta*" are the commoner √*mad*-derived terms for drunk intoxication or substance-induced intoxication. This state is sometimes contrasted with madness (e.g., *matto madanīyadrayvena*, *unmatta unmādena pañcavidhena*, Vijñāneśvara on YVS 2.32, as quoted by Hyne-Sutherland 2015, 80. Also see Cup 7, note 2 at start).
19. *Dārimukha Jātaka* (#378). As noted by Collins (2015, 199).
20. For an analysis of the concept of madness in India, including Sanskrit terminology, see Hyne-Sutherland 2015. Also Collins 2015.
21. Sedgwick 1994.
22. Sedgwick 1994.
23. Sedgwick 1994, 132.
24. See Hickman 2014 on this rhetoric.
25. Lemon 2018, x.
26. Lemon 2018, xi.
27. Lemon 2018, xi.
28. Here I bracket Indian philosophical discussions of desire, attachment, and intention, referring to general patterns we see in literary, medical, legal, and other genres.
29. There's nothing to stop us translating this into the language of addiction. After all there is an attachment to going back to an object. Yet this loses something of the differences: an emphasis on desire and attachment on the part of the subject, alongside a discourse of self-control.
30. Mukharji 2014, 65.
31. Mukharji 2014, 65.
32. Mitra 1872a.; Mitra 1873. On Mitra see Asiatic Society 1978 and Sur 1974.
33. Mitra 1872b.
34. Mitra 1873, 2.
35. Mukherjee 1978, 62.
36. Prakash 1987. Also Prakash 1961; Achaya 1994; Achaya 1998.
37. Agrawala 1963; Handiqui 1968; Shastri 1969. The importance of P. K. Gode's work on cultural history goes without saying.
38. Kolhatkar 1999. Also Kolhatkar 1987. I have not cited this work at every point in my discussion of Vedic *surā* as I would probably have done so in every note.
39. Chatterjee 2005.
40. HDŚ.
41. Aalto 1959; Hellwig 2012.
42. See Habighorst, Reichart, and Sharma 2007.
43. See the Appendix on *Soma* for some bibliography. I cite studies on drugs in the sections on various drugs.
44. Clark 1983. E.g., Dietler 1990; Dietler 2001; Dietler and Herbich 2006. Dietler 2006 has also been very useful.
45. Steinkraus 1996.

46. E.g., McGovern 2009.
47. Marshall 1951, vol. 2, 420–421; vol. 3, pl. 125.
48. Allchin 1977; Allchin 1979; Mahdihassan 1972; Mahdihassan 1979.
49. See McHugh forthcoming b.
50. Also, some of the translations, for example of recipes, are reproduced both in the articles and this book. For the drinks see McHugh 2020a.; forthcoming c.; forthcoming d.; forthcoming e. I thank the editors of these journals for allowing me to summarize those articles here. I have also published some of the translations from this book in short survey articles aimed at a variety of more general audiences: McHugh 2020b.; forthcoming a. McHugh 2020c. is a journalistic online visual essay on this topic, also using some of the translations in this book, aimed at a popular audience. At an extremely early stage of this project I published a survey of alcohol in early India (McHugh 2013), though that article is largely superseded by my later research.

Aperitif

1. For example, in the *Arthaśāstra* the "Superintendent of *Surā*" oversees many drinks. Medhātithi (on Manu 8.159) notes this usage of *surā* explaining *saurika*, or *surā*-related [debts] as follows: "'*Saurika*' means caused by drinking *surā*, and this usage of *surā* has the generic sense of intoxicating beverage." (*surāpānanimittaṃ saurikaṃ surāgrahaṇaṃ madyopalakṣaṇārthaṃ*).
2. One exception: a "*sura*" is made in Himachal Pradesh today (Tamang 2010, 212). Also there is a medical preparation called *surā* (see Cup 9). Many *surā*-like drinks are still made in South Asia but are largely absent from urban bars.
3. *Jātaka* (Pali), *Kumbha Jātaka* (512). References to the Pali *Jātaka*s are to Fausbøll's ed.
4. On the development of the Pali *Jātaka* collection see von Hinüber 1998a. For a recent analysis of the *Jātaka*s see Appleton 2010.
5. *Terminalia chebula.*
6. *Phyllanthus emblica.*
7. Meulenbeld quotes a number of authorities regarding *śāli*, which seems to be winter rice (1974, 509).
8. One ms. tradition has *rasaṃ* here, so a red juice/liquid.
9. Literally "tree-dog" and no doubt the palm-civet. As for the term "tree-dog" in this sense, compare to Malayalam *marappaṭṭi*, "tree-dog," and similar terms from South India.
10. I deliberately use the most neutral translation.
11. I accept the attested extra *ca*. As we shall see in Chapter 7, in Pali Vinaya texts the difference between the *sambhāra* and the grains matters (note there is no *kiṇṇa/kiṇva* here). *Cāṭi* (f.) occurs in Pali but is not, as far as I am aware, attested in Sanskrit. This word has a Dravidian origin—compare Tamil *cāṭi* "jar." (Turner 1966, s.v. *cāṭī). Perhaps *cāṭi* implied a large jar for brewing or was a cognate of a vernacular term for a brewing vessel.

12. In the *Arthaśāstra* cats are used as protection against rats in storage buildings (AŚ 2.5.6; 4.3.21).
13. H. T. Francis translates "And when the liquor fermented and began to escape, the cats drank the strong drink that flowed down from the inside of the jars . . ." (*Jātaka* trans. Francis et al., vol. 5, p. 7). Fausbøll's edition does not support this, though there are several variants for this line, which has possibly been unclear to traditional scholars too. One problem is the inclination to read the *te paccitvā* as somehow connected with the brewing or fermentation of the drink. One source, Fausbøll's B2, has the cats getting free (*muñcitvā*) and stretching their bodies (*uttānakāye*) to get the drink.
14. I prefer the attested reading: *suraṃ deva, madhuraṃ devā ti* as opposed to Fausbøll's *suraṃ detha, madhuraṃ dethā 'ti*. Given the men are being executed for a crime they have not committed and wish to explain themselves this is a more likely exclamation. Also, when the cats revive, the king contrasts poison (*visa*) with a "sweet" thing (*madhura*), the term here implying a state of being free from noxious matter, like English "sweet (water)." Taking *madhura* as "innocuous" also explains why the word suddenly crops up in the brewers' plea *in addition* to the word *surā*. Finally, we might remember that *surā* is a new type of drink for the king and his superintendents, so just shouting "It's *surā*, sir!" would not be helpful according the internal logic of the narrative.
15. *Kumbha Jātaka* (512), ed. Fausbøll. I am grateful to Phyllis Granoff for comments on this passage. All errors are my own.
16. In the version in the *Dhammapadaṭṭhakathā* (XI. *Jarāvaggo*, 1) the women have made this *surā*, their husbands have celebrated, and then afterward they too are keen to celebrate.
17. *Kumbha Jātaka* (512).
18. Possibly "masters" but more likely "husbands."
19. By uttering the canonical verse *Dhammapada* 146
20. See Cup 6 on Balarāma.
21. Braidwood et al. 1953.
22. See Patrick McGovern on early alcohol (e.g., 2009).
23. Later we will see how *surā* is contrasted with "gruel" as ends of a spectrum of desirability.

CUP 1

1. Of course if you only have one type of alcoholic drink and it is, for example, beer, your generic word for "liquor" and "beer" are one and the same. As for "*surā*," Mayrhofer (EWA Part 2, s.v. *súrā-*) suggests that a connection to the root √*sav* (to press out, i.e., express a juice or liquid) and to the word *soma* (a pressed-out but not fermented drink) are most plausible, perhaps implying that solid-state fermentation is an ancient practice, as such fermentation often requires pressing as one sees with Japanese *sake*. For Avestan *hurā* see Brough 1971, 331. On another early Persian

drink, **wašak*, that is paired in a certain Pahlavi text with *hur* (*surā*) see Henning (1955).

2. For simplicity I use "sugar," "starch," "yeast," "alcohol," etc. instead of technical terms. This usage hides the complexity of types of sugars, etc. involved. Yeast can, of course, act on something like wheat flour to rise it, given small amounts of sugars available in the flour.
3. For a survey of traditional alcoholic fermentations using grains see Steinkraus 1996, 363–508.
4. See McGovern 2009.
5. Pegu 2013.
6. I would like to thank Baidar Murmu of the Santhal community, as well as Dr. Purusottam Pattanail and Nilamadhaba Kanhar at the Tribal Museum Bhubaneswar for arranging for me to see the production of *handia* in Bhubaneswar in the fall of 2014.
7. Steinkraus 1996, 432–433.
8. This section is a very much abridged version of McHugh forthcoming c.
9. Please see McHugh forthcoming c for more on this process, the texts, dates, and other details. Also see Kolhatkar 1987 and 1999.
10. On the relative dates of the *Ṛgveda* and *Atharvaveda* see *Ṛgveda*, trans. Jamison and Brereton, Vol. 1, p. 5.
11. On dating these texts see Gonda 1977, 476–487. On the relative early date of the *Baudhāyana Śrauta Sūtra* see Gonda 1977, 514. For a date of around 500 BCE see Witzel 1989, 142–143.
12. ĀŚS XIX 5.11.
13. For references and translations pertinent to this description see McHugh forthcoming c.
14. For a discussion of the *kārotara*, *parisrut*, and *kīlāla* see also McHugh forthcoming c.
15. The householder's fire in which the foods to be offered in sacrifices are prepared.
16. For the mantras of the *Sautrāmaṇī* see Cup 6.
17. The offertorial fire.
18. BŚS 17.31–32. I am not a scholar of Vedic ritual texts and have adapted Dandekar's translation of this text as given in the *Śrautakośa* with brewing-reading changes (*Śrautakośa*, vol. I, part 2, 903–905). I am grateful to Stephanie Jamison for comments on this passage. All errors are my own.
19. Caland (1903, 6–7) suggests this section, the *karmānta* that clarifies points of the ritual, is later than the main text. Though this is still an early usage of the word *kiṇva*.
20. BŚS 26.22. Caland's edition; my translation, indebted to Dandekar's in the *Śrautakośa*. The final description here of the hide and the *kārotara* is tricky: *carmaṇā tv evābhividi*. I have used Dandekar's translation, but this is far from certain. At the most we might assume the hide is somehow involved with this object.
21. BŚS 17.34.
22. *Atharvaveda Paippalāda* 5.10, ed. and trans. Lubotsky.
23. Here I differ from Oort 2002—for a detailed response see McHugh forthcoming c and McHugh forthcoming b.

24. Damerow 2012, 6.
25. I thank Andrea Gutierrez for comments about the history of *sambar*.
26. AŚ, ed. and trans. Kangle. Also trans. Olivelle.
27. Drawing on the work of Schlingloff who compared the descriptions of building forts with archaeological evidence, Olivelle accepts that this text is an accurate description of practice in at least one realm of activity. *Arthaśāstra*, trans. Olivelle, 7.
28. AŚ, trans. Olivelle, 28.
29. AŚ, trans. Olivelle, 37–38.
30. AŚ, trans. Olivelle, 51–52. Though note Yaśodhara (on KS 1.4.23 in the Devadatta Shastri, 1964 ed.) quotes the *āsava* and *maireya* recipes from the AŚ with minor variations in the thirteenth century CE.
31. Possibly betelnut, though uncertain given other early references to the nut are to "*pūga*," and this word is attested earlier in other senses. See the section on betel in Cup 2.
32. AŚ 2.25.16–18.
33. The herbs starting with *moraṭā* in line 33 of this. Perhaps a known brewing mixture.
34. A herb, some variety of sugar, or a type of limestone paste, see HIML IB, 323, n. 112.
35. AŚ 2.25.26–28, Olivelle's translation, modified.
36. AŚ 2.25.31, Olivelle's translation, modified.
37. AŚ 2.25.35–36, trans. Olivelle.
38. As noted by Kangle on this line. Note that the *Gaṇapāṭha* of Pāṇini V.4.3 has words for what are apparently types of liquor, *avadātikā*, probably white or clear (*surā*), and *kālikā*, which may be black, seasonal, or perhaps "on credit" (Agrawala 1963, 121).
39. See Kangle and Olivelle, along with their notes, on AŚ 2.25.32.
40. This is probably the *bīja* described in AŚ 2.25.30. *Bīja* is also apparently a synonym for *kiṇva* elsewhere. See, later in this chapter, "Medical Sources on Surā" and also the *Mānasollāsa* discussion in "*Surā* for Pleasure in the Twelfth Century.
41. AŚ 2.25.32.
42. AŚ 2.25.33–34.
43. Referring to Olivelle's Appendix on weights and measures (AŚ trans. Olivelle, 455–459).
44. Mayrhofer suggests from **kṛṇva*- "acting, effecting." (EWA Part 1, s.v. *kiṇva*-).
45. AŚ 2.25.1.
46. AŚ 2.25.38. Or possibly even "*kiṇva* for *surā*." I thank Patrick Olivelle for suggesting the latter possibility (p.c. July 2020).
47. *Sarvadarśanasaṃgraha*, *Ānandāśramasaṃskṛtagranthāvali* ed. 51, p. 1. See also Bhattacharya on the fragmentary Cārvāka aphorisms that include the same line (Bhattacharya 2002, 604).
48. For betel, see the *Sarvasiddhāntasaṃgraha*, trans. Radhakrishnan and Moore (1957, 235). On the Cārvākas and the *trivarga* see Bhattacharya 2002, 618–619.
49. Paraphrasing Jain's translation of the *Sarvārthasiddhi* on *Tattvārthasūtra* VIII.2.
50. Though note the word here, *rasa*, refers to alcoholic drinks in some Jain sources, such that this could theoretically be *rasabīja*, so "alcohol-seed"; see the section in Jainism in Chapter 7. See later in this chapter for *bīja* as a starter.

51. *Tattvārthavārtikam* (*Rājavārikam*) of Akalaṅka on *sūtra* VIII.2 (Part II, p. 566). As discussed by Dundas (2002, 97).
52. For references to *surā* in medical literature see Meulenbeld 1974, 514–516. For the *Caraka* and *Suśruta* I have used the eds of Jādavji Trikamji Acharya, referring also to the editions and translations of Priya Vrat Sharma. I indicate any significant differences in readings in the notes.
53. See HIML IA, 351. Also see Wujastyk's discussion (2003, 63–64).
54. SS. Sū. XLV.170–216. For Ḍalhaṇa I have used the edition of Jādavjī Trivikramjī Ācārya.
55. By contrast, in the *Caraka*, at CS Sū. XXVII.188, grape juice liquor comes later in the list of liquors, being a type of *āsava* (grape-*āsava*) listed along with a sugarcane juice one (or this may be *āsava* made from grapes *and* sugarcane), which is compared to honey mead. Thus the grape-containing liquor is less prominent in the CS than in the SS.
56. On the date of Ḍalhaṇa see HIML IA, 378–379.
57. Meulenbeld (1974) lists several possibilities, possibly *Boerhavia repens* L., or *Trianthema portulacastrum* L.
58. See HIML IA, 193–194.
59. The fact that barley *saktu* is specified suggests that this is indeed not just flour but rather roasted like modern *sattū* flour.
60. SS. Sū. XLV.170–182ab.
61. See HIML IIA, 206–207.
62. HIML IIA, 196–210.
63. Śārṅg 2.10.5–6. My translation.
64. Grierson (1885, 78), records that "*baksa*" was used in Gaya for the refuse left in a distillation boiler.
65. Someśvara III reigned 1124–1138 CE. See G. K. Shrigondekar's discussion of these dates in the introduction to volume one of the *Mānasollāsa* of Someśvara (vol. I, 6–7).
66. A word that can refer to many plants, though I think this may be the best option here. See Meulenbeld 1974, 578.
67. Probably the grain, though let us not forget the sugary juice of sweet sorghum.
68. *Mānasollāsa*, Viṃ. 5, Adhy. 10, stanzas 431bc–437ab. Spaces added for clarity.
69. *Yava* commonly refers to barley. However, as the bark or rind is said to be used here I am not certain that this is a good translation in this context.
70. A similar form, *ghoṇṭā* is a synonym for *badarī*, the jujube (*Ziziphus jujube*). Note that *ghoṇṭāphala* can refer to the areca nut palm.
71. This can refer to a number of plants. Meulenbeld 1974.
72. Despite the uncertainties regarding the terms here (I am not even fully confident of how to separate the start of the compound), the most important thing is that these are no doubt plant names and this is a herbal preparation.
73. The text says "three nights and five nights (*ca*)" but I assume this means three or five.
74. *Mānasollāsa* Viṃ. 5, Adhy. 10, stanzas 437bc–442ab.
75. Also see the description in Chapter 9 of making a distilled rice drink where the mold was black in Cuttack in the early twentieth century.

76. Mr. Jai Chacko of Mankotta, Kerala, informs me that he heard of a drink being made from fermented rice in Kerala about fifty years ago for domestic consumption (personal communication, November 2014). Made from rice in a manner similar to *handia* this was apparently fermented for several months in large jars and then filtered through cotton bags to produce a strong, clear liquor.
77. For *handia* see Panda et al. 2014, 154–155. For sake see Steinkraus 1996, 439–447.
78. Rām III.45.40. Though attested in many manuscript traditions and the choice of the editor P. C. Divanji, the editor of this volume of the critical edition, there are variants, such as *suvṛṣti-*. Nevertheless the *surā* option is well attested and the perfect contrast with a fermented gruel.
79. See Meulenbeld 1974.

CUP 2

1. *Mānasollāsa*, Viṃ. 5, Adhy. 10, verses 442–449ab.
2. I cite the relevant articles in the section on the drink in question.
3. This section both reproduces parts of and summarizes, minus most of the notes, McHugh 2020a.
4. Mintz 1985, ch. 3.
5. On sugar in India see Roy 1918; Gopal 1964; von Hinüber 1971. Also Daniels 1996.
6. Daniels 1996, 374.
7. AŚ 2.25.39.
8. On the date of the *Mahābhārata* see Van Buitenen trans., *The Mahabharata:1. The Book of the Beginning*, xxv. For the *Rāmāyaṇa* see Goldman, trans. and introduction, *The Rāmāyaṇa of Vālmīki*, vol. I: *Bālakāṇḍa*, 23.
9. Rām 5.9.22. All translations of the *Rāmāyaṇa* refer to the critical edition.
10. Rām 5.9.29.
11. Rām 6.62.8.
12. Rām 5.9.18.
13. My translation of *kṛtasurā* is conjectural. It seems to be contrasted with the clear variety. There are quite a few variants for this line.
14. The critical edition provides the readings of commentators who understand *mādhvīkā* here as honey mead and alternatively grape wine (one suggesting a reading of *mārdvīkā*). For flower *āsava*, commentaries have a drink made of mahua flowers (*madhūkapuṣpa*) etc. Given the chronology here I am very cautious of reading *mādhvīkā* as a reference to grape wine. If this is grape wine this is a notable early reference but not utterly out of the possible chronological scheme I discuss later. There are many textual variations for the final lines.
15. Rām 5.9.19.
16. MBh 8.27.77; 8.30.33. See McHugh 2020a. for all these references.
17. SS Sū. 45.182–191.

18. *Raghuvaṃśa* 16.52 (*Bombay Sanskrit Series* ed.). *Pāṭala* may be *Stereospermum suaveolens* (Roxb.) DC = *S. Chelonoides* (L.f.) DC.
19. See the description of the seasonal regimen for drinking in Cup 5.
20. *Bālarāmāyaṇa*, Act 7. Also in *Subhāṣitaratnakoṣa* (Poem 963).
21. *Purāṇamadhu. Padmaprābhṛtaka* ed. Dezsö and Vasudeva, 3.70 (my trans.). This could refer to old honey, but I think that less likely, especially in this bawdy play.
22. As I also write in McHugh 2020a: Daniels (1996, 375) reports that a text from Dunhuang dated provisionally from the ninth or tenth century CE contains the first reference to making sugarcane wine in China, though sugarcane wine may have been made there at an earlier period (Daniels 1996, 58–59), yet it is not a prominent alcoholic drink in early Chinese texts. Sugarcane was consumed in China from early periods, with the earliest reference in Chinese literature dating from 241 BCE, and pharmacopoeias mention various sugarcane sugars from the sixth century CE (Daniels 1996, 58, 88). Sugarcane wine appeared quite early in peninsular and insular Southeast Asia, with one Chinese reference to it being produced on the Malay peninsula dating from between 581–618 CE (Daniels 1996, 88).
23. MBh 5.58.5.
24. *Kapittha*, *Feronia elephantum* Corrêa = *Feronia limonia*, Hindi *kaith*.
25. AŚ 2.25.19–21. My translation.
26. AŚ 2.25.29.
27. AŚ 2.25.35. Measurements as given in Olivelle's translation, Appendix 2—note that *prastha* is also a measure of volume: *karṣa* = approx 151g.

    tulā = approx 37.76 kg.

    prastha = approx 0.6 kg.

28. The etymology of *ariṣṭa*, meaning whole, unbroken, may hint at this usage in the long term (EWA s.v. Part 1, REŚ).
29. For an early Chinese drink using juices and honey see McGovern 2009, 38.
30. For example, in the *Carakasaṃhitā* one *āsava* is made, fermented with *dhātakī* (*dhātakyā 'bhiṣuto.* CS Sū 27.188ab).
31. There is considerable scientific literature on this herb that I cannot consider here.
32. See also the other definitions in Meulenbeld 1974.
33. Śārṅg II.10.1.
34. Śārṅg II.10.2.
35. See for example the list of *āsava*s at CS Sū 25.49.
36. SS Sū 44.28–30ab. Meulenbeld (1974) on "*āsava*" highlights the interest of the commentary on this recipe.
37. Buddhologists might be familiar with the *āsava* in the sense of a defiling outflow. In Sanskrit *āsava* (drink) and *āśrava/āsrava* (Buddhist term) differ, but the two words are the same in Pali. Buddhaghosa discusses this double meaning in the *Atthasālinī*, explaining the "outflows" are like long stored (or infused?) liquors (*cirapārivāsikā madirādayo āsavā*, *Atthasālinī* 127, ed. Müller, p. 48).
38. For *surāsava* see SS Sū 45.187bc–88ab.
39. As is clear from the work of Patrick McGovern for regions other than South Asia.

40. In this section I summarize McHugh forthcoming e.
41. Regulation EC 110/2008.
42. See Chapter 7 on Buddhism, and also McHugh forthcoming e.
43. *Mānava Gṛhyasūtra* II.14.28: *maireyapānaṃ surāpānaṃ*. For more details and a discussion of the dating of this text see McHugh forthcoming e.
44. Mbh 4.67.27; 14.58.12; 14.91.36.
45. Most likely the three myrobalans, *āmalakī* (*Phyllanthus emblica* L.), *vibhītakī* (*Terminalia bellirica* [Gaertn.] Roxb.), *and harītakī* (*Terminalia chebula* Retz.). On this standard mixture see Meulenbeld 1974, 468.
46. AŚ 2.25.22. My translation.
47. For the identification, see Meulenbeld, *The Mādhavanidāna*, 591. On the property of the leaves see Ambasta (2000 s.v. *Gymnema sylvestre*). I agree with Achaya that we are not told the main sugar here, and the jaggery is a sweetening after-addition. Achaya 1991, 126. This also explains the distinctive technical term *pratīvāpa* for some sort of "additional additive."
48. *Aṣṭādhyāyī* VI.2.70. Or the secondary sugar might be variable—though the vinegar I discuss here suggests it is the base.
49. *Syzygium cumini* (L.) Skeels.
50. AŚ 2.15.17.
51. E.g., Ḍalhaṇa on SS Sū 45.189.
52. Rām. 2.85.13.
53. Rām 2.85.65. For more examples of *maireya* in the *Rāmāyaṇa* see McHugh forthcoming e.
54. Rām. 2.85.18c.
55. Rām 2.85.49a.
56. Rām 2.85.77.
57. E.g., McGovern 2009, 39.
58. As with the *madhu-maireya* Rāma offers to Sītā at Rām 7.41.13, another example of *maireya* as a prestige drink. For more examples see McHugh forthcoming e.
59. E.g., *Amara* 2.10 (*Śūdravarga*) 42.
60. This section is a very concise summary of McHugh forthcoming d, which readers should consult for many more details and references.
61. AŚ 2.25.24–25. My translation.
62. See Olivelle's note on this line in his translation of the AŚ. Also McHugh forthcoming d, where I discuss other secondary literature on these locations.
63. AŚ 2.15.16. Given the classification with honey, perhaps grape *madhu*, "grape nectar," was sometimes sweet, somewhat like an alcoholic (or fermentable non-alcoholic) defrutum or vino cotto.
64. *Mānasollāsa* Viṃ. 5, Adhy. 10, verses 442bc–443ab.
65. For the details of grape and wine chronology see McHugh forthcoming d.
66. *Raghuvaṃśa* IV.65.
67. See McHugh forthcoming d and also Tomber 2007 for a recent review of evidence of amphorae.
68. *Vikramāṅkadevacarita* 18.72. I thank Whitney Cox for this reference.

69. See Falk 2009.
70. See Carter 1982, 250.
71. Perhaps with *muddikā* and *caṣaka*. See KEWA (s.v. *cáṣakaḥ*, *mṛdvīkā*) and EWA (Part 3, s.v. *caṣaka*, *mṛdvīkā*). See McHugh forthcoming d for details.
72. Personal interview October 2014. I am also grateful to Mr. Kumar for introducing me to toddy tappers and showing the tapping process.
73. See Meulenbeld, appendix to Das 1988, 440.
74. CITD, Inscription 30, part II, pp. 94–95. Also, there are two technical terms relating to toddy production used in some south Indian inscriptions: *ēṇi-k-kāṇam*, a "ladder tax evidently levied on toddy-drawers" and a *taḷai-k-kāṇam*, the "fee or tax on the *taḷai* or foot-binding used by toddy tappers." The tapper was thus taxed on the tools of his trade, for the sheer fact of being an active tapper. It is unclear whether at this stage they were taxed per tree or by volume of toddy (SITI, vol. III, part 2, glossary of terms.).
75. Sircar 1965, 399.
76. Sircar 1965, 396, 397.
77. Sircar 1965, 402, 403. Sircar 1966, 404. EI XXVIII, p. 326–327 (no. 59).
78. Karttunen 1997, 137–138. There do not appear to be any classical European references to toddy.
79. Karttunen 1997, 137–138.
80. MBh 9.33.2 (*tāladhvaja*) and MBh 9.40.35 (*tālaketu*).
81. E.g., Mārīca, struck by an arrow leaps as high as a *tāla*, *tālamātram* (Rām 3.42.13). In the *Buddhacarita* (13.23) some of Māra's demons are the size of palmyras, *tālapramāṇāḥ*.
82. HV 57 (critical ed.)
83. HV 57.6.9.
84. I thank Kathleen Eagan Murray for this observation.
85. HV 57.16–17.
86. Here I disagree with Parpola and Janhunen (2012, 87).
87. SS Sū 45.144–45ab.
88. *Raghuvaṃśa* (Kale) IV.42. This is how Mallinātha takes it as well as Kale, but if the drinking place was fashioned from betel leaves that would in fact parallel the bower made from vines they use in Persia. An echo of this line occurs at *Rājataraṅgiṇī* IV.155 where Lalitāditya's soldiers rest at the foot of *tālītarus* drinking "waves of coconut-*surā*." (*-ācāntanārikerasurormayaḥ*).
89. See "Later Dharmaśāstra Texts" in Cup 7. The *Pulastyasmṛti* fragment there mentioning toddy may be the earliest, possibly mid–late first millennium.
90. For *vāruṇī* as a grain drink *or* toddy see also the *Bhāvaprakāśa*, *Pūrvakhaṇḍa*, *Madyavarga* 24. Cf. Manu 11.147; AH Sū 5.86.
91. Śārṅg II.10.7ab.
92. *Hārītasaṃhitā* (ed. Raison) I.19.4, 12. Perhaps taking the second form of the word here as meaning palmyra scrum/foam/ferment. Twelve drinks are described here under a *fourfold* classification of *surā* (*Hārītasaṃhitā* I.19.1): *gauḍī*, *mādhvī*, *paiṣṭī*, and *niryāsā*, and thus we find yet another reworking of Manu's threefold

surā formula (on which see Cup 7). Grape wine (*mṛdvīkārasasaṃbhūtā*) is given along with *tāḍamaṇḍī* as the two types of *niryāsā* drinks. Therefore presumably the drinks in the *mādhvī* class (called by the usual tricky *madhv*-esque names in the expanded verse on them) here are honey based (i.e., *not madhu* as wine), and maybe also *madhūka* based. In this respect, this fourfold *surā* (sugar, honey, grain, grape wine) resembles that seen in some Tantric sources (See "Abhinavagupta on Liquor" in Cup 8). For the date of this text and the uncertainty surrounding its printed form see HIML IIA, 60.

93. See previous note.
94. *Mānasollāsa*, Viṃ. 5, Adhy. 10, verses 443cd–444ab.
95. Meulenbeld (appendix to Das 1988) gives *Phoenix paludosa* Roxb.
96. A synonym of *tamāla*, which can refer to many plants, notably *Cinnamomum tamala*, as well as species of *Garcinia* (Meulenbeld, appendix to Das 1988). However, I suspect it should also be a type of palm tree, so the text may be corrupt or else this term (or the original version) refers to a type of palm, possibly in local plant terminologies.
97. Probably *Phoenix sylvestris*.
98. *Mānasollāsa*, Viṃ. 5, Adhy. 10, verses 447cd–449ab.
99. AŚ 2.15.40, 2.17.4. *Madhuka* (short "u") is also mentioned in the AŚ but it is notable that Kangle's edition differentiates between the two forms—probably *madhuka* here means liquorice.
100. See Asouti and Fuller (2008, 23, 84) on early human distribution of the mahua tree.
101. See EWA (Part. 2) and KEWA on this word (under *madhu*), attested from the *sūtra* literature onward. At *Śaṅkhāyana Gṛhya Sūtra* 1.12.9 in the wedding the bridegroom ties *madhūka* flowers (*madhūkāni*) to the bride reciting the mantra RV IV.57.3, "Honeyed the plants . . ." (Jamison and Brereton trans.) Mahua stands for sweetness here, yet, being a flower, it is suitable for adorning, like garlands.
102. Pali Vinaya, *Mahāvagga* VI.35.6.
103. See the "Law Code of Manu" section in Cup 7.
104. *Mānasollāsa*, Viṃ 5, Adhy. 10, verses 444bc–445ab.
105. SS Sū 45.191.
106. SS Sū 45.169.
107. *Harṣacarita*, (Kane) *Ucchvāsa* 7 (p. 124). There is alliterative play on minerals/ores, *dhātu-*, which may be influencing the choice of words.
108. *Madhūkāsavamadyaprāyaiḥ*. Or possibly, "mahua *āsava* and intoxicating drink." *Harṣacarita*, *Ucchvāsa* 7 (p. 124).
109. For the date of Aruṇadatta see HIML IA, 663–664.
110. Aruṇadatta on AH *Sūtrasthāna* 5.75. See also "Kashmiri Śaiva Exegesis on Liquor" in Cup 8.
111. *Mānasollāsa*, Viṃ. 5, Adhy. 10, verses 445cd–446ab.
112. Steinkraus 1996, 398.
113. AŚ 2.15.17. See earlier discussion on *maireya*.
114. In England for 1200–1400 Clark observes that "spring or river water, *often drunk in the past by poor labourers and their families*, may have started to become polluted in

towns and areas affected by the growth of rural industries." (1983, 32; also see 112–113. My emphasis). One does not actually have to prove that ale was safer/healthier (or perceived to be so) to explain the ubiquity of ale drinking—it could well just be a matter of preference or something else, especially given the calorific value of these drinks. The common notion that beer was *thought to be* safer than water (or *actually was* safer—a completely different argument) deserves further research, including reflection on the popular appeal of the idea. Perhaps the attraction lies in a perceived irony that says more about us than about the past: "Those medieval monks drank beer every day! History is fun!" Not to mention the ubiquitous passion for applying "scientific" hygiene-evolutionary arguments to the "weird" habits of people in the ancient past.

115. SS Sū 46.421.
116. *Mānasollāsa*, Viṃ. 3, Adhy. 13, verses 1581–1584.
117. *Mānasollāsa*, Viṃ. 3, Adhy. 13, verses 1601–1629.
118. *Mānasollāsa*, Viṃ. 3, Adhy. 13, verse 1615.
119. To prevent palm sap fermenting one must smear lime (mineral) in the vessel or collect the sap cold.
120. In the BKŚS Sānudāsa, shipwrecked, is washed ashore where he quenches his thirst with coconut water (*nārikelajala* BKŚS 18.345c)
121. *Mānasollāsa*, Viṃ. 3, Adhy. 13, verses 1619–1620.
122. *Nāla*. I am not sure if these tubes/reeds/pipes are spouts, handles, drinking straws, pipes for siphoning the water, or filters of some sort. On straws, see also "The Ideal Manner of Drinking" in Cup 4.
123. *Mānasollāsa*, Viṃ. 3, Adhy. 13, verses 1624–1626.
124. *Mānasollāsa*, Viṃ. 3, Adhy. 13, verses 1627–1628.
125. For a bibliography on betel in premodern South Asia, see Ali 2018. Also Gutierrez 2015 and the papers on betel in Gode 1960a.
126. For the early history including archaeology and words for betel in India see Zumbroich 2007, 87–140. While the evidence for a Proto-South-Dravidian form of one word for the areca nut seems convincing (though an old word does not mean an old thing—consider American English "corn"), references to betel at Aśoka's consecration in a text probably composed just after 350 CE are no more indicative of betel being used at the time of Aśoka than the mechanical clock in Shakespeare's Julius Caesar is evidence for such clocks in ancient Rome. A seemingly early reference to betel in the *Baudhāyana Dharmasūtra* is a red herring. This passage (BDS 1.8.39) deals with the ritual purification of certain items, explaining that goat's wool blankets are to be purified with *ariṣṭas*, which could mean the fermented drinks discussed already, or more likely, the soapberry. Note that early references that clearly refer to betel-chewing are to *tāmbūla* and *pūga*, which complicates how we read the references to *kramuka* in the *Arthaśāstra* (e.g., 2.25.18) and elsewhere, for this term might not always refer to betel nut, especially in very early sources. For example, at CS Sū 25.49 *kramuka-āsava* is one of the four **bark** *āsavas*. *Pūga* can likewise be tricky as it also has the sense of a mass/quantity and is attested early in that sense, for example in the *Mahābhārata*.

127. The leaves made into toothsticks are *nāgalatā-*. (*Dīpavaṃsa* V 6.4), which could be another plant even though attested as betel. The compound here could perhaps be betel vine and toothsticks, as Zumbroich suggests. Either way the leaves are classified with items of oral hygiene and adornment. The nuts are *pūga* (*Dīpavaṃsa* V 6.10). For the date see von Hinüber 1997, 89.
128. As noted by Gutierrez 2015, 121. The word used is *tiṃpura*. Burrow 1940, documents no. 77, 721. Also see Baums and Glass, s.v. *tiṃpura* (Accessed May 1, 2021) On the date of these texts see Hansen 2012, 44.
129. The KS on betel will be discussed later. On the date in relation to the *Arthaśāstra*, see Scharfe 1993, 4–5.
130. CII, vol. III, *Inscriptions of the Early Gupta Kings and Their Successors*, Inscription 18.
131. CII, vol. III, Inscription 18, lines 2–3.
132. CII, vol. III, Inscription 18, line 11.
133. *Raghuvaṃśa* (Kale) IV.44b.
134. *Raghuvaṃśa* IV.67, 74, 81.
135. For the aromatics see McHugh 2012, 166–173. There are also references to betel (*tāmbūla-*) in the *Pādatāḍitaka* (p. 57, p. 109 in Dezsö and Vasudeva ed.) another text that is probably early, possibly fifth/sixth century (Dezsö and Vasudeva, xvii–xix).
136. *Mahāsīlava Jātaka* (51) and *Aṇḍabhūta Jātaka* (62).
137. *Aṇḍabhūta Jātaka*, ed. Fausbøll, vol. 1, p. 290.
138. *Aṇḍabhūta Jātaka*, ed. Fausbøll, vol. 1, p. 291.
139. KS 1.4.4.
140. CS Sū V.76bc–77.
141. SS Sū 46.279–280. SS Sū 46.485–487.
142. Bhaṭṭotpala's commentary has cloves.
143. Varāhamihira give a recipe for a perfume called *pārijāta* in verse 27 of this same chapter, yet Bhaṭṭotpala gives nutmeg, *jātīphalam*, for the term *pārijāta* in the line quoted previously. Perhaps Bhaṭṭotpala is updating this text to include flavorings that were commoner at the time, so tenth-century Kashmir? On the date of Bhaṭṭotpala see Pingree 1970-, Series A, vol. 4, p. 270.
144. *Bṛhatsaṃhitā*, ed. Tripathi, 76.35–37.
145. Goodman 1995, 121–141.
146. See Cup 7 on "Kodo Millet."
147. Gutierrez 2015. Gode 1960b.
148. Gutierrez 2015, 119, 120.
149. See the passages Gutierrez quotes (2015, 120).
150. See my notes on Jainism and betel in Cup 7.
151. Gode 1960c.
152. Acharya suggests the passage quoted here might also an even later interpolation (*Mṛcchakaṭikā*, trans. Acharya, xx–xxvi).
153. The nature of these *prastaras* of saffron is unclear. The commentary of Pṛthvīdhara (mid-thirteenth century; for the date, see *Mṛcchakaṭikā*, trans. Acharya, xxvi and note) explains that they are hide-pouches containing saffron.

154. The gloss as *kastūrikā* has no connection, phonetically, with the Prakrit *selajjaam*. Sanskrit *śaileya* can mean a lichen used in perfumery, like oak-moss. Or maybe the form is related to *śaila-*, benzoin or bitumen? Pṛthvīdhara explains that "musk is being wetted," connecting the word to "*śalya*," arrow, because it is used in *vedha*, the perfumery process of adding perfumery ingredients to moist (or maybe, less technically, because it is *piercing* in odor), as well as being like "*ājya*," ghee, so "pungent-butter." Also, one word for civet perfume is *śālija* (and the animal is sometimes *śāli*), and although this is maybe not a good candidate for this Prakrit form, in my experience words for materia medica do not always conform to neat linguistic rules. How we understand the verb somewhat depends on the nature of the aromatic.
155. My translation of *Mṛcchakaṭikā*, 4.194 (Clay). Referring also to Acharya's translation.
156. See Baldissera's edition, translation, and study.
157. *Narmamālā* 1.124. Possibly we should read the compound as *-drākṣāmadhughaṭā-*, so more explicitly grapes. Note that wine is transported to the house in a (clay) jar/pot.
158. This may be a rare reference to more solitary drinking. *Narmamālā* 1.131, trans. Baldissera.
159. *Narmamālā* 1.136, trans. Baldissera, modified.
160. *Narmamālā* 1.138, trans. Baldissera.
161. *Narmamālā* 1.142d. My translation; Baldissera has "chewing," which is possible, but betel preparation involves leaf cutting.
162. *Narmamālā* 1.147, trans. Baldissera, modified.
163. *Narmamālā* 2.6cd, my translation.
164. *Narmamālā* 2.19, trans. Baldissera.
165. *Śukasaptati*, ed. Tripathi, p. 2, 8. Also see the translation by Haksar.
166. Ali 2018.
167. *Rājataraṅgiṇī* of Kalhaṇa, trans. and ed. Stein.
168. *Rājataraṅgiṇī* IV.425–427, trans. Stein.
169. Ali 2018, plates.
170. Ali 2018, 535–539.
171. *Kādambarī*, Book 1, trans. Smith, pp. 468–469.
172. *Kādambarī*, Book 1, trans. Smith, pp. 390–391.
173. *Maireyamattayā* (*Rājataraṅgiṇī* IV.435), an example of a later usage of the word *maireya*, when it was possibly more of a lexical option than a common drink.
174. Dietler 2006, 232.
175. See Curley 2003 and Sangar 1981.
176. *Rājataraṅgiṇī* VII.787–788, trans. Stein. See also VIII.71 where King Uccala exceeds Harṣa's extravagance in offering betel (*tāmbūladāna-*).
177. See the section on "Drink as a Vice" in Cup 7.
178. Compare to kola nut in Africa, which likewise has to be used fresh and was previously costly, in part due to limited supply and complex methods of transporting it, which were nevertheless possible before rapid transport and refrigeration. (Lovejoy 1995).

179. *Rājataraṅgiṇī* VII.193.
180. *Rājataraṅgiṇī* VII.194. My translation.
181. Stein takes this as meaning he sold leaves together with the unidentified *nāgarakhaṇḍa* substance, etc. I prefer to read this as implying a costly type of leaf, particularly as this man is a leaf-merchant.
182. *Rājataraṅgiṇī* VIII.1947. My translation.
183. Benn 2015, 43–44.
184. Benn 2015, 43–44.
185. Adapting Bottéro 1995, 31.

CUP 3

1. Clark 1983, 5–6.
2. Unfortunately, it was only as this book was well into the production stage that I read Amy Langenberg's (2020) excellent reflections on what we can (and cannot) do with such texts as ancient Vinayas, and sadly I do not have any time to reflect on her study and incorporate it here.
3. Clark 1983, 198.
4. RV I.191.10. See McHugh forthcoming c on this reference. As Stephanie Jamison pointed out to me (personal communication) this may be a precursor to the *surā* banner (for which, see the section on "The Drinking-House Banner" later in this chapter).
5. VS 30.11. On this sacrifice, see Dumont (1963), who translates a similar list from the *Taittirīya Brāhmaṇa*.
6. On *kīlāla* see McHugh forthcoming c.
7. See "*Surā* in Vedic Sources" in Chapter 1. For more details of *parisrut* see McHugh forthcoming c.
8. See HDŚ II.ii, 1206–1212.
9. GGS II.1.10, trans. Oldenberg.
10. ŚGS 1.11.2, trans. Oldenberg.
11. ŚGS 1.11.5, trans. Oldenberg.
12. ĀGS 2.5.5. AŚ 11.1.24.
13. AŚ 2.25. I refer here to Olivelle's new translation of this passage, which I have paraphrased in places. I also refer to Kangle's translation, notes, and edition.
14. *Pānoddeśāni*. Kangle takes this as "drinking bars." Olivelle suggests this must be *bahuvrīhi* compound qualifying drinking-houses that "advertise drinking," The term *uddeśa* could imply a place, so some sort of "drinking-areas," which may contrast with furnished, possibly private rooms in which patrons could stay. Or, as I have translated, this might also be some sort of menu of drinks available or a tally of drinks consumed.
15. AŚ 2.25.11–15. My translation, very closely following Kangle and Olivelle.

16. Sanskrit *śauṇḍika* (vintner), and related forms such as *śuṇḍā* (drink shop or liquor), *śauṇḍa* (fond of liquor, drunk), are neatly translated by forms of "tipple" in English. Like the Sanskrit words, "tipple" can mean drink, and "tippler" can mean both someone who sells ale and someone who habitually drinks it. The disadvantage is that "tipple" is rather archaic nowadays, especially in the sense of person who sells drink.
17. AŚ 2.36.8. This same group of traders also hawk drugged food and liquor on credit or cheaply to poison enemies. See the section on "Drink on Credit" later in this chapter. Religious rest houses, craftsmen, and merchants should also provide lodgings (AŚ 2.36.5–7).
18. See Ferstl for an assessment of the date and authorship of this text (2011, 10).
19. *Mattavilāsaprahasana*, ed. Gaṇapatiśāstrī, p. 8, my translation.
20. My translation. (*Majjhima Nikāya* I.6, ed. V. Trenckner, vol. 1, 374). I thank Erik Braun for telling me about this passage.
21. Mayrhofer writes that the origin of *śuṇḍā* and related forms is unclear (EWA, Part 2, s.v. *śuṇḍā*). The word is attested early, for example at Pāṇini 4.3.76.
22. *Saṃyutta Nikāya* IV.6 (*Sappo*), ed. Feer, vol. 1, 106.
23. According to the *Pali Text Society Dictionary*, *dhutta*, meaning "rogue," is attested in compound with a variety of typical vices—such as dice, *akkha-dhutta*, as well as *surādhutta*.
24. The following discussion of the *surā* banner is adapted and abridged from McHugh 2017.
25. Olivelle 2011, 28.
26. BDS 1.18.17–18. On the dating of this text I rely on Olivelle (*Dharmasūtras*, translation, 4–10).
27. For references see McHugh 2017, 463–465.
28. Medhātithi on *Manu* 11.93. For more references see McHugh 2017, 462–465.
29. Chaucer, *Canterbury Tales* I (A) 666–667.
30. Clark 1983, 29, 67. Note that Viennese Heurige still have pine branches as a sign (as pointed out to me by Stephanie Jamison, p.c).
31. Bennett 1996, 21.
32. Clark 1983, 68.
33. MBh 5 Appendix. 1, no 9, 11.8–9.
34. On this episode, the similar *Jātaka*, related verses, and the cat-observance in general see Söhnen-Thieme 2005. The story also occurs at *Pañcatantra* III, Story 2.2 (In Olivelle's translation). Note that neither the Pali version of this verse, nor that at Manu 4.195, mention the *surā* sign. See also *Mānavadharmaśāstra*, trans. Olivelle, p. 275, n. 4.195.
35. AŚ, trans. Olivelle, 46. Another practice associated with drinking, gambling, is also regulated (AŚ 3.20).
36. AŚ 2.25.1.
37. AŚ 2.25.1.
38. AŚ 2.25.2.
39. AŚ 2.25.3.
40. AŚ 2.25.3. Quoting and paraphrasing Olivelle.

41. AŚ 2.25.5. *Pāna* here has a similar sense to our "let's get a drink." Compare to BKŚS 13.32–35 and several other examples of this usage discussed later in the chapter.
42. Working from Olivelle's table of weights and measures in his trans. of AŚ, where weights are given for these measures—nevertheless, the measures are at the smaller end of the scale.
43. AŚ 2.22.6–7.
44. AŚ 2.25.39.40. See Olivelle's note. Also see AŚ 2.6.2 where liquor is classified as a product of the "fort" for revenue.
45. AŚ 2.25.1. The Superintendent of *Surā* causes the business to be done (-*vyavahārān . . . kārayed*), though it is not clear if those experts who did the work of brewing, etc. were to have any degree of economic independence within this (supposedly) regulated system.
46. AŚ 2.25.6. On the English alehouse as a site for trading stolen goods see Clark (1983, 85, 145–47).
47. AŚ 2.25.7–8 for this regulation and those on sales.
48. AŚ 2.25.9–10.
49. Dietler 1990, 365–368.
50. AŚ 2.29.43; 2.30.18; 2.31.13. And Olivelle's note on 2.29.43. Also AŚ 4.13.15–17, a passage that Olivelle thinks is out of place, describes what a man offers to an elephant when he wishes to be killed by it, and the offerings include liquor (*madya*). The elephant Nāḷāgiri is given *surā* to enrage him in the *Cullahaṃsa Jātaka* (533). In that story, he is usually given eight pots (*ghaṭa*) of *surā* but Devadatta, who wishes to kill the Buddha, has them give him sixteen pots of strong *surā* (*tikhiṇasurāya soḷasa ghaṭe*) to enrage/intoxicate him (*mattakaṃ katvā*), so he will kill the Buddha—a plan that fails. (Fausbøll's ed. vol. 4, 334). Elephants are, of course, often associated with states of *mada/matta* and the substance musth, *mada*.
51. Edgerton 1931, 100, translating *Mātaṅgalīlā* 11.32. The drinks are *vāruṇī* (i.e., *surā*) and *prasannā*, clear *surā*.
52. *Vālodaka Jātaka* (183).
53. AŚ 2.25.35.
54. Exactly what is implied is unclear. Kangle writes that commentators explain it covers making, drinking, and selling *surā*. Olivelle writes that given the previous sentence, it definitely covers manufacture.
55. AŚ 2.25.37.
56. In addition to the discussion here and the materials on Kalyapālas (see later in this chapter), some other inscriptional references to liquor, though less to liquor regulation, are as follows. There is a reference to a donation of the "five *kaṣāyas*" in a tenth-century CE inscription from modern Madhya Pradesh, and the translator renders this as "the five spirituous liquors" but, grouped just before donations by betel-leaf merchants, I am not so inclined to read *kaṣāyapañcake* as referring to alcohol—it could be a liquid extract of some sort, or even a perfume product (especially grouped with the betel). Meulenbeld (1974, 453) notes there are five types of *kaṣāya* infusion in medical texts. (CII, vol. IV, *Inscriptions of the Kalachuri-Chedi Era*, part 1, Inscription 42, pp. 186–195.) *Surā* sellers/brewers (*śauṇḍaka*) are mentioned along with weavers

and milkmen as subjects that that formed part of a land grant, in an early medieval inscription from modern Odisha. (EI 29, "Santirama Grant of Dandimahadevi," pp. 86–89. Also see Sircar 1965, 398.) Also see the grants involving trees in the discussions of toddy and mahua in Chapter 2.

57. Transliterated by Sircar, EI 30 (1953–54), "Charter of Vishnushena."
58. Clark 1983, 108; 184–184. For one Indian example, see the story of the woman who set up a profitable drinking house. Also the section on "Later Developments: Kalyapālas and the Rise of Distillation."
59. For the quoted statutes, I use the translation of Wiese and Das (2019: 106–113; 125–127), modifying some terms (e.g., "barrel").
60. *Sandhayato*, for someone who ferments things.
61. The exact nature of the *dhārmika* charge is unclear; see Lubin 2015, 234 n. 35. See also Wiese and Das (2019, 84).
62. I will provide a full discussion of this word later. Lubin (2015) does not translate this term. Kosambi (1959, 288) has "distillery-*vārika*." Sircar (1966, s.v. *kalvapāla*) takes the term to be a "spirit distiller," as an equivalent of *kalyapāla*.
63. Combining the insights of Lubin with those of Wiese and Das. As for the *kāca* load, I think the two measures in statute 57 are probably two varieties of human-carried load or modes of human carrying, one being mentioned again here. Wiese and Das write that it is hard to know if the *kela* is an agricultural product or a measure.
64. *Periplus* section 49, in Casson 1989. Also see McHugh forthcoming d on this text and wine.
65. As at ṚV I.191.10. On this skin see McHugh forthcoming c.
66. AŚ 2.25.38, my translation.
67. AŚ 3.4.22.
68. Manu 9.13.
69. KS 4.1.35.
70. MBh 4.14–15.
71. Again, there are quite a few variants here.
72. MBh 4.14.7, 4.15.5. Also, Kīcaka tries to offer some *madhumādhavī*, no doubt mead, when she arrives (4.15.3).
73. Thus the passage in some traditions of the Sanskrit *Rāmāyaṇa* where Sītā promises the Ganges that she will offer her *surā* is far from incongruous. On this episode see Jha 2002, 97; 108.
74. Falk 1986, 89–90.
75. *Dhammapadāṭṭhakathā* XI.1. Burlingame's translation. I have replaced "strong drink" with "*surā*". (*Buddhist Legends*, pt. 2, 328–329). On this text see Hinüber 1997, 132–135.
76. Drunkenness and possession are frequently compared, though here actual possession takes place, which somewhat exonerates the women of their shameful behavior.
77. *Dhammapada* 146. My translation.
78. I am grateful to Professor Gregory Schopen for sharing his translation with me. *Mūlasārvāstivāda Vinaya Kṣudrakavastu. Derge 'dul ba Da* 182b.3–184a.3.
79. Huang 2000, 176–177.

80. In contrast to the "women's work" of brewing ale in fourteenth-century England, .which, though requiring skill, only required very low skill. See Bennett 1996, 33.
81. *Mūlasārvāstivāda Vinaya Kṣudrakavastu, Derge Da* 156a.3–b.7. Again, I think Professor Schopen for sharing his translation of this passage with me.
82. Gamburd 2008, 101.
83. See Bennett 1996. Also, Dietler 2006, 236.
84. Bennett 1996, 33. Bennett's emphasis.
85. AŚ 12.4.8.
86. GDS 12.41 (*-madya-*); VDS 16.31 (*saurikaṃ*). See "The Vice of Drinking" in Cup 7.
87. Manu 8.159.
88. Clark 1983, 80–82.
89. *loṇasakkharā*, "salt and sugar" is less likely.
90. In the story of the present for the *Vāruṇi Jātaka* (47). My translation.
91. A description of drinking in one medical text is perhaps an exception, and there the foods may be prescribed to balance the drinking as a doctor is present. See the *Heart of Medicine* in "A Perfect Drinking Session" in Cup 5.
92. Though I do not know whether the modern tradition of snacks with drinks is a continuity with ancient traditions.
93. *Gūthapāna Jātaka* (227). My translation.
94. *Kāka Jātaka* (145); *Sigāla Jātaka* (113). As noted by Bloomfield 1920a.
95. Compare to Hemacandra's description of the drunkard (Chapter 7 on Jainism). In the speech of Sakka in the Pali *Kumbha Jātaka* the drinker is said to think "The whole world is *mine*!" (Fausbøll ed., stanza 43)
96. KS 1.4.23.
97. Probably the seeds of *Brassica juncea.*
98. *Kesaraiḥ*. I have opted for saffron.
99. *Mayūramāriṇī* means "peacock killer," and *mayurāri* ("peacock enemy") would seem to refer to a type of lizard or chameleon.
100. Maybe the same as *karpūraharidrā*, *Curcuma amada* Roxb.?
101. *Harītakī*. Or "fresh *harītakī*," and no ginger. *Terminalia chebula* Retz. chebulic myrobalan.
102. *Amorphophallus paeoniifolius* (= *A. campanulatus*)? See HIML vol. IA, 461, n. 713.
103. Taking *velu* as a Dravidian "finger" word.
104. *Śatāvarī*, *Asparagus racemosus* Willd. Here the shoots are used, not the roots as are often used in Āyurveda.
105. *Karīra*, *Capparis decidua* (Forssk.) Edgew.
106. Tentative translation of *laghuvarjitān*.
107. The editor has emended *tujī* to *tugā*. Neither is easy, though *tugākṣīrī* is tabashir, edible but not a tasty condiment.
108. Possibly clearing nut?
109. Emended by editor from *kaṭajaṃ*. Possibly *Holarrhena pubescens* Wall. ex. G. Don (*H. antidysenterica*), which has an astringent tonic bark.

110. *Aegle marmelos*, probably the fruit here. This is a spicy, salty astringent drink or mixture, maybe even a pickle? Perhaps served on the other snacks, a sort of wet chaat masala?
111. I am uncertain about this line.
112. I cannot make sense of this compound, unless one reads as *balā*, *laghu*, which is also rather tricky.
113. *Ajājī*, which can also be nigella.
114. *Harika*. Translation rather uncertain but *hari* can refer to these lentils. Maybe a local variety of lentils—we should bear in mind that our lentil categories, culinary and botanical, might well not be the same as the ones used here.
115. Tentative translation: *-kṛtāvāsa* "lodging."
116. On the *pūraṇa* see "poli" in Achaya 1998. Also Prakash 1987, part II, 274.
117. *Mānasollāsa*, Viṃ. 5, Adhy. 10, verses 449bc–464.
118. *Vikramāṅkadevacarita* 6.85, ed. Bühler, my translation. I thank Whitney Cox for this reference.
119. For the debates surrounding the date see Dezsö and Vasudeva's introduction (2009), which I have also used as my primary source.
120. See KS 1.4.32 and Yaśodhara's commentary on the *viṭa*. I do not take "*tadupajīvī*" at KS 1.4.32 as implying that he is a pimp, but rather a parasite. Also see *Pādatāḍitaka*, ed. Dezsö and Vasudeva, pp. 22–23.
121. *Pādatāḍitaka*, pp. 34–39. The same word for a drinking place as that used in the *Arthaśāstra*. I give my own translation of this particular line for consistency of terminology, though the translation and notes of Dezsö and Vasudeva have been invaluable.
122. *Pādatāḍitaka*, pp. 36–37.
123. Dezsö and Vasudeva's translation, modified with regards to some drinking vocabulary, and also the garments. *Pādatāḍitaka*, p. 39. For *apavartikā* Böhtlingk & Roth note that one commentator on the KŚS glosses this as *nīvi*, loincloth, or waist-cloth. Possibly the *madya-bhājana* implies more a jar than a cup here, which is an even more extreme image.
124. *Mattavilāsaprahasana*, ed. Śāstrī, p. 9.
125. *Nānacchanda Jātaka* (289). My translation.
126. The story of the present in the *Puṇṇapāti Jātaka* (53). My translation.
127. KS 6.1.9.
128. AŚ 13.3.56.
129. See "Cellar-Keepers and Connoisseurship" in Chapter 4.
130. *Amarakośa* 2.10.39bc–43.
131. AŚ 2.4.11.
132. *Śakuntalā* of Kālidāsa, ed. Somadeva Vasudeva, VI.40 (p. 265). My translation.
133. Clark 1983, 132.
134. See Clark 1983, 148, 157: "free from the involvement of the well-to-do."
135. At *Anabhirati Jātaka* (65), where they are like *pānāgāra*, rivers, roads, etc. (Fausbøll ed., vol. 1, p. 302). In the *Mahāhaṃsa Jātaka* (534, Fausbøll ed., vol. 5, p. 367) women are said to be common to all, *sādhāraṇa*, like drinkers' *surā* houses (*surāghara*).

136. Zin and Schlingloff 2007, 69–78. I thank Dr. Zin for answering my questions about this image and providing images.
137. See Zin and Schlingloff (2007, 69–70) for several examples of the narrative in Pali texts, from the *Jātaka* and commentarial literature.
138. *Dhammapadaṭṭhakathā* II.7, ed. Norman, vol. I, part 2, p. 272. Burlingame's translation adds "careless" for *pamajjati*, part 1, p. 319.
139. Cohen 1995, 116.
140. Schlingloff suggests another image is the *Kumbha Jātaka*, but it is fragmentary (1987, 147–148).
141. *Jātakamālā*, *Kumbhajātaka*, XVII. 22. My translation.
142. From the *Sāratthappakāsinī* as quoted in Zin and Schlingloff 2007, 70, n. 202.
143. My translation of the German. Zin and Schlingloff 2007, 74–75.
144. Schlingloff notes that there is no distillation, just cooking. He also thinks the evidence for distillation at this period is not convincing (Zin and Schlingloff 2007, 75–76).
145. Yaśodhara glosses *Kaumudī* as *Kojāgara*, the night of the full moon in the month *Āśvina* (September/October).
146. KS 5.5.11–12. My translation.
147. KS 3.5.25. Note that in that case the woman is given a *madanīyam*, not *surā* or *madya*—and quite likely this term has a sense of "a narcotic drug." For more on such narcotics see "Kodo Millet" in Cup 7.
148. Dietler and Herbich 2006, 405–406. My emphasis.
149. See Mitra 1872a.
150. MBh 1.211. See Chapter 6 for their self-destruction.
151. Also *kṣīva*. Mayrhofer (EWA, s.v. *kṣība*) believes the origin of this term is unclear. On Balarāma see Chapter 6.
152. MBh 1.211.7–9.
153. MBh 1.212.20.
154. MBh 1.213.53.
155. MBh 1.214.17–25.
156. Outside these more literary references, there is a reference to a drinking party (*madyaprahavaṇa*) at the forest edge (*vanānte*) in the *Arthaśāstra* (3.12.38).
157. MBh 1.76.1–3. The word is a good example of how even in early texts the precise naming of drinks is inflected by alliterative choices. I do not read *madhu* as wine in the absence of other clear references to grapes or grape drinks in this epic.
158. For the full narrative see Rām 5.59–61.
159. Rām 5.60.8–9. The monkeys manhandle the *madhūni* (honeys) that are the size of trough-measures (*droṇamātrāni*), and throw around the honey-leavings: wax, (*madhūcchiṣṭa*).
160. Rām 5.59.11.
161. Thus I do not really see a difficulty with this monkey *madhu*. On this question see also Bapat 1966.
162. Rām 5.59.14.
163. Rām 5.59.15–17.

164. See Chapter 2, "Maireya." Also McHugh forthcoming e.
165. On *vānaras* in this part of the *Rāmāyaṇa* see R. Goldman and S. Goldman, *Rāmāyaṇa*, vol. 5, pp. 62–64. I would argue that they are more human-like here than it might seem on first appearances.
166. For the earliest inscriptions there is not enough context to show clearly that *kalyapāla*-like words refer to brewers. Lüders discussed *kālavāḷa* as found in Mathura inscriptions, writing that "the exact meaning of *kālavāḷa* is unknown." He suggests it might also denote some high official, denying the possibility of a connection to the *kalyapāla* words. ("Seven Brahmi Inscriptions from Mathura and its Vicinity." EI 24, 204–206). Sircar writes that *kālavāḷa* and so on are a "designation of uncertain meaning if it is not the same as Sanskrit *Kalyapāla*, a vintner." (1966, 139. As discussed by Quintanilla 2007, 268, 286). Other terms Quintanilla lists for professions in Mathura inscriptions are attested early in more illuminating contexts (e.g., *gaṇikā*), which is not the case for *kalyapāla/kālavāla* (Quintanilla 2007, 286). Quintanilla notes *kālavāla* may perhaps mean baldheaded, as for example, *kālavalīkṛta* at ŚBr II.2.4.3.
167. See EWA Part 3, s.v. *kalyā*; *kaḍaṅga*. Turner gives many modern forms (1966): s.v. kalya[4]. Also see Burrow and Emeneau 1984, s.v. kaḷ.
168. Excluding inscriptions in note 166, the earliest clear usage with a definition of a Sanskritized form (here: *kalyapāla*) I am aware of is in Viśvarūpa's commentary (probably ninth century) on the *Yājñavalkyasmṛti*. Here *kalpāla* is a gloss on *śauṇḍika*. (YVS, *Vyavahara*, verse 50. As noted by Sircar 1959 [EI 30, p. 176.] On Viśvarūpa see Olivelle 2010, 52.) Hemacandra (twelfth century) gives *kalyapāla* as a synonym of some other words for people who make and sell drink: *kalyapālaḥ surājīvī śauṇḍiko maṇḍahārakaḥ | vārivāsaḥ pāṇavanik dhvajo dhvajy āsutībalaḥ ||*. (*Abhidhānacintāmaṇi*, *Martyakāṇḍa* 3, verse 565). He also gives *kalya* in a list of terms for intoxicating drinks (*Abhidhānacintāmaṇi*, *Martyakāṇḍa* 3 verse 566). Medinikara (thirteenth century) gives *kalyā* in the sense of *madya* (*Medinīkośa*, *Yāntavarga* 8–9). For the dates of lexica see Vogel 1979.
169. An inscription from Arthuna in Rajasthan records the foundation and endowment of a temple of Śiva by the Paramāra king Chāmuṇḍarāja in the late eleventh century CE. As part of the endowment, duties for commodities sold in the market (*haṭṭe*) are recorded, including "on (each) vuṃvaka of the *kalyapālas* (*kalyapālānāṃ*) four rūpakas." (EI 14 [no. 21], pp. 295–310, "Arthuna Inscription of the Paramara Chamundaraja: Vikrama Samvat 1136," verse 74. Lionel Barnett's translation, though I have changed "distillers" to "*kalyapālas*.") In this inscription, a duty for the temple is also imposed on the gambling house (*dyūte*). (Arthuna Inscription, verse 75).
170. An inscription from 1209 from what is the modern Saurashtra region recording certain land grants includes a certain *kalya-śr[e]ṣṭi*, a leader (or "banker" or "guild-foreman") of the *kalya[pālas]* whose name was Kheta, and who was no doubt an important figure in the community as he was called on to act as a witness for this grant. (IA vol. 18 [no. 176], "Grant of Bhimadeva II Vikrama Samvat 1266," lines 53–54.)

171. EI, vol. 1 (1892) "Siyadoni Inscription" no. 11, line 19. At line 13 there is mention of a shop in the *prasannahaṭṭa*, a *prasanna*-market. Is this the same Kallapāla *surā* market or something else? (Note it is not *prasannā*).
172. EI, vol. 1 (1892) "Siyadoni Inscription" no. 4, lines 8–10; no. 11, lines 18–20. As discussed by Chattopadhyaya (1994, 141; 148–149). Both donations mention what seems to be a measure, a *tālī* (is there any relation to toddy?). Donation 11 mentions a *surā*(-*bhāṇḍaṃ*), likely used in the generic sense.
173. E.g. EI, vol. 1 (1892) "Siyadoni Inscription" no. 8, line 15.
174. *Līlāvatīsāra* 2.119, ed. and trans. R. C. C. Fynes.
175. Clark 1983, 20–21.
176. *Rājataraṅgiṇī* IV.677–678. This *kalyapāla* origin is reiterated in the summary of reigns at the end of the chronicle, VIII.3426.
177. *Rājataraṅgiṇī* IV.685.
178. *Rājataraṅgiṇī* V.206. Stein's translation, modified.
179. E.g., King Kṣemagupta is portrayed as ruined by drink. In him the fever of wealth and youth is increased by indulging in *āsavas* (*āsavāsevanotsikta*, *Rājataraṅgiṇī* VI.150–154). See also the episode involving a drink king setting a fire in the section on "Vices" in Cup 7.
180. McHugh forthcoming b. My brief comments here mirror those on this topic in McHugh forthcoming c.
181. Marshall 1951, vol. 2, 420–421; vol. 3, pl. 125.
182. Allchin 1977, 1979.
183. E.g., Mahdihassan 1972.
184. Kolhatkar 1987, 44.
185. HIML IIA, 218–219. Meulenbeld notes the importance of this passage.
186. A jar normally used for ghee or one that has been used for ghee? Might the use of a former ghee jar help seal the clay, for the jars all used here were no doubt unglazed?
187. *Vimudrya*. Apte gives *vimudra* as unsealed, opened, but here the opposite sense, "especially sealed," is better.
188. *Gadanigraha*, *Prayogakhaṇḍa Āsavādhikāra* 269bc–272 (p. 388).
189. For more attestations of this form see Cup 9.
190. Habib 1985, 205. I thank S. R. Sarma for this reference. Also see Habib 2011, 55–56.
191. Habib 1985, 207–208. What was this substance? Either way we have distillers who know their way around wine here.
192. Habib 1985, 208.
193. Habib 1985, Chatterjee 2005.

CUP 4

1. *Gandhamātram* (mere-odor) indicating "the smallest trace." The cups are called *vāruṇīcaṣaka*, so "*surā* cups," though *vāruṇī* is a quite flexible word, especially in literature. *Dhūrtaviṭasaṃvāda* (Dezsö and Vasudeva ed., p. 322). My translation.

2. Martin 2011.
3. Martin 2011, 31.
4. Olivelle (2019, 385) writes that *kāma* along with *dharma* and *artha* were not generally conceived of as three "goals/aims of life" or "goals of a person" but rather as a set of beneficial pursuits, or *areas of activity* pertinent to the good life.
5. Ali 2004, 20.
6. KS 1.4.4. Unless noted otherwise I use the KS edition of Devadatta Shastri.
7. See Gode 1960d.
8. KS 2.10.1. My translation.
9. Yaśodhara on KS 1.4.14. *Saraka* can also mean a cup, as well as liquor. Perhaps this sense of intimate drinking developed from the vessel, like "[to share] a loving cup." The terms for communal drinking simply imply a general coming-together to drink.
10. KS 2.10.4.
11. KS 2.10.6.
12. Yaśodhara: *bījapūram īṣadapanītacukraṃ khaṇḍaśaḥ kṛttaṃ śarkarāyuktam*. "Citron (*Citrus medica*) with the sour juice somewhat removed, cut into pieces and mixed with sugar."
13. KS 2.10.7–8. My translation.
14. Carter 1968, 128–129.
15. MBh 1.92.9–10.
16. There are, for example, several images of this posture in Cave 3 at Badami. I also think the "drunken courtesan" from Mathura is most certainly this sort of counterpart to literary descriptions. For a theory of this image as related to the *Mṛcchakaṭikā* see Stadtner 1996.
17. Kenneth Zysk (unpublished draft kindly shared with the author) has made the intriguing suggestion that there may be a connection between the *samāpānaka* and the Greek symposium. Now, as with imported wine itself there may indeed have been some interactions with Hellenistic cultures (though not forgetting Iranian ones and possibly others), such as drinking iconographies, forms of vessels, possibly the offering of drink on the ground (see the discussion later in this chapter, and also Chapter 5), but, most respectfully, I am not at all convinced that any of the varieties of drinking *gatherings* as seen in this and the previous chapter are in any way Indianized developments or otherwise of symposiums, linguistically or otherwise. First, although our evidence for very early periods is sparse it does seem there was a complex and quite ancient Indian culture of various types of communal drinking (and several extremely distinctive local types of drink). Second, the primary and more common word for the gathering is arguably *āpānaka*, *samāpānaka* being evidently an extension of that form. Also, that an occasion of drinking alcohol in India might involve several people drinking together, and that such an event might be named using a drink-word etymologically related to the word used to denote *drinking* gatherings in ancient Greek are not facts that require an explanation in terms of outside influences. Communal drinking, and also the association of drink with such factors as conversation, music, sexuality, special drinking places, and distinctive vessels and foods, are all historically present in many cultures that produce alcoholic drinks and have no connection at all

with Hellenized cultures. Thus, ultimately, the *caṣaka* is half empty for me, and I do not see enough unusual and striking similarities between these two types of drinking gatherings to suppose a notable connection of any sort between them.

18. KS 1.4.14.
19. KS 1.4.22–24.
20. See Cup 5.
21. See Classical Drunken Behavior.
22. For an example, see Zin (2003, vol. 1, 119).
23. For the bowls, see the images in this chapter. For the chalice shape, see for example the Mathura sculpture of Balarāma at the Norton Simon Museum in Los Angeles (F.1975.15.1.S). For the "mug" at Mathura see Carter (1992, 253). For shallow bowls with a foot, see Zin (2003, vol. 2, p. 129).
24. On the word *caṣaka* see McHugh forthcoming d.
25. See the references to the *śukti* in the *Mānasollāsa* and the BKŚS, discussed later.
26. See Pal 2007, 174, 177–178. Pal does not give a date for this bowl, but discusses it among ancient and early medieval materials. Pal notes that this may be the style of bowl seen in an eighth-century Kashmiri stone relief of Kāmadeva drinking with his celestial court, an image quite typical for drinking posture and content: the god of love having a drink with a lover. (Pal 2007, fig. 106).
27. See Kolhatkar (1999, 77) for Indra taking *soma* with a straw (*nāḍī*).
28. *Naḷapāna Jātaka* (20). Note that the half verse (= older text) mentioning drinking through a straw was not attested in any of the manuscripts of the *Jātaka* itself.
29. They use the trunk *nālavat*, "like a reed/tube." *Saduktikarṇāmṛta* 1564 (late twelfth, early thirteenth century) attributed to Jayadeva. See Knutson (2014, 143). See also "Non-Alcoholic Drinks" in Chapter 2 for a possible reference to drinking straws in the *Mānasollāsa*.
30. See the image of group drinking from Pattadakal (Figure 4.3). Also the famous scene of a couple seated drinking from Cave 17 at Ajanta.
31. KS 1.3.15. Yaśodhara explains that the "drinkable" *peya*, is of two types, prepared with fire (soups, broths) and not prepared with fire. The latter are of two types: fermented (*saṃdhānakṛtam*) and the opposite. What appear to be the unfermented drinks are also of two types (note that, confusingly, Yaśodhara treats these first, which should make them the fermented ones "*tatrādyaṃ* . . ."). There are liquefied, dissolved (*drāvitam*) drinks made from water mixed with jaggery, tamarind etc.—presumably dissolved to make what is called drink (*pānaka*). Probably these are more like today's cordials. And the unliquefied drinks, called "juices" (*rasa*), are prepared by mixing palmyra or *moca* [= banana?] fruits with insoluble herbs. He states that the reference to *āsava* in the *sūtra* implies fermentation, noting that this can be done using mild, medium, or intense fermentation.
32. For example, see *Dhūrtaviṭasaṃvāda*, ed. Dezsö and Vasudeva, pp. 393, 403; *Āgamaḍambara* 2.140.
33. BKŚS 19.205.
34. *Āgamaḍambara* 1.88. Also see *Śiśupālavadha* 8.52 where a ruddy lotus lake and *surā* are compared as they both redden the face and contain lotuses.

35. *Dhūrtaviṭasaṃvāda*, p. 330. My translation.
36. *Dhūrtaviṭasaṃvāda*, ed. Dezsö and Vasudeva, pp. 391–395.
37. *Dhūrtaviṭasaṃvāda*, ed. Dezsö and Vasudeva, p. 393. My translation.
38. *Harṣacarita Ucchvāsa* 6 (Kane ed., p. 106). So common is the motif of drinking from a lover's mouth that it seems quite reasonable to assume the *gaṇḍūṣa* is from her mouth. At the very least we can assume they have the same cup.
39. On this and other *dohadas*, see Bloomfield 1920b.
40. *Kāvyādarśa* 1.16. For a discussion of *mahākavya* including Daṇḍin's definition, see Peterson 2003, 7–9.
41. Peterson 2003, 7–9.
42. See Dundas's translation of the *Śiśupālavadha* (possibly seventh century CE), chapter 10 for the main drinking episode. For Mankha's *Śrīkaṇṭhacarita* (twelfth century CE), see the translation with analysis by Walter Slaje. Maṅkha refers to *hārahūraka* and *kāpiśāyana* wine, though these may just be fossilized terms for good wine by this point. There is an interesting reference to attendants pouring some drink, here called *āsava*, from one big jar (*pṛthubhāṇḍa*) into another smaller vessel (*anyalaghubhājanodare*, *Śrīkaṇṭhacarita* 14.4). This process makes a resounding noise and perhaps gives us as sense of the initial preparations involved in serving drinks stored in jars. Wine, *madhu*, is called a guru of the teachings of Love here (*Śrīkaṇṭhacarita* 14.1). In the *Kirātārjunīya*, as will be discussed later, we likewise see drink as imparting instructions on matters of love, something also seen at *Śiśupālavadha* V 9.87. For a list of terms for drinks Maṅkha uses, see the translation and analysis of Slaje 2015, 134. On grapes and wine in Kashmir see Slaje 2015, 27–28.
43. *Buddhacarita*, ed. Olivelle, pp. xix–xxiii.
44. BC 3.63; 4.1.
45. All translations of the BC from this point are Olivelle's. BC 4.26.
46. BC 4.27.
47. BC 4.31, 33–35, 41, 43, 54.
48. All translations from KA are from Peterson's translation (2016). I have changed some drink names for consistency within this book. For the date of this text see Peterson's translation, p. ix.
49. KA 9.3.
50. KA 9.35.
51. KA 9.36.
52. KA 9.42.
53. KA 9.51–53, 55–60.
54. KA 9.63.
55. KA 9.70–71.
56. On this concept see Ali 2004, 98–99.
57. *Mānasollāsa*, Viṃ. 5, Adhy. 10, verses 426bc–428. This translation was also published in McHugh 2013.
58. *Mānasollāsa* Viṃ. 5, Adhy.10, verses 449bc, 465ab.
59. The text has *ratharambhā-*. I am not sure how to take the *ratha*. Possibly it is another leaf or a type of plantain.

60. Means both "water vessel" and "coconut," so possibly a smaller pot or a larger coconut shaped cup?
61. Finot 1896, 134: "the color of cow urine."
62. *Madhu* here seems to have a more generic sense of "liquor."
63. *Mānasollāsa*, Viṃ. 5, Adhy. 10, verses 465bc–470ab.
64. See Mitra and Dalal (2005) on finds of glass from the Middle East at the site of Sanjan in Gujarat.
65. *Yathāmānam*, which I read not as relating to size but "according to their honor."
66. I take the editor's suggestion of *strībhiḥ* in preference to *tribhiḥ*.
67. Reading as *bahuvidhān*.
68. This line is unclear; I am taking *skandha* here as division, department, section.
69. Or maybe the *madya* was stored or kept, *sthita*, in these vessels.
70. One could also read this as placing dots of the *surā* on their heads.
71. Emending to *śuklāṃ pāṇḍurasāṃ svāduṃ kṛṣṇāṃ kaṭukaṣāyikām*.
72. Given the recipes provided earlier, and the reference to both "pale" and "black" in these two lines, I have decided to translate the *pāda*s as describing different varieties of *surā*, possibly taken here in the broadest sense of this word as "intoxicating drink."
73. *Mānasollāsa*, Viṃ. 5, Adhy. 10, verses 470bc–485.
74. *Mānasollāsa*, Viṃ. 5, Adhy. 10, verse 487b.
75. *Mānasollāsa*, Viṃ. 5, Adhy. 10, verses 489bc–491ab.
76. *Mānasollāsa*, Viṃ. 5, Adhy. 10, verses 492–493.
77. *Mānasollāsa*, Viṃ. 5, Adhy. 10, verses 497bc–499ab.
78. *Mānasollāsa*, Viṃ. 5, Adhy. 10, verses 499–500.
79. *Mānasollāsa*, Viṃ. 5, Adhy. 10, verses 500–502.
80. *Mānasollāsa*, Viṃ. 5, Adhy. 10, verses 502–503.
81. *Mānasollāsa*, Viṃ. 5, Adhy. 10, verse 504.
82. *Mānasollāsa*, Viṃ. 5, Adhy. 10, verse 512.
83. *Mānasollāsa*, Viṃ. 5, Adhy. 10, verse 513ab.
84. *Mānasollāsa*, Viṃ. 5, Adhy. 10, verses 513–514.
85. On the creation of literary Kannada see Pollock (2006, 303–304).
86. Available in an English translation by James Mallinson. For consistency with the rest of my translations I have translated the passages from this text. I have also consulted Lacôte's edition, notes, and French translation.
87. For the date, Lacôte suggests around the eighth or ninth century CE (Lacôte 1908, 147). Winternitz (1920, vol. 3, 316, n. 1) dismisses this as conjecture. Agrawala (1974, 229) proposes it was composed "sometime in the Gupta period."
88. BKŚS 12.79.
89. The word *anusvāde* is Lacôte's conjecture, and this is a new term, but I agree with him this makes good sense here as a following-on taste.
90. BKŚS 13.3–18. My translation. Extracts of these translations have also been published in McHugh 2020b.
91. As noted by Lacôte.
92. A tricky line with so many forms of *svad*, but I wish to keep the abundance of forms of the verb here in the translation too.

93. BKŚS 13.32–37.
94. BKŚS 19.118, 122.
95. The other guardians of the directions differ between Buddhism and Hinduism. See Zin 2015, 128. For the northern drinkers see Zin 2003, vol. 1, 286–293. For Kubera drinking, see Zin 2003, vol. 1, 282.
96. Zin 2015, 130; 141 n. 47 and 48, referring to *Abhidharmakośa* III.64 and *Divyavadāna* XVII.
97. See Zin 2015, 131. For a more detailed discussion of *yakṣas*, Kubera, and these northern drinkers at Ajanta and elsewhere see Zin 2003, vol. 1, 251–293.
98. Red adornments and garments occur in many iconographic schemes, but I see no connections to other such uses of red in this case.
99. BKŚS 15.60.
100. BKŚS 15.63.
101. I have expanded the translation for clarity. BKŚS 15.62.
102. BKŚS 18.
103. BKŚS 18.11–12.
104. *Sadoṣam yadi pānaṃ ca svayaṃ mā pibas tataḥ* (BKŚS 18.34ab) As in many other texts *pānaṃ* is here the generic word for "drink," implying an alcoholic drink.
105. BKŚS 18.38.
106. BKŚS 18.43.
107. BKŚS 18.45–50.
108. Taking there to be an implied *lakṣayitum* per Lacôte's suggestion.
109. BKŚS 18.51–56.
110. Quite notable is the description of him passing time with his friends, happy (*prasannaḥ*), along with his happy woman (*prasannayā*) as also with some *prasannā*, clear, *surā* (*prasannayā*) (BKŚS 18.93), another example of how in literary sources the form of the word could override technicalities, as elsewhere these people drink grape wine (see Ch. 4, note 117).
111. *Rājataraṅgiṇī* I.42, trans. Stein. Also see Stein's notes on grapes in Kashmir (*Rājataraṅgiṇī* vol. II, p. 429).
112. Extracts from *Rājataraṅgiṇī* VIII.1866. My translation.
113. *Līlāvatīsāra* 9.2–7.
114. See BKŚS 18.640.
115. See also the praise of friends at drinking gatherings (*āvāṇaesu*) at *Mudrārākṣasa* 6.5.
116. See the following note.
117. Sānudāsa later (BKŚS 18.86) learns he drank grape wine (*drākṣāmadhu*), not blue-lotus nectar (*puṣkaramadhu*), which would be fine, technically, in *dharmaśāstra* for anyone but a Brahmin (note his father is a merchant called Mitra Varman at BKŚS 18.4). I am certain the extremely scholarly Sānudāsa was supposed to be aware of this, so he is avoiding drink as a vice.
118. *Yasyāṃ yakṣāḥ . . . Meghadūta, Uttaramegha* 5.
119. In the edition of E. Hultzsch with Vallabhadeva's commentary, this is verse 66.

120. I have not been able to find other references to this text beyond this quotation. K. S. Ramamurti discusses this passage briefly (1971, 30), though he sheds no more light on this lost text.

121. The best readings for this comment are in the Bombay Nirnaya-Sāgara Press edition of 1890, ed. Godbole and Parab (in this text the line is *Uttaramegha*, stanza 3 on p. 53). The meter is *Śārdūlavikrīḍita*. The recipe is as follows. I have made one emendation, in bold (*daru* to *dāru*), that has no effect on the meter:

*Tālakṣīrasitāmṛtāmalaguḍonmattāsthikālāhvayā**dār**vindradrumamoraṭekṣuka dalīgugluprasūnair yutam |*
itthaṃ cen madhupuṣpabhaṅgyupacitaṃ puṣpadrumūlāvṛtaṃ kvāthena smaradīpanaṃ ratiphalākhyaṃ svādu śītaṃ madhu ||
iti madirārṇave ||

The first line is a list of substances and herbs, the identity of some of which is uncertain, and even the grouping of some of the elements in this compound is uncertain. Moreover, the terms *sitā* and *amṛtā* can both refer to an alcoholic drink. As best as I can determine, the "recipe" breaks down as follows:

tālakṣīra = palmyra-milk = palm toddy? Tabashir?
sitā = white sugar
amṛta/-ā = "nectar" but the word can refer to many plants
amala = can be "pure" or also as *amalā*: the emblic "Indian gooseberry"
guḍa = jaggery
unmatta = possibly datura?, bone/fruit-stone/pip? (*asthi*)
kāla or kālā = can refer to many plants and trees, *-āhvayādārv* (= "the tree called kālā")
indradruma = "Indra tree," is *Terminalia arjuna*
moraṭa/ā = a common name, numerous options
ikṣu = sugar cane
kadalī = plaintain
guglu = uncertain, but resembles *guggulu*, a type of Indian myrrh
prasūna = flowers/buds

The preceding terms are all in the instrumental plural, and the next term, "mixed with" (*yutam*), refers something being mixed with these materials.

The next line seems to contain:

madhupuṣpa = mahua flowers?

bhaṅgi/ī = uncertain. Bhang? Some manner of preparing the flowers?
upacitam = increased, abundant with.
So some sort of mass of mahua flowers?
puṣpadru = "flower-tree" uncertain, maybe mahua?
mūla = root, so the root of the previous tree.
āvṛtam = surrounded with.
So somehow covered in, surrounded by the roots of the flower tree?
kvāthena = with a decoction, or "by boiling."

122. Both published in *Kāmakuñjalatā*. For the relationship of the two see the end of the *kārikā* text. Both have been translated with an introduction by Eva-Maria Schinzel (2014).
123. Saṃvat 1866. Descriptive Catalogue of the Sanskrit Manuscripts of the Asiatic Society, vol. XIV, Calcutta 1955, pp. 2–4. Mss. 10348, 10347. On the date also see Schinzel (2014, 4). The works quoted in the commentary on the *sūtra* are all early: the commentary on *sūtra* 5 of the *Kādambarasvīkaraṇasūtra* refers to the work of Māgha, the "*Kirāta*," and the *Raghuvaṃśa* in the context of the association of drinking and successful intercourse (Schinzel 2014, 15). The *Kādambarasvīkaraṇakārika* contains elements associated with yogic and esoteric anatomy (Schinzel 2014, 5–6). The use of the word *kāpiśāyana* in the commentary indicates little, given the lexically varied style (*Kādambarasvīkaraṇasūtra*, introducing *sūtra* 9). Perhaps scholars of *śāstric* style and of *kāmaśāstra* might be able to help refine our sense of the dates of these texts.
124. Schinzel 2014, 106.
125. *Kādambarasvīkaraṇakārikā* verse 1.
126. *Kādambarasvīkaraṇasūtra* 1–4. My translation.
127. I base these and the following comments on Schinzel's translation.
128. Note both texts start with the injunction to drink for sex. The commentary to the *Kādambarasvīvaraṇasūtra* concludes with verses that suggest this same rationale for the text: "It is taught as a rule one must drink liquor (*sīdhu*, sugar-cane wine) at the time of sex . . .," which, we are told in the same verses, along with studying *kāmaśāstra*, will lead to pleasure for the woman, the man, and to the creation of offspring.
129. *Harṣacarita* ed. Kane, *Ullāsa* 2 (p. 32): "In his discussions, he rained wine/sweet conversation (*madhu*), though he had given it up." Taking *madhu* as either sweet (conversation) or wine. Is this permanent temperance? At another point the king's breath is compared to the day of the mythical churning of the ocean when various items, including liquor, arose (*Harṣacarita* ed. Kane, *Ullāsa* 2, p. 34). Yet, arguably, this passage is driven more by an extended metaphor than a desire to portray the king as a drinker. Thus, although there is drinking at festive events in this text, the king himself is most certainly not prominently represented as a drinker.
130. There are very few references to kings drinking in that text, though see the incident with the drunk fire-setting king in the "Vices of Kings" in Cup 7. Also see the discussion of the Kashmiri Kalyapāla dynasty in Cup 3.
131. Handiqui 1968, 2.
132. My translation, *Yaśastilaka* part II, *Āśvāsa* 4 (p. 126). As noted and translated by Handiqui 1968, 324.
133. My comments here are adapted from Douglas (1987, 3–15).
134. Pemberton and Duffy 1934, 303.
135. Dietler 2001, 85.
136. I am inspired here by Maria Heim's reflections on action, intention, and narrative in Buddhism. Heim 2013, ch. 4.
137. Bakhtin 1984, 122.

138. As noted, the *Bṛhatkathāślokasaṃgraha* presents the interesting case of a literary text that inverts all the conventions of drinking (the woman gets the man intoxicated; parents secretly encourage their moral sons to drink). This is indeed life turned inside out (Bakhtin 1984, 122). Though, again, this confused-confusion follows all the (inverted) conventions quite perfectly, and *this* inverted-drinking is, quite naturally, productive of the very sorts of things that drink usually destroys: economic success and the family.

CUP 5

1. E.g., Carroll 2015.
2. Wujastyk 2003, 193. HIML IA, 597–656.
3. AH *Nidānasthāna 6; Cikitsasthāna 7.*
4. AH *Cikitsitasthāna* 7.72: *vaidyavikatthanām*, glossed by Aruṇadatta as *kadarthanāṃ*, "torments." All translations from Vāgbhaṭa in this chapter are mine.
5. AH *Cikitsitasthāna* 7.73.
6. *Āśritopāśritahitaṃ*. In other words, the drinker-patient here, and physicians who manage and prescribe it. I thank Dr Vitus Angermeier for pointing out to me that something quite specific along these lines must be implied here. The commentator Indu suggests a sense of the drink being good for dependents and dependents of dependents.
7. AH *Cikitsitasthāna* 7.74.
8. My headings in brackets.
9. *Āvaneya*, "earthern." Indu (probably late twelfth century CE, HIML IA, 674) gives "a particular type of vessel" (*bhāṇḍaviśeṣa*) for *āvareya*, which the editor also gives as another reading. Aruṇadatta glosses the term as *ḍoluṅgaka*, which I have not been able to find elsewhere. Made of gold and stones, and wrapped in cooling wet silk, these things are presumably some sort of larger vessel.
10. Indu: the breezes are very cooling because these items have sandalwood water and other cooling substances applied to them.
11. Aruṇadatta explains these as gods (*devas*), anti-gods/asuras (*dānavas*), *kūṣmāṇḍa* (in the sense of some sort of impish being?) and others.
12. Referring to Yaśodhara's definition of *saraka*, which fits well here. See "The Man About Town" in Cup 4.
13. AH *Cikitsitasthāna* 7.75–93. Ed. B. H. P. Vaidya.
14. AH *Nidānasthāna* 6.10bc–11ab.
15. There is an excellent translation of this section by Wujastyk (2003, 217–224). I retranslate as I want to play close attention to the terminology.
16. AH *Sūtrasthāna* 3.11cd.
17. The commentaries of Aruṇadatta and Hemādri mention *asana* (*Terminalia tomentosa* Wight & Arn.) and other heartwoods, such as sandalwood (in

Aruṇadatta). Compare to the pink herbal water drunk in Kerala nowadays, flavored with sappan wood chips.

18. AH *Sūtrasthāna* 3.21–23ab.
19. AH *Sūtrasthāna* 3.29ab.
20. *Kāvyamīmāṃsā*, *Adhyāya* 18 (p. 108). My translation.
21. AH *Sūtrasthāna* 3.45cd. The slowing of digestive fire in this season is stated at the start of this section (3.42).
22. It is tempting to understand this as "excess intoxication" given the derivation from *ati* √*i*, though in both Apte's *Practical Sanskrit Dictionary* and Monier-Williams's the majority of senses for *atyaya* in English are on the lines of perishing, danger, distress (though the sense of transgression/overstepping is also given). *Atyāya* is given in the sense of excess in both dictionaries. Nevertheless, as seen in this chapter the condition is not equivalent to modern "alcoholism" (from alcoholismus, first coined in Sweden by Huss in 1849 in a paper on chronic alcoholism, OED, s.v. "alcoholism") and is by no means always produced from excessive drunkenness, nor is it particularly a form of addiction as we understand it. Thus for *madātyaya* Monier-Williams (2000) gives a "disorder" not an excess; Böhtlingk and Roth (1855–1875, s.v. *madātyaya*) give a "krankhafter Zustand in Folge von Trunkenheit"; and Apte (2003) gives "any distemper resulting from drunkenness."
23. As for some other texts, briefly: the *Suśrutasaṃhitā* (*Uttaratantra* 47) on *pānātyaya* (not *madātyaya*), is less detailed that in the *Caraka*. The focus is on diagnosis and treatment, with formulae for medicines and less attention to "correct drinking." The *Aṣṭāṅgahṛdaya* divides the topic into symptoms/diagnosis (*nidāna*) and therapy (*cikitsā*), and is more detailed and complex in presentation than both the *Caraka*- and *Suśrutasaṃhitā*, with the praise of liquor and the account of ideal drinking placed *after* the sections on diagnosis and therapy. The foregrounding of the defense of liquor in the *Carakasaṃhitā* (in its current form) is striking and might be a counterblast to brahminical tendencies of a certain time and place, which presumably would seek to diminish the respectable use of liquor?
24. CS *Cikitsāsthāna* 24.20.
25. Cakrapāṇidatta was a Hindu who lived in the Bengal area and composed his works in approximately the third quarter of the eleventh century CE. (HIML IIA, 92–93).
26. Falk 2010, 100.
27. On foreign wine, drinking imagery, and drinking terminology (e.g., *caṣaka*, *madhu*, *mṛdkvīkā*) in early India see McHugh forthcoming d.
28. HDŚ II.2, 745–747.
29. See Wujastyk (2003, xl–xliv) for a discussion of this term and possible translations. Meulenbeld (1974, 469) has "morbific entity."
30. CS *Cikitsāsthāna* 24.22.
31. CS *Cikitsāsthāna* 24.24.
32. CS *Cikitsāsthāna* 24.25. Cakrapāṇidatta states the latter two drinks and humors are in reverse order and the bilious should have grape wine.

33. The listing of grapes and honey together here raise the possibility that Manu's "*mādhvī*" may be deliberately ambiguous? Recall also the explicit definition of *madhu* as honey *or* grape-related thing (i.e. wine) in the *Arthaśāstra*.
34. CS *Cikitsāsthāna* 24.26–28. My translation.
35. CS *Cikitsāsthāna* 24.29.
36. Gonda 1952, 45. As discussed in Wujastyk 2003, xl.
37. Or possibly just the senses: *buddhīndriya*.
38. CS *Cikitsāsthāna* 24.35–36.
39. CS *Cikitsāsthāna* 24.37.
40. CS *Cikitsāsthāna* 24.
41. Taking the reading in the ed. of Jādavji Trikamji Acharya.
42. CS *Cikitsāsthāna* 24.39–51.
43. There are other descriptions of drunkenness in this text but there is no room to discuss them here.
44. *Nāṭyaśāstra* 7.38. My translation.
45. *Nāṭyaśāstra* 7.39–43. My translation.
46. Taking *sattva* as mind as suggested by Cakrapāṇidatta, though the term can also mean "character" or "living being." CS *cikitsāsthāna* 24.73.
47. CS *Cikitsāsthāna* 24.53.
48. E.g., CS *Śārīrasthāna* 1.18–20. On CS 1.18–20 as likely reflecting Nyāya Vaiśeṣika ideas see Hellwig 2009b. Given the complexity of this text as a whole it would require more work to say what sort of *manas* we are dealing with here.
49. CS *Cikitsāsthāna* 24.57.
50. CS *Cikitsāsthāna* 24.59
51. Taking the alternative reading of *balam* in Jādavji Trikamji Acharya's edition. CS *Cikitsāsthāna* 24.61.
52. CS *Cikitsāsthāna* 24.62–67.
53. CS *Cikitsāsthāna* 24.68–69.
54. I take the reading *anākūlam*, as given by P.V. Sharma.
55. Going with Cakrapāṇidatta's interpretation of this as implying there to be no risk of the third stage.
56. CS *Cikitsāsthāna* 24.74–78.
57. Even where in the *Kāmasūtra* the woman has already drunk before meeting the man, this (possibly solitary) drinking took place to facilitate an encounter with another person.
58. CS *Cikitsāsthāna* 24.80–82.
59. CS *Cikitsāsthāna* 24.88.
60. CS *Cikitsāsthāna* 24.92–93.
61. CS *Cikitsāsthāna* 24.94.
62. CS *Cikitsāsthāna* 24.107–109.
63. CS *Cikitsāsthāna* 24.115–116.
64. Zimmermann 1987.
65. Possibly the elephant apple, *Dillenia indica* L.
66. *Parūṣaka* = *Grewia asiatica* L. Hindi *phālsā*.

67. CS *Cikitsāsthāna* 24.136–137.
68. I am not sure how to read this, but it is clearly a system for producing cold air.
69. CS *Cikitsāsthāna* 24.152–159ab.
70. CS *Cikitsāsthāna* 24.195–198.
71. Setting aside the list of contents.
72. CS *Cikitsāsthāna* 24.206.
73. In other words, this material is not at odds with legal discourse.

CUP 6

1. The study of Vedic texts and rituals is specialized, so I rely on previous scholarship. See Kolhatkar (1999) for a thorough study of this ritual. I am interested here in the mature form of the sacrifice, not its development. Kolhatkar suggests that *surā* may have entered the ritual realm in connection with the Kṣatriya being allowed to perform sacrifice, with the reservation that he drink *surā*, "considered to be the soma-drink of the kṣatriya sacrificer." (Kolhatkar 1999, p. 185). See Steiner (2001) for a critique of Kolhatkar, especially the assumption that the classical *varṇa* system was present in very early periods.
2. I.e., described using forms of √*mad*.
3. JBr 3.228. Section 202 in Caland's edition and translation. As mentioned by Oberlies (1998, vol. 1, 294).
4. Malamoud (1992, 28) quoting ŚBr V.1.2.10 and ŚBr V.1.5.28. In later texts one of the dangers of drink is that it makes people reveal secrets: "in vino veritas." So why is *surā* falsehood? In the Vedic case this most human drink, *surā*, has qualities associated with the *human* realm, such as lying. And routine lying is, of course, essential to "in vino veritas."
5. Jamison, online *Ṛgveda* commentary on RV I.191.
6. Malamoud 1992.
7. I shall not undertake a detailed description and analysis of the whole ritual here, but rather I focus on selected aspects. On this ritual, in addition to Malamoud (1992) see Kolhatkar (1999); Jamison (1991, 98–103); Oberlies (1998, 293–295).
8. Jamison 1991, 98.
9. Jamison 1991, 99.
10. Jamison 1991, 98–99.
11. Oberlies 1998, 293.
12. I rely on Bloomfield 1893. Also Oldenberg 1893.
13. Bloomfield's translation of *Taittiriya Brāhmaṇa* I.7.1.6. At Bloomfield 1893, 147.
14. Bloomfield 1893, 152.
15. ŚBr XII.7.1.1–14. I quote Eggeling's translation of ŚB XII.7.7. Also see Weber's ed. As Kolhatkar explains, in this myth Indra beheads Viśvarūpa who has three heads, one of which eats *soma*, one *surā*, and one food. Viśvarūpa's father Tvaṣṭṛ is angered and does a *soma* sacrifice to which Indra is not invited. But Indra takes *soma* that was not

offered to him (in some versions using a straw). This *soma* flows out of his body, becoming the components of the *Sautrāmaṇī*, which is used to cure him after this purging. (Kolhatkar 1999, ch. 6). For a discussion of this productive disintegration see Malamoud (1992, 27).

16. As Oldenberg notes regarding ŚBr V.5.4.7. (1893, 346).
17. Malamoud 1992, 28.
18. RV X.131.2 as used in the *Kaukilī Sautrāmaṇī* of the *Taittirīya Brāhmaṇa* 2.6.1. See Dumont 1965, 311–312, and n. 7.
19. RV X.131, trans. Jamison, in *Ṛgveda*, trans. Jamison and Brereton (2014). My comment in parentheses. I have capitalized the vocative "O" in verse 4 for consistency within this book.
20. Note that the recipe in Chapter 1 was from the *Caraka* form of the ritual as described in the *Baudhāyana Śrautasūtra*, which belongs to the *Taittirīya Brāhmaṇa* school. Dumont (1965) presents the mantras for the *Kaukilī* version of the ritual from the *Taittirīya Brāhmaṇa*. The mantras I quote here from Dumont (1965) are identical to those used in the *Caraka* version of the *ritual* in the *Taittirīya Brāhmaṇa* apart from the omission in the *Caraka* version of "... *mádhumatīṃ mádhumatā* ..." Gonda writes that this particular mantra occurs in four variant forms (1980, 79). For the relation of the mantras to ritual actions see the *Caraka Sautrāmaṇī* in the *Śrautakośa* (vol. 1, pt. 2, 904).
21. TB 2.6.1, trans. Dumont 1965, 311. My clarifications in brackets.
22. TB 2.6.4, trans. Dumont 1965, 316. I have altered and added to some of Dumont's parenthetical glosses, also adding some Sanskrit.
23. Gonda (1980,124): "In these Stanzas the gods—the Aśvins and Sarasvatī, assisted by Savitar and Varuṇa—ritually heal the bodily form of Indra, 'weaving' his inner shape and lovely figure by means of the ingredients and utensils used in preparing the surā."
24. Jamison 1986, 172–178.
25. Malamoud 1989.
26. Malamoud 1992, 29. My translation. See also the locations and *varṇa* associations of *surā* houses in *The Ambience* in Ch. 7.
27. Malamoud 1992, 30–31. My translation.
28. Kuiper writes that later "Daitya" "Dānava" and "Asura" are "nearly or entirely synonyms," and "if there was a distinction at all, it must have been very small." (Kuiper 1979, 76).
29. For the various versions of this myth see Bedekar 1967. Also Dumézil 1924, 39–46.
30. MBh 1.15.12–13, trans. Van Buitenen.
31. MBh 1.16.13, 15–16, trans. Van Buitenen.
32. MBh. 1.16.26–27, trans. Van Buitenen.
33. MBh. 1.16.33–37.
34. Rām. 1.44.21–23, trans. Goldman.
35. See "A Painting of a *Surā* Shop?" in Chapter 3.
36. For the date of this text see Bryant 2002.
37. BhP 8.8.9, ed. Śāstrī.
38. BhP 8.8.30. My translation.

39. BhP 8.8.30.
40. See the discussion and table in Bedekar 1967, 45–47. The version where she goes to Ananta is in the *Padmapurāṇa, Uttarakhaṇḍa*. For the partial incarnation of Śeṣa (=Ananta) as Balarāma see MBh 1.61.91ab.
41. The word *madirá* is found in the *Ṛgveda* in the sense of exhilarating (e.g., II.14.9d), being derived from *mádati*. We see the word in this feminine form in Manu (11.149ab) where it is probably a synonym of *surā*, being used along with *vāruṇī*. (This section is probably a redactorial excursus—see Manu, ed. and trans. Olivelle, 60). Note that *surā*, *vāruṇī*, and *madirā* all have different metrical properties. Commentators Sarvajñanārāyaṇa and Kullūka gloss *madirā* at Manu 11.149ab as *surā*. Yet unlike *surā* and *madhu*, which are used in the sense of a specific type of drink as well as in the sense of "drink in general," *madirā* arguably often lies more on the more generic end of the semantic spectrum, though in pharmacological texts it is presented as a specific variety of *surā* (see Chapter 1).
42. AŚ 2.4.17. I am aware of at least one temple to Surā Devī in India today (near Dehradun) though I have been unable to find anything about it. There is also a village called Suradevi near Nagpur.
43. The situation is confusing. Madirā may sometimes be identified with Surā, sometimes connected, and sometimes we do not know. Scharfe writes that Madirā is the wife of Vasudeva in the *Harivaṃśa*, and the wife (not the daughter) of Varuṇa in the *Viṣṇupurāṇa* (1993, 88). She is also mentioned as Vasudeva's wife in the *Mausalaparvan* (MBh. 16.8.18). Harihara Śāstri notes that another text, the *Īśānaśivagurudevapaddhati* has the goddess Jyeṣṭhā in place of Madirā in a passage very similar to that in the installation of Madirā in the city in the *Arthaśāstra*. (1956–1957, 107–113. As noted by Olivelle: AŚ p. 506). Vettam Mani notes that Jyeṣṭhā is an inauspicious goddess who arose in the churning of the Milk Ocean according to the Tamil *Rāmāyaṇa* of Kamban, and she is called Jyeṣṭhā (elder sister) as she emerged prior to Lakṣmī—so Jyeṣṭhā may be Surā-as-Fortune's-elder-sister in this tradition, possibly also in others where she emerges first? (Mani 1979, s.v. Jyeṣṭhā 1). Later in this chapter, however, we will meet Jyeṣṭhā as the *wife* of Varuṇa in the MBh, the mother of Surā! (Though this is compatible with the versions where Madirā is Vasudeva's wife). Bedekar (1967) writes that Madirā emerges in the version of the churning myth in the *Matsya Purāṇa* and the *Skandamahāpurāṇa* (at least in the editions he was using). Notably, in the *Matsya Purāna*, as reported by Bedekar, Madirā emerges in a secondary churning, having been preceded by Surā, which redundancy perhaps suggests the Madirā passage may be a later addition or belongs to a separate tradition.
44. Evoking Jonathan Z. Smith's terminology. Smith 1978, 101.
45. In her study of the concepts of purity and impurity, where she defines dirt as "matter out of place." (Douglas 2002 [1966], 44).
46. MBh. 1.60.51. My translation.
47. Some more references: there is also a reference to Surādevī in the Buddhist *Lalitavistara* (c. fourth century CE) as one of eight divine maidens who inhabit the northern quarter of Kubera (*Lalitavistara*, ed. Lefmann, ch. 24, part 1, p. 391, line

104). On a possible Greek reference to Surā as a god (Soroadeios, m.) see Humbach (2007), who argues, on sophisticated philological grounds, that this is not a reference to a Surā Deva. (Though he seems unaware of the prominence of Surā Devī in some Indic sources. Also, with respect to Humbach's paper, *surā* is a flexible word, and is it quite plausible that Greeks might construe a grain-*surā* as wine: compare "rice wine.")

48. On this role see Ali 2004, 45–46.
49. *Pādatāḍitaka*, ed. Dezsö and Vasudeva, pp. 112–113. My translation.
50. *Mattavilāsaprahasana*, ed. Śāstrī, p. 8. My translation.
51. Trevelyan 1876, vol. 2, 183.
52. *Atharvaveda Saṃhitā* (*Śaunaka*) 4.34.6a.
53. This could be an early stock list of tasty liquids.
54. According to the Jain *Sarvārthasiddhi* commentary on the *Tattvārthasūtra* of Umāsvāti, after the *Lavaṇoda* ("Salt"), *Kāloda* ("Black"), and *Puṣkara* ("Lotus") Oceans there are: the *Vāruṇīvara*, *Kṣīravara* ("Milk"), *Ghṛtavara* ("Ghee"), and *Ikṣuvara* ("Sugar Cane") Oceans (*Sarvārthasiddhi*, trans. S. A. Jain, on *Tattvarthasūtra* III.7, p. 89). Most notable is the *Vāruṇīvara* or *Vāruṇoda* Ocean (*Varuṇoa*), which according to Kirfel tastes like "rum" (*sīdhu*?), though I have not located the text containing this description (Kirfel 1920, 253). The name of this ocean is apparently connected to the fact that it is the abode of the gods Vāruṇī and Vāruṇakānta (Kirfel 1920, 253). In addition to these oceans, the Jain continent called the *Dhātakīkhaṇḍa* is named after the profusion of *dhātakī* plants there (Kirfel 1920, 251). The Jains were aware that (red) *dhātakī* was a component of alcoholic drinks and the trade in *dhātakī* is forbidden. (See the section on Jainism in Cup 7). Imagine a continent said to be filled with hops to get a sense of the connotations. *Dhātakī* continent does not border the *Vārunīvara* Ocean, however, but the Black one.
55. See the useful table in Kirfel (1920, 57). For a more detailed account see Kirfel 1920, 112–128.
56. Kirfel's "Group 1." There are variant names for these oceans—I only give one example of each here.
57. Kirfel 1920, 58.
58. Kueny 2001, 13–17. Though I do not suggest any connection between the two.
59. As discussed, the nuances of "*mada*" are hard to capture, and the sense no doubt changed over time, but this seems a good rough translation. I have relied here on Hopkins (1905). In the MBh critical edition the seer is Cyavana. RV I.116 10, a hymn to the Aśvins, alludes to the fact they rejuvenated Cyavāna.
60. Apparently *mada*, intoxication, *already* exists.
61. MBh 3.122.8–10. My translation.
62. MBh 3.123.22.
63. MBh 3.124.9a. According to a Vedic version this lack of access to *soma* is what renders them incomplete, and thus less desirable than the seer in the contest to win the princess (Hopkins 1905, 46).
64. MBh 3.124.10–12.
65. MBh 3.124.19–24. My translation.
66. MBh 3.125.8. My translation.

67. JBr 3.160, trans. Hopkins 1905, 66–67 (I have changed "brandy" to Surā).
68. MBh 14.9.37.
69. JBr 3.160, trans. Hopkins 1905, 66.
70. *Kalāvilāsa*, ed. and trans. Somadeva Vasudeva. See Vasudeva's introduction, as well as Sternbach (1974, 77–78).
71. *Kalāvilāsa* 6.10. See Vasudeva's notes on this verse that uses medical imagery. The whole of this chapter is well worth reading in Vasudeva's translation, along with his insightful notes.
72. *Kalāvilāsa* 6.15. My translation.
73. *Kalāvilāsa* 6.16–17. My translation. Compare to *Bhagavad Gītā* 5.18, 6.8 (As pointed out by Vasudeva in his ed. and trans., 363–364).
74. *Kalāvilāsa* 6.18, and see Vasudeva's note (p. 364).
75. *Kalāvilāsa* 6.28.
76. *Kalāvilāsa* 6.33. My translation. The whole list being 6.29–32.
77. Echoing *Kalāvilāsa* 6.28. For another list of types of *mada* see the Introduction to Cup 7.
78. MBh 1.71.
79. MBh 1.71.6.
80. MBh 1.71.26.
81. MBh 1.71.31.
82. MBh 1.71.33. My translation.
83. MBh 1.71.52–55. My translation.
84. *Saṃjñānāśaṃ*: another reading is that his understanding was destroyed. I take this to mean his state on drinking, not his temporary death.
85. On these myths and others see Goldman 1977.
86. Goldman 1977, 93.
87. Joshi 1979, 48–49.
88. AŚ 13.3.54.
89. For a study of Balarāma in the *Mahābhārata*, with extensive bibliography, see Bigger 1998.
90. *Kādambarasvīkaraṇakārikāmañjarī* verse 1.
91. Probaby *Neolamarckia cadamba* (Roxb.) Bosser (=*Anthocephalus indicus* var. glabrescens H.L.Li).
92. I have used Nīlakaṇṭha's commentary on this passage. If we accept a tentative date of the version in the critical edition as around 300 CE, then maybe this passage in the vulgate was created some time after that? (On the date see Hein 1986, 296, n. 1).
93. I have used *Harivaṃśa*, vulgate, with commentary of Nīlakaṇṭha, *Viṣṇuparvan* 41.5–23. (In the critical edition this is at Appendix 1, No. 18, 516–553).
94. Carter 1968, 130–131; Carter 1982, p. 254, fig. 13.
95. I translate literally as this is a neat example of the odor+wind+sense theory of olfaction.
96. Nīlakaṇṭha here explains that it is by means of cups of *surā* that are drunk in sacrifices such as the *Vājapeya* and *Sautrāmaṇī* that men manage to drink the nectar of immortality, and that it is therefore (in these cases) pure, fit for sacrifice (*medhyā*).

97. My translation of *Harivaṃśa*, vulgate, with commentary of Nīlakaṇṭha, *Viṣṇuparvan* 41.5–23. (In the critical edition this is at: Appendix 1, No. 18, 516–553).
98. Sanford 2005, 98. Sanford relates that in the Dauji (Balarāma) temple in Baldeo *bhāṅg prasād* is served (2005, 93). As we shall see, cannabis was a more acceptable intoxicant in upper caste law and society than alcohol, so his taste in intoxicants here is more acceptable to orthodox caste Hinduism (strong as *bhāṅg* may be).
99. MBh 1.213.54a.
100. In D4, "Devanāgarī Composite Version" (Tanjore) inserted after MBh 1.213.52a.
101. See McHugh forthcoming d on this word.
102. Or a different region, or a tradition with a different lexicon, though I think a diachronic explanation is likely.
103. He is only said to be *kṣība*, drunk, on two occasions in the MBh (Bigger 1998, 37–41).
104. *Śiśupālavadha* 2.16, 20, trans. Dundas.
105. Though the iconography of the one earring was not always followed (Joshi 1979, 39–40).
106. MBh 11.25.40.
107. MBh 16.2.4–10.
108. MBh 16.2.18–19. My translation of all the passages here.
109. MBh 16.3.21.
110. Possibly they are said here to be "attached to sugarcane wine" (*sīdhuṣu saktāś* 16.4.8a), though the editor notes many variants. In the *Bhāgavata Purāṇa* version they drink sweet *maireya* (BhP 11.30.12).
111. MBh 16.4.13.
112. MBh 16.4.14.
113. MBh 16.4.16–27.
114. MBh 16.4.31.
115. MBh 16.4.34.
116. MBh 16.4.40–41.
117. MBh 16.4.42–44.
118. MBh 16.5.

CUP 7

1. MBh 5.34.41. I translate literally to show the misalignment with *doing*.
2. The first three being *mattaḥ pramatta unmattaḥ* . . . , "the drunk, the careless, the mad . . ." (MBh 5.33.82).
3. MBh 5.34.42.
4. MBh 5.34.42. Vidura also states that the *mada* of supremacy/power (*aiśvaryamada*) is worse than that from drink, etc., for the one drunk on power does not wake up without first falling down. MBh 5.34.51.
5. Clark 1983, 20.

6. RV, trans. Jamison and Brereton, intro., 5.
7. RV X.107.9, trans. Jamison and Brereton.
8. See "Brewing and the *Surā* Trade in the Earliest Sources" in Chapter 3.
9. RV VII.86.6ab. Trans. Jamison and Brereton. I have capitalized the vocative O for stylistic consistency in this book. Also see Jamison 2007, 98–99.
10. See also Jamison's commentary on this line. Jamison, Online Commentary to RV, accessed March 4, 2016.
11. RV VIII.2.12 (622), trans. Jamison and Brereton.
12. See "Surā in Vedic Sources" in Chapter 1.
13. Jamison and Brereton, on RV VIII.21.
14. RV VIII. 21.14ab, trans. Jamison and Brereton.
15. For *surā* and dice in the *Atharvaveda* see later in this section. For dice as a cause of *mada* see ṚV X.34.1. See also my comments on drinking in the *sabhā* in "Female Brewers" in Chapter 3.
16. AVŚ 6.69.1, trans. Whitney, modified. According to Whitney the meaning of *aragárāṭas* is uncertain.
17. AVŚ 9.1.18.
18. Tsuchiyama 2005, 56.
19. AVŚ 6.69, AVŚ 6.19 (on purification), and AVŚ 9.1.18 accompany the pouring, according to the *Vaitāna Sūtra*, as noted by Whitney in his comment on AVŚ 6.69.
20. AVŚ 14.1.36, 36, trans. Whitney.
21. AVŚ 14.1.36, trans. Whitney, notes.
22. AVŚ 6.70.1. Only the attachment of the man's mind to the woman is explicitly stated, but one assumes the entities in the first line are likewise objects of attachment.
23. MS II.4.2. As also given in Kolhatkar 1999, 3, who notes the same statement in *Kāṭhaka Saṃhitā* XII.12.
24. ŚBr XII.8.1.5–6. Eggeling's translation with my annotations in brackets.
25. ŚBr XII.8.1.5–6. Eggeling's translation with my annotations in brackets.
26. See Kolhatkar 1999, 2–4, 103–105. Also Bloomfield, 1893, 152–153. Also Malamoud 1992, 22, 28 on KŚS XIX.3.18–24.
27. See Kolhatkar 1999, 103.
28. MS II.4.2; *Kāṭhaka Saṃhitā* XII.12, as noted by Kolhatkar (1999, 3), who includes a reference to *surā* giving pleasure to the Kṣatriya from the *Aitareya Brāhmaṇa* XXXIX.6,
29. ŚBr XII.7.3.20, trans. Eggeling.
30. ŚBr V.1.2.10.
31. See Bodewitz 2007.
32. Bodewitz 2007, 336.
33. MBh 5.33.73–74.
34. Manu 7.45–46. On the date of Manu see the section on "The Law Code of Manu."
35. At Manu 7.46 it is said that the problems arise when the king is attached to, devoted to (*prasakta*) to the vices—presumably well-regulated enjoyment is acceptable.
36. The chapter on vices is AŚ 8.3.

37. Probably sometimes between 175–300 CE. AŚ, trans. Olivelle, introduction, referring to the work of McClish.
38. AŚ 8.3.61. My translation. Compare to BKŚS (cantos 16,17) where skill in playing the *vīṇā* is vital in winning a certain woman's hand. Displaying the loincloth (*kaupīna*) is another problem associated with drink in the *Arthaśāstra*, which recalls in particular the flailing son of a Bactrian.
39. Bühnemann 2017, 239.
40. AŚ 8.3.55–64.
41. AŚ 8.3.57.
42. AŚ 1.16.28.
43. AŚ 1.17.36. Also see AŚ 1.18.15 where the vices are used to ruin a prince in disfavor.
44. AŚ 3.16.9.
45. On this text see the introduction to Knutson's translation (Knutson and Kāmandaki forthcoming). I am very grateful to Jesse Knutson for his detailed comments on my translation of this text and for allowing me to consult his own translation.
46. *Nītisāra*, *Sarga* 15.
47. *Nītisāra*, *Sarga* 15, verses 7–8. My translation.
48. *Vyasana*.
49. *Nītisāra*, *Sarga* 15, verses 60–66. My translation.
50. *Yogayātrā* 2.4–7. As noted by Shastri (1969, 214–215). On this text see Geslani 2016. Like Manu, he has ten vices from lust and eight from anger.
51. *Patnīyaty api mātaraṃ* . . . *Yogayātrā* 2.5.
52. *Yogayātrā* 2.7. *Aprakāśam*, though note that Kern has *āprakāmam*.
53. The discussion here is based on Book I, after the end of Story 3. Edgerton's edition, vol. 1 (1924), pp. 61–62. Trans. Olivelle, p. 26.
54. Manu 7.49. Though the king is said to be attached, *prasakta*, to both the desire and anger vices (Manu 7.46).
55. There is indeed a similarity between *vyasana*-as-*prasaṅga*, attachment, and the early modern English notion of addiction as encompassing devotion (see Lemon 2018, Intro.). Also, we should also bear in mind that writers of some Sanskrit-English dictionaries would have had a different understanding of "addiction" than we do today.
56. There are contexts where the object sought in vice has agency to tempt and overpower, such as with courtesans and in the famous *Ṛgvedic* gambler hymn (X.34), yet in general the *vyasana* lies in the unsated desire, greed, attachment of the subject, as the author of the *Pañcatantra* understood.
57. *Arthapāruṣyam*, one of the anger-vices, is defined in the *Pañcatantra* as "lusting after the property of others without compassion" (trans. Olivelle, p. 26; for the Sanskrit see *Pañcatantra*, ed. Edgerton, vol. 1, p. 62).
58. *Rājataraṅgiṇī* IV.320.
59. Manu 11.55.
60. On this also see Jacobi, *Jaina Sutras* (pt. I, pp. xxii–xxix). Also, von Hinüber 1997, 11.
61. Bodewitz notes that for some of great sins the Brahmin is the victim and not the agent, whereas for the vices the king is always the agent, and for this reason he thinks the vice list is not the counterpart of the Brahmininal sin list (2007, 324). Despite this

and other variables, I suggest there is some structural similarity between the sins and the vices.

62. "Give or take a century or so" as Olivelle notes in discussing this date (*The Early Upaniṣads*, 12). For this section, I have largely relied on *The History of Dharmaśāstra* by P. V. Kane. (Vol. II, pt. 2, pp. 791–799). I use the term "Hindu" as an umbrella term, though much of the material is literally Brahminical.
63. *Chāndogya Upaṇiṣad* 5.10.9, trans. Olivelle.
64. All references to the *Dharmasūtras* are from Olivelle's edition, with my translation in some cases where noted.
65. On the dates of the *Dharmasūtras* see Olivelle's edition and translation, 4–10.
66. *Dharmasūtras*, ed. and trans. Olivelle, 15.
67. *Dharmasūtras*, ed. and trans. Olivelle, 1.
68. *Dharmasūtras*, ed. and trans. Olivelle, Introduction.
69. Olivelle 2006, 171.
70. See Olivelle 2006, 14–16. Also, Davis 2010, Ch. 1. Along with killing Brahmins, the prohibition on *surā* was an exemplary injunction of a worldly (*laukika*) variety for the grammarians Kātyāyana and Patañjali of the last three centuries BCE (Olivelle 2006, 174–175). While a statement not to drink *is* in fact given in the Vedas, for these authors rules about drinking are exemplary worldly injunctions, as opposed to Veda-derived ones. Olivelle notes that in this context "worldly" likely implies *dharmaśāstric* (Olivelle 2006, 174–175). That the injunction not to drink *surā* is located in the worldly realm, *despite the existence* of several Vedic statements on this matter, strengthens Olivelle's argument that the earliest authority for *dharma* in a Brahminical context was customary norms and practices of actual communities (Olivelle 2006, 177).
71. Olivelle proposes this is the student who has returned home in his edition. In McClish's proposed structure the passage concerns the graduate. McClish 2019.
72. ĀDS 1.17.21. My translation. All ĀDS translations, and other translations from the *Dharmasūtras*, are based on the editions in *Dharmasūtras*, ed. and trans. Olivelle.
73. ĀDS 1.17.25. My translation.
74. On *kīlāla* see McHugh forthcoming c.
75. ĀDS 1.20.12.
76. Black pepper is in the *surā* the hunter discovers in the *Kumbha Jātaka*, and these two ingredients feature in one of the *saṃbhāras* in the *Arthaśāstra*.
77. ĀDS 1.21.8.
78. ĀDS 1.25.3. My translation.
79. Olivelle 2011, 24.
80. See Brick 2012.
81. ĀDS 1.25.10.
82. Brick 2012, 11.
83. GDS 2.20.
84. GDS 23.1.
85. GDS 23.2.
86. GDS 23.6.
87. GDS 24.10.

88. GDS 15.16 (*-madyapa-*)
89. Olivelle, *Dharmasūtras*, 10.
90. GDS 11.20 states these regional variations are only legal if not in conflict with sacred scriptures.
91. BDS 1.2.4.
92. BDS 1.18.18.
93. BDS 2.1.21. As Olivelle notes, the concept of the "twice-born" is used increasingly frequently in these somewhat later *dharmasūtras*. Olivelle, *Dharmasūtras*, 8–9. For observations on how to read "twice-born," see Lubin 2005, 87–88.
94. BDS 2.4.7. See also "The Ms" in Chapter 8.
95. AŚ 3.3.20.
96. BDS 1.9.
97. BDS 1.9.3.
98. VDS 1.20.
99. VDS 20.19–22. My translation.
100. VDS 20.22. My translation.
101. VDS 20.44.
102. Olivelle 2011, 36.
103. VDS 3.59.
104. VDS 21.11, 15, trans. Olivelle, modified. Olivelle notes the first of these verses is corrupt.
105. BDS 3.6.1–13.
106. HDŚ V.ii, 1348. I thank Patrick Olivelle for this reference (personal communication, June 2020).
107. Manu, ed. and trans. Olivelle, 19.
108. Manu, ed. and trans. Olivelle, 18–25, 37–41.
109. Manu, ed. and trans. Olivelle, 4.
110. Manu 11.55.
111. Manu 11.67. Recall the association of courtesans and drinking, and drinking and sex in general.
112. Manu 11.68.
113. Along with Medhātithi, I read this as a *dvandva*.
114. Manu 11.91–98. Olivelle's translation, modified.
115. Nārāyaṇa: "'In folly' means from passion, and not out of ignorance." (*mohāt rāgāt na tv ajñānāt*). I have used Mandlik's edition for all commentaries. For Medhātithi I also refer to Jhā's translation.
116. So Medhātithi on XII.92. Also Kullūka and Rāghavānanda on the same verse.
117. Note that at *Taittirīya Brāhmaṇa* 1.3.3.16 *surā* is said to be the supreme *anna* for humans, while *soma* is the supreme *anna* for the gods. (Cited by Steiner 2001, 375).
118. Of course Manu may have been drawing on an older tradition of defining types of *surā*.
119. Medhātithi takes this as applying to all drinks derived from sugar cane.
120. The principal variant is the more ambiguous *dvijājibhiḥ* (Olivelle ed.), so there may have been other interpretations of this text, as we see later.

121. Medhātithi, my translation.
122. VaiDh 5.100. Also AŚ 4.13.1–2.
123. If deliberately ambiguous it could imply the "*mārdvīkaṃ mādhavaṃ ca*" we see in the *Caraka Saṃhitā* (see "Drinking, Intoxication, Disease, and Health According to Caraka's Compendium" in Cup 5)
124. Medhātithi (Manu 11.95) explains this is fermented grape juice and that unfermented grape juice is not forbidden, and the same applies to grains and water that have not fermented: "There is no prohibition of recently produced grape juice so long as it has not attained a state of being intoxicating." (*na sadyo jātasya mṛdvīkārasasya pratiṣedho yāvan madyāvasthām aprāptasyeti*). If Medhātithi was from Kashmir then wine might have been a more culturally important drink for him. (On Medhātithi and Kashmir see HDŚ I.i, 574–575). Nārāyaṇa here has: "*Mādhvī* is made with grape juice according to some. Or it is made with mahua flowers, or with honey." (*mādhvī drākṣārasakṛteti kecit. madhūkapuṣpeṇa madhunā vā kṛtā*). Kullūka has "The *madhuka* tree is called *madhu*, that made from its flowers is *mādhvī*." (*madhukavṛkṣo madhuḥ tatpuṣpaiḥ kṛtā sā mādhvī*). Rāmacandra has "'*Mādhvī*' means of mahua flowers." (*mādhvī madhūkapuṣpasya*).
125. People possessed by *rākṣasa*s and *piśāca*s are said to enjoy liquor in the *Aṣṭāṅgahṛdayasaṃhitā* (6.4.26c–34b). (See Smith 2006, 496).
126. See Olivelle's note (Manu, 342). Some commentators take this as mispronunciation or recitation when impure, but Olivelle prefers Nandana's explanation that this is recitation in the presence of people who are forbidden to hear the Veda.
127. Manu, ed. and trans. Olivelle, 16–17; 59–60.
128. Manu 11.147, trans. Olivelle, modified. Compare to BDS 2.1.21. The word for the drink is *vāruṇī* in both verses dealing with unintentional drinking. Also see Bühler's translation of Manu, 460. (As cited in Manu, ed. and trans. Olivelle, 343).
129. Manu 11.148ab, 11.150.
130. See Jhā's translation of Medhātithi on Manu 11.147 (11.146 in Jhā's translation)
131. Manu 5.56, trans. Olivelle, modified.
132. Whatever the social context of ĀDS 1.17.21, it is a rule about *madya*-avoidance at a particular stage of life, and the line is not given in the context of sin and penances.
133. Manu also writes of wives drinking *madya*, again suggesting incontinent indulgence rather than Brahminical pollution by *surā* (Manu 9.80, 9.84).
134. Though the BDS is the first to explicitly list these *varṇa*s in a drink context.
135. I follow Olivelle's assessment. See VaiDh, ed. and trans. Olivelle, Introduction.
136. VaiDh, ed. and trans. Olivelle, 20–21.
137. Made from *ṭaṅka*, which Nandapaṇḍita gives as a type of *kapittha*, the wood-apple, *Feronia elephantum*.
138. *Kaula* "made from kola" = *badara* = *Ziziphus jujuba* Mill.
139. Nandapaṇḍita takes this as date fruit (as opposed to date palm toddy), and given the grouping with jackfruit (not a toddy tree) I agree.
140. Nandapaṇḍita has this made from the tree, as opposed to the date fruit.
141. VaiDh 22.82–84, ed. Olivelle. My translation.

142. *Dvijātibhiḥ* is a variant in some traditions of Manu too (see Olivelle's ed.), so maybe this version is from a tradition that had a stronger interpretation of Manu's prohibition for all three twice born *varṇas*. Nandapaṇḍita in his commentary on the VaiDh quotes the Manu version as "*brahmavādibhiḥ*," which Nandapaṇḍita takes as implying three *varṇas*.
143. "But for Kṣatriyas and Vaiśyas there is no offence in touching this. Touching implies drinking (*sparśaḥ pānopalakṣaṇam*)." Nandapaṇḍita on VaiDh 22.84.
144. *Hārītasaṃhitā* I.19, ed. Raison.
145. *Mitākṣarā* on *Yājñavalkyasmṛti, Prāyaścitta*, 253 (Chowkhamba 1929 ed., fasc. 10, p. 959).
146. The quote from the VaiDh given in Khiste and Hośiṅga's edition of the *Mitākṣarā* differs from Olivelle's edition, most notably for the two drinks *ṭāṅkaṃ* and *kaulaṃ*, given in the *Mitākṣarā* version as *sairaṃ* (given in Pulastya too) and *tālaṃ* (toddy).
147. Kane suggests a date of between the fourth and seventh centuries CE. (HDŚ I.i, 516–517.) Also see the similar list in the *Hārītasaṃhitā* where all the drinks are subsets of a fourfold *surā*. *Hārītasaṃhitā* I.19, ed. Raison.
148. Nandapaṇḍita has *sirā sindīvṛkṣa*, though he also explains *maireya* as made from *mirā*! I am not sure what *saira* could be.
149. Quoted in *Mitākṣarā* on III.253–255. Nandapaṇḍita quotes part of this passage in his commentary on VaiDh 12.83–84.
150. On *Yājñavalkyasmṛti, Prāyaścitta*, 253. The quote following this paragraph is also from the same section of commentary.
151. *Mīmāṃsāsūtra* 1.1.2, trans. in McCrea (2012, 2). I have relied on McCrea's description of this system here. I thank Christopher Fleming for some observations on Kumārila's project.
152. Using Olivelle's translation of "*smṛti*," as used in Olivelle (2016), which contains (pp. 88–104) a lucid introduction to Mīmāṃsā.
153. *Tantravārtika* I.III.4, ed. Sastri. See Jha's translation. Although an excellent translation, his slippage between "wine" and "*surā*" as well as "*madhu*" and "*sīdhu*" is sometimes confusing in this case.
154. Olivelle 2016, 96.
155. MBh 5.58.
156. MBh 5.58.5. In the critical edition the part of the line concerning the drinks has no variants.
157. As cited by Kumārila, Manu 11.95 reads "*na peyā brahmavādibhir*" which latter term he explains as implying Brahmins.
158. Kumārila refers to *madhu* and *sīdhu* as not prohibited for Kṣatriyas and Vaiśyas (I.III.4), which suggests he understands these as equivalent to Manu's *mādhvī* and *gauḍī*. He presumably understands *āsava* in the epic and *gauḍī* in Manu as *sīdhu*. It is likely, given his date, that he understands *madhu* as wine. In a period when grape wine was prominent, what was probably originally "honey-*āsava*" in earlier periods was understood as (grape wine) + (sugar-*āsava*, *sīdhu*), which are easily equated with Manu's two non-grain *surās*.
159. The passage resembles *Maitrāyaṇī Saṃhitā* 2.4.2.

160. Given with no attribution at *Subhāṣitaratnabhāṇḍāgāra*, p. 259, verse 337. My translation. As quoted in Pandey's translation and commentary of *Hārīta Saṃhitā* (vol. 1, p. 613).
161. Verpoorten's (2009) survey is excellent, and I agree that drinking is not an *enormously* important theme in (Indian) Buddhism as a whole, particularly in terms of morality and the law—at least when compared with Brahminical materials. For drinking within Buddhist ethics see Harvey (2000, 77–79). For Pali materials and their reception in modern Buddhism see Trafford 2009.
162. Bodewitz suggests ascetic abstinence may be the primary form, remarking of the drink rule in Hindu law that "The drinking of alcohol . . . can hardly be regarded as a capital sin of all the classes. The whole series makes and impression of a Brahmanical adaptation of the rules of life of the ascetics." (2007, 325). Given the apparent antiquity of the separation of Brahmins and *surā*, however, and the ancient notion of *surā* as enticing and socially damaging, I think the picture is more complicated. Also, for an exploration of the concept "brahman" (i.e. Brahmin in my usage in this book) as used by several groups in very early periods, see McGovern 2018. Perhaps anyone "brahminical" (in McGovern's sense) was to avoid *surā*, and that might imply various ascetic groups too? (also see the following note).
163. An early Buddhist Pali text, the *Upakkilesasutta* (*Anguttara Nikāya* 4.50) mentions drinking *surā* and *meraya*, along with sex, accepting silver and gold, and wrong livelihood as obstructions/defilements (*upakkilesa*) for ascetics and Brahmins. Although the list differs from the precepts, we see that abstinence from sex and alcohol constitutes an essential component of the ethos for such persons, "leaders in religious life" as the *Pali Text Society Dictionary* translates the compound "ascetics and brahmans." I thank Beatrice Chrystall for this reference.
164. I quote the less commonly seen Sanskrit. From the *Abhidharmakośabhāṣya* 4.34 (which will be discussed later).
165. In the *Mahāprajñāpāramitāśāstra* attributed to Nāgārjuna (c. second century CE), which exists only in a Chinese translation made in year 404 or 405 CE (see Lamotte 1944, vol. 1, preface). In a discussion of the five *śīla*s there is a discussion of liquor (Chapter XXII.5, trans. Lamotte, vol. 2, pp. 816–819, as mentioned by Verpoorten 2009, 36). Explaining the virtue of abstention the author states there are three types of liquor: *surā* from grains, fruit liquor, and herb liquor. An example of the fruit one is that made from grapes and also what appear to be *ariṣṭa*s (*a li tcha* = *ariṣṭaka*). The "herb" one is defined as any herb or plant mixed with ground rice or sugarcane juice. Liquor made from fermented milk, especially that of hooved animals, is also mentioned in this "herb" category—to my knowledge this is the only place milk-liquor is mentioned in Indic sources apart from the use of milk in some Vedic *surā*s. Could this threefold classification be a response to Manu's threefold version or vice versa? (Note I am working from a French translation, seemingly somewhat expanded for clarity, from a Chinese translation of the Indian text). This text also lists thirty-five faults of liquor, which resemble the dangers of drink in texts on vice and in medical texts. Then there follow some verses, again along the lines of others we have seen: the drinker loses intelligence, beauty, shame, memory, families are broken

apart, he laughs and cries when he should not, and so on. Lamotte notes that the list of thirty-five faults is also given in the *Nandikasūtra*. (For that list see Feer 1883, 247–248).

166. Though I understand the compound as implying "the intoxicants *surā* and *maireya*" as does Vasubandhu (see "Buddhist Scholastic Analysis of Drink and Drink Rules" later in this chapter). One might also read it as "*surā*, *maireya*, and intoxicants."
167. Trafford (2009, 11–12) notes that the compound can imply that a person abstains from drinks "which are occasions of heedlessness" or "when they are occasions of heedlessness." (Citing Gombrich 1991, 298). Collins (2015, 204–205) likewise notes the two possible readings of the Pali precept: one undertakes to refrain from consuming certain drinks "because they are the occasion for negligence . . ., or that one does so only in so far as they are an occasion for negligence."
168. *Vinaya* (Pali), *Culla Vagga*, ed. Oldenberg, 1.13.1–2. As mentioned by Ali (1998, 177).
169. The word *majja* is used here, not the *surāmeraya* of the rule. Is this another example of *madya* as liquor-as-worldly-indulgence?
170. Ali 1998, 177.
171. See Heim 2013, 145.
172. On the form of the precept see von Hinüber 1998b. 257–260.
173. On this structure, see von Hinüber 1997, 13.
174. See Ch'en 1945. Also see *Divyāvadāna* (13), where we also read of liquor given to elephants (Bloomfield 1920, 336).
175. All the passages on this rule given here are from *Vinaya* (Pali) *Suttavibhaṅga Pācittiya* 51 (Oldenberg ed.). My translations. Also see Horner's translation.
176. In the narrative portion, prior to stating the rule, the Buddha refers to Sāgata drinking *majja* (*madya*).
177. *Āmalakaphāṇite.*
178. *Kāpotaka* means a grey-white color; *kapota* is a pigeon, and *kapi* a monkey, and these words may be related to Sanskrit words for colors: grey, brown, or perhaps reddish for *kāpotikā*. PTS dictionary, s.v. *kāpotikā*, *kāpotaka*, *kapota*, *kapi*.
179. The PTS dictionary compares this word to *Kāpiśāyana* (wine), which appellation of origin (from Kāpiśī) also resembles *kapiśa*, "reddish brown," writing "a kind of intoxicating drink, or a reddish color." *Kāpotikā* is the also name of the drink in the *Surāpāna Jātaka* (81) version. Might rare *Kāpotikā surā* be a satire on the name of Kāpiśāyana wine, parodying the color/toponym associations of "*Kāpiśāyana*"? Compare: if Canary wine (from the Canary Islands) were still popular, then in a satire someone might describe a glass "overflowing with precious Budgie wine," from the (fictional) Budgerigar Islands.
180. Vinaya (Pali), *Mahāvagga* VI.14.1—2 (Oldenberg's ed.) The term here is *majjam*.
181. Note the Buddhist prohibition of alcohol plays a role in the history of tea in China. (Benn 2015).
182. As described in the *Sāsanavaṃsa*, ed. Bode. See introduction, 26, and text, 80–81. Translated by Law (1952, 88–89). The *Sāsanavaṃsa* was translated into Pali in 1861 from a Burmese text composed in 1831 (von Hinüber 1997, 3).

183. Toddy does not usually require additives, and both *surā* and *maireya* are defined in terms of *sambhāra* in the Pali monastic rule. In early Buddhism, whether monks could drink "*jalogi*" was an important question. Whether *sambhāra* had been added was relevant to some discussions of that question. In the course of writing this book I have not come across anything that can help us understand the word *jalogi* (unless the drink called *jagala* is somehow related, but it probably is not). On the *jalogi* debate, see Verpoorten (2009, 37). Also de la Vallée Poussin 1908, 94–95.
184. See Kieffer-Pülz's study (2005).
185. This also applies for the Theravada texts Kieffer-Pülz analyzes, where there was also discussion as to whether or not drinking was a *paṇṇativajja/paññativajja* (offence of breaking a rule). Questions of intention or mental state when drinking are also important in these texts. Kieffer-Pülz concludes the Theravada commentarial materials that classify drinking as *paṇṇativajja* (breaking a rule) may come from Sri Lanka. The contrary theory applies in South India, and it "is therefore to be assumed that the drinking of alcohol by monks was more strongly rejected in South Indian society than in Sri Lanka." (2005, 174). Though see my comments on this theory later.
186. As Cabezón explains (2017, 180–182).
187. On Vasubandhu see Gold 2018.
188. I have used Pradhan's edition, and my translation and interpretation owes a lot to that of Louis de la Vallée Poussin from the Chinese (including notes by Palmyr Cordier). At an extremely late stage of editing this book I became aware of another extant Sanskrit commentary on this passage, by Sthiramati, who is dated to the sixth century (Kano and Kramer 2020). That commentary (and Kano and Kramer's article) is largely in agreement with my discussion here. I particularly look forward to seeing the later part of that commentary when published, explaining *surā*, *maireya*, and betel/kodo millet. I thank Sonam Kachru for drawing my attention to this piece (personal communication, December 2020).
189. Tatz 1985, 6.
190. *Abhidharmakośabhāṣya* IV.34cd and comments.
191. These terms from common law are a useful comparison: *malum prohibitum* is "wrong merely because it is proscribed; made unlawful by statute." See Garner 1985. I thank Mathew Wrenshall for this observation (personal communication, June 2019).
192. See de la Vallée Poussin's translation for the details of the quotations here.
193. De la Vallée Poussin quotes a passage from the *Sumaṅgalavilāsinī* that describes how when fed a mixture of milk and liquor they only take the milk.
194. Also, at AK *bhāṣya* IV.29 Vasubandhu breaks the eight precepts for days of enhanced lay abstinence into eight limbs in three groups (4+1+3), and there the precept on drinking is the sole *apramādāṅga*.
195. Vasubandhu then explains how liquor leads to a bad rebirth/hell.
196. Some of the comments here are also included in McHugh forthcoming e.
197. The *Vyākhyā* commentary gives "made from sugarcane juice etc." (as quoted by Palmyr Cordier in de la Vallée Poussin's notes). Pradhan's edition gives *dravāsava* which probably implies an *āsava* made from liquids, such as juices as opposed to

solid grains. Here we should recall the class of drinks said to be *drāvita*, "liquified" in Yaśodhara's commentary on *Kāmasūtra* 1.3.15. (See note 31 in "The Ideal Manner of Drinking" in Cup 4). Either way, Vasubandhu understands the words in broad terms. When fully published, the commentary of Sthiramati (see Kano and Kramer 2020) on this passage may clarify this word.

198. Medhātithi discusses the same issues on Manu 11.94.
199. De la Vallée Poussin's translation has that the substances "are called *surā* and *maireya* when they intoxicate." I prefer to read this as limiting the abstinence to liquor and not involving betel and *kodrava*.
200. D'Mello 1997, 307. There is much literature on kodo millet toxicity that I cannot cite here.
201. Meulenbeld (1974, 72) quotes the *Aṣṭāṅgahṛdaya* (*sūtrasthāna* 13.26) where some authorities state that immature matter (*āma*) arises from the humors that are "extraordinarily excited by their mutual coalescence (*anyonyamūrcchanāt*), (in the same way) as a poison arises from *kodrava* grains." (Meulenbeld's translation. The commentary explains the coalescence as *parasparamiśrībhāvāt*).
202. AŚ 4.3.28. Also see AŚ 14.1.9, 13, 16, 22, where it is used in poisons and narcotics. There we also find reference to the straw/stalks (*-palāla*), decoction (*-kvātha*) and powder (*-cūrṇa*) of *madanakodrava*. Olivelle takes the word as a *dvandva* compound, which is reasonable given the separate use of the word *madana* elsewhere, but I believe these other references to intoxicating *kodrava* make a case for reading it as narcotic/stupefying kodo millet.
203. *Haramekhalā* IV.276–279 (Kathmandu ed. which is clearer in this case).
204. *Madhukośa* on *Mādhavanidāna Jvaranidāna* 10–11, ed. Jadavji Tricumji Acharya. My translation. Also see Meulenbeld 1974, 72, 95, 546.
205. *Śārṅg.* I.7.203.
206. Geeta and Gharaibeh 2007.
207. Geeta and Gharaibeh 2007.
208. KS 7.1.25; 7.2.44. Geeta and Gharaibeh mention (2007, 1235) a reference to datura in the *Arthaśāstra*, but in Kangle's edition the word does not occur, though *pattūra* (a known herb) does (at AŚ 2.25.33. And *dhattūra* is not among the variants Kangle gives). Datura is also mentioned at a quite early date, along with *madanakodrava*, in the *Suśrutasaṃhitā* (*cikitsāsthāna* 17.37) though the dating of that text is a complex matter.
209. See previous note.
210. See the usage of datura in the rituals of the *Vajramahābhairava Tantra* (Siklós 1994). Davidson provides a lengthy list of references to datura in Tantric texts (2002, 201, 386 n. 103). No doubt there are many more.
211. See Chapter 9 for datura as *surā* and for the addition of datura to a fermented drink.
212. Hellwig (2012) has some comments on datura. Also see Sangar 1981, 206–207.
213. Kieffer-Pülz 2005, 174.
214. *Jātakamālā*, ed. Kern. My translations of this text. Also see the translation and introduction by Khoroche 1989.
215. On this iconography see Appleton (2017, 28–29).

216. For Borobudur see Krom (1920–, vol. 1: Reliefs, Serie 1.(B).a. Plaat VII, image 59). I thank Sonya Rhie Quintanilla and Katie Blaser at the Cleveland Museum of Art for sharing an image of this scene from a Nepalese *thangka* (Accession no. 1973.69. Right hand border, sixth vignette from the top. Also illustrated in Huntington and Bangdel 2003, 146–149). For a possible image at Ajanta see Schlingloff 1987, 148. Lilian Handlin also kindly shared with me an image of the scene from Pagan, where there are several such images.
217. *Jatakamālā*, *Kumbha Jātaka*, ed. Kern, p. 100, lines 21–22.
218. *Jatakamālā*, *Kumbha Jātaka*, ed. Kern, p. 101, verse 3, lines 1–2.
219. *Jatakamālā*, *Kumbha Jātaka*, ed. Kern, p. 101, verse 4bc, line 5.
220. *Jatakamālā*, *Kumbha Jātaka*, ed. Kern, p. 101, line 9.
221. *Jatakamālā*, *Kumbha Jātaka*, ed. Kern, p. 102, verse 12.
222. *Jātaka* (Pali), *Kumbha Jātaka* (512), ed. Fausbøll, vol. 5, pp. 15–17, verses 37–54.
223. Though in terms of textual history, these verses are earlier than the prose part.
224. The drunken destruction of the clan of Kṛṣṇa and Baladeva is also related in the Pali *Ghata Jātaka* (454) and alluded to in the *Saṃkicca Jātaka* (530). The episode is also mentioned the *Life of the Buddha* (*Buddhacarita* 11.31) of Aśvaghoṣa, where the Buddha-to-be, in a speech condemning passions and sense pleasures, asks what self-possessed person would delight in pleasures (*kāmeṣu*), which led to the destruction (*vināśam*) of various figures, including the Vṛṣṇis and Andhakas.
225. My translation. I translate the third-person singular as "you."
226. Possibly a Jain.
227. Khoroche notes several manuscripts have *paṇyatām* (*upagatā*) here (1987, 40).
228. *Jātakamālā*, *Kumbha Jātaka*, ed. Kern, verses 14–16. My translation.
229. This is a reorganization of the speech from the Pali version (as we possess it), where the epic and mythological references are placed at the end.
230. Compare *Bhagavad Gītā* 1.41 for women as an essential link in scenarios of social decline.
231. Khoroche (1987) notes several manuscripts give *vismṛta* (not *vismita*).
232. *Jātakamālā*, *Kumbha Jātaka*, ed. Kern, verses 17–19. My translation.
233. *Jātakamālā*, *Kumbha Jātaka*, ed. Kern, verse 23.
234. *Jātakamālā*, *Kumbha Jātaka*, ed. Kern, verse 26ab.
235. *Jātakamālā*, *Kumbha Jātaka*, ed. Kern, verse 27.
236. *Jātaka* (Pali), *Kumbha Jātaka* (512), ed. Fausbøll, vol. 5, p. 20.
237. If we consider these speeches and also the lists of thirty-five evils of drink.
238. I largely rely on Williams 1963.
239. See *Ācārāṅga Sūtra* II.1.8.8 for prohibition on accepting *majja* (*madya*). In a Jain context when *mahu*/*madhu* is forbidden this would (always?) be honey, prohibited owing to the bees killed in collecting it. The *Ācārāṅga Sūtra* (II.1.8.1) contains a list of drinks (*pāṇaga*) made from fruit that monks may not accept (*aphāsuya*), including grapes (*muddiyā*), date (*khajjūra*), pomegranate (*dālima*), and coconut (*nāliera*). If this passage dates from the first or second century BCE then this is yet another rather early reference to grapes (wine?), dating approximately from the period when the other early references appear. Also, is the coconut one toddy or coconut water drink? On the date of the *Ācārāṅga Sūtra* see Dundas 2002, 23.

240. K. R. Chandra's *Prākṛta-Hindī Koś* has *soṃḍā*. See Jacobi (*Jaina Sūtras*, 1968, 93 n. 2) on the "*saṃkhaḍi*," which seems to be connected with the preparation of food, yet this is clearly a type of event that monks should avoid, possibly some sort of "feast" in the broadest sense of that word. Schubring translates as a "general/public feeding" (1935, 173).
241. Jacobi's translation. *Ācārāṅga Sūtra* II.1.3.2. For the Prakrit see Jacobi's edition.
242. On the great vows see Dundas 2002, 158–159.
243. In the clause about liquors and seasoned foods *pāṇīyarasabhoyaṇabhoī* is mentioned in vow 4, clause 4, *Ācārāṅga Sūtra* II.15 (ed. Jacobi, Part 1, p. 135). Jacobi, who knew these texts very well, translates the first part of the compound as "liquors" though it is notable that the form used is not (a Prakrit form of) *madya*, *surā*, or something else explicitly intoxicating (*Ācārāṅga Sūtra*, trans. Jacobi, Part 1, 208). There is no room here to consider other Jain texts on ascetic conduct.
244. In one Jain classification of types of food, into ten *vikṛtis* (transformed foods), we read of *madya* of two types, that made from sugarcane juice, and that made from grains—a more limited classification than Manu's three-fold one, but similar to the Buddhist interpretations of *surā* and *maireya* (Williams 1963, 39–40). Drinking is also a *vyasana*, one of seven that include eating meat (Williams 1963, 54).
245. Jain authorities distinguish between things used once or internally, such as garlands and food, called *upabhogas* by the Śvetāmbaras, though Hemacandra, along with the Digambaras, calls these items *bhogas*, which are contrasted with things used repeatedly or externally, called *paribhogas* by the Śvetāmbaras. Hemacandra, along with the Digambaras, calls these latter things *upabhogas*. See Williams (1963, 102).
246. Though betel in Jainism is not straightforward. As it is forbidden to take at night, the implication is that it is accepted in the day (Williams 1963, 108). Yet Āśādhara forbids the eating of areca nuts (Williams 1963, 112–113). Haribhadra advises against *excessive* betel (Williams 1963, 129). Devagupta classes eating betel as a useful type of harmful action, along with eating (Williams 1963, 130) and betel is generally classed as a type of food, though sometimes as an adornment (Williams 1963, 143). In observing a vow called the *sāmāyika vrata* a king or rich man has to lay aside his betel (Williams 1963, 133), implying they otherwise use it. For Hemacandra, one of the fields (*kṣetras*) of generosity (*dāna*) is laymen, one's co-religionists to whom one can give betel (Williams 1963, 165). Betel is offered in some Jain *pūjas* (Williams 1963, 223, 224), and distributed in certain life cycle rites (Williams 1963, 277, 280).
247. Williams 1963, 11–12.
248. *Yogaśāstra* of Hemacandra (with *Svopajñavritti* commentary), ed. Muni Jambuvijaya (Delhi: Motilal Banarsidass, 2009). I have also referred to Quarnström's translation.
249. Williams 1963, 11, 26.
250. On this distinctive use of the word *rasa* in the sense of alcohol (and these other materials for Hemacandra) see Williams 1963, 119.
251. *Yogaśāstra* of Hemacandra, III.107–108. My translation.
252. Or *bāhya*-, external souls?
253. Hemacandra quotes several *śloka* verses at the end of his commentary on *Yogaśāstra* III.8–17, the first of which states: "Numerous living beings are produced of alcoholic

drink (*rasa*), therefore one afraid of the sin of inflicting violence should not drink intoxicating drink."

254. Hemacandra glosses this as *madirā*.
255. Although Hemacandra explains the verse thus, I suspect there is a hint of the drunk, naked man exposing his private parts (*gūḍha*).
256. Hemacandra glosses this as *madyapāna*.
257. Hemacandra glosses this as *surā*.
258. The poison produced at the churning of the ocean. According to Apte (2003) *hālahalī* and *hālāhalī* can refer to liquor. Coincidentally (or maybe not) Hālāhalā (f.) is a character in another Jain story involving liquor that I should also mention: Makkhali Gosāla was a former pupil of Mahāvīra, the most recent Jain Fordmaker, who became his arch-enemy. Gosāla was proud and jealous, wielding magic powers he had learned from Mahāvīra, and proclaiming himself an omniscient being. He even tried to turn these powers, a special "heat," on Mahāvīra but they literally bounced back, after which Gosāla's days were numbered. Then he returned to the house of a potter woman called Hālāhalā where he began to act very strangely, drinking liquor (Hemacandra's version: *madyaṃ*), singing, dancing, joining his hands in respect, and smearing himself with clay. A follower who visited him was disturbed by this behavior and in response to this Gosāla's disciples diplomatically and pragmatically explained that this behavior was actually a sign of Gosāla attaining enlightenment. Thus a damaged, proud, heretical teacher's bizarre, drunken swan-song was proclaimed a sign of enlightenment by this misguided group. My account is based on Hemacandra's version, *Triṣaṣṭiśalākāpuruṣacarita* 10.8.434–470, Prasārakasabhā Sanskrit ed. Also see Johnson's translation, vol. VI, 220 for the death. See the earliest version in the *Viyāhapannatti* (summary by Deleu, 218). On the eight "finalities," as understood by this sect, which include the five delirious actions, see Basham (1981, 61–62, 68, 254–255). I thank Surendra Bothra for this reference (personal communication, Jaipur, January 2017).
259. *Yogaśāstra* III.8–17. My translation.
260. On the date and work of Āśādhara see Williams 1963, 26–28. On writers emphasizing the *hiṃsā* involved in making and drinking liquor see Williams 1963, 54.
261. A less common word for intoxicating drink, given also in Amara (2.10.40). Apte (2003) gives the derivation from *kaśā*, "whip," so "fit to be whipped," and referring to intoxicating drink as well as to a horse's flank.
262. *Sāgaradharmāmṛta* of Āśādhara II.4–5. As discussed in Williams 1963, 54.
263. Certain other fermented foods are prohibited for the same reason: non-clarified butter (*navanīta*) and fermented gruels (Williams 1963, 105–106, 112. Also *Yogaśāstra* III.34–35.) Sexual activity is likewise given a micro-organismic interpretation and said by several authorities to kill myriads of tiny living creatures inside the bodies of women (Williams 1963, 91–92).
264. *Yaśastilaka* of Somadeva. On Somadeva see Williams 1963, 21. For the materials on alcohol see Williams 1963, 54. On this text as a whole see Handiqui 1968. For the materials on alcohol also see Handiqui (1968, 262), and for these two narratives see Handiqui 1968, 418–419.

265. Williams 1963, 50–55.
266. *Yaśastilaka Āśvāsa* 7, *Uttarakhaṇḍa* (vol. 2, p. 327 in *Yaśastilaka*, ed. Śivadatta and Paṇaśikar). My translation.
267. The story is also mentioned in the verses Hemacandra quotes at the end of his commentary on *Yogaśāstra* III.8–17 (verse 6 of quoted verses).
268. These two narratives are given at *Yaśastilaka Āśvāsa* 7 (vol. 2, pp. 327–329). Handiqui summarizes them (1968, 418–419).
269. Another list of sinful transgressive Ms. Note there is also a Jain stock list—*māṃsa* (meat), *madhu* (honey), and *madya* (liquor)—explicitly known as the three *makāras* (Williams 1963, 53–54).
270. Part of the text would appear to be missing but the sense is clear.
271. See also *Yaśastilaka Āśvāsa* 4 (vol. 2, p. 118) where Yaśodhara argues, against his mother, that Hindu scriptures are self-contradicting in similar language.
272. Though recall that for Hemacandra Jains are forbidden to trade in *dhātakī* flowers.
273. AH *Cikitsasthāna* 7.57: *madhumādhavamaireyasīdhugauḍāsavādi-*.
274. AH *Cikitsasthāna* 7.54–57.
275. On the date of Dṛḍhabala see HIML IA, 139–141. On this passage as composed by Dṛḍhabala see HIML IA, 132–133.
276. CS *Cikitsāsthāna* 24.3–10. My translation, consulting Cakrapāṇidatta's commentary.
277. Cakrapāṇidatta on CS *Cikitsāsthāna* 24.7 has "in the form of . . . ," *-rūpeṇa*.
278. According to MW, Puṣṭi is also deified, but if Nirvṛti is so personified she is not, to my knowledge, as prominent a figure as Surā and Rati et al.
279. CS *Cikitsāsthāna* 24.207.
280. *Mattavilāsaprahasana* of Mahendravikramavarman, ed. Gaṇapatiśāstrī. For the whole play see Lorenzen's translation.
281. See Ferstl, "Overlooked Material" (forthcoming).
282. A term he uses later in the scene. *Mattavilāsaprahasana*, ed. Gaṇapatiśāstrī, p. 16.
283. *Mattavilāsaprahasana*, ed. Gaṇapatiśāstrī, p. 12.
284. *Mattavilāsaprahasana*, ed. Gaṇapatiśāstrī, p. 12.
285. *Piḍäaputthaesu* = *piṭakapustakeṣu*.
286. *Aviṇaṭṭhamūḷapāṭhaṃ* = *avinaṣṭamūlapāṭhaṃ*.
287. *Mattavilāsaprahasana*, trans. Lorenzen p. 89. Gaṇapatiśāstrī ed., p. 12.
288. *Mattavilāsaprahasana*, trans. Lorenzen p. 92.
289. Modifying Lorenzen's translation, p. 92. *Mattavilāsaprahasana*, ed. Gaṇapatiśāstrī, p. 20.
290. *Madhu* is said to be bee's honey (*makkhikāmadhu*). *Vinaya* (Pali), *Nissaggiyā Pācittiyā* 23. ed. Oldenberg, vol. 3, p. 251.
291. *Vinaya* (Pali), *Mahāvagga*, *Bhesajjakkhandhaka* VI.35, ed. Oldenberg, vol. 1, p. 246.
292. *Samantapāsādikā* of Buddhaghosa, on *Mahāvagga Bhesajjakkhandhaka* VI.35, ed. Takakusu and Nagai, p. 1102.
293. *Āgamaḍambara* of Jayanta Bhaṭṭa, 1.84–85. My translation.
294. *Dhūrtaviṭasaṃvāda*, pp. 399–411.
295. *Dhūrtaviṭasaṃvāda* (p. 408). My translation.
296. BKŚS 16.74b. My translation.

297. *Bhāvaprakāśa, Pūrvakhaṇḍa, Madyavarga*, 35.
298. *Strychnos potatorum* Linn.
299. *Haramekhalā Pariccheda* 1.45. Kṛṣṇaprasāda Śarma ed. My translation.
300. The verses on qualities other than color may be from a later date. See Alsdorf (1966, 215–220) on this passage as a later expansion/addition of the older verses that give only colors. If we understand *mahu* as grape wine, that might help date the additions to around the time of the *Arthaśāstra* references? Assuming *mahu* here is not honey or mead.
301. *Uttaradhyāyanasūtra* 34.16.
302. Compared to orpiment and turmeric (*Uttaradhyāyanasūtra* 34.8ab), thus implying a color we would call "yellow" in English.
303. *Uttaradhyāyanasūtra* 34.14. My translation. See also Jacobi's translation (1968). I read the text's *mahu* as *madhu*, hence the tentative translation as "wine."
304. Böhtlingk und Fritze 1880, vol. 3, no. 7562, 7563. As quoted in Aalto (1959, 27). I have not been able to trace this proverb further.
305. Jamison 2019, 19.
306. Davis 2011, 162.
307. Olivelle 2012, 172. I thank Patrick Olivelle for drawing my attention to this matter (personal communication, June 2020).
308. Olivelle 2012, 172–173.
309. Olivelle 2012, 176.
310. *Chāndogya Upaṇiṣad* 5.11.5. This is the only such utopia I am aware of in Hindu sources.
311. Xuanzang, trans. Li Rongxi, 55.
312. On this realm of the law, see Davis 2005.
313. See Boyd White (1985) on law as constitutive rhetoric.

CUP 8

1. *Mattavilāsaprahasana*, ed. Gaṇapatiśāstrī, p. 11.
2. *Mattavilāsaprahasana*, ed. Gaṇapaṭiśāstrī, p.9.
3. *Mattavilāsaprahasana*, trans. Lorenzen, 83.
4. Ferstl 2011 and Ferstl forthcoming. I thank Shaman Hatley for pointing out that we do have evidence of female Atimārga Kāpālikā initiates—the female character, Devasomā, in the *Mattavilāsaprahasana* is such an initiate.
5. Based on Sanderson 2018 (lecture and handout). Also Sanderson 2015b.
6. On ascetics in the Mantramārga, see Sanderson 2015b, 16.
7. Sanderson 1991, 3–5.
8. Cf. Sanderson 2015b.
9. *Khārjūrī ripunāśinī. Kulārṇava Tantra* 5.33ab. The fifth *Ullāsa* is this text deals with the five Ms (about which more later), including *madya*, intoxicating drink. This particular drink could be date-palm toddy or date-fruit liquor.
10. Sanderson 1988, 660.

11. On *ali* see Ch. 8, note 59.
12. The last word being conjectural. Sanderson's translation of *Niśisaṃcāra* fol. 7v1–3, given in Sanderson 2005, 112–113, n. 63. I have changed the translation of the word *ali* (on which more later) for the sake of consistency in my own translations.
13. In the context of Tantric Buddhism we also see how liquor may be forbidden but not repellant. Christian Wedemeyer quotes a text where the accomplished Tantric Buddhist practitioner is said to transcend dualities. Such a person perceives the loved and hated as alike: "As oneself, so an enemy . . . As urine, so liquor (*madya*) . . ." Wedemeyer 2007, 404. I have changed Wedemeyer's "wine" to liquor. He is quoting the *Pañcakrama* of Nāgārjuna.
14. *Jayadrathayāmala*, *Ṣaṭka* 4, fols. 206v3–207v5 (*Vīratāṇḍavavidhipaṭala* vv. 5–30b). As quoted and translated in Sanderson 2007, 284–287, and see 280–288 for a discussion of this form of worship in other texts.
15. Sanderson 2007, 287.
16. Sanderson (2007, 280–282) notes a reference in the *Rājataraṅgiṇī* to a certain Brahmin ascetic being punished for such worship.
17. See Sanderson 1995, 78–83 for some of the uses of liquor in a variety of rituals.
18. As collected in Törzsök 2007.
19. Törzsök's translation modified for drink terminology (2007, 466).
20. As noted by Törzsök (2007, 466): *Kulasāra* (fol. 70r) *sautrāmaṇyaṃ surāpānaṃ*. . . .
21. *Tantrāloka* 4.264ab, as noted by Törzsök (2007, 467).
22. The text later defines *mādhavī* as twofold, from grapes (*drākṣī*), and from dates (*khārjūrikā*). See following note for citation.
23. *Brahmayāmala*. National Archives Kathmandu manuscript no. 3-370 (Nepal-German Manuscript Preservation Project microfilm reel A42/6). Transcription courtesy of Shaman Hatley. This passage is verse 131ab of chapter 24, the *Guhyāmṛtapaṭala*, in Hatley's transcription, which section also contains the recipes for liquors.
24. "[W]ithout definitely ruling out the sixth and ninth." Hatley 2018, 139. The *Hārītasaṃhitā*, a medical text, likewise unpacks the details of a manyfold *surā*, though that presents an expanded fourfold *surā*. *Hārītasaṃhitā* (ed. Raiṣon) I.19.
25. The *five* Ms are described for example in the *Kulārṇavatantra*. For a translation of selections see Brooks 2000, 350–351, 354–355.
26. See Jayaratha on TĀ 29.98bc, which notes the three "labials," i.e., Ms. Also Jayaratha on TĀ 15.170.
27. Manu 5.56. Olivelle's translation, modified.
28. Jayaratha on TĀ 29.98bc. See also Sanderson 2013a, 18–19; Sanderson 2015a, 166–167, n. 27.
29. For example the observance of the widow in BDS 2.4.7 (See "Dharmasūtras" in Chapter 7). In the *Śāntiparvan* of the *Mahābhārata* in a discussion of non-violence we find the following statement with some Ms: "meat, honey, *surā*, fish, *āsava*, and sesame-rice—this was instigated by rogues—it is not intended in the Vedas." *māṃsaṃ madhu surā matsyā āsavaṃ kṛsaraudanam | dhūrtaiḥ pravartitaṃ hy etan naitad vedeṣu kalpitam* || (MBh. 12.257.9). On this line, see Aldorf 2010, 41.
30. *Yaśastilaka Uttarakhaṇḍa*, *Āśvāsa* 7 (vol. 2, p. 327 in Śivadatta and Paṇaśikar ed.).

31. For an accessible short introduction to the life and works of Abhinavagupta, see Sanderson 1987.
32. On the date of Jayaratha, see Sanderson 2007, 418–419.
33. Sanderson 1995, 16.
34. Sanderson 1995, 47.
35. Sanderson 1995, 17. I have removed the Sanskrit terms from this quotation.
36. Sanderson 1987, 9.
37. Sanderson (1995, 78–83) gives many references to Abhinavagupta on liquor and drinking.
38. TĀ 4.246ab. As quoted by Sanderson 2013b.
39. Sanderson 1995, 84. My clarifications in brackets.
40. Sanderson 1995, 48.
41. Sanderson 1995, 87.
42. TĀ 15.163cd; 167cd–168ab. As translated in Sanderson (2013a, 18–19).
43. TĀ 15.170 ab.
44. TĀ 29.10–13. My translations of TĀ and commentary unless otherwise stated. I have consulted Gnoli's TĀ translation, and also the analysis and translations in Dupuche (2003). I thank Shaman Hatley for comments on some of my translations. All mistakes and misunderstandings are my own.
45. An esoteric name for alcohol according to Gnoli in his translation here.
46. Gnoli suggests *bhairava* is an adjective here, though the texts Jayaratha quotes might suggest otherwise. Also, liquor is sometimes worshiped as Bhairava, Madyabhairava or Ānandabhairava, in ritual (see Sanderson 2007, 286; Bühnemann 2017, 247).
47. Dupuche (2003, 186 n. 9) citing Minoru Hara, notes that "beloved of the gods" can also mean "legitimate, or blood-related to god." Citing Hara 1969.
48. See also the entry on *kṛtrima* in the *Tāntrikābhidhānakośa*.
49. See "Grape Wine" in Cup 2.
50. This is also supported by the fact that when the orders of the drinks in Abhinavagupta (grain, honey, jaggery = f., n., m.) are rearranged in the verse quoted by Jayaratha (grain, jaggery, honey = f., m., n.), the genders listed are rearranged in the same order. Also, in terms of raw materials *kṣaudram* in the sense of honey is neuter, and *guḍaḥ*, jaggery, is masculine. Grain *surā* is almost always feminine: *prasannā*, *paiṣṭī*, *vāruṇī*, etc. This form is apparently the most powerful of the three—and is the most forbidden in *dharmaśāstra*.
51. Dupuche 2003, 88. Also citing Gnoli 1985, 292.
52. Though the praise of wine here may be derived from the Tantra Jayaratha quotations, which I have not been able to identify (nor can Dupuche). In any case wine was prestigious, if *not* a source of local pride, even outside Kashmir.
53. E.g., Bilhaṇa, *Vikramāṅkadevacarita* 18.72. I thank Whitney Cox for this reference (personal communication).
54. Possibly a variety of plantain (which are often said to be dark), though bananas/plantains are not associated with the region. Gnoli (TĀ trans., p. 639) is also uncertain.
55. TĀ 37.42–44. My translation, referring closely to Gnoli's translation. I translate *madya* as wine given the context.

56. *Gurunāthaparāmarśa*, verse 4. As quoted by Gnoli, TĀ trans., p. lxxvii. *Saraka* is the editor's emendation and the reading *-karaka* is attested in two manuscripts. *Karaka* would be some sort of small jar/jug, which would work perfectly well too.
57. A third type of drinking "penance" is mentioned in humorous literary texts. In the *Dhūrtaviṭasaṃvāda* some *madirā* is offered to a woman as a *prāyaścittam* (Dezsö and Vasudeva ed., pp. 350–351). Likewise in the *Pādatāḍitaka* a *mayda-prāyaścitta* is prescribed (though Dezsö and Vasudeva note this line in their edition is conjectural). (pp. 148–149).
58. As quoted by Jayaratha for TĀ 29.11–13.
59. *Ali* means "bee" and also "alcoholic drink." S.v. *ali* in *Tāntrikābhidhānakośa*. I have not seen this word in this sense outside Tantric texts and lexica. For example, Böhtlingk and Roth (1855–1875, s.v. *ali*) note the word as attested in this sense in several lexica, e.g., *Medinīkośa* (*Lāntavarga* 2) where has it in the sense of *surā*. Bhattacharya notes the word *ali* and similar forms in the sense of liquor in Munda languages (1966, 31). Note also that Burrow and Emeneau (1984, s.v. *ari* 219) have *ari* in Tamil in the sense of fermented liquor or toddy.
60. I rely here on Sanderson 2009.
61. As quoted by Sanderson 2009: *Cintyaviśya* quoted in *Dīkṣādarśa* of Vedajñana II. A (Institut français de Pondichéry [IFP] Transcript 76), p. 24; B (IFP Transcript 153), p. 38.
62. As noted by Sanderson 2009. For example: *Parākhya* cited by Trilocanaśiva in *Prāyaścittasamuccaya* (IFP Transcript 284), p. 141.
63. Quoted by Sanderson 2009. The *kalyapāla* called Māhila from Kundāpura in Oḍḍadeśa is apparently mentioned in the *Nityāhnikatilaka* of Muktaka NAK MS 3-384 (palm-leaf; Newari script; 1453 CE), fols. 17v5–24r2. A *karavālaḥ* called Jayadeva from Vahapura is listed in the *Ciñciṇīkaulānāṃ gurusaṃtatiḥ* (in NAK MS 4-304).
64. On the representation of Tantra in the *Rājataraṅgiṇī* see Törzsök 2012.
65. A general background sense of Brahminical abstinence is also the basis for the symbolism, or more specifically, the "connotative semiotics," of alcohol in Tantric Buddhist rituals in Christian Wedemeyer's account (Wedemeyer 2012). Though as we saw above, liquor is clearly forbidden in Buddhist texts too.
66. Sanderson 2013b.
67. Though in some rituals unappetizing substances may correspond to the appetites of certain fierce beings.
68. My discussion complements Bühnemann's paper (2017). The passage I quote is not an iconographic program or visualization but a narrative, explanatory account of her deeds (and she could not hand out the drinks if she were holding all the attributes given in many of Bühnemann's sources.)
69. My principal source is the edition of Kak and Śāstrī, *Paṭala* 19. Also the same text with a Hindi translation by Kapiladeva Narayana. Finally, the greater part of the *Devīrahasya* passages I translate here are quoted in the *Haṃsavilāsa* of Haṃsamiṭṭhu (pp. 309–313), and notable variants in that version are marked as "H." I will not attempt a critical edition of this passage here, though.

70. Sanderson writes that this text "which was well known in Kashmir, contains no trace of the terminology of Kashmirian non-dualism and appears to be East Indian in character, though it was probably composed or revised in Kashmir since it has integrated the local Kashmirian goddesses into its pantheon." (2007, 408). Also see Sanderson 2014, 81–82.
71. Published in Losty 2019, 72–73. I thank Siddhartha Shah for alerting me to this image (personal communication). There are quite a few differences from the iconography given in the text here, but the nine cups and nine jars carried by a Śaiva goddess emerging from the water is telling. Also, tellingly, Losty writes that an image that seems to be from the same format-series depicts Sadāśiva (Losty 2019, 72).
72. That is not to say that the longer narrative appeared for the first time in this this text. Parts of this may have originated elsewhere, but I am interested here in this as an attested text read in the light of the culture and discourses of alcohol, and less in textual history within Tantra.
73. H. *smaraṇa*-.
74. Often translated as "vessel" this is a likely a drinking cup here, filled up from the larger jars (*kumbha*) in the other arms.
75. H. *ratnāṅgulīya*-. The other texts, *raktā*-.
76. *Devīrahasya*, 19.1–7.
77. For a French translation of one version of this gemstone origin-myth see Finot 1896, 4–6.
78. *Khadira* is *Acacia catechu*, the source of an astringent resin used in betel-wraps.
79. *Tryūṣanādya*: dried ginger, black pepper, and long pepper and other spices relevant in this context.
80. On the ten goddesses called the Mahāvidyās in this text see Sanderson 2007, 408, n. 588.
81. I am not sure how to take the word *bhadantī* here. H. has *tadante*.
82. *Devīrahasya*, 19.8–16ab.
83. *Nāgavallarī* is a name for the betel-leaf vine—though that primordial plant, *ahivallarī*, is connected to the wrong drugs here.
84. By way of comparison, the Tantric Buddhist *Saṃvarodayatantra* contains another classification of intoxicating drink that is worth quoting (26.31–33):

> According to how it arose on the surface of the earth, it is made from substances (*dravyajā*), from roots, from jaggery, ground-grains, and made from *madhva*, made from trees, and made from sugarcane.
>
> It is said that there are five types of *mādhvī* (grape-wine/honey/mahua—probably wine), and taught that grain-based [*surā*] is eightfold, and there are seven varieties of jaggery-based [*surā*]—this list is established.
>
> They originate in various lands and there is the designation "*madya*" ("intoxicating drink").
>
> It is strong, bitter, pungent, sweet, and unctuous.

Compare *dravyajā* to the Vasubandhu's *dravyāsava* in "Buddhist Scholastic Analysis of Drink and Drink Rules" in Cup 7. My translation using the Sanskrit edition in Tsuda 1970.

85. *Devīrahasya* 19.16bc–19ab. The last line is absent from H. See the next section, "Enter Cannabis," for this line.
86. Unclear, possibly honey-based drinks?
87. *Devīrahasya* 19.19bc–21ab.
88. *Phyllanthus emblica* L.
89. *Devīrahasya* 19.21bc–23ab.
90. Several other authorities state *guḍapuṣpa* is *madhūka*; see HIML IIB, 104, n. 94.
91. Taking the text in H. which has *bādāmaka*; the other editions have *bhādāmaka*.
92. *Devīrahasya* 19.23bc–29.
93. *Devīrahasya* 19.30–35.
94. Emending *pañcavyomaśarīriṇāṃ to -śarīriṇā*, this term referring to Śiva/Bhairava. I thank Shaman Hatley for this suggestion.
95. The feminine equivalent of a *mantra* (m.) is called a *vidyā*. This particular *vidyā* was also a goddess associated with early and Tantric traditions of snakebite curing. See Slouber (website) on *bheruṇḍa*.
96. *Devīrahasya* 22.1–32ab.
97. The probable reference to cannabis in a play, the *Dhūrtasamāgama*, is an exception, though the consumer there is a religious ascetic. See Wujastyk 2002, 60–61. Also see the discussion later in this section.
98. Wujastyk 2002, 47.
99. Principally: Meulenbeld 1989; Wujastyk 2002; Hellwig 2012; Sangar 1981; Dutt 1922.
100. Meulenbeld 1989, 59–70, 60–61. Also see *bhaṅgā* in Meulenbeld 1984, 104.
101. Meulenbeld 1989, 61, n. 2.
102. Meulenbeld 1989, 61, n. 3. According to Wujastyk (2002, 56) cannabis the drug is always feminine in Sanskrit.
103. Meulenbeld 1989, 62.
104. On this date: HIML IIA, 228.
105. See Wujastyk 2002 and Meulenbeld 1989.
106. Wujastyk 2002, 56–59.
107. Meulenbeld 1989, 64. Wujasyk 2002 expands the list of clear early references. Also see Dutt on cannabis (1922, 236–242), and Sanderson (see the following paragraph).
108. Hellwig 2012, 464–465.
109. Hattox 1985. And we should not assume that finds such as that reported by Ren et al. (2019) from 500 BCE in the Eastern Pamir region are evidence of widespread usage that is not reported elsewhere.
110. Sanderson 2003, n. 43. Sanderson's note is a mine of useful information.
111. I am grateful to James Mallinson for providing me with a .pdf of this play, though I am unable to say the origin of this particular edition (and during the COVID19 epidemic it has proved impossible to access a printed version). Also see Wujastyk 2002, 60–61.
112. See Wujastyk (2002, 63) for a list of types of users from the *Ānandakanda*. On the date of this text see HIML IIA, 592.
113. On the date of the text in question, see Rosenthal 1971.
114. Or 1463 CE—see Rosenthal 1971, 146–147.

115. Rosenthal 1971, 177–179; 155.
116. Shahnavaz 1984.
117. Sanderson 2003, n. 43.
118. Sanderson 2003, n. 43, discussing *Sarvollāsa* 30.47–48.
119. Sanderson 2003, n. 43.
120. Sanderson 2003, n. 43, discussing Bhaṭṭārakasvāmin's *Spandapradīpikā*.
121. Dutt 1922, 239. As quoted in Wujastyk 2002, 65–66.
122. Carstairs 1979, 305. I will not consider other references to modern uses of *bhāṅg*, such as in Holi.
123. Mallinson 2007, 7–8.
124. Mallinson 2007, 171, n. 34.
125. See Ch. 8, note 118.
126. Sanderson 2014, 26, n. 97.
127. *Sarvollāsa* of Sarvānandanātha 16.2.
128. Though the picture is complex, as one would expect in a large compendium. Still, as Pratapaditya Pal presents this material it is clear that according to this text Brahmins were not to use liquor in rituals (Pal 1981, 16–17).
129. As noted by Hellwig (2012, 467). Also Wujastyk 2002, 66. A lexicon of *materia medica*, the *Rājavallabhanighaṇṭu*, also mentions the arising of *vijayā* in the churning of the ocean of milk. See Wujastyk 2002, 64.
130. *Ānandakanda* 1.15.318.
131. *Ānandakanda* 1.15.319–321.
132. *Ānandakanda* 1.15.322.
133. *Ānandakanda* 1.15.322–330.
134. The word *varṇa* is used primarily in the sense of "color" here, and the social *varṇa*s are not mentioned. In the *Sarvollāsa*, however, a text we saw earlier, we find another classification of cannabis by *varṇa*, and these plants are indeed the same colors, white, red, yellow, and black, commonly associated with the human *varṇa*s. *Sarvollāsa* 30.43–44.
135. *Ānandakanda* 1.15.331–335ab.
136. *Ānandakanda* 1.15.335bc–336ab.
137. For the full list see Hellwig 2012, 467.
138. *Ānandakanda* 1.15.385–484
139. *Ānandakanda* 1.15.485–486ab. Wujastyk lists all the stages.
140. *Ānandakanda* 1.15.492.
141. *Haṃsavilāsa*, pp. 314–317. I have not been able to find this in an edition of the *Padmapurāṇa* itself.
142. *Haṃsavilāsa*, p. 314, verse 2.
143. Or "his knowledge gone to darkness and inertia."
144. *Padmapurāṇa* as quoted in *Haṃsavilāsa*, p. 316, verses 31–35. My translation.
145. The āyurvedic pharmaceutical qualities were also well established—see Wujastyk 2002.
146. For example, it is mentioned by Mādhavakavi, probably in the twelfth century CE, which Meulenbeld believes is one of the earliest references (HIML IIA, 189–191;

HIML IIB, 220). Meulenbeld appears to be noncommittal regarding P. V. Sharma's claim that opium is mentioned in the *Gadanigraha* (HIML IIA, 216), but this makes little difference to the date in this case. See also Meulenbeld 1984, 95–96. Vaṅgasena (1050–1100) compares cannabis to opium, Wujastyk 2002, 57.

147. *Ānandakanda* 2.1.292.
148. As Mayrhofer writes this is ultimately from Greek *opion* via Arabic *afjūn* (and probably other intermediary forms). EWA, Part 3, s.v. *ahiphena*.
149. Note the word in my edition is in fact *aphena*. *Ānandakanda* 2.1.287–288. As noted by Meulenbeld (HIML IIA, 590). Also see Hellwig 2012, 467.
150. Cox 2017, 169–170.
151. Davidson 2002, 257–262.
152. As quoted in the *Haṃsavilāsa* (p. 308). As discussed and also translated by Vasudeva 2012, 250. I provide my own re-translation for liquor-term-consistency.
153. SII, vol. III, parts 1–4, 1929. No. 66, "Inscription at Kolar," pp. 136–139.
154. Of course liquor is used in many rituals less regulated by any sort of Sanskritic traditions, but I cannot consider these here. Such worship must be ancient. For example, in the Pali *Jātaka* collection we read of *surā* offered left in the open (*-bali-*) on the seashore along with milk, rice pudding, fish, and meat for divine serpent beings, *nāgas*. Recall here that Balarāma, Kṛṣṇa's brother who is known to like a drink, has a close connection to *nāgas*. Another *Jātaka* mentions people in a city leaving offerings (*-bali-*) for *yakṣas* (*yakkhas*) consisting of meat and fish and *surā* in small bowls. (*Kāka Jātaka* [146]; *Sigāla Jātaka* [113]).

CUP 9

1. From the *Metamorphosis of Tobacco* (1602) as quoted in *Wine, Beere, Ale, and Tobacco* (p. 51, n. 559).
2. See HIML IIA, 467–470. Also Meulenbeld 1981.
3. See "Later Developments" in Chapter 3.
4. See "Later Developments" in Chapter 3 for *Gadanigraha*. Also *Arkaprakāśa* I.80 (p. 15 of the Tripāṭhī ed.). The unpublished *Anup Gandhasāra* (folio 22b.) of uncertain date (mid-second millennium? See McHugh 2012, 117–118) has two recipes using the term, for example the perfume called *covā*: ". . . *sarvaṃ ekatra kṛtvā tāmrapātre nidhāya pātālayantreṇa jalaṃ niṣkāsya covā rājayogyo bhavati*," though I am uncertain whether the distilled water is discarded. Note that the "essence" produced by distillation is also known as a *sattva* in alchemical texts (Hellwig 2009a, 349, 373).
5. Orta 1913, *Colloqy* 16, p. 140.
6. E.g., Mitra 1873, 16.
7. HIML IIA, 333–336.
8. *Bhaiṣajyaratnāvalī* 74.386.

9. *Bhaiṣajyaratnāvalī* 74.372–386. Mitra also quotes this recipe but does not give his source, and his version, while it shares some stanzas with that in my edition of the *Bhaiṣajyaratnāvalī*, is different. (1873, 19–20). I am not aware of earlier versions of this recipe.
10. Ray 1906. J. C. Ray was based at Ravenshaw College, Cuttack (Anonymous 1907, 308–309).
11. Ray 1906, 130.
12. Ray 1906, 134.
13. Ray adds that the previous year "preparation of rice spirit has been discontinued," so in 1905 (Ray 1906, 130).
14. *Haṃsavilāsa* of Haṃsamiṭṭhu. Vasudeva 2012.
15. I summarize Vasudeva's account of the system here.
16. Vasudeva 2012, 245.
17. *Haṃsavilāsa*, p. 314, line 1.
18. Liquor was made of fire in the TĀ, as discussed earlier, but not necessarily because it burns.
19. For the date of around 1400, see Sanderson 2014, 81. Goudriaan and Gupta (1981, 146–147) place the compiler in the sixteenth century.
20. Khandelwal translates as *gāñjā*. The drug is also mentioned at *Sarvollāsa* 30.13 in a quotation from the *Bhāvacuḍāmaṇi* where it is explained that *saṃvidā* imparts sattvic bliss, *madya* (intoxicating drink) imparts rājasic bliss, and *tvaritā* imparts tamasic bliss.
21. *Sarvollāsa* 16.18–19.
22. Ray 1909; 1911.
23. Meulenbeld (HIML IIB, 373) is skeptical about *tāmrakūṭa* as tobacco, as discussed by Ray (1911, 40) with regard to its usage in the *Kulārṇava Tantra*. While I agree that this occurrence is not evidence of early Indian knowledge of tobacco, or for the transformation of an ancient Sanskrit word *tāmrakūṭa* into modern Indic words for tobacco, nevertheless it is plausible that the passage is a later addition to these texts. N. B. Divatia (1921, vol. 1, 71) makes a similar point in contesting Ray's theories of the early use of tobacco in India: "as a result of being a comparatively recent foreign importation, various artificial Sanskrit forms for the word have been coined . . ."
24. Ray 1911, 40. Sanderson (2014, 78) says this text has a date after the twelfth century. I have not been able to find the verses Ray quotes in the printed edition, and Goudriaan and Gupta write that quotations attributed to this text are not always traceable (1981, 93).
25. According to the *Bengali Historical Dictionary* the word is first attested in 1850. I thank Dr. Thibaut d'Hubert for this reference.
26. This paragraph is taken from McHugh forthcoming a.
27. The material I provide here is from the *Yogaratnākara*, 16; for the date see HIML IIA, 351–352.
28. Manohar 2004.
29. Gode 1960e; 1960f. Also Gode 1960a, chs. 47 and 48.

30. Gode 1960e, 412.
31. The "drugs" and perfumes, possibly included under the *śarbatkhānā* are: *Rājavyavahārakośa*, *Bhogyavarga* 87–94 (coffee is at 87ab). Liquor is *Bhogyavarga* 95ab, and betel 95bc–97ab. Medicines then follow.
32. Meulenbeld (1974, 453–54) explains that *kaṣāya*s are by no means always decoctions, but can also be expressed juice, cold infusions, and other types of liquid extract.

Digestif

1. Alluding to David Courtwright's (2001) idea of a psychoactive revolution over the past five hundred years.
2. James 1902, 387.

Appendix

1. Lockwood 2021, 52.
2. Taillieu and Boyce 2003. Also see Brough 1971; 1973.
3. For the earlier scholarship on *soma* see Doniger 1968.
4. Hawkes 1967, 174.
5. Smith 1972.
6. Houben (2003) is a good review of the Indic case. Taillieu and Boyce (2003) on *Haoma* is easily available and short. Matthew Clark (2017) offers an accessible survey. I do not necessarily agree with his conclusion, but then again there is no point in writing something bland about *soma*. Nevertheless, I find Clark's acceptance of multiple *somas* (ch. 13), and *soma* as (possibly) a mixture quite sensible. Clark (2017) also contains a thorough bibliography.
7. Smith 1972, 480.
8. "[I]t was made with the expressed juice of a creeper (*Asclepias acida*, or *Sarcostemma viminalis*) diluted with water, mixed with barley meal, clarified butter, and the meal of wild paddy (*nivàra*), and fermented in a jar for nine days. The juice of the creeper is said to be of an acid taste, but I have not heard that it has any narcotic property; I am disposed to think therefore, that the starch of the two kinds of meal supplied the material for the vinous fermentation . . ." Mitra 1873, 21–22.
9. Mitra got the idea of the *soma* as fermented from John Stevenson's translation of the *Sāma Veda* (1842), as cited by Mitra (1873, 22). There, references to adding barley to cups of *soma* led him to think this was a beer or sorts (Stevenson 1842, 5–6). Evidently it was difficult to shake off a very European model of the production of intoxicants, such that the presence of barley strongly suggested beer making.

Stevenson also confuses *soma* and *surā*—suggesting that Śukra got drunk on *soma* (Stevenson 1842, 5–6).

10. See Doniger's (1968) survey of early *soma* theories. Also Havell's (1929) theory of *soma* as rāgi millet, a theory based on correlating physical and practical descriptions of *soma* with a plant known to be used to make an intoxicant in South Asia.
11. Aalto, "The alcohol percentage cannot have been high." (1959, 18).
12. Doniger 1968, 115–118.
13. Oldenberg 1894, 366. My translation from the German. Also see Doniger 1968, 123.
14. Oldenberg 1894, 366–367.
15. Dumézil 1924, 90. Also see Doniger 1968, 130.
16. E.g., Witzel 2000, 27.
17. But were these nineteenth-century scholars wrong? In the world of their informants *soma* was now regarded as a certain plant.
18. RV trans. Jamison and Brereton, vol. 3, 1234. For a similar point see Houben 2003, 18.
19. In this I agree with Houben (2003, 17, 23).
20. Clark 2017.
21. See "Words" in the Introduction for more on this term. In some later Vedic texts Mada personified is directly associated with *surā*—see Chapter 6 for this myth.
22. RV trans. Jamison and Brereton, vol. 1, 31–32. For a good example of confusion born of attachment to a modern and limited concept of "intoxicant" alongside the categories of modern pharmacology and botany, Flattery and Schwatz write (1989, 4, my emphasis): "the '*soma*' which *Sarcostemma* has directly replaced, however, seems not to have been the original plant but an *Ephedra*, a **nonintoxicating** plant . . ." Who are *we* to say the perceived effects of a divine *soma*-ephedra drink could not have been connected to the concept of *mada*?
23. RV X.119. Another "experiential" one is RV VIII.48.
24. RV trans. Jamison and Brereton, vol. 3, 1589. Referring to Thompson (2003).
25. RV X.119, trans. Jamison and Brereton, vol. 3, 1590.
26. Houben 2003, 23–24.
27. From the poem commonly known as "Seven Cups of Tea" by Lu Tong as translated and discussed in Benn 2015, 90–92.
28. On kava, see Lebot, Merlin, and Lindstrom 1992.
29. Lebot, Merlin, and Lindstrom 1992, 1–3.
30. Sherratt 1997, 408.
31. Houben 2003, 16.
32. Houben 2003, 22.
33. See McHugh 2012, ch. 8.
34. Sarianidi 1994a; 1994b; 1998.
35. Houben 2003, 27.
36. Bakels 2003.
37. Also, it is quite conceivable that an alcoholic drink might contain intoxicating herbs (and that a brew of intoxicating herbs might be fermented to become alcoholic).

38. Dietler 1990; Goodman 1995.
39. Elizarenkova 1996, 14.
40. Malamoud 1989, especially 54–56.
41. Whitaker 2011, 151.
42. Whitaker 2011, 152.
43. RV IX.17.3–4 (729), trans Jamison and Brereton, vol. 3, 1251–1252.

Bibliography

Abbreviations for works frequently cited

AK	*Abhidharmakośa of Vasubandhu*
ĀDS	*Āpastamba Dharmasūtra*
AH	*Aṣṭāṅgahṛdaya of Vāgbhaṭa*
AŚ	*Arthaśāstra*
ĀŚS	*Āpastamba Śrauta Sūtra*
AVŚ	*Atharvaveda Śaunaka*
BC	*Buddhacarita* of Aśvaghoṣa
BDS	*Baudhāyana Dharmasūtra*
BhP	*Bhāgavata Purāṇa*
BKŚS	*Bṛhatkathāślokasaṃgraha* of Budhasvāmin
BŚS	*Baudhāyana Śrauta Sūtra*
CII	*Corpus Inscriptionum Indicarum*
CITD	*A Corpus of Inscriptions in the Telingana Districts of H.E.H. the Nizam's Dominions*
CS	*Caraka Saṃhitā* (Sū = *Sūtrasthāna*)
EI	*Epigraphia Indica*
EWA	Mayrhofer, Manfred. 1986
GDS	*Gautama Dharmasūtra*
GGS	*Gobhila Gṛhya Sūtra*
H.	*Haṃsavilāsa* of Haṃsamiṭṭhu
HDŚ	*History of Dharmaśāstra*. See Kane 1930–1962
HIML	*History of Indian Medical Literature*. See Meulenbeld 1999–2002
HV	*Harivaṃśa*
IA	*Indian Antiquary*
JBr	*Jaiminīya Brāhmaṇa*
KA	*Kirātārjunīya* of Bhāravi
KEWA	Mayrhofer, Manfred. 1956
KS	*Kāmasūtra of Vātsyāyana*
Manu	*Mānavadharmaśāstra*
MBh	*Mahābhārata*
MS	*Maitrāyaṇī Saṃhitā*
MSV	*Mūlasārvāstivāda Vinaya*
MV	*Mattavilāsaprahasana* of Mahendravikramavarman
MW	*Monier-Williams' A Sanskrit-English Dictionary. See Monier William 2000*
OED	*Oxford English Dictionary*
PTS	Pali Text Society

Rām	*Rāmāyaṇa* of Vālmīki
RV	*Ṛgveda*
ŚBr	*Śatapatha Brāhmaṇa*
Śārṅg	*Śārṅgadharasaṃhitā* of Śārṅgadhara
ŚGS	*Śāṅkhāyana Gṛhya Sūtra*
SII	*South Indian Inscriptions*
SITI	*South Indian Temple Inscriptions*
SS	*Suśrutasaṃhitā* (Sū = *Sūtrasthāna*)
TĀ	*Tantrāloka* of Abhinavagupta
TB	*Taittirīya Brāhmaṇa*
VaiDh	*Vaiṣṇava Dharmaśāstra*
VDS	*Vasiṣṭha Dharmasūtra*
VS	*Vājasaneyi Saṃhitā*
YT	*Yaśastilaka* of Somadeva
YVS	*Yājñavalkyasmṛti*

Inscriptions

Corpus Inscriptionum Indicarum. Archaeological Survey of India, 1877–.

A Corpus of Inscriptions in the Telingana Districts of H.E.H. the Nizam's Dominions. Ed. P. Sreenivasachar. (1940-1956). Hyderabad: The Nizam's Government.

Epigraphia Indica. Vols 1–42 (1892–1978). Delhi: Archaeological Survey of India.

Indian Antiquary. (1872–1933; 1964-1971). Bombay, Education Society's Press. Continued by *The New Indian Antiquary* (1938-1947).

South Indian Temple Inscriptions. Ed. T. N. Subramanian. 3 vols. in 4 parts. Madras Government Oriental Series, nos. 104-121, 131, and 157. Madras: Government Oriental Manuscripts Library, 1953-1957.

South Indian Inscriptions. Vols. 1–24 (1890–1982). Mysore: Archaeological Survey of India.

Primary Sources Including Editions, Commentaries, and Translations

Abhidhānacintāmaṇi of Hemacandra. Bombay: Nirnayasagara Press, 1889.

Abhidharmakośa of Vasubandhu. Ed. P. Pradhan. Patna: K. P. Jayaswal Research Institute, 1967.

Abhidharmakośa of Vasubandhu. Trans. Louis de la Vallée Poussin. Paris: Paul Geuthner, 1924.

Ācārāṅga Sūtra. Ed. Hermann Jacobi. Pali Text Society Publications 3. London: Pub. for the Pali Text Society by H. Frowde, 1882.

Ācārāṅga Sūtra. Trans. in Jacobi 1968 (1884).

Āgamaḍambara of Jayanta Bhaṭṭa. Ed. and trans. Csaba Dezső. *Much Ado About Religion*. New York: New York University Press, JJC Foundation, 2005.

Amarakośa (Nāmaliṅgānuśāsana) of Amarasiṃha with the Commentary of Maheśvara. Ed. V. Jhalakikar and R. G. Bhandarkar. Delhi: Eastern Book Linkers, 2002.

Ānandakanda. Ed. S. V. Radhakrishna Sastri. Tanjore Saraswati Mahal Series 15. Tanjore: TMSSM Library, 1952.

Aṅguttara Nikāya. Various editors. Pali Text Society Publications 10, 20, 35, 44, 46, 66. London: Pub. for the Pali Text Society by H. Frowde, 1885.

Āpastamba Dharmasūtra, see *Dharmasūtras.*

Arkaprakāśa of Rāvaṇa. Ed. Indradeva Tripāṭhī. Kṛshṇadāsa āyurveda Sīrīja 37. Vārāṇasī: Kṛṣṇadāsa Akādamī, 1995.

Arthaśāstra of Kauṭalya. Ed. and trans. R. P. Kangle. Bombay: University of Bombay, 1963.

Arthaśāstra of Kauṭalya. Trans. Patrick Olivelle. *King, Governance, and Law in Ancient India: Kautilya's Arthasastra: A New Annotated Translation.* New York: Oxford University Press, 2013.

Aṣṭādhyāyī of Pāṇini. Trans. Srisa Chandra Vasu. Allahabad: Indian Press, 1891.

Aṣṭāṅgahṛdaya of Vāgbhaṭa. Collated by K. R. Ś. Navare and A. M. Kuṇṭe, ed. B. H. P. Vaidya with the commentaries of Aruṇadatta and Hemādri. 7th ed. Jaikrishnadas Ayurveda Series 52. Vārāṇasī: Caukhambhā Oriyaṇṭāliyā, 1982.

Aṣṭāṅgahṛdaya of Vāgbhaṭa. Trans. K. R. Srikantha Murthy 1st ed. Kṛshṇadāsa āyurveda Sīrīja 27. Varanasi: Krishnadas Academy, 1991.

Atharvaveda Paippalāda, Kāṇḍa Five. Ed. and trans. Alexander Lubotsky. Harvard Oriental Series, Opera Minora 4. Cambridge, Mass.: Department of Sanskrit and Indian Studies, Harvard University, 2002.

Atharvaveda Śaunaka. TITUS version online. On the basis of the editions: *Gli inni dell' Atharvaveda* (Saunaka), trasliterazione a cura di Chatia Orlandi, Pisa 1991; and *Atharva Veda Sanhita,* herausgegeben von R. Roth und W. D. Whitney, Berlin 1856. Entered by Vladimir Petr und Petr Vavroušek, Praha 1996; TITUS version by Jost Gippert, http://titus.uni-frankfurt.de/texte/etcs/ind/aind/ved/av/avs/avs.htm

Atharvaveda. Trans. Maurice Bloomfield. Sacred Books of the East 42. Oxford: Clarendon Press, 1897.

Atharvaveda. Trans. William Dwight Whitney. Harvard Oriental Series 7, 8. Cambridge, Mass.: Harvard University, 1905.

Atthasālinī: Buddhaghosa's Commentary on the Dhammasaṅgaṇī. Ed. Edward Muller. London: Pali Text Society, 1897.

Āśvalāyana Gṛhya Sūtra. Ed. P. Śāstri Rāṇaḍe. Ānandāśramasaṃskṛtagranthāvaliḥ 105. Poona: Ānandāśrama mudraṇālya, 1936.

Bālarāmāyaṇa of Rājaśekhara. Ed. Jīvānanda Vidyāsāgara. Calcutta: New Valmiki Press, 1884.

Baudhāyana Dharmasūtra, see *Dharmasūtras.*

Baudhāyana Śrauta Sūtra. Ed. Willem Caland. Bibliotheca Indica 163. Calcutta: Asiatic Society of Bengal, 1904-1924.

Bhāgavatapurāṇa, with Thirteen Commentaries. Ed. Kṛṣṇa Śaṅkara Śāstrī et al. Varanasi: Śrīvidyāhitanidhisadasyāḥ, 1965-.

Bhaiṣajyaratnāvalī of Govindadāsa. Ed. and enlarged Brahmashankar Mishra. Chaukhambha Sanskrit Bhawan Series 67. Varanasi: Chaukhambha Sanskrit Bhawan, 2006.

Bhāvaprakāśa of Bhāvamiśra. Ed. Srī Brahma Śankara. Vārāṇasī: Caukhambā Saṃskṛta Sīrīja Āphisa, 1961.

Brahmayāmala Tantra. National Archives Kathmandu manuscript no. 3-370 (Nepal-German Manuscript Preservation Project microfilm reel A42/6). Transcription courtesy of Shaman Hatley.

Bṛhatkathāślokasaṃgraha of Budhasvāmin. Ed. and trans. Félix Lacôte. Paris: Imprimerie Nationale, 1908–1929.

Bṛhatkathāślokasaṃgraha of Budhasvāmin. Trans. James Mallinson. *The Emperor of the Sorcerers*. New York: New York University Press, JJC Foundation, 2005.

Bṛhatsaṃhitā of Varāhamihira. Ed. Sudhākara Dvivedi. Benares: Lazarus & Co., 1895–1897. Reprinted, A. V. Tripathī. Sarasvatī Bhavan Granthamālā 97. Varanasi: Varanasey asaṃskṛtaviśvavidyālaya, 1968.

Buddhacarita of Aśvaghoṣa. Trans. Patrick Olivelle (with Sanskrit text). *Life of the Buddha*. New York: New York University Press, JJC Foundation, 2008.

Caraka Saṃhitā. Text and trans. P. V. Sharma. Varanasi: Chaukhambha Orientalia, 1981.

Carakasaṃhitā with commentary of Cakrapāṇidatta. Ed. Jādavji Trikamji Acharya. New Delhi: Munśirāma Manoharalāla. 1981.

Cullavagga. Trans. T. W. Rhys Davids and Hermann Oldenberg. Sacred Books of the East 13, 17, 20. Delhi: Motilal Banarsidass, 1965 (1882).

Chāndogya Upaniṣad. Ed. and trans. in Patrick Olivelle, *The Early Upanisads: Annotated Text and Translation*. New York: Oxford University Press, 1998.

Devīrahasya. Ed. Harabhaṭṭa Śāstrī and Ram Chandra Kak. Vadodara: Butala, 1985

Devīrahasya. Ed. and trans. [Hindi] Kapiladeva Narayana. Caukhambā Surabhāratī Granthamālā 456. Vārāṇasī: Caukhambā Surabhāratī Prakāśana-a, 2009.

Dhammapadaṭṭhakathā. Ed. Harry Campbell Norman and Lakshmana Shastri Tailang. Pali Text Society Publications 59, 64, 68, 71, 74, 78. London: Pub. for the Pali Text Society by H. Frowde, 1906.

Dhammapadaṭṭhakathā. Trans. Eugene Watson Burlingame. *Buddhist Legends*. Cambridge, Mass.: Harvard University Press, 1921.

Dharmasūtras. Ed. and trans. Patrick Olivelle. *Dharmasūtras: The Law Codes of Āpastamba, Gautama, Baudhāyana, and Vasiṣṭha*. Delhi: Motilal Banarsidass, 2000.

Dhūrtaviṭasaṃvāda. Ed. and trans. "Rogue and Pimp Confer." In Dezsö and Vasudeva 2009.

Dīghanikāya. Ed. J. Estlin Carpenter and T. W. Rhys Davids. *The Dīgha-nikāya*. London: Pub. for the Pali Text Society by H. Frowde, 1890.

The Dîpavaṃsa: An Ancient Buddhist Historical Record. Ed. Hermann Oldenberg. London: Williams and Norgate, 1879.

Gadanigraha of Śrī Vaidya Soḍhala. Kashi Sanskrit Series 182. Varanasi: Chowkhamba Sanskrit Series Office, 1968.

Gautama Dharmasūtra, see Dharmasūtras.

Gobhila Gṛhya Sūtra. Trans. Hermann Oldenberg. Sacred Books of the East 29, 30. Oxford: Clarendon Press, 1886.

Gurunāthaparāmarśa of Madhurāja. Ed. P. N. Pushp. Kashmir Series of Texts and Studies 85. Srinagar: J & K Government, 1960.

Haṃsavilāsa of Haṃsamiṭṭhu. Eds Swami Trivikrama Tirtha and Mahamahopadhyaya Hathibhai Shastri. Gaekwad's Oriental Series 81. Baroda: Oriental Institute, 1937.

Haramekhalā of Mādhuka. Ed. Kṛṣṇaprasāda Śarma. Kathmandu: Nepālarāṣṭriyābhilekhālaya, 1972/73.

Haramekhalā of Mādhuka. Ed. K. Sāmbaśivaśāstri. Śrī Citrodayamañjari 13. Trivandrum: Printed by the Superintendent, Government Press, 1936.

Hārītasaṃhitā. Ed. and trans. Alix Raison. *La Hārītasaṃhitā: Texte Médical Sanskrit*. Publications De L'Institut Français d'Indologie 52. Pondichéry: Institut Français d'Indologie, 1974.

Hārītasaṃhitā. Text with English commentary, Gyanendra Pandey. *Hārīta Saṃhitā*. Banaras Ayurveda Series 76. Varanasi: Chowkhambha Sanskrit Series Office, 2014.

Harivaṃśa. Critical ed. P. L. Vaidya. Poona: Bhandarkar Oriental Research Institute, 1969.

Harivaṃśa. Vulgate with commentary of Nīlakaṇṭha. Bombay: Venkatesvara Steam Press, 1897.

Harṣacarita of Bāṇa. Ed. Pāṇḍuraṅga Vāmana Kane. 1st ed. Bombay: Author, 1918. Reprinted, Delhi: Motilal Banarsidass, 1997.

Jaiminīya Brāhmaṇa. Ed. Raghu Vira and Lokesh Chandra. Sarasvati-vihara Series 31. Nagpur: International Academy of Indian Culture, 1954.

Jaiminīya Brāhmaṇa. Trans. and ed. Willem Caland. Amsterdam: J. Müller, 1919.

Jātaka (Pali). Ed. V. Fausbøll and Dines Andersen. London: Trübner, 1875.

Jātaka (Pali). Trans. H. T. Francis, Edward B. Cowell, Robert Chalmers, W. H. D. Rouse, and Robert Alexander Neil. Cambridge: Cambridge University Press, 1895.

Jātakamālā of Āryaśūra. Ed. Hendrik Kern. Harvard Oriental Series 1. Boston: Published for Harvard University by Ginn, 1891.

Kādambarī of Bāṇa. Text and trans. David Smith. *Clay Sanskrit Library*. New York: New York University Press, 2009.

Kalāvilāsa of Kṣemendra. Trans. Somadeva Vasudeva (with Sanskrit text). In Nīlakaṇṭha Dīkṣita, Kṣemendra, and Bhallaṭa. *Three Satires*. 1st ed. Clay Sanskrit Library. New York: New York University Press, JJC Foundation, 2005.

Kāmakuñjalatā. Ed. Ḍhuṇḍhirāja Śāstri. Caukhambā-Saṃskṛta-granthamālā 493–496, Grantha Saṇkhya 92, Bis. Vārāṇasī: Chaukhambā Saṃskṛta Sīrīja Āfisa, 1967.

Kāmandakīya Nītisāra of Kāmandaki. Forthcoming. Trans. Jesse Knutson. *The Essence of Politics*. Murty Classical Library of India 28. Cambridge, Mass.: Harvard University Press

Kāmasūtra of Vātsyāyana with the commentary of Yaśodhara. Ed. Damodar Lal Gosvami. Haridas Sanskrit Granthamala 29. Benares: Jai Krishnadas-Haridas Gupta, 1929.

Kāmasūtra of Vātsyāyana with the commentary of Yaśodhara. Ed. Devadatta Shastri. Varanasi: Chaukhambha Sanskrit Sansthan, 1964. *Unless otherwise stated references to Kāmasūtra are to this edition.*

Kāmasūtra of Vātsyāyana. Trans. Richard Schmidt. *Das Kāmasūtram des Vātsyāyana*. Berlin: H. Barsdorf, 1907.

Kāvyādarśa of Daṇḍin. Ed. R. R. Shastri. Government Oriental Series 4. Poona: Bhandarkar Oriental Research Institute, 1938.

Kāvyamīmāṃsā of Rājaśekhara. Ed. C. D. Dalal. Gaekwad's Oriental Series 1. Baroda: Central Library, 1916.

Kirātārjunīya of Bhāravi. Trans. Indira Viswanathan Peterson (with Sanskrit text). *Arjuna and the Hunter*. Cambridge, Mass.: Harvard University Press, 2016.

Kulārṇava Tantra. Ed. Tārānātha Vidyāratna. Tantrik Texts 5. London: Luzac, 1917.

Lalitavistara. Ed. Salomon Lefmann. Halle A. S.: Buchhandlung Des Waisenhauses, 1902.

Līlāvatīsāra of Jinaratnasūri. Trans. R. C. C. Fynes (with Sanskrit text). *The Epitome of Queen Līlāvatī*. 1st ed. Clay Sanskrit Library. New York: New York University Press, JJC Foundation, 2005.

Mādhavanidāna of Mādhavakara with *Madhukośa*. Ed. Vaidya Jadavji Tricumji Acharya. Bombay: Nirnaya Sagar, 1920.

Mahābhārata. Critically edited in 19 volumes. General editor, Vishnu Sitaram Sukthankar. Poona: Bhandarkar Oriental Research Institute, 1933–1959.

Mahābhārata, book 1. Trans. J. A. B. Van Buitenen. *The Mahabharata. 1. The Book of the Beginning*. Chicago: University of Chicago Press, 1973.

Maitrāyaṇī Saṃhitā. Ed. Leopold von Schroeder. Wiesbaden: F. Steiner, 1970–1972 (1881–1886).

Majjhima Nikāya. Ed. V. (Vilhelm) Trenckner, Robert Chalmers, Mabel Haynes Bode, and Caroline A. F. Rhys Davids. London: Pub. for the Pali Text Society by H. Frowde, 1888.

Mānasollāsa of Someśvara. Ed. G. K. Shrigondekar. Gaekwad's Oriental Series 28, 84, 138. Baroda: Oriental Institute, 1925–1961.

Mānavadharmaśāstra. Trans. Georg Bühler. *The Laws of Manu*. Sacred Books of the East 25. Oxford: Clarendon Press, 1886.

Mānavadharmaśāstra. *The Commentary of Govindarája on Mánava-Dharma Śástra (Being a Supplement to Mánavadharmaśástra with the Commentaries of Medhátithi, Sarvajñanáráyana, Kulluka, Rághavánanda, Nandana, and Rámachandra)*. Edited with notes by V. N. Mandlik. 2 vols. Bombay: Ganpat Krishnaji's Press, 1886.

Mānavadharmaśāstra with the *Manubhāṣya* of Medhātithi. Trans. Mahāmahopādhyāya Gangānātha Jhā. Allahabad: University of Calcutta, 1926.

Mānavadharmaśāstra with the *Manubhāṣya* of Medhātithi. *Manusmṛti Medhātithibhāṣyasamalaṅkṛtā*. Kalakattā: Udayācal Press, 1967–1971.

Mānavadharmaśāstra. Ed. and trans. Patrick Olivelle. *Manu's Code of Law: A Critical Edition and Translation of the Mānava-Dharmaśāstra*. Oxford: Oxford University Press, 2005.

Das Mānava Gṛhya Sūtra. Ed. Friedrich Knauer. St Petersburg: Académie Impériale des Sciences, 1897.

Mātaṅgalīlā of Nīlakaṇṭha. Ed. T. Gaṇapati Śāstrī. Trivandrum Sanskrit Series 10. Trivandrum: Travancore Govt. Press, 1910.

Mattavilāsaprahasana of Mahendravikramavarman. Ed. T. Gaṇapatiśāstrī. Anantaśayana saṃskṛtagranthāvaliḥ 55. Trivandrum: Printed by the Govt. Press, 1917.

Mattavilāsaprahasana of Mahendravikramavarman. Trans. David N. Lorenzen, "A Parody of the Kapalikas in the Mattavilasa." In *Tantra in Practice*, ed. David Gordon White, 81–96. Princeton Paperbacks. Princeton, N.J.: Princeton University Press, 2000.

Medinīkośa of Medinikara. Ed. Jagannatha Shastri Hoshinga. Kāśī Saṃskṛta Granthamālā 41. Vārāṇasī: Caukhambā Saṃskṛta Sīrija Āphisa, 1940.

Meghadūta of Kālidāsa with commentary of Mallinātha. Ed. Nārāyaṇa Bālakṛishṇa Godbole and Kāśinātha Pāṇḍuraṅga Paraba. 3rd ed. Bombay: Nirnaya-Sāgara Press, 1890.

Meghadūta of Kālidāsa with commentary of Vallabhadeva. Ed. E. Hultzsch. Prize Publication Fund 3. London: Royal Asiatic Society, 1911.

Mṛcchakaṭikā of Śūdraka. Trans. Diwakar Acharya (with Sanskrit text). *The Little Clay Cart*. 1st ed. Clay Sanskrit Library. New York: New York University Press, JJC Foundation, 2009.

Mṛcchakaṭikā of Śūdraka. Ed. M. R. Kale with the commentary of Pṛthvidhara. Bombay: Sri Krishna Publishing, 1924.

Mudrārākṣasa of Viśākhadatta. Trans. Michael Coulson (with Sanskrit text). *Rākṣasa's Ring*. New York: New York University Press, JJC Foundation, 2005.

Mūlasārvāstivāda Vinaya. Sections as translated by Gregory Schopen, *Kṣudrakavastu. Derge 'dul ba Da* 182b.3–184a.3; *Kṣudrakavastu, Derge Da* 156a.3–b.7.

Narmamālā of Kṣemendra: Critical Edition, Study and Translation. Ed. and trans. Fabrizia Baldissera. Beiträge Zur Südasienforschung. Würzburg: Ergon, 2005.

Nāṭyaśāstra of Bharata. Ed. Rāmakṛṣṇa Kavi. Gaekwad's Oriental Series 36, 68, 124, 145. Baroda: Central Library, 1956.

Nītisāra of Kāmandaka. Ed. Gaṇapatiśāstrī. Anantaśayanasaṃskṛtagranthāvaliḥ 14. Trivandrum: Printed at the Travancore Govt. Press, 1912.

Pādatāḍitaka of Śyāmilaka, in Dezsö and Vasudeva 2009.

Padmaprābhṛtaka of Śūdraka, in Dezsö and Vasudeva 2009.

Pañcatantra. Ed. Franklin Edgerton. The Panchatantra Reconstructed: An Attempt to Establish the Lost Original Sanskrit Text of the Most Famous of Indian Story-collections On the Basis of the Principal Extant Versions. New Haven, Conn.: American Oriental Society, 1924.

Pañcatantra. Trans. Patrick Olivelle. New York: Oxford University Press, 1997.

Raghuvaṃśa of Kālidāsa. Ed. Shankar Pandurang Pandit. Bombay Sanskrit Series 5, 8, 13. Bombay: "Indu-Prakash" Press, 1872–1897.

Raghuvaṃśa of Kālidāsa with the Commentary Sañjīvanī of Mallinātha. Cantos I–V. Ed. and trans. M. R. Kale. Delhi: Motilal Banarsidass, 1997.

Rājataraṅgiṇī of Kalhaṇa: A Chronicle of the Kings of Kaśmīr. Trans. and ed. Aurel Stein. Westminster: A. Constable, 1900.

Rājavyavahārakośa of Raghunatha Pandit. 1st ed. Delhi: Vidyanidhi Prakashan, 2007.

Rāmāyaṇa of Vālmīki. Critical edition. General editors G. H. Bhatt and U. P. Shah. Baroda: Oriental Institute, 1960–1975.

Rāmāyaṇa of Vālmīki. Trans. Robert P. Goldman, Sally J. Sutherland Goldman, Rosalind Lefeber, and Sheldon I. Pollock. Princeton, N.J.: Princeton University Press, 1984–2017.

Ṛgveda. Ed. Barend A. Van Nooten and Gary B. Holland. *Rigveda: A Metrically Restored Text*. Harvard Oriental Series 50. Cambridge, Mass.: Dept. of Sanskrit and Indian Studies, Harvard University Press, 1994.

Ṛgveda. Trans. Karl Friedrich Geldner. *Der Rig-Veda. Harvard Oriental Series* 63. Cambridge, Mass.: Dept. of Sanskrit & Indian Studies; Harvard University Press, 2003 (1951).

Ṛgveda. Trans. Stephanie W. Jamison and Joel P. Brereton. *The Rigveda: The Earliest Religious Poetry of India*. New York: Oxford University Press, 2014.

Śakuntalā of Kālidāsa. Ed. and trans. Somadeva Vasudeva (with Sanskrit text). *The Recognition of Shakúntala*. Clay Sanskrit Library. New York: New York University Press, JJC Foundation, 2006.

Sāgaradharmāmṛta of Āśādhara. Ed. K. Chandra Shastri. Jñānapīṭha Mūrtidevī Granthamālā 47. New Delhi: Bharatiya Jnanpith Publication, 1978.

Samantapāsādikā of Buddhaghosa. Ed. Junjirō Takakusu and Makoto Nagai. Pali Text Society Publications 96, 102, 109, 116–117, 126. London: Pub. for the Pali Text Society by Oxford University Press, 1924.

Saṃyutta Nikāya. Ed. Léon Feer and Caroline A. F. Rhys Davids. *The Saṃyutta-nikâya of the Sutta-piṭaka*. London: Pub. for the Pali Text Society by H. Frowde, 1884.

Śaṅkhāyana Gṛhya Sūtra. On the basis of the editions by Hermann Oldenberg, *Indische Studien* XV, 1878, and S. R. Sehgal, Delhi, 1960. Electronically edited by Thomas Zehnder, Freiburg (Breisgau) 1997; corrections by Matthias Ahlborn, TITUS version by Jogh Gippert, Frankfurt a/M. Online version at: http://titus.uni-frankfurt.de/texte/etcs/ind/aind/ved/rv/sankhgs/sankh.htm

Śaṅkhāyana Gṛhya Sūtra. Trans. Hermann Oldenberg. *The Grihya-sûtras: Rules of Vedic Domestic Ceremonies*. Sacred Books of the East 29, 30. Oxford: Clarendon Press, 1886.

Śārṅgadharasaṃhitā of Śārṅgadhara with commentary of Aḍhamalla and Kāśirāma. Ed. Paraśurāma Śāstri. Jaikrishnadas Ayurveda Series 53. Vārāṇasī: Caukhambhā Oriyanṭāliyā, 1983 (1931).

Śārṅgadharasaṃhitā of Śārṅgadhara. Text and trans. Śārṅgadhara and K. R. Srikanthamurthy. Varanasi: Chaukhambha Orientalia, 1984.

Sarvadarśanasaṃgraha of Mādhava. Ānandāśramasaṃskṛtagranthāvali 51. Pune: Ānandāśrama Press, 1977.

Sarvollāsa of Sarvānandanātha. Ed. S. N. Khandelwal. Varanasi: Chaukhamba Surbharati Granthmala, 2003.

Sāsanavaṃsa. Ed. Mabel Haynes Bode. Pali Text Society Publication 41. London: Pub. for the Pali Text Society by H. Frowde, 1897.

Sāsanavavaṃsa. Trans. Bimala Churn Law. *The History of the Buddha's Religion = Sāsanavaṃsa*. Sacred Books of the Buddhists 17. London: Luzac, 1952.

Śatapatha Brāhmaṇa. Ed. Albrecht Weber. *The Śatapatha Brāhmaṇa in the Mādhyaṃdina-Śākhā*. Berlin: F. Dümmler, 1855.

Śatapatha Brāhmaṇa. Trans. J. Eggeling. *The Śatapatha-Brāhmaṇa According to the Text of the Mādhyandina School, Part V*. Sacred Books of the East 44. Oxford: Clarendon Press, 1900.

Śiśupālavadha of Māgha. Trans. Paul Dundas (with Sanskrit text). *The Killing of Shishupala*. Cambridge, Mass.: Harvard University Press, 2017.

Śrautakośa. Ed. Dhuṇḍirāja Gaṇeśa Dīkshita Bāpaṭa and Chintaman Ganesh Kashikar and R, N. Dandekar (translator of vol. 1, English Section). Vaidika Saṃśodhana Maṇḍala. Poona: Vaidika Saṃśodhana Maṇḍala, 1958–1970.

Śrīkaṇṭhacarita of Maṅkha with the commentary of Jonarāja. Ed. Durgaprasada and Paraba. Kāvyamālā 3. Bombay: Nirṇaya-Sāgara Press, 1887.

Subhāṣitaratnakoṣa of Vidyākara. Ed. D. D. Kosambi and Vasudeo Vishwanath Gokhale. *The Subhāṣitaratnakoṣa*. Harvard Oriental Series 42. Cambridge, Mass.: Harvard University Press, 1957.

Subhāṣitaratnakoṣa of Vidyākara. Trans. Daniel H. H. Ingalls. *An Anthology of Sanskrit Court Poetry*. Harvard Oriental Series 44. Cambridge, Mass.: Harvard University Press, 1965.

Subhāṣitaratnabhāṇḍāgāra. Ed. Kāśīnātha Pāṇḍuraṅga Paraba. *Subhâshita-ratna-bhâṇḍâgâram; Or, Gems of Sanskrit Poetry: Being a Collection of Witty, Epigrammatic, Instructive and Descriptive Verses*. 2nd rev. and enl. ed. Bombay: Printed and published by Jâvajî Dâdâjî and Janârdana Mahâdeva Curjara, 1886.

Śukasaptati. Ed. R. Tripathi. Haridas Sanskrit Series 269. Varanasi: Chowkhamba Sanskrit Series Office, 1966.

Śukasaptati. Trans. A. N. D. Haksar. *Shuka Saptati: Seventy Tales of the Parrot*. New Delhi: HarperCollins Publishers, 2000.

Suśrutasaṃhitā. Ed. Vaidya Jādavjī Trivikramjī Ācārya and Nārāyaṇ Rām Ācārya Kāvyatīrtha. Krishnadas Ayurveda Series 51. Varanasi: Krishnadas Academy, 1998.

Suśrutasaṃhitā: with English Translation of Text and Ḍalhaṇa's Commentary along with Critical Notes. Ed. Priya Vrat Sharma. Varanasi: Chaukhambha Visvabharati, 1999–2001.

Tantrāloka of Abhinavagupta. Ed. Rājānaka Jayaratha, Mukunda Rama Shastri, and Mad husūdanakaulaśāstrī. Kaśmīrasaṃskṛtagranthāvaliḥ XXIII, XXVIII–XXX, XXXV–XXXVI, XL. Allahabad: Printed at the Indian Press, 1918.

Tantrāloka of Abhinavagupta. Trans. Raniero Gnoli. *Luce Delle Sacre Scritture (Tantrāloka)*. 2nd ed. Classici Delle Religioni. Sezione Prima, Religioni Orientali. Torino: Unione Tipografico-editrice Torinese, 1980.

Tantravārtika of Kumārila. Ed. Gangadhara Sastri. *The Tantravârtika, a Gloss on Ṡabara Svâmî's Commentary on the Mîmâmsâ Sûtras by Bhaṭṭa Kumârila*. Benares Sanskrit Series 3. Benares: Braj B. Das, 1903.

Tantravārtika of Kumārila. Trans. Ganganatha Jha. *Tantravārttika: A Commentary on Śabara's Bhāṣya on the Pūrvamīmāṃsā Sūtras of Jaimini*. Bibliotheca Indica 161. Calcutta: Asiatic Society of Bengal, 1924.

Tattvārthavārtikam (*Rājavārikam*) of Akalaṅka. Ed. Mahendra Kumar Jain. Kāśī: Bhāratīya Jñānapīṭha, 1953.

Tattvārthasūtra of Umāsvātī, with Sarvārthasiddhi commentary. Trans. S. A. Jain. *Reality*. Calcutta: V. S. Sangha, 1960.

Triṣaṣṭiśalākāpuruṣacarita of Hemacandra. Bhavnagar: Prasārakasabhā, 1905–1909.

Triṣaṣṭiśalākāpuruṣacarita of Hemacandra. Trans. H. M. Johnson. Gaekwad's Oriental Series 51, 77, 108, 125, 139, 140. Baroda: Oriental Institute, 1931.

Uttarādhyayanasūtra. Ed. Jarl Charpentier. Uppsala: Appelbergs Boktryckeri Aktiebolag, 1922.

Vaiṣṇava Dharmaśāstra. Ed. V. Krishnamacharya *Viṣṇusmṛti, with the Commentary Keśavavaijantī of Nandapaṇḍita*. Adyar Library Series 93. Madras: Adyar Library and Research Center, 1964.

Vaiṣṇava Dharmaśāstra. Ed. and trans. Patrick Olivelle. *The Law Code of Viṣṇu: A Critical Edition and Annotated Translation of the Vaiṣṇava-Dharmaśāstra*. Harvard Oriental Series 73. Cambridge, Mass.: Department of Sanskrit and Indian Studies, Harvard University: Distributed by Harvard University Press, 2009.

Vājasaneyi Saṃhitā. Ed. Albrecht Weber. *The White Yajurveda. The Vājasaneyi-Saṃhitā in the Mādhyaṃdina- and Kāṇva Śākhā*. Berlin: F. Dümmler, 1852–1859.

Vasiṣṭha Dharmasūtra, see *Dharmasūtras*.

Vikramāṅkadevacarita of Bilhaṇa. Ed. Georg Bühler. Bombay Sanskrit Series 14. Bombay: Government Central Book Depot, 1875.

Vinaya (Pali). Ed. Hermann Oldenberg. London: Williams and Norgate, 1879–1883.

Vinaya (Pali). Trans. I. B. Horner. *The Book of the Discipline (Vinaya-piṭaka)*. Sacred Books of the Buddhists 10–11, 13–14, 20, 25. London: Pub. for the Pali Text Society by Luzac & Co., 1969.

Viyāhapannatti, Bhagavaī: The Fifth Aṅga of the Jaina Canon. Study by Jozef Deleu. 1st Indian ed. Delhi: Motilal Banarsidass, 1996.

Wine, Beere, Ale, and Tobaco, a Seventeenth Century Interlude. Ed. James Holly Hanford. *Studies in Philology* 12.1, 1915.

Xuanzang. *The Great Tang Dynasty Record of the Western Regions*. Trans. Li Rongxi. Berkeley, Calif.: BDK America, 1996.

Yājñavalkyasmṛti with commentary of Viśvarūpa. Ed. T. Gaṇapati Sāstrī. *The Yâjnavalkyasmriti: With the commentary Bālakrīda of Visvarûpâchârya*. Anantaśayana saṃskṛtagranthāvaliḥ 74, 81. Trivandrum: Printed by the Govt. Press, 1922.

Yājñavalkyasmṛti with *Mitākṣarā* commentary of Vijñāneśvara. Ed. Nārāyaṇaśāstrī Khiste and Jagannātha Śāstrī. Caukhambā-Saṃskṛta-granthamālā 62. Varanasi: Caukhambā Saṃskṛta Sīriza Āphisa, 1930.

Yaśastilaka of Somadeva. Ed. M. P. Śivadatta and V. L. Ś. Paṇaśikar. Kāvyamālā 70. Mumbayyāṃ: Nirṇayasāgarākhyamudraṇayantrālaye, 1916.

Yogaratnākara. Ed. Chimnājī Āpte. Poona: Māhādeva, 1888.

Yogaśāstra of Hemacandra. Ed. Muni Jambūvijaya. Delhi:Motilal Banarsidas; Ahmedabad: Śrī Siddhibhuvanamanohara Jaina Ṭrasṭa; Bhavnagar: Śrī Jaina Ātmānanda Sabhā, 2009.

Yogaśāstra of Hemacandra. Trans. Olle Quarnström. *The Yogaśāstra of Hemacandra: A Twelfth Century Handbook on Śvetāmbara Jainism*. Harvard Oriental Series 60. Cambridge, Mass.: Dept. of Sanskrit and Indian Studies, Harvard University, Distributed by Harvard University Press, 2002.

Yogayātrā of Varāhamihira. Ed. Rāmacandra Jha. Kāmeśvara Siṃha Granthamālā 23. Darabhaṅgā: Kāmeśvarasiṃhadarabhaṅghāsaṃskṛtaviśvavidyālaya, 1986.

Secondary Sources

Aalto, Pentti. 1959. "Madyam Apeyam." In *Johannes Nobel Commemoration Volume*, ed. C. Vogel, 17–37. New Delhi: International Academy of Indian Culture.

Achaya, K. T. 1991. "Alcoholic Fermentation and its Products in Ancient India." *Indian Journal of the History of Science* 26: 122–129.

———. 1994. *Indian Food: A Historical Companion*. Delhi: Oxford University Press.

———. 1998. *A Historical Dictionary of Indian Food*. Delhi; New York: Oxford University Press.

Agrawala, Vasudeva Sharana. 1963. *India as Known to Pāṇini: A Study of the Cultural Material in the* Ashṭādhyāyī. Varanasi: Prithvi Prakashan.

———. 1974. *Bṛhatkakathāślokasaṃgraha: A Study*. Varanasi: Prithivi Prakashan.

Ali, Daud. 1998. "Technologies of the Self: Courtly Artifice and Monastic Discipline in Early India." *Journal of the Economic and Social History of the Orient* 41.2: 159–184.

———. 2004. *Courtly Culture and Political Life in Early Medieval India*. Cambridge: Cambridge University Press.

———. 2018. "The Betel-Bag Bearer in South Indian History: A Study from Inscriptions." In *Clio and Her Descendants: Essays for Kesavan Veluthat*, ed. Manu Devadevan, 524–546. Delhi: Primus Books.

Allchin, F. Raymond. 1977. *Evidence of Early Distillation at Shaikhân Dherî*. Ed. Maurizio Taddei. Naples: South Asian Archaeology, 755–797.

———. 1979. "India: The Ancient Home of Distillation." *Man*, New Series 14.1: 55–63.

Alsdorf, Ludwig. 1966. *The Arya Stanzas of the Uttarajjhaya. Abhandlungen der Geistes- und Sozialwissenschaftlichen Klasse*, Jahrg. 1966, Nr.2. Mainz: Akademie der Wissenschaften Und der Literatur in Kommission Bei F. Steiner, Wiesbaden.

———. 2010. *The History of Vegetarianism and Cow-Veneration in India*. London; New York: Routledge Advances in Jaina Studies. Taylor and Francis.

Ambasta, S. P. ed. 2000. *The Useful Plants of India*. New Delhi: National Institute of Science Communication, Council of Scientific & Industrial Research.

Anonymous. 1907. "Rice Spirit." *Indian Engineering* 40: 308–309.

Appleton, Naomi. 2010. *Jataka Stories in Theravada Buddhism: Narrating the Bodhisatta Path*. Burlington: Ashgate Pub.

———. 2017. *Shared Characters in Jain, Buddhist and Hindu Narrative: Gods, Kings and Other Heroes*. Abingdon, Oxon: Routledge.

Apte, V. S. 2003. *The Practical Sanskrit-English Dictionary*. Rev. and enl. ed. Delhi: Motilal Banarsidass.

Asiatic Society, Calcutta. 1978. *Rajendralal Mitra 150th Anniversary Lectures*. Calcutta: Asiatic Society.

Asouti, Eleni, and Dorian Q. Fuller. 2008. *Trees and Woodlands of South India: Archaeological Perspectives*. Walnut Creek, Calif.: Left Coast Press.

Bakels, C. C. 2003. "Report Concerning the Contents of a Ceramic Vessel Found in the 'White Room' of the Gonur Temenos, Merv Oasis, Turkmenistan." *Electronic Journal of Vedic Studies* 9.

Bakhtin, Mikhail. 1984. *Problems of Dostoevsky's Poetics: Mikhail Bakhtin*. Ed. and trans. Caryl Emerson; introduction by Wayne C. Booth. Minneapolis: University of Minnesota Press.

Bapat, G. V. 1966. "Madhu-Drinking: An Interesting Episode and Problem from the Ramayana." *Bulletin of the Deccan College Research Institute* 25: 59–64.

Basham, A. L. 1981. *History and Doctrines of the Ajivikas, a Vanished Indian Religion*. Delhi: Motilal Banarsidass (reprint).

Baums, S., and A. Glass. *A Dictionary of Gāndhārī*. Online resource available at https://gandhari.org/n_dictionary.php

Bedekar, V. M. 1967. "Legend of the Churning of the Ocean in the Epics and Purāṇas: A Comparative Study." *Purāṇa* 9: 7–61.

Benn, James A. 2015. *Tea in China: A Religious and Cultural History*. Honolulu: University of Hawai'i Press.

Bennett, Judith M. 1996. *Ale, Beer and Brewsters in England: Women's Work in a Changing World, 1300–1600*. New York: Oxford University Press.

Bhattacharya, R. 2002. "Cārvāka Fragments: A New Collection." *Journal of Indian Philosophy* 30.6: 597–640.

Bhattacharya, S. 1966. "Some Munda Etymologies." In *Studies in Comparative Austroasiatic Linguistics*, ed. N. H. Zide, 28–40. The Hague: Mouton.

Bigger, Andreas. 1998. *Balarāma im Mahābhārata: Seine Darstellung im Rahmen des Textes und Seiner Entwicklung*. Beiträge Zur Indologie 30. Wiesbaden: Harrassowitz Verlag.

Bloomfield, Maurice. 1893. "Contributions to the Interpretation of the Veda: The Story of Indra and Namuci." *Journal of the American Oriental Society* 15: 143–188.

———. 1920a. "Notes on the Divyāvadāna." *Journal of the American Oriental Society* 40: 336–352.

———. 1920b. "The Dohada or Craving of Pregnant Women: A Motif of Hindu Fiction." *Journal of the American Oriental Society* 40: 1.

Bodewitz, H. 2007. "Sins and Vices: Their Enumerations and Specifications in the Veda." *Indo-Iranian Journal* 50.4: 317–339.

Böhtlingk, Otto von, and Roth, Rudolph. 1855–1875. *Sanskrit-wörterbuch heraugegeben von der Kaiserlichen Akademie der Wissenschaften*. St. Petersburg: Buchdr. der K. Akademie der Wissenschaften.

Böhtlingk, Otto von, and Ludwig Fritze. 1880. *Indische Sprüche*. Leipzig: P. Reclam.

Bottéro, Jean. 1995. "Le vin dans une Civilization de la Bière: la Mésopotamie." In *In Vino Veritas*, ed. O. Murray and M. Tecusan, 21–34. London: British School in Rome.

Boyd White, James. 1985. "Law as Rhetoric, Rhetoric as Law: The Arts of Cultural and Communal Life." *University of Chicago Law Review* 52: 684–702.

Braidwood Robert, J. et al. 1953. "Symposium: Did Man Once Live by Beer Alone?" *American Anthropologist* 55.4: 515–526.

Brick, David. 2012. "Social and Soteriological Aspects of Sin and Penance in Medieval Hindu Law." In *Sins and Sinners*, ed. Phyllis Granoff and Koichi Shinohara, 7–30. Numen Book Series 139.

Brooks, Douglas Renfew. 2000. "The Ocean of the Heart: Selections of the *Kularnava Tantra*." In Tantra in Practice, ed. D. White, 347–360. Princeton, N.J.: Princeton University Press.

Brough, John. 1971. "Soma and *Amanita muscaria*." *Bulletin of the School of Oriental and African Studies* 34.2: 331–362.

———. 1973. "Problems of the 'Soma-Mushroom' Theory." *Indologica Taurinensia* 1: 21–32.

Bryant, Edwin. 2002. "The Date and Provenance of the Bhāgavata Purāṇa and the Vaikuṇṭha Perumāl Temple." *Journal of Vaishnava Studies* 11.1: 51–80.

Bühnemann, Gudrun. 2017. "Churned from the Milk Ocean, Invoked into a Skull Cup: The Goddess Vāruṇī in Nepal." *Berliner Indologische Studien* 23: 215–264.

Burrow, T. 1940. *A Translation of the Kharoṣṭhi Documents from Chinese Turkestan. James G. Forlong Fund Series* 20. London: Royal Asiatic Society.

Burrow, T., and M. B. Emeneau. 1984. *A Dravidian Etymological Dictionary*, 2nd ed. Oxford: Clarendon Press.

Cabezón, José Ignacio. 2017. *Sexuality in Classical South Asian Buddhism. Studies in Indian and Tibetan Buddhism*. Somerville, Mass.: Wisdom Publications.

Caland, W. 1903. *Über das Rituelle Sūtra des Baudhāyana. Abhandlungen für die Kunde des Morgenlandes*, Bd. 12, 1. Leipzig: Brockhaus.

Carroll, Aaron, E. 2015. "Alcohol or Marijuana? A Pediatrician Faces the Question." *New York Times*, March 16, 2015.

Carstairs, G. M. 1979. "Daru and Bhang, Cultural Factors in the Choice of Intoxicant." In *Beliefs, Behaviors, & Alcoholic Beverages: A Cross-cultural Survey*, ed. Mac Marshall, 297–312. Ann Arbor: University of Michigan Press.

Carter, Martha, L. 1968. "Dionysiac Aspects of Kushan Art." *Ars Orientalis* 7: 121–146.

———. 1982. "The Bacchants of Mathura: New Evidence of Dionysiac Yaksha Imagery from Kushan Mathura." *The Bulletin of the Cleveland Museum of Art* 69.8: 247–257.

———. 1992. "Dionysiac Festivals and Gandharan Imagery." In *Banquets d'Orient*, ed. R. Gyselen, *Res Orientales*, v. 4, 51–60. Bures-sur-Yvette: Leuven (Belgique): Groupe Pour l'Étude de la Civilisation du Moyen-Orient; Diffusion, Peeters Press.

Casson, L. 1989. *The Periplus Maris Erythraei: Text with Introduction, Translation, and Commentary*. Princeton, N.J.: Princeton University Press.

Chandra, K. R. 1987. *Prākṛta-Hindī-Koś*. Ahmedabad: Prakrit Jain Vidya Vikās Fund.

Chatterjee, P. 2005. "The Lives of Alcohol in Pre-colonial India." *The Medieval History Journal* 8: 189–225.

Chattopadhyaya, B. 1994. *The Making of Early Medieval India*. Delhi; New York: Oxford University Press.

Chaucer, Geoffrey. *The Riverside Chaucer* (3rd ed.). Boston, Mass.: Houghton Mifflin, 1987.

Ch'en, Kenneth. 1945. "A Study of the Svagata Story in the Divyavadana in Its Sanskrit, Pali, Tibetan, and Chinese Versions." *Harvard Journal of Asiatic Studies* 9: 207–314.

Clark, Matthew. 2017. *The Tawny One: Soma, Haoma, and Ayahuasca*. London: Muswell Hill Press.

Clark, Peter. 1983. *The English Alehouse: A Social History, 1200–1830*. London; New York: Longman.

Cohen, Richard Scott. 1995. "Setting the Three Jewels: The Complex Culture of Buddhism at the Ajanta Caves." Ph.D. Thesis, University of Michigan.

Collins, Steven. 2015. "Madness and Possession in Pāli Texts." *Buddhist Studies Review* 31.2: 195–214.

Courtwright, David T. 2001. *Forces of Habit: Drugs and the Making of the Modern World.* Cambridge, Mass.: Harvard University Press.

Cox, Whitney. 2017. *Modes of Philology in Medieval South India.* Philological Encounters Monographs 1. Leiden; Boston: Brill.

Curley, David. 2003. "'Voluntary' Relationships and Royal Gifts of Pān in Mughal Bengal." In *Robes of Honour: Khil'at in Precolonial and Colonial India*, ed. Stewart Gordon, 50–79. Delhi: Oxford University Press.

Damerow, Peter. 2012. "Sumerian Beer: The Origins of Brewing Technology in Ancient Mesopotamia." *Cuneiform Digital Library Journal* 2012.2: 1–20.

Daniels, Christian. 1996. *Science and Civilization in China*, vol. 6, pt. 3, *Agro-Industries: Sugarcane Technology.* Cambridge: Cambridge University Press.

Das, Rahul, Peter. 1988. *Das Wissen von der Lebensspanne der Bäume: Surapālas Vṛkṣāyurveda.* Ed. and trans. Rahul Peter Das. Alt- und Neu-Indische Studien 34. Stuttgart: Franz Steiner Verlag Wiesbaden Gmbh.

Davidson, Ronald M. 2002. *Indian Esoteric Buddhism: A Social History of the Tantric Movement.* New York: Columbia University Press.

Davis, Donald R. 2005. "Intermediate Realms of Law: Corporate Groups and Rulers in Medieval India." *Journal of the Economic and Social History of the Orient* 48.1: 92–117.

———. 2010. *The Spirit of Hindu Law.* Cambridge; New York: Cambridge University Press.

———. 2011. "Matrilineal Adoption, Inheritance Law, and Rites for the Dead among Hindus in Medieval Kerala." In *Religion and Identity in South Asia and Beyond: Essays in Honor of Patrick Olivelle*, ed. Steven E. Lindquist, 147–164. London/New York/Delhi: Anthem Press.

Descriptive Catalogue of the Sanskrit Manuscripts of the Asiatic Society, vol. XIV, Calcutta, 1955.

Dezsö, C. and Vasudeva, S, ed. and trans. 2009. *The Quartet of Causeries.* Clay Sanskrit Library. New York: New York University Press, JJC Foundation.

Dietler, Michael. 1990. "Driven by Drink: The Role of Drinking in the Political Economy and the Case of Early Iron Age France." *Journal of Anthropological Archaeology* 9: 352–406.

———. 2001. "Theorizing the Feast: Rituals of Consumption, Commensal Politics, and Power in African contexts." In *Feasts: Archaeological and Ethnographic Perspectives on Food, Politics, and Power*, ed. M. Dietler and B. Hayden, 65–114. Tuscaloosa: University of Alabama Press.

———. 2006. "Alcohol: Anthropological/Archaeological Perspectives." *Annual Review of Anthropology* 35: 229–249.

———, and Ingrid Herbich. 2006. "Liquid Material Culture: Following the Flow of Beer Among the Luo of Kenya (with Ingrid Herbich)." In *Grundlegungen, Beiträge zur europäischen und afrikanischen Archäologie für Manfred K.H. Eggert*, ed. Hans-Peter Wotzka, 395–408. Tübingen: Francke Verlag.

Divatia, Narsinhrao Bholanath. 1921. *Gujarāti Language and Literature.* London: Macmillan.

D'Mello, J. P. Felix. 1997. *Handbook of Plant and Fungal Toxicants.* Boca Raton: CRC Press.

Doniger, Wendy. 1968. "The Post-Vedic History of the Soma Plant." In Wasson 1968, 95–147.

Douglas, Mary. 2002 [1966]. *Purity and Danger*. London: Routledge and K. Paul.

———, and International Commission on Anthropology of Food and Food Problems. 1987. *Constructive Drinking: Perspectives on Drink from Anthropology*. Cambridge; New York; Paris: Cambridge University Press; Editions de la Maison des sciences de l'homme.

Dumézil, Georges. 1924. *Le festin d'immortalité*. Paris: Libraries Orientaliste Paul Geunthner.

Dumont, Paul-Emile. 1963. "The Human Sacrifice in the Taittirīya-Brāhmaṇa: The Fourth Prapāṭhaka of the Third Kāṇḍa of the Taittirīya-Brāhmaṇa with Translation." *Proceedings of the American Philosophical Society* 107.2: 177–182.

———. 1965. "The Kaukilī-Sautrāmaṇī in the Taittirīya-Brāhmaṇa: The Sixth Prapāṭhaka of the Second Kāṇḍa of the Taittirīya-Brāhmaṇa with Translation." *Proceedings of the American Philosophical Society* 109.6: 309–341.

Dundas, Paul. 2002. *The Jains*. 2nd ed. London: Routledge.

Dupuche, John R. 2003. *Abhinavagupta: The Kula Ritual, As Elaborated in Chapter 29 of the Tantrāloka*. Delhi: Motilal Banarsidass.

Dutt, Uday, Chand. 1922. *Materia Medica of the Hindus*. Rev. ed. with additions and alterations. Calcutta: Adi-Ayurveda Machine Press.

Edgerton, F. 1931. *The Elephant-Lore of the Hindus; The Elephant-Sport (Matanga-lila) of Nilakantha*. New Haven: Yale University Press.

Elizarenkova, Tatiana. 1996. "The Problem of Soma in the Light of Language and Style of the Ṛgveda." In *Langue, Style et Structure dans le Monde Indien: Centenaire de Louis Renou: Actes du Colloque International (Paris, 25–27 Janvier 1996)*, ed. Nalini Balbir, Georges-Jean Pinault, Jean Fezas, and Louis Renou, 13–31. Paris: Librairie H. Champion.

Falk, Harry. 1986. *Bruderschaft und Würfelspiel: Untersuchungen zur Entwicklungsgeschichte des Vedischen Opfers*. Freiburg: H. Falk.

———. 2009. "Making Wine in Gandhara under Buddhist Monastic Supervision." *Bulletin of the Asia Institute* 23: 65–78.

———. 2010. "Libation Trays from Gandhara." *Bulletin of the Asia Institute*, New Series, 24: 89–113.

Feer, Léon. 1883. *Fragments, Extraits du Kandjour. Annales du Musée Guimet*, T. 5. Paris: E. Leroux.

Ferstl, Christian. 2011. "Mahendravikramavarmans Mattavilāsaprahasana im kultur- und literaturgeschichtlichen Kontext." M.Phil Thesis. Universität Wien.

———. Forthcoming. "Overlooked Material for the Study of Pāśupata Śaivism: The Satirical Play Mattavilāsaprahasana." Available on academia.edu, accessed November 3, 2020: https://www.academia.edu/12332050/Overlooked_Material_for_the_Study_of_Pāśupata_Śaivism_The_satirical_play_Mattavilāsaprahasana

Finot, Louis. 1896. *Les Lapidaires Indiens*. Paris: É. Bouillon.

Fischer-Tiné, Harald, and Jana Tschurenev, eds. 2014. *A History of Alcohol and Drugs in Modern South Asia: Intoxicating Affairs*. London; New York: Routledge, Taylor & Francis Group.

Flattery, David Stophlet, and Martin Schwartz. 1989. *Haoma and Harmaline: The Botanical Identity of the Indo-Iranian Sacred Hallucinogen "soma" and Its Legacy in Religion, Language, and Middle-Eastern Folklore*. Berkeley: University of California Press.

Gamburd, Michele Ruth. 2008. *Breaking the Ashes: The Culture of Illicit Liquor in Sri Lanka*. Ithaca, N.Y.: Cornell University Press.

Garner, Bryan A. 1995. *A Dictionary of Modern Legal Usage*. 2nd ed. New York: Oxford University Press.

Geeta, R., and Gharaibeh, Waleed. 2007. "Historical Evidence for a Pre-Columbian Presence of Datura in the Old World and Implications for a First Millennium Transfer from the New World." *Journal of Biosciences* 32.7: 1227–1244.

Geslani, Marko. 2016. "Astrological Vedism: Varāhamihira in Light of the Later Rituals of the Atharvaveda." *Journal of the American Oriental Society* 136.2: 305–323.

Gnoli, Raniero. 1985. *Il Commento Di Abhinavagupta Alla Parātriṃśikā (Parātriṃśikātattvavivaraṇam): Traduzione E Testo*. Serie Orientale Roma 58. Roma: Istituto Italiano per Il Medio Ed Estremo Oriente.

Gode, P. K. 1960a. *Studies in Indian Cultural History*, vol. 1. Hoshiarpur: Vishveshvaranand Vedic Research Institute.

———. 1960b. "The Attitude of Hindu Dharmaśāstra towards Tāmbūla-Bhoga." In Gode 1960a, 131–138.

———. 1960c. "History of the Verse about the Thirteen Qualities of Tāmbūla—Between A.D. 1200 and 1900." In Gode 1960a, 145–148.

———. 1960d. "History of the Spittoon in India." In Gode 1960a., 181–190.

———. 1960e. "Reference to Tobacco in Some Sanskrit Works between A.D. 1600 and 1900." In Gode 1960a, 410–417.

———. 1960f. "References to Tobacco in Marathi Literature and Records between A.D. 1600 and 1900." In Gode 1960a, 418–426.

Gold, Jonathan C. 2018. "Vasubandhu." *The Stanford Encyclopedia of Philosophy* (Summer 2018 Edition), ed. Edward N. Zalta. https://plato.stanford.edu/archives/sum2018/entries/vasubandhu/

Goldman, Robert P. 1977. *Gods, Priests, and Warriors: The Bhṛgus of the Mahābhārata*. Studies in Oriental Culture 12. New York: Columbia University Press.

Gombrich, Richard F. 1991. *Buddhist Precept and Practice: Traditional Buddhism in the Rural Highlands of Ceylon*. 2nd ed. with minor corrections. Delhi: Motilal Banarsidass.

Gonda, J. 1952. *Ancient-Indian Ojas, Latin *augos and the Indo-European Nouns in -es-/-os*. Utrecht: A. Oosthoek, 1952.

———. 1977. *The Ritual Sūtras*. Wiesbaden: Harrassowitz.

———. 1980. *The Mantras of the Agnyupasthāna and the Sautrāmaṇī*. Amsterdam; New York: North-Holland Pub. Co.

Goodman, Jordan. 1995. "Excitantia: or, How Enlightenment Europe Took to Soft Drugs." In Goodman et al. 1995, 126–148.

———, Paul E. Lovejoy, and Andrew Sherratt. 1995. *Consuming Habits: Drugs in History and Anthropology*. London; New York: Routledge.

Gopal, L. 1964. "Sugar-Making in Ancient India." *Journal of the Economic and Social History of the Orient* 7.1: 57–72.

Goudriaan, Teun, and Gupta, Sanjukta. 1981. *Hindu Tantric and Śākta Literature. A History of Indian Literature*, vol. 2, fasc. 2. Wiesbaden: Harrassowitz.

Grierson, George Abraham. 1885. *Bihār Peasant Life*. Calcutta; London: The Bengal Secretariat Press; Trübner and Co.

Gutierrez, Andrea. 2015. "Modes of Betel Consumption in Early India: *Bhoga* and *Abhoga*." *Scripta Instituti Donneriani Aboensis* 26: 114–134.

Habib, I. 1985. "Medieval Technology: Exchanges between India and the Islamic World." *Aligarh Journal of Oriental Studies* 1.2: 197–222.

———. 2011. *Economic History of Medieval India, 1200–1500*. History of Science, Philosophy, and Culture in Indian Civilization, vol. VIII, Economic History of India Pt. 1. New Delhi: Pearson Education.

Habighorst, Ludwig V., P. Reichart, and Vijay Sharma. 2007. *Love for Pleasure: Betel, Tobacco, Wine, and Drugs in Indian Miniatures*. Koblenz, Germany: Ragaputra Edition.

Handiqui, Krishna Kanta. 1968. *Yaśastilaka and Indian Culture*. 2nd ed. Jīvarāja Jaina Granthamālā; Pushpa 2. Sholapur: Jaina Saṁskṛti Saṁrakshaka Sangha.

Hansen, Valerie. 2012. *The Silk Road: A New History*. New York: Oxford University Press.

Hara, Minoru. 1969. "A Note on the Sanskrit Phrase *devānāṃ priya*." *Indian Linguistics* 30: 13–26.

Harihara Sastri, G. 1956–1957. "Notes on the Arthaśāstra of Kauṭalya." *The Journal of Oriental Research* (Madras) 26: 107–113.

Hartman, Louis F., and A. Leo Oppenheim. 1950. *On Beer and Brewing Techniques in Ancient Mesopotamia*. Supplement to the *Journal of the American Oriental Society*. Baltimore: American Oriental Society.

Harvey, Peter. 2000. *An Introduction to Buddhist Ethics: Foundations, Values, and Issues*. Cambridge; New York: Cambridge University Press.

Hatley, Shaman. 2018. *The Brahmayāmalatantra or Picumata. Volume I: Chapters 1–2, 39–40 & 83. Revelation, Ritual, and Material Culture in an Early Śaiva Tantra*. Collection Indologie N° 133; Early Tantra Series N° 5. Institut Français De Pondichéry/Ecole Française D'Extrême-Orient/Asien-Afrika-Institut, Universität Hamburg, 2018.

Hattox, Ralph S. 1985. *Coffee and Coffeehouses: The Origins of a Social Beverage in the Medieval Near East*. Seattle; London: University of Washington Press.

Havell, E. B. 1920. "What Is Soma." *Journal of the Royal Asiatic Society of Great Britain and Ireland* 52.3: 349–351.

Hawkes, Jacquetta. 1967. "God in the Machine." *Antiquity* 41.163: 174–180.

Heim, Maria. 2013. *The Forerunner of All Things: Buddhaghosa on Mind, Intention, and Agency*. New York: Oxford University Press.

Hein, N. 1986. "A Revolution in Krsnaism: The Cult of Gopala." *History of Religions* 25.4: 296–317.

Hellwig, Oliver. 2009a. *Wörterbuch der Mittelalterlichen Indischen Alchemie*. Eelde, Netherlands: Barkhuis.

———. 2009b. "The Theory of the *Puruṣa* in *Carakasaṃhitā, Śārīrasthāna* 1.1 and Its Connection with the Early History of Indian Philosophy." *Studien zur Indologie und Iranistik* 28: 27–69.

———. 2012. "Intoxication." *Brill's Encyclopedia of Hinduism*. Leiden; Boston: Brill.

Henning, Walter Bruno. 1955. "The Middle-Persian Word for 'Beer.'" *Bulletin of the School of Oriental and African Studies* 17.3: 603–604.

Hickman, Timothy A. 2014. "Target America: Visual Culture, Neuroimaging, and the 'Hijacked Brain' Theory of Addiction." *Past & Present* 222, No. Suppl. 9: 207–226.

Hopkins, E. 1905. "The Fountain of Youth." *Journal of the American Oriental Society* 26.1: 1.

Houben, Jan, E. M. 2003. "The Soma-Haoma Problem: Introductory Overview and Observations on the Discussion." *Electronic Journal of Vedic Studies* 9.1: 1–47.

Huang, H. T. 2000. *Science and Civilization in China*. Fermentations and Food Science vol. 6, pt. 5. Cambridge: Cambridge University Press.

Humbach, Helmut. 2007. "The Indian God of Wine." In *Iranian Languages and Texts from Iran and Turan: Ronald E. Emmerick Memorial Volume*, ed. M. Macuch, M. Maggi, and W. Sundermann, 135–142. Wiesbaden: Harrassowitz Verlag.

Huntington, John C., and Dina Bangdel. 2003. *The Circle of Bliss: Buddhist Meditational Art*. Chicago, Ill.: Serindia Publications.

Hyne-Sutherland, Amy Louise. 2015. "Speaking of Madness: A Comparative Analysis of Discourses on Pathologized Deviance in Contemporary and Classical India." Ph.D. Thesis, University of Texas at Austin.

Jacobi, Hermann. 1968 (1884, 1895). *Jaina Sutras*. Sacred Books of the East 22, 45. Delhi: Motilal Banarsidass.

Jain, S. A. 1992. *Reality: English Translation of Shri Pujyapada's Sarvarthasiddhi*. Madras: Jwalamalini Trust.

James, William. 1902. *The Varieties of Religious Experience*. New York: Longmans, Green, and Co.

Jamison, Stephanie W. 1983. *Function and Form in the -áya-formations of the Rig Veda and Atharva Veda*. Ergänzungshefte Zur Zeitschrift Für Vergleichende Sprachforschung 31. Göttingen: Vandenhoeck & Ruprecht.

———. 1986. "Brāhmaṇa Syllable Counting, Vedic *Tvác* 'Skin', and the Sanskrit Expression for the Canonical Creature." *Indo-Iranian Journal* 29.3: 161–181.

———. 1991. *The Ravenous Hyenas and the Wounded Sun: Myth and Ritual in Ancient India*. Ithaca, N.Y.: Cornell University Press.

———. 2007. *The Rig Veda between Two Worlds = Le R̥gveda Entre Deux Mondes: Quatre Conférences au Collège de France en Mai 2004*. Paris: Collège de France.

———. 2019. "The Term Gr̥hastha and the (Pre)history of the Householder." In *Gr̥hastha: The Householder in Ancient Indian Religious Culture*, ed. P. Olivelle. New York: Oxford University Press.

———. Online commentary on Rig Veda translation. http://rigvedacommentary.alc.ucla.edu/ Accessed May 1, 2021.

Jha, D. N. 2002. *The Myth of the Holy Cow*. New Delhi: Navayana Publishing, 2009.

Joshi, N. P. 1979. *Iconography of Balarāma*. 1st ed. New Delhi: Abhinav Publications.

Kane, P. V. 1930–1962. *History of Dharmaśāstra (Ancient and Mediaeval Religious and Civil Law in India)*. Poona: Bhandarkar Oriental Research Institute.

Kano, Kazuo, and Jowita Kramer. 2020. "The Fourth Chapter of the *Tattvārthā Abhidharmakośaṭīkā*: On Forbidding Intoxicating Liquor." In *Sanskrit Manuscripts in China III: Proceedings of a Panel at the 2016 Beijing International Seminar on Tibetan Studies August 1 to 4*, ed. Birgit Kellner, Jowita Kramer, and Li Xuezhu, 107–136. Beijing: China Tibetology Publishing House.

Karttunen, Klaus. 1997. *India and the Hellenistic World*. Studia Orientalia 83. Helsinki: Finnish Oriental Society.

Kern, Hendrick. 1913. "Die Yogayatra des Varahamihira, Adhyaya 1–9." *Verspreide Geschriften*, Vol. 1, 99–168. Hague.

Khoroche, Peter. 1987. *Towards a New Edition of Ārya-Śūra's Jātakamālā*. Bonn: Indica et Tibetica.

Khoroche, Peter, and Wendy Doniger. 1989. *Once the Buddha Was a Monkey: Ārya Śūra's Jātakamālā*. Chicago: University of Chicago Press.

Kieffer-Pülz, Petra. 2005. "Die Klassifizierung des Alkoholverbots in der Buddhistischen Rechtsliteratur der Theravādin." In *Im Dickicht der Gebote. Studien zur Dialektik von Norm und Praxis in der Buddhismusgeschichte Asiens*, ed. P. Schalk, 153–223. Uppsala: Universitet.

Kirfel, Willibald. 1920. *Die Kosmographie der Inder, nach den Quellen Dargestellt*. Bonn U. Leipzig: K. Schroeder.

Knutson, Jesse. 2014. *Into the Twilight of Sanskrit Court Poetry: The Sena Salon of Bengal and Beyond*. Berkeley: University of California Press.

Kolhatkar, Madhavi. 1987. "The Method of Preparing Surā According to the Vedic Texts." *Bulletin of the Deccan College Research Institute* 46: 41–45.

———. 1999. *Surā, the Liquor and the Vedic Sacrifice*. New Delhi: D.K. Printworld.

Kosambi, D. 1959. "Indian Feudal Trade Charters." *Journal of the Economic and Social History of the Orient* 2.3: 281–293.

Krom, Nicolaas Johannes, and Theodoor van Erp. 1920–1931. *Beschrijving Van Barabudur Samengesteld*. 's-Gravenhage: M. Nijhoff.

Kueny, Kathryn. 2001. *The Rhetoric of Sobriety: Wine in Early Islam*. Albany: State University of New York Press.

Kuiper, Franciscus Bernardus Jacobus. 1979. *Varuna and Vidūṣaka: On the Origin of the Sanskrit Drama*. Verhandelingen Der Koninklijke Nederlandse Akademie Van Wetenschappen, Afd. Letterkunde; Nieuwe Reeks, D.100. Amsterdam; New York: North-Holland Pub.

Lacôte, Félix. 1908. *Essai sur Guṇāḍhya et la Bṛhatkathā, Suivi du Texte Inédit des Chapitres XXVII à XXX du Nepāla-māhātmya, par Félix Lacôte*. France: E. Leroux.

Lamotte, Etienne. 1944. *Le Traité de la Grande Vertu de Sagesse (Mahāprajñāpāramitāśāstra)*. Bibliothèque Du Muséon v. 18. Louvain: Bureaux Du Muséon.

Langenberg, Amy Paris. 2020. "On Reading Buddhist Vinaya: Feminist History, Hermeneutics, and Translating Women's Bodies." *Journal of the American Academy of Religion* 88.4: 1121–1153.

Lebot, Vincent, Mark David Merlin, and Lamont Lindstrom. 1992. *Kava: The Pacific Drug*. New Haven, Conn.: Yale University Press.

Lemon, Rebecca. 2018. *Addiction and Devotion in Early Modern England*. Philadelphia: University of Pennsylvania Press.

Lockwood, Patricia. 2021. *No One Is Talking About This*. New York: Riverhead Books.

Losty, J. P. 2019. *Rajput Paintings from the Ludwig Habighorst Collection*. London: Francesca Galloway.

Lovejoy, Paul E. 1995. "Kola Nuts: The 'Coffee' of the Central Sudan." In Goodman et al. 1995, 98–120.

Lubin, Timothy. 2005. "The Transmission, Patronage, and Prestige of Brahmanical Piety from the Mauryas to the Guptas." In *Boundaries, Dynamics and Construction of Traditions in South Asia*, ed. Federico Squarcini, 77–103. Firenze, Italy: Firenze University Press and [New Delhi]: Munshiram Manoharlal.

———. 2015. "Writing and the Recognition of Customary Law in Premodern India and Java." *Journal of the American Oriental Society* 135.2: 225–259.

———, Donald R. Davis, Jr., and Jayanth K. Krishnan, eds. 2010. *Hinduism and Law: An Introduction*. Cambridge: Cambridge University Press.

Mahdihassan, S. 1972. "The Earliest Distillation Units of Pottery in Indo-Pakistan." *Pakistan Archaeology* 8: 159–168.

———. 1979. "Distillation Assembly of Pottery in Ancient India." *Vishveshvaranand Indological Journal* 17: 264–266.

Malamoud, Charles. 1989. *Cuire le Monde: Rite et Pensée dans l'Inde Ancienne*. Paris: La Découverte.

———. 1992. "Le soma et sa contrepartie: remarques sur les stupéfiants et les spiritueux dans les rites de l'Inde ancienne." In *Le Ferment Divin*, ed. Dominique Fournier and Salvatore D'Oonofrio, 19–33. Paris: Éditions de la Maison des sciences de l'homme.

Mallinson, James. 2007. *The Khecarīvidyā of Ādinātha: A Critical Edition and Annotated Translation of an Early Text of Haṭhayoga*. Routledge Studies in Tantric Traditions. London; New York: Routledge.

Mani, Vettam. 1979. *Purāṇic Encyclopaedia*. Delhi: Motilal Banarsidass.

Manohar, P. Ram. 2004. "Smoking and Ayurvedic Medicine in India." In *Smoke: A Global History of Smoking*, ed. S. L. Gilman et al., 68–75. London: Reaktion Books.

Marshall, John Hubert. 1951. *Taxila: An Illustrated Account of Archaeological Excavations Carried Out at Taxila under the Orders of the Government of India between the Years 1913 and 1934*. Cambridge: Cambridge University Press.

Martin, Meredith. 2011. *Dairy Queens: The Politics of Pastoral Architecture from Catherine De' Medici to Marie-Antoinette*. Harvard Historical Studies 176. Cambridge, Mass.: Harvard University Press.

Mayrhofer, Manfred. 1956–. *Kurzgefasstes Etymologisches Wörterbuch des Altindischen. Indogermanische Bibliothek* II Reihe, Wörterbücher. Heidelberg: Winter.

———. 1986–. *Etymologisches Wörterbuch des Altindoarischen. Indogermanische Bibliothek* II Reihe, Wörterbücher. Heidelberg: C. Winter.

McClish, Mark. 2009. "Political Brahminism and the State: a Compositional History of the Arthaśāstra." PhD diss., University of Texas at Austin, 2009.

———. 2019. "A Thematic Analysis of the *Āpastamba Dharmasūtra*." Lecture and handout at the American Oriental Society Meeting, Chicago, March 16, 2019.

McCrea, Lawrence J. 2012. "Mīmāṃsā." *Brill's Encyclopedia of Hinduism*. Leiden: Brill.

McGovern, Nathan. 2019. *The Snake and the Mongoose: The Emergence of Identity in Early Indian Religion*. New York: Oxford University Press, 2019.

McGovern, Patrick E. 2009. *Uncorking the Past: The Quest for Wine, Beer, and Other Alcoholic Beverages*. Berkeley: University of California Press.

McHugh, James. 2012. *Sandalwood and Carrion: Smell in Indian Religion and Culture*. Oxford; New York: Oxford University Press.

———. 2013. "Alcohol in Pre-Modern South Asia." In *A History of Alcohol and Drugs in Modern South Asia: Intoxicating Affairs*, ed. H. Fischer-Tiné and J. Tschurenev, 29–44. London; New York: Routledge.

———. 2017. "Material Culture and Society: The Ancient Indian Alestake." In *The Oxford History of Hinduism: Hindu Law*, ed. Patrick Olivelle and Donald R. Davis, 455–465. New York: Oxford University Press.

———. 2020a. "Sīdhu (Śīdhu): The Sugar Cane 'Wine' of Ancient and Early Medieval India." *History of Science in South Asia* 8: 36–56.

———. 2020b. "Varieties of Drunk Experience in Early Medieval South Asia." *South Asia* 43.2: 345–354.

———. 2020c. "Intoxicating Transformations: Alcohol Theory in Pre-modern India." In *Fluid Matter(s): Flow and Transformation in the History of the Body*, ed. Natalie Köhle and Shigehisa Kuriyama. Asian Studies Monograph Series 14. Canberra: ANU Press: https://press.anu.edu.au/publications/series/asian-studies/fluid-matters

———. forthcoming a. "Mind Altering Drugs in Premodern India." Forthcoming in *The Oxford Handbook to Drug History*, ed. Paul Gootenberg. New York: Oxford University Press.

———. forthcoming b. "Too Big to Fail: The Idea of Ancient Indian Distillation." Forthcoming in *Drink of Immortality: Essays on Distillation and Alcohol Use in Ancient India*, ed. D. N. Jha.

———. forthcoming c. "The Ancient Indian Alcoholic Drink Called *Surā*: Vedic Evidence." Accepted by *Journal of the American Oriental Society*.

———. forthcoming d. "Grape Wine in Ancient and Early Medieval India: The View from the Centre." Accepted by the *Indian Economic and Social History Review*.

———. forthcoming e. "Theorizing Alcoholic Drinks in Ancient India: The Complex Case of *Maireya*." Accepted by *The Social History of Alcohol and Drugs*.

Meulenbeld, G. Jan. 1974. *The Mādhavanidāna and Its Chief Commentary, Chapters 1–10*. Orientalia Rheno-traiectina 19. Leiden: Brill.

———. 1981. "Observations on the Arkaprakāśa, a Medical Sanskrit Text Ascribed to Rāvaṇa." In *Les Médecines Traditionelles d'Asia*, ed. G. Mazars, 111–139. Strasbourg: Université Louis Pasteur.

———. 1984. "The Surveying of Sanskrit Medical Literature." In *Proceedings of the International Workshop on Priorities in the Study of Indian Medicine*. Groningen, Rijsuniversitaet te Groningen.

———. 1988. "Additions to Sanskrit Names of Plants and their Botanical Equivalents." In *Das Wissen von der Lebensspanne der Bäume: Surapālas Vṛkṣāyurveda* (appandix), ed. and trans. Rahul Peter Das, 425–465. Alt- und Neu-Indische Studien 34. Stuttgart: Franz Steiner Verlag Wiesbaden Gmbh.

———. 1989. "The Search for Clues to the Chronology of Sanskrit Medical Texts, as Illustrated by the History of *bhaṅgā*." *Studien zur Indologie und Iranistik* 15: 59–70.

———. 1999–2002. *A History of Indian Medical Literature*. Groningen: E. Forsten.

Mills, James H. 2003. *Cannabis Britannica: Empire, Trade and Prohibition, 1800–1928*. Oxford; New York: Oxford University Press.

Mintz, Sidney Wilfred. 1985. *Sweetness and Power: The Place of Sugar in Modern History*. New York: Viking.

Mitra, Rajendralal. 1872a. "A Picnic in Ancient India." *Journal of the Asiatic Society of Bengal* 41: 340–353.

———. 1872b. "Beef in Ancient India." *Journal of the Asiatic Society of Bengal* 41: 174–196.

———. 1873. "Spirituous Drinks in Ancient India." *Journal of the Asiatic Society of Bengal* 42.1: 1–23.

Mitra, R., and K. Dalal. 2005. "A Report on the Glass Vessels from Sanjan, 2002." *Journal of Indian Ocean Archaeology* 2: 62–68.

Monier-Williams, M. 2000 (1899). *A Sanskrit-English Dictionary*. New ed. Oxford: Oxford University Press.

Mukharji, Projit. 2014. "Vishalyakarani as E. Ayapana: Retro-Botanizing, Embedded Traditions and Multiple Historicities of Plants in Colonial Bengal, 1890–1940." *Journal of Asian Studies* 73.1: 65–87.

Mukherjee, B. N. 1978. "Rajendra Lal Mitra and His Contemporaries." In Asiatic Society 1978, 48–69.

Oberlies, Thomas. 1998. *Die Religion des Ṛgveda*. Wien: Institut für Indologie der Universität Wien.

Oldenberg, H. 1893. "Indra und Namuci." *Nachrichten von der Königl. Gesellschaft der Wissenschaften und der Georg-Augusts-Universität zu Göttingen*: 342–349.

———. 1894. *Die Religion des Veda*. Berlin: Wilhelm Hertz.

Olivelle, Patrick. 2006. "Explorations in the Early History of the Dharmaśāstra." In *Between the Empires*, ed. P. Olivelle, Chapter 7. Oxford; New York: Oxford University Press, 2006.

———. 2010. "Dharmaśāstra: A Textual History." In Lubin, Davis, Jr., and Krishnan 2010: 28–57.

———. 2011. "Penance and Punishment: Marking the Body in Criminal Law and Social Ideology of Ancient India." *The Journal of Hindu Studies* 4.1: 23–41.

———. 2012. "Aśoka's Inscriptions as Text and Ideology." In *Reimagining Aśoka, Memory and History*, ed. Patrick Olivelle, Janice Leoshko, and Himanshu Prabha Ray, 157–183. New Delhi: Oxford University Press.

———. 2016. *A Dharma Reader: Classical Indian Law*. New York: Columbia University Press.

———. 2019. "From *Trivarga* to *Puruṣārtha*: A Chapter in Indian Moral Philosophy." *Journal of the American Oriental Society* 139.2: 381–396.

Oort, Marianne S. 2002. "Surā in the Paippalāda Saṃhitā of the Atharvaveda." *Journal of the American Oriental Society* 122.2: 355–360.

Orta, Garcia de. 1913. *Colloquies on the Simples & Drugs of India*. New ed. (Lisbon, 1895) Edited and annotated by the Conde De Ficalho. Trans. with an Introduction and Index by Sir Clements Markham. London: Henry Sotheran.

Oxford English Dictionary Online. OED Online, Oxford University Press.

Pal, Pratapaditya. 2007. *The Arts of Kashmir*. New York; Milan: Asia Society; 5 Continents.

———. 1981. *Hindu Religion and Iconology According to the Tantrasāra*. Los Angeles: Vichitra Press.

The Pali Text Society's Pali-English Dictionary. Ed. T. W. Rhys Davids, William Stede, and the Pali Text Society. Chipstead, Surrey: Pali Text Society, 1921.

Panda, S. K., et al. 2014. "Process Characteristics and Nutritional Evaluation of Handia—A Cereal-Based Ethnic Fermented Food from Odisha." *Indian Journal of Traditional Knowledge* 13.1: 149–156.

Parpola, A., and Janhunen, J. 2012. "On the Asiatic Wild Asses and Their Vernacular Names." In *Current Studies on the Indus Civilization*, ed. T. Osada and H. Endo, vol. 9, 59–124. New Delhi: Manohar Publishers & Distributors.

Pegu, R. et al. 2013. "Apong, an Alcoholic Beverage of Cultural Significance of the Mising Community of Northeast India." *Global Journal of Interdisciplinary Social Sciences* 2.6: 12–17.

Pemberton, Murdock, and P. G. Duffy. 1934. *The Official Mixer's Manual*. New York: Blue Ribbon Books.

Peterson, Indira Viswanathan. 2003. *Design and Rhetoric in a Sanskrit Court Epic: The Kirātārjunīya of Bhāravi*. Albany: State University of New York Press.

Pingree, David. 1970–. *Census of the Exact Sciences in Sanskrit*. Series A. Philadelphia: American Philosophical Society.

The Plant List, a working list of all plant species, a collaboration between The Royal Botanical Gardens, Kew and Missouri Botanical Garden: http://www.theplantlist.org/

Pollock, Sheldon. 2006. *The Language of the Gods in the World of Men: Sanskrit, Culture, and Power in Premodern India*. Berkeley: University of California Press.

Prakash. Om. 1961. *Food and Drinks in Ancient India: From Earliest Times to c. 1200 A.D.* Delhi: Munshi Ram Manohar Lal.

———. 1987. *Economy and Food in Ancient India*. Delhi: Bharatiya Vidya Prakashan.

Poussin, L. de la Vallée. 1908. "The Buddhist Councils." *Indian Antiquary* 37: 1.

Ray, Ganapati. 1909. "Was Tobacco in Vogue in 1600?" Letter in *Indian Antiquary* 38: 176.

———. 1911. "Is Tobacco Indigenous to India?" Letter in *Indian Antiquary* 40: 37–40.

Ray, Jogesh Chandra. 1906. "On the Hindu Method of Manufacturing Spirit from Rice, and its Scientific Explanation." *Journal of the Asiatic Society of Bengal* 2.4: 129–142.

Ren, Meng, Zihua Tang, Xinhua Wu, Robert Spengler, Hongen Jiang, Yimin Yang, and Nicole Boivin. 2019. "The Origins of Cannabis Smoking: Chemical Residue Evidence from the First Millennium BCE in the Pamirs." *Science Advances* 5.6: 1–8.

Quintanilla, Sonya Rhie. 2007. *History of Early Stone Sculpture at Mathura, ca. 150 BCE–100 CE*. Leiden; Boston: Brill.

Radhakrishnan, S., and Charles Alexander Moore. 1957. *A Source Book in Indian Philosophy*. Princeton, N.J.: Princeton University Press.

Ramamurti, K. S. 1971. "Medical Lore—a Few References in Medieval Sanskrit Literature." *Sri Venkateswara University Oriental Journal* 14.1: 27–32.

Rosenthal, Franz. 1971. *The Herb: Hashish versus Medieval Muslim Society*. Leiden: Brill.

Roy, R. B. J. C. 1918. "Sugar Industry in Ancient India." *Journal of the Bihar and Orissa Research Society*, December: 435–454.

Sanderson, Alexis. 1985. "Purity and Power among the Brāhmans of Kashmir." In *The Category of the Person: Anthropology, Philosophy, History*, ed. M. Carrithers, S. Collins, and S. Lukes, 190–216. Cambridge: Cambridge University Press.

———. 1987. "Abhinavagupta." In *The Encyclopedia of Religion*, ed. Mircea Eliade and Charles J. Adams. New York: Macmillan, 1987.

———. 1988. "Saivism and the Tantric Traditions." In *The World's Religions*, ed. S. Sutherland, 660–704. London: Routledge and Kegan Paul.

———. 1991. "Tantric Śaivism: An Unpublished Summary of 24 Lectures Delivered at the École Pratique des Hautes Études, Section 5, Paris, from April to June 1991." Published online at: https://www.academia.edu/6312650/Tantric_Śaivism_an_unpublished_summary_of_24_lectures_delivered_at_the_École_Pratique_des_Hautes_Études_Section_5_Paris_from_April_to_June_1991

———. 1995. "Meaning in Tantric Ritual." In *Essais sur le Rituel III*, ed. A.-M. Blondeau and K. Schipper, 15–95. *Bibliothèque de l'École des Hautes Études*, Sciences Religieuses, Volume CII. Louvain-Paris: Peeters.

———. 2003. "The Śaiva Religion Among the Khmers, Part I." *Bulletin de l'Ecole française d'Extrême-Orient* 90–91: 349–463.

———. 2005. "A Commentary on the Opening Verses of the Tantrasāra of Abhinavagupta." In *Sāmarasya: Studies in Indian Arts, Philosophy, and Interreligious Dialogue in Honour of Bettina Bäumer*, ed. Sadananda Das and Ernst Fürlinger, 89–148. New Delhi: D. K. Printworld.

———. 2007. "The Śaiva Exegesis of Kashmir." In *Mélanges tantriques à la mémoire d'Hélène Brunner/Tantric Studies in Memory of Hélène Brunner*, ed. Dominic Goodall and André Padoux, 231–442 and bibliography 551–582. Pondicherry: IFI/EFEO.

———. 2009. "Tantric Śaivism and Caste." Handout from lecture delivered at the Institut für Südasien-, Tibet-, und Buddhismuskunde Universität Wien, June 7, 2009.

———. 2013a. "Pleasure and the Emotions in Tantric Śaiva Soteriology." Handout from lecture, University of Hamburg, June 18, 2013. Published online at: https://www.academia.edu/6389439/Pleasure_and_the_Emotions_in_Tantric_Śaiva_Soteriology._Lecture_University_of_Hamburg_18_June_2013_Handout_21_pp

———. 2013b. Abhinavagupta on the Subjective Nature of Brahmanical Values: Śākta Fundamentalism Against the Absorption of Śaivism into "Hinduism." Handout, 15 Jan. 2013, Tokyo (Department of Indian Philosophy and Buddhist Studies, University of Tokyo).

———. 2014. "The Śaiva Literature." *Journal of Indological Studies* (Kyoto), Nos. 24 & 25 (2012–2013), 2014, pp. 1–113.

———. 2015a. "Tolerance, Exclusivity, Inclusivity, and Persecution in Indian Religion During the Early Mediaeval Period." In *Honoris Causa: Essays in Honour of Aveek Sarkar*, ed. and foreword by John Makinson, 155–224. London: Allen Lane.

———. 2015b. "How Public Was Śaivism?" Revised from a transcript of the lecture at the Symposium Tantric Communities in Context, Vienna, February 5, 2015, pre-publication text available online at: https://www.academia.edu/37106741/How_Public_Was_Śaivism

———. 2018. "The Śākta Transformation of Śaivism" Lecture presentation and handout, 17th World Sanskrit Conference, Vancouver, B.C., July 10, 2018. Handout available online at: https://www.academia.edu/37198020/The_Śākta_Transformation_of_Śaivism._Keynote_Lecture_Handout._WSC_Vancouver_2018.pdf).

Sanford, A. Whitney. 2005. "Holī through Daūjī's Eyes: Alternative Views of Krishna and Balarāma in Daūjī." In *Alternative Krishnas: Regional and Vernacular Variations on a Hindu Deity*, ed. Guy L Beck, 91–112. Albany: State University of New York Press.

Sangar, S. P. 1981. "Intoxicants in Mughal India." *Indian Journal of the History of Science* 16.2: 202–214.

Sarianidi, Viktor. 1994a. "New Discoveries at Ancient Gonur." *Ancient Civilizations from Scythia to Siberia* 2.3: 289–310.

———. 1994b. "Temples of Bronze Age Margiana: Traditions of Ritual Architecture." *Antiquity* 68: 388–397.

———.1998. *Margiana and Proto-Zoroastrianism*. Athens: Kapon Editions.

Scharfe, Hartmut. 1993. *Investigations in Kauṭalya's Manual of Political Science*. 2nd, rev. ed. Wiesbaden: Harrassowitz.

Schinzel, Eva-Maria. 2014. "The Kādambarasvīkaraṇasūtra with Commentary and the Kādambarasvīkaraṇakārikā Two Indian Treatises on Erotics." MA Thesis. Ludwig-Maximilians-Universität, München.

Schlingloff, Dieter. 1987. *Studies in the Ajanta Paintings: Identifications and Interpretations*. Delhi: Ajanta Publications: Distributors, Ajanta Books International.

Schubring, Walther. 1935. *Die Lehre der Jainas*. Berlin; Leipzig: W. de Gruyter & co.

Sedgwick, Eve Kosofsky. 1994. "Epidemics of the Will." In *Tendencies*, by E. K. Sedgwick, 130–142. London: Routledge.

Shahnavaz, S. 1984. "Afyūn." *Encyclopædia Iranica* I.6, 594–598. An updated version is available online at http://www.iranicaonline.org/articles/afyun-opium.

Shastri, Ajay Mitra. 1969. *India as Seen in the Bṛhatsaṁhitā of Varāhamihira*. Delhi: Motilal Banarsidass.

Sherratt, Andrew. 1997. "Sacred and Profane Substances: The Ritual Use of Narcotics in Later Neolithic Europe." In *Economy and Society in Prehistoric Europe*, ed. Andrew Sherratt, 403–430. Princeton, N.J.: Princeton University Press.

Sibum, Heinz Otto. 1995. "Reworking the Mechanical Value of Heat: Instruments of Precision and Gestures of Accuracy in Early Victorian England." *Studies in History and Philosophy of Science. Part A* 26.1: 73–106.

Siklós, Bulcsu. 1994. "Datura Rituals in the *Vajramahabhairava Tantra*." *Acta Orientalia Academiae Scientiarum Hungaricae* 47.3: 409–416.

Sircar, Dineschandra. 1965. *Indian Epigraphy*. Delhi: Motilal Banarsidass.

———. 1966. *Indian Epigraphical Glossary*. Delhi: Motilal Banarsidass.

Slaje, W. 2015. *Bacchanal im Himmel Und Andere Proben Aus Maṅkha*. Veröffentlichungen Der Indologischen Kommission Bd. 3. Wiesbaden: Harrassowitz Verlag.

Slouber, Michael. "Bheruṇḍa" at http://www.garudam.info/bheruṇḍa/. Accessed January 22, 2019.

Smith, Frederick M. 2006. *The Self Possessed: Deity and Spirit Possession in South Asian Literature and Civilization*. New York: Columbia University Press.

Smith, Huston. 1972. "Wasson's Soma—A Review Article." *Journal of the American Academy of Religion* 40.4: 480–499.

Smith, Jonathan Z. 1978. *Map Is Not Territory: Studies in the History of Religions*. Studies in Judaism in Late Antiquity 23. Leiden: Brill.

Söhnen-Thieme, Renate. 2005. "Buddhist Tales in the Mahābhārata." In *Parallels and Comparisons*. Ed. P. Koskikallio. Zagreb: Croatian Academy of Sciences and Arts.

Southworth, Franklin C. 2005. *Linguistic Archaeology of South Asia*. London: Routledge Curzon.

Stadtner, Donald. 1996. "'The Little Clay Cart' in Early Mathura." *Orientations* 27.1: 39–46.

Steiner, K. 2001. "Madhavi Bhaskar Kolhatkar, Surā: The Liquor and the Vedic Sacrifice." *Indo-Iranian Journal* 44.4: 372–377.

Steinkraus, Keith H. ed. 1996. *Handbook of Indigenous Fermented Foods*. 2nd ed., rev. and exp. New York: Marcel Dekker.

Sternbach, Ludwik. 1974. *Subhasita, Gnomic and Didactic Literature. History of Indian Literature*, vol. 4, fasc. 1. Wiesbaden: O. Harrassowitz.

Stevenson, John. 1842. *Translation of the Sanhita of the Sama Veda*. London: Oriental Translation Fund.

Sur, Shyamali. 1974. "Rajendralal Mitra as a Historian: A Revaluation." *Proceedings of the Indian History Congress* 35: 370–378.

Taillieu, Dieter, and Boyce, Mary. 2003. "Haoma." *Encyclopedia Iranica*, vol. XI, fasc. 6, pp. 659–667; an updated version is available online at: http://www.iranicaonline.org/articles/haoma Accessed online November 27, 2018.

Taittirīya Brāhmaṇa. Trans. in Dumont 1965.

Tamang, Jyoti Prakash. 2010. *Himalayan Fermented Foods: Microbiology, Nutrition, and Ethnic Values*. Boca Raton: CRC Press.

Tāntrikābhidhānakośa. Wien: Verlag der Österreichischen Akademie der Wissenschaften, 2000.

Tatz, Mark. 1985. *Difficult Beginnings: Three Works on the Bodhisattva Path*. 1st ed. Boston: New York: Shambhala; distributed in the U.S. by Random House.

Thompson, George. 2003. "Soma and Ecstasy in the Ṛgveda." *Electronic Journal of Vedic Studies* 9.1.

Tomber, Roberta. 2007. "Rome and Mesopotamia - Importers into India in the First Millennium AD." *Antiquity* 81.314: 972–988.

Törzsök, Judit. 2007. "The Search in Śaiva Scriptures for Meaning in Tantric Ritual." In *Mélanges Tantriques à la Mémoire D'Hélène Brunner*, 485–516. Collection Indologie 106. Institut Français de Pondichéry Ecole Française D'Extrême Orient.

———. 2012. "Tolerance and Its Limits in Twelfth Century Kashmir: Tantric Elements in Kalhaṇas Rājataraṅgiṇī." *Indologica Taurinensia* 38: 1–27.

Trafford, Paul. 2009. "Avoiding *Pamāda*: An Analysis of the Fifth Precept as Social Protection in Contemporary Contexts with Reference to the Early Buddhist Teachings." MSt in Study of Religions thesis, Oxford University, 2009.

Trevelyan, G. O. 1876. *The Life and Letters of Lord Macaulay*. Leipzig: Bernhard Tauchnitz.

Tsuchiyama, Y. 2005. "*Abhiṣeka* in the Vedic and in the Post-Vedic Rituals." In *From Material to Deity: Indian Rituals of Consecration*, ed. S. Einoo and J. Takashima, 51–93. New Delhi: Manohar.

Tsuda, Shinichi. 1970. "*Saṃvarodaya-tantra*: Selected Chapters." PhD thesis, Australian National University.

Turner, R. L. 1966. *A Comparative Dictionary of the Indo-Aryan Languages*. London; New York: Oxford University Press. Online version at: https://dsalsrv04.uchicago.edu/dictionaries/soas/

Vasudeva, Somadeva. 2012. "The Transport of the Haṃsas: A Śakta Rāsalīlā as Rājayoga in Eighteenth-Century Benares." In *Yoga in Practice*, ed. David Gordon White, 242–254. Princeton, N.J.: Princeton University Press.

Verpoorten, J. 2009. "Le bouddhisme et l'ivresse." *Acta Orientalia Belgica* 22: 35–40. Louvain-la-Neuve, Belgium.

Vogel, Claus. 1979. *Indian Lexicography*. Wiesbaden: Harrassowitz.

von Hinüber, Oskar. 1971. "Zur Technologie der Zuckerherstellung im Alten Indien." *Zeitschrift Der Deutschen Morgenländischen Gesellschaft* 121.1: 93–109.

———. 1997. *A Handbook of Pali Literature*. New Delhi: Munishiram Manoharlal.

———. 1998a. *Entstehung und Aufbau der Jātaka-Sammlung*. Mainz: Akademie der Wissenschaften und der Literatur.

———. 1998b. "Structure and Origin of the Pātimokkhasutta of the Theravādins." *Acta Orientalia Academiae Scientiarum Hungaricae* 51.3: 257–265.

Wasson, R. Gordon. 1968. *Soma: Divine Mushroom of Immortality*. New York: Harcourt, Brace, Jovanovich.

Watkins, Calvert. 2011. *The American Heritage Dictionary of Indo-European Roots*. 3rd ed. Boston: Houghton Mifflin Harcourt.

Wedemeyer, Christian K. 2007. "Beef, Dog, and Other Mythologies: Connotative Semiotics in Mahāyoga Tantra Ritual and Scripture 1." *Journal of the American Academy of Religion* 75.2: 383–417.

———. 2012. *Making Sense of Tantric Buddhism History, Semiology, and Transgression in the Indian Traditions*. New York: Columbia University Press, 2012.

Whitaker, Jarrod. 2011. *Strong Arms and Drinking Strength: Masculinity, Violence, and the Body in Ancient India*. New York: Oxford University Press.

Wiese, Harald, and Sadananda Das. 2019. *The Charter of Viṣṇuṣeṇa*. Studia Indologica Universitatis Halensis 11. Halle an Der Saale: Universitätsverlag Halle-Wittenberg.

Will, Elizabeth. 1991. "The Mediterranean Shipping Amphoras from Arikamedu." In *Rome and India: The Ancient Sea Trade*, ed. R. D. de Puma and V. Begley, 151–156. Wisconsin Studies in Classics. Madison, Wis.: University of Wisconsin Press, 1991.

Williams, R. 1963. *Jaina Yoga; a Survey of the Mediaeval Śrāvakācāras*. London; New York: Oxford University Press.

Winternitz, M. 1920. *Geschichte der Indischen Litteratur*. Vol. 3. Leipzig: C. F. Amelang Verlag.

Witzel, Michael. 1989. "Tracing the Vedic Dialects." In *Dialectes dans les littératures indo-aryennes*, ed. Collete Caillat, 97–264. Paris: Institut de Civilisation Indienne.

———. 2000. "The Languages of Harappa." www.people.fas.harvard.edu/~witzel/IndusLang.pdf

Wujastyk, Dominik. 2002. "Cannabis in Traditional Indian Herbal Medicine." In *Ayurveda at the Crossroads of Care and Cure*, ed. Ana Salema, 45–73. Lisbon: Centro de História de Além-Mar.

———. 2003. *The Roots of Ayurveda*. Rev. ed. London: Penguin Books.

Zimmermann, Francis. 1987 (1982). *The Jungle and the Aroma of Meats: An Ecological Theme in Hindu Medicine*. Trans. Janet Lloyd. Berkeley: University of California Press.

Zin, M. 2003. *Ajanta: Handbuch der Malereien* part 2 *Devotionale und ornamentale Malereien*. Wiesbaden: Harrasowitz Verlag.

———. 2015. "Pictures of Paradise for Good Luck and Prosperity: Depictions of Themes Irrelevant for Enlightenment in the Older Buddhist Tradition (with special reference to the paintings of Ajanta)." In *Mani-Sushma*, vol. 1, 125–147. Delhi: B. R. Publishing Corporation.

———, and Dieter Schlingloff. 2007. *Saṃsāracakra: Das Rad der Wiedergeburten in der indischen Überlieferung* (*Buddhismus-Studien* 6). Düsseldorf: Veröffentichung des EKŌ-Haus der Japanischen Kultur.

Zumbroich, Thomas. 2007. "The Origin and Diffusion of Betel Chewing: A Synthesis of Evidence from South Asia, Southeast Asia and Beyond." *eJournal of Indian Medicine* 1 (2007–2008): 87–140.

Zysk, Kenneth. n.d. "A Study of Male Social Gatherings in Ancient India and Ancient Greece with Special Reference to Sanskrit *samāpānaka*, *goṣṭhī*, and Greek *symposion*." Unpublished draft.

Index

I have added some basic, simple definitions of certain Sanskrit terms in parentheses below for the assistance of readers from other fields.

I have also provided in parentheses a glossary of brief definitions of the various drinks and brewing related terms in Sanskrit.

Page ranges given **in bold** indicate sections primarily concerned with given topics.

Abhidharmakośa and *-bhāṣya* (of Vasubandhu), 219–222, 224
  Sthiramati's commentary on, 345n188
Abhinavagupta
  life and works, 251–252
  See also *Tantrāloka*
Ācārańga Sūtra, 228
addiction
  in early-modern England, 9, 338n55
  Eve Sedgwick on, 9
  modern concept of, 9–10
  as translation of Sanskrit words, 10, 193, 196
Afghanistan, 53
Africa, brewing in, 28
Āgamaḍambara (of Bhaṭṭa Jayanta), 119, 237
Āgamarahasya, 277
agarwood, 49
aging of drinks, 47, 150
ahiṃsā and drink, 230–232
ahiphena. *See* opium
Ajanta caves, 99–103, 131
ākṣikī (*surā* made with *vibhītaka*, *Terminalia bellirica*), 38
alcohol
  no concept of in early Indic texts, 8, 32, 35, 44
alcoholism, 11, 23, 145, **151**, 161, 329n22
ale
  changing sense of English word, 7
alehouse, English, 4
ali ("liquor," a word mostly used in Tantric texts), 247, 259, 354n59
āmalaka/*-kī*, emblic myrobalan, 20, 217, 265
Amarasiṃha, lexicon of, 100
amphoras, 54
amṛta (nectar of immortality), 183, 234, 335n96
  at churning of ocean, 102, 170–173, 274
  liquor compared to, 138, 152–153, 157
  in Tantra, 247, 253–254, 263, 265
anaesthetic, liquor as, 146
Ānandakanda, 271, 274, 276
Andhakas and Vṛṣṇis (clans)
  at drinking bout, 105, 184
  as example in moral texts, 195, 227, 232, 347n224
  mutual slaughter of, 143, **186–187**
  See also Balarāma; Kṛṣṇa
animals, and drink, 85, 94–95
āpānaka. *See under* drinking: social nature of
Āpastamba Dharmasūtra
  on drinking, 199–200
Apsarases, 122–125
areca nut. *See* betel
ariṣṭa (medicinal herbal drink, sometimes said to be made with decoction), **47–50**, 150, 210, 217
  in *Arthaśāstra*, 33, 34, 86
Arjuna (hero in the *Mahābhārata* epic), 105, 122, 206
Arjuna and the Hunter. See *Kirātārjunīya*
arka (arrack), 109, 281, 285
Arkaprakāśa (of Rāvaṇa), 109, 280–281
arrack. See *arka*
artha (power, wealth), 119
Arthaśāstra, 116, 226, 282
  *āsava*s and *ariṣṭa*s in, 48
  date of, 33
  drinking-house in, 78–79, 100
  drugged liquor in, 78, 93, 99, 182
  kodo millet as narcotic in, 222
  mahua in, 60
  maireya in, 51
  regulation of liquor commerce in, 83–86, 243
  surā in, 33–35
  vices in, 193–194
  wine in, 53
  women collecting brewing materials in, 89
Aruṇadatta (commentator on AH), 61

āsava (generic word for liquor, often sugar-based; medical drink *not* made with decoction), **47–50**, 97, 105, 184, 186, 305n37
in *Arthaśāstra*, 33, 48
as generic word, 60, 61, 217
in *Kāmasūtra*, 89, 95, 116
lists of types, 46
Aśoka, King, 65
dharma of, 241–242
Aṣṭāṅgahṛdaya (of Vāgbhaṭa), 61
on ideal drinking, **145–150**
praise of Surā in, 233–234
Asuras (anti-gods), 267–268
Asura/Daitya/Dānava terminology, 332n28
Buddhist myth of, 100–103
and churning of the ocean, 170–173, 234, 258, 274
Mada (Intoxication) as, 176
Namuci as, 166–167
and Śukra story, 179–181
Aśvaghoṣa. See *Buddhacarita*
Aśvins (twin gods prominent in Vedas), 165–170, 175–176, 234
Atharvaveda, 174
date of, 29
surā in, 28, 29, 31, 190–191
āyurveda (system of medicine), **145–161**, 281
āsavas and *ariṣṭas* in, 47–50
benefits of drink in, 146, 157
doctors in, 148, 195
maireya in, 52
praise of *surā* in, 233–235
surās made from grain in, 37–39

Bactria, 46, 98, 201
Bakhtin, 143, 328n138
bakkasa. *See* dregs
bakula tree, 120
Balarāma, 117, 152, **182–185**, 234
and churning myth, 172
Dauji temple, 336n98
in *Mahābhārata*, 105, 186–187
and palm trees, 57–58
stammering drunken verse, 1
Bālarāmāyaṇa (of Rājaśekhara), 47
bamboo
in fermentation structures, 28, 29, 30, 40
as tube for transporting drink, 20
Bāṇa, 61
banner (*dhvaja*), for *surā* shop, 80, **81–83**, 100–103
bar (structure in modern pubs), 77
bark, 40, 230
used for *surā* in *Kumbha Jātaka*, 21
barley, 27, 203, 290
grain *surā*, as used in, 30, 38, 40, 166, 168
sattū, 160, 303n59
basi (sugarcane drink of Philippines), 47
Baudhāyana Dharmasūtra, 82, 201–203, 251
Baudhāyana Śrauta Śūtra
date of, 29
surā brewing in, 29–30
beer
changing meaning of English word, 7
German, 27, 50
betel, **64–73**, 235–236, 257, 285
areca trees in inscriptions, 56–57
Cārvākas on, 36
date appears in texts, 65
as intoxicating, 222–223, 273
in Jainism, 136, 229, 348n246
in *Kāmasūtra*, 113, 114
kramuka as word for areca nut, 33, 302n31
morality of, 67–68
in *Rājataraṅiṇī*, 108
sensuality and, 68–70
spittoon for, 114
as *surā* in Tantric texts, 263–264, 273, 283
Bhagavad Gītā, 176, 178
Bhāgavata Purāṇa
churning myth in, 172
Bhairava, 248, 255, 257, 274
Bhaiṣajyaratnāvalī (of Govindadāsa), 281
bhāṅg/bhaṅgā. *See* cannabis
Bhāravi. See *Kirātārjunīya*
Bhāvaprakāśa, 238
Bhṛgus, 181
bīja (word for starter), 34, 39, 40, 282, 302n40
Bilhaṇa, 55
black pepper, *Piper nigrum*: *marica*, 96
as additive to drinks, 20, 34, 51, 199, 339n76
Borobudur, 225
Brahmā (Hindu god), 265, 267
Brahmayāmala Tantra, 249–250, 254
Brahmins (a *varṇa*: priests, Veda scholars), 177, 186, 245
as domestic ascetics, 240
as general term in early periods, 343n162
myth of why *surā* prohibited for, 179–181, 258
prohibition of *surā* for, in *Dharmasūtras*, 198–203
and Sautrāmaṇī ritual, 139, 165
and *surā* in Vedas, 191–192
See also *Dharmaśāstra*
brewers, 20–21, 77, 81, 93–94
female, 88–92

as mobile, 99
See also *śuṇḍā*
brewing
as assembling, 29, 168, 255–256
European style of, 27, 32
exertion of, 80–81
inspection of, 86–88
Japanese, 29, 30, 41
Korean, 29
saṃdhāna as a word for in Sanskrit, 29
scientific rationale for, 32
skills, 91
temperature regulation, 91
terminologies for, 7, 28, 29
unstated, embodied practices of, 5
in Vedic sources, 28–32, 77, 167–168
vessels for (see *cāṭi*; jars)
by women, **89–92**
See also fermentation
Bṛhatkathāślokasaṃgraha (of Budhasvamin), 119, 129–137, 238
Bṛhatsaṃhitā (of Varāhamihira)
betel in, 66–67
Buddha (also the Buddha-to-be), 81, 91, 221
attends party in *Buddhacarita*, 121–122
prohibits liquor for monks, 216–217
uses straws in previous birth, 117
See also Buddhism
Buddhacarita (of Aśvaghoṣa), 121–122
Buddhism, 81, 90–92, 142, 268
and Asuras banished from heaven for drinking, 102, 171
in Burma, 218
discovery of *surā*, according to (*Kumbha Jātaka*), 19–23
drinks forbidden in, 60, 119
medicine permitted in, 217–218, 237
and morality of drinking, 213–228
precepts on drinking, 214–215, 219–222, 224, 236, 345n194
and prohibition of drinking to monks, 216–217
Tantric Buddhist text on liquor (*Saṃvarodayatantra*), 355n84
threefold liquor definition in, 343n165
and Vinaya rule on drinking, 215–219
See also *Abhidharmakośa*; monks, Buddhist; nuns, Buddhist
Burma, 218

camphor, 66, 237
cannabis, 73, **269–276**, 282, 283, 285
added to rice liquor, 282
archaeology of ancient, 356n109
bag (*jhaulika*), 271
bhāṅg as *prasād*, 336n98
colors of, 274
date when mentioned as drug in South Asia, 14, 270–272
in *Dhūrtasamāgama* play, 271
in eastern Indian Tantra, 272
and Islam, 271–272
names of, 264, 274
origin myth of, 264, 274
plants as sexed, 274
preparation of, 275
as substitute for liquor, 273–274
Carakasaṃhitā
betel in, 66
date of, 151
on drinking and health, 150–161
praise of Surā in, 234–235
cardamom, 63, 66
carnival, and Bakhtin, 104, 143
Cārvāka (materialist school of Indian philosophy), 36
caṣaka. See under cups
catechu, 64
cāṭi. See under jars
cats, as guards for *surā* jars, 21, 300n12
Central Asia, 65
Champagne, 51
as gay drink, 141
Chāndogya Upaniṣad
early version of four great sins in, 198
Chartreuse
mauve, 218
Château d'Yquem, 113
chebulic myrobalan, *Terminalia chebula*: *harītakī*, 20, 96
chickpeas, 96–97, 127
China, 243, 343n165
alcohol in, 5, 74–75, 91
history of noodles in, 4
sugarcane products in, 47
tea in, 55, 72
translation of word for "wine," 6
yellow wine (*huangjiu*), 27, 42–43
churning of the ocean, myth, 102, **170–173**, 234, 249, 283
in Tantric text, 260–269, 274, 276
Cikitsāsārasaṃgraha, 270
citron, *Citrus medica*: *mātuluṅga*, 114, 115, 136, 257, 321n12
clarification of *surā*, 34–35
See also *prasannā*; settling

coconut, 265, 347n239
  toddy from, 55–60, 209, 210, 281
  water, 63, 64, 309n120
coffee, 285
color, 148
  black *surā*, 39–41, 127–129, 282
  of non-alcoholic drink, 63
  pale *surā*, 39–41
  red *surā*, 20, 31, 37
  of *sīdhu*, 47
  white *surā*, 34–35, 38, 127
  See also drunkards: with red eyes and faces
consecration, royal, 169, 190
cosmopolitan (drink), 128
country liquor (IMIL), 110, 280–282
courtesans, 95, 97, 119–120, 173, 190
cows, 190
credit, drink obtained on, 85, **93–94**
cups, 115
  betel leaves as, 58
  caṣaka, 64, 97, 114, 117, 124–127, 144, 147, 149, 184, 307n71
  garnished with flowers, 110, 124, 127, 147, 237
  karaka (also "pot"), 68, 126, 127
  lotus leaves as, 134
  mouth used as, 119–120, 124, 150
  pātras as, 69, 261
  saraka as, 111, **114**, 116, 133–135, 321n9
  shapes of, 117
  silver, 69
  skull-cups, in Tantra, 245, 247–248
  śukti ("oyster shell"), 64, 117, 126–127, 147
curds, 96, 174, 290
Cyavana/Cyāvana (a seer), 175–177

da Orta, Garcia de, 281
Ḍalhaṇa, 37–38, 49–50
dancing, associated with drink, 98, 99, 116, 128, 173, 215
date palm, 109, 160, 246, 347n239
  jaggery, 56, 273
  liquor made with fruit, 37, 209
  toddy, 56, 59, 283
datura, **222–224**, 264, 282, 283
  See also drugged preparations, as used for nefarious means
debts, 10, 93, 194
Delhi Sultanate, distillation in, 109
Delight of the Mind. See *Mānasollāsa*
Devas (gods), 102–103, 170–173, 179–181
Devīrahasya, 261–269
Dhammapadaṭṭhakathā, 90–91
Dhanvantari (god of medicine), 171
dharma (rightousness, duty, law), 180
  Aśokan, 241–242
  compatible with drink, 139, 146
  definitions of, 198–199
  disturbed by drink, 187, 188
  Hindu *dharma* of drinking, 198–213
  history of concept, 199
  regional variation in, 200–201, 239
  sources of, 199, 212–213
  tradition versus texts, 244
  in *trivarga*, 321n4
  See also morality
Dharmaśāstra
  on *surā* and drinking, 203–213
  See also *Mānavadharmaśāstra*
Dharmasūtras, 82. *See also* individual names of *Dharmasūtras*
  on *surā* and drinking, 198–203, 240
dhātakī (flowers used in fermentation), *Woodfordia fruticosa*, **49**, 59, 60, 61
  Jain references to, 229–230, 233, 334n54
Dhūrtaviṭasaṃvāda (*Conversation of Rogue and Rake*), 111, 119, 237–238, 354n57
Dhūrtasamāgama (of Jyotirīśvara), 271, 356n111
dhvaja. See banner
dice, 90, 93, 131, 189, 190
  See also vice
dictionaries
  translations in, 6–7
Dīpavaṃsa, 65
diseases and drink. See *madātyaya*
distillation, 39, 74, **108–110**, 210–211, 257, **280–283**
  and archaeology in South Asia, 14
  John Marshall's theory of ancient Indian, 14
  Sanskrit vocabulary for, 109, 281, 358n4
  surā as not distilled in early periods, 31
doctors. *See* Āyurveda: doctors
dohada (craving), of bakula tree, 120
doṣas ("humors," "morbific entities," in medical theory), 151–161, 329n29
Draupadī, 89–90
dregs (*bakkasa*), 37–39
drinking
  actions preceding, 117, 127, 147, 151–152
  age permitted, 132, 139
  āpanaka, samāpānaka (group drinking bout), **114**, 116, 133, 146, 158, 184, 187, 325n115
  medical regulation of, 145–161
  private nature of some, 116, 127, 133, 142
  public nature of some, 116, 141
  saraka ("loving cup"), 111, **114**, 116, 133–135, 321n9

social nature of, 158
of wealthy, as prescribed in Āyurveda, 146–148
See also drinking establishments; festivals; parties; weddings
drinking establishments, **76–110**, 84, 116, 141
in *Arthaśāstra*, 79
banner for, 80, 81–83
conduct in, 97–100
as open to all, 100
painting of, at Ajanta, 100–103
snacks and food in, 93–94
drinks, alcoholic. *See* liquor
drinks, non-alcoholic, 62–64
in Buddhism, 237
drugged preparations, used for nefarious means, 93, 98–99, 120, 222–223
in *Arthaśāstra*, 78, 194, 222
in *Kāmasūtra*, 104
drugs
Western views on Indian, 2
drunkards
animals as, 94–94, 314n50
as like possessed people, 69, 128, 178, 230
neglecting dharma, 188
with red eyes and faces, 31, 120, 125, 128, 131
typical behavior of in texts, 95, 120–129, 142
as violent, 31
women, 22, 114–118
Drunken Games (play). See *Mattavilāsaprahasana*
drunkenness. *See* drunkards; intoxication
Dumézil, Georges
on *soma*, 290

elephants, 95, 128
drinking liquor, 85, 314n50
and *mada*/*matta*, 105, 185
trunks used as drinking straws, 119
emblic myrobalan, *Phyllanthus emblica*: *āmalaka*, 20, 265
England
alewives in, 92
drinking establishments in, 76, 82–83
entheogen
as loaded concept, 8
enzymes, for fermentation, 27, 32
Epitome of Queen Līlāvatī, Līlāvatīsāra (of Jinaratnasūri), 107, 136, 320n174
ergot, 222, 289
Essence of Politics. See *Nītisāra*

female brewers and drinkers. *See* women
fermentation, 49
as assembling, 29
duration of, 30–31, 35, 40, 49–50
as philosophical model, 35–37
saṃdhāna as term for, 29
scientific rationale for, 32
from starches, 27–28
temperature regulation, 49–50, 91
See also brewing; ferment starters; *kiṇva*
ferment starters, **35–37**, 281–282
ranu (in Odisha), 28
See also brewing; fermentation; *kiṇva*
festivals, **103–106**, 116, 141, 186, 195
drink at, in *Arthaśāstra*, 86, 99
of *surā*, in Buddhist sources, 22, 90–91
filtration, of drinks, 29, 31, 40, 81
fish, 94, 100, 235, 239, 250, 358n154
flag, for *surā* shop. *See* banner
flavors
descriptions of ("wine talk"), 127–128, 130–132, 135–136
of drinks, 32–33, 40, 51, 120, 124, 127
of *leśyās* in Jainism, 238–239
of snacks, 93–97, 115, 127
of *surā*, 40, 42
flowers
as garnishes, 111, 119, 124, 127, 136, 147, 150, 237
France, drinking culture, 112

Gadanigraha (of Soḍhala), 109, 281
gambling. See dice; vice
Gandhāra, 55, 152
Gandharvas, 122–125, 235
gardens, drinking gatherings in, 116, 121–122, 134, 142
gauḍī (jaggery-based liquor), 152
gauḍa liquor, 149
in Manu, 205–206
in Tantra, 249, 254–255, 263
Gautama Dharmasūtra
drinking in, 200–201
ghee, 109, 127, 148, 170, 174, 237
ginger, 96–97, 127, 148, 150
glass, 96, 117, 126
gods. *See* Devas; *names of individual gods*
goṣṭhī. See salons
grains, 27–43. *See under individual types of grains*
grapes, 160, 237, 238, 290, 347n239
āsava, 54
as dried, 54
in Tantra, 254–257, 263
wine and, 53–55, 127, 136, 184, 206, 209–210
See also Kashmir; *mārdvīkam*; wine

Greece. *See* Hellenistic
Gṛhyasūtras, 51
surā as funeral libations in, 78
surā at weddings in, 78, 189
gruels, 40–41, 42–43, 115, 203
gruit, 32
guṇas (three metaphysical principles), 154
definition of, 158
Gupta period, 65, 89, 113, 144
Gurunāthaparāmarśa (of Madhurāja), 257
Gymnema sylvestre, *meṣaśṛṅgī*, 51

hālāhala (a poison), 230, 276
character in Jain narrative, 349n258
Haṃsavilāsa (of Haṃsa Miṭṭhu), 275, 282–283
handia (drink), 28, 41–42
Hanumān, 46, 105–106
haoma, 289, 293–294
Hārahūraka wine, 53, 323n42
Haramekhalā (of Mādhuka), 222–223, 238
haria (drink). See *handia*
harīṭakī (Pali). See *harītakī*
harītakī, chebulic myrobalan, 20, 96
Hārītasaṃhitā, 59, 210, 307n92
Harivaṃśa, 182–184
Harṣacarita (of Bāṇa), 61, 120, 140, 327n129
heart, 153–154, 178, 189, 207
heaven, 102–103, 174, 238
Hellenistic culture, 55, 74, 152, 333n47
Hemacandra. See *Yogaśāstra*
honey, 167, 190, 223, 237, 250, 254, 265
in *Arthaśāstra*, 54
āsava made of, 48, 184
forbidden to Jains, 229–230, 347n239
forest of, in *Rāmāyaṇa*, 105–106
maireya made of, 52, 217
mead, 61–62, 209, 210, 254
ocean of, 174
preparation of jar with, 49
and soma, 290
widows to avoid, 201
See also *madhu*; *mādhvī*
householders, 34, 85, 148, 240
humors, medical. See *doṣas*
hunting. *See* vices

IMIL (Indian Manufactured Indian Liquor). *See* country liquor
impurity, ritual
in dharma texts, 201, 206, 209
in Tantra, 247–248, 253–254
Indra, 102, 117, 234, 265
in *Kumbha Jātaka*, 21, 224–228
and myth about Mada (Intoxication), 175–179
reviled by *surā* drinkers, 190
Indra Sutrāman in Sautrāmaṇī ritual, 166–167, 191
inns. *See* drinking establishments
inscriptions, 314n56
on Kalyapālas, 107
liquor for temples in, 278
Mandasor, on betel, 65
on trees, 56–57
Viṣṇuṣena Charter, 86–88, 278
intoxication, 180
āyurvedic theory of, 152–161
bad type, in Vedas, 189
multifarious nature of in Indian texts, 11
performance of according to *Nāṭyaśāstra*, 155–156
personified (*see* Mada)
three stages of alcoholic, 154–156
translating Sanskrit words for, 8–12
See also drunkards; *mad*; *mada*
Islam
betel and, 71

jackfruit, 52, 62, 209–210
jagala (type of grain *surā*), 38
jaggery. *See* sugarcane
Jainism, 136, 140–141
betel in, 348n246
fermentation compared to karmic matter in, 37
leśyā flavor compared to liquor, 238–238
Makkhali Gosāla narrative in, 349n258
morality of drinking in, 228–233
jalogi (a liquor in Buddhist texts), 345n183
James, William, 287
jars, 91, 147
amphoras, 54
as banner for shop, 82
bhājana, 86–88, 98
cāṭi (Pali), 20–21, 93, 299n11
fumigation of, 49, 282
ghaṭa, 40
ghee, 109
image of, 102
kalaśa, 68, 237
karaka, 68, 126
kumbha, 30, 261
torpedo, 54
for water, 64
Jātaka texts (stories of Buddha's previous births), 100, 116, 117
betel in, 66

date of, 20
Gūthapāna Jātaka, 94–95
Naḷapāna Jātaka, 117–118
rogues in, 98–99
Vāruṇī Jātaka, 93–94
See also *Kumbha Jātaka*

Jātakamālā (of Āryaśūra), 102, 224–228
Java, 225
Jiri Jakl on, 13
Jayadrathayāmala, 248
Jayaratha, commentator on *Tantrāloka*, 251–259
date of, 251
Jyeṣṭhā (goddess), 173, 333n43

Kaca, 179–180, 267
See also Śukra
Kadamba tree, 182–183
Kādambarasvīkaraṇasūtra (of Purārvas), 138–139, 149
Kādambarasvīkaraṇakārikā (of Bharata), 138–139
Kādambarī/kādambara (flexible word for liquor), 100, 182
as grain *surā*, 38
as grape wine, 138
personified as goddess, 182–184
in Tantra, 253
kalā. *See* sixty four arts
Kalāvilāsa (of Kṣemendra), 177–179
Kali age (our current cosmic era), 267
Kālidāsa (poet, c. fourth century CE), 47, 54, 58, 65, 100
See also *Raghuvaṃśa*; *Śakuntalā*
Kalvar (caste). *See* Kalyapāla
Kalyapāla (brewer, distiller caste), 87, **106–110**, 259
kāma (desire, lust, also personified as a god)
as god, 138, 140, 147, 234–235, 257
as Madana, 123
as root of some vices, 193–196
in *trivarga*, 321n4
in Vedic texts, 78
Kāmandaki. See *Nītisāra*
Kāmaśāstra
Texts on drinking as adjuncts to, 138–139
Kāmasūtra (of Vātsyāyana), 113–117, 144, 216
betel in, 65–66
brewers in, 99
date of, 65
datura in, 223
festivals in, 104
sixty four arts, include mixing drinks, 119
snacks in, 95, 115
wife managing household liquor in, 89
Kane, P. V., 13
Kapiśa, 53
Kāpiśāyana wine, 53, 131–132, 184, 344n179
karma and *karmic* rewards, 119, 134
kārotara (rigid fermentation container in Vedic brewing), 30, 168
kaṣāya, translation of, 360n32
Kashmir, 117, 177–179, 237
grapes and wine in, 55, 135–135, 206, 256–257, 325n111
in *Narmamālā* satire, 68–70
saffron in, 55, 136, 256–257
kaśya (word for liquor), 231, 349n261
kava root, 31, 292–293
Kāvyādarśa (of Daṇḍin), 120
kāvya (Sanskrit belles lettres) drink and drunks in, 110–144
khārjūram (date wine), 37
See also date palms
Khecarīvidyā, 273
Kīcaka, 89
The Kick. See *Pādatāḍitaka*
kīlāla (*surā*-related drink, perhaps sweet), 29–30, 77, 199
kilañjā-basket, 81
kings. *See* Kṣatriyas
kiṇva (ferment starter for grain *surā*), 32–33, **35–37**, 44, 255, 281
as analogy for the origin for mind in Cārvāka school, 36
bīja as possible term for, 34, 39
in Buddhist monastic rule, 217
recipe for, 34
regulation of, 83, 85, 199
Vedic reference to, 30
Kirātārjunīya (of Bhāravi), 120, **122–125**, 327n123
kiss. See mouth
kodo millet and kodua poisoning, 40, 222–224
kodrava. *See* kodo millet
kohala (type of grain *surā*), 38
Kolhatkar, Madhavi Bhaskar, 13, 108, 331n1
Kolkata, Shaw's Bar, 1
Kṛṣṇa (Hindu god, "Krishna"), 105, 182, 184
destruction of Andhakas and Vṛṣṇis and, 186–187
drunk with Arjuna in *Mahābhārata*, 48, 206, 211, 212–213, 244
king compared to in *Mānasollāsa*, 128

Kṣatriyas (a *varṇa*: kings, warriors), 258
compared to Brahmins, 177
in *Dharmaśāstra*, 204–213
permitted to drink, 139, 187, 258
sabhā-culture and, 90
in Vedic texts, 192
and vice of drinking, 192–197
See also *varṇa*
Kṣemendra, 68–70, 177–179, 188
kṣība (drunk), 65, 69, 105, 108, 196
Kubera (god associated with yakṣas, wealth, and the Northern direction), 130–132, 333n47
Kulārṇava Tantra, 246, 284
Kulasāra, 249
Kumārila
on dharma and drinking, 212–213
Kumbha Jātaka (Buddhist "Previous Birth Story of the Jar"), 20–22, 116, 182
date of, 20
images of, 347n216
speech of Indra, 224–228
See also *Jātakamālā*

Lalitavistara, 333n47
Laṅkā, 46
law
commercial, 83–88
See also dharma; *dharmaśāstra*; morality
Law Code of Manu. See *Mānavadharmaśāstra*
leather, as used for brewing and storage, 30, 77, 87–88
Life of the Buddha (text). See *Buddhacarita*
Līlāvatīsāra. See *Epitome of Queen Līlāvatī*
lime, mineral, 56, 64, 302n34
liquor. See also *madya, surā*
aged, 47, 150
color of (*see under* color)
medical benefits of, 146
morality of in Vedic text, 189–192
offered to gods, 130, 151–152
off-premises consumption, 84, 98
ontology of in Indian texts, 11
perfuming of, 46, 69
ritual uses, 78, 165–170 (*see also* Tantra)
as safer than water, 62, 308n114
served garnished, 111, 119, 127
as shared, 111
smell of, 131–132, 136, 238
storage of, 73–74, 89, 131
as a teacher/guru, 124, 323n42
texts devoted to, 137–139
trade in, 78–79, 89
transport of, 84, 87–88
variety of, 44
as vice, 192–197
as wages, 85
Little Clay Cart. See *Mṛcchakaṭikā*
long pepper, *Piper longum*, 49, 51, 96, 199

Ma-kāras (lists of acts and substances that begin with "m" in Sanskrit)
in *Baudhāyana Dharmasūtra*, 201, 251
in Jainism, 232, 250, 350n269
in Manu, 207, 250
in Tantra, 250–251, 351n9, 352n29
mad (verb root)
applied to Balarāma and elephants, 185
scope of use, 8
and *soma*, 291
translation into English, 8
from Proto-Indo-European, 297n17
See also *mada*; *madya*
mada ("intoxication"), 90, 152, 188
in *Avesta*, 297n17
bad, in *Ṛgveda*, 189
contrasted with madness, 298n18
as elephant musth, 105
of gambling in *Ṛgveda*, 297n17, 338n56
in *Gṛhya Sūtra* wedding rite, 78
of narcotic drugs, 222–224
personified, 123, 175–179
of power, 336n4
of *soma*, 291–292
as transient emotion (*vyabhicāribhāva*) in literary theory, 140, 155–156
madātyaya (liquor-intoxication malady), 159–161
translation of word, 151, 329n22
madhu (honey, mead, wine, nectar, *soma*), 90, 152, 254–255
ambiguities of word, 54, 134–135, 254
as grape wine, 33, 53–54, 71, 95, 116, 131, 134–135, 150, 213, 226
as honey, 61–62, 105–106
Proto-Indo-European origin of word, 297–298n17
soma as, 290
widows to avoid, 201
See also honey; *mādhvī*; mead
Madhuca longifolia. *See* mahua
madhūka, mahua trees, 57, 60
See also mahua
Madhukośa (of Vijayarakṣita), 223
madhūlakam (a type of grain *surā*), 38
Madhurāja. See *Gurunāthaparāmarśa*
Madhuvana (Honey Forest), 105–105

mādhvī (category of threefold-*surā*), 152, **205–206**, 330n33, 341n123, **341n124**
mādhavī variant in Tantric source, 249
as mahua, 60
as wine in Tantric text, 263
madirā (often a generic word for liquor), 182–183, 333n41
as generic word, 37, 52, 119, 120, 123
as goddess, 172, 182–183, 333n43
Madirārṇava (*Ocean of Liquor*), 137–138, 326n121
madness, 223
contrasted with intoxication, 298n18
drunkenness as form of in Buddhist text, 8
etymology of English word, 297n17
scholarship on concept in India, 298n20
madya (intoxicating drink), 37, 135, 152, 259
legal term, 200, 203, 205–206, **208**
as an "m" in Tantra, 250
translation issues, 8
Madyabhairava, 248
Māgha. See *Śiśupālavadha*
Mahābhārata (a Sanskrit epic), 61, 89–90, 115
Andhakas and Vṛṣṇis in, 186–187
Balarāma in, 105, 184–185, 186–187
churning myth in, 170–171
date of, 46
dharma speech of Vidura, 188
festivals in, 105
myth of Mada/Intoxication in, 175–179
myth of Śukra in, 179–181
sabhā (assembly hall) in, 90
sīdhu in, 46, 336n110
surā banner in, 83
vices (*doṣa*) in, 193
mahāpātakas (great sins that cause loss of caste), 200
early version in *Chāndogya Upaniṣad*, 198
vices compared to, 197
See also dharma; morality; vices
Mahāprajñāpāramitāśāstra (of Nāgārjuna), 343n165
mahua flowers and liquor (made with flowers of *Madhuca longifolia*)
flowers, used in wedding ritual, 78
forbidden as drink for Buddhists, 237
liquor, **60–61**, 137, 209, 210, 341n124
sīdhu, variety of, 46
in Surā myth, 265
See also *madhu*; *madhūka*; *mādhvī*
maireya (variable-sugar-based, spiced liquor with secondary fermentation), **50–53**, 238
in *Arthaśāstra* drink list, 33
in Buddhism, 214–215, 217, 221–222, 226, 244
in *Kāmasūtra*, 95, 116
in legal texts, 209, 210
Makkhali Gosāla, 349n258
Mallinātha, 137–138
malted grains, 27, 29–31, 44
man-about-town. See *nāgaraka*
manas (mind), 156
Mānasollāsa (of Someśvara III)
coconut water in, 59
jackfruit wine in, 62
mahua in, 60
non-alcoholic drinks in, 63–64
party in, **125–129**, 248
snacks in, 95–96
surās (grain) in, 39–41, 282
toddy in, 59
water in, 63
wine in, 54, 255
Mānavadharmaśāstra (*Law Code of Manu*), 93, **203–208**, 243, 249
date and composition of, 204
on the six woman-corrupters, 89
on *surā* banner, 82
on vices, 193
See also *surā*: threefold
Mānava Gṛhyasūtra, 51
maṇḍa (top layer of liquid). *See* settling
Mandasor Silk Weavers' Inscription, 65
mango, 34, 57, 64, 110, 136, 150, 237
Maṅkha. See *Śrīkaṇṭhacarita*
mantras
in Sautrāmaṇī ritual, 167–168, 332n20
Manu. See *Mānavadharmaśāstra*
mārdvīkam (grape wine), 37, 54, 136, 150, 257
See also grapes; *madhu*; *mādhvī*; wine
marica/*marīca*. *See* black pepper
Marshall, John, 108
māṣa (urad dal), 34
māsara (liquid infusion of toasted grains in Vedic brewing), 29–31, 168
material culture, 3–6, 77, 143–144
Mathura, sculpture from, 55, 321n16
Matsyendrasaṃhitā, 273
Mattavilāsaprahasana (of Mahendravikramavarman), 173
Buddhist monk in, 235–237
description of *surā* shop in, 80, 98
Kāpālika ascetic in, 245–246
Mausalaparvan of *Mahābhārata*, 186–187
McGovern, Patrick, 13, 28

mead, 46, **61–62**, 105, 150, 152, 254–255
Indo-European origin of word, 297–298n17
in Tantra, 254
See also *madhu*; *mādhvī*; honey
meat, 100, 159
in Buddhism, 235, 237
connected to drinking, 20, 52, 94, 97, 127, 136, 148, 190
in Jainism, 232
morality of, in Manu, 205–207
in Tantra, 247, 250
medaka (type of grain *surā*), 33, 38
Medhātithi, 82, 206, 207
Meghadūta (of Kālidāsa), 137–139
meṣaśṛṅgī, *Gymnema sylvestre*, 51
Mesopotamia, 32, 74
translating terminology for drinks and brewing in, 7
microorganisms. See *yeast*; *molds*
milk, 63, 170–171, 174, 343n165
millets (various types of grain), 40
Mīmāṃsā. *See* Kumārila
Mitākṣarā (of Vijñāneśvara), 210–211
Mitra, Rajendralal
biography of, 12
on *soma*, 290
mold, in fermentation, 27, 282
See also ferment starters; *kiṇva*
monkeys. *See* Vānaras
monks, Buddhist, 119
satire of, in *Mattavilāsaprahasana*, 235–237
and Vinaya on drinking, 215–218
morality of drink and drinking
in Buddhist sources, 215–228
drink as vice, 192–197
in Jain sources, 228–233
in Vedic sources, 189–192
See also *Dharmaśāstra; Dharmasūtras*; vice
moringa, 95
mouth
as colored, 114, 125
as cup, 119–120, 124, 185
as dry after drinking, 183
as perfumed/fragrant, 114, 125, 148, 150
Mṛcchakaṭikā (of Śūdraka), 68, 321n16
Much Ado About Religion. See *Āgamaḍambara*

nāgaraka (man-about-town), 95, 113–117
nāgas (semi-divine serpent beings), 95, 358n154
Ananta, 170, 172, 182, 187
Vāsuki, 170, 276
nagnahu (additive, perhaps a starter, in Vedic era brewing), 29–31, 168
Namuci (an Asura), 166–167
Naṇḍapaṇḍita, 209–210
Narmamālā (of Kṣemendra), 68–70
Nāṭyaśāstra (of Bharata)
intoxication, performance described in, 155–156
nectar of immortality. See *amṛta*
Niruttara Tantra, 283
Nītisāra (of Kāmandaki)
on vices, 194–195
Niya (site), 65
Northeast regions of India, 28
nudity, associated with drink, 98, 121–122, 194, 230, 240, 338n38
nuns, Buddhist, 91–92
nutmeg, 66, 265

ocean
asuras falling into, 102
myth of churning (*see* churning of the ocean)
of *surā* and other edible liquids, 173–175
vāruṇīvara ocean in Jainism, 334n54
Ocean of Liquor (text). See *Madirārṇava*
Odisha, brewing *handia* in, 28, 41–42, 281–282
ojas (vital energy substance), 148, **153–154**, 234
opium, 276, 283–285
etymology of Sanskrit word for, 358n148
oranges, in Kashmir, 256

pachwai (a type of liquor), 282
Pādatāḍitaka (of Śyāmilaka), 97, 173
Padmaprābhṛtaka, 47
Padmapurāṇa, 275
paiṣṭī (ground grain based *surā*), 152, 154, **205–206**, 207, 211, 249, 263
See also *surā*: threefold
palm trees, 12, 44, 55–60, 182, 273
areca, 64
Balarāma and, 57–58
fruit of palmyra, 58, 322n31
leaves as fans, 147
See also coconut; inscriptions: on trees; toddy
pān. *See* betel
pāna, as general word for liquor, 8, 89, 120, 131, 176, 193, 194
pānaka (cordials, flavored non-alcoholic drinks), 322n31
pānātyaya. See *madātyaya*
Pañcatantra, 313n34
on vices, 195–196
Pāṇini, 51, 52
parisrut (liquefied *surā*-mash; unfiltered *surā*), 29, 36, 78, 89–90, 168

parties, 103–106, 158
  Tantric, orgiastic, 248
  See also drinking: social nature of; festivals; weddings
Pārvatī (Hindu goddess), 280
pasteurization, lack of, 44
Pattadakal, 117, 118, 133
penances for drinking, 81–82, 200–203, 204–207, 354n57
  in Tantra, for not drinking, 257
pepper. *See* black pepper; long pepper
perception, intoxicated changes in, 10, 128, 130–131, 135–136, 142
perfume, 69, 114
  classed with betel, 66
  use in scenting drinks, 46, 125, 136
Persia, 54, 65
phāṇita (sugarcane syrup), 35
Philippines, 47
piṣṭa (ground grain), 33, 40, 254–255
plants, translating Sanskrit names of, 11–12
  See also names of individual plants
poison, 152–153
  kālakūṭa, 284
  See also drugged preparations; *hālāhala*
pomegranate, 347n239
postures, when drinking or drunk, 98–99, 103, 114–116, 117, *118*, *133*, 147, *225*
Prakash, Om, 12
prasannā ("clear" grain *surā*), 33–35, 38–39, 46, 217, 325n110
  acchasurā variant word, 149
precepts, Buddhist. *See* Buddhism, precepts
priyaṅgu (foxtail millet), 40
pūga (areca nut). *See* betel
Pulastyasmṛti, 210
pulque, 56
punishments, 81–82
purity. *See* impurity

Raghuvaṃśa (of Kālidāsa), 58, 65, 327n123
raisins. *See* grapes: as dried
Rājaśekhara, 47
Rājataraṅgiṇī of Kalhaṇa
  betel in, 70–71
  chapter nomenclature, 16
  grapes and wine in, 136
  Kalyapālas in, 108
  kings drinking/abstaining in, 140, 196
  Tantric rituals in, 259
  wine in, 136
Rājavyavahārakośa, 285
rake (stock character). See *viṭa*
rākṣasa, 46, 235, 267, 341n125
Rāma, 42, 105
Rāmāyaṇa (Sanskrit epic), 42, 46
  churning myth in, 171–172, 283
  date of, 46
  drinks in, 46
  Madhuvana (Honey Forest) episode, 105–106
  maireya in, 51, 52
  sīdhu in, 46
ratiphala (drink recipe), 137–138, 326n121
Rāvaṇa, 42, 105
  drinks in palace of, 46
  purported author of *Arkaprakāśa*, 280
refrigeration, lack of, 44
Ṛgveda
  hymn to Indra Sutrāman, 166–167
  mada in, 297n17
  soma in, 289, 291–292, 295
  surā in, 77, 189–190
rice
  nature of *śāli*/*sāli* variety, 299n7
  in *surā* brewing, 30, 33, 40
  as *surā* ingredient in *Kumbha Jātaka* story, 20–21
  taṇḍula, 20
River of Kings of Kalhaṇa. See *Rājataraṅgiṇī*
Rome, 54
roses, 285

sabhā (assembly hall), 90
saccharification, 27–28, 44
Sadāśiva, 261, 266–268, 355n71
saffron, 55, 65, 68, 96, 136, 257, 285
saira (a type of liquor), 210, 342n146, 342n148
sake (Japanese drink), 29, 50
Sakka. *See* Indra
Śakra. *See* Indra
Śakti, 255
Śakuntalā (of Kālidāsa), 100
saliva, use in fermentation, 27
salons (*goṣṭhī*), 116
salt, 83, 93–94, 96, 97
  ocean, 174
samāpākana. *See* drinking: social nature of
Sāmaveda, 177
Sāmba, 105, 186–187
sambhāra/*saṃbhāra* (herbal additive mixture for various drinks)
  for *āsava* in *Arthaśāstra*, 48
  in Buddhist monastic rule, 217–218, 345n183
  as cognate with *sambar*, 32
  for *maireya*, 51
  for *surā* in *Arthaśāstra*, 33–34
  for *surā* in *Kumbha Jātaka*, 21
saṃdhāna ("brewing, fermentation"), 322n31
  as assembling ingredients, 29, 168

saṃsāra (eternal realm of rebirth), 128, 148, 157–158
 Buddhist wheel image of, 100–101
 drunkard as image of, 178
Saṃvarodayatantra, 355n84
sandalwood, 63
saraka (shared cup, couple drinking). *See* drinking: social nature of
Sarasvatī (goddess), 165–170, 234
Śārṅgadharasaṃhitā
 āsavas and *ariṣṭas* defined in, 49
 grain *surā* in, 38
 mada of narcotics in, 223
Sarvollāsa Tantra, 273, 283
śaṣpa (sprouted grains in Vedic brewing), 29–31, 168
Śatapatha Brāhmaṇa, 191–192
śauṇḍika. See *śuṇḍā*
Sautrāmaṇī ritual, **165–170**, 190, 234–235
 disposal of *surā* in, 191
 Jain critique of, 232–233
 and royal consecration, 169
 Tantra references to, 249, 252, 258
 See also mantras
Schopen, Gregory, 2, 315n78, 316n81
seasons
 drinks prescribed varying with, 47, 149–150
 fermentation time varying with, 49
sediment. *See* dregs; settling
servants, 112, 114, 119, 131, 147
set of three. See *trivarga*
settling, of *surā* layers to produce varieties, 38–39
sex
 drink as connected with, 130–137, 148, 155, 277
 preparations (*saṃskāras*) for as including drink, 114, 123, 138–139
 in Tantra, 247–248, 250, 277
 as violence, in Jainism, 349n263
shared drinks. *See* liquor: as shared
sīdhu/*śīdhu* (sugarcane wine), **45–47**, 123, 148, 150, 213, 226, 253, 336n110
 aged, 47
 bakula tree craves, 120
 in inscription, 87
 regional drink, 46, 201
sin, drinking as. See *mahāpātakas*
Śiśupālavadha (of Māgha), 120, 185, 322n34, 323n42, 327n123
Sītā, 42, 105, 315n73
Śiva (Hindu god, "Shiva"), 172, 245, 251, 254, 257, 258, 267
sixty four arts (*kalās*), 119
smell
 of liquor reveals drinking, 131, 238
 smelling *surā* as sin, 191, 200, 204
 smelling *surā* in Sautrāmaṇī, 191
smoking, 285
 See also tobacco
snacks. See *upadaṃśa*
social-history, reflections on, 3–6, 77, 112
soldiers, as drinking, 52, 65, 106
soma (plant, god, and psychoactive, crushed-plant infusion in Vedas), 31–32, 75, 117, 174, **289–295**
 as alcoholic drink, 290–291, 360n8, 360n9, 361n10
 archaeology and, 293–294
 Aśvins permitted to drink, 175–176
 compared to *surā*, 30–32, 165, 169, 191
 effects of, in *Ṛgveda*, 291–292, 297n17
 gender of word, 169
 substitutes for, 293
Somadeva (Jain author), 140–141
Someśvara III, King. See *Mānasollāsa*
sorghum, 28, 40, 294
spittoon, 114
Śrauta Sūtras, 28–32
Śrī (Fortune, goddess), 171–172, 183–184
Śrīkaṇṭhacarita (of Maṅkha), 120, 323n42
Sri Lanka, 65, 90, 92. *See also* Laṅkā
starch, 27–28
starters, for fermentation. See *ferment*; *kiṇva*
still (for distillation). *See* distillation
storage. *See* liquor: aged; liquor: storage
straws, for drinking, 64, 117–119
Śūdra (a *varṇa*: servants), 100, 258
sugarcane products, 45, 47
 crystal (*śarkarā*), 45, 46, 160, 263
 jaggery (*guḍa*), 45, 51, 56, 205–206, 209–210, 254, 263
 juice (*ikṣurasa*), 45, 52
 -juice ocean, 174
 mahua products classed with, 61
 massecuite (*matsyaṇḍikā*), 45
 mollasses (*kṣāra*), 45
 processing, 45
 soft brown (*khaṇḍa*), 45
 syrup (*phāṇita*), 35, 48, 49
 See also *gauḍī*
sugars. *See also* sugarcane products
 as base for fermentation, 44
 as produced from grains in fermentation, 27–28
Śukra, 173, 281

myth where prohibits/curses *surā*, 179–181, 195, 258, 267

śuṇḍā (and related forms), 93, 99, 100, 228
  meaning of, and of cognate forms, 81, 313n16
  etymology of, 313n21

sura ("god" = deva)
  traditional etymology connected to *surā*, 171–172

surā (grain-based drink; liquor in general; threefold-liquor, **27–43**, 149, 203, 233, 281. *See also* Surādevī
  arising at churning of ocean, 170–172, 249, 261, 283
  bad *mada* of in *Ṛgveda*, 297n17
  barley based, 38
  black, 40–41, 127–129, 282
  Buddhist narrative of discovery in *Kumbha Jātaka*, 19–23
  color of, 20, 31, 34–35, 37–38
  and distillation (*see* distillation)
  as falsehood, 165, 331n4
  filtering of, 31
  flavor of, 40, 42, 159
  gender of word, 169
  as generic word for liquor, 299n1
  the goddess Surā (*see* Surādevī)
  grain based (see also *paiṣṭī*):
    in *Arthaśāstra*, 33–35
    in *Mānasollāsa*, 39–41
    in medical sources, 37–39
    in Vedic sources, 28–32
  kapotikā variety, 217–218, 344n179
  -*kara* (maker), 77
  as *kṛtrimā*, fabricated, in Tantra, 255–256
  Mada (Intoxication) placed inside it, myth of, 176
  and *maireya*, 51, 214–215, 217
  many meanings of word, 19, 27
  mṛtasañjīvanī surā (medicine), 281
  ocean of, 173–175
  origin of word from man's name, according to *Kumbha Jātaka*, 20
  praise of in medical texts, 233–235
  in *Rāmāyaṇa*, 42, 46
  soma compared to, 165, 169
  strength of, 41
  Śukra prohibts for brahmins, 179–181
  in Tantric sources, 249, 254–257, 263–266
  as threefold, 152, **204–206**, 243, 249, 254–256, 263, 266, 269, 330n33
  varieties derived from settling layers, 38–39
  Vedas, status in, 165, 169–170, 189–192
  white, 34–35, 38, 127
  See also Surādevī

Surādevī (goddess, deified liquor), 151, **170–173**, 233–235, 245, *262*
  in Buddhist text, 333n47
  in Greek text, possible reference, 333n47
  iconography of, 260–261, 355n71
  kin of, 173
  in Tantric texts, **260–269**
  temple to, 333n42

Suśrutasaṃhitā
  āsava recipe in, 49
  betel in, 66
  date of, 37
  grain-*surā* in, 37–38
  mahua in, 61
  water in, 62

Suśruta's Compendium. See *Suśrutasaṃhitā*

śyāmāka. See millets

symposium, Hellenistic, compared to Indian drinking, 321n17

syrup. *See* sugarcane

tāmbūla (betel quid). *See* betel

taṇḍula. *See* rice

Tantra, 142–143, **245–279**
  Hindu, simple definition of, 246–247
  ma-kāras in, 250–251, 352n29
  surā defined in, 249
  See also Abhinavagupta; Jayaratha; *Tantrāloka*

Tantrāloka (of Abhinavagupta), 251–260
  aesthetics in, 252–253
  date of, 251
  Kula ritual in, 253–259
  philosophy in, 251–252
  See also Abhinavagupta; Jayaratha

Tantravārttika. *See* Kumārila

taverns. *See* drinking establishments

taxation, 85–88

tejas (an element: light, fire)
  as nature of liquor in Tantric sources, 254, 257, 283

temperature. *See under* fermentation; seasons

temples, liquor used in, 278

thirst, as after effect of drinking, 183

toasts before drinking. *See* drinking: actions preceding

tobacco, 67, 280, **283–285**

toddy, 55–60, 283
  and Buddhism in Burma, 218
  as distilled, 110, 281
  in legal texts, 210
  main palm species tapped in South Asia, 56
  tappers, 56–57

tokman (sprouted/malted grains in Vedic brewing), 29–31, 168, 199
trade. *See* liquor: trade in
translation
author's reflections on, 15
transport of liquor. *See* liquor: transport
trees, legal and economic aspects, 56–57
triphalā mixture, 51, 64, **306n45**
trivarga, 148
definition of, 321n4

upadaṃśa (drinking snack), 82, **94–97**, 98, 114–115, 120, 126–127, 148
salt as, 93
urad dal (*māṣa*), 34

Vaiṣṇava Dharmaśāstra, 209–210
Vaiśya (a *varṇa*: trade, agriculture), 100, 192, 258
Vājapeya, Vedic ritual, 78
Vānaras (monkey-beings in *Rāmāyaṇa*), 105–105
Varāhamihira. See *Bṛhatsaṃhitā*; *Yogayātrā*
varcas, 190
varṇas (classes or "estates" of classical Indian social theory), 100, 139, 243
and drink in Manu, 204–207, 243
roman transliteration of, 15–16
in Tantra, 258, 259
"twice born," 201
Vedic antecedents and drink, 191–192
See also individual *varṇas*
Varuṇa (god associated with order and with waters), 173, 183, 189, 249
vāruṇī (=*surā*), 93, 150, 249, 320n1, 333n41
origin of word in man's name in *Kumbha Jātaka*, 20
personified (=Surā), 139, 171, 173, 260, *262*
See also *surā*; Surādevī
Vāruṇi Jātaka, 93–94
Vasiṣṭha Dharmasūtra
on drinking, 201–203
Vasubandhu. See *Abhidharmakośa*
Vātsyāyana. See *Kāmasūtra*
Vedas/Vedic, 205–207, 268
brewing methods in, 28–32
mantras for brewing, 167–168, 332n20
prohibition of *surā* for Brahmins in, 191
sacrifice compared to *surā* shop, 80
Sautrāmaṇī ritual, 28–32, **165–170**
Vājapeya ritual, 78
See also *soma*
vetiver, 63
vices, 90, 189, **192–197**, 226
addiction compared to, 193, 196
in *Arthaśāstra*, 193–194
called *doṣas* in *Mahābhārata*, 193
class of vice-like woman-corrupting acts, 89
drink as, in *Bṛhatkathāślokasaṃgraha*, 130, 325n117
Mada (Intoxication) placed in, myth of, 176–179
in Manu, 193
in *Nītisāra*, 194–195
in *Rājataraṅgiṇī*, 196
"sins" compared to, 197
in *Yogayātrā*
See also dice
Vidura
speech on dharma, 188
vijayā. *See* cannabis
Vikramāṅkadevacarita, 96, 317n118, 353n53
vīṇā (a string instrument)
and drink, 193
Vinaya (Buddhist monastic discipline texts)
Mūlasarvāstivāda, 91–92
Pali, 60, 214–219
violence
from drinking, 31, 186–187, 189–190, 192
Virūpa (Buddhist saint), 277
Viṣṇu (Hindu god), 264, 267
Viṣṇuṣena, Charter of. *See* inscriptions
viṭa (stock character, rake-parasite), 97–98
vyasana. *See* vices

water
for drinking, 62–64, 150
ocean of, 174
weddings, 78, 91–92, 103–106, 189
wheat, 40, 263
wine (grape), 46, **53–55**, 85, 290, 325n117
broad usage of English word, 6, 50
in *Kāmasūtra*, 95
in Kashmir, 136, 256–257
in legal texts, 206, 209, 210, 212–213
in *Mānasollāsa*, 54, 127
in medical texts, 37, 150, 160
in Tantra, 254–257
See also grapes
wine talk. *See* flavor: descriptions of
women, 147, 227, 238
as brewers and traders, 22, **88–92**, 99, 100–103
drunk, in literary texts, 120–129, 143
groomed to join harem in *Kāmasūtra*, 104
in Hindu law, 201, 202
as objectified in some Sanskrit texts, 14–15

permitted to drink with men in connection with sex, 114–117, *115*, *118*, 139
rape of intoxicated (*paiśāca* marriage), 104
sexual availability of, compared to drinking houses, 100
surā as funerary libation for, 78
in Tantra, 247
washed with *surā* at weddings, 78
working in drinking houses, 79
See also courtesans; nuns, Buddhist; sex; Surādevī
wood apple, *Feronia elephantum*, 48, 209
Woodfordia fruticosa. See *dhātakī*
words
diachronic change in meaning, 7
for drinks in Sanskrit, 6–12 (*see also names of individual drinks*)

Xuanzang
on drink culture in India, 243

Yādavas. *See* Andhakas and Vṛṣṇis
yakṣas and *yakṣīs* (supernatural beings), 95, 130–132, 152, 205, 206, 235, 358n154
yaśas, 190
Yaśastilaka (of Somadeva), 140–141, 250
Yaśodhara (commentator on *Kāmasūtra*), 95, 114
yava. *See* barley
yavanāla. *See* sorghum
Yayāti, 105, 179
yeast, 27
See also ferment starters; *kiṇva*
yoga, 282
as word for "mixture" in *Arthaśāstra*, 34
Yogaratnākara, 285
Yogaśāstra (of Hemacandra), 229–231
Yogayātrā (of Varāhamihira)
on vices, 195

Zoroastrianism, *haoma* in, 289, 293–294